INTERNATIONAL COMMERCIAL ARBITRATION IN SWEDEN

INTERNATIONAL COMMERCIAL ARBITRATION IN SWEDEN

PROF. DR KAJ HOBÉR

Partner, Mannheimer Swartling Advokatbyrå

OXFORD

UNIVERSITY PRESS

OXFORD

UNIVERSITY PRESS

Great Clarendon Street, Oxford OX2 6DP

Oxford University Press is a department of the University of Oxford.
It furthers the University's objective of excellence in research, scholarship,
and education by publishing worldwide in

Oxford New York

Auckland Cape Town Dar es Salaam Hong Kong Karachi
Kuala Lumpur Madrid Melbourne Mexico City Nairobi
New Delhi Shanghai Taipei Toronto

With offices in

Argentina Austria Brazil Chile Czech Republic France Greece
Guatemala Hungary Italy Japan Poland Portugal Singapore
South Korea Switzerland Thailand Turkey Ukraine Vietnam

Oxford is a registered trade mark of Oxford University Press
in the UK and in certain other countries

Published in the United States
by Oxford University Press Inc., New York

British Library Cataloguing-in-Publication Data
Data available

Library of Congress Cataloging-in-Publication Data
Data available

Typeset by Glyph International, Bangalore, India
Printed in Great Britain
on acid-free paper by
CPI Antony Rowe, Chippenham, Wiltshire

ISBN 978–0–19–921852–3

PREFACE

When I started out in private practice in March 1982, I was fortunate enough to become involved in international arbitration from day one, and fortunate enough also to be working with the late Dr J. Gillis Wetter, one of the leading international arbitration lawyers in Sweden at the time. Soon I became involved in the preparation of the second edition of *Arbitration in Sweden*, which was published in 1984. The first edition of that book, published in 1977, was the first comprehensive account in the English language of Swedish arbitration law. Ever since the publication of the second edition of *Arbitration in Sweden*, I have struggled to find time to prepare a follow-up to that book, particularly after the adoption of the 1999 Swedish Arbitration Act. Other commitments and projects, however, made this impossible. I am therefore happy to finish the work now that I started so many years ago.

At the beginning of the 1980s arbitration was still a rather exotic practice area for most business lawyers. Today the situation is radically different: virtually all leading law firms in most jurisdictions are involved in international arbitration, private and public. Throughout these decades of radical expansion of international arbitration, Sweden has continued to play a central role as a leading arbitration centre, particularly with respect to disputes involving entities from the former Soviet Union and China. During the first decade of the new century, Stockholm has also established itself as a centre for investment treaty arbitration, particularly under the Energy Charter Treaty.

The purpose of this book is to analyse and describe Swedish arbitration law as per 1 December 2010. It is primarily addressed to non-Swedish lawyers, with some basic knowledge and understanding of international arbitration. I have chosen to approach the topic from a practical point of view, but providing theoretical analysis and discussion where necessary. The book is to a large extent a condensed account of my experience—both practical and theoretical—as an international arbitration lawyer. I have refrained, however, with a few exceptions, from expressing my personal views on the various issues discussed in the book.

The book deals only with international *commercial* arbitration. There is thus no discussion of investment treaty arbitration, even though I do refer to some investment arbitration awards. I do this, however, for illustrative purposes only. Notwithstanding the fact that there is a high degree of overlap between the two forms of arbitration, they are best treated separately.

In preparing this book, I have benefitted greatly from the assistance and advice of many colleagues at Mannheimer Swartling Advokatbyrå. I thank them all. Of the many who have assisted me, I would like to give special thanks to Pontus Ewerlöf, now with the Cederquist firm, and to Nils Eliasson, partner in our Hong Kong office. Special thanks are also due to my secretary, Cristina Manzoni, and to Egle Breskute Öfverhus, paralegal in our dispute resolution practice group. They have both been of invaluable assistance in completing the book.

I need hardly add that responsibility for errors and shortcomings lies solely with me.

As usual my greatest thanks go to my wife Britt and our sons David and Jakob.

Kaj Hobér
Uppsala, February 2011

CONTENTS

Table of Cases   xv
Table of Legislation   xxiii

1 Introduction   1

  1.1   History of Arbitration in Sweden   1.01

  1.2   The Swedish Legal System   1.18
      1.2.1   General   1.18
      1.2.2   The courts and the judiciary   1.21
         1.2.2.1   The courts   1.21
         1.2.2.2   The judiciary   1.29
      1.2.3   The legal profession   1.35

  1.3   The Arbitration Institute of the Stockholm Chamber of
Commerce   1.46

  1.4   Sovereign Immunity and International Commercial
Arbitration in Sweden   1.52
      1.4.1   Sovereign immunity in general   1.52
         1.4.1.1   Introduction   1.52
      1.4.2   National legislation   1.57
      1.4.3   The UN Convention   1.75
         1.4.3.1   Immunity from jurisdiction   1.80
         1.4.3.2   Arbitration   1.85
      1.4.4   Sovereign immunity and Swedish law   1.94

  1.5   Sovereign Immunity and Arbitration   1.122
      1.5.1   General observations   1.122
      1.5.2   Sovereign immunity and arbitration under Swedish law   1.131

2 Applicable Law   33

  2.1   Introduction   2.01

  2.2   *Lex Arbitri*—The Law Governing the Arbitration   2.05

  2.3   Party Autonomy—Choice of Law by the Parties   2.14
      2.3.1   Introduction   2.14
      2.3.2   The content of party autonomy   2.24
      2.3.3   Exercising party autonomy   2.42
      2.3.4   Restrictions on party autonomy   2.51
         2.3.4.1   General comments   2.51

	2.3.4.2 No reasonable connection	2.55
	2.3.4.3 National public policy	2.59
	2.3.4.4 Mandatory rules of municipal law	2.71
	2.3.4.5 International public policy	2.89
	2.3.4.6 The function of international public policy	2.92
	2.3.4.7 The content of international public policy	2.93
2.4	No Choice of Law by the Parties	2.97
	2.4.1 Introduction	2.97
	2.4.2 Swedish conflict of laws rules	2.103
	2.4.2.1 The 1964 Act on the Law Applicable to International Sales of Goods	2.106
	2.4.2.2 The centre of gravity test	2.118
	2.4.2.3 The 1980 Rome Convention	2.144
	2.4.2.4 The Rome I Regulation	2.163
2.5	Issues Not Covered by the *Lex Contractus*	2.173
	2.5.1 *Lex corporationis*	2.174
	2.5.2 Agency	2.181
	2.5.3 Negotiable instruments	2.185
	2.5.4 Torts	2.186
	2.5.5 Property	2.192
2.6	Classification Rules	2.198
2.7	The Law Governing the Arbitration Agreement	2.201
3	**The Arbitration Agreement**	**89**
3.1	Introduction	3.01
3.2	The Validity of an Arbitration Agreement	3.04
	3.2.1 General remarks	3.04
	3.2.2 Requisites of a valid arbitration agreement	3.05
3.3	Concluding the Arbitration Agreement	3.06
	3.3.1 Arbitration agreement in writing	3.06
	3.3.2 Oral arbitration agreement	3.12
	3.3.3 Arbitration agreement by conduct	3.14
	3.3.3.1 Arbitration agreement as a result of party usage	3.23
	3.3.3.2 Arbitration agreement by 'inactivity'	3.28
3.4	Interpretation of Arbitration Agreement	3.31
3.5	Unenforceability of Arbitration Agreements due to the Swedish Contracts Act	3.37
3.6	The Doctrine of Separability	3.42
	3.6.1 Introduction	3.42
	3.6.2 Application of doctrine of separability	3.48
	3.6.3 Should the application of the doctrine of separability be limited?	3.53
	3.6.3.1 No agreement in the first place	3.55

3.6.3.2 The principal agreement is void *ab initio*, voidable, or has been declared invalid   3.60

3.7 Invalidity of the Arbitration Agreement   3.74

3.8 Arbitrability   3.77
- 3.8.1 Disputes capable of settlement   3.81
- 3.8.2 The existence of factual circumstances   3.86
- 3.8.3 Filling gaps   3.92
- 3.8.4 Consumer and labour disputes   3.95
- 3.8.5 Civil law effects of competition law   3.98

3.9 Effects of Arbitration Agreement   3.111
- 3.9.1 Bar to court proceedings   3.112
  - 3.9.1.1 Respondent has failed to cooperate in arbitration   3.118
  - 3.9.1.2 Respondent has disregarded the agreement in previous court proceedings   3.121
  - 3.9.1.3 The subject matter of the dispute is non-arbitrable   3.123
- 3.9.2 Assistance by courts   3.126
- 3.9.3 Rules of organization and procedure   3.127
- 3.9.4 Authority of arbitrators   3.128
- 3.9.5 Effect of arbitration agreement on third parties   3.130
  - 3.9.5.1 Party substitution   3.131
  - 3.9.5.2 Guarantee agreements   3.142
  - 3.9.5.3 Conduct by third parties, including the 'group of companies' doctrine   3.146
- 3.9.6 Confidentiality   3.164

3.10 Termination of Arbitration Agreement   3.168
- 3.10.1 Introduction   3.168
- 3.10.2 Termination with respect to existing dispute   3.171
  - 3.10.2.1 By understanding   3.171
  - 3.10.2.2 Events during proceedings   3.172
  - 3.10.2.3 Judgment   3.173
  - 3.10.2.4 Expiration of award period   3.175
  - 3.10.2.5 Award   3.176
- 3.10.3 Complete termination   3.178

3.11 Drafting of Arbitration Clauses   3.182

4 The Arbitrators   145

4.1 Appointment of Arbitrators   4.01
- 4.1.1 Introduction   4.01
- 4.1.2 Appointment of arbitrators under the SAA   4.04
  - 4.1.2.1 Arbitrators not specifically named in agreement   4.06
  - 4.1.2.2 Arbitrators specifically named in agreement   4.11
  - 4.1.2.3 Arbitrators in multi-party arbitrations   4.13
- 4.1.3 Rules   4.18
  - 4.1.3.1 SCC   4.18
  - 4.1.3.2 Other rules   4.36

4.2 Qualifications of Arbitrators   4.39

4.3 Powers and Duties of Arbitrators   4.46

4.4 Relation of Arbitrators to the Parties   4.52

4.5 Challenge and Replacement of Arbitrators   4.62
    4.5.1 The SAA   4.62
       4.5.1.1 Grounds for challenge. Disclosure   4.62
       4.5.1.2 Procedure   4.85
       4.5.1.3 Replacing arbitrators   4.87
    4.5.2 Rules   4.91

4.6 Compensation of Arbitrators   4.103
    4.6.1 Fees and expenses   4.103
    4.6.2 Value Added Tax (VAT) on arbitrators' compensation   4.126
    4.6.3 Rules   4.130

5 Jurisdiction of the Arbitral Tribunal   **183**

5.1 Introduction   5.01

5.2 Issues Affecting the Jurisdiction of the Arbitrators   5.07

5.3 The Arbitrators' Determination of their Jurisdiction   5.13

5.4 Court Review of the Arbitrators' Jurisdiction   5.19
    5.4.1 Situations in which a court may consider a declaratory
       action with respect to the jurisdiction of the arbitrators   5.21
       5.4.1.1 Jurisdiction of the Swedish courts   5.21
       5.4.1.2 Requirements with respect to declaratory judgments   5.34
    5.4.2 Potential effects of a declaratory action with respect
       to the jurisdiction of the arbitrators   5.36

5.5 Anti-suit Injunctions   5.38

5.6 Rules   5.43

6 The Procedure before the Arbitral Tribunal   **197**

6.1 Introduction   6.01

6.2 General Principles of Swedish Judicial Procedure   6.16

6.3 Basic Principles of Arbitration Procedure   6.29
    6.3.1 Party autonomy   6.30
    6.3.2 Impartiality, practicality, speed   6.31
    6.3.3 *Audi alteram partem*   6.32

6.4 Commencing the Arbitration Proceedings   6.35
    6.4.1 Request for arbitration   6.35
       6.4.1.1 SCC Rules   6.42
    6.4.2 Service of the request for arbitration, the award, and
       other documents   6.44
       6.4.2.1 Proof of notification and methods of service   6.48

	6.4.2.2 'Notices' clauses	6.52
	6.4.2.3 Persons authorized to accept service	6.54
	6.4.2.4 Particular rules for service of documents outside Sweden	6.57
	6.4.2.5 SCC Rules	6.58
6.5	Conduct of the Arbitration	6.64
	6.5.1 General	6.64
	6.5.2 Written submissions	6.71
	6.5.2.1 Prayers for relief	6.73
	6.5.2.2 Legal grounds	6.76
	6.5.2.3 Facts and circumstances	6.77
	6.5.3 Post-hearing briefs	6.87
	6.5.4 Evidence	6.89
	6.5.4.1 Introduction	6.89
	6.5.4.2 Powers of the arbitrators	6.97
	6.5.4.3 Admissibility of evidence	6.101
	6.5.5 Documentary evidence and production of documents	6.109
	6.5.5.1 Documentary evidence	6.109
	6.5.5.2 Production of documents	6.112
	6.5.6 Witnesses and experts	6.122
	6.5.6.1 Hearing of witnesses	6.122
	6.5.6.2 Written witness statements	6.145
	6.5.6.3 Experts	6.150
	6.5.6.4 Inspection of the subject matter of the dispute	6.160
	6.5.6.5 Evaluation of evidence	6.162
	6.5.7 Evidence taken with court assistance	6.170
	6.5.8 Hearings	6.184
	6.5.8.1 Introduction	6.184
	6.5.8.2 The main hearing	6.218
7	**The Award**	255
7.1	Introduction	7.01
7.2	Principles of Decision	7.02
	7.2.1 Decision according to law	7.04
	7.2.2 Keeping within Authority	7.08
	7.2.3 Dealing with all matters	7.09
7.3	Deliberations and Voting	7.10
7.4	Different Kinds of Awards and Decisions	7.22
	7.4.1 Award or decision?	7.22
	7.4.2 Separate awards	7.27
	7.4.3 Interim awards	7.36
	7.4.4 Consent awards	7.38
	7.4.5 Default awards	7.42
7.5	Formalities	7.43
7.6	Reasons and Dissenting Opinions	7.57

7.7	Interest and Costs	7.71
	7.7.1 Interest	7.71
	7.7.2 Costs	7.78
7.8	Rendering the Award	7.84
7.9	Effects of the Award	7.92
	7.9.1 Execution	7.93
	7.9.2 Time starts running	7.94
	7.9.3 Termination of arbitration agreement	7.96
	7.9.4 *Res judicata*	7.104
	7.9.4.1 Application of the principles of *lis pendens* and *res judicata* in Swedish arbitration law	7.108
	7.9.4.2 *Res judicata* and *lis pendens* in international arbitration	7.120
7.10	Correction and Interpretation of the Award	7.137
	7.10.1 General	7.137
	7.10.2 Correction of arbitral awards	7.140
	7.10.3 Amendment of arbitral awards	7.146
	7.10.4 Interpretation of arbitral awards	7.149
	7.10.5 SCC Rules	7.152
8	**Setting Aside Arbitral Awards**	**293**
8.1	Invalid and Challengeable Awards	8.01
	8.1.1 General remarks	8.01
	8.1.2 Principle of *in dubio pro validitate*	8.09
	8.1.3 Burden of proof	8.12
	8.1.4 Other means of recourse	8.15
	8.1.5 Jurisdiction of Swedish courts	8.19
8.2	Invalid Arbitral Awards	8.26
	8.2.1 Grounds for invalidity	8.27
	8.2.1.1 Non-arbitrability	8.29
	8.2.1.2 Violation of public policy	8.33
	8.2.1.3 Formal requirements of the arbitral award	8.47
	8.2.2 Non-statutory grounds for invalidity	8.50
	8.2.2.1 Situations where an 'award' may not be characterized as an arbitral award	8.51
	8.2.2.2 The party against whom the award was made was not a party to the arbitration proceedings	8.53
	8.2.2.3 An award too obscure to enforce	8.56
	8.2.3 Invalidity of part of the award	8.57
8.3	Challenge of Arbitral Awards	8.58
	8.3.1 Grounds for challenging an award	8.58
	8.3.2 No arbitration agreement	8.63
	8.3.3 Excess of mandate	8.65
	8.3.3.1 Award after the expiration of a time limit for rendering of the award	8.66
	8.3.3.2 Excess of mandate	8.69

8.3.4 The arbitration should not have taken place in Sweden   8.109
8.3.5 Improper appointment of arbitrators   8.112
8.3.6 One of the arbitrators should have been disqualified   8.114
8.3.7 Other procedural irregularities   8.118
    8.3.7.1 The irregularities to which the general clause applies   8.118
    8.3.7.2 Probable influence on the outcome of the dispute   8.176
    8.3.7.3 The procedural irregularity must not have been caused by the fault of the challenging party   8.182

8.4 Waiver of Right to Challenge   8.184
    8.4.1 Implied waiver   8.185
    8.4.2 Exclusion agreements   8.187

8.5 Remission of Arbitral Awards   8.193

8.6 Review of Jurisdictional Awards   8.205
    8.6.1 Introduction   8.205
    8.6.2 Scope of application   8.209
    8.6.3 Scope of the review   8.211
    8.6.4 Application of section 36 of the SAA in practice   8.215

9 Recognition and Enforcement of Arbitral Awards   355

9.1 Enforcement of Swedish Awards   9.02
    9.1.1 Enforcement in Sweden   9.02
    9.1.2 Enforcement abroad   9.06

9.2 Enforcement of Foreign Awards   9.07
    9.2.1 Nationality of award   9.08
    9.2.2 Recognition and enforcement   9.09
    9.2.3 The New York Convention v the Swedish Arbitration Act   9.11
    9.2.4 Separate, partial, and interim awards   9.14
    9.2.5 Grounds for refusing recognition and enforcement   9.17
        9.2.5.1 Lack of capacity of the parties and invalidity of arbitration agreement   9.23
        9.2.5.2 Violation of procedural due process   9.26
        9.2.5.3 Excess of mandate   9.31
        9.2.5.4 Improper composition of the arbitral tribunal or improper arbitral procedure   9.34
        9.2.5.5 Arbitral award not binding   9.38
        9.2.5.6 Non-arbitrability   9.52
        9.2.5.7 Public policy   9.53
    9.2.6 Procedures for recognition   9.64

Appendix 1   The Swedish Arbitration Act   375
Appendix 2A   Arbitration Rules of the Arbitration Institute of the Stockholm Chamber of Commerce (2010)   388
Appendix 2B   Rules for Expedited Arbitrations of the Arbitration Institute of the Stockholm Chamber of Commerce (2010)   402

Contents

Appendix 3   Procedures and Services under the UNCITRAL
              Arbitration Rules   415
Appendix 4   UNCITRAL Model Law on International
              Commercial Arbitration (1985)   417
Appendix 5   UNCITRAL Arbitration Rules (1976)   429
Appendix 6   UNCITRAL Arbitration Rules (2010)   441
Appendix 7   Requests to set Aside Arbitral Awards on the Basis of
              Section 33 and/or Section 34 of the SAA   456
Appendix 8   Review of Arbitral Awards on Jurisdiction   465
Appendix 9   Enforcement of Arbitral Awards   467

Index   469

TABLE OF CASES

References are to chapter and paragraph numbers. Footnotes are indicated by *n* e.g. 8.60*n*

AB Akron-Maskiner v N-GG, NJA 2002 p377 . . . . .8.60*n*
AB Electrolux v G Rejving i Stockholm, NJA 1963 A 23 . . . . .8.134*n*
AB Hans Osterman v Stockholms Automobilhandlarförening and
    AB Autostandard, NJA 1943 p527 . . . . .8.54
AB Skånska Cementgjuteriet v Motoraktiebolaget i Karlstad,
    NJA 1953 p751 . . . . 7.104*n*, 7.106*n*, 8.89*n*, 8.150, 8.180
AJ v Ericsson, NJA 2007 p841 . . . . .4.71
Åkesson v Nordiska ömsesidiga olycksfallsförsäkringsföreningen
    Bore, NJA 1905 p23 . . . . .3.89
Aktiebolaget H v Grästorps kommun, NJA 1961 p658 . . . . .3.19
Aktiebolaget Pergaco v AC Pais Lde, NJA 1992 p823 . . . . 2.134–2.139
Aktiebolaget Sandviken Steel v Peter H, AD 43/1997 . . . . .3.39*n*
Alcatel CITSA v The Titan Corporation, RH 20051 . . . . .6.187*n*
Ali Shipping Corporation v Shipyard Trogir [1998] 1 Lloyd's Rep 643 . . . . .3.164*n*
Alingsås kommun v Luftteknik Mellin & Selling, RH 1982:102 . . . . .3.05*n*
Allianz SpA et al v West Tankers Inc., Case C-185/07 (ECJ) 5.38*n*, 5.41, 5.42
Altinel v Sudoimport, RH 1991:15 . . . . 8.52*n*, 8.186*n*
Archangelskoe Geologodobychnoe Predpriyatie v Archangel Diamond
    Corporation, Case No T 2277-04, 15 November 2005 . . . . 8.215–8.216
Åsbacka Trävaruaktiebolag v E. Hedberg, NJA 1924 p569 . . . . .3.12*n*
Återförsäkringsbolaget Patria v Trygg-Hansa Försäkringsaktiebolag,
    Case No 677-99 . . . . .8.186

Bäckman v Platzer Bygg Aktiebolag, NJA 1976 p706 . . . . 3.39*n*, 3.75*n*
Barmer Ersatzkasse v Försäkringsaktie bolaget Skandia, NJA 1990 p724 . . . . 2.131–2.133
Beckman (Carin) and Åke Beckman v People's Republic of China,
    NJA 1957 p195 . . . . 1.100, 1.101*n*
Björklund et al v Lundqvist, NJA 1955 p500 . . . . 3.14*n*, 3.35*n*
Boliden Chemtrade Services AB v Western Tankers AB, RH 1986:162 . . . . .3.12*n*
Bostadsrättsföreningen x 13 v Kingdom of Belgium (2753–07) 1.114
Bostadsrättsföreningen Korpen v Byggnads AB Åke Sundvall,
    Case No T 1649-04, 16 February 2007 . . . . .8.61*n*
Bostadsrättsföreningen Mossviolen 1 v Folkhem Försäljnings AB,
    NJA 1992 p143 . . . . .3.41*n*
British Petroleum Company (Libya) Ltd v The Government of the
    Libyan Arab Republic, Award 19 October 1973 . . . . 2.38, 3.67
Buckeye Check Cashing Inc v John Cardegna et al, 546 US (2006)
    No 04-1264 . . . . .3.63*n*
Bulgarian Foreign Trade Bank Ltd (Bulbank) v A.I. Trade
    Finance (AIT), NJA 2000 p538 . . . . 2.204–2.205, 3.165–3.167, 3.180
Byggnadsaktiebolaget Holger Preislers v H Palén, NJA 1913 s 191 . . . . .3.139*n*

C (Ingela) v Kommunernas Försäkringsaktiebolag, NJA 1981 p1205 . . . . .8.117
Caparo Group Ltd v Fagor Arrastate Sociedad Cooperative
    (Commercial Court) QBD, 7 August 1998. . . . . .3.153*n*
Case No Ä 7145-04 . . . . 4.84*n*, 4.96*n*
Case No T 10321-06 . . . . .4.84*n*
Case Ö 280–09, 11 March 2009. . . . . .4.134*n*
CD Distribution Sverige Aktiebolag v Niclas H J, AD 165/1987. . . . . .3.39*n*
(The) *Charente*, NJA 1942 p 65 . . . . .1.98, 1.121, 1.139
Chromalloy Aero Services v Arab Republic of Egypt, 939 F Supp 907 . . . . .9.42*n*
Civilekonomernas Riksförbund v Bankinstitutens
    Arbetgivarorganisationen et al., AD 28/1994 . . . . .3.39*n*
CME Czech Republic BV v Czech Republic, 13 September 2001 . . . . .7.121–7.123, 7.125, 7.128,
    8.101, 8.153, 8.154
Commandante Marine Corp v Pan Australia Shipping Corp
    [2006] FCAFC 192 . . . . 3.63*n*, 3.71
Commonwealth of Australia v Cockatoo Dockyard Pty Ltd
    [1995] 26 NSWLR 662 . . . . .3.164*n*
Connection SA Aktiebolag v Exsped Transport Aktiebolag, RH 1990:7. . . . . .3.23*n*
Consafe IT AB v Auto Connect Sweden AB, Case Ö 280–09, 11 March 2009. . . . . .7.37*n*
Creighton v Qatar, Court of Cassation 6 July 2000 (France) 1.127
Czech Republic v CME Czech Republic BV, RH 2003:55. . . . . 7.16, 7.106*n*, 7.120,
                                  8.101–8.104, 8.152, 8.165

D (Dan) v Småföretagarnas Arbetsgivarorganisation, AD 120/1994 . . . . .3.39*n*
Datema v Forenade Cresco Finans, NJA 1992 p733 . . . . .9.44*n*
Decision of the Tribunal Fédéral of 28 April 1992, [1992]
    ASA Bull 368 (Switzerland) 3.101*n*
DHL Express AB v Nordic Logistic Service Oy's bankruptcy estate,
    NJA 2005 Not note 8. . . . . 3.07*n*, 3.08*n*
Dow Chemical France et al v Société Isover-Saint-Gobain (1983) 110JDI 899 . . . . .3.149
Dutco case, Cour de Cassation, Première chamber civile, 7 January 1992 (France). 4.30

E (Lars) v Hem Films Scandinavia Aktiebolag, AD 181/1988 . . . . .3.39*n*
E (Richard) v Monimpex, NJA 1993 C56. . . . . .9.30*n*
ECO Swiss China Time Ltd v Benetton International NV, Case C-126/97
    (1999) ECR I-3055 . . . . 2.75*n*, 3.104–3.110, 8.41
Eisenberg Export Company Ltd et al v The Republic of Kazakhstan,
    SCC cases 38/1997 and 39/1997 . . . . .3.145*n*
Eisenberg Export Company Asia House Ltd v Republic of Kazakhstan, RH 2003:61. . . . . . .3.145*n*
El Nasharty v J Sainsbury plc [2007] EWHC 2618 (Comm). 3.63*n*
Elf Aquitaine Iran (France) v National Iranian Company, Award 14 June 1982 . . . . .3.69*n*
Embassy of the Russian Federation v Compagnie Noga d'importation et d'exportation,
    Case No 2000/14157, Paris Court of Appeal, 1st Chamber, Section A. 1.128
(The) *Emja*, NJA 1997 p866. . . . . .3.21, 3.135–3.136
Esselte AB v Allmänna Pensionsfonden, NJA 1998 p189. . . . . .6.05*n*, 7.104*n*, 7.106*n*, 7.108*n*,
                              7.118*n*, 7.119*n*, 7.125, 8.07*n*, 8.89, 8.150, 8.180
Esso Australia Resources Ltd and others v The Honourable
    Sidney James Plowman and others (1995) 183 CLR 10. . . . . .3.164*n*

F (Stig) v Rohman & Söner Byggnads AB, NJA 1982 p800. . . . . 3.39*n*, 3.75*n*
Fastigheten Preppen v Carlsberg, RH 2009:91 . . . . .8.61*n*

Fiona Trust & Holding Corporation & ors v Yuri Privalov & ors [2006]
  EWHC 2583 (Comm) 3.63
Five Seasons Fritidsaktiebolags Konkursbo (bankruptcy estate) v Five Seasons
  Försäljningsaktiebolag, NJA 1993 s 641 . . . . 3.83*n*, 3.139
Fløjstrup v Madsen, NJA 2008 N32. . . . . .9.19*n*
Forenede Cresco AS v Datema AB, NJA 1992 p733 . . . . 9.47–9.51
Försäkringsaktiebolaget Fylgia and Brand- och livförsäkringesaktiebolaget
  Svea brandförsäkring v AE, NJA 1937 p120 . . . . 8.159, 8.178
Försäkringsaktiebolaget Skandia v Riksgäldskontoret, NJA 1937 p1 . . . . .2.104, 2.119–2.122
Forsman v Inovius, NJA 1973 p480 . . . . .3.35*n*

G (Karl Gustaf) v Nils S, NJA 1984 p215. . . . . .6.85*n*
G (Robert) v Johnny L, NJA 2002 C45. . . . . 9.55–9.63
Göranzon (Carleric) v Skandinaviska Aluminiumprofiler AB,
  NJA 1979 p666 . . . . 3.39*n*, 3.75*n*
Götaverken Arendal AB (Sweden) v General National Maritime
  Transport Company (Libya), NJ 1979 p527 . . . . .9.13, 9.33, 9.36, 9.39–9.46
Government of Kuwait v American Independent Oil Company
  (Aminoil) 21 ILM (1982) 976 . . . . .2.31*n*, 2.39–2.40
Government of the Federative Socialist Soviet Republic of Russia v
  Compagnie NOGA d'Importation et d'Exportation (Switzerland),
  Case No T 925-98-80. . . . . .7.115*n*
Gummesson (Rolf) AB v Securitas Teknik AB, NJA 1998 p829 . . . . .6.110*n*
Gustafson v Länsförsäkringar, Case No T 8090-99 . . . . .8.85*n*

H (Brigitte) v Skandinaviska Färginstitutet AB, NJA 2000 p335 . . . . 8.145, 8.147
H (Conny) v Extraversion Aktiebolag, AD 95/1988 . . . . .3.39*n*
H (David) v Trygg-Hansa AB, NJA 2000 p202 . . . . .3.131*n*
H (Göran) v Fritidsbolaget MCB AB, AD 1976 no 54 . . . . 3.159–3.163
Halotron Inv v Jan A. and AB Bejaro Product, RH 1995:123 . . . . .3.115*n*
Harbour Assurance Co (UK) Ltd v Kansa General International
  Insurance Co Ltd [1993] 1 Lloyds Law Report 455 . . . . 3.61, 3.63
Hermanson v Asfaltsbeläggningar, NJA 1976 p125 . . . . 3.49, 3.64*n*
Hilmarton Case, Cass 1e civ, 10 June 1997 (France) 9.42*n*
Himpurna California Energy v Indonesia, Int'l Art Rep 39 (2000) 5.40*n*

ICC Case No 1110. . . . . 2.94*n*, 3.85*n*
ICC Case No 1703. . . . . .2.127*n*
Icon AB v Göran W and Björn H., RH 1991:16 . . . . 3.35*n*, 3.154*n*
If Skadeförsäkring AB v Securitas AB et al, Case No T 8016-04, 3 November 2005 . . . . 8.71, 8.92*n*
International News Service v The Associated Press, 248 US 215
  (US Supreme Court 1918) 8.45*n*

J (Bengt) v Telia Aktibolag, AD 111/1994. . . . . .3.39*n*
J (Christer) v Svenska Kommunalarbetarförbundet, NJA 1982 p853. . . . . 3.39*n*, 3.41*n*
Jansson v Reprotype AB, NJA 1975 p536 . . . . .7.56*n*, 8.09*n*, 8.136, 8.145, 8.210*n*
Jansson (Gunnar) v the estate of Oscar Jansson, NJA 1965 p384 . . . . . . 8.133, 8.161, 8.172, 8.179
Johansson (Tore) med firma Svenska Maskinagentur v Handelsbolaget
  Maskinfirma Hafo, NJA 1949 p609 . . . . .3.30*n*
Joint Stock Company Acron v Yara International ASA, Case T 7200–08, 7 April 2009 . . . . . .7.24*n*
JSC Aeroflot Russian Airlines v Russo International Venture Inc and MGM
  Productions Group Inc, Case No T 1164-03. . . . . .8.96

KIS France SA v SA Société Générale (France), Cour d'Appel, Paris, 31 October 1989......3.153*n*

Klatzkow Konsult AB v Pevaeche SA, NJA 1989 C22 ....9.30*n*

Kontorscenter Ynglingagatan Aktiebolag v RG Kungshuset Aktiebolag, NJA 1991 p319.....3.31*n*

Köpper v Carlstein, NJA 1930 p692............................2.199*n*

Korsnäs Aktiebolag v AB Fortum Värme, T 156–09, 9 June 2010 .... 4.7222–4.73, 4.84*n*, 8.115*n*

Kronan v Lindroth, NJA 1922 p135............................3.142*n*

Kvarnabo Timber v Cordes GmbH & Co, NJA C 26 ....9.55*n*

L (Christine) och Sven A, NJA 1999 p300 .... 6.54*n*, 6.55

L (Lars) v Acard Sverige AB, NJA 1992 p290 ....3.39*n*

L (Ulla) v Österlen-Hus AB, NJA 1987 p639 ....3.39*n*

Lauder v Czech Republic, 3 September 2001........... 7.121–7.123, 7.125, 7.128, 8.153, 8.154

Lena Goldfields Ltd v Union of Soviet Socialist Republics,
    Cornell Law Quarterly (1950) 42............................2.31*n*

Lenmorniiproekt OAO v Arne Larsson & Partner Leasing AB,
    Supreme Court Case No Ö 13-09, 16 April 2010 .... 6.51, 6.53, 6.63, 9.28

LIAMCO v State of Libya, Svea Court of Appeal 1979 ....1.135–1.139

LIAMCO (Libyan American Oil Company) v Government of the
    Libyan Arab Republic, Award 12 April 1977............................ 2.38, 3.68

Lönnström Oy v Convexa AB, RH 1985:137 ....3.143*n*

Luftteknik Mellin & Selling AB v Allingsås kommun, RH 102:82............................3.04*n*

M (Kurt Wilhelm) v Aktiebolaget Ragnar J, NJA 1965 p94............................7.112

M (Nils) v Södra Skogsägarna Aktiebolag, NJA 1986 p388............................ 3.39*n*, 3.75*n*

Medicinalstyrelsen v Jonson, NJA 1916 p100............................3.142*n*

Megafon case 2.180*n*

Mitsubishi Motors Corp v Soler Chrysler-Plymouth Inc, 473 US 614,
    105 SCt 3346 (1985) 3.100, 3.103*n*, 3.109, 3.110

Mors/Labinal, Cour d'appel de Paris, 19 May 1993............................3.101*n*

Mostaza Claro v Centro Móvil Milenium SL (2006), Case c 168/05 ....3.109*n*, 8.42–8.43

MS 'Emja' Braack Schiffahrts v Wärtsilä Diesel AB, NJA 1997 p866..........3.21, 3.135–3.136

Nagel v the Czech Republic, Case No T 9059-03, 30 May 2005 .... 8.218–8.222

National Housing and Construction Corporation of Uganda v
    Solel Boneh International Ltd, NJA 1989 p143............................8.20, 8.187–8.189

NCC Aktiebolag v Dykab i Luleå Aktiebolag, Case No T 3863-01,
    20 June 2002 .... 8.82*n*, 8.173–8.175, 8.183*n*

NEMU Mitt i Sverige AB v JH et al, NJA 1998 p574 .... 4.107, 4.111*n*

Norrköpings Trikåfabrik v Persson, NJA 1936 p521 .... 3.49, 3.64*n*

Norsa v Baggå AB, NJA 1925 p557 (I and II) 3.83*n*

Norsolor case, 9 *Yearbbok Commercial Arbitration* (1984) 110 & 159 ....2.31*n*

Nykvarnas Skyltaktiebolag v Esselte Dymo AB, NJA 1982 p738................ 3.35*n*, 3.115*n*

Nylund v Sveriges Verkstandsförening and Gylling, ADD No 27............................3.89

O (Kenneth) v Motor Union Assuransfirma AB, NJA 1993 p308 ....6.49*n*

Omnium de Traitement et de Valorisation (OIV) v Hilmarton Ltd,
    Cass 1e civ, 10 June 1997 (France) 9.42*n*

Orsjö Församling v Gustafsson, NJA 1896 p136............................3.142*n*

Östgöta Enskilda Bank v Folksam, RH 1994:103 ....3.143*n*

Pabalk Ticaret Ltd v Norsolor SA, 9 *Yearbook Commercial Arbitration* (1984) 110 & 159.....2.31*n*

Peterson Farms, Inc v C & M Farming Limited [2004] EWHC 121 (Comm) 3.153*n*

Petrobart Limited v the Republic of Kirgizistan, NJA 2008 p406;
  Case No T 3739-03, 13 April 2006 . . . . 3.35*n*, 3.36*n*, 8.223–8.228
Petroleum Development (Trucial Coast) Ltd v The Sheikh of Abu Dhabi,
  International and Comparative Law Quarterly (1952) 247 . . . . .2.31*n*
Petterson (Kjell) v Förvaltningsbolaget Gamlestaden, Ö 4497/94 .3.143*n*
Philips Petroleum Co v the Islamic Republic of Iran, Iran-US Claims Tribunal,
  29 June 1989, 21 Iran-US CTR 79 . . . . .3.69*n*
Premium Nafta Products Ltd v Fili Shipping Company Ltd [2007] UKHL 40. . . . . .3.63*n*
Prima Paint Co v Flood Conklin Manufacturing Corp, 388 US 395 (1967) 3.63*n*
Profura AB v Stig Blomgren, Case T 2863–07, 19 March 2008 . . . . 3.57–3.58

Restaurangprodukter i Tyresö AB v KF/Procordia International AB,
  NJA 1996 s751. . . . . .8.61*n*
REW v Byggfirman Oscarsson & Söderberg, NJA 1931 p647 . . . . .3.83*n*
Rich (Marc) & Co AG v Società Italiana Impianti SpA,
  C-190/89 [1991] ECR 1-3855 . . . . C- 5.31*n*, 8.19*n*
Rizaeff Freres v The Soviet Mercantile Fleet (China) 1.70
Rockwool AB and Gullfiber AB v Byggma Syd AB's bankruptcy estate,
  NJA 1982 p244 . . . . 3.17–3.18
Russian Federation v RosInvestCo UK Ltd, Case No Ö 2301-09,
  12 November 2010. . . . . 5.30, 5.33*n*, 5.35, 8.25

3S Swedish Special Supplier AB v Sky Park AB, NJA 2000 p773 . . . . 4.134*n*, 7.37*n*
S & E Contractors, Inc v United States, 92 S Ct 1411 (US Supreme Court 1972) 8.45
Saab-Scania AB v Edgard B, NJA 1977 p92 . . . . 3.20, 3.28*n*
Sapphire International Petroleum Ltd v National Iranian
  Oil Company, ILR (1967) 136 . . . . 2.31*n*, 2.36
Saudi Arabia v Arabian American Oil co, (Aramco), ILR, Vol 27(1963) 117 . . . . .2.09*n*
SCC Case 108/1997, SIAR 2001, p57 . . . . .2.209*n*, 3.21, 3.149*n*
SCC Case 17/1998, SIAR 1999, Vol 2, p42 . . . . .2.01*n*
SCC Cases 80/1998 and 81/1998, SIAR 2002, Vol 2, p45 . . . . .2.98*n*, 2.115, 2.209*n*
SCC Case 46/1999, SIAR 2001, p73 . . . . .2.209*n*
SCC Case 60/1999. . . . . 4.95*n*, 4.96*n*
SCC Case 10/2000. . . . . .4.96*n*
SCC Case 87/2000. . . . . .4.96*n*
SCC Case 60/2001. . . . . .4.95*n*
SCC Case 096/2001, SIAR 2003, Vol 2, p47 . . . . .2.193*n*
SCC Case 12/2002, SIAR 2004, Vol 1, p93 . . . . .2.209*n*
SCC Case 24/2002, SIAR 2004, Vol 2, p165 . . . . .2.209*n*
SCC Case 172/2003. . . . . .4.96*n*
SCC Case 148/2003. . . . . .4.96*n*
SCC Case 14/2004. . . . . 4.84*n*, 4.96*n*
SCC Case 7/2005, SIAR 2007, Vol 1, p155 . . . . .2.01*n*
SCC Case 10/2005, SIAR 2007, Vol 2, p235 . . . . .2.209*n*
SCC Case V 053/2005. . . . . .4.95*n*
SCC Case V 002/2006. . . . . .4.96*n*
SCC Case V 019/2006. . . . . .4.96*n*
SCC Case V 046/2007. . . . . .4.95*n*
SCC Case V 081/2007. . . . . .4.95*n*
SEE v Yugoslavia. 2.09*n*
Shipping Partnership for M/S Red Sea v Götaverken Sölvesborg AB,
  NJA 1990 p419 . . . . 8.140, 8.183, 8.210*n*

Siemens AG and BKMI Industrieanlagen GmbH v Dutco Consortium Construction
  Co, Cour de Cassation, Première chambre civile, 7 January 1992 (France)............4.30
Société Générale de l'Industrie du Papier Rakta v Parsons and Whittemore
  Overseas Company, Inc, ICC Case No 1703................................2.127*n*
Société Isover-Saint-Gobain v Dow Chemical France et al [1984]
  Rev Arb 98, 100–101......................................3.151*n*
Société Planavergne SA v KB i Stockholm AB, NJA 2003 p379................3.23–3.27, 9.13
Sodemaco SA v Gräsås Trävaru AB, NJA 1986 C89............................9.18*n*
Soyak International Construction & Investment Inc v
  Hochtief AG, NJA 2009 p128......................7.49*n*, 7.50, 8.88, 8.158, 8.164
Soyak v WM et al, NJA 2008 p1118............................4.124
State of Ukraine v Norsk Hydro ASA, Case No T 3108-06, 17 December 2007...........3.29*n*
Stockholm stad v Knut T, AD 104/1997..................................3.39*n*
Sven v Z v ABV Rock Group Kommanditbolag, AD 34/1995......................3.39*n*
Svensk Ekonomibyrå AB v Lena E, AD 135/1995............................3.39*n*
Svenska Kreditförsäkringsaktiebolagets konkursbo (bankruptcy estate) v
  [41 reinsurance companies], NJA 2003 p3.......................... 3.83*n*, 3.139*n*
Svenska Pontohamnar AB v Precon AB, RH 1989:51.........................3.23*n*
Sveriges Pälsdjursuppfödares Riksförbund och AB Nordiska
  Skinnauktioner mot Dansk Pelsdyravlerforening, NJA 1994 C48.................6.174
Swedish Marin Equipment AB v Bo J., RH 1985:90.............................3.154*n*
Swembalt v Republic of Latvia, NJA 2002 C62................................ 9.44, 9.55*n*
Sydkraft v Skandia, NJA 1998 p448.....................................3.30*n*
Systembolaget AB v V & S Vin & Sprit Aktiebolag, Case No
  T 4548-08, 1 December 2009....................6.220*n*, 8.80–8.83, 8.108, 8.175*n*

Taisto L v R E Wahlgren Ingenjörsbyrå Aktiebolag, RH 1989:1.....................3.04*n*
TBB Tekniska Byggnadsbyrån v Kronan, NJA 1973 p740......................8.167, 8.179
Tekno-Pharma AB v State of Iran, NJA 1972 C No 434 ....1.132–1.134, 1.138
Texas Overseas Petroleum Company and California Asiatic Oil
  Company of Libyan Arab Republic.....................................2.38
Titan Corporation v Alcatel CIT S.A., Case No T 1038-05......................8.21–8.22
Tureberg-Sollentuna Lastbilscentral ekonomisk förening v
  Byggnadsfirman Rudolf Asplund AB, NJA 1980 p46........3.05*n*, 3.07*n*, 3.08, 3.29, 3.39
TV3 Broadcasting Group Ltd v Kanal, NJA 2000 p435 ....3.84*n*

U (Ragne) v Kvissberg & Backström Byggnads AB, NJA 1981 p711.............. 3.39*n*, 3.75*n*
Uganda Case, NJA 1989 p143......................................8.20, 8.187–8.189
Ukraine v Norsk Hydro ASA, Case T 3108–06, 17 December 2007 ....3.59
Urhelyi (Rita) v Arbetsmarknadens försäkringsaktiebolag, NJA 1974 p573.............3.41*n*

V 2000, Paris Court of Appeal, 7 December 1994...............................3.16*n*
Västerås Kommun v Republic Iceland, NJA 1999 p821 .... 1.103, 1.112*n*
Venantius AB v Innovativ Informationsteknologi i Sverige Aktiebolag,
  Case No T 7483-02, 21 April 2004 ....8.105*n*
von Hoffman v Trier, Case C-145/96 (ECJ) 16 September 1997 ....4.127

W (Ken) v Luleå Basketklubb, AD 61/1996................................3.39*n*
Wall v Försäkringsaktiebolaget Fylgia, NJA 1918 p478.........................3.89
Walter Ray Neusser Oel und Fett AG v (1) Cross Pacific Trading Ltd (2)
  Orbis Commodities Pty Limited [2005] FCA 955 ....3.63*n*
West Tankers Case, Case C-185/07 (ECJ)............................5.38*n*, 5.41, 5.42

Will-Drill Resources, Inc. v Samson Resources co, 2003, WL 22809197,
   5th cir, 26 November 2003 . . . . .3.56
Wirgin Advokatbyrå handelsbolag v If Skadeförsäkring AB,
   Case No T 4390-04, 12 September 2005 . . . . .8.47

Xcaret Confectionery Sales AB v Concorp Scandinavia AB, case Ö 1634–09 . . . . .3.155n

TABLE OF LEGISLATION

References are to chapter and paragraph numbers. Footnotes are indicated by *n* e.g. 3.172*n*

Swedish legislation

Act on Commercial Agency 1991 . . . . . .2.142
 s 3 . . . . .2.139
Act on Foreign Arbitration
  Agreements and Arbitral
  Awards 1929. . . . . 1.01, 1.08, 6.01, 9.11
Act on Immunities and Privileges
  in Certain Cases 1976. . . . . .1.94*n*
Act on International Sales 1987 . . . . . . .2.110
Act on the Law Applicable to
  International Sales of
  Goods 1964 . . . . .2.105–2.118,
                                 2.127, 2.165
 s 3 . . . . .2.111
 s 4 . . . . .2.111, 2.112,
                                 2.113, 2.114
Arbitration Act 1887 . . . . . . .1.01, 1.05, 1.06
Arbitration Act 1929 . . . . .1.01, 1.07,
                          3.164, 3.175, 6.01, 7.52,
                          8.137*n*, 8.145*n*, 8.177,
                          8.179, 8.210*n*, 8.185
 s 8(2) 3.172*n*
 s 9(1) 3.172*n*
 s 16 . . . . .3.172*n*
 s 18 . . . . .8.136*n*
 s 21 . . . . 8.118, 8.139, 8.171, 8.177*n*
 s 22 . . . . .8.56
Arbitration Act 1999 . . . . . . 1.01, 1.09–1.12,
                          2.07, 2.208, 3.142,
                          3.164, 3.175, 6.01
 full text. . . . . Appendix 1
 s 1 . . . . 3.05, 3.78, 3.102, 4.04
 s 1(1) 3.06, 3.79, 3.86, 3.89
 s 1(2) 3.79, 3.92
 s 1(3) 3.79
 s 2 . . . . .3.46, 3.47*n*, 5.04, 5.14,
                          5.16*n*, 5.19, 5.35
 s 2(1) 3.46*n*, 5.36*n*
 s 2(2) 5.16, 5.20, 7.24*n*, 8.16*n*
 s 3 . . . . 3.44, 5.14
 s 3(1) 3.51, 3.64
 s 4 . . . . 3.77, 3.112
 s 4(2) 3.113*n*
 s 4(3) 6.210*n*

 s 5 . . . . 3.118, 3.120, 4.117, 5.04*n*
 s 5(2) 4.05, 4.09
 s 6 . . . . 3.03*n*, 3.39, 3.76, 3.95
 s 7 . . . . .4.39, 4.40, 8.114
 s 8 . . . . 4.39, 4.40, 4.62, 4.63, 4.64*n*,
                          4.65, 4.71, 8.114, 8.115, 8.116
 s 8(1) 4.66
 s 8(2) 4.66
 s 8(3) 4.67
 s 8(4) 4.68, 4.105
 s 9 . . . . .4.39, 4.40, 4.70
 s 10 . . . . .4.85
 s 10(1) 4.04
 s 10(3) 4.85
 s 11 . . . . 4.85, 4.102
 s 12 . . . . .4.06
 s 12(3) 4.16, 4.33
 s 13 . . . . .4.05, 4.06, 6.191*n*
 ss 14–17 . . . . .4.33
 s 14 . . . . 4.87, 6.41
 s 14(1) 4.05, 4.07
 s 14(2) 4.05, 4.07
 s 14(3) 4.07, 4.09
 s 15 . . . . .3.120*n*, 4.05, 4.87
 s 15(1) 4.10
 s 15(2) 4.10
 s 16 . . . . 3.172, 4.05, 4.87, 4.92
 s 17 . . . . .4.69
 s 18 . . . . .4.09
 ss 19–26 . . . . .6.02
 s 19 . . . . . . 4.07*n*, 6.35*n*, 6.44*n*, 6.45, 6.65
 s 19(2) 6.35, 6.36, 6.37
 s 20 . . . . 6.65, 6.191
 s 21 . . . 4.50*n*, 4.88, 5.36, 6.02, 6.30, 6.31,
                          6.175, 7.52*n*, 8.73, 8.126
 s 22 . . . . 4.48, 6.189
 s 22(2) 8.22
 s 23 . . . . .6.37*n*, 6.65, 8.146
 s 23(2) 6.81, 6.82
 s 24 . . . . .6.32, 6.65, 6.226
 s 24(1) 6.218, 6.226, 8.124
 s 24(3) . . . 3.120*n*, 6.32, 6.225, 6.227, 7.42
 s 25 . . . . 6.112, 6.183
 s 25(1) 6.93, 6.97

Arbitration Act 1999 (*cont.*)
s 25(2) 6.34*n*, 6.103, 8.132
s 25(3) 4.49, 6.126
s 25(4) . . . 3.129, 6.209, 6.215, 6.217, 7.36
s 25(6) 6.101*n*
s 26 . . . . 6.170, 6.172, 6.173, 6.175
s 26(1) 6.126*n*, 6.177, 8.134
ss 27–32. . . . . .7.01
s 27 . . . . .6.65, 6.86, 7.22
s 27(1) 8.205
s 27(2) 7.38, 7.40
s 27(4) 4.46, 7.97, 7.138
s 28 . . . . .6.86
s 29 . . . . 7.27, 7.30
s 30 . . . . 3.172, 7.15
s 30(1) 7.10
s 30(2) 7.10
s 30(3) 6.33
s 31 . . . . .3.172, 4.50*n*, 6.65, 7.44,
7.85*n*, 7.87, 8.47, 8.163
s 31(1) 9.03
s 31(2) 7.88*n*
s 31(3) 7.89
s 32 . . . . 3.176, 4.46, 7.09, 7.86, 7.89,
7.94, 7.97, 7.100, 7.115, 7.137,
7.138, 7.139, 7.140, 7.142, 7.149,
7.150, 7.157, 8.47, 8.60, 8.198
s 32(1) 4.109, 7.146
s 32(3) 7.145
s 33 . . . . . . 3.103, 5.07*n*, 5.08, 5.21, 7.45,
7.88, 7.101, 7.106, 8.02, 8.04,
8.11*n*, 8.18, 8.26, 8.27, 8.29, 8.30,
8.36, 8.40, 8.47, 8.49, 8.50, 8.191,
8.214, Appendix 5
s 33(1) 7.101, 8.30
s 33(2) 7.101, 8.57
s 34 . . . . . . 3.103, 4.41, 4.71*n*, 5.07*n*, 5.09,
5.21, 6.46, 6.73, 7.09, 7.16,
7.24*n*, 7.88, 7.89, 7.94, 7.106,
8.02, 8.04, 8.08, 8.11*n*, 8.18,
8.26, 8.30, 8.48, 8.55, 8.62,
8.63, 8.66, 8.69, 8.77, 8.85, 8.106,
8.109, 8.110, 8.114, 8.120, 8.145,
8.146, 8.190, 8.214, 9.05,
Appendix 5
s 34(1) 5.34, 5.37, 7.08, 8.36, 8.58,
8.118, 8.128, 8.157, 8.158
s 34(2) . . . 3.14*n*, 3.46*n*, 5.09, 5.13, 5.16*n*,
5.37, 6.73, 7.08, 7.56, 8.81, 8.185
s 34(3) 3.128, 8.03
s 34(5) 4.85
s 34(6) 5.37*n*, 8.108
s 35 . . . . . . 3.177, 4.46, 7.99, 7.102, 8.15,
8.48, 8.56*n*, 8.193, 8.196, 8.198,
8.199, 8.201, 8.204

s 36 . . . . 3.57*n*, 5.18, 5.21, 6.86, 7.23,
7.26, 7.88, 8.146, 8.205, 8.206–
8.212, 8.215, 8.217, 8.222, 8.225
s 36(2) 8.213
s 37(1) 4.103, 4.118
s 37(2) 4.103, 4.111, 4.112, 4.114,
4.119, 4.126
s 38 . . . . 4.115, 4.116
s 38(1) 4.116, 4.117
s 38(2) 4.114
s 39 . . . . .4.103
s 39(2) 4.68*n*, 4.104
s 40 . . . . 4.115, 7.89
s 41 . . . . . 4.119, 4.120, 4.124, 6.46, 7.86,
7.88, 7.94, 8.212
s 41(1) 4.122
s 41(2) 4.121
s 42 . . . . 4.105, 6.83*n*
s 43 . . . . 5.21, 7.88, 8.06, 8.20*n*
s 44 . . . . 4.07*n*, 5.21
s 44(2) 6.173
s 44(3) 4.85, 6.174
s 46 . . . . 2.06, 2.11–2.12, 6.190
s 47 . . . . 5.10*n*, 8.58, 8.110, 8.111
s 48 . . . . .2.177, 2.178, 2.202–2.203,
2.209*n*, 8.30*n*, 8.64
s 49 . . . . 3.77, 3.124
s 51 . . . . . . 4.41*n*, 5.14*n*, 8.189–8.192
ss 52–60. . . . . .3.46*n*, 9.01, 9.07
s 52 . . . . .3.128*n*, 9.08, 9.45
ss 53–59. . . . . 9.08–9.09
ss 53–60. . . . . .8.192
s 53 . . . . .9.09
s 54–60 . . . . .9.09
s 54 . . . . 7.107, 9.07, 9.09, 9.12, 9.17,
9.19, 9.22–9.24, 9.26–9.28, 9.31,
9.32, 9.34, 9.35, 9.38, 9.42
s 54(1)(2) 6.51
s 55 . . . 7.107, 9.07, 9.09, 9.17, 9.18, 9.19,
9.35, 9.52, 9.53
s 56 . . . . .9.64
s 57 . . . . .9.64
s 58 . . . . .9.64
s 58(2) 9.44
s 59 . . . . 3.128*n*, 9.66

Code of Judicial Procedure *see* Procedural Code
Competition Act
Chapter 2, s 6. . . . . .3.102*n*
Chapter 3, S 25. . . . . .3.102*n*
Contracts Act
Chapter 3. .3.82
s 6(1) 3.28*n*
s 4(2) 3.28*n*
s 6(2) 3.28, 3.29

s 9 . . . . .3.28*n*
s 36 . . . . 3.01, 3.37–3.38, 3.40–3.41,
3.75, 7.04

Enforcement Code
Chapter 3, s 15 . . . . .9.03
Chapter 3, s 16 . . . . .9.04
Chapter 3, s 18(2) 9.04
Chapter 16, ss 11–16 . . . . .6.210*n*
Chapter 18, s 2 . . . . .9.03*n*
Enforcement Code 1734 . . . . .1.04
Enforcement Statute 1669 . . . . .1.03

Foreign Arbitration Act
Art 7, para 1 . . . . .9.40*n*
s 9, para 2 . . . . 9.45

Interest Act
ss 3, 4, 6, 9 .7.73*n*

Labour Dispute Act 1974
s 1(3) 3.96, 3.97*n*

Procedural Code 1948 . . . . .1.18, 4.17,
6.04–6.05, 6.08–6.09,
6.16, 6.20–6.22, 6.114,
6.122, 8.117
Chapter 10 . . . . .5.25
Chapter 10, s 1 . . . . .5.26*n*
Chapter 10, s 3 . . . . .5.27*n*
Chapter 10, s 4 . . . . .5.27*n*
Chapter 10, s 8 . . . . .5.27*n*
Chapter 10, s 18 . . . . .5.28
Chapter 13, s 2 . . . . 3.87*n*, 5.34, 5.35
Chapter 13, s 3 . . . . .7.111
Chapter 14 . . . . .4.14*n*
Chapter 15, s 3 . . . . 6.210*n*, 7.36*n*
Chapter 15, s 3(2) 7.36*n*
Chapter 15, s 7 . . . . .6.210*n*
Chapter 17 . . . . .6.17
Chapter 17, s 11 . . . . .7.113
Chapter 18 . . . . .7.78*n*
Chapter 18, s 6 . . . . .7.80*n*
Chapter 32, s 8 . . . . .3.116
Chapter 34, s 2 . . . . .3.113*n*
Chapter 35, s 2 . . . . .7.07*n*
Chapter 36, ss 5–6 . . . . .6.117*n*
Chapter 36, s 17(1) 6.135*n*
Chapter 36, s 17(2) 6.139*n*
Chapter 36, s 17(5) 6.135*n*, 6.139*n*
Chapter 38, s 2 . . . . .6.110, 6.112*n*,
6.117*n*
Chapter 42, s 2 . . . . .6.75*n*
Chapter 43, s 14 . . . . .6.88*n*
Chapter 58, s 1 . . . . .8.17*n*

Rules of the Arbitration Institute of the
Stockholm Chamber of
Commerce *see* SCC Rules

Sale of Goods Act
s 3 . . . . .3.23
SCC Rules 2.42, 2.154, 2.177, 3.127,
4.17, 4.18–4.35, 4.92, 4.102,
6.01, 8.68
full text . . . . Appendix 2
Art 2 . . . . 6.42, 6.65*n*
Art 3 . . . . .6.43
Art 4(1) 4.27
Art 4(4) 4.27
Art 5 . . . . 6.43, 6.65*n*
Art 8 . . . . .6.61
Art 8(2) 6.62
Art 8(3) 6.63
Art 9 . . . . 2.209, 4.134
Art 9(3) 4.27
Art 9(4)(i)–(iii) 4.27
Art 10 . . . . .4.134
Art 10(1) 5.43, 5.45
Art 11 . . . . .3.190*n*, 4.29, 4.34
Art 12 . . . . 4.18, 4.23
Art 13 . . . . .6.65*n*
Art 13(2) 4.18
Art 13(3) 6.191*n*
Art 13(4) 3.190*n*, 4.28, 4.30, 4.38*n*
Art 13(5) 4.18
Art 14 . . . . .4.91
Art 14(1) 4.62*n*
Art 14(3) 4.91
Art 15 . . . . .6.235
Art 15(1) 4.29*n*
Art 15(2) 4.93
Art 15(3) 4.93
Art 15(4) 4.93
Art 16(1) 4.98
Art 17(1) 4.99
Art 17(2) 4.99
Art 18 . . . . .6.234
Art 19(1) 6.30*n*
Art 19(2) 5.36*n*, 6.31*n*, 6.32*n*
Art 20 . . . . .2.209
Art 20(1), (2) 6.186
Art 20(3) 6.187
Art 22(1) 2.20*n*, 2.29
Art 22(1) 2.99
Art 22(2) 2.43
Art 24 . . . . .2.194
Art 24(1) 2.152, 6.65*n*
Art 24(2) 6.65*n*, 6.81*n*
Art 24(3) 6.65*n*
Art 25 . . . . 6.81*n*, 6.82*n*

SCC Rules (*cont.*)
Art 26. . . . . 6.181, 6.182
Art 26(1) 6.34*n*
Art 26(2) 6.182
Art 26(3) 6.112*n*
Art 27(1) 6.65*n*, 6.218*n*
Art 28. . . . . .6.181
Art 28(1) 6.182
Art 29. . . . . 6.181, 6.183
Art 29(1) 6.183
Art 30. . . . . .6.32*n*
Art 30(3) 6.165
Art 32. . . . . . . 6.217*n*, 6.234, 7.36*n*, 7.153
Art 34. . . . . 6.81*n*, 6.88*n*
Art 35(2) 6.191*n*
Art 36(1) 6.65*n*, 7.49*n*, 7.50*n*, 8.164*n*
Art 36(3) 7.10*n*
Art 36(4) 6.60*n*
Art 37. . . . . 3.175*n*, 5.36, 7.52*n*, 7.53
Art 41. . . . . .7.99*n*, 7.152, 7.153
Art 41(1) 7.153
Art 41(2) 7.154
Art 42. . . . . . . 7.100*n*, 7.152, 7.155, 7.157
Art 43. . . . . 4.130*n*, 4.134, 4.136,
7.78*n*, 7.79*n*, 7.81*n*
Art 43(3) 4.135
Art 44. . . . . .7.78*n*, 7.79*n*, 7.81*n*
Art 45. . . . . .4.134
Art 45(4) 4.134, 7.37, 9.15
Art 46. . . . . .3.166*n*
Art 48. . . . . .4.60
App II. 6.43*n*
App III, Art 3 . . . . .4.131

Statute Book 1734 . . . . 1.04, 1.18
Swedish Arbitration Act (SAA)
see Arbitration Act 1999

Trade Secrets Act 1990 . . . . .3.84

VAT Act
Chapter 1, s 2. . . . . .4.129*n*
Chapter 5, s 5. . . . . 4.128*n*, 4.129*n*

Other jurisdictions

China
Civil Procedural Code 1991
Art 5. . . . . .1.70*n*
Law on Judicial Immunity from
Measures of Constraint for the
Property of Foreign
Banks 2005 . . . . .1.69
Law on the Territorial Sea and
the Continuous Zone 1992. . . . . . . .1.68

England
Arbitration Act 1996
s 7 . . . . .3.47*n*
State Immunity Act 1978 . . . . 1.57, 1.101
s 3(3) 1.55*n*
Foreign Limitation Period
Act 1984 . . . . .2.199*n*

France
Arbitration Rules of the French
Arbitration Association
Art 13. . . . . .6.236*n*
Nouveau Code de procedure civile
Art 1502(2) 4.31*n*

Italy
Rules for International Arbitration 1994
of the Italian Association
for Arbitration
Arts 2, 8 . . . . .6.236*n*

Russian Federation
Arbitration Rules 1995 of the
International Commercial
Arbitration Court at the Chamber
of Commerce and Industry of
the Russian Federation 6.236*n*
Civil Procedural Code
Art 124(1) .1.62
Art 127. . . . . .1.62
Art 401. . . . . .1.61
Code of Arbitrazh Procedure of
5 May 1995 . . . . .1.62
Art 251(1) .1.61

Switzerland
Federal Law on International Private Law
Art 103. . . . . .2.194
Rules of International Arbitration
Art 26. . . . . .6.236*n*

United States
Foreign Sovereign Immunities Act 1976 . 1.57,
1.101, 1.140
s 1603(d) 1.55*n*

Roman law

Codex Iustinianus 2:55. . . . . .1.02
Digesta 4:8. . . . . .1.02
Novellae 87:11 . . . . .1.02

International legislation and agreements

AAA/ICDR Arbitration Rules
Art 37. . . . . .6.235

Agreement on Cultural Co-operation
between Denmark, Finland,
Iceland, Norway and Sweden
(1971) 1.105, 1.106, 1.109, 1.110
Agreement on Nordic Common
Education at the Upper
Secondary School Level
(1992) 1.105, 1.106, 1.109

Brussels I Regulation (Council
Regulation (EC) No 44/2001 of
22 December 2000 on Jurisdiction
and the Recognition and
Enforcement of Judgments in
Civil and Commercial
Matters) 5.22n, 5.29, 5.41, 8.19
Art 1.2(d). 5.31, 5.32, 5.33, 8.19n
Art 2.1 . . . . .5.30
Chapter I, Art 2(1) 5.29n
Chapter II, Arts 2–7 . . . . .5.30
Chapter III, Art 31 . . . . 5.41ni
Brussels Convention (1968) 5.22n, 5.41,
8.19n
Brussels Convention on State-Owned
Vessels (1929). 1.94

EC Treaty
Art 81 (ex Art 85) 3.107, 3.108, 3.109
Art 101. . . . . .8.41n
EU VAT Directive (Council
Directive 2008/8/EG) 4.128
European Convention on
International Commercial
Arbitration 1961
Art VII 2.20
European Convention on State
Immunity (1972) and
Additional Protocol 1.101

Geneva Convention 1927. . . . . .1.08
Geneva Convention for resolving
conflicts of laws regarding
bills of exchange (1930) 2.185
Geneva Convention for resolving
conflicts of laws regarding
cheques (1931). 2.185
Geneva Protocol 1923 . . . . .1.08
Art 2. . . . . .2.05

Hague Convention on the Law
Applicable to International
Sales of Goods
(15 June 1955) 2.105, 2.108,
2.109, 2.165

IBA Rules on the Taking of Evidence
in International Commercial
Arbitration 6.96, 6.107
Art 3(3) 6.115
Art 4(3) 6.124, 6.135n
Arts 5, 6 . . . . .6.157
Art 9(2) 6.107
Art 9(5) 6.164
ICC Rules (1955). . .3.127, 4.18n, 4.30, 4.32,
4.38, 4.61, 6.236, 8.188, 9.39, 9.41
Art 6(4) 3.47n
Art 7(1) 4.62n
Art 7(2) 4.80n, 4.91n
Art 8(1) 4.38
Art 8(4) 4.38
Art 9(5) 4.38
Art 10. . . . . .4.17n
Art 10(1) 4.38
Art 10(2) 4.32n, 4.38
Art 11(1) 4.101
Art 11(3) 4.101
Art 21. . . . . .9.36
Art 23(1) 7.37n
Art 24. . . . . .1.127
Art 24(1) 7.52n
Art 25(2) 7.133
Art 28(6) 7.133
Art 29. . . . . 7.152n, 8.187
Art 30. . . . . .4.137
Art 31. . . . . .4.137
Art 31(3) 7.79n
App I, Art 6 . . . . .3.166n
App II, Art 1. . . . . .3.166n
ICSID Rules
Chapter VI, Rule 46 . . . . .7.52n
International Convention on Civil
Liability for Oil Pollution
Damage 1969. . . . . .1.68
International Law Association Draft
Convention
Art IC. 1.55n
International Law Commission
Draft Articles on State Immunity
Art 2(1)(g) .1.55n

LCIA Rules. 4.61, 7.52n
Art 5.2 . . . . .4.62n
Art 5.3 . . . . .4.91n
Art 8. . . . . .4.17n
Art 23.1 . . . . .3.47n
Art 27. . . . . .7.152n
Art 28. . . . . .7.79n
Art 28.4 . . . . .7.80n
Art 30. . . . . .3.166n

Lugano Convention (1988) 5.22*n*,
            5.29, 5.41, 8.19
    Chapter 2, Art 2 . . . . .5.29*n*

New York Convention on the Recognition
    and Enforcement of Foreign Arbitral
    Awards (1958) 3.05, 3.09, 6.30,
        6.226, 7.37, 9.06, 9.07–9.13, 9.19,
            9.20, 9.27, 9.29, 9.39
    Art II 3.05*n*, 3.10, 3.13, 9.25
    Art II(1) 3.09
    Art II(2) 3.10*n*
    Art IV 9.64
    Art V 3.46*n*, 8.192, 9.11, 9.12
    Art V(1) 9.12, 9.17
    Art V(1)(a) 3.13, 9.24, 9.25
    Art V(1)(b) .6.51*n*
    Art V(1)(c) 9.31
    Art V(1)(d) 9.34, 9.35
    Art V(1)(e) 9.38, 9.40*n*
    Art V(2) 2.82, 9.17
    Art V(2)(a) 8.30*n*, 8.31
    Art V(2)(a) 9.52
    Art V(2)(b) 9.53
    Art VI 9.44
    Art VI(1)(a) .9.25
    Art VI(1)(b) .9.26
    Art VII(1) 3.10*n*, 9.21

Rome I Regulation (Regulation (EC)
    No 593/2008) 2.18, 2.104, 2.105,
            2.144, 2.163–2.172, 2.209
    Art 3 . . . . .2.167
    Art 4 . . . . 2.168–2.170
    Art 7 . . . . .2.172
    Art 9 . . . . .2.172
    Art 25 . . . . .2.165
Rome II Regulation (Regulation (EC)
No 864/2007 on the Law Applicable
    to Non-Contractual
    Obligations) 2.186–2.191
    Art 4(1) 2.187
Rome Convention on the Law Applicable
    to Contractual Obligations
    (1980) 2.18, 2.104, 2.105,
        2.129–2.131, 2.138, 2,143–2.164,
            2.166, 2.209
    Art 1(2) 2.145
    Art 3 . . . . 2.44*n*, 2.75*n*
    Art 3(1) 2.17, 2.46, 2.47*n*, 2.146
    Art 3(3) 2.147
    Art 3(4) 2.48*n*, 2.148
    Art 4 . . . . .2.149, 2.156, 2.157
    Art 4(1) 2.149
    Art 4(2) 2.128, 2.150, 2.156

Art 4(5) 2.130*n*
Art 7 . . . . .2.158
Art 7(1) 2.72*n*, 2.83
Art 9(1) 2.160
Art 9(2) 2.160
Art 14 . . . . .6.168
Art 15 . . . . .2.162
Art 16 . . . . .2.161

Statute of the International Court
    of Justice
    Art 38.1(c) 2.32

Treaty of Lisbon 3.107*n*

UN Convention on Contracts for the
    International Sale of Goods
    (1980) 2.194, 2.195
UN Convention on Jurisdictional
    Immunities of States and Their
    Property 1.57, 1.74, 1.75–1.93,
            1.95, 1.117, 1.119, 1.130
    Art 1 . . . . 1.77*n*, 1.85*n*
    Art 2(1)(c) 1.83
    Art 3 . . . . .1.77*n*
    Art 5 . . . . .1.78*n*
    Art 7 . . . . .1.81
    Art 8 . . . . .1.81
    Art 9 . . . . .1.81*n*
    Art 10 . . . . 1.82–1.83
    Art 10(3) .1.84
    Art 17 . . . . 1.86–1.87
    Arts 18, 19 . . . . .1.88–1.89, 1.140*n*
    Art 18(c) 1.90*n*, 1,91*n*
    Art 20 . . . . .1.89*n*
    Art 28 . . . . .1.76*n*
    Art 30(1) .1.76*n*
UN Convention on the Law of the
    Sea 1982 .1.68
UNCITRAL Arbitration Rules
    (1976) 1.13, 1.47, 3.127, 3.184, 3.185,
            4.10, 4.18*n*, 4.36–4.37, 6.101*n*
    full text . . . . .Appendix 3,
                        Appendix 4
    Art 5 . . . . .4.36
    Arts 6–8 . . . . .4.36
    Arts 9–12 . . . . .4.100
    Art 13 . . . . .4.36
    Art 14 . . . . .4.36
    Art 20 . . . . .6.82*n*
    Art 21(2) .3.47*n*
    Art 24 . . . . .6.168
    Art 35 . . . . .7.152*n*
    Art 36 . . . . .7.152*n*
    Arts 38–41 .4.137

UNCITRAL Model Law on
International Commercial
Arbitration 1.11, 1.12, 2.08, 4.65, 6.01,
8.04, 8.215, 9.01
   Art 7 . . . . 3.10, 3.11
   Art 7(5) 3.15
   Art 12 . . . . .4.64*n*
   Art 12(2) 4.80*n*, 8.116
   Art 15 . . . . 4.87*n*, 4.99*n*
   Art 16(1) 3.47*n*
   Art 16(3) 3.47*n*
   Art 17 . . . . 6.213*n*, 6.215
   Art 18 . . . . .6.32*n*
   Art 23(2) 6.82*n*
   Art 28(1) 2.20, 2.29
   Art 28(2) 2.99
   Art 31 . . . . .7.52*n*
   Art 31(2) 7.49*n*
   Art 34 . . . . 3.46*n*, 8.15*n*
   Art 34(2) 8.12
   Art 34(2)(b) .8.04
   Art 34(4) 8.196
   Art 36 . . . . .3.46*n*

UNIDROIT Principles of
International Commercial
Contracts 1994 . . . . 2.31*n*, 2.152
   Art 1.9(1) 3.23*n*
   Art 2.1.1 . . . . .3.16*n*
   Art 2.1.11 . . . . 3.15*n*, 3.28*n*
   Art 5.2.1 . . . . .3.157*n*
US-USSR Optional Clause
   Agreement (1977) 1.13–1.16

Vienna Convention on Diplomatic
   Immunity (1961) 1.94, 1.120
Vienna Convention on Diplomatic
   Immunity (1963) 1.94
Vienna Convention on the
   International Sale of Goods
   (1980) 2.110, 2.155

Washington Convention on the
   Settlement of Investment
   Disputes between States and
   Nationals of other States (1965)
   Art 25 . . . . .3.69

1

INTRODUCTION

1.1 History of Arbitration in Sweden   1.01

1.2 The Swedish Legal System   1.18

    1.2.1 General   1.18

    1.2.2 The courts and the judiciary   1.21

      1.2.2.1 The courts   1.21

      1.2.2.2 The judiciary   1.29

    1.2.3 The legal profession   1.35

1.3 The Arbitration Institute of the Stockholm Chamber of Commerce   1.46

1.4 Sovereign Immunity and International Commercial Arbitration in Sweden   1.52

    1.4.1 Sovereign immunity in general   1.52

      1.4.1.1 Introduction   1.52

    1.4.2 National legislation   1.57

    1.4.3 The UN Convention   1.75

      1.4.3.1 Immunity from jurisdiction   1.80

      1.4.3.2 Arbitration   1.85

    1.4.4 Sovereign immunity and Swedish law   1.94

1.5 Sovereign Immunity and Arbitration   1.122

    1.5.1 General observations   1.122

    1.5.2 Sovereign immunity and arbitration under Swedish law   1.131

1.1 History of Arbitration in Sweden

1.01 On 1 April 1999 the new Swedish Arbitration Act (SAA) entered into force. It replaced the 1929 Arbitration Act and the 1929 Act on Foreign Arbitration Agreements and Arbitral Awards.

1.02 Arbitration is an ancient phenomenon. It has existed as long as mankind. References to arbitration can be found in Roman law and in ancient Greek law— and even before. In Roman law, for example, where agreement to submit a dispute to arbitration was called a *compromissum*, provisions on arbitration may be found in Digesta 4:8, Codex Iustinianus 2:55 and Novellae 87:11.

1.03 Commercial arbitration also has a long tradition in Sweden. It was not until 1887, however, that the first comprehensive Arbitration Act was adopted. It is believed that the first time that arbitration is referred to in a statutory text is in the Visby city law from the 14th century.[1] The Visby city law had a statute dealing with disputes

---

[1] Visby was at that time a member of the Hanseatic League and as such played an important role for Hanseatic trade in the Baltic Sea area.

submitted by the parties to so-called entrusted persons.[2] Arbitration provisions are also to be found in the 1669 Enforcement Statute.[3]

1.04 In 1734 the first major Statute Book—ie a compilation of the most important statutes—was published in Sweden. In the Enforcement Code of the 1734 Statute Book there is a provision dealing with arbitration to the effect that if parties had referred a dispute to entrusted persons, and agreed to abide by their decision, such decision was enforceable. No other provisions on arbitration were, however, included in the 1734 Statute Book.

1.05 In 1826 a committee presented a proposal for general civil law legislation in Sweden. The proposal included a procedural code, one chapter of which was devoted to 'arbitration'. This proposal was the first step of many in the preparation of the first Swedish Arbitration Act: the 1887 Arbitration Act. It is noteworthy that two fundamental features of modern arbitration were codified already in the first Arbitration Act. First, it was laid down that a valid arbitration agreement is a bar to court proceedings. Second, the arbitral award was final and binding, unless the parties had made reservations in this respect.

1.06 In 1918 voices were raised for a thorough review of the 1887 Arbitration Act. It was said that it did not live up to expectations. In particular it was said that the provisions of the Act did not sufficiently prevent parties from obstructing the proceedings. This criticism led to a partial amendment of the 1887 Act in 1919.

1.07 In 1927 a legislative committee was once again charged with the task of reviewing the 1887 Act. This eventually resulted in the 1929 Arbitration Act, which, although a new legislative act, built on the same principles as the 1887 Act.

1.08 During the 1920s, the League of Nations adopted two international instruments of great importance for international arbitration, viz, the Geneva Protocol of 1923 and the Geneva Convention of 1927. As a result of Sweden's accession to these two instruments, the Swedish legislator adopted the 1929 Act on Foreign Arbitration Agreements and Arbitral Awards.

1.09 Even though there were minor changes in the 1929 Acts over the years, it was not until 1999 that Swedish arbitration legislation was thoroughly revised, resulting in the SAA.

1.10 Given the increase in the number of arbitrations in Sweden—both domestic and international—since the 1970s, it was felt that the time had come to revise Swedish arbitration legislation. Another reason prompting a revision was the fact that during the last few decades Sweden had become the selected place of arbitration for a significantly increasing number of international arbitrations in which both, or all,

---

[2] SOU 1994: 81, p 55.
[3] Ibid.

parties were non-Swedish. The legitimate expectations and requirements of such users ought to be met by creating an efficient, up-to-date and easily comprehensible legislative framework for the resolution of disputes. At the suggestion of the Arbitration Institute of the Stockholm Chamber of Commerce,[4] in 1992 the Swedish Government issued instructions for the preparation of a new Arbitration Act, and, pursuant to legislative tradition in Sweden, appointed a committee of experts to prepare a draft Act.[5]

The report of the committee, including a draft Arbitration Act was presented in **1.11** June 1994.[6] In drafting the report, the committee took three decisions on principles which were implemented throughout its work, viz:

1. The Act should essentially be an adaptation and improvement of the present Act to arbitral practice and case law. It should, like the present Act, apply equally to domestic and international arbitrations.
2. As a consequence of the first decision, the Committee decided that the UNICITRAL Model Law should not be used as a blueprint for drafting the Act. This notwithstanding, the utmost attention was given to each provision of the Model Law, and it will be seen that in substance there are few major or essential differences between the Act and the Model Law.
3. The Act should be easily accessible and comprehensible to foreign users which have widely divergent legal and professional traditions. Hence the statutory text should be brief and written in simple language. Moreover, the Act should to the extent possible be self-contained and comprehensive in the sense that it should include a minimum number of references to other Swedish legislation. In particular, a clear demarcation ought to be made between the Act and the Procedural Code which applies in litigations before Swedish courts; the currently prevailing uncertainty as to the possibly analogous application of certain provisions of the Procedural Code therefore has been removed by the addition of new provisions in the Act.[7]

In accordance with Swedish legislative practice, the Ministry of Justice referred the report for comments to a number of Swedish Government bodies, courts, universities, and interest groups. Based on such comments and the expert report, the Ministry of Justice prepared a so-called Government Bill which was introduced to Parliament in 1998.[8] The Arbitration Act was adopted by Parliament on 4 March 1999 and entered into force on 1 April 1999.

The 1999 Act replaces both the 1929 Acts, but builds on the same basic principles, **1.12** due account taken of subsequent developments—domestic as well as international—in

---

[4] For a discussion of the Arbitration Institute and its role for arbitration in Sweden see para 1.46.
[5] The Committee was chaired by Bo Broomé, Appeals Court President; the experts were Ulf Franke, Lars Heuman, Kaj Hobér, Göran Ramberg, Hans-Gunnar Solerud, and J Gillis Wetter.
[6] The Swedish abbreviation of such a report is 'SOU'; the reports always have a year and a number. The report of the expert committee is known as 'SOU 1994:81'.
[7] Wetter, *The Draft New Swedish Arbitration Act. A Presentation* (1984) 7–8
[8] Govt Bill 1998/99:35.

arbitration legislation and arbitral practice. While not formally adopting the UNCITRAL Model Law on International Commercial Arbitration, the Model Law has served as an important source of inspiration for the 1999 Act. In fact there are no provisions in the Act which deviate from, let alone contradict, the approach taken by the Model Law. It should be noted, however, that the 1999 Act applies equally to domestic and international arbitrations.

1.13   As mentioned above, commercial arbitration has a long tradition in Sweden. This notwithstanding, it was not until the late 1970s that the number of cases started to grow significantly. An important factor in this development was the conclusion of the 1977 US-USSR Optional Clause Agreement between the American Arbitration Association and the USSR Chamber of Commerce and Industry. The agreement designated Sweden as the place of arbitration for disputes between parties from the two countries.[9] Under this agreement the arbitration was to be conducted under the 1976 UNCITRAL Arbitration Rules by an arbitral tribunal consisting of three arbitrators. The agreement introduced a so-called list procedure for the appointment of the third and presiding arbitrator when the two party-appointed arbitrators could not agree thereon. In an appendix to the agreement the parties had agreed on a joint panel of arbitrators which was to be reviewed annually by the American Arbitration Association and the USSR Chamber of Commerce and Industry.

1.14   The abbreviated form[10] of the clause reads:

> Any dispute, controversy or claim arising out of or relating to this contract, or the breach, termination or invalidity thereof, shall be settled by arbitration in accordance with the 'Optional Arbitration Clause for use in contracts in USA-USSR Trade 1997' (prepared by American Arbitration Association and USSR Chamber of Commerce and Industry).

1.15   The Optional Clause Agreement confirmed Sweden's, and Stockholm's, role as a leading forum for the settlement of disputes between East and West. Following the disintegration of the USSR, the agreement was renewed and signed by the Russian Chamber of Commerce and Industry.

1.16   In preparation for the negotiations of the Optional Clause Agreement, a group of Swedish lawyers prepared a comprehensive study of Swedish arbitration law which was subsequently published as the first edition of *Arbitration in Sweden* in 1977. A second edition was published in 1984.

1.17   Shortly after the Optional Clause Agreement was concluded, China International Economic and Trade Arbitration Commission (CIETAC) expressed an interest in

---

[9] For an analysis of the agreement, see Lebedev, 'The 1977 Optional Clause For Soviet-American Contracts', 27 *American Journal of Comparative Law* (1979) 469–478.

[10] The full text of the US-USSR Optional Clause Agreement is reproduced as Appendix 5 in *Arbitration in Sweden* (2nd edn, 1984).

learning more about arbitrating in Sweden. These contacts have developed and deepened over the years, as a result of which a significant number of China-related arbitrations are now conducted in Sweden.[11]

1.2 The Swedish Legal System[12]

1.2.1 General

Sweden is a civil law jurisdiction, although as far as procedural law is concerned the **1.18** Swedish legal system shares many traits with common law. Statutes are the most important source of law. Important parts of the statutes have been brought together in the so-called Statute Book. It is divided into codes, or books, each covering a specific area of Swedish law, eg land law, criminal law, procedural law etc. Although the Statute Book officially bears the year of 1734, it consists almost exclusively of recent legislation. The Procedural Code, for example, was adopted in 1948, but has of course been modernized and otherwise amended.

If no statute gives a clear answer to a specific question, reported judicial decisions, **1.19** the *travaux préparatoires* of the statute, and scholarly writings are important secondary sources of law.[13] It is worthwhile noting that there is no *stare decisis* doctrine under Swedish law. Consequently, decisions of higher courts are not binding in the formal sense on lower courts. Needless to say, however, in practice the judgments and decisions rendered by the Supreme Court are followed by lower courts.

Traditionally, the *travaux préparatoires,* particularly the Government Bill, have **1.20** played an important role in interpreting and trying to understand statutes, even though the *travaux préparatoires* are not binding. As a consequence of Sweden's membership of the European Union this is now gradually changing, since more and more of Swedish legislation is based on directives and regulations from the European Union.

1.2.2 The courts and the judiciary

1.2.2.1 The courts

Sweden has three levels of general courts; Courts of First Instance or District Courts, **1.21** Courts of Appeal, of which there are six in number, and the Supreme Court. Generally speaking, these courts adjudicate cases which have not expressly been

---

[11] Cf Moser, Ulf Franke, 'Stockholm Arbitration and the Bridge to China', in Hobér-Magnusson-Öhrström (eds), *Between East and West, Essays in Honor of Ulf Franke* (2010) 343.
[12] Section 1.2 draws on the chapter on Sweden, prepared by the author, in *Encyclopedia of International Commercial Litigation* (2008).
[13] The *travaux préparatoires* consist of the Committee Report ('SOU'), which precedes most major legislative acts, as well as the Government Bill; see notes 6 and 8.

excluded from their jurisdiction. The jurisdiction of the special courts is limited to matters enumerated in the relevant empowering statute.

1.22   The District Courts have jurisdiction over civil and criminal matters regardless of the circumstances of the case or the character of the crime. The District Courts vary greatly in size. The smallest have only a few legally trained judges, whereas the largest, the Stockholm District Court, is served by a large number of judges. The smallest courts naturally have limited experience in large civil cases, since most commercial disputes are handled by the courts in the areas where the large companies are located.

1.23   The most important decisions by the Supreme Court appear in a publication called Nytt Juridiskt Arkiv cited as NJA. Swedish cases are generally not cited by reference to the names of the parties but only to the publication where the case is reported, the year of publication and the page, for example, NJA 1952 p 8. In this book, however, citations include also the names of the parties, for example *A v B* (NJA 1952 p 8). Other decisions by the Supreme Court, which are not given a full report, but a shorter one, a so-called note, are cited by reference to the year, number, and letter, for example NJA 1954 C 733.

1.24   There is also a similar reporting system with respect to decisions by the Courts of Appeal. Again, reports are published of the more important Court of Appeal decisions. Citations are to the publication—the Swedish abbreviation of which is RH—year and number, for example, RH 1985:15. In this book reference will be made to the names of the parties also with respect to these cases. Occasionally reference is made also to cases which are not reported. The citation is then to the docket number, for example T4567/97, where 'T' indicates that it is a civil case, then the number of the case, '4567' and the year, '97', ie 1997, when it was filed with the court in question. Since none of the case reports is available in English, court decisions are sometimes reported extensively in this book.

1.25   Courts whose jurisdiction is specifically restricted to certain categories of disputes are referred to as special courts. Such special courts include the Labour Court, the Market Court, and the administrative courts.

1.26   The Labour Court exercises jurisdiction in disputes involving the application and interpretation of labour law, including disputes regarding termination of employment contracts and related issues. The Market Court has exclusive jurisdiction over disputes concerning marketing law and is the court of last resort in respect of certain competition law matters.

1.27   Certain special courts constitute an integral part of the District Courts, such as land courts dealing with disputes concerning real estate, expropriations, and the like, and Environmental Courts. There are also certain special courts which constitute integral parts of the Courts of Appeal, such as the Environmental Court of Appeal.

There are also three levels of administrative courts; Administrative County Courts, **1.28** Administrative Courts of Appeal, of which there are four in number, and the Supreme Administrative Court. These courts have jurisdiction over administrative matters mainly between private parties and public authorities. The administrative courts handle all tax disputes.

1.2.2.2 The judiciary

Even though the pattern is gradually changing, a permanent judge is generally **1.29** recruited from a position as associate judge and seldom from other branches of the legal profession. Judges are not appointed on political merits. A permanent judge is appointed by the Government and is, under the Constitution, irremovable, except for reasons of serious criminal acts or retirement.

About one-third of the graduates from law school spend two years as law clerks and **1.30** junior judges in courts of first instance. This is considered a very good training for a legal career, whether within the court system or in private practice.

If a junior judge continues his or her career within the courts, he or she will serve as **1.31** assistant and deputy judge in District Courts and appellate courts for about ten years before qualifying for appointment as a permanent judge.

As a whole, the Swedish judiciary is considered to be competent and capable. **1.32** Naturally, a judge at a District Court in a small town will typically be less experienced in commercial matters than a judge at one of the larger District Courts.

Sweden is a small jurisdiction. The number of legal scholars and the volume of legal **1.33** scholarship is therefore considerably less than in many other countries. The preference to solve commercial disputes by arbitration has limited the number of decisions of the Supreme Court dealing with central areas of commercial law. As a consequence, it is not uncommon for it to be impossible to give a definitive answer to a particular question of law because the question has never been dealt with by a court or exhaustively addressed in legal writings.

On the other hand, if there is guidance to be found in the *travaux préparatoires* of a **1.34** specific Act, academic commentary, or Supreme Court decision, the degree of predictability will usually be high. A considerable number of judges, including Justices of the Supreme Court, are appointed after having served for a long time in the Ministry of Justice or in various legislative commissions. This, among other things, has resulted in a propensity to follow very closely the suggestions and directions in the legislative history of the Act in question when a statutory provision is interpreted. If there is no legal precedent or if the legislative history is silent on a particular matter, suggestions put forward in academic writings are often followed by the court. In general, there has been little 'judge-made' law in Sweden, even from the Supreme Court. Swedish courts tend to restrict themselves to interpreting the law as it stands rather than creating new principles.

1.2.3 The legal profession

1.35 The structure of the legal profession is different from that of most other European countries. The main reason is that there is no unified legal profession, as members of the Swedish Bar Association have no monopoly in respect of their professional activities. Prescribed qualifications for legal practice do not exist. Neither do general limitations exist on the right to practice as legal consultants, to give legal advice, nor to appear in any court, or before any other authority, save for very limited exceptions.

1.36 The Swedish Bar Association is the organization for the majority of private practitioners. Its members are called *advokat,* advocate. This title is exclusively reserved for members of the Bar Association. While others may do the same work, it is a criminal offence for others to use the title of *advokat.*

1.37 There are normally separate career structures for judges and public prosecutors. It is still unusual, but not unheard of, for advocates to be appointed judges or prosecutors or for persons holding such positions to become members of the Bar.

1.38 Advocates may practice alone, in association with other advocates who share overhead expenses, in partnership with other advocates, or within a corporate structure provided that all the shares of the corporation are owned by advocates. They are not allowed to practice in partnership or in a corporate structure with persons other than advocates.

1.39 Advocates, generally speaking, bear unlimited liability towards clients, even if the practice is carried out in the form of a limited liability company.

1.40 The Ethical Rules of the Swedish Bar Association contain specific regulations on the advocate's relations towards the courts and other authorities and the opposing party in a matter. Generally, advocates have a duty towards the courts to ensure that existing procedural and other rules are followed. Although having no general duty to investigate the correctness of statements made by clients, an advocate must not make statements to a court which the advocate knows to be untrue and must not repudiate a statement by the opposing side which the advocate knows to be true.

1.41 It is not permitted for an advocate to communicate directly with a party who has retained counsel, except under certain circumstances. Communication between advocates on matters relevant to the client must as a matter of principle be disclosed to the client. This follows from the advocate's general relationship of trust with the client.

1.42 In respect of confidentiality, advocates, and their employees, are bound to observe confidentiality in relation to all information relating to clients which is disclosed to them in the course of their work, except insofar as they may be specifically directed by a court to disclose the same.

1.43 Advocates can as a general rule not be heard in court as witnesses on matters relating to their clients.

The Bar Association has not established any rules concerning fees chargeable for **1.44** work performed. The Ethical Rules stipulate that all fees charged by an advocate must be reasonable. Fees are normally charged on the basis of several factors such as the importance and complexity of the matter, the time spent on the matter in question, the responsibility of the advocate and the outcome. Contingency fees are in general prohibited. Estimates of legal fees may be given to the client but the advocate is not under an obligation to provide them.

If an itemized bill is requested by the client, the advocate is required to submit a **1.45** written account of the legal services rendered in the matter.

1.3 The Arbitration Institute of the Stockholm Chamber of Commerce

The Stockholm Chamber of Commerce (SCC) Institute is the leading arbitration **1.46** institution in Sweden and one of the leading institutions at the international level

The SCC Institute is an organization within the Stockholm Chamber of **1.47** Commerce, which has maintained an entity for dispute resolution since 1917. Even though the SCC Institute forms part of the Chamber of Commerce it has an independent status. The decisions of the Board of the SCC Institute are final and not subject to any form of review or control by the Chamber. The primary task of the SCC Institute is to administer and manage arbitrations under its own rules, the SCC Rules.[14] It also accepts to act in accordance with other rules and to perform other functions as per the agreement of parties. In particular, it acts as appointing authority under the UNCITRAL Rules.[15] As mentioned above, the SCC Institute has for decades played a leading role with respect to institutional arbitrations in East–West disputes, including China-related disputes.

The Board of the SCC Institute consists of six Swedish members and eight non- **1.48** Swedish members from Egypt, Hong Kong, China, Russia, Switzerland, the United Kingdom, and the United States. Board meetings take place as a rule at least once a month. The Board members are appointed by the Board of the Stockholm Chamber of Commerce. The primary task of the Board is to take decisions with respect to the appointment of arbitrators, challenges of arbitrators, jurisdiction of the SCC Institute, place of arbitration, if not determined by the parties, as well as the advance deposit to be paid by the parties.

The day-to-day management and administration of cases is handled by the Secretariat **1.49** which is headed by the Secretary General of the SCC Institute. The Secretariat also

---

[14] See Appendix 2.
[15] See Appendix 3, SCC Procedures and Services under the UNCITRAL Arbitration Rules.

prepares materials and presentations for the meetings of the Board of the SCC Institute. The Secretary General is assisted by a Deputy Secretary General.

1.50 The Secretariat is divided into three sections each consisting of a lawyer and an assistant.

1.51 There is a quorum if two members of the Board are present. Even though Board meetings take place every month, emergencies occur from time to time. Such matters are usually handled by the chairman of the Board together with another member of the Board. It should also be mentioned that the Board has delegated the decision-making to the Secretariat with respect to certain matters, eg determination of the award period and the determination of arbitration costs. This means that such decisions can be taken expeditiously and without the involvement of the Board.

1.4 Sovereign Immunity and International Commercial Arbitration in Sweden

1.4.1 Sovereign immunity in general

1.4.1.1 Introduction

1.52 State and State enterprises are to an increasing degree participating in international trade and commercial, economic and financial transactions. This is true also with respect to international commercial arbitration in Sweden. This fact leads to potential problems relating to sovereign immunity.

1.53 The question of State immunity and international arbitration is not a new issue. It has been addressed by practitioners and scholars alike on many occasions.[16] This notwithstanding, many aspects of this issue remain unresolved. Most of the unresolved issues do not *directly* concern the arbitration proceedings. Typically, they arise only when the award has been rendered and when the winning side is seeking to enforce the award.[17] While arbitrators generally aspire—some commentators would even say they have a duty—to render a valid and enforceable award, once an award has been rendered, measures taken with respect to the award are typically beyond the control and authority of the arbitrators. On the other hand, there are situations when questions of State immunity arise also for the arbitrators. Given the fact that State immunity is one of the most traditional topics of public international law, and also of private international law, it is perhaps surprising that it still presents problems in international arbitrations. This is probably explained by the fact that, as mentioned above, many aspects of State immunity remain unresolved

---

[16] For a comprehensive discussion of State immunity, see eg Badr, *State Immunity: An Analytical and Prognostic View* (1984); Schreuer, *State Immunity: Some Recent Developments* (1988). Fox, *The Law of State Immunity* (2002); Hafner *et al* (eds), *State Practice Regarding State Immunity* (2006).
[17] See para 1.122.

and also by the fact many newly independent States are inexperienced in matters concerning State immunity, also with respect to international arbitrations.

State immunity is based on the concept of sovereignty in the sense that a sovereign **1.54** may not be subjected, without its approval, to the jurisdiction of another sovereign. In most Western and industrialized countries today the notion of restrictive State immunity is broadly endorsed. In the former Soviet Union, certain other former socialist States, and in some developing countries, however, the opposite and historically the more traditional view was usually adhered to, viz the doctrine of absolute State immunity.[18]

The theory of *restrictive State immunity* rests on the distinction between commercial **1.55** activities (*acta jure gestionis*) and sovereign activities (*acta jure imperii*). Pursuant to this theory a State enjoys immunity only for the latter category of acts. In other words, if a State engages in commercial activities it does not enjoy immunity with respect to such activities. Even though the principle of restrictive immunity is easily formulated and nowadays generally accepted, a number of open questions remain. One such question is to what extent immunity is, or perhaps should be, restricted when it comes to execution of court judgments and arbitral awards against assets of the State.[19] Also, it is not always easy to distinguish between commercial and sovereign acts. In fact, much of the debate during the last decades has focused on how to make this distinction.[20]

The theory of *absolute State immunity* is based on the idea that no suit may be brought **1.56** against a State without its consent. As far as Soviet law was concerned, this theory was based on the assumption that the State, the sovereign, is always one: it is always one single subject, although the manifestations of its legal personality may be manifold. It does not lose its sovereignty by entering into commercial transactions, be they in the form of contracts, or otherwise. The State continues to act as a sovereign.

1.4.2 National legislation

As of today, there is no comprehensive international treaty dealing with sovereign **1.57** immunity. This means that whenever issues relating to state immunity arise they will be decided on the basis of the relevant national legislation, usually the law of the country before whose courts the issue in question is tried as well as on customary international law as understood and interpreted by such courts. Over the years

---

[18] With respect to the former Soviet Union, see eg Boguslaviskij, *Mezhdunarodnoe chastnoe pravo* (*Private International Law*) (1989) 148–154, 178–182.

[19] See para 1.127.

[20] See eg Badr, *op cit* at 34 *et seq* and Schreuer, *op cit* at 10 *et seq*—several attempts have been made in municipal codifications, and otherwise, to define 'commercial acts', see eg section 3(3) of the British State Immunity Act; section 1603(d) of the US Foreign Sovereign Immunities Act; Article 2(1)(g) of the International Law Commission Draft Articles on State Immunity; and Article IC of the Draft Convention prepared by the International Law Association.

many attempts have been made to agree on an international convention on state immunity. The International Law Commission first took up the subject in 1977 at the suggestion of the UN General Assembly. This initiative eventually resulted in the United Nations Convention on Jurisdictional Immunities of States and Their Property which was adopted by the UN General Assembly on 2 December 2004 but has not yet entered into force.[21] It will enter into force when thirty states have deposited their instruments of ratification and approval with the UN Secretary General. This means that for the time being, issues of sovereign immunity in international commercial arbitration are governed by national legislation. The UN Convention adopts, generally speaking, the theory of restrictive immunity. This approach has long since been accepted by several leading trading nations. Examples include the 1976 US Foreign Sovereign Immunities Act[22] and the 1978 UK State Immunity Act.[23]

1.58 Many arbitrations taking place in Sweden involve Russian and Chinese State organs and entities. It is therefore of particular interest, however briefly, to look at the approaches taken in these countries to issues of sovereign immunity.

1.59 In the *Russian Federation* and other former socialist States there is a clear trend away from the theory of absolute immunity towards restrictive immunity. In many of the former socialist States, as well as in developing countries, the law of State immunity remains, however, shrouded in mystery.

1.60 As far as the former Soviet Union is concerned, with the exception of the three Baltic States, it is, generally speaking, fair to say that former republics closely follow the development of Russian law and often adopt solutions identical, or similar, to those adopted by the Russian legislator. It is therefore of particular interest to monitor the development of Russian law. While there is a clear trend away from the absolute theory of State immunity in Russian law, as will be explained in the following, the Russian legislator has still not adopted any legislative act in this field which confirms that the restrictive theory has been adopted.[24] The situation is similar in most other former republics. This means that the traditional approach—absolute immunity—continues to colour the thinking of lawyers and State officials, since it has not been officially repealed, nor officially replaced by the theory of restrictive immunity.

1.61 There are two basic provisions in Russian law addressing State immunity, viz, Article 401 of the Civil Procedural Code of the Russian Federation and Article 251(1) of the Code of Arbitrazh Procedure of 5 May 1995.[25]

---

[21] See para 1.75

[22] Foreign Sovereign Immunities Act of 1976, Pub L No 94-583, 90 Stat 2891 (1976), (codified at 28 USC §§ 1330, 1332(a)(2)–(4), 1391(f), 1441(d), 1602–1611 (1976).

[23] State Immunity Act 1978, c 33.

[24] It should be noted, however, that the Russian Federation has signed but not ratified the UN Convention.

[25] It must be noted that the Arbitrazh courts, whose activities are governed by the Code of Arbitrazh Procedure, have nothing to do with arbitration, but are rather specialized State courts for commercial and economic disputes.

While the wording—and possibly the scope—of these provisions is different, **1.62** they are both based on the theory of absolute State immunity. Article 124(1) of the Russian Civil Code could be viewed as heralding a new approach in that it stipulates that the Russian Federation 'shall act in relations regulated by civil legislation on equal principles with the other participants of these relations—citizens and juridical persons'. Article 127 of the Civil Code also provides for a law on State immunity to be adopted. As mentioned above, however, no such law has been adopted. On the other hand, two draft laws on State immunity have been prepared. Both drafts are based on the theory of restrictive immunity.[26] The trend away from absolute immunity was also confirmed by President Yeltsin in May of 1998 in an opinion on a draft law sent to the chairman of the State Duma.[27] The opinion was prepared with respect to a Draft Law on the Administration of State Foreign Financial Assets inherited by the Russian Federation. While the opinion is not a wonder of clarity, it is clear that the approach taken in it is based on the theory of restrictive State immunity. The most recent confirmation of the aforementioned trend is a so-called information letter issued by the Presidium of the Supreme Arbitrazh Court of the Russian Federation.[28] In the information letter comments are provided with respect to two actual court cases involving embassies in Moscow. In effect the Presidium of the Supreme Arbitrazh Court has accepted the theory of restrictive immunity. This is particularly interesting since the Code of Arbitrazh Procedure, as mentioned above, prescribes absolute immunity.

It follows from the brief account above that Russian law seems to be moving away **1.63** from the theory of absolute State immunity.

It is reasonable to assume that other former republics will, sooner or later, follow **1.64** suit. For the time being, however, the law of State immunity is in a transitional stage.

As far as China is concerned, the situation seems to be the following. **1.65**

To date, there is no Chinese substantive law or procedural law specifically dealing **1.66** with State immunity. Nor are there any relevant cases from the People's Courts dealing with State immunity.

In practice, however, it is commonly known and consistently argued by **1.67** Chinese scholars that China has traditionally been adhering to the doctrine of

---

[26] For a discussion of the two drafts, see Bykhovskaya, 'State Immunity in Russian Legislation and Judicial Practice', in *Uppsala Yearbook of East European Law* (2003) 271–309.

[27] Ibid, 4–9.

[28] Ibid, 16–19—Information Letters are regularly issued by the two Supreme Courts of the Russian Federation, ie, the Russian Supreme Court and the Supreme Arbitrazh Court. Such letters are mainly of an explanatory nature. They include overviews of recent decisions of the Supreme Courts and provide lower courts with instructions on how to interpret and apply statutory provisions.

absolute immunity. The Chinese position on the principle of State immunity has been summarized as follows:

   (i)   Based on the sovereign equality of all States, sovereign immunity of States and their property is a principle of international law;

  (ii)   Unless a State voluntarily and expressly waives its immunity, all acts of a State *per se* or conducted on its behalf should be absolutely immune from foreign jurisdictions;

 (iii)   A State-owned enterprise is an independent legal entity and should not enjoy immunities for its activities;

 (iv)   Negotiations and international treaties should be utilized to deal with the differences among nations in relation to the issues of State immunity; and

  (v)   China reserves its rights to take counter-measures if any foreign State infringes upon sovereign immunities enjoyed by China and its property.[29]

1.68 There is, however, a limited number of laws and regulations dealing with specific instances of State immunity. The 1992 Law on the Territorial Sea and the Continuous Zone provides that jurisdictional immunity will not be granted to foreign governmental vessels for commercial purposes, which is consistent with the relevant provisions in the 1969 International Convention on Civil Liability for Oil Pollution Damage, to which China is a party and the relevant provisions in the 1982 UN Convention on the Law of the Sea, which was ratified by China in 1996.[30]

1.69 The Law on Judicial Immunity from Measures of Constraint for the Property of Foreign Central Banks of 2005 (2005 Law of Judicial Immunity[31]) is probably the first law in China concerning the more general issue of State immunity. This Act was adopted to grant judicial immunity from constraint measures directed at the property of foreign central banks in the Hong Kong Special Administration Region (SAR), with a view to maintaining and strengthening the position of the Hong Kong SAR as an international financial centre after the handover of the sovereignty over Hong Kong to China. Although this law was passed at the request of the Hong Kong SAR, it is also applicable in mainland China as well as in the Macao SAR. Article 1 of the 2005 Law of Judicial Immunity provides that the PRC grants judicial immunity from constraint measures, namely, the attachment of or the execution measures with respect to the property of foreign central banks, unless the foreign central banks or the governments of their States waive such

---

[29] See Dahai QI, 'State Immunity, China and Its Shifting Position', 7(2) *Chinese Journal of International Law* (2008) 315–316.

[30] See Xixiang Song and Lu Xie, 'Changing from Adjusting Domestic Law to International Convention on Jurisdictional Immunities of State and Their Property', 1 *Politics & Law* (2007) 41.

[31] See Lijiang Zhu, 'State Immunity from Measures of Constraints for the Property of Foreign Central Banks: the Chinese Perspective', 6(1) *Chinese Journal of International Law* (2007) 67–81.

immunity in writing, or the property is allocated to be used for the constraint measures.

Given the scarcity of Chinese domestic legislation on State immunity, when **1.70** dealing with civil lawsuits with a foreign element in the Chinese courts, the principle of reciprocity is the dominant approach.[32] There are very few court cases on State immunity where a Chinese court has dealt with the issue of immunity of a foreign State entity from its jurisdiction. One pre-revolution case, *Rizaeff Freres v The Soviet Mercantile Fleet,* has so far been cited by some scholars as the only recorded case decided by a Chinese court on the issue of State immunity, in which the Chinese court applied the doctrine of absolute immunity.[33]

It is believed that the Supreme People's Court will consult with the Ministry of **1.71** Foreign Affairs (MFA) as soon as a foreign State is involved in Chinese court proceedings, and that the MFA will never suggest jurisdiction over foreign States or execution of their property.[34]

Except for judicial immunity from measures of constraint for the property of **1.72** foreign central banks in China provided in the 2005 Law of Judicial Immunity as set out above, there are no Chinese laws or regulations on State immunity from execution. Moreover, the 2005 Law of Judicial Immunity only serves to confirm a widely recognized international practice. It does not deal with jurisdictional State immunity in general, and therefore, does not shed more light on China's overall position on State immunity, nor could it serve as a legal basis for the People's Courts to deal with a lawsuit in China, or arbitral proceedings in China involving a foreign state or a foreign state entity.

It is worth mentioning that the Chinese Government has, on several occasions, **1.73** reiterated that a waiver of immunity from jurisdiction does not amount to a waiver by the State of immunity from measures of constraint. A specific express consent of the State is necessary in this respect.[35]

China's position on the doctrine of absolute immunity did not significantly **1.74** change until 14 September 2005, when China became a signatory to the 2004 United Nations Convention on Jurisdictional Immunities of States and Their Property.[36] This move has been described as a 'probable shift of China's position

---

[32] Article 5 of the 1991 Civil Procedural Code (CPL) provides that '... should the courts of a foreign country impose restrictions on the civil litigation rights of the citizens, legal persons, or other organizations of the People's Republic of China, the People's Court of the People's Republic of China shall follow the principle of reciprocity regarding the civil litigation rights of the citizens, enterprises, or organizations of that foreign country'.

[33] See Dahai QI, above note 29, 321.

[34] Ibid, 317–318.

[35] See Lijiang Zhu, above note 31, 77.

[36] See <http://treaties.un.org/Pages/ViewDetails.aspx?src=UNTSONLINE&tabid=2&mtdsg_no= III-13&chapter=3&lang=en#Participants > (accessed 15 April 2010).

on the principle of State immunity from the absolute doctrine to the restrictive doctrine'.[37] However, since the UN Convention has not entered into force and has not been ratified by China, such change and shift are yet to be introduced in Chinese domestic legislation and to be implemented in judicial practice.

1.4.3 The UN Convention

1.75 On 2 December 2004, the UN General Assembly adopted the UN Convention on Jurisdictional Immunities of States and Their Property (the 'Convention').[38] The Convention is the first modern multilateral instrument to adopt a comprehensive approach to issues of sovereign immunity from suits in foreign courts.

1.76 The Convention, which has not yet entered into force, was open for signature by all States until 17 January 2007.[39] It was signed by 28 States.[40] So far eight States have ratified the Convention.[41] Thirty ratifications are required for the Convention to enter into force.[42]

1.77 The Convention applies to the immunity of a State and its property from the jurisdiction of the courts of another State.[43] The Convention does not apply to the immunities enjoyed by a State with respect to its diplomatic and consular missions or persons connected with them. Nor does it apply to immunities accorded heads of States *ratione personae* or to immunities enjoyed with respect to aircraft or space objects owned or operated by a State.[44]

1.78 The Convention codifies the basic customary international law principle that a 'State enjoys immunity, in respect of itself and its property, from the jurisdiction of the courts of another State'.[45]

1.79 The importance of the Convention is that it clarifies the exceptions to this principle. In particular, it embraces the restrictive theory of sovereign immunity, according to which governments are subject to essentially the same jurisdictional rules as private entities in respect of their commercial transactions.

---

[37] See Dahai QI, above note 29, 307–337.

[38] The Jurisdictional Immunities Convention was adopted during the 65th plenary meeting of the General Assembly by resolution A/59/38 of 2 December 2004.

[39] See Article 28 of the Jurisdictional Immunities Convention.

[40] Austria, Belgium, China, Czech Republic, Denmark, Estonia, Finland, France, Iceland, India, Iran (Islamic Republic of), Japan, Kazakhstan, Lebanon, Madagascar, Mexico, Morocco, Norway, Paraguay, Portugal, Romania, Russian Federation, Senegal, Sierra Leone, Slovakia, Sweden, Switzerland, Timor-Leste, and United Kingdom of Great Britain and Northern Ireland.

[41] Austria, Iran (Islamic Republic of), Kazakhstan, Lebanon, Norway, Portugal, Romania, and Sweden.

[42] See Article 30(1) of the Convention, which provides: 'The present Convention shall enter into force on the thirtieth day following the date of deposit of the thirtieth instrument of ratification, acceptance, approval or accession with the Secretary-General of the United Nations'.

[43] Article 1 of the Convention.

[44] Ibid, Article 3.

[45] Ibid, Article 5.

1.4.3.1 Immunity from jurisdiction

As indicated above, the general rule of the Convention is that a foreign state is **1.80** entitled to immunity from the jurisdiction of the forum state, and the forum state must refrain from exercising that jurisdiction in a proceeding before its courts, unless one of the stated exceptions to that immunity applies. These exceptions are described below.

Waiver of jurisdictional immunity   Article 7 of the Convention sets forth the **1.81** basic principle that a State may validly waive its right to immunity from jurisdiction. Article 7 provides that:

> A State cannot invoke immunity from jurisdiction in a proceeding before a court of another State with regard to a matter or case if it has expressly consented to the exercise of jurisdiction by the court with regard to the matter or case: (a) by international agreement; (b) in a written contract; or (c) by a declaration before the court, or by means of a written communication in a specific proceeding.

Nor may a State, according to Article 8, invoke immunity from jurisdiction in a proceeding before a court of another state if it has itself instituted the proceeding in question, intervened in that proceeding, or 'taken any other step relating to the merits'. Moreover, a State instituting a proceeding before a court of another State cannot invoke immunity from the jurisdiction of the court in respect of any counterclaim arising out of the same legal relationship or facts as the principal claim.[46]

The exception for commercial transactions   One of the most important, if **1.82** not the most important, exception from immunity under the Convention is the exception for commercial transactions. Article 10 of the Convention provides that:

> If a State engages in a commercial transaction with a foreign natural or juridical person and, by virtue of the applicable rules of private international law, differences relating to the commercial transaction fall within the jurisdiction of a court of another State, the State cannot invoke immunity from that jurisdiction in a proceeding arising out of that commercial transaction.

Article 10 must be read together with Article 2(1)(c), which provides that: **1.83**

> 'commercial transaction' means:
> (i) any commercial contract or transaction for the sale of goods or supply of services;
> (ii) any contract for a loan or other transaction of a financial nature, including any obligation of guarantee or of indemnity in respect of any such loan or transaction;
> (iii) any other contract or transaction of a commercial, industrial, trading or professional nature, but not including a contract of employment of persons.

---

[46] Ibid, Article 9.

1.84 To a large extent commercial activities of a State are carried out by its State-owned companies or other forms of commercial enterprises. The Convention, however, does not expressly regulate the status of State-owned commercial enterprises. Article 10(3) provides that when a State enterprise (or other entity established by a State) that has an independent legal personality and is capable of suing and being sued, and of acquiring, owning or possessing, and disposing of property (including by state authorization), is involved in a proceeding that relates to a commercial transaction in which that entity is engaged, the immunity from jurisdiction enjoyed by that State shall not be affected. However, the question whether a State-owned enterprise enjoys derivative immunity by virtue of their State ownership or interest is not regulated by the Convention. This should not cause practical problems, since even if such a State-owned enterprise would be deemed to enjoy derivative immunity, the exception for commercial transactions in Article 10 would apply. However, given the extent to which State-owned enterprises, State pension funds, sovereign wealth funds, and similar entities are involved in international trade, it would nevertheless have been beneficial to have the status of such enterprises clarified by the Convention.

1.4.3.2 Arbitration

1.85 According to Article 1, the Convention applies only to the 'immunity of States and its property from the jurisdiction of the *courts* of another State' (emphasis added). Thus, the Convention does not address the question of *immunity from the jurisdiction of arbitral tribunals*. Being a consensual and private form of dispute settlement, the conclusion of an arbitration agreement by a State, is widely considered to constitute a waiver of any objections of immunity by such State before an arbitral tribunal constituted in accordance with such arbitration agreement.[47] In fact, since arbitrators are private citizens who cannot exercise any governmental authority, there is nothing to be immune from. This principle, however, has not been codified by the Convention.

1.86 The Convention does, however, provide one important clarification regarding the effect of an arbitration agreement with respect to supervisory jurisdiction over the arbitral proceedings by foreign courts. Article 17 of the Convention provides that:

> If a State enters into an agreement in writing with a foreign natural or juridical person to submit to arbitration differences relating to a commercial transaction, that State cannot invoke immunity from jurisdiction before a court of another State which is otherwise competent in a proceeding which relates to:
>
> (a) the validity, interpretation or application of the arbitration agreement;
>
> (b) the arbitration procedure; or
>
> (c) the confirmation or the setting aside of the award, unless the arbitration agreement otherwise provides.

---

[47] Cf eg Shaw, *International Law* (2nd edn, 1988) 373.

Thus, Article 17 reflects the widely accepted principle that a valid consent to **1.87**
arbitration constitutes a waiver of immunity in relation to the supervisory
jurisdiction over the arbitral proceedings by foreign courts that are competent
in the matter.

Immunity from execution   The Convention also includes provisions dealing with **1.88**
the possibility of seeking execution of judgments, orders, arbitral awards etc against
properties or assets belonging to foreign States. The Convention uses the term
'measures of constraint' to describe the variety of mechanisms available under
domestic law for enforcing such judicial orders. It addresses pre- and post-judgment
measures in separate articles, Articles 18 and 19, respectively.

In accordance with these provisions the basic rule in either case is that no measures **1.89**
of constraint may be taken against State property unless, and to the extent that,
the State has *expressly* consented to such measures by international agreement,
by an arbitration agreement or in a written contract, or by a declaration before
the court or in a written communication after a dispute has arisen, or if the State
has allocated or earmarked property for the satisfaction of the claim that is the object
of the proceeding.[48] It is important to keep in mind, however, that the mere
waiver of immunity from jurisdiction, or the inclusion of a regular arbitration
clause in the contract, does not imply consent to pre-judgment or post-judgment
measures of restraint under Articles 18 and 19. For a State to be deemed to have
waived its immunity from execution, the waiver of immunity from jurisdiction
clause or the arbitration clause must contain additional wording according
to which the State expressly consents to being subjected to measures of
constraint.[49]

Importantly, however, with respect to post-judgment measures of constraint, the **1.90**
Convention provides for an additional exception from immunity from execution,
viz, the Convention permits post-judgment measures of constraint with regard to
property in the territory of the forum State that is specifically in use or intended for
use by the State for other than government non-commercial purposes, provided
that post-judgment measures of constraint may only be taken against property that
has a connection with the entity against which the proceeding was directed.[50] Thus,
the Convention recognizes that judgments and arbitral awards may be executed
against 'commercial assets' of a State. It must be emphasized, however, that with
regard to arbitral awards, the Convention only comes into play after such an award
has been found enforceable in the forum State.[51]

---

[48] Articles 18 and 19 of the Convention.

[49] Articles 18 and 19 require that the State has 'expressly consented to the taking of such measures'.
Moreover, Article 20 of the Convention further provides that: '[w]here consent to the measures of
constraint is required under articles 18 and 19, consent to the exercise of jurisdiction under article 7
shall not imply consent to the taking of measures of constraint'.

[50] Article 18(c) of the Convention.

[51] See Chapter 9.

1.91 A significant limitation of the possibility to execute judgments or awards against 'commercial assets' of the unsuccessful State, however, is that the measures of constraint 'may only be taken against property that has a *connection with the entity against which the proceeding was directed*' (emphasis added).[52] This qualification thus prevents the successful party from seeking enforcement against *any* commercial assets of the State in question. The assets must have a *connection* with the specific *entity* against which the underlying court proceedings or arbitral proceedings were directed. According to the Annex to the Convention:

> The expression 'entity' in subparagraph (c) means the State as an independent legal personality, a constituent unit of a federal State, a subdivision of a State, an agency or instrumentality of a State or other entity, which enjoys independent legal personality.
>
> The words 'property that has a connection with the entity' in subparagraph (c) are to be understood as broader than ownership or possession.

1.92 Article 19 does not pre-judge the question of 'piercing the corporate veil', ie questions relating to a situation where a State entity has deliberately misrepresented its financial position or subsequently reduced its assets to avoid satisfying a claim.

1.93 The requirement of a *connection* between the state entity against which the proceedings were directed and the assets against which enforcement is sought is thus somewhat softened by the clarification that connection shall have a broader meaning than ownership. Furthermore, the Convention does not exclude the possibility of 'piercing the corporate veil' if the entity in question has deliberately been 'shielded' from execution by the respondent State.

1.4.4 Sovereign immunity and Swedish law

1.94 As of today there is no general legislation in Sweden on sovereign immunity. There is, however, a statute of 1938 which implements the 1929 Brussels Convention on State-owned vessels. There is also legislation implementing the 1961 and 1963 Vienna Conventions on Diplomatic Immunity, as well as other treaties concerning diplomatic immunities.[53]

1.95 On 23 December 2009 Sweden ratified the UN Convention on Jurisdictional Immunities of States and Their Property. If and when the Convention enters into force, the text of the Convention will be incorporated into Swedish law, as a Swedish statute.[54] As mentioned above, the Convention will automatically enter into force when it has been ratified by thirty States. As of today it has been ratified by eight states, including Sweden.

---

[52] Article 18(c) of the Convention.
[53] The 1976 Act On Immunities and Privileges in Certain Cases, as amended.
[54] Govt Bill 2008/2009:204, p 109.

The foregoing means that Swedish law on sovereign immunity remains non-statutory **1.96** and is still essentially based on cases decided by Swedish courts and views expressed in scholarly writings.

As far as Swedish case law is concerned, it is important to keep in mind that the total **1.97** number of sovereign immunity cases decided by the Supreme Court is around ten—ie a very small number—almost half of them decided prior to the Second World War.

For many years, the leading case was *The Charente*,[55] in which the Supreme Court **1.98** stated that Swedish law historically had recognized the immunity of foreign States. The Court held:

> Further, it is of the utmost importance that the principle of sovereign immunity is recognized without any modifications, or with only minor modifications, by most countries, including such major and highly culturally developed nations, which are close to Sweden, such as Germany, France and the United Kingdom, as well as the United States. Having regard to the significance of the problem to international commerce it cannot be assumed, unless compelling reasons are presented—which in fact are entirely missing—that Swedish law takes a different position on the principle as such of recognition of sovereign immunity.[56]

The significance of this statement is that in the view of the Supreme Court Swedish **1.99** law should be adapted—and presumably changed, if need be—to developments in law in other countries which from a political, legislative, and cultural point of view are similar to Sweden.

The next immunity case decided by the Supreme Court was *Carin Beckman and* **1.100** *Åke Beckman v People's Republic of China* (NJA 1957 p 195), where China was granted immunity in a dispute concerning China's purchase of an embassy building in Stockholm.

It was not until 1999 that the Supreme Court had the occasion again to rule on **1.101** sovereign immunity in general,[57] and then again in 2009.[58] Prior to these two recent Supreme Court cases, it is fair to say that Swedish law accepted the general principle of sovereign immunity, but with significant and important exceptions,[59] viz:

(a) *Waiver.* The foreign State may waive its immunity.
(b) *Counterclaim.* If the foreign State has itself commenced proceedings, it cannot plead immunity against a counterclaim raised by the opponent provided that there is a certain connection between the two claims.

---

[55] *The Charente*, NJA 1942 p 65, was one of ten attachment cases concerning as many vessels which had been requisitioned by the Government of Norway and chartered by it to the British Government.

[56] NJA 1942 p 65, at 74–75.

[57] Decisions by courts dealing with immunity and arbitration are discussed at para 1.131.

[58] For a discussion of these two cases, see para 1.109 *et seq.*

[59] *Arbitration in Sweden* (2nd edn, 1984) 11–13.

(c) *Activities jure gestionis.* Did Sweden accept the restrictive theory of sovereign immunity, such that immunity was available with respect only to truly sovereign actions (*jure imperii*) and not with respect to normal commercial actions engaged in by a sovereign (*jure gestionis*)? The courts had not been directly confronted with the issue. However, as the above-quoted passage from *The Charente* indicates, a crucial factor for the Supreme Court in 1942 was the recognition of such principle by other important jurisdictions. In the course of the following decades, major foreign jurisdictions adopted the restrictive theory. Most important in this respect were the US Foreign Sovereign Immunities Act of 1976[60] and the UK State Immunity Act of 1978.[61] Among international agreements in the area, the 1972 European Convention on State Immunity and the Additional Protocol[62] were important even though Sweden did not ratify them. All of these international instruments incorporated the restrictive theory of sovereign immunity.

(d) *Real property.* Disputes concerning Swedish immovable property could be entertained by the courts notwithstanding a plea of immunity. There might have been an exception to this rule, however, in the case of property used for the purposes of a diplomatic mission.[63]

1.102 A distinction was generally made between immunity from jurisdiction and immunity from enforcement. It was thought not to be not a necessary consequence of the fact that a court or other authority could exercise jurisdiction over a foreign State that such court or authority could take measures of enforcement against assets or property of such foreign State located within its territorial jurisdiction. Therefore, it was not clear if the abovementioned exceptions extended to the execution stage of judgments obtained against the foreign State. If the judgment was made under the abovementioned statute of 1938 relating to State-owned vessels it is clear that the judgment could be executed within the limits laid down by the statute. A judgment could probably be executed in many other cases falling under (c) and (d) above. In cases falling under (a) and (b) it was deemed conceivable that the foreign State had, as it were, a second line of defence so that a separate waiver was necessary if a judgment obtained against it was to be executed.[64]

1.103 As mentioned above, in 1999 the Supreme Court for the first time in many decades had the opportunity to address questions of sovereign immunity. In *Västerås kommun v Republic Iceland* (NJA 1999 p 821) the Supreme Court concluded that

---

[60] Foreign Sovereign Immunities Act of 1976, Pub L No 94-583, 90 Stat 2891 (1976), (codified at 28 USC §§ 1330, 1332(a)(2)–(4), 1391(f), 1441(d), 1602–1611 (1976).

[61] State Immunity Act 1978, c 33.

[62] Europ. T.S.74.

[63] The Supreme Court so held in *Carin Beckman and Åke Beckman v People's Republic of China* (NJA 1957 p 195).

[64] See Karlgren, *Kortfattad Lärobok i Internationell Privat- och processrätt* 166 (5th edn, 1974).

that the Republic of Iceland was entitled to rely on immunity. Many regarded this as a surprising and disappointing decision.[65]

The origin of the dispute was a contract (the 'Contract') dated 1 December 1992, **1.104** between the Icelandic Ministry of Education and Culture ('Icelandic Ministry') and the Local Authority responsible for schools in the Swedish town district of Västerås. According to Article 3 of the Contract, the Local Authority undertook to give flight-technician education to Icelandic students and to examine them at the end of their studies. The Icelandic Ministry agreed according to the same article, to 'defray any possible costs of educating Icelandic students, which are not covered by the Swedish Government according to the Agreement between the Nordic countries concerning education at the upper-secondary-school level'. Article 7 of the Contract provided that disputes concerning the Contract were to be settled according to Swedish law.

The agreement between the Nordic countries referred to in the Contract is the 1992 **1.105** Agreement on Nordic Common Education at the Upper Secondary School Level (1992 Agreement), which had been signed by all Nordic States on 4 March 1992. This Agreement, which entered into force on 16 January 1993 was based on a previous 1971 Agreement on Cultural Co-operation between Denmark, Finland, Iceland, Norway and Sweden ('1971 Agreement'). The subject matter of the 1971 Agreement was broad. Cooperation in the field of education was mentioned only in general terms.

The 1992 Agreement, which refers to Article 3 of the 1971 Agreement, was adopted **1.106** specifically in order to provide for education, particularly professional education, in the upper secondary schools. Article 2 states: 'Parties to this agreement and their school authorities shall refrain from demanding compensation from each other for education that is given to applicants from other Nordic countries who study at the upper-secondary-school level'.

Education at upper secondary school level in Sweden is financed by the local authority **1.107** of the town district where the student resides.

In total 260 students received flight-technician education in Västerås between **1.108** 1992 and 1994. Thirty-three were Icelandic students. In 1994 the Local Authority requested full compensation from the Swedish Government for the education of the Icelandic students. The Government compensated approximately 35 per cent of the costs but refused to pay the rest.

The Local Authority referred to Article 3 in the Contract and requested the Icelandic **1.109** Ministry to pay the rest of the costs. The ministry refused, arguing that it was the obligation of the Swedish Government or the National School Authority to pay in

---

[65] For comments on the case see, Mahmoudi, in 95 *American Journal of International Law* (2001) 192–197.

accordance with Article 2 of the 1992 Agreement. Negotiations did not resolve the problem. The Local Authority then brought an action against Iceland in the Västerås District Court on 10 April 1996. Iceland claimed immunity from suit.

1.110 In ruling on the defence of immunity, the District Court first determined whether the Contract was a public law or private law contract. The Court concluded that the Contract was to a certain extent of a private law character. It also noted that the Contract had a public law character, emphasizing that both parties to the contract were public law entities engaged in education activities regulated in public law instruments. The public law character of the Contract combined with the fact that it was viewed as an extension of the 1971 Agreement led the District Court to conclude that the dispute concerned a public act and that Iceland enjoyed immunity.

1.111 The Svea Court of Appeal affirmed the decision of the District Court.

1.112 In its decision the Supreme Court recognized the doctrine of restrictive immunity by confirming that a State can rely on immunity only with respect to sovereign acts. The Court went on to discuss the difficulties involved in characterizing acts as either sovereign or commercial, referring, *inter alia,* to the nature of the act and the purpose of the act. It concluded, however, that it was difficult to articulate criteria which would be applicable in all circumstances. The practical approach suggested by the Court was to make an overall assessment of all circumstances in each individual case. In performing this overall assessment the Court concluded that the Contract concerned 'a subject which is typically of a public law nature and which has also been regulated by an intergovernmental agreement mentioned in the contract'.[66] On that basis the Supreme Court found that the Contract was to be characterized as a sovereign act and that Iceland enjoyed immunity.

1.113 Given, in particular, the nature of the Contract, its purpose, as well as the intention of the parties, an appropriate application of the principle of restrictive immunity would—and probably should—have resulted in a denial of sovereign immunity. The Supreme Court seems to have given too much weight to the fact that both parties to the Contract were public entities.

1.114 In the most recent decision on state immunity—*Bostadsrättsföreningen x 13 v Kingdom of Belgium* (2753-07)[67]—the Supreme Court has taken a welcome step towards applying the principle of restrictive immunity as it is being applied in many other countries. The claimant in the case was an apartment house cooperative in Stockholm which had signed a lease contract with Belgium with respect to an apartment to be used as part of the Belgian Embassy. In one of the exhibits to the lease contract, Belgium undertook to refurbish the apartment in question and to

---

[66] *Västerås Kommun v Republic of Iceland* (NJA 1999, p 821) at 825.
[67] The decision of the Supreme Court was rendered on 30 December 2009.

bear the costs thereof. The cooperative commenced a court action in the Stockholm District Court asking the Court for a declaratory judgment to the effect that Belgium was under an obligation to refurbish the apartment and to bear the costs thereof. In the District Court, Belgium raised the defence of State immunity.

The District Court granted immunity. The cooperative appealed to the Svea Court **1.115** of Appeal which affirmed the decision of the lower court on 15 June 2007.

The Supreme Court reversed the decision of the Court of Appeal in its decision of **1.116** 30 December 2009, thus denying immunity and sending the case back to the District Court.

In its reasons the Supreme Court endorses the principle of restrictive immunity. In **1.117** so doing it refers to and discusses the UN Convention on Jurisdictional Immunities of States and their Property.[68] The Supreme Court explains that the method used in the UN Convention to distinguish between sovereign and commercial acts corresponds to an approach that Sweden is prepared and willing to take.[69] It goes on to say that—given the developments in State practice that have taken place over the last several decades—when characterizing an act, as sovereign or commercial the focus should be on the nature of the act, adding that sometimes also the purpose of the act should be taken into account.[70]

With respect to the case before it, the Court had no difficulty in characterizing the **1.118** contract as a private law—ie commercial—act. The lease contract, the Court said, is of a private law character which could have been entered into also by private law entities.

Belgium had emphasized that the lease contract concerned premises to be used as **1.119** an embassy. Referring to the legislative history of the UN Convention, the Court concluded that this fact could not change the commercial character of the contract, nor lead to acceptance of the sovereign immunity defence raised by Belgium.[71]

In its decision, the Court also addressed the issue of diplomatic immunity. **1.120** Discussing the purpose of the 1961 Vienna Convention on Diplomatic Immunity, the Court concluded that it ensures the inviolability of diplomatic premises from execution measures directly linked to the premises. The provisions of the Vienna Convention do not, however, so the Court held, mean that the sending State is entitled to immunity before the courts of the receiving State with respect to the contractual obligations of the sending State. Consequently, Belgium could not rely on diplomatic immunity.

As mentioned above, the approach taken by the Supreme Court with respect to **1.121** immunity from jurisdiction of courts is in line with the approaches of other

---

[68] See para 1.75. As mentioned, the UN Convention has not entered into force.
[69] Ö 2753-07, p 5.
[70] Ibid, pp 5–6.
[71] Ibid, p 7.

countries which subscribe to the theory of restrictive immunity. The reasoning in this 2009 case very much echoes the approach taken in the 1942 *Charente* case, viz, Swedish law should adapt to developments in the leading trading nations.[72]

1.5 Sovereign Immunity and Arbitration

1.5.1 General observations

1.122 Surprising as it may sound, it is not unusual that States, and State entities involved in international commercial arbitrations, or counsel representing them, rely on State immunity seeking to avoid the arbitration. The argument is that the arbitrators lack jurisdiction since the State enjoys immunity.

1.123 While such arguments and objections may require a certain amount of time to address and resolve, today they do not constitute a problem from a legal point of view. It is long since accepted that arbitrators derive their authority from the arbitration agreement entered into by the parties. The arbitrators sit there because the parties have agreed to put them there. Arbitrators do not represent any sovereign nor the interests of any sovereign. In most legal systems arbitrators do not, and cannot, exercise any State authority, but only the authority given to them by the parties. Arbitration is thus an entirely private dispute settlement mechanism and the proceedings before the arbitrators have nothing to do with the exercise of State authority. Consequently, for a sovereign State involved in international arbitration, there is simply nothing to be immune from. Accordingly, if a sovereign State, which has entered into a contract providing for arbitration, pleads immunity before an arbitral tribunal, such an objection must be rejected. The resulting award will not be either void or challengeable because of such rejection.

1.124 In addition to the simple fact that there is nothing to be immune from, the conclusion mentioned above also follows from the well-known Latin maxim *pacta sunt servanda* ('agreements must be kept') In many, if not most, jurisdictions, an arbitration clause is regarded as an implicit waiver of immunity from suit. The commitment made by the sovereign State when accepting arbitration is thus binding and irrevocable. To put it in somewhat dramatic terms: a sovereign State must be sovereign enough to make a binding promise. Accepting that a promise to arbitrate requires 'confirmation' by the sovereign State before the tribunal would in fact be to undermine the sovereignty.

1.125 In international commercial arbitration today it is not a bold statement to say that a valid arbitration clause constitutes a waiver of State immunity in relation to most forms of court proceedings, including so-called ancillary proceedings, ie proceedings

---

[72] See para 1.98.

where a court of law is asked to come to the assistance of the arbitration proceedings, eg to appoint and replace arbitrators. The arbitration clause would also constitute a waiver with respect to challenge proceedings before courts. If the State has won an award which is being challenged by the other party, the State would not be in a position successfully to raise a jurisdictional objection based on sovereign immunity. This is also the case with respect to recognition proceedings, ie proceedings brought in a court of law to have the award recognized and to obtain *exequatur*, ie leave to enforce it.

There is yet another situation where the issue of State immunity may become   **1.126** relevant in international arbitrations. The situation is the following: let us assume that the State has made an objection as regards the validity of the arbitration agreement before the arbitral tribunal. The other party may then wish to have the validity issue determined by a court of law, either before or after the tribunal has ruled on the issue. Under many systems of law a party to an arbitration agreement may at any time submit the issue of the validity of an arbitration agreement to a court of law, even while the arbitration proceedings are going on.[73] Such a court action often does not *automatically* mean that the arbitration proceedings must be stayed, awaiting the decision of the court. This is a decision to be taken by the arbitrators. If the arbitrators decide to continue with the arbitration proceedings they do, of course, take a risk in the sense that time and money may have been spent in vain, if the court were to conclude that the arbitration agreement is invalid. It is quite possible that the State in question will raise the defence of State immunity in such court proceedings, arguing that it is immune from suit. In such a situation the arbitrators must evaluate the possibility of the State being successful in raising the question of State immunity before the court. If the State is indeed successful, it means that the court of law in question will not be able to try the objection, which in most cases means that it will be for the arbitrators to try it. On the other hand, if the State is not successful, the court of law will proceed with the case, in which case the arbitrators must assess the likelihood of the claimant being successful on the merits of the claim. As far as the immunity aspect is concerned, it follows from what has been said above that an arbitration agreement will in most legal systems be viewed as a waiver of immunity from suit. It is thus unlikely that a plea of immunity will be accepted by a court of law in the situation described above.

An important issue in this context is the exact scope of a waiver of State immunity.   **1.127** As mentioned above the generally held view today is that an arbitration clause constitutes waiver of immunity from the jurisdiction of foreign courts exercising their ancillary role in international arbitration and that the ancillary role extends to the declaration of enforceability of an arbitral award. In several legal systems it is, however, still an open question whether such waiver should extend also to the *execution* of an arbitral award. On this issue, French courts have issued two decisions

---

[73] See discussion at para 5.21 *et seq.*

which are of particular interest. In *Creighton v Qatar*[74] the French Court of Cassation ruled that a State, by signing an ICC arbitration clause—including the undertaking to carry out the award in accordance with the terms of Article 24 of the ICC Rules of Arbitration—has, at least implicitly, waived immunity from execution. Article 24 of the ICC Rules of Arbitration (then in force) provided in its second paragraph that 'by submitting the dispute to arbitration by the International Chamber of Commerce, the parties shall be deemed to have undertaken to carry out the resulting award without delay and to have waived their right to any form of appeal insofar as such waiver can validly be made'.[75] Generally speaking, the decision in *Creighton v Qatar* well illustrates the impact of State immunity on international commercial arbitration from the very beginning of the proceedings until and including the enforcement of the resulting award. Also, it is probably fair to assume that the outcome corresponds to the expectations of most participants in international arbitrations.

1.128 The other French decision is that of the Paris Court of Appeal in *Embassy of the Russian Federation v Compagnie Noga d'importation et d'exportation*.[76] In this case the Russian Federation had signed not only an arbitration clause—providing for arbitration at the Stockholm Chamber of Commerce—but also an express waiver 'of any right of immunity'. This notwithstanding, the Paris Court of Appeal ruled that such an explicit waiver did not extend to the immunity from execution guaranteed by the 1961 Vienna Convention on Diplomatic Relations and by customary international law on diplomatic immunities. Consequently, the Court of Appeal ordered the lifting of the arrest orders obtained by Noga with respect to bank accounts opened in the name of the Russian Embassy and other diplomatic entities of the Russian Federation.[77]

1.129 In 1998 Mr Sedelmayer, a German citizen, won an investment treaty arbitration against the Russian Federation.[78] For many years Mr Sedelmayer tried to enforce the award against assets of the Russian Federation, primarily in Germany.[79] For a long period of time the Russian Federation was successful in raising the sovereign immunity defence against such enforcement measures. Eventually, however, Mr Sedelmayer found real estate in the city of Cologne owned by the Russian Federation, but used for commercial purposes.[80]

---

[74] The decision was rendered on 6 July 2000, An English translation appears in Mealey's International Arbitration Report, September 2000 at A-I.

[75] A similar provision is found in Article 28 of the revised ICC Rules which took effect on 1 January 1998.

[76] Case No 2000/14157, Paris Court of Appeal, 1st Chamber, Section A. The decision was rendered on 10 August 2000. See 1 *Revue D'Arbitrage* (200 l) 114–134, and *ICCA Yearbook Commercial Arbitration* (2001) 273–276.

[77] In a decision of 12 May 1999, the Cour de Cassation overturned the decision of the Court of Appeal, but it did accept that Court's reasoning with respect to the relationship between a waiver of immunity from execution and diplomatic immunity.

[78] The award is reproduced and discussed in Hobér, *Investment Arbitration in Eastern Europe: In Search of a Definition of Expropriation* (2007) 46 *et seq*, Appendix 1.

[79] For an overview of the court proceedings in Germany, see Stumpe, SIAR 2008:2, p 167 *et seq*.

[80] As will be discussed at para 1.141. Mr Sedelmayer is now also trying to execute the award in Sweden.

As far as international arbitration is concerned, the only immunity issue which is **1.130**
still open seems to be that of immunity against execution. To a certain extent the
issue is addressed in the UN Convention.[81] In many, if not most, legal systems, it is
still, however, an open question whether, and to what extent, an arbitration clause
constitutes a waiver of immunity also with respect to execution.

1.5.2 Sovereign immunity and arbitration under Swedish law

It is generally accepted under Swedish law that a valid arbitration clause constitutes **1.131**
a waiver of sovereign immunity, with the possible exception for immunity from
execution. So far, there are only two reported court cases dealing specifically with
the question of immunity and arbitration.

The first case, *Tekno-Pharma AB v State of Iran* (NJA 1972 C No 434), was decided **1.132**
in 1972. It addressed the questions of implied waiver and the extent of the waiver.

Tekno-Pharma claimed compensation from Iran under a tenancy agreement **1.133**
pursuant to which Iran had rented its embassy. The agreement included an arbitration clause. Iran refused, however, to appoint an arbitrator and pleaded
immunity in proceedings brought by the claimant to cause such arbitrator to
be appointed. The authority which at that time was authorized to make
appointments of arbitrators accepted the plea of immunity. The case went on
appeal to the Svea Court of Appeal which dismissed the appeal stating that it
did not 'consider the arbitration clause relied on to be equivalent to an express
waiver of immunity'. The Supreme Court, to which the matter was finally
appealed, affirmed the decision of the Court of Appeal without further
discussion.

The terse judgment of the Supreme Court in *Tekno-Pharma* could possibly be **1.134**
interpreted to mean that under Swedish law a waiver of immunity made in an
agreement is revocable.[82] It is submitted, however, that the record in the case
does not warrant such a conclusion. Indeed, if any conclusion may be drawn
from the case it is that an express waiver would be a sufficient (but not necessarily
the only) means of relinquishing immunity, and that the particular arbitration
clause in the case did not amount to an express waiver. The summary form of the
Supreme Court decision, however, and the fact that the case did not receive a full
report, are clear indications that the question to what extent an arbitration clause
implies a waiver of immunity was still open as far as the Supreme Court is
concerned.

The second case, *LIAMCO v State of Libya*, was decided by the Svea Court of Appeal **1.135**
in 1979. The Libyan American Oil Company (LIAMCO) brought a case against
Libya to obtain recognition and enforcement of an arbitral award rendered in a

---

[81] See para 1.75 *et seq.*
[82] Melander, 'Hävande av immunitet', 60 SvJT (1975) 81.

dispute concerning Libya's nationalization of LIAMCO's oil concessions. Libya argued that it enjoyed immunity against the jurisdiction of Swedish courts.

1.136 The Svea Court of Appeal granted the application by Liamco and accordingly declared the award to be enforceable in the same manner as a Swedish court judgment. Libya appealed the decision to the Supreme Court, but before the Court ruled on the question the dispute was settled. The application of Liamco was accordingly withdrawn and the decision of the Svea Court of Appeal never became *res judicata*. In a technical sense, the question of immunity in recognition proceedings is thus still unresolved by Swedish courts. However, the decision of the Svea Court of Appeal represents the latest pronouncement as to the state of Swedish law on the question of such immunity and arbitration and therefore merits attention. The majority of the Court (three out of five judges, including the President of the Court) granted the request for enforcement of the award and stated with respect to the question of immunity:

> By accepting the arbitration clause contained in Article 28 of the concession agreements Libya—which otherwise in its capacity as a sovereign State enjoys extensive rights to immunity from the jurisdiction of the courts of Sweden—must be deemed to have waived its right to invoke immunity. The facts transpiring thereafter do not lead to a different conclusion. The issues decided by the award are arbitrable under Swedish law. No circumstance exist which would make the implementation of the award manifestly incompatible with the fundamental principles of Swedish law. The request for enforcement shall therefore be granted.[83]

1.139 One of the judges submitted a concurring opinion which is of interest to quote in this context:

> It has become ever more common during recent years that states and state-owned organs act as parties to agreements of a commercial nature. If such agreements provide for arbitration, it is shocking per se that one of the contracting parties later refuses to participate in the arbitration or to respect a duly rendered award. When a state party is concerned, it is therefore a natural interpretation to consider that said party, in accepting the arbitration clause, committed itself not to obstruct the arbitral proceedings or their consequences, by invoking immunity.
>
> Swedish commentary and practice have given states extensive rights of immunity, but it is not clear whether, and if so to what extent, these rights should be deemed to have certain limits. In prior case law, it has been assumed that a foreign state, even in the event that the dispute concerns an agreement containing an arbitration clause, may invoke immunity. The latest case appears to be that reported at Nytt Juridiskt Arkiv 1972, note C 434. Abroad, however, case law in several countries has accepted that arbitration clauses, at least as concerns contracts with a commercial background, have the effect of neutralizing immunity. In my opinion, the position which according to the just mentioned case seems to have been taken by the courts of Sweden cannot be maintained. The principle or immunity should not, in a case like this, be allowed to

---

[83] Quoted from the English translation printed in 20 ILM (1981) 895–896.

keep fundamental principles of contract law from being applied. I therefore take the view that execution of the arbitral award should be allowed.[84]

Employing language from *Tekno-Pharma,* a minority of the Court voted to dismiss the application, basing their decision on the immunity of Libya. **1.138**

It is regrettable that the Supreme Court did not have the opportunity to pronounce its views on the question of immunity in *LIAMCO.* Again we can sense the approach taken in the 1942 *Charente* case.[85] It is submitted that the decision of the Svea Court of Appeal represents the present state of Swedish law. Accordingly, an arbitration clause is deemed to constitute a waiver of immunity in judicial proceedings aimed at the recognition and enforcement of a foreign arbitral award in Sweden. Such a waiver would extend to all judicial proceedings that may be instituted in connection with the arbitration in question. **1.139**

As pointed out above, a distinction is generally made between immunity from jurisdiction and immunity from attachment and execution. It is still an open question whether an arbitration agreement would be construed by Swedish courts so as to constitute waiver of immunity in attachment and execution proceedings. It could be argued that it is one thing to pronounce a judgment or an award against a foreign sovereign State and thus bring moral pressure upon it, but quite another to use force against the property of that State. Generally speaking, it is universally recognized that greater caution must be exercised in this field than in relation to the assumption of jurisdiction. Internationally, however, there seems to be a trend in favour of limiting the scope for pleading immunity with respect to attachment and execution. Thus, the US Foreign Sovereign Immunities Act of 1976 provides that a waiver of immunity from enforcement is irrevocable and makes available for execution any property of the foreign State used by the foreign State in a commercial activity in the United States.[86] **1.140**

This key issue is now pending before the Swedish Supreme Court. In his attempts to enforce his arbitral award against the Russian Federation, Mr Sedelmayer is now seeking to freeze real estate in Stockholm, the registered owner of which is the Russian Trade Representation. In March 2005 the Enforcement Agency in Stockholm rejected Mr Sedelmayer's application on the basis that the Russian Federation enjoyed immunity. This decision was appealed to the relevant District Court which affirmed the decision. Mr Sedelmayer then appealed to the Svea Court of Appeal which refused to grant immunity to the Russian Federation. This decision was then appealed to the Supreme Court which granted *certiorari* on 8 March 2010.[87] One of the issues argued in the case is the extent to which the real estate in question was, or is being, used for commercial purposes. **1.141**

---

[84] Ibid.
[85] See para 1.98.
[86] 28 USC §§ 1605, 1610 (1976). See also Articles 18 and 19 of the UN Convention discussed at para 1.88 *et seq.*
[87] Ö 170–10.

2

APPLICABLE LAW

2.1 Introduction   2.01

2.2 *Lex Arbitri*—The Law Governing the Arbitration   2.05

2.3 Party Autonomy—Choice of Law by the Parties   2.14
     2.3.1 Introduction   2.14
     2.3.2 The content of party autonomy   2.24
     2.3.3 Exercising party autonomy   2.42
     2.3.4 Restrictions on party autonomy   2.51
         2.3.4.1 General comments   2.51
         2.3.4.2 No reasonable connection   2.55
         2.3.4.3 National public policy   2.59
         2.3.4.4 Mandatory rules of municipal law   2.71
         2.3.4.5 International public policy   2.89
         2.3.4.6 The function of international public policy   2.92
         2.3.4.7 The content of international public policy   2.93

2.4 No Choice of Law by the Parties   2.97
     2.4.1 Introduction   2.97
     2.4.2 Swedish conflict of laws rules   2.103
         2.4.2.1 The 1964 Act on the Law Applicable to International Sales of Goods   2.106
         2.4.2.2 The centre of gravity test   2.118
         2.4.2.3 The 1980 Rome Convention   2.144
         2.4.2.4 The Rome I Regulation   2.163

2.5 Issues Not Covered by the *Lex Contractus*   2.173
     2.5.1 *Lex corporationis*   2.174
     2.5.2 Agency   2.181
     2.5.3 Negotiable instruments   2.185
     2.5.4 Torts   2.186
     2.5.5 Property   2.192

2.6 Classification Rules   2.198

2.7 The Law Governing the Arbitration Agreement   2.201

2.1 Introduction

2.01   It goes without saying that in international commercial arbitration—which typically has its origin in an international transaction—questions relating to applicable law play an important role. The fact that the parties to the disputed contract come from different countries indicates that questions concerning the law applicable to different aspects of the dispute may arise. It is therefore no surprise that applicable law in international arbitration is one of the classic issues of international arbitration law and that it has generated significant scholarly interest.[1] At the same time, however,

---

[1] Cf eg Lew, *Applicable Law in International Commercial Arbitration* (1978); Stern, 'Trois arbitrages, un même problème, trois solutions', 1 *Revue de l'Arbitrage* (1980) 2; Baxter, 'International Conflict of Laws and International Business' 34 *International and Comparative Law Quarterly* (1985)

many disputes before arbitrators are determined without any analysis of issues relating to the applicable law, with perhaps only a formal reference to the law applicable to the contract.[2] This is so because many, if not most, disputes turn on matters of fact. In such cases, the task of the arbitrators is to determine the issues of fact and relate the facts to the contract. Disputes of this kind may then be determined without applying any particular statute or legal principle, but simply by applying the provisions of the contract. There are other cases, however, where the arbitrators may not need to apply any particular statute, or legal principles, but where they must *interpret* the contract. Experience shows that not all contracts are crystal clear. Which rules of interpretation are the arbitrators to apply in such a situation? This is clearly a question relating to the applicable law in the dispute. Yet again, there are cases where the governing law of the disputed contract is an issue from the very beginning. It is probably correct to assume that questions relating to applicable law are not the most central problem of international commercial arbitration today. Notwithstanding this, such problems do arise frequently. When they do arise, they are mostly complicated and are frequently decisive for the outcome of the entire dispute.

2.02 As mentioned above, international commercial arbitration, will—almost by definition—usually involve more than one system of law, or of legal rules. These laws and rules may in turn cover different aspects of the dispute. This chapter deals with the law governing the arbitration itself (the *lex arbitri*), primarily the procedural and formal aspects of it. The chapter also addresses the law and/or legal rules governing the substantive issues in dispute. The most important issue in this respect is the law governing the disputed contract, the *lex contractus*, but sometimes issues arise which are not governed by the *lex contractus*. Finally, this chapter deals with the law applicable to the arbitration agreement.

2.03 This book focuses on arbitrations taking place in Sweden. Even though arbitrators sitting in Sweden are under no obligation to apply Swedish conflict of laws rules,[3] it would seem to be a reasonable starting point to look at Swedish law in these respects. This is done in para 2.4.2.[4] The traditional ball-and-chain of scholarly research in the area of applicable law in international commercial arbitration is the fact that arbitration is a private and confidential method of settling disputes and that awards and decisions are typically published only with the consent of the parties to the dispute. The general conflict of laws rules of most jurisdictions, and their application and interpretation, are readily available in the form of statutes,

---

538; Redfern-Hunter, *Law and Practice of International Commercial Arbitration* (1986) 70 *et seq*, von Mehren, 'International Commercial Arbitration and Conflict of Laws', in *Ius Arbitrale Internationale, Essays in Honor of Hans Smit* (1993) 57; Grigera Naón, *Choice-of-Law Problems in International Commercial Arbitration* (1992); Chukwumerije, *Choice of Law in International Commercial Arbitration* (1994).

   [2] Cf eg SCC Case 17/1998, in SIAR 1999, Vol 2, p 42; SCC Case 7/2005, in SIAR 2007, Vol 1, p 155.

   [3] See para 2.97 *et seq*.

   [4] See para 2.103 *et seq*.

scholarly writings, and case law reports.[5] Their application and interpretation by arbitrators are not. During the last decade the situation has improved significantly since many arbitral institutions and publications do publish decisions and awards in anonymized and redacted versions.[6] Notwithstanding this, the fact remains that we do not have the full picture when it comes to applicable law in international commercial arbitration.

This chapter is based on statutes, scholarly writings, and the practice of arbitral tribu- **2.04** nals sitting in Sweden. In this latter respect, account is also taken of arbitral awards rendered in Sweden which have been challenged before the courts of Sweden. In such challenge proceedings the award must be submitted to the court. It thereby becomes a document in the public domain. Even though the question of applicable law may not have been the reason for the challenge of a particular award, the award in question may shed light on how arbitrators have dealt with the question of applicable law.[7]

---

[5] Swedish conflict of laws rules are discussed and analysed, *inter alia*, in the following non-Swedish publications: *Arbitration in Sweden* (2nd edn, 1984) 44 *et seq*; Beckman, 'Das internationale Privat- och Prozessrecht in der schwedischen Rechtsprechung und Literatur', 25 *Zeitschrift für ausländisches und intenationales Privatrecht* (1960) 496; Bogdan, 'Application for Foreign Rules on Non-Possessory Security Rights in Sweden Private International Law', 47; *Nordisk Tidskrift for International Ret, Acta Scandinavica juris gentium* (1978) 14; Bogdan-Hobér, 'Chronique de jurisprudence suédoise (1996–2004)', *Journal du Droit International* (No 2, 2006) 719; Bogdan, 'Some Arbitration—Related Problems of Swedish Private International Law', *Yearbook of the Arbitration Institute of the Stockholm Chamber of Commerce* (1990) 70; Eek, 'Conflict of Laws in Swedish Courts', 20 ICLQ (1971) 605; Eek, 'Coup d'oeil sur l'histoire du droit intenational privé en Suède', 1 *Melanges Séfériades* (1961) 29; Eek, 'The Contractual Forum Scandinavia', 173 *American Journal of Comparative Law* (1964); Eek, *The Swedish Conflict of Laws* (1965); Eek, 'Peremptory Norms and Private International Law', Academie de droit intenational, 139 *Rec. des Cours* (1973) 1; Hjerner, 'Choice of Law Problems in International Arbitration with Particular Reference to Arbitration in Sweden', *Yearbook of the Arbitration Institute of the Stockholm Chamber of Commerce* (1982) 18; Hobér, 'Das anzuwendende Recht beim internationalen Schiedsverfahren in Schweden, Recht der intenationalen Wirtschaft', September 1986/ Heft 9, 68; Hobér, 'International Commercial Arbitration in Sweden: Two Salient Problem Areas', in *Liber Amicorum Lars Hjerner* (1990) 236; See Hobér, *In Search for the Centre of Gravity, Swedish and International Arbitration* (1994) 32–33; Nial, American-Swedish Private International Law, 1965; Nial, 'Selected Problems of Private International Law', 101 Académie de droit international, 101 *Receuil des Cours*, (1961); Michaeli, *Internationales Privatrecht* (1948); Strömholm, *Torts in the Conflict of Laws. A Comparative Study* (1961); Welamson, 'Conflict of Laws in the Field of Evidence According to Scandinavian Law', in 88 *Congreso Internationale di diritto processuale civile* (1968); and Wetter, 'Choice of Law in International Arbitration Proceedings in Sweden', *Yearbook of the Arbitration Institute of the Stockholm Chamber of Commerce* (1984) 19 *et seq*.

[6] As far as awards rendered in Sweden are concerned some are nowadays reported and commented on in the Stockholm International Arbitration Report (SIAR) which was previously known as Stockholm Arbitration Report (SAR).

[7] When an award is challenged in a Swedish court, the award must be submitted to the court, as of which moment the award is in the public domain under Swedish law. Thus, in such a situation it would be possible to learn how the arbitrators have addressed issues concerning applicable law. It is uncertain, however, to what extent, if any, a court of law may review the arbitrators' decision in such matters. The only possible exception is when the arbitrators have not applied a law chosen by the parties, in which case an award could probably be challenged on the ground that the arbitrators have acted beyond the matters submitted to them, or that an irregularity of procedure has occurred, see Hobér, 'Svensk domstolspraxis i skiljedomsrätt 1987–1990', *Yearbook of the Arbitration Institute of the Stockholm Chamber of Commerce* (1991) 26; see discussion at para 8.93 *et seq*.

2.2 *Lex Arbitri*—The Law Governing the Arbitration

2.05   As will be discussed in detail below,[8] the principle of party autonomy is one of the cornerstones of international commercial arbitration. Generally speaking, under the principle of party autonomy the parties are free themselves to select the law to govern their relationship. There are, however, certain limitations and restrictions on party autonomy.[9] It would seem that the principle of party autonomy enjoys general acceptance and application in the field of international commercial arbitration.[10] This is above all explained by the fact that arbitral tribunals owe their allegiance only to the parties, and to the arbitration agreement entered into by them, and typically not to any national law as do national courts with respect to their respective national laws. The arbitrators derive their competence and authority from the arbitration agreement. By applying the law chosen by the parties, the arbitrators simply carry out the function entrusted to them by the parties. This does *not* mean, however, that arbitral tribunals exist in a legal vacuum. Arbitral tribunals are ultimately dependant on a national law permitting the very existence of arbitration and arbitral tribunals in the territory of which the arbitration takes place. This national law is the law of the place, or the seat, of the arbitration, or in other words, the *lex arbitri*. While party autonomy thus plays an exceedingly important role, the ultimate benchmark is always the *lex arbitri*.[11] This was recognized already in the 1923 Geneva Protocol, Article 2 of which states:

> The arbitral procedure, including the constitution of the arbitral tribunal, shall be governed by the will of the parties and by the law of the country in whose territory the arbitration takes place.

2.06   As far as arbitrations taking place in Sweden, or rather where the seat of arbitration[12] is in Sweden, are concerned, the *lex arbitri* is Swedish arbitration law, primarily consisting of the Swedish Arbitration Act (SAA) and case law based on it. This approach is enshrined in section 46 of the SAA which reads: 'This Act shall apply to arbitral proceedings which take place in Sweden notwithstanding the fact that the dispute has an international connection'.

2.07   Swedish arbitration law fully accepts the principle of party autonomy. In addition, the provisions of the SAA which govern the actual conduct of the arbitration proceedings are few in number. Consequently, there is ample room for the parties to agree on supplementary rules, institutional or otherwise. Moreover, most of the provisions of the SAA are non-mandatory. The parties are thus free to agree on other rules.

---

[8] See para 2.14 *et seq.*
[9] See para 2.51 *et seq.*
[10] See para 2.21 *et seq.*
[11] See Mann, *Lex Facit Arbitum, in International Arbitration, Liber Amicorum for Martin Domke* (1967) 157–183.
[12] For a discussion of the seat of arbitration, see para 6.185 *et seq.*

As mentioned above, the law of the place or seat of arbitration is the *lex arbitri*. This **2.08** concept is not only important for purposes of providing the ultimate theoretical benchmark for international commercial arbitration. The *lex arbitri* may also have important practical consequences. This is explained by the fact that the arbitration law of one State typically differs from that of other States. For example, the categorization of disputes as arbitrable and non-arbitrable may differ. If such categorization is mandatory under the law of the place of arbitration, the provisions dealing with arbitrability must be complied with. It is not a matter of choice for the parties. Even though the UNCITRAL Model Law[13] has brought about a relatively far-reaching streamlining of national arbitration legislation, there are still differences. Consequently, the choice of the seat of arbitration—and thereby the *lex arbitri*— does still matter.

Despite continuing harmonization of arbitration laws, and desirable as it may be **2.09** from an international commercial point of view to free international arbitration from limitations that may exist in national laws, it is submitted that differences in national legislation will continue to exist. The *lex arbitri* will therefore continue to play a critical role. Over the years attempts have been made to free international commercial arbitration from national constraints and to minimize the importance of the seat of arbitration. These attempts are usually referred to as the delocalization theory, the ideological underpinning of which is the principle of party autonomy, ie the fact that the agreement of the parties to arbitrate is the *sine qua non* for the entire arbitral process.[14] The ultimate purpose of the delocalization theory was to

---

[13] Model Law On International Commercial Arbitration, adopted by UNCITRAL on 21 June 1985. Revisions of the Model Law were adopted in 2006; see Appendix 4.

[14] For a thorough discussion of this and related issues, see Toope, *Mixed International Arbitration* (1990). Toope uses the term 'delocalisation' both with respect to procedural law and to substantive law; in the latter respect Toope defines the problem as the possibility to apply to the substance of a dispute a system of law not connected with any single national system of law. (See Toope, ibid, at 17–18). Much of the discussion concerning delocalization has been confusing, but the ultimate objective seems to be to free international arbitration from any limitations which may exist in various countries with a view to minimizing the legal significance of the place of arbitration. See eg Fouchard, *L'Arbitrage Commercial International* (1956) 22–27; Goldman, 'Arbitrage', in 128 *Droit International Privé* 195. See also Paulsson, 'Arbitration Unbound: Award Detached from the Law of its Country of Origin', *International and Comparative Law Quarterly* (1981) 358; Paulsson, 'Delocalisation of International Commercial Arbitration: When and Why it Matters', *International and Comparative Law Quarterly* (1985) 53.

The theory of delocalized awards seems to have its origins largely in considerations of immunity in connection with arbitrations in which one party is a sovereign State. One example is *Saudi Arabia v Arabian American Oil Co (Aramco)*, ILR, Vol 27 (1963) 117, which took place in Geneva. The arbitral panel invoked rules of public international law on sovereign immunity to conclude that a sovereign State would not be subject to the law of another State, and found that Swiss law could therefore not be applied in the arbitration. For a thorough discussion of the origin and development of the theory, see Blackaby and Partasides with Redfern and Hunter, *Redfern and Hunter on International Arbitration* (5th edn, Oxford University Press, 2009).

Despite the lively discussion that has taken place on delocalized awards, it must be very rare in practice for parties to state expressly that an arbitration and a resulting award should be delocalized or a-national. An instructive example of the difficulties such an arbitration can create is the infamous

do away with the dual system of control over international arbitration—ie first by the courts at the seat of arbitration[15] and then by the courts at the place of enforcement of the award[16]—and replace it with only one form of judicial supervision, viz, at the place of enforcement of the award.

2.10 From a practical point of view, it would seem clear that the advocates of the delocalization theory have not won many supporters. Moreover, from an almost logical point of view, delocalization is possible only if the *lex arbitri* permits it. Even international commercial arbitration must have a 'legal starting point': it cannot exist in a legal vacuum.

2.11 As explained above, the position in Sweden is clear: with respect to arbitrations taking place in Sweden, section 46 of the Arbitration Act explicitly states that the *lex arbitri* is Swedish arbitration law, which in turn is based on the principle of party autonomy.

2.12 From time to time the question has been discussed whether parties may subject an arbitration in one country to the procedural law of another country. Is it possible to have an arbitration in Sweden under German procedural law? From a practical point of view, it is difficult to understand why parties would wish to complicate matters in this way. Luckily it seems to very seldom happen. In the Government Bill introducing the SAA, the following statement is made:

> It follows from [section 46] that the Act is always applicable to arbitrations taking place in Sweden. This means that the parties cannot in general agree that an arbitration taking place in Sweden shall follow foreign law in so far as the actual procedure is concerned. The parties are not, however, precluded from agreeing on other rules with respect to issues where the act is not mandatory, which rules may of course be based on foreign law.[17]

2.13 In other words, the parties would *not* be free to subject the arbitration to German procedural law in general, but could incorporate specific provisions of German law in their arbitration agreement.

---

award in the *SEE v Yugoslavia* case, which, thirty years after being rendered remained the subject of a challenge for voidness. An overview of all proceedings in connection with this case appears in van den Berg, *The New York Convention of 1958* (1981) 41–43. The debate on delocalized arbitration has found a new question to focus on, viz, whether or not an arbitral award which has been set aside by a court in the country where the arbitration took place can nevertheless be enforced in another country; commentators in favour of enforcement include Gaillard, 'Enforcement of a Nullified Foreign Award', *New York Law Journal* (1997) 3; Paulsson, 'The Case for Disregarding LSAs (Local Standard Annulments) under the New York Convention', *American Review of International Arbitration* (1996) 99; idem, 'Rediscovering the New York Convention: Further Reflections on Chromalloy', *Mealey's International Arbitration Report* (September 1996) 22; commentators against enforcement include *Schwartz*, 'A Comment on Chromalloy: Hilmarton à l'americaine', Journal of International Arbitration (1997) 125; Charavi, 'Chromalloy: Another View', *Mealey's International Arbitration Report* (January 1997) 21, idem, 'A Nightmare Called Hilmarton'.

[15] Cf para 3.01 *et seq*, where challenges of arbitral awards are discussed.

[16] Cf para 9.01 *et seq*, for a discussion of the enforcement of foreign arbitral awards.

[17] Govt Bill 1998/99; 35 at p 244.

2.3 Party Autonomy—Choice of Law by the Parties

2.3.1 Introduction

As mentioned above, in international commercial transactions, the agreements **2.14** entered into by the parties are usually detailed to such an extent that arbitrators may be able to decide the dispute simply by applying the provisions of the agreement in question.[18] Agreements do not, however, exist in a legal vacuum. Generally speaking, they are based on, or supported by, a law, usually referred to as the 'governing law of the contract', or the 'proper law of the contract', or simply the '*lex contractus*'. This law will be relevant for purposes of interpretation of the contract, as well as for the validity of the contract, the rights and obligations of the parties, the mode of performance and the consequences of breaches of the contract. The relevant aspects of the *lex contractus* will be dealt with in this section. The law governing the substance of the dispute is in the majority of cases the *lex contractus*. There are, however, other aspects of an international commercial dispute which raise issues of applicable law. For example, the legal capacity of parties to enter into agreements, the right to represent legal entities and other issues of legal representation often generate complicated issues in this respect. Such issues do not fall under the *lex contractus*. They are dealt with in Section 2.5.

The principle of party autonomy is today considered to be one of the cornerstones **2.15** of international commercial arbitration. This principle was eloquently explained in 1971 by Professor Pierre Lalive in the following way:

> There are few principles more universally admitted in private international law than that referred to by the standard terms of the 'proper law of the contract'—according to which the law governing the contract, is that which has been chosen by the parties, whether expressly or (with certain differences or variations according to the various systems) tacitly.
>
> The differences which may be observed here between different national systems relate only to the possible limits of the parties' power to choose the applicable law or to certain special questions or to modalities, but not to the principle itself, which is universally accepted.[19]

As far as international commercial arbitration is concerned, there is ample proof of **2.16** the existence of the parties' freedom to choose the law applicable to their contract.

National courts in most countries accept the principle of party autonomy in the **2.17** choice of the *lex contractus*. The principle has also been enshrined in the 1980 Rome Convention on the Law Applicable to Contractual Obligations, which is applicable to contracts entered into by Member States of the European Union.[20] Article 3(1) of

---

[18] See para 2.01.

[19] Quoted from ICC Award No 1512, doc 410/1935, dated 24 February 1971.

[20] The Convention entered into force on 19 June 1980. For a discussion of the Rome Convention, see para 2.144 *et seq.*

the Convention reads: 'A contract shall be governed by the law chosen by the parties'.

2.18 The 1980 Rome Convention has been replaced by the Rome I Regulation which also continues this principle.[21]

2.19 If national courts are prepared to accept and recognize the principle of party autonomy, there does not seem to be any reason for arbitral tribunals not to do so.

2.20 For example, the 1961 European Convention on International Commercial Arbitration stipulates that: '[t]he parties shall be free to determine, by agreement, the law to be applied by the arbitrators to the substance of the dispute'.[22] The 1985 UNCITRAL Model Law in Article 28(1) also recognizes party autonomy.[23] In addition, the rules of most arbitration institutions have provisions confirming the principle of party autonomy.[24]

2.21 The principle of party autonomy enjoys almost universal recognition in municipal law, by national courts, in international conventions on arbitration, in arbitration rules, and by arbitral tribunals.[25] The advantages of the principle are clear enough: it achieves certainty, predictability, and uniformity. By allowing the parties to choose themselves the law governing their contract they can be certain of what law will be applied to their dispute. The effect and interpretation of their contract become predictable and a uniform resolution of their dispute is ensured irrespective of who will decide the dispute. Needless to say, different arbitrators may apply and interpret the designated law differently. Also, as will be discussed below,[26] there are certain limitations and restrictions on the principle of party autonomy which may influence the desired certainty, predictability, and uniformity. Even so, however, party autonomy eliminates the potential complication of having the arbitrators determine the applicable law.

2.22 There is one additional advantage that should be mentioned. By allowing the parties to choose the law to be applied to their dispute, they are barred from

---

[21] Regulation (EC) No 593/2008 of the European Parliament and of the Council of 17 June 2008 on the law applicable to contracted obligations, (Rome I). Article 3(1) of the Regulation stipulates: 'A contract shall be governed by the law chosen by the parties'. For a discussion of the Regulation, see para 2.163 *et seq.*

[22] Article VII of the 1961 European Convention on International Commercial Arbitration.

[23] The first sentence of this Article reads: 'The arbitral tribunal shall decide the dispute in accordance with such rules of laws as are chosen by the parties as applicable to the substance of the dispute'.

[24] Suffice it in this context to refer to the SCC Rules, Article 22(1) of which stipulates: 'The Arbitral Tribunal shall decide the merits of the dispute on the basis of the law or the rules of law agreed on by the parties'.

[25] The following discussion is a condensate of generally accepted rules and principles of international arbitration. It is submitted that it fairly reflects the position of Swedish arbitration law, at least insofar as international commercial arbitration is concerned. Given the consensual and confidential nature of arbitration, and given the fact that questions relating to applicable law seldom reach the courts, it is not surprising that there are few published decisions on the meaning, scope, and limitation on party autonomy.

[26] See para 2.51 *et seq.*

arguing, once the award has been rendered, that it was decided on the basis of an unjust or unfair law. This will typically help to ensure the final and binding effect of an arbitral award. By the same token, failure by the arbitrators to apply the law chosen by the parties may put the voluntary compliance with the resulting award at risk.

More importantly, however, the award may be set aside by a national court of law, **2.23** if the arbitrators have failed to apply the law chosen by the parties.[27] This is explained by the fact that the principle of party autonomy means that the arbitrators have an obligation to apply the law chosen by the parties. This in turn is the necessary consequence of the consensual nature of arbitration: the arbitrators derive their authority from the agreement of the parties and must follow their instructions.[28] In this connection it is essential to distinguish between the *failure*, or *refusal*, to apply the chosen law and the arbitrators' *erroneous* application of such law. Only the former can lead to the setting aside of an arbitral award.[29]

2.3.2 The content of party autonomy

Experience shows that in international commercial arbitration parties mostly **2.24** choose a *national* law to govern their contract, to the extent that they make a choice of law at all. The principle of party autonomy, does not, however, require the parties to choose a national law. In fact, the principle allows the parties to choose any set of rules, or principles—whether they be characterized as 'law', 'rules of law', or something else—to serve as the basis for resolving their disputes, subject of course to any limitations and restrictions on party autonomy that may exist. This is evidenced by the fact that parties are allowed to agree that arbitrators may decide their disputes as *amiables compositeurs*, or *ex aequo et bono*, ie without applying any law, or rules of law, at all. There are no generally accepted detailed definitions of these two concepts. Generally speaking, however, they mean that arbitrators may disregard legal and contractual requirements with a view to arriving at an equitable and just resolution of the dispute, provided that the parties have authorized the arbitrators so to act. The theoretical foundation underlying this possibility is, again, the consensual nature of arbitration. It is based on the agreement of the parties and this agreement constitutes the sole authority for the arbitrators.

As mentioned above, the principle of party autonomy relates to the *lex contractus*, ie **2.25** the law applicable to the contract. As mentioned above, there are, however, other substantive aspects of a dispute which may not relate directly to the contract, including, for example, capacity, power of representation, third party interests, torts etc, as well as issues concerning the mode of performing contractual obligations, but

---

[27] For a discussion of whether the failure by arbitrators to apply the law chosen by the parties may lead to the setting aside of an award, see para 8.93 *et seq.*
[28] See para 2.05.
[29] See para 8.93 *et seq.*

which may be important to the outcome of the dispute. Such aspects are covered by other conflict of laws rules which are discussed in Section 2.5 below.

2.26 Given the nature of party autonomy, it is clear that the parties have a large variety of options in exercising their autonomy.

2.27 The options include the following:

    (i) The national law of either of the disputing parties;

    (ii) The national law of a third, neutral country;

    (iii) Several systems of law, or combinations of rules from several systems of law, or the principles common to more than one system of law;

    (iv) General principles of law, either separately, or in combination with one or several national laws;

    (v) Public international law, either separately, or in combination with one or several national laws;

    (vi) International trade law (*lex mercatoria*);

    (vii) *Amiables compositeurs* or *ex aequo et bono*.

2.28 Many of the options mentioned above have generated an abundance of scholarly comment. Suffice it, at this point, to make a few comments of practical importance.

2.29 First, it is important again to point out that there is no requirement that the parties choose a national law. This is confirmed, *inter alia*, by the UNCITRAL Model Law, Article 28(1) of which refers to 'rules of law', rather than to 'the law'. Similar language is found in the rules of most arbitration institutions today. For example, Article 22(1) of the SCC Rules, stipulates:

> The Arbitral Tribunal shall decide the merits of the dispute on the basis of the law or the rules of law agreed upon by the parties. In the absence of such agreement, the Arbitral Tribunal shall apply the law or rules of law which it considers to be most appropriate.

2.30 Secondly, parties should, needless to say, familiarize themselves with the national law(s), rules of law, or principles of law in question. Despite ambitious and valuable work to harmonize rules and laws relating to international transactions, differences in national laws do remain.

2.31 Thirdly, also with respect to *lex mercatoria* the parties may experience difficulties in predicting the practical effect of such a choice of rules. As far as party autonomy is concerned, it is clear that the parties are entitled to agree on such rules, principles, and provisions in statutes and treaties which in their opinion form part of an international trade law. If they simply refer to *lex mercatoria*, however, it is uncertain what practical effect such a choice will have, but they certainly have the right to make such a choice.[30]

---

[30] In an important contribution to the debate, Mustill, 'The New Lex Mercatoria: The First Twenty-Five Years', in Brownlie and Bos (eds) *Liber Amicorum for the Rt Hn Lord Wilberforce* (1987) 149, made a survey of norms which have been claimed to form part of *lex mercatoria*. He was able to

Fourthly, the reference to general principles of law is typically *not* a reference to 'the **2.32** general principles of law recognized by civilized nations' found in Article 38.1(c) of the Statute of the International Court of Justice. The general principles referred to in the Statute form part of public international law as one of several *sources* of such law. They are typically not intended to be applied as a separate set of rules, or as a system of law. Notwithstanding this, there are a number of arbitral awards—typically between States and private entities—where 'the general principles of law' have been applied.[31] State contracts—ie contracts between a State, or a State-owned entity, and a private entity—sometimes have choice of law clauses providing for the application of 'general principles of law'. This is a perfectly acceptable way of exercising party autonomy. Such a clause is indeed valid. It may, however, cause problems when the arbitrators are to apply it.[32] Generally speaking, it is probably fair to say

find some twenty such rules, seven of which were at a very high level of abstraction, the remaining thirteen being of a more detailed nature. Mustill found this to be 'rather a modest haul for twenty-five years of international arbitration' (p 177). With respect to the question whether *lex mercatoria* could be chosen as 'the law' to be applied to the substance of a dispute he suggested that 'the answer must surely be no' (p 160). Mustill also notes that there are very few arbitral awards, at least reported awards, where *lex mercatoria* has in fact been applied. One of the most well-known examples is the so-called *Norsolor* case, *Pabalk Ticaret Ltd v Norsolor SA*; the award was rendered on 26 October 1979 and reprinted in 9 *Yearbook Commercial Arbitration* (1984) 110, where an ICC arbitral tribunal sitting in Vienna applied *lex mercatoria* in a dispute between a Turkish and a French company. The award was set aside by an Austrian Court of Appeal. This decision was reversed, however, by the Austrian Supreme Court and the award was eventually enforced in France. The decision of the Austrian Supreme Court (Oberster Gerichtshof) was rendered on 18 November 1982 and reprinted in 9 *Yearbook Commercial Arbitration* (1984) 159. The Court of Appeal in Vienna which set aside the award characterized *lex mercatoria* as 'world law of doubtful validity' ('Weltrecht fraglicher Geltung'). The Supreme Court, however, said that the principle of 'good faith'—which the tribunal had found to be one of the guiding principles of *lex mercatoria*—was 'inherent in the private law systems which in no way is contradictory to strict legal resolutions of the country concerned'. Since then UNIDROIT (The International Institute for the Unification of Private Law) has issued its Principles of International Commercial Contracts in 1994. The publication suggests in seven chapters—starting with general provisions and ending with rules on non-performance—'the best solutions' for international commercial contracts. In the Introduction it is stated, *inter alia*, that the UNIDROIT Principles 'reflect concepts to be found in many, if not all, legal systems. Since, however, the Principles are intended to provide a system of rules especially tailored to the needs of international commercial transactions, they also embody what are perceived to be the best solutions, even if still not generally adopted', *Principles of International Commercial Contracts* (1994) vii. In the Preamble it is stated that the Principles 'may be applied when the parties have agreed that their contract be governed by general principles of law', the '*lex mercatoria* or the like', idem at 1.

[31] The better known awards include *Petroleum Development (Trucial Coast) Ltd v The Sheikh of Abu Dhabi*, published in *International and Comparative Law Quarterly* (1952) 247 (in that case the sole arbitrator said, *inter alia*, the following: 'The terms of that clause invite, indeed prescribe, application of principles rooted in the good sense and common practice of the generally of civilized nations—a sort of "modern law of nature"'. Idem at 250); *Sapphire International Petroleum Ltd v National Iranian Oil Company*, reprinted in ILM (1967) 136 (the contract in question did not contain any choice of law clause); *Government of the State of Kuwait v The American Independent Oil Company*, reprinted in ILM (1982) 976; and *Lena Goldfields Ltd v Union of Soviet Socialist Republics*, reprinted in *Cornell Law Quarterly* (1950) 42; for an interesting discussion of the latter, see Veeder, 'The Lena Goldfields Arbitration: The Historical Roots of Three Ideas', *International and Comparative Law Quarterly* (1998) 747.

[32] Such a clause would seem to raise two major concerns, viz, (i) what are these principles?, and (ii) the risk of confusing such general principles with the general principles referred to in the Statute of the International Court of Justice.

that the 'general principles of law' are not sufficiently developed and detailed to provide hard and fast rules for the resolution of detailed and complex legal issues.

2.33 As mentioned above, in international commercial arbitrations most choice of law clauses seems to indicate a national law. For the parties the choice of a national law will provide a certain degree of predictability and certainty, even though the parties are as a rule deemed to have accepted future changes in that legal system. Very often this is straightforward. There may be problems in this respect, however, when the contract has been signed with the State or with a State-owned, or controlled, entity. This is particularly common in the natural resources sector and other sectors where long-term contracts are used. For the private, non-State, party the potential problem is that the State, as legislator, may change the law and thereby the terms and conditions of the contract. Parties have tried various methods to protect themselves from changes in the local law, where the local law is the *lex contractus*. One approach is to include so-called freezing clauses, the objective of which is to freeze the national law as of the date of signing the contract. The purpose is thus to insulate the contract from any subsequent changes in the local law. Variations on this general theme often come in the form of *force majeure* clauses, hardship clauses, or revision clauses. In oil concession contracts these clauses often come in the form of so-called stabilization clauses. The general idea is the same: to ensure that the contracting State will not change the terms and conditions of the contract by changing the local law.

2.34 The problem with these kinds of clauses, however, is that the State may still introduce a new law—valid in its own territory—forbidding precisely such clauses.

2.35 Parties have also tried to deal with this problem by including specific language in the choice of law clauses in their contracts. It is then for the arbitrators to interpret, and apply, the choice of law made by the parties.

2.36 A well-known illustration of how arbitral tribunals have tried to deal with the application of local law to State contracts is the *Sapphire Arbitration*[33] from 1963. In that case there was no explicit choice of law clause in the contract. Since the contract was for an oil concession in Iran, it would seem natural that Iranian law was a potential *lex contractus*. The arbitrator, Judge Pierre Cavin, took a different view. He said the following:

> It is quite clear from the above that the parties intended to exclude the application of Iranian law. But they have not chosen another positive legal system and this omission is on all evidence deliberate. All the connecting factors cited above, point to the fact that the parties therefore intended to submit the interpretation and performance of their contract to principles of law generally recognised by civilised nations, to which article 37 of the agreement refers, being the only clause which contains an express reference to an applicable law.[34]

---

[33] *Sapphire International Petroleums Ltd v National Iranian Oil Co*, reprinted in ILR (1967) 136.
[34] Ibid, 175.

The question of protecting the private party to a State contract from changes in the **2.37**
local law also came up in the Libyan oil nationalization arbitrations.[35] The governing
law clause was the same in all three oil concession contracts. It read as follows:

> This concession shall be governed by and interpreted in accordance with the principles
> of law of Libya common to the principles of international law and, in the absence of
> such common principles, then by and in accordance with the general principles of law,
> including such of those principles as may have been applied by international tribunals.

This clause was interpreted by three different tribunals, with different results.

In *Texas Overseas Petroleum Company and California Asiatic Oil Company (TOPCO) v* **2.38**
The Government of Libyan Arab Republic, the sole arbitrator, Professor Dupuy, seems
to have interpreted the clause primarily as a choice of public international law,
whereas in *British Petroleum (Libya) Ltd v The Government of the Libyan Arab*
Republic, Judge Lagergren appears to have regarded it as a choice of general principles.
In the third arbitration, *Libyan American Oil Company v The Government of the*
Libyan Arab Republic, Dr Mahassani held that Libyan law was applicable, excluding
such provisions which were in conflict with the principles of the international law.

The three awards illustrate the difficulties in trying to protect the private party **2.39**
against changes in the local law in general, and by agreeing on specific language in
the arbitration clause in particular.[36] Another illustration of these difficulties is the
Aminoil Award[37] decided in March 1982. In that case, the arbitrators had been
given wide discretion to determine the applicable substantive law. Article III(2) of
the arbitration agreement of 23 June 1979 read as follows:

> The law governing the substantive issues between the Parties shall be determined by
> the Tribunal, having regard to the quality of the Parties, the transnational character of
> their relations and the principles of law and practise prevailing in the modern world.

The tribunal held that prima facie the contract should be governed by Kuwaiti law. **2.40**
The tribunal also concluded that Kuwaiti law—as a modern legal system—
incorporated international law and that international law incorporated general
principles of law. Thus, for the tribunal the general principles of law constituted the
source of law to be applied by it.[38]

The debate about the internationalization of State contracts is largely gone today, **2.41**
pre-empted as it has been by the growth of investment treaty arbitration. Claims
by private parties that the State has breached a State contract often fall under the

---

[35] See Stern, note 1, above; see also Greenwood, 'State Contracts in International Law—The
Libyan Oil Arbitrations', 17 ILM (1982) 14.

[36] For an in-depth discussion of attempts to 'internationalize', or 'delocalize' arbitrations concerning State contracts, see Toope, *op cit* at 17–97. For a general discussion of problems relating
to stability in the energy sector, see Cameron, *International Energy Investment Law. The Pursuit of*
Stability (2010).

[37] *The Government of Kuwait v American Independent Oil Company (Aminoil)*, 21 ILM (1982) 976.

[38] See note 37, above at 1000–1001.

jurisdiction of investment protection treaties, bilateral as well as a multilateral. The argument is that the State has breached an international obligation resulting from the treaty in question. Most investment protection treaties have arbitration clauses which usually provide a forum for the private investor.

2.3.3 Exercising party autonomy

2.42 The most common form of exercising party autonomy is for the parties to include a choice of law clause in their contract. Such clauses come in many different forms depending on the circumstances in the individual case and the wishes of the parties. Most arbitration institutions provide, together with their rules, standard clauses on choice of law. For example, the SCC Rules have the following standard clause: 'This contract shall be governed by the substantive law of [insert jurisdiction]'.

2.43 Such a clause would typically be sufficient for many, if not most contracts. In this context it should be pointed out that the choice of the law of an identified jurisdiction is understood as *excluding* the conflict of laws rules of that jurisdiction. Generally speaking, this is the case even if there is no reference to the 'substantive law', but simply to 'the law' of a given State. For example, Article 22(2) of the SCC Rules stipulates:

> Any designation made by the parties of the law of a given state shall be deemed to refer to the substantive law of that state and not to its conflict of laws rules.

2.44 In most cases the parties agree on the applicable law when they enter into the contract in question. The generally held view, however, is that the law to be applied is the law at the time of the dispute.[39] In other words, the parties are deemed to have agreed to accept changes in the law that take place between the execution of the contract and the commencement of the arbitration. It should be pointed out that parties may strictly speaking agree on the applicable law at any time: in the contract, by changing the choice of law clause in the contract, by separate agreement, even during the arbitration. Needless to say, late changes in the applicable law, for example, during the proceedings, may create practical problems. It is clear, however, that the principle of party autonomy allows the parties to do this.

2.45 Even if the parties have not made an *explicit* choice of law in the form of a governing law clause in the contract, or in a separate agreement, it may be possible to infer such a choice from the terms of the contract, or from the circumstances surrounding the case (implicit choice of law).

2.46 For example, Article 3(1) of the 1980 Rome Convention recognizes the possibility of an implied choice of law. This provision stipulates that a choice of law must be 'expressed or demonstrated with reasonable certainty by the terms of the contract or the

---

[39] For example, Article 3 of the Rome Convention provides that a choice of law, or a variation of a choice of law, can be made at any time after the conclusion of the contract by agreement between the parties.

circumstances of the case'. It goes without saying that it is problematic to select a law for the parties, pretending that it is their choice, when in fact in most cases they have not given any thought to the question of applicable law. As indicated by the language of Article 3(1) of the 1980 Rome Convention, caution must be exercised when attributing an implied choice of law to the parties. One factor which may be taken into account when trying to attribute a choice of law to the parties is their choice of forum. This is, however, but one of several factors which may be taken into account. The generally held view is that the choice of forum alone cannot constitute an implied choice of substantive law.[40] There may be many reasons why parties choose a particular forum for the settlement of their dispute, reasons which may have nothing to do with the applicable law to the substance of their dispute.

It follows from what has been said above that the parties may agree to have one law **2.47** apply to certain aspects of the contract, but another law to other aspects. The conflict of laws term for this is *dépeçage*. In the Swedish conflict of laws this was traditionally not accepted. It is, however, explicitly recognized in the 1980 Rome Convention and has therefore since 1995 been part of the Swedish conflict of laws.[41]

Should the validity or the interpretation of a choice of law clause be challenged **2.48** separately—which seems to be rather unusual—the question arises which law to apply to resolve the disputed issue. The generally held view seems to be that the law indicated in the challenged clause should be used.[42] This solution is, of course, circular, but the only practical and realistic solution.

When a contract has unclear and seemingly contradictory choice of law provisions, **2.49** the arbitral tribunal will be required to construe the contract provisions in question with a view to determining the intention of the parties. Factors which will be taken into account include the wording of the provisions as well as the context in which they appear. The following case illustrates this.[43]

A dispute arose out of an agreement concerning trade in Russian securities, entered **2.50** into between a Bahamian investor and a Cypriot broker. The investor initiated arbitration against the broker, alleging that the broker had failed to comply with the investor's instructions by not selling securities when requested. The broker asserted that the claim was without merit, claiming that under Russian law he had been entitled to discharge his obligations under the agreement by depositing the securities with a public notary. The agreement contained two applicable law clauses. Article 5 stated that the parties 'assume amenability in accordance with the current legal acts of Russia and this Agreement clause for non-execution or improper execution of the terms of this Agreement . . .'. Article 7.2 provided for arbitration in Stockholm

---

[40] Cf eg Lew, *op cit*, at 190.
[41] Article 3(1) of the 1980 Rome Convention.
[42] Cf Article 3(4) of the 1980 Rome Convention.
[43] SAR 1999:2 p 42.

and further stated that '[t]he applied law is under the law of Sweden'. The arbitral tribunal—composed of three arbitrators of Swedish nationality—noted that Article 7.2 was in itself clear. The article laid down that Swedish substantive law was to be applied. The arbitral tribunal further noted that, by contrast, Article 5 made reference to current legal acts of Russia. The article as a whole dealt with liability. The arbitral tribunal found that 'in context and considering the wording', it seemed unlikely that Article 5.1 could have been intended as a general provision on applicable law. The arbitral tribunal further noted that under all circumstances Article 5.1 was far too ambiguous to override the plain meaning of Article 7.2. Accordingly, the arbitral tribunal held that Swedish law applied.

2.3.4 Restrictions on party autonomy

2.3.4.1 General comments

2.51 Party autonomy enjoys almost universal acceptance as far as international commercial arbitration is concerned. At the same time, however, there are certain, at least potential, restrictions on party autonomy. What are these restrictions, if any? The focus here is to answer the question of which circumstances may cause arbitrators to set aside, or ignore, a choice of law made by the parties. Consequently, the possible influence of these potential restrictions on courts, and their decision-making, will not be discussed. An international arbitral tribunal does not have a *lex fori* in the private international law sense of the term. Even if *lex arbitri* could—to a very limited extent—be equated with *lex fori*, it is very difficult, if not impossible, and usually not very fruitful, to approach issues concerning applicable law and party autonomy in the same way as is done when national courts are involved. The lack of a *lex fori* has important consequences for the applicable law in international commercial arbitrations, viz, that there is no such thing as a 'foreign' law, but the laws of all countries are put on an equal footing and no single law *a priori* enjoys any priority over any other law. The obvious exception to the foregoing is, however, the law chosen by the parties.

2.52 The starting point is—again—the consensual nature of arbitration in the sense that it is the will of the parties who have agreed to arbitrate which, as a matter of principle, must be decisive.

2.53 Theoretically speaking there are four categories of circumstances which may constitute restrictions and limitations on party autonomy:

- the chosen law has no reasonable connection with the transaction in question, nor with the parties involved in it;
- national public policy;
- mandatory rules of municipal law; and
- international public policy.

2.54 There are not necessarily always clear borderlines between the different categories enumerated above. This is particularly true with respect to the three latter categories.

It should be emphasized that the term 'public policy' will be used to cover what is understood by the civil law term *ordre public*, as well as the common law term 'public policy'.[44]

2.3.4.2 *No reasonable connection*

In the private international law rules of some municipal legal systems, while accepting **2.55** the principle of party autonomy, there are provisions to the effect that the law chosen must have a reasonable connection to the parties, or to the transaction in question; if not, the law chosen by the parties will not be accepted by the national courts.

The rationale behind this potential limitation on party autonomy would seem to be **2.56** the presumed existence of a forum law (*lex fori*) and the desire to uphold the supremacy of the *lex fori*. As mentioned above, however, in international arbitration there is no *lex fori* for the arbitrators. Consequently, arbitrators have no obligation to uphold the *lex fori* of any national jurisdiction. On the contrary, their obligation is to apply the law chosen by the parties.

The generally held opinion today is that this potential limitation on party auton- **2.57** omy does not apply to international commercial arbitration.[45] In fact, in many international contracts a neutral law is chosen precisely because it does *not* have any connection with the parties, or the transaction.[46]

It would seem clear that the law chosen by the parties in an international commercial **2.58** arbitration does not need to have a reasonable connection, nor indeed any connection, with the parties or with the transaction.

2.3.4.3 *National public policy*

Generally   The concept and meaning of national public policy is fraught with **2.59** uncertainty and ambiguity. A totally comprehensive definition has never been offered. Generally speaking, however, it is clear that public policy reflects the

---

[44] The two terms are today in practice often used interchangeably and as referring to the same phenomenon. As a theoretical matter, however, it is clear that their meaning and application differ.

[45] See Lew, *op cit,* at 105; Delaume *op cit,* at 109; Holtzman and Neuhaus, *A Guide to the UNCITRAL Model Law on International Commercial Arbitration: Legislative History and Commentary* (1989) 765; David, *Arbitration in International Trade* (1985) 343; von Hoffman, *Internationale Handelsschiedsgerichtbarkeit* (1970) 67 *et seq*; Craig, Park, and Paulson, *International Chamber of Commerce Arbitration* (1984) Part III § 17.04 at 86. This is also confirmed by arbitral practice where virtually no awards can be found when arbitrators have refused to apply the law chosen by the parties, see Lew, *op cit,* at 105. Strictly speaking, this follows already from the conclusion drawn at para 2.31, viz, that parties have the possibility to instruct the arbitrators to act *ex aequo et bono,* or as *amiables compositeurs.*

[46] One example is the contract practice which evolved in East–West trade—particularly prior to 1989—where the parties normally agree to apply the substantive law of a third, neutral country such as for example Sweden or Switzerland. As far as the application of Swedish law is concerned, see Hobér, *International Commercial Arbitration in Sweden: Two Salient Problem Areas,* in *Studies in International Law, Liber Amicorum for Lars Hjerner* (1990) 236–238.

fundamental legal, economic, and moral standards of any given State.[47] When public policy is held to apply, an otherwise applicable foreign law will not be applied or enforced. It will be replaced by another substantive law. In the practice of national courts that other law is mostly the *lex fori*.

2.60 The focus here is on the so-called negative function of the public policy mechanism, ie the rejection of a foreign law which would otherwise have been applicable and its replacement with another law.

2.61 As regards national public policy in international commercial arbitration a distinction must be made between the public policy of the *lex contractus* and the public policy of national laws other than the *lex contractus*.

2.62 In international commercial arbitration there is no *lex fori* in the private international law sense of the term. As regards applicable substantive law, this means, *inter alia*, that an international arbitrator is under no obligation to apply any national law *a priori*, with the exception of course of the law chosen by the parties. The absence of a *lex fori* also means that the laws of all different nations have the same value and that none of them has a privileged status in relation to any other law. The primary allegiance of the international arbitrator is to the *lex contractus* as determined by the parties.

2.63 *Public policy of lex contractus*   In discussing the public policy of the *lex contractus* different considerations apply depending on whether *lex contractus* has been chosen by the parties or determined by the arbitrators.

2.64 *(i) Lex contractus determined by the parties*   An international arbitrator has an obligation to apply the law determined by the parties. The starting point must therefore be that the parties' discretion is unrestricted in so far as the choice of the applicable law is concerned. Not only do the parties have the discretion to choose any law or rules they wish, but they may also *exclude* the application of any national law by referring, for example, to the general principles of law, or to *ex aequo et bono*. In addition, the parties may restrict the field of application of the national law selected by combining it with the general principles of law, freeze that law at a given date, and so on. They may also exclude from the applicable law selected provisions that would otherwise make certain contractual clauses void.

2.65 It follows from the foregoing that the parties are the masters of the law or rules to be applied and also over the public policy of the law they may have chosen. After all, they can single out exactly what provisions of the law of a particular country they want to apply. From this, one can draw two important conclusions.

2.66 First, any conflict between the wording of the contract and the public policy of the law chosen by the parties must be resolved by the international arbitrator in the

---

[47] Under Swedish law the *ordre public* test is whether or not foreign law would be patently incompatible with the basic principles of Swedish law; cf Bogdan, *Svensk internationell privat- och processrätt* (7th edn, 2008) 76 *et seq*. This is obviously a very high standard.

light of the wording of the contractual clause relating to the applicable law. For example, a clause providing that 'all questions not covered by the contract shall be governed by Swiss law' puts the arbitrators under an obligation to give effect to all the contractual stipulations even if these would be void by virtue of Swiss public policy. It is important to underline again that as far as the international arbitrator is concerned there is no natural hierarchy between the municipal laws of different countries. To the contrary: a law is only applied if the parties have chosen it, and even then only within the limits of the will of the parties.

2.67 Secondly, if the parties have *not* created any hierarchy between the contractual provisions and the applicable law, the situation is different. If the parties simply refer to the law of a specific country as the applicable law—eg by stipulating that 'this contract shall be governed by and construed in accordance with Swedish substantive law'—the natural interpretation of the will of the parties would seem to be that the parties wish to apply Swedish law in its entirety, including its public policy rules. However, since the ultimate test is the will of the parties, other interpretations *may* be possible, depending on the circumstances of the individual case.

2.68 *(ii) Lex contractus determined by the arbitrators*   The situation is different if the arbitrators determine the applicable law where the parties have not specified it. In such a case, it is submitted that the arbitrators must apply that law as it stands. It is difficult to see that the arbitrators have the right to exclude one provision or another from the law determined by them, on the basis that such provision is contrary to the will of the parties as manifested in the contractual clauses. It is of course possible to envisage cases where the arbitrators take the view that the parties had the intention not to subject the contract to the public policy provisions in question, but this would presuppose that the parties' intention on this point could somehow be ascertained. This is typically unlikely to happen in a situation where the parties themselves have failed to agree on, or to specify, the applicable law.

2.69 *Public policy of other national laws than the lex contractus*   The primary allegiance of an international arbitrator is to the *lex contractus* as determined by the parties or by the arbitrator. With respect to the applicable substantive law in a dispute, there is typically no reason for him to look to the public policy of any national law other than the *lex contractus*. It has been said at times that an international arbitrator should take account of the public policy of certain other national laws, for example, in order to ensure that the resulting award does not offend the public policy of the place where enforcement may be sought. This may be advisable from a practical point of view. It is submitted, however, that an international arbitrator is under no *obligation* to respect the public policy of any national law, except as described above.[48]

2.70 Needless to say, it is of utmost importance for the parties to obtain a valid and enforceable arbitral award. In fact the entire arbitral process is geared towards

---

[48] See discussion at para 2.59 *et seq.*

this goal. Should the resulting award be unenforceable because it violates the public policy of the country where enforcement is sought, the parties would have spent time, money, and energy in vain. It is probably fair to assume that most arbitrators do their utmost to ensure that the award will be enforceable. In real life this is, however, easier said than done, because it will in many, if not most, cases be impossible for the arbitrators to know in which country, or countries, enforcement will ultimately be sought. Given the widespread acceptance of the 1958 New York Convention, enforcement will often be sought not only in the home country of the losing party, but in any jurisdiction where he may have assets. The practical considerations underlying the desire to render an enforceable award cannot and do not create any *legal obligation* for the arbitrator to apply, or to take account of, the public policy rules of countries where enforcement may ultimately be sought.

2.3.4.4 *Mandatory rules of municipal law*

2.71 **Generally** Mandatory municipal law rules are usually defined as rules which are deemed to be so essential from the viewpoint of an individual State that their application may *never*—in the view of the State in question—be set aside by foreign laws.[49] The scope of application of mandatory rules is mainly determined with regard to their *objective* rather than with regard to the *result* of their application. As opposed to the public policy rules of any given State—which come into play only on the basis of the circumstances of an individual case—mandatory rules are *always* to be applied, irrespective of which foreign law is applicable to the contract and irrespective of which results such application produces.[50]

2.72 The concept of mandatory rules has evolved on the basis of the legal status of particular rules in the *lex fori*. Such rules—which are sometimes referred to as public policy laws (*lois d'ordre public*), or *lois de police*[51]—are different from the public policy mechanism in that they are deemed so essential as to be applied under any and all circumstances even if the foreign law in question does not violate the public policy of *lex fori*.[52] In the practice of national courts such rules often aim to protect the weaker

---

[49] See eg Eek, *Lagkonflikter i tvistemål II* (1978) 107–110; Bogdan, *Svensk internationell privat- och processrätt* (7th edn, 2008) 84–85; Pålsson, *Romkonventionen—Tillämplig lag för avtalsförpliktelser* (1998) 114–115 and, generally, Cordero Moss, *International Commercial Arbitration and Mandatory Rules* (1999).

[50] In Sweden, for example, labour law legislation and consumer protection legislation are sometimes mentioned as such mandatory rules, Cf Bogdan, *op cit*, at 84–85.

[51] Another term often used in French legal literature is *lois d'application immédiate*, see Francescakis, 'Lois d'application immédiate et règles de conflit', 3 *Revue critique de droit international privé* (1967) 691–697. Another way to describe such laws is to characterize them as 'positive' public policy rules, where the positive function of public policy is to insist on the immediate application of certain rules whereby such rules replace the ordinarily applicable conflicts rules of *lex fori* rather than the foreign law in question, cf Eek, *Lagkonflikter i tvistemål II* (1978) 107.

[52] Cf Article 7(1) of the 1980 Rome Convention on the Law Applicable to Contractual Obligations, which stipulates: 'When applying under this convention the law of a country, effect may be given to the mandatory rules of the law of another country with which the situation has a close connection, if and so far as, under the law of the latter country, those rules must be applied whatever the law applicable

party in a contractual relationship. While there seems to be general acceptance that such mandatory rules exist within the conflict of laws rules of the *lex fori*, the situation is much more complicated with respect to international commercial arbitration.

An international arbitrator need not take account of the distinction between **2.73** mandatory rules of the forum and foreign mandatory rules. The distinction that he has to make is between mandatory rules of the *lex contractus* and mandatory rules of other national legal systems.

In discussing mandatory rules of municipal law, we must distinguish between such **2.74** rules of the *lex contractus* and mandatory rules of other national laws than the *lex contractus*. Furthermore, we must distinguish between situations when the parties have chosen the *lex contractus* and when the *lex contractus* has been determined by the arbitrators.

Mandatory rules of the lex contractus
(i) Lex contractus determined by the parties This situation resembles the situa- **2.75** tion discussed above with respect to national public policy when the *lex contractus* has been chosen by the parties. This means, as a matter of principle, that party autonomy reigns supreme. There is nothing to prevent the parties from deciding to restrict the application of the law chosen to certain specific issues, or the other way around, to exclude certain contractual provisions from being subject to the *lex con-tractus* which would otherwise have rendered such provisions invalid. Ultimately, the parties could have chosen another law which would not have rendered the contractual provisions in question invalid. The ultimate test, however, is the will of the parties. To determine the will of the parties, the arbitrators must interpret the relevant contractual provisions. Thus, if the parties have simply stated that 'this contract shall be governed by the substantive laws of France', the arbitrators must also apply the mandatory rules of French law. The generally held opinion seems to be that the arbitrators must apply the mandatory rules of the *lex contractus*, provided that the parties have not exercised their autonomy so as to exclude the mandatory rules of the *lex contractus*.[53] This would mean, for example, that to the extent that

---

to the contract. In considering whether to give effect to these mandatory rules, regard shall be had to their nature and purpose and to the consequences of their application or non-application'. For a general discussion of Article 7 of the Convention, see Pålsson, *op cit*, at 114–126. While mandatory rules may express the public policy of the *lex fori*, there is no automatic link between the two categories. Technical rules of law, eg in the administrative law field, typically have little to do with upholding fundamental values of the legal system in question but would rather seem to be prompted by considerations of legal efficiency and order, cf Böckstiegel, 'Public Policy and Arbitrability', in *Comparative Arbitration Practice and Public Policy in Arbitration*. VIIIth International Arbitration Congress, New York, 4–6 May 1986 (1987) 183.

[53] Cf eg Lazareff, 'Mandatory Extraterritorial Application of National Law', *Arbitration International* (1995) 135, where it is said—without distinguishing between the situation when the parties have chosen *lex contractus* and when it has been determined by the arbitrators—that '[t]here is no doubt that the mandatory rules of the *lex contractus* should be applied by the arbitrator, whether or not invoked by the parties'. The latter part of the quoted language raises a crucial issue of—predominantly—a procedural character, viz, whether or not an arbitrator may apply a law, or

EC competition rules form part of the *lex contractus*, and have not been excluded by the parties, the arbitrators must apply such rules. Some commentators take the view, however, that antitrust rules must always be applied and cannot be 'set aside' by virtue of a choice of law by the parties, nor ignored by arbitrators acting as *amiables compositeurs* or deciding *ex aequo et bono*.[54]

2.76 The application of EC competition rules is a complicated question that has generated much discussion. There is a fundamental rule of the arbitral process which plays a decisive role in this connection, viz, the prohibition on arbitrators acting *ultra petita* and going beyond the authority bestowed upon them by the parties; as Roman law puts it with characteristic economy: *arbiter nihil extra compromissum facere potest*. This means, it is submitted, that unless at least one of the parties has raised the issue of EC competition law the arbitrators cannot raise that issue *ex officio*. They have neither the right nor the obligation to do so. On the other hand, if that issue has been raised by at least one of the parties, then the arbitrators must address it, otherwise they would be acting *infra petita*, which could result in the award being set aside.[55]

2.77 *(ii) Lex contractus determined by the arbitrators*   It would seem that in cases where the arbitrators determine the *lex contractus*, the arbitrators will also have to apply the mandatory rules of the *lex contractus*. For the same reasons as those discussed above with respect to public policy, it is difficult to see why the arbitrators should have the right to exclude certain provisions of the *lex contractus* in this situation.[56]

2.78 *Mandatory rules of other national laws than the lex contractus*   The situation becomes even more complicated when the question of applying mandatory rules of national laws other than *lex contractus* must be answered. Against the background of the foregoing discussion—which proceeds from the assumption that it is the will of the parties which must be decisive—one is inclined to ask if there is any reason at all for the arbitrator to apply rules which have nothing to do with the *lex contractus*.

provisions of a law, even if neither of the parties has relied on such law, or provisions, in the arbitration. As pointed out by Lazareff, Mayer has taken the view that an arbitrator has an obligation to apply the mandatory rules of the *lex contractus* only if the parties have not excluded the application of such rules and provided that at least one of the parties has relied on such rules, see Mayer, 'Mandatory Rules of Law in International Arbitration', *Arbitration International* (1986) 280.

[54] See eg Dalhuisen, 'The Arbitrability of Competition Issues', *Arbitration International* (1995) 161. Dalhuisen refers, *inter alia*, to the 1980 Rome Convention on the Law Applicable to Contractual Obligations, Article 3 of which stipulates that mandatory rules of a country cannot be contracted out of when all the elements connected with the situation are relevant to that country; see also Weigand, 'Evading EC Competition Law by Resorting to Arbitration?' *Arbitration International* (1993) 251–252. The relationship between EC competition rules and international commercial arbitration was discussed in a much debated judgment rendered by the European Court of Justice in *Eco Swiss China Ltd v Benetton International NV*, C-126/97. In this case the European Court concluded that national courts of law must set aside arbitral awards which violate the EC competition rules, provided that the national legislation in question stipulates that arbitral awards which violate public policy may be set aside.

[55] See discussion at para 8.76 *et seq.*

[56] See para 2.59 *et seq.*

Generally speaking, there would seem to be two potential grounds for the arbitrator to do so, viz, (i) that the mandatory rules in question form part of international public policy, and (ii) that the arbitrator has a duty to ensure that the resulting award is enforceable. If one were to accept the first proposition, it would seem that the ultimate ground is that the rules form part of international public policy, rather than constituting mandatory rules of any municipal law system. With respect to the second proposition, it has already been suggested that the arbitrator is under no such obligation. Needless to say, such a position may result in an award not being enforceable, if for example, such mandatory rules are deemed to form part of the public policy of the country where enforcement is sought. It is submitted, however, that it must be up to the parties, rather than the arbitrators, to decide how they wish to address such a potential risk.

In discussing this issue, it would once again seem necessary to distinguish between the situation where the parties have and have not, respectively, chosen the *lex contractus*. **2.79**

(i) Lex contractus determined by the parties The arbitrators are bound to apply the law chosen by the parties. This principle is really all it takes for them not to apply mandatory rules of a national legal system other than the *lex contractus*. **2.80**

There seems to be a school of thought suggesting that arbitrators have a *duty* to apply mandatory rules other than those found in the *lex contractus*.[57] **2.81**

This school of thought seems to be based on assumptions the correctness of which is doubtful. For example, one of the assumptions seems to be that arbitration as an institution must exercise a certain amount of self-restraint so as not to end up in disrepute in the eyes of national judiciaries and enforcement authorities. It is submitted, however, that there is no evidence that arbitrators are under such an obligation as a matter of law. As far as public policy is concerned, it would seem that States having doubts in this respect should avail themselves of Article V(2) of the New York Convention which allows them to refuse recognition and enforcement precisely on public policy grounds. **2.82**

Reference is sometimes made in this connection to Article 7(1) of the 1980 Rome Convention on the Applicable Law to Contractual Obligations. Suffice it to point out that the Article stipulates that 'effect *may* be given to the mandatory rules of the law of another country . . .' (emphasis added). This means that courts in States **2.83**

---

[57] Cf eg Werner, 'Application of Competition Laws by Arbitrators. The Step Too Far', *Journal of International Arbitration* (1995) 23–24. See also Grigera Naon, *Choice of Law Problems in International Commercial Arbitration* (1992) 69; Blessing, 'Mandatory Rules of Law versus Party Autonomy in International Arbitration', *Journal of International Arbitration* (1997) 23; Craig, Park, and Paulsson, *International Chamber of Commerce Arbitration* (2nd edn, 1990) 307; Schiffer, *Normen ausländischen 'öffentlichen' Rechts in internationalen Handelsschiedsverfahren* (1990) 65–67, 169–170; Drobnig, 'Internationale Schiedsgerichtsbarkeit und wirtschaftsrechtliche Eingriffsnormen', in *Festschrift für Kegel* (1987) 95, 112, 117.

which have ratified the Convention are not under an *obligation* to do so, but that they may. Moreover, it is unclear exactly what the words 'effect may be given to' mean. This language does not necessarily mean 'apply', but could simply mean 'consider', or 'take into account'.[58]

2.84 In order to apply mandatory rules other than those of the *lex contractus*, it would, generally speaking, seem to be necessary for the transaction in question to have some connection with the country whose mandatory rules are relied upon. If that is the case, the country concerned could be said to have an interest in having its mandatory rules applied by arbitrators. If such laws were *not* applied by the arbitrators, and if the resulting award were to be enforced in that country, there could be a risk that the mandatory rules in question would be deemed to form part of the public policy of that country, which is a ground on which refusal to enforce the award could be based. Such a line of reasoning brings us back to the question whether or not the arbitrator has an obligation to ensure that the award is enforceable. It is difficult to see that the arbitrator has any obligation *per se* to safeguard the interests of the State whose mandatory rules are relied upon. The only allegiance which the arbitrators have is in relation to the parties; it is their will that the arbitrator must comply with. However, there may—at least theoretically—exist one reason for the arbitrator to apply such mandatory rules, viz, if non-application would violate international public policy.

2.85 *(ii) Lex contractus determined by the arbitrator* An international arbitrator should proceed from the assumption that all national laws have the same weight, as long as the parties have not determined that one or several of them should be applied to the substance of the case. Consequently, there is theoretically nothing to prevent an arbitrator from applying mandatory rules of another law than the *lex contractus*, if the parties have made no choice of law. From a practical point of view, such application seems to be most frequently resorted to in relation to the mandatory rules of the State where the contract is to be performed. It should be pointed out, however, that there seems to be no consensus among arbitrators, nor among writers, as to the applicability of mandatory rules foreign to the *lex contractus* when this law has not been chosen by the parties. It would seem that several arbitrators and commentators tend to favour application of mandatory rules of the place of performance of the contract.

2.86 Arbitral practice presents a rather mixed picture. The only conclusion one can draw is that sometimes arbitrators do apply mandatory rules of other municipal laws than the *lex contractus* and that they usually refer to some strong and purportedly legitimate interest of the State whose mandatory rules are concerned as justifying the application of such rules.

2.87 In discussing the application of mandatory rules foreign to the *lex contractus* it is important to distinguish between the following two situations, viz,

---

[58] See Pålsson, *op cit*, at 122–125.

(a) application of mandatory rules, and
(b) consideration of mandatory rules as factual circumstances.

It is possible, for example, to take account of or to consider foreign mandatory rules   **2.88** such as currency control regulations, import and export regulations, and the like without *applying* such rules in the sense that such rules do not form the legal basis for the decision of the arbitrators. Assume for example that a contract is subject to the laws of the state of New York and that a debtor invokes the exchange control regulations of his home country as a ground for his non-payment of a certain sum, since the regulations lead to the invalidity of the contract in the given situation. To accept such an argument does not necessarily mean that the exchange control regulations are being *applied* in the legal-technical sense, but could mean that they are merely taken into account as a factual circumstance in deciding whether or not the agreement should be declared invalid under the laws of New York. All the legal conclusions as to the validity of the contract are thus to be drawn on the basis of the laws of New York. This does not mean that the arbitrator *applies* the exchange control regulations, but that he evaluates their effect on the performance of the contract, an evaluation which is done on the basis of the *lex contractus*.

2.3.4.5 International public policy

Introduction   The discussion above concerning national public policy and   **2.89** mandatory rules of municipal law has shown that there are no clear cut lines to be drawn between these two concepts. The concept of international public policy is even more difficult to define and to distinguish from the other two concepts. There is one distinctive feature, however, pertaining to international public policy, viz, that it is not connected with any particular *national* system of law. Rather, it is based on and stems from notions and policies purportedly generally accepted by the international community as a whole. In that sense one could perhaps characterize international public policy as the lowest common denominator of all legal systems of the world. There is, however, at least one troubling theoretical aspect with the concept of international public policy. Since it is not based on any municipal law, nor on any supra-national rule, it is not possible to regulate, to enforce, or to apply any sanctions should international public policy have been deviated from. In practice, it would seem likely that if application of any law or rule would be deemed to be contrary to international public policy such application would in all likelihood also violate the national public policy of one or several States. Consequently, in such a situation the same result could be achieved by applying the national public policy of a State, rather than by referring to international public policy. In this perspective, it would seem difficult to characterize international public policy as an *additional* restriction on party autonomy. Already for this reason, the field of application of international public policy must necessarily be very restricted. Nevertheless, there may, at least theoretically, be situations where an arbitrator would consider himself prevented from applying the national public policy of any given State and would therefore want to rely on international public policy.

2.90 Generally speaking, there seems to be a consensus that international public policy *does* exist in international commercial arbitration and that it *does* have a role to play. However, this consensus seems to exist mostly at the conceptual level, rather than at the practical level when it comes to implementation of the concept. There are two aspects which continue to vex scholars and practitioners alike, viz, (i) what is the *function* of international public policy in international commercial arbitration, and (ii) what exactly is the *content* of international public policy? Before these two issues are discussed, there is a very fundamental issue to be answered with respect to international commercial arbitration: if there is such a thing as international public policy, why must the international arbitrator apply it? We are faced again with the fact that the international arbitrator is, it is submitted, the servant of the parties only and has no allegiance to any State, nor to any municipal law system.

2.91 The fact remains, however, that the concept of international public policy has been mentioned and discussed in a number of arbitral awards and is cited with approval in the legal literature. Thus, even though a sound theoretical base for the concept may be lacking, international public policy does play a certain role in modern international commercial arbitration.

2.3.4.6 The function of international public policy

2.92 As mentioned above, the function of national public policy is to replace a law—which would otherwise have been applied—with another law. Traditionally, this has *not* been the function ascribed to international public policy. Rather, its role has generally been considered to be of a positive character, in the sense that its effect has been said *directly* to influence the arbitrators in resolving a given dispute.[59] In this sense the traditional function of international public policy could perhaps be said to be parallel to that of mandatory rules of municipal law.[60] While the positive function of international public policy is still considered to be its main function, it has been suggested that it may also have a *negative* function. This negative function may take two forms: first to exclude the application of laws and rules which would normally be applicable, and second to exclude the application of the national public policy of a given State, in case such public policy would contradict international public policy. In all likelihood the latter situation would in practice be an unusual one, but theoretically possible.

2.3.4.7 The content of international public policy

2.93 Since most international arbitrations are typically based on one or several contracts, the central question is to determine the extent to which international public policy may influence the validity of the disputed contract(s). This brings us to the most difficult question of all in this connection, viz, to determine the *content* of international

---

[59] Lew, *op cit*, at 539.
[60] See para 2.71 *et seq*.

public policy. It goes almost without saying that there is no generally accepted comprehensive definition of what constitutes international public policy. Rather one has to search for the constituent parts of international public policy in various sources of law and in other norms. Despite the lack of a general definition, there seems to be a consensus as to certain occurrences which are deemed to form part of international public policy.

One classic example is bribery and corruption. The landmark case in this sphere is **2.94** an award rendered by Judge Gunnar Lagergren in 1963.[61] In that case a claim was made for payment of a commission for a contract obtained by a British company in Argentina. Pursuant to the agreement between the parties the claimant was to receive 10 per cent of the value of the contract. Although both parties agreed to submit their dispute to arbitration and have the arbitrator decide on the merits of the dispute, Judge Lagergren felt compelled to dismiss the case *ex officio* on the basis that such a claim was not arbitrable, as a consequence of which the arbitrator did not have jurisdiction over the dispute. Judge Lagergren explained, *inter alia*, in his award that 'it cannot be contested that there exists a general principle of law recognized by civilized nations that contracts which seriously violate *bonos mores* or international public policy are invalid or at least unenforceable and that they cannot be sanctioned by courts or arbitrators'.[62]

Judge Lagergren's characterization and rejection of bribery and corruption has not **2.95** changed over the years. However, the conclusions to be drawn from this rejection have changed, such that the prevailing view today seems to be that the arbitrator ought not to decline jurisdiction. Rather, an arbitrator should rule on the merits of the dispute in question, even if bribery and corruption are involved and thus deny such claims, based as they are on contractual clauses which are null and void, because they violate international public policy.[63] Irrespective of which approach is used, there is general agreement that contractual provisions concerning bribery and corruption are invalid since they violate international public policy.

---

[61] This award is probably one of the most frequently cited awards in the literature of international arbitration. The first comprehensive summary of award was published by Lew, *op cit*, at 553–555. It was not until 1994, however, that the full text of the award was published, see Wetter, 'Issues of Corruption before International Arbitral Tribunals: The Authentic Text and True Meaning of Judge Gunnar Lagergren's Award in ICC Case No 1110', *Arbitration International* (1194) 277. This is the first known arbitration where an arbitrator has applied international public policy to refuse enforcement of a contract involving bribes.

[62] 48) Quoted from Wetter, note 61, at 293.

[63] See eg El Kosheri and Leboulanger, 'L'arbitrage face à la corruption et aux trafics d'influence', *Revue de l'Arbitrage* (1984) 3; Lew, 'Determination of Arbitrators' Jurisdiction and the Public Policy Limitations on that Jurisdiction', in Lew (ed), *Contemporary Problems in International Arbitration* (1986) 82–85, Böckstiegel, note 53 at 200–202; Goldman, 'The Complementary Roles of Judges and Arbitrators in Ensuring that International Commercial Arbitration is Effective', in *ICC Court of Arbitration 60th Anniversary* (1984) 272; Oppetit, 'Le Paradoxe de la corruption à l'epreuve du Droit Du Commerce International', *Journal du droit international* (1987) 5; Rubino-Sammartano, *International Arbitration Law* (1989) 317–321; Eriksson, 'Arbitration and Contracts Involving Corrupt Practices: The Arbitrator's Dilemma', *American Review of International Arbitration* (1993) 407–411.

2.96 Other areas where there seems to be a consensus—at least in scholarly writings— that they form part of international public policy include drug traffic, slavery, racial, religious and sexual discrimination, violation of human rights, kidnapping, murder, piracy, and terrorism. Consequently, contractual provisions aimed at facilitating such practices would typically be held invalid as violating international public policy, irrespective of which law the parties have chosen to govern their contract.

2.4 No Choice of Law by the Parties

2.4.1 Introduction

2.97 In situations where the parties have not made any choice of law, the arbitrators must address the question of applicable law. In doing so, they are faced with the initial question of *how* to determine the applicable law. There are two aspects of this issue, viz, (i) must the arbitrator use a conflict of laws system to find the applicable law, and (ii) assuming that the answer to the first aspect is in the positive, which conflict of laws system should he apply?

2.98 For many years one view often expressed was that arbitrators should use a conflict of laws system to find the applicable law. Every developed system of national law has rules for the conflict of laws, sometimes referred to as private international law rules. The suggestion was often made that the arbitrators should apply the conflict of laws rules of the place of arbitration.[64]

2.99 The more modern view is that arbitrators need not go through a conflict of laws system to find the applicable law. Rather, they can directly determine the law applicable to the merits of the dispute. For example, in the UNCITRAL Model Law, Article 28(2), the revised version thereof, authorizes the arbitrators to apply the law which they consider to be appropriate. Many arbitration rules have provisions to the same effect. For example, Article 22(1) of the SCC Rules stipulates that the tribunal 'shall apply the law or rules of law which it considers to be most appropriate'.

2.100 This modern view makes sense. It is in full harmony with the desire to give an arbitral tribunal considerable flexibility in making its choice of law. It is seldom meaningful to have the arbitrators first find a conflict of laws system in order to find the applicable law.

2.101 The approach suggested above means that there is no need to address the second aspect mentioned above, ie which conflict of laws system should the arbitrators

---

[64] For example, in the second edition of *Arbitration in Sweden* (1984) 46–47, it was suggested that Swedish conflict of laws rules should be applied when the parties had agreed on Sweden as the place of arbitration. Cf SCC Cases 80/1998 and 81/1998 in SIAR 2002, p 45, where the tribunal found that an arbitral tribunal sitting in Sweden is not obliged to apply Swedish conflict of laws rules, but is recommended to do so when the parties have agreed on Sweden as the place of arbitration.

apply? If arbitrators nevertheless are faced with this aspect, the modern view today is that there should be no preference for the conflict of laws rules of the place of arbitration. As far as Swedish arbitration law is concerned, there is indeed no *requirement* that Swedish conflict of laws rules be applied in an arbitration taking place in Sweden. The rationale underlying this approach is that parties cannot be presumed to have accepted the conflict of laws rules of the place of arbitration simply because they have chosen a specific place for the arbitration. This does not mean, however, that the conflict of laws rules of the place of arbitration cannot, and do not, play a role in the selection of the applicable law.

Generally speaking, it would be reasonable to assume that for arbitrators sitting in **2.102** Sweden—Swedish as well as non-Swedish—the Swedish conflict of laws rules will often serve as a point of departure in their search for the applicable substantive law.

2.4.2 Swedish conflict of laws rules

In the commercial law field, the Swedish conflict of laws rules were until relatively **2.103** recently by and large uncodified. The rules were based on case law and scholarly writings.[65] It is important to note that case law concerning Swedish conflict of laws rules is sparse. This can be explained due to the fact that a very large proportion of commercial disputes in Sweden are resolved through arbitration rather than court litigation. Needless to say, choice of law issues are often addressed in commercial arbitration. Since arbitral awards are not published on a regular basis, however, decisions on applicable law by arbitrators are usually not available. During the last decade the situation has changed somewhat, such that more and more awards are being published. Such awards thus provide some guidance with respect to choice of law issues in arbitrations conducted in Sweden.

The development of modern Swedish conflict of laws rules in the commercial law **2.104** field can be divided into three time periods.[66] The first period starts in 1937 with a well-known case decided by the Swedish Supreme Court, *Försäkringsaktiebolaget Skandia v Riksgäldskontoret*.[67] In this case the Supreme Court introduced the centre of gravity test. This approach to choice of law issues in contractual matters was predominant until 1998, when the second period started. In that year Sweden adopted the 1980 Rome Convention on the Law Applicable to Contractual Obligations by adopting a statute incorporating the Rome Convention. It should be noted that the Rome Convention is not applicable in Sweden to contracts entered into prior to 1 July 1998. With respect to such contracts the centre of gravity test is

---

[65] See eg note 5.
[66] The three time periods are relevant to the situation where the parties have *not* agreed on the applicable law. The principle of party autonomy has always been accepted as a fundamental principle of Swedish private international law. The discussion in para 2.14 *et seq* is consequently highly relevant also from a more narrow Swedish perspective.
[67] NJA 1937 p 7.

still applied, at least as a matter of principle. The third period started on 17 December 2009 as of which date the Rome I Regulation came into force. It will be applicable to contracts entered into after 17 December 2009. Both the centre of gravity test and the 1980 Rome Convention will thus continue to be of importance for the foreseeable future.

2.105   There is one statute which runs through all three time periods mentioned above, viz, the 1964 Act on the Law Applicable to International Sales of Goods. This Act is based on the Hague Convention of 15 June 1955 on the Law Applicable to International Sales of Goods, of which Sweden is a member.[68] It follows from both the 1980 Rome Convention and the Rome I Regulation that these two instruments do not affect the application of previously adopted conventions by EU Member States. Consequently, the 1964 Act continues to be applicable as part of Swedish conflict of laws rules.

2.4.2.1 The 1964 Act on the Law Applicable to International Sales of Goods

2.106   Sweden is a party to the Hague Convention of 15 June 1955 on the Law Applicable to International Sales of Goods, which was incorporated into Swedish municipal legislation by the 1964 Act on the Law Applicable to International Sales of Goods.

2.107   The 1964 Act is of general application, ie it applies also with respect to States which have not ratified the Hague Convention.

2.108   The main principle of the Hague Convention is that when parties to an international contract of sale have not agreed on a choice of law, the contract will be governed by the law of the jurisdiction where the seller was domiciled at the time he received the order. As will be discussed, however, the law of the purchaser might be applied, for example, when the seller receives the order in the jurisdiction of the purchaser.

2.109   The fact that the 1964 Act forms part of the Swedish conflict of laws rules, and is of general application, raises the question whether it is reasonable, and in conformity with the expectations of the parties, to apply the provisions of the Act when two non-Swedish parties have agreed to arbitrate in Sweden and the parties come from States which have not ratified the 1955 Hague Convention. It could perhaps be argued that the 1964 Act should *not* be applied in such a situation. Similar considerations apply when only one of the parties comes from a State which has ratified the Convention. At least in the latter situation arbitration practice would seem to have accepted application of the 1964 Act. In one arbitration from the late 1980s conducted in Stockholm, the arbitral tribunal applied the 1964 Act leading to the application of Soviet law, despite the fact that the Soviet Union had not ratified the 1955 Hague Convention. This issue was not squarely addressed by the tribunal because none of the parties raised any objection to application of the 1964 Act.

---

[68] The convention has also been ratified by Belgium, Denmark, Finland, France, Italy, Nigeria, Norway, and Switzerland.

In this connection, it is important to mention the 1987 Swedish Act on International **2.110** Sales. Sweden has acceded to the 1980 Vienna Convention on the International Sale of Goods. The 1987 Act became effective as of 1 January 1989. The Act, just like the Convention, regulates various *substantive* aspects of international sales such as the rights and obligations of sellers and purchasers, termination, and damages. If a dispute concerns an international sales transaction as defined in the Convention, and the parties have chosen Swedish (substantive) law, the 1987 Swedish Act will be applied.

The starting point under the 1964 Act is the principle of party autonomy. Section 3 **2.111** of the Act confirms that the parties are free to agree on the applicable law. Failing such choice of law, section 4 stipulates that that the law of the place where the seller is domiciled at the time of receipt of the order is to be applied. If the order has been received at a *permanent place of business* of the seller, the law of that place is applied. It should be noted that it must be a permanent place of business of the seller, which probably means that receipt by a permanent agent/agency is not sufficient.

The law of the seller is thus the main principle enshrined in the 1964 Act. The rationale **2.112** is that typically the performance of the seller is the most characteristic performance under a sales contract. There are situations, however, where the 1964 Act prescribes the application of the law of the buyer, ie the law of his domicile. Section 4, paragraph 2 stipulates that the law of the buyer is to be applied if the seller, or his authorized representative, receives the order at the *domicile of the buyer*, or the law of the country where the *buyer has a permanent place of business* if the order is placed there.

In an arbitration decided in 1987 the application of the 1964 Act, in particular the **2.113** exception to the main rule in section 4, was dealt with by the tribunal.[69]

(a) The dispute arose between a French company (the 'Company') and a Soviet foreign trade organization (the 'Organization') concerning the sale of certain manufacturing equipment. The French company sold such equipment to the Organization. The contract of sale (the 'Contract') which was signed in Moscow contained an arbitration clause providing for arbitration in Stockholm. The clause also stipulated that the award was to be rendered pursuant to such 'rules of law as may be applicable pursuant to the conflict of laws rules of the country where the tribunal has its seat'. The parties were in agreement that the applicable conflict of laws rules were those contained in the 1964 Act. The parties were also in agreement that the Contract had been signed in Moscow.

(b) The Organization argued that since the Contract had been signed in Moscow, the seller had received the order in Moscow, as a consequence of which Soviet law had to be applied. The Company, on the other hand, took the position that the order was made through a letter from the Organization to the Company. In a further letter, the Company accepted the order. This was done at the domicile of the Company, ie in France, as a consequence of which French substantive law had to

---

[69] See Hobér in *Search for the Centre of Gravity, Swedish and International Arbitration* (1994) 32–33.

be applied. This letter stipulated, *inter alia*, that the Contract was to be negotiated. In the opinion of the Company, this exchange of letters constituted the order and that only the *means* of fulfilling the agreement between the parties were the subject of negotiations in Moscow. The Company also maintained that a further reason for applying French substantive law was that such law had the closest link with the dispute. The Company did not, however, elaborate on this point.

(c) The Organization replied with respect to the two letters relied on by the Company that the first letter constituted a solicitation of an offer and that the second letter was the offer thus requested. As a consequence of this no legal and binding commitments existed prior to the signing in Moscow of the Contract. In addition, said the Organization, all addenda which were subsequently made to the Contract were likewise signed in Moscow.

(d) In its decision the tribunal started by saying that it was clear from the submissions of the parties that the Contract had been negotiated and signed in Moscow. It went on to say that the Contract constituted the final and legally binding agreement between the parties. According to the legal history of the 1964 Act, signing of the Contract in the buyer's country would for purposes of applying that Act be considered as tantamount to the seller having received the order there. Consequently, the tribunal said, the substantive law of the country in which the buyer is domiciled shall apply. In the case at hand this meant that the substantive law of the Soviet Union had to be applied and in particular the law of the RSFSR where the seat of the Organization was situated.

2.114 In this case, the tribunal thus applied the exception to the main rule laid down in section 4 of the 1964 Act, ie the law of the buyer when the order had been received at the buyer's domicile. As the tribunal pointed out, when a contract is signed in the presence of both parties at the domicile of the buyer, this means that the order must be deemed to have been received at his domicile.

2.115 In a more recent case,[70] a tribunal concluded that it was not under an obligation to apply Swedish conflict of laws rules—in particular the 1964 Act, since the disputed contract concerned the international sale of goods—because the place of arbitration had not been agreed by the parties, but had been selected by the Arbitration Institute of the Stockholm Chamber of Commerce. The tribunal concluded that it should first apply conflict of laws rules to find the governing substantive law. It also concluded that the essential issue was to determine the legal system with which the transaction had its closest connection. The tribunal found that this system was the law of the seller. In reaching this conclusion, the tribunal referred to the 1964 Act—which had been relied on by the claimant—but did not *apply* the 1964 Act. Rather it applied international and generally accepted standards for deciding the closest connection of a contract.[71]

---

[70] SCC Cases 80/1998 and 81/1998, SIAR 2002, vol 2, 45.
[71] Ibid, 54.

The 1964 Act is not applicable to sales concerning registered ships and aircraft, nor **2.116** to securities or sales organized by judicial bodies. Sales of real estate, services, intellectual property rights, and electricity are also excluded. It should also be noted that questions concerning the form of the agreement, the legal capacity of the parties, as well as *in rem* aspects are not covered by the 1964 Act.[72]

As far as purchases at exchanges and auctions are concerned, the law to be applied is **2.117** the law of the place where the exchange is located, or where the auction takes place.

2.4.2.2 The centre of gravity test

The main principle of the Swedish conflict of laws rules in the field of contracts— **2.118** when no choice of law has been made, and when the 1964 Act is inapplicable—used to be that the applicable law was that of the jurisdiction with which a contract had its closest connection, or where its centre of gravity was.[73]

The centre of gravity test was laid down by the Swedish Supreme Court in a case **2.119** from 1937, *Försäkringsaktiebolaget Skandia v Riksgäldskontoret*.[74]

The case concerned United States dollar bonds sold in New York by the Kingdom **2.120** of Sweden acting through the National Debt Office (*Riksgäldskontoret*). The bonds did not have any choice of law clause and the question was whether the bonds were governed by Swedish law or by the law of the state of New York. The Supreme Court concluded, on the basis of a number of connecting factors, that the bonds belonged to the American market. The Supreme Court consequently applied New York law. In reaching its conclusion, the Court made an analysis of various elements in the contractual documents with a view to establishing as governing law the law of the country with which the contract had its closest connection.

For the Supreme Court the most significant such elements were not only the **2.121** form of the bonds, but also the fact that they were exclusively payable in New York in United States dollars. The Court did take account of the fact that the issuer of the bonds was the sovereign Swedish State, a fact which at the time would normally have prompted application of the traditional *lex domicilii debitoris* rule.[75] However, the Court took the position that other connecting factors outweighed this element.

Skandia was a landmark case in that it replaced the previously existing theory of the **2.122** so-called hypothetical will of the parties. The underlying philosophy of this theory was the attempt to establish the will of the parties, as if they had thought of the question of

---

[72] See para 2.173 *et seq.*
[73] See Hobér, note 69. For a critical analysis of the centre of gravity principle, see Göransson, 'A Swedish Centre of Gravity Test?—Law, Fact and Fiction on the Individualizing Method', in *Essays in Honour of Lennart Pålsson* (1997) 47.
[74] NJA 1937 p 1.
[75] Cf Nial, note 5, *Selected Problems of Private International Law*, 43–44.

applicable law when they entered into the contract. The search for the hypothetical will of the parties was thus a subjective method. By contrast, the centre of gravity test represented a move away from the subjective approach and introduced an objective approach, in that it prescribes the weighing of *all objective elements* of a legal relationship with a view to finding the law of the country with which the relationship had its closest connection. The classification of the centre of gravity test as an objective method would typically mean that such aspects as the well-founded assumptions of the parties and what they had reasonable grounds to believe with respect to applicable substantive law ought to be disregarded. However, the difference between the two approaches—one subjective, the other objective—should not be exaggerated as far as the results are concerned because the hypothetical will of the parties would in most cases typically coincide with the law of the country with which the contract has its closest connection. This is so because even if one tries to establish the hypothetical will of the parties in question, it will in practice mostly prove impossible; the search for the hypothetical will therefore usually boil down to the following question: what would two reasonable businessmen have done in the same situation? In answering this question, one is very close to applying the centre of gravity test.

2.123   Generally speaking, when applying the centre of gravity test *all* connecting factors relating to the contract in question must be taken into account. This means that the *domicile* and the *nationality* of the disputing parties must be considered, as well as the place where the contract *was signed* and the *place of performance*. Other factors include the *language* of the contract and the *currency* to be used pursuant to the contract. In addition to these traditional connecting factors, a court of law would seem to be free to take account of any other elements of the contract it deems appropriate in determining the centre of gravity of the contract. It must be emphasized, however, that the weighing of the various connecting factors can never be a mechanical exercise in the sense that a court will simply count the number of such factors. Rather, a court must determine the relative weight and importance of the connecting factors in light of the actual circumstances of the individual case.

2.124   In fact, this means that a subjective element is inherent also in the centre of gravity test, which is therefore better characterized as a quasi-objective rather than an objective approach. Since there is no fixed benchmark for each of the connecting factors, the ultimate determination will depend on the discretion of the courts. Needless to say, this inescapable fact raises not only theoretical difficulties in explaining the distinctive features of the centre of gravity test, but also practical difficulties for parties in that it is difficult for them to predict what the governing substantive law will be in any given situation when they have not agreed on the governing law. For this reason the centre of gravity test has been criticized for amounting to nothing more than reading the Kremlin tea leaves, or alternatively, reading the runes. There is certainly a grain of truth in such criticism. The centre of gravity test undoubtedly provides for some uncertainty. Notwithstanding this, the method seems to have been accepted in many legal systems. The explanation for this acceptance seems to be twofold. First, in practice it is often possible to determine—in advance—the centre of gravity of a contractual relationship by taking account of and weighing the various connecting factors at hand in the individual case: in other words the feared unpredictability is mostly exaggerated. Secondly, the method provides for a degree of flexibility which is necessary in modern commercial life. Indeed the centre of gravity test was seen as a reaction against the rigidity of the previously existing conflict of laws rules, which often prescribed fixed choice of law rules for different kinds of contracts.

As far as Swedish law is concerned the relative unpredictability of the centre of gravity **2.125** test is further alleviated by the application of so-called *in dubio* rules. The *in dubio* rules are non-binding. They are rather to be characterized as recommendations which may be relied upon, if and when the centre of gravity test fails to give an unambiguous result.

It is important to keep in mind that the *in dubio* rules are subsidiary to the centre of **2.126** gravity text, in the sense that the *in dubio* rules may not be resorted to immediately, but come into play only when the centre of gravity test has failed to give a clear answer.[76]

Separate *in dubio* rules have been developed with respect to different categories of **2.127** contracts. Even though the rules have not found statutory expression, and although there is a certain amount of controversy surrounding them, below are some of the more commonly accepted *in dubio* rules.

• International sales transactions are usually governed by the *lex domicilii* of the seller; this is the main rule enshrined in the 1964 Act and also applies as an *in dubio* rule with respect to sales transactions which are not covered by the 1964 Act, eg securities. As far as registered vessels and aircraft—which are also excluded from the 1964 Act—are concerned, however, the law of the country of registration is usually applied;
• Unilateral monetary obligations (loans, guarantees, securities, and gifts) are *in dubio* subject to the *lex domicilii debitoris*;[77]
• Standard contracts of a mass bargaining character, typically concluded with banks, insurance companies, transportation companies, and the like, are governed by the *lex domicilii* of the enterprise providing the standardized service in question;[78]
• Transactions and contracts entered into at markets, fairs, auctions, stock exchanges etc, are governed by the *lex loci actus*;[79]
• Contracts for labour and services (eg construction contracts and turn-key contracts); it has traditionally been considered that such contracts should *in*

---

[76] This is at any rate the theoretical role attributed to the *in dubio* rules in the centre of gravity test. In practice, however, there seems to be a temptation for judges and arbitrators to regard such rules not as subordinated to the general test, but rather to put them on an equal footing with the centre of gravity test proper, even to a point where the *in dubio* rules are applied as if they were the actual centre of gravity test.

[77] See eg Karlgren, *Kortfattad Lärobok i Internationell Privat- och processrätt* (1974) at 101; Nial, note 5, *Selected Problems of Private International Law*, at 55–56 and 61–63.

[78] Bogdan, note 49 at 234.

[79] Karlgren, note 77 at 101.

dubio be governed by the law of the country where the work is carried out. This view is based on the following pronouncement:

- With respect to construction contracts (ie agreements for the construction of roads, buildings, etc) it is natural to assume that the law of the place where the works are executed ought to apply *in dubio*. It is true that such an agreement may relate to the sale of certain goods, but since it also involves the erection of eg machinery, it appears natural to attach particular importance in doubtful cases to the law of the place where the construction occurs at least where the construction part of the transaction is predominant. This may also be explained by the fact that the construction arbitration work involves local employment contracts, agreements with subcontractors, and possibly agreements concerning real estate which under a 'certain' rule should be subjected to the law of the place where the real estate is located[80]

- However, given the ever increasing complexity of, in particular, turn-key contracts the time has probably come to take a more differentiated view on this issue. A modern turn-key contract is typically a 'mixed' contract, combining distinctive features of supply, licensing, employment, and construction contracts. The know-how and technology provided by the exporter/supplier usually play a vital role and often include the financing of the transaction, management skills, and educational elements. The mixed character and the complexity may render impossible any attempt to find any single law which in a reasonable way takes account of all aspects of the transaction. In such situations it may be worthwhile to consider application of different laws to different issues; for example, the law of the exporter to issues relating to the supply of know-how, the law of the country where construction is carried out to issues relating to construction matters, the law of the exporter to the supply of goods and machinery, etc.

- Licensing agreements are usually governed by the law of the country where the right in question is to be exercised, with the exception of copyright, where the *lex domicilii* of the copyright holder is usually recommended.[81]

---

[80] Eek, *Exporträtt 4* (1978) 58–59, 62. See also the confirmation of this *in dubio* rule in an award rendered in 1980 by a tribunal sitting in Stockholm: 'Pursuant to the doctrine of the closest connection, the various elements of each contract are to be examined with a view to determining its centre of gravity, or, in the words of the Swedish Supreme Court (in the *Skandia* case cited above) to what legal system the agreement essentially belongs. Under both contracts here at issue, the goods were to be delivered to the [buyer's country], both [plants] were to be erected and commissioned there. It does not appear from the text of the contracts in what location they were signed, but the tribunal holds that the circumstances are immaterial. The aforementioned basic characteristic of the contracts are such that their most intimate territorial connection is with the [buyer's country]. It was held by an arbitration tribunal acting in Sweden and applying Swedish conflict of laws in ICC Case No 1703, *Société Générale de l'industrie du Papier Rakta v Parsons and Whittemore Overseas Company, Inc,* a case which bore many similarities with the present—that the law of Egypt applied to a contract which provided for the erection of a plant in that country'. Quoted in Wetter, 'Choice of Law in International Arbitration Proceedings in Sweden', 2 *Arbitration International* (1986) 301–302.

[81] Bogdan, *Patent- och varumärke i svensk internationell privat- och processrätt*, NIR (1980) 281–285.

It has sometimes been said that the common denominator of the *in dubio* rules is that **2.128** they recommend application of the law of the country where the party who is to perform the most characteristic act under the contract in question is domiciled. As the brief enumeration above suggests, this is not always the case.[82] It is noteworthy that the concept of the most characteristic performance has found its way into the 1980 Rome Convention, in so far as the concept forms the basis for the legal presumption laid down in Article 4(2) of the Convention. Even though there is no generally accepted definition of what is meant by the most characteristic performance under a contract, it is usually said that the payment of money is *not* the most characteristic performance.[83]

As mentioned above, the centre of gravity test prevailed until 1998 when Sweden **2.129** incorporated the 1980 Rome Convention. It has sometimes been suggested that this marked the introduction of a new era in Swedish conflict of laws rules. In the formal sense this is correct. As far as the practical results are concerned, however, it is doubtful that the differences between the two approaches are significant.

The 1980 Rome Convention also proceeds from the concept of a close connection **2.130** of the contractual relationship with a specific country. Instead of *in dubio* rules, however, it refers to legal presumptions. On the other hand, it is explicitly stated that the legal presumptions must be disregarded when the circumstances taken together point to another law as having the closest connection with the contract in question.[84] One might argue that the difference between the *in dubio* rules and legal presumptions, such as those laid down in the Convention are minimal, indeed a question of semantics rather than substance. There are, however, differences both at the practical and theoretical levels. One such difference is that—at least from a legal technical point of view—a presumption must be rebutted, otherwise it will prevail.

It is possible that two Supreme Court decisions prior to the incorporation of the **2.131** Rome Convention could be interpreted as a first step towards accepting the approach in the Convention and as a first step away from the centre of gravity test

---

[82] In the case of licensing contracts, for example, reference is made to the law of the country where the right is to be exercised, which in many cases, in practice is equal to the law of the licensee. With respect to licensing contracts, it would seem, however, that in many cases the most characteristic act to be performed is that of the licensor and not the licensee whose primary obligation is typically to pay a royalty fee or similar remuneration to the licensor. With an oversimplification the licensor could be regarded as the seller—of the right to use the know-how, patent or trademark etc in question—and the licensee as the purchaser.

[83] In the Giuliano-Lagarde Report, the concept of characteristic performance is described in the following way: 'Identifying the characteristic performance of a contract obviously presents no diffi-culty in the case of unilateral contracts whereby the parties undertake mutual reciprocal performance, the counter-performance by one of the parties in a modern economy usually takes the form of money. This is not, of course, the characteristic performance of the contract. It is the performance for which payment is due, ie depending on the type of contract, the delivery of goods, the granting of the right to make use of an item of properly, the provision of a service, transport, insurance, banking operations, security, etc, which usually constitutes the centre of gravity and the socio-economic functions of the contractual transaction'; *Official Journal of the European Union* [1980] C282, p 20.

[84] Article 4(5) of the 1980 Rome Convention.

as described above. In the first case, *Barmer Ersatzkasse v Försäkringsaktiebolaget Skandia*,[85] decided in 1990, the Court addressed the question of the law applicable to claims filed by a German insurance company for recovery of compensation disbursed by it as a result of a traffic accident in Sweden.

2.132 The insurance contract between the Barmer Ersatzkasse and the insured was governed by German law. It is noteworthy that there was no contractual relationship between Barmer and Skandia, but pursuant to certain provisions of German law, Barmer had the right to recover compensation disbursed by it. These provisions of German law constituted the basis for Barmer's claim. Even though Skandia acknowledged *per se* that Barmer had a right to recover compensation disbursed by it, Skandia argued that Swedish law was applicable as the *lex loci delicti commissi*. Both the District court and the Court of Appeal concluded that Swedish law was applicable, since the accident had occurred in Sweden, ie the *lex loci delicti commissi* was applied. The Supreme Court, however, ruled that German law was to be applied with respect to Barmer's right to recover compensation. In reaching this conclusion, the Supreme Court noted that parties to an insurance contract in all likelihood assume that the right to recover compensation is governed by the law applicable to the insurance contract and that insurance premiums are probably determined on the basis of this assumption.

2.133 In addition, the Court said that such a solution—to apply the law governing the insurance contract also to issues concerning the right to recover disbursed compensation—would be in conformity with Article 13 of the 1980 Rome Convention.[86]

2.134 The second case, *Aktiebolaget Pergaco v A C Pais Lde*,[87] decided in 1992, concerned the question of the law applicable to an agency contract.

2.135 The agent (Pergaco) filed suit against the principal (Pais) and asked for commission for sales effected after termination of the contract. Under Swedish law an agent was under certain circumstances entitled to such commission. The agent had its place of business in Sweden and the greater part of its commercial activities were carried out in Sweden. However, activities were also carried out in Norway and Finland. The principal argued that the law of Portugal had to be applied. He stated, *inter alia*, that it had been the understanding between the parties—at least implicitly—that Portuguese law would apply, and that the contract was entered into in Portugal.

2.136 The District court found that Swedish law was applicable. In reaching this conclusion the court applied one of the *in dubio* rules under the centre of gravity test, since the test

---

[85] NJA 1990 p 724.

[86] Article 13, which deals with subrogation, reads: 'Where a person ("the creditor") has a contractual claim upon another ("the debtor"), and a third person has a duty to satisfy the creditor, or has in fact satisfied the creditor in discharge of that duty, the law which governs the third person's duty to satisfy the creditor shall determine whether the third person is entitled to exercise against the debtor the rights which the creditor had against the debtor under the law governing their relationship and, if so, whether he may do so in full or only to a limited extent'.

[87] NJA 1992 p 823.

itself had not produced an unambiguous result. The Court of Appeal, however, took the position that the law of Portugal was applicable. The Court of Appeal, in applying the centre of gravity test, weighed the connecting factors differently than the Court of first instance. The Court of Appeal pointed out that the agency originally covered only Finland, but was later enlarged to cover Norway and Sweden as well, and that the agent frequently visited the principal in Portugal together with customers, during which visits the customers often placed the final order with the principal.

In its decision, the Supreme Court said that under Swedish private international **2.137** law questions concerning agency are normally governed by the law of the country where the agent has its place of business, at least if the major part of his activities are carried out in such country. In explaining this conclusion, the Supreme Court said that such a rule was well-founded not only because of the connection with the country of operation, but also due to social considerations, since the relationship between the principal and the agent resembled that of employer and employee; in such situations it was appropriate to grant the weaker party the advantage of a simple and clear choice of law rule. The aforementioned principle should also apply when the agent and the principal had equal bargaining positions. The Court characterized this principle—the law of the country of the agent—as a presumption and said that this presumption could be set aside if the contractual relationship had a significantly stronger connection with another country. In the case at hand, the Supreme Court found, after weighing all the connecting factors, that those point-ing to the application of Portuguese law were not strong enough. Consequently, the Court applied Swedish law.

It is interesting to note that the Court characterized the principle 'the law of the **2.138** country of the agent' as a presumption, which, although the Court did not refer to the Rome Convention, may have been inspired by the terminology of the Rome Convention. In referring to this presumption, the Court may have chosen a different approach than the lower courts. They clearly referred to the centre of gravity test, albeit the court of first instance and the Court of Appeal reached different results.

Another interesting aspect of the Court's reasoning is the fact that the assumption **2.139** referred to by the Court has apparently been inspired by a statement in the Government Bill introducing the existing law on commercial agents, to the effect that the law of the country of the agent is to be applied, at least if the agent performs most of his activities there.[88] In that Government Bill reference is made to the social concerns mentioned by the Supreme Court. Social and similar concerns have in different ways influenced the Swedish legislation on agency. It has sometimes been said that the Swedish rules on agency are mandatory in the sense that they are always to be applied even if the parties have chosen the law of another country.[89]

---

[88] Govt Bill 1990/91:63, p 24 *et seq.*
[89] Cf eg Eek, *Lagkonflikter i tvistemål II* (1978) 93–94, with further references; see discussion at para 2.71 *et seq.*

This line of reasoning is now reflected in section 3 of the 1991 Act on Commercial Agency.[90]

2.140 Both cases have their peculiarities, which makes it difficult to evaluate them in relation to the centre of gravity test.

2.141 In the first case, there was no contractual relationship between the two disputing parties, which probably led the lower courts to characterize the dispute rather as a tort action and to apply the *lex loci delicti commissi*, the traditional Swedish conflict of laws rule for such cases.[91] Furthermore, the Supreme Court treated the right to recover disbursed compensation—which was based on statutory provisions of German law—as ancillary to the insurance contract rather than a contractual right in and of itself.

2.142 As far as the second case is concerned, it must be borne in mind that the Swedish legislation on agency is at least partially permeated by social considerations that have eventually led to a specific provision to the effect that under certain circumstances Swedish law must always be applied. It is difficult to escape the impression that the Supreme Court has been influenced by this special character of agency contracts, which generally speaking, sets such contracts apart from other international commercial contracts. In its reasoning the Supreme Court refers to the Government Bill on the basis of which the 1991 Act on Commercial Agency has been promulgated. In addition, it would seem reasonable to assume that, had it been the objective of the Supreme Court to do away with the centre of gravity test in a general fashion, it would probably have deemed it appropriate to address this issue in its reasons. It did not.

2.143 It is conceivable that the two cases did represent a first step away from the centre of gravity test. As of 1 July 1998, however, the 1980 Rome Convention replaced the centre of gravity test with respect to contracts entered into subsequent to that date.

2.4.2.3 The 1980 Rome Convention

2.144 As previously mentioned, the 1980 Rome Convention is applicable to contracts entered into between 1 July 1998 and 17 December 2009.[92] Contracts signed as of the latter date are covered by the Rome I Regulation.

2.145 The Rome Convention applies, as a matter of principle, to all contractual obligations. Article 1(2) enumerates a number of exceptions, however. For example, obligations

---

[90] Section 3 reads: 'A provision which pursuant to the act may not be set aside to the detriment of the agent, may not be set aside to his detriment through an agreement on the application of foreign law to the legal relationship, if such legal relationship would otherwise be subject to this act'.

[91] See para 2.185 *et seq*.

[92] The Convention has generated a multitude of commentary and scholarly writings, see eg Plender-Wilderspin, *The European Contracts Convention—The Rome Convention and the Choice of Law for Contracts* (2nd edn, 2001); Fletcher, *Conflict of Laws and European Community Law* (1982); Kage, *The New Private International Law of Contract of the European Community* (1993). The report prepared by Professors Giuliano and Lagarde—see note 83—is of particular importance in understanding and interpreting the Convention.

arising under bills of exchange, cheques, promissory notes, and other negotiable instruments are excluded. So are arbitration agreements and questions governed by the *lex corporationis* (eg creation, registration, legal capacity of legal entities). Another important exception in the commercial field is the question whether an agent can bind the principal, or whether an organ of a company can bind the company, or body corporate in relation to a third party. Also certain contracts of insurance are excluded from the Rome Convention.

The starting point under the Convention is party autonomy. Article 3(1) stipulates **2.146** that a contract shall be governed by the law chosen by the parties. This provision explicitly recognizes *dépeçage*, ie that the parties can select the law applicable to parts of the contract or to the entire contract.

Article 3(3) sets forth a limitation on party autonomy. The provision stipulates that **2.147** when the parties have chosen one law, but all other circumstances relevant at the time of the choice are connected with another country only, the mandatory rules of that other country may still be applied. This provision deals with so-called single-country contracts, which occur when both contracting parties are of the same nationality. Therefore from a practical point of view, as far as international commercial arbitration is concerned, the provision is typically of little relevance. The choice of law made by the parties is valid, but may be limited by the mandatory rules of the country where the parties are domiciled.

It follows from Article 3(4) that the validity of a choice of law clause is determined **2.148** by the law selected through that choice of law. As previously mentioned, this is strictly speaking circular, but is the only practical and realistic solution.[93]

The central provision of the 1980 Rome Convention is Article 4 which deals with **2.149** the applicable law in *the absence of a choice* by the parties. In such situations, Article 4(1) stipulates that the contract shall be governed by the law of the country with which it is most closely connected. By way of exception, however, a severable part of the contract may be governed by the law of another country, if that part has a closer connection with that other country.

Article 4(2) supplements the preceding paragraph by introducing a presumption to **2.150** the effect that the contract is deemed to be most closely connected with the country where the party who is to effect the performance which is characteristic of the contract has his habitual residence, or in the case of a body corporate, or unincorporated, its central administration. If the contract is entered into in the course of that party's trade or profession that country shall be the country in which the principal place of business is situated.

In practice it is often difficult to determine with which country the contract has **2.151** its closest connection, also when the 'most characteristic performance' test is

---

[93] See discussion at para 2.48.

taken into account. As illustrated below this may be the case with licence agreements.

2.152 A dispute arose under a cross licensing agreement between a Chinese company and a European company.[94] The agreement provided for arbitration in Sweden in accordance with the SCC Rules but did not have any provisions as regards the applicable law. As a consequence, the parties requested that this question be dealt with in a partial award. In accordance with Article 24(1) of the SCC Rules, the arbitral tribunal—composed of two Swedish arbitrators and one Chinese arbitrator—stated that, in the absence of agreement between the parties, the law or rules which the tribunal considered most appropriate should be applied. Since the arbitration was to be held in Sweden, the tribunal concluded that Swedish conflict of laws rules were, *in dubio,* applicable and were considered by the tribunal when determining the most appropriate law. Under the Rome Convention, the governing rule is that the applicable law shall be the law of the country with which the agreement has the closest connection. The fact that the agreement had been signed and negotiated in China was not considered sufficient to result in the application of Chinese law. Equally, however, the choice of Sweden as the forum could not imply a choice of Swedish law as the applicable substantive law. In such circumstances, the tribunal decided that the UNIDROIT Principles of International Commercial Contracts were to apply, supplemented by Swedish law if and to the extent the UNIDROIT rules did not give guidance on a particular issue.

2.153 It is worth noting the tribunal's decision not to apply substantive Swedish law despite this being the easiest option. The tribunal pointed out that the choice of forum is usually based on practical considerations generally not having any bearing on the issue of applicable law.[95] Sweden and the SCC Institute have traditionally been chosen as a neutral and adequately regulated place for arbitration proceedings and not necessarily on the basis of a preference for Swedish substantive law. It is also interesting to note the tribunal's endorsement of the UNIDROIT principles as the rules of law best placed to capture the international character of the case.

2.154 In other situations it is a lot easier to determine the country with which the contract has its closest connection. In one case,[96] a Russian company undertook, under two contracts, to sell industrial materials to a United Kingdom company. The general terms of the parties' contracts contained an arbitration clause, pursuant to which disputes were to be resolved by arbitration under the Rules of the SCC Institute. The Russian company filed a request for arbitration with the SCC Institute, claiming sums alleged to be due to it under the contracts. The United Kingdom company raised a counterclaim for damages. In an interim award, the arbitral tribunal—composed of a Swedish arbitrator, a Russian arbitrator, and an English arbitrator—addressed the issue of applicable law with respect to the merits and the scope of the arbitral tribunal's

---

[94] SAR 2002:1 p 59.
[95] See para 2.46.
[96] SAR 2002:2. 45.

jurisdiction with regard to the counterclaim. The arbitral tribunal held that an arbitral tribunal sitting in Sweden was not under an obligation to apply Swedish conflict of laws rules, although it was recommended to apply such rules if the parties had fixed the seat to be Sweden. In this case, however, the seat of the arbitration had been fixed by the SCC Institute, not by the parties. Thus, the arbitral tribunal considered itself entitled to decide the issue of the governing substantive law of the contract without being bound by Swedish conflict of laws rules. The arbitral tribunal noted that, in international arbitration, the question whether to apply, in the first place, a set of conflict of laws rules by which the applicable substantive law is decided, or to decide the substantive law directly, had been solved differently. The arbitral tribunal found that is was in favour of first applying conflict of laws rules and then noted that the essential question to be determined was to identify the system of law with which the transaction had its closest and most real connection.

The tribunal referring to international and generally accepted standards for deciding **2.155** the closest connection of a sales contract, found that the country with the closest connection to the contract was the seller's country, ie Russia. Consequently, Russian law, more precisely the 1980 Vienna Convention on the International Sale of Goods, which forms part of Russian law, was applied to the merits of the case.

An exception from the presumption in Article 4(2) is made in paragraph 3 for **2.156** contracts the subject matter of which are rights in immovable property, or a right to use immovable property. With respect to such contracts the presumption is that the contract is most closely connected with the country where the immovable property in question is situated. Another exception is made in paragraph 4 of Article 4 regarding contracts for the carriage of goods. A further important modification of the presumption in paragraph 2 is laid down in paragraph 5. It stipulates that if the characteristic performance cannot be determined, the presumptions set forth in paragraphs 2–4 shall be disregarded, provided that it appears from the circumstances as a whole that the contract is more closely connected with another country.

The net effect of Article 4 of the Rome Convention thus seems to be very close to **2.157** the centre of gravity test with its *in dubio* rules. The difference seems to be one of form and approach rather than of content.

Article 7 of the 1980 Rome Convention deals with mandatory rules of law of a **2.158** country other than the country whose laws the parties have chosen.[97] This Article

---

[97] The provision refers to mandatory rules in general. It must be noted, however, that the provision covers only those mandatory rules which—in their country of origin—are intended to be applied, irrespective of which law is otherwise applicable to the contract.

These mandatory rules are different from, but related to, the *ordre public* exception in Article 16. A refusal to apply a foreign law based on *ordre public* requires an examination of the foreign law in question given the circumstances of the individual case. Article 7, however, presupposes that certain rules are *a priori* so vital to their country of origin that they can never be replaced by a foreign law; see discussion at para 2.78 *et seq*.

has been controversial from the very beginning, not only in relation to international commercial arbitration, but also with respect to court proceedings. Article 7 stipulates that 'effect may be given'—which is not the same thing as to apply the law—to the mandatory rules of the other country, with which the 'situation'—ie not the contract—has a close connection. In considering whether to give effect to such rules, the provision goes on to say that regard shall be had to their nature and purpose and to the consequences of their application or non-application.

2.159 It is believed that this provision has been applied to a very limited extent, if at all, in international commercial arbitration in Sweden.

2.160 Another important aspect addressed in the 1980 Rome Convention is the formal validity of contracts. Article 9 sets forth the two basic rules in the Convention. Article 9(1) stipulates that a contract entered into between two persons in the *same* country is valid as to form *either* if it meets the formal requirements of the law governing it under the Convention, ie the *lex contractus*, or, of the law of the country where it is concluded, ie the *locus regit actum* principle. The other rule deals with the situation when the contracting persons are in *different* countries. For this situation, Article 9(2) prescribes that the contract is valid as to form *either* if it meets the formal requirements of the *lex contractus*, as determined by the provisions of the Convention, *or* the formal requirements of the law of *one* of the countries where the contract was concluded.

2.161 The Convention has a traditional *ordre public* clause in Article 16, ie that the application of a rule of the law of any country pursuant to the provision of the Convention may be refused if such application would be 'manifestly incompatible' with the public policy (*ordre public*) of the forum.[98]

2.162 Article 15 is probably of more practical relevance. It excludes *renvoi*. In other words, the application of the law of a country under the Convention excludes the conflict of laws rules of that country.

2.4.2.4 The Rome I Regulation

2.163 As mentioned above, the Rome I Regulation will be applied to contracts entered into after 17 December 2009. Contracts entered into prior to that date will continue to be covered by the 1980 Rome Convention, or the centre of gravity test, as the case may be.

2.164 The Rome I Regulation is to a large extent based on the 1980 Rome Convention. Commentaries and case law concerning the Convention will therefore continue to be relevant also with respect to the Regulation. It is important to note that the Regulation is directly applicable in Swedish courts and that the European Court of Justice will ultimately decide how to interpret and understand the Regulation.

2.165 Article 25 of the Regulation stipulates that the Regulation does not affect treaties already entered into. This means that the 1964 Act on the Law Applicable to the

---

[98] See para 2.59 *et seq.*

International Sale of Goods continues to be relevant, since it is based on the 1955 Hague Convention.[99]

The scope of application of the Rome I Regulation, laid down in its Article 1, coincides with the corresponding provision of the Rome Convention. **2.166**

Just like the Rome Convention, the Rome I Regulation is based on the principle of party autonomy. Accordingly, Article 3 of the Regulation provides that a contract shall be governed by the law chosen by the parties. Article 3 sets forth certain limitations on party autonomy, which correspond to the limitations in Article 3 of the Rome Convention. Paragraph 4 of Article 3 in the Rome I Regulation is a new provision. The intention of the provision is to protect the application of EU legislation. The choice by the parties of the law of a non-Member State shall not prevent the application of Community law, provided that all elements relevant to the situation at the time of the choice are located in one or more Member States. **2.167**

The central provision of the Rome I Regulation is Article 4 which deals with applicable law in the absence of a choice by the parties. In contrast to the Rome Convention, the Rome I Regulation provides for a number of fixed choice of law rules in paragraph 1, viz, items a–h. It is noteworthy that there is considerable overlap between these fixed choice of law rules and the *in dubio* rules used in the centre of gravity test.[100] Thus, for example, contracts for the sale of goods are governed by the law of the seller (item a); service contracts by the law of the service provider (item b); contracts concerning *in rem* rights in immovable property by the law where the property is located (item c), etc. **2.168**

Paragraph 2 of Article 4 provides for a subsidiary rule in situations where a contract is not covered by paragraph 1 or where more than one of the fixed rules can be applied to the contract in question. In this situation the contract shall be governed by the law of the country where the party required to effect the characteristic performance of the contract has his habitual residence. **2.169**

Paragraphs 3 and 4 of Article 4 stipulate that if a contract is more closely connected with another country than would follow from paragraphs 1 and 2, and where the applicable law cannot be determined based on these paragraphs, the contract shall be governed by the law of the country with which it is most closely connected. **2.170**

Separate provisions of the Rome I Regulation address contracts of carriage, consumer contracts, and individual employment contracts. **2.171**

Article 9 of the Rome I Regulation addresses so-called overriding mandatory provisions. It corresponds to Article 7 of the Rome Convention. Paragraph 2 of Article 9 stipulates that nothing in the Regulation shall restrict the application of the overriding **2.172**

---

[99] See para 2.105 *et seq.*
[100] See para 2.125 *et seq.*

mandatory provisions of the law of the forum. It is important to note that no reference is made to mandatory rules of any other law than the law of the forum. In this respect the Regulation differs from the Rome Convention. However, paragraph 3 of Article 9 raises the same concerns as Article 7 of the Rome Convention.[101] This provision refers to the law of the country where the obligations arising out of the contract are to be, or have been, performed. The mandatory rules of such law 'may be given effect' pursuant to paragraph 3.

2.5 Issues not Covered by the *Lex Contractus*

2.173 The discussion above has focused on the law applicable to contracts in dispute. Since international commercial arbitration by definition is based on contracts, determining the *lex contractus* is the central choice of law issue. There are, however, a number of other conflict of laws issues which often arise in international commercial arbitration. The most frequent issues are briefly discussed below.

2.5.1 *Lex corporationis*

2.174 The majority of international commercial arbitrations are between legal entities of different nations. This fact gives rise to a number of issues relating to the legal status etc of legal entities. Most issues of this kind are governed by the so-called personal law—the *lex corporationis*—of the entity in question. This is the case under Swedish conflict of laws rules, as well as under the rules of most other jurisdictions.[102] The *lex corporationis* is usually the law of the country where the legal entity in question has been registered, provided registration is required for the creation and existence of a legal entity. If registration is not required, the law of the seat of the legal entity is mostly the *lex corporationis*. This usually means the seat of the Board of the legal entity.

2.175 The question of whether a legal entity has been validly established is determined by the *lex corporationis* as is the question of whether the entity has been liquidated, or otherwise dissolved. Questions relating to the merger and demerger of legal entities are also decided by the *lex corporationis*. As a result, company and privatization legislation of many East European countries—including the former Soviet Union— has in this way played an important role in many international arbitrations during the 1990s. With respect to the former Soviet Union, for example, many disputes arose out of contracts signed by foreign trade organizations operating under the then foreign trade monopoly system.[103] When these organizations were subsequently privatized issues arose with respect to the fate of such contracts. Was the

---

[101] See discussion at para 2.78 *et seq.*
[102] Bogdan, *op cit*, at para 161 *et seq.*
[103] For a discussion of the Soviet foreign trade monopoly, see Hobér, *Joint Ventures in the Soviet Union* (1989).

new privatized legal entity bound by the contracts entered into by the foreign trade organization? To determine the effect of the privatization, and the status of the new legal entities, Russian privatization and company legislation must be applied.

The application of *lex corporationis* to similar issues is illustrated by the following **2.176** case.[104]

A German company requested arbitration against a Chinese respondent under **2.177** the Rules of the SCC Institute, claiming compensation for non-payment under a contract and remuneration for certain works under an additional agreement. The Chinese respondent objected, *inter alia*, that neither the claimant nor the respondent were parties to the contract containing the arbitration clause relied on by the claimant. The claimant responded that the parties were the same legal entities that had signed the contract, although their corporate names had subsequently been changed. With respect to the respondent, the claimant also submitted, alternatively, that the respondent was at least a legal successor to the contracting party and that the respondent had, at any rate, by its subsequent actions entered into the contract. In a separate award, the sole arbitrator—of Swedish nationality—addressed the issue whether he had jurisdiction to adjudicate the case. The parties had not made an explicit choice of law. The arbitrator noted that, pursuant to section 48 of the SAA, an arbitration agreement shall in such cases be governed by the law of the country where the arbitral proceedings are taking place.[105] However, the arbitrator found that this section did not apply to the issue whether a party was authorized to enter into an arbitration agreement or whether the party was duly represented. The applicable law for such issues must be established by applying general Swedish conflict of laws rules. The same reasoning applied, according to the arbitrator, with respect to the issues relevant in this case, ie the legal identity of the contracting parties and whether or not they were parties to the proceedings. The arbitrator noted that, according to Swedish conflict of laws rules, the issues regarding the correct use of company names and/or a possible legal succession on the respondent's side were to be determined by the law of the country where the company in question was domiciled (*lex corporationis*). Thus, the arbitrator held that with respect to the German claimant this issue was to be governed by German law, whereas the same issue with respect to the Chinese respondent was to be governed by Chinese law. However, the issue whether the respondent by its subsequent actions had entered into the contract related to the existence and validity of the agreement. This issue was, according to the arbitrator, to be decided under the law applicable to the agreement. The arbitrator noted that, in the absence of a choice of law, an agreement is governed by the law of the country with which it is most closely connected and it is presumed that the closest connection is with the country where the party who is to effect the characteristic performance is domiciled.

---

[104] SAR 2003:1 p 119.
[105] See para 2.200 *et seq* for a discussion of the law applicable to the arbitration agreement.

The characteristic performance in this case, ie the performance in kind, was to be performed by the German claimant. Thus, the arbitrator held that the contract was governed by German law and that, accordingly, the issue whether the respondent by its actions had entered into the contract was to be decided under German law. Applying the rules of law thus identified, the arbitrator held that the respondent was not a proper party to the contract and that the arbitrator therefore lacked jurisdiction to hear the case.

2.178   Although section 48 of the SAA provides that the law of the place of arbitration is to apply to the arbitration agreement,[106] this does not cover all issues relating to the arbitration agreement. As illustrated by this decision issues concerning legal identity and corporate legal succession are governed by the *lex corporationis*.

2.179   Another important issue determined by the *lex corporationis* is the question of who is authorized to represent the legal entity in question. If a party argues, for example, that the disputed contract has not been signed by an authorized representative of the entity in question, the *lex corporationis* must be applied to resolve this issue. Other issues determined by the *lex corporationis* include the validity of decisions taken by the various organs of the entity in question, and of course in more general terms, the legal capacity of the entity.

2.180   The *lex corporationis* may sometimes play a role also with respect to shareholders' agreements. The agreement as such is governed by the *lex contractus*. There may, however, be a tension between the scope of application of the *lex contractus* and the *lex corporationis*, respectively. Put differently: to what extent can the parties to a shareholders' agreement deviate from rules and regulations governing the legal entity in question concerning eg voting at shareholders' meetings, dividend policy, etc?[107] The *lex corporationis* may also become relevant with respect to transactions involving shares in joint stock companies and publicly traded companies. For example, responsibility for information in prospectuses issued in connection with the public offering of securities is probably regulated by the *lex corporationis*.[108] The transfer, assignment and collateralization may also be governed by the *lex corporationis* in certain situations.[109]

---

[106]   See discussion at para 2.201 *et seq.*

[107]   From time to time these issues have been raised with respect to Russian joint stock companies in situations where a shareholders' agreement has been governed by a law other than Russian law. In the well-known *Megafon* case, the Federal Arbitration Court of Western Siberia declared a shareholders' agreement governed by Swedish law, and entered into between shareholders in the Russian open joint stock company OAO Megafon, invalid on the basis that it violated Russian public policy. This case, and other similar cases, led to an intensive debate about Russian law and shareholders' agreements. The debate resulted in an amendment to the Russian Joint Stock Companies Act to the effect that shareholders' agreements are now recognized as such. It is still an open question, however, whether such agreements may be governed by a foreign law.

[108]   Cf Hobér, 'Tillämplig lag på utländska företags emissionsprospekt i Sverige, jämte något om amerikanska bestämmelser om emissionsprospekt', SvJT (1987) 582.

[109]   See Ooi, *Shares and Other Securities in the Conflict of Laws* (2003).

2.5.2 Agency

As far as *agency* is concerned, it is necessary to distinguish between the internal **2.181** relationship between the agent and the principal, on the one hand, and the external relationship between the agent and third parties, on the other. As far as the internal relationship is concerned, it may be based on an employment contract or some other contractual arrangement between the agent and the principal. The law governing this internal relationship is the *lex contractus* of the contractual arrangement in question. The external relationship, however, is mostly governed by the law of the country where the agent is performing his activities.[110] The external relationship includes issues such as the scope of the agency, its effect in relation to third parties when the agent exceeds his authority, and the termination of the agency.

The law applicable to the authority of an agent to bind his principal was discussed **2.182** in the following case.[111]

A French company (A) and a Chinese company (B) entered into a contract for the **2.183** sale by the French company of machinery. The contract referred to a second Chinese company (C) as an alternative signatory party to an inspection certificate concerning the goods as a beneficiary under an irrevocable letter of guarantee. C was also mentioned as a party in annexes to the contract.

Relying on an arbitration clause providing for arbitration at the Arbitration **2.184** Institute of the Stockholm Chamber of Commerce, A filed a request for arbitration against both B and C requesting payment for deliveries under the contract. C denied being a party to the contract or having entered into any arbitration agreement with A and also asserted that B did not act as an agent for C. Addressing the issue of which law to apply when deciding whether C was bound by the arbitration agreement, the sole Swedish arbitrator noted that the issue in question did not concern the merits of the dispute, nor did it concern the validity and interpretation of the arbitration agreement. Instead, the issue of C's acquiescence to the arbitration agreement concerned the status or liability of C as a contracting party and raised issues of legal competence, or authority, to enter into binding agreements. The arbitrator noted that the authority of an agent to bind his principal is normally governed by the law of the country where the agent acted. In this case, the country where the alleged agent B had acted was the People's Republic of China. The arbitrator thus found Chinese law applicable to the question whether B as an agent had bound C to the contract and the arbitration clause. Applying Chinese law, the arbitrator concluded that A had not shown that there was an arbitration agreement between A and C. A's request for arbitration against C was therefore dismissed.

---

[110] See eg Bogdan, *op cit*, at 280.
[111] SAR 2002:2 p 111.

2.5.3 Negotiable instruments

2.185 Choice of law issues concerning bills of exchange, cheques, promissory notes and other negotiable instruments are also not covered by the principle of party autonomy. They are governed by international conventions, viz, the 1930 Geneva Convention for resolving conflicts of laws regarding bills of exchange,[112] and the 1931 Geneva Convention for resolving conflicts of laws concerning cheques.[113]

2.5.4 Torts

2.186 Under Swedish conflict of laws rules it is generally accepted that issues related to or arising out of torts, whether committed intentionally, negligently, or without fault, fall outside the autonomy of parties. The generally accepted view has been that such issues are governed by the law of the place where the alleged tort was committed (the *lex loci delici commissi*).[114] As of January 2009, tort issues are governed by Regulation (EC) 864/2007 on the Law Applicable to Non-Contractual Obligations, the so-called Rome II Regulation. The Regulation is applicable to occurrences after 20 August 2007 when it entered into force. It establishes conflict of laws rules for torts, unjust enrichment, and *culpa in contrahendo*.

2.187 The general rule of the Rome II Regulation is that 'the law of the country in which the damage occurs' is the applicable law, 'irrespective of the country or countries in which the indirect consequences of that event occur' (Article 4(1)). The rule is known as the *lex loci damni.*

2.188 There are some important exceptions, however.

2.189 First, parties are in most cases entitled to opt out of both the general rule and the exceptions listed below by agreement. That is, two parties can agree—either before an injury takes place or afterwards—to submit their dispute to the law of their choice. This is a novelty for Swedish conflict of laws rules according to which torts have traditionally fallen outside party autonomy. However, parties cannot opt out of certain mandatory laws, including those governing cases of unfair or restricted competition and cases involving intellectual property.

2.190 Secondly, the Rome II Regulation does not apply at all to cases involving breach of contract; defamation (or other issues relating to privacy or personality); marriages, family wills, trusts, and estates; or instances where the Government has caused injury in the course of exercising governmental authority.

2.191 The Regulation also makes exceptions to the general rule in a number of particular circumstances. The major exceptions are:

---

[112] SÖ 1933:27.
[113] SÖ 1933:30.
[114] Bogdan, *op cit*, at 282 *et seq*.

- Where both victim and injurer habitually reside in the same country, the law of that country generally applies;
- Where both victim and injurer have a pre-existing relationship—as when they are preparing to conclude a contract with one another or when they already have a contractual relationship separate from the injury—the law governing that pre-existing relationship generally applies;
- As far as product liability is concerned, determining the applicable law involves a combination of multiple factors, particularly where the product was marketed. Generally, if the product was marketed in the victim's country of residence, the law of that country applies;
- With respect to environmental damage, a plaintiff may elect to have applied either the law of the country in which the damage occurred (the general rule) or the law of the country in which the event giving rise to the damage occurred;
- In cases involving intellectual property rights, the law of the country where the protection is sought generally applies;
- Finally, a court has the discretion not to follow the general rule in special cases where an injury or wrongdoing is 'manifestly more closely connected' with a country other than the one in which the damage occurred.

2.5.5 Property

It is a well-established principle under Swedish conflict of laws rules, as well as under similar rules of other jurisdictions, that with regard to real estate the law of the jurisdiction where the property is located (*lex rei sitae*) determines rights and duties with respect to such property, both between the parties and in relation to third parties.[115] This is the most natural and practical approach to solve problems related to real estate and probably the only possible approach for achieving uniform and consistent solutions. **2.192**

As far as movables are concerned, relations between one of the parties and third persons are also governed by the *lex rei sitae*. Accordingly, the rights of the buyer in the property as against the creditors of the seller are governed by the law of the jurisdiction in which the goods sold are located at the time of the execution of the contract. In the same fashion, the rights of the seller in the property as against creditors of the buyer are governed by the *lex rei sitae*. In practice the most important question in this respect relates to retention of title clauses. The proper law of the contract—the *lex contractus*—decides whether the seller is entitled in relation to the buyer to recover the property should the buyer fail to pay. The effect of a retention of title clause in relation to the buyer's creditors is determined by the law of the place where the property is located when that issue is raised and not when the contract is executed.[116] Related issues were discussed in the case described below.[117] **2.193**

---

[115] See eg Bogdan *op cit*, at 297 *et seq.*
[116] Ibid.
[117] Cf SCC Case 096/2001 in SIAR 2003:2, p 47.

2.194 A Swiss company initiated arbitration before the Arbitration Institute of the Stockholm Chamber of Commerce against a company incorporated in the Republic of Uzbekistan, arguing that the parties had entered into an agreement for delivery of certain equipment, that the respondent had failed to make payment of the agreed purchase sum and that, under the contract, the claimant was to retain title to the equipment delivered until the entire purchase sum had been paid. The claimant requested an award establishing that the equipment delivered was the property of the claimant and ordering the respondent to restore the equipment to the claimant. The claimant also asked for interim measures. In an order with respect to the application for interim measures, the arbitral tribunal—composed of three arbitrators of Swedish, Swiss, and Russian nationality—addressed the question of the governing law. The arbitral tribunal noted that, pursuant to Article 24 of the Rules of the Arbitration Institute of the Stockholm Chamber of Commerce, the arbitral tribunal shall decide the merits of the dispute on the basis of the law or rules of law agreed by the parties. In the absence of such an agreement, the arbitral tribunal shall apply the law or rules of law which it considers most appropriate. In this case, the parties had not agreed on the applicable law. The arbitral tribunal, proceeding on the basis of the aforementioned rule, found that the 1980 United Nations Convention on Contracts for the International Sale of Goods (CISG) was the appropriate choice in this case. The arbitral tribunal found that the claimant had established a prima facie case with respect to one of its claims and granted the interim measures requested. In the final arbitral award, the arbitral tribunal was again faced with the issue of applicable law. Addressing the enforceability of the retention of title clause, the arbitral tribunal noted that the general view held in most jurisdictions seems to be that the enforceability of such clauses as between the parties is governed by the *lex contractus* whereas the enforceability in relation to third parties is governed by the *lex rei sitae*. The arbitral tribunal found this principle reasonable and applied it to the case. The arbitral tribunal reiterated that the appropriate choice of the *lex contractus* in this case was CISG. However, CISG did not offer any guidance as to the enforceability of the retention of title clause. Thus, a different *lex contractus* would have to apply on this point. The arbitral tribunal applied the principle that the law to which the relevant provision has the closest connection should be chosen and noted that there seemed to be almost universal agreement that sale of goods contracts should be governed by the law of the country where the seller is domiciled. For these reasons the arbitral tribunal found that the law of the seller's country, ie Switzerland, should apply. However, with regard to movable property destined for export, Article 103 of the Swiss Federal Law on International Private Law provided that retention of title was to be governed by the law of the State of destination of the goods. Therefore, in this particular case, although Swiss law was applicable as a matter of principle, the arbitral tribunal found that Uzbeki law would in fact govern the retention of title clause. Applying Uzbeki law, the arbitral tribunal found that the retention of title clause was enforceable as between the parties and rendered a ruling in favour of the claimant.

As highlighted by this award, the law or rules of law chosen by the arbitral tribunal **2.195** do not necessarily have to be a national law. In this case, the arbitral tribunal, without referring to any national legal system, found that the *lex contractus* was CISG, ie an international convention. However, since this Convention did not contain any rules on the enforceability of retention of title clauses, the arbitral tribunal in this respect had to find a different *lex contractus*. Thus, the award also illustrates that an arbitral tribunal may subject a contract to two different *leges contractae*, governing different aspects of the contract (ie *dépeçage*). It is also worth noting that the arbitrators seem to have accepted the concept of *renvoi*, which is in principle not used in Swedish private international law.

The *lex rei sitae* also applies with respect to security interests in property.[118] To establish a **2.196** security interest that is valid in relation to third parties, it is necessary to satisfy the requirements in the jurisdiction where the property is located at the time when the security interest is granted. Notwithstanding this, if a valid security interest has been created in one jurisdiction without transfer of possession and the property is subsequently moved by the debtor or a third party to a jurisdiction whose laws provide that the validity of a security interest is dependent upon possession by the secured party, the security interest may be extinguished when the property is moved to the new jurisdiction.

Special rules apply with respect to *res in transitu*.[119] Typically, the *lex rei sitae* is of less **2.197** importance with respect to such goods. Many different suggestions have been made in this area, but no well-established rules seem to exist.

2.6 Classification Rules

In an international setting, the classification of rules and concepts is usually regarded **2.198** as forming part of the conflict of laws rules. This is the case in Sweden as in most other jurisdictions. This is indeed one of the classical theoretical issues of private international law.[120] To the extent that Swedish conflict of laws rules are applied by courts, such application includes the classification rules. Generally speaking, the traditional choice is between classification pursuant to the *lex fori* or pursuant to the *lex causae*. The prevailing view in Sweden is that classification is to be made pursuant to the *lex fori*, at least as a rule.[121]

To the extent that arbitrators sitting in Sweden apply Swedish conflict of laws **2.199** rules, the expectation is that they will also apply Swedish classification rules.[122]

---

[118] Bogdan, ibid.
[119] Ibid.
[120] For an in-depth discussion of this issue see eg Gihl, *Den internationella privaträttens historia och allmänna principer* (1951) 335 *et seq*; Svenné Schmidt, *Kvalifikationsproblemet i den internationale privatrett* (1954); Dicey and Morris, *The Conflict of Laws* (13th edn 2000) ch 35.
[121] See Bogdan, *op cit*, at 66 *et seq*.
[122] Cf *Arbitration in Sweden, op cit*, at 55.

Unnecessary problems would probably arise of they were to apply Swedish conflict of laws rules but the classification rules of another jurisdiction. On the whole, however, in practice classification issues seldom seem to cause major problems in international commercial arbitrations. There are probably two explanations for this. First, as far as commercial transactions are concerned, in contrast perhaps to family law and inheritance law issues, there seem to be few legal concepts which nowadays are characterized in a radically different way in different jurisdictions. Issues concerning interest, damages, and also statutes of limitation are now mostly characterized as substantive law issues and thus governed by the *lex causae* rather than by any other law.[123]

2.200 Secondly, as has been discussed above,[124] it is increasingly common for arbitral tribunals to determine the applicable law without going through a conflict of laws system. Arbitrators are given a large margin of discretion and flexibility in this respect. The same seems to apply to classification rules and rightly so. When the parties have chosen the applicable law themselves the natural approach is to apply the classification rules of that law—ie the *lex causae*—if this should prove necessary. Since arbitral tribunals do not have a *lex fori* in the way that national courts have,[125] applying the classification rules of the *lex causae* seems to be the only practical and realistic approach.

2.7 The Law Governing the Arbitration Agreement

2.201 As will be discussed below, the arbitration clause in a contract constitutes a separate and independent agreement.[126] Generally speaking, it leads a life of its own. This means, among other things, that the arbitration agreement may be governed by another law than the law governing the main contract. This also means that a choice of law clause in the main contract does not automatically extend to the arbitration agreement.

2.202 Section 48 of the Swedish Arbitration Act deals with the law applicable to the arbitration agreement. As would be expected, party autonomy is accepted, which means that any law chosen by the parties will be applied. It must be observed that reference is made to a specific choice of law with respect to the arbitration agreement. Generally speaking, it is unusual that parties make a separate choice of law with respect to the arbitration agreement. In practice therefore, the subsidiary rule in

---

[123] In England issues related to the statutes of limitation (extinctive prescription) were traditionally classified as procedural. By the introduction of the 1984 Foreign Limitation Period Act, the position of England has changed such that the *lex causae* is to apply; cf Hobér, *Extinctive Prescription and the Applicable Law in Interstate Arbitration* (2001) 257–262. Under Swedish law, issues concerning limitation are classified as substantive issues—and thus governed by the *lex causae*—following on old Supreme Court Case, *Köpper v Carlstein* (NJA 1930 p 692).

[124] See para 2.99.

[125] As explained at para 2.05 *et seq*, the *lex arbitri* cannot be equated to the *lex fori*.

[126] See para 3.46 *et seq*.

Section 48 is more important. It stipulates that when the parties have made no choice of law, the law of the place of arbitration will govern the agreement, provided that the parties have agreed on a place of arbitration in their arbitration clause.

Section 48 raises primarily two questions, viz, (i) how to deal with a choice of law **2.203** clause in the main contract in relation to the arbitration clause, and (ii) which law should be applied when the parties have not agreed on a place of arbitration.

As far as the first issue is concerned, it could perhaps be argued that it would be **2.204** natural to extend the choice of law clause in the main contract to the arbitration agreement. After all, it would not be unreasonable to assume that this would be in conformity with the expectations of the parties and that the choice of law clause in the main contract should be viewed as an implied term of the arbitration agreement. The position of Swedish law is different, however, at least when the parties have agreed on a place of arbitration. In the so-called *Bulbank* case,[127] the contract entered into between the parties was governed by Austrian law pursuant to the agreement of the parties.

The parties had also agreed on Stockholm as the place of arbitration. The central **2.205** issues in the case concerned confidentiality and alleged breach of the arbitration agreement. The Supreme Court concluded, without much discussion, that since the parties had agreed on Stockholm as the place of arbitration, Swedish law was to be applied to the arbitration agreement. It is possible that a general choice of law clause would—and perhaps should—be given more importance if the parties have not agreed on a place of arbitration.

In one of the cases discussed above,[128] the tribunal concluded that Russian law was **2.206** applicable to the substance of the dispute. The tribunal also had to address the question of the law applicable to the arbitration agreements.

Turning to the issue of whether the arbitral tribunal had jurisdiction with respect to **2.207** the counterclaim raised by the respondent, the arbitral tribunal noted that, although it had found that the applicable substantive law for the contracts in dispute was Russian law, it did not follow from this that the same law was applicable also in respect of matters concerning the validity or scope of the arbitration agreements. The arbitral tribunal found that the law of the place of arbitration was the most correct and suitable law to govern the arbitration agreements. Since the arbitral tribunal was sitting in Sweden, the arbitral tribunal concluded that it would apply Swedish law when deciding whether or not it had jurisdiction over the counterclaim. Considering that the counterclaim—a claim for damages in respect of an alleged failure to deliver goods under the contract—was based on the contract in dispute, the arbitral tribunal held that the claim fell within the scope of the arbitration

---

[127] *Bulgarian Foreign Trade Bank Ltd (Bulbank) v A I Trade Finance (AIT)* (NJA 2000 p 538)
[128] SAR 2002:2 p 44 at para 2.154.

clause of the contract. Thus, the arbitral tribunal had jurisdiction to try the counterclaim as well.

2.208   This leads us to the second question raised above, ie how to determine the applicable law when the parties have made no choice of law and no agreement has been reached as to the place of arbitration. In the Government Bill introducing the 1999 Arbitration Act it is simply suggested that in such a situation, one should apply the general conflict of laws rules.[129]

2.209   As discussed above, both the Rome Convention and the Rome I Regulation exclude arbitration agreements from their respective scope of application. It would thus seem that the centre of gravity test must be applied, but where does an arbitration agreement have its centre of gravity? If the parties have agreed on institutional arbitration, the institution in question will often determine the place of arbitration. For example, Articles 9 and 20 of the SCC Rules stipulate that the Board of the SCC Institute will determine the seat of the arbitration if the parties have failed to do so. If the institution in question does not have provisions of this kind, it would nevertheless seem reasonable to apply the law of the country where the institution has its seat. As indicated above, another solution would be to extend a general choice of law clause in the contract to the arbitration agreement.[130]

---

[129]   Govt Bill 1998/99:35, p 245.

[130]   Reported decisions by arbitral tribunals by and large seem to follow the rule laid down in section 48 of the Arbitration Act, even though there are occasional deviations:

- SCC Case 10/2005, in SIAR 2007, Vol 2, p 235 (Swedish law based on the parties' choice of 'the Arbitration Committee of Sweden' as the forum. No place of arbitration was agreed).
- SCC Case 24/2002, in SIAR 2004, Vol 2, p 165 (English law based on the parties' choice of English law as the governing law of the contract, despite the fact that the parties had agreed on Sweden as the place of arbitration).
- SCC Case 12/2002, in SIAR 2004, Vol 1, p 93 (Swedish law applied to the transfer of the arbitration agreement based on the fact that the arbitration had been instituted in Sweden under the SCC Rules).
- SCC Cases 80/1998 and 81/1998, in SIAR 2002, Vol 2, p 45 (Swedish law, despite the absence of choice of law and choice of place of arbitration).
- SCC Case 108/1997, in SIAR 2001, p 57 (Swedish law, as the agreed *lex arbitri*, was applied to determine whether a parent company is bound by an arbitration agreement entered into by a subsidiary).
- SCC Case 46/1999, in SIAR 2001, p 73 (Swedish law as the agreed *lex arbitri* to determine whether an arbitration agreement between a creditor and debtor extends to a pledge to whom the creditor has pledged its claims).

3

THE ARBITRATION AGREEMENT

3.1 **Introduction** 3.01

3.2 **The Validity of an Arbitration Agreement** 3.04

  3.2.1 General remarks 3.04

  3.2.2 Requisites of a valid arbitration agreement 3.05

3.3 **Concluding the Arbitration Agreement** 3.06

  3.3.1 Arbitration agreement in writing 3.06

  3.3.2 Oral arbitration agreement 3.12

  3.3.3 Arbitration agreement by conduct 3.14

    3.3.3.1 Arbitration agreement as a result of party usage 3.23

    3.3.3.2 Arbitration agreement by 'inactivity' 3.28

3.4 **Interpretation of Arbitration Agreement** 3.31

3.5 **Unenforceability of Arbitration Agreements due to the Swedish Contracts Act** 3.37

3.6 **The Doctrine of Separability** 3.42

  3.6.1 Introduction 3.42

  3.6.2 Application of doctrine of separability 3.48

  3.6.3 Should the application of the doctrine of separability be limited? 3.53

    3.6.3.1 No agreement in the first place 3.55

    3.6.3.2 The principal agreement is void *ab initio*, voidable, or has been declared invalid 3.60

3.7 **Invalidity of the Arbitration Agreement** 3.74

3.8 **Arbitrability** 3.77

  3.8.1 Disputes capable of settlement 3.81

  3.8.2 The existence of factual circumstances 3.86

  3.8.3 Filling gaps 3.92

  3.8.4 Consumer and labour disputes 3.95

  3.8.5 Civil law effects of competition law 3.98

3.9 **Effects of Arbitration Agreement** 3.111

  3.9.1 Bar to court proceedings 3.112

    3.9.1.1 Respondent has failed to cooperate in arbitration 3.118

    3.9.1.2 Respondent has disregarded the agreement in previous court proceedings 3.121

    3.9.1.3 The subject matter of the dispute is non-arbitrable 3.123

  3.9.2 Assistance by courts 3.126

  3.9.3 Rules of organization and procedure 3.127

  3.9.4 Authority of arbitrators 3.128

  3.9.5 Effect of arbitration agreement on third parties 3.130

    3.9.5.1 Party substitution 3.131

    3.9.5.2 Guarantee agreements 3.142

    3.9.5.3 Conduct by third parties, including the 'group of companies' doctrine 3.146

  3.9.6 Confidentiality 3.164

3.10 **Termination of Arbitration Agreement** 3.168

  3.10.1 Introduction 3.168

  3.10.2 Termination with respect to existing dispute 3.171

    3.10.2.1 By understanding 3.171

    3.10.2.2 Events during proceedings 3.172

    3.10.2.3 Judgment 3.173

    3.10.2.4 Expiration of award period 3.175

    3.10.2.5 Award 3.176

  3.10.3 Complete termination 3.178

3.11 **Drafting of Arbitration Clauses** 3.182

3.1 Introduction

3.01 An agreement by the parties to submit disputes to arbitration is the starting point, indeed the *sine qua non*, for any commercial arbitration today. Without a valid arbitration agreement there can be no valid arbitration. As will be discussed below, without a valid arbitration agreement, the dispute may end up in court, rather than before a tribunal of arbitrators. Also, at the other end of the arbitration process, lack of a valid arbitration agreement may lead to the setting aside of an arbitral award and to refusal of enforcement of the award.

3.02 International commercial arbitration is based on the agreement of the parties, on their consent to resolve disputes through arbitration. Arbitration is thus consensual in nature and is based on the free will—and autonomy—of the parties to agree on how to settle disputes. An arbitration agreement is just as binding as any other agreement. Once consent has been given, a party cannot unilaterally withdraw its consent.

3.03 There are two basic forms of arbitration agreements: the arbitration clause, which is included in the commercial contract and the submission agreement. Generally speaking, the arbitration clause deals with disputes in the future, ie disputes arising out of, or in connection with, the contract in question. Most international commercial arbitrations conducted in Sweden fall into this category. Submission agreements, by contrast, look to the past. This is an agreement to submit an existing dispute to arbitration. At one time, the submission agreement was in many jurisdictions the only form of arbitration agreement that was accepted. In modern Swedish arbitration law, the distinction between existing and future disputes has not been maintained, as far as commercial disputes are concerned.[1]

3.2 The Validity of an Arbitration Agreement

3.2.1 General remarks

3.04 Under Swedish law, an arbitration agreement is generally speaking not different from other agreements in respect of its validity. Accordingly, there is no particular form prescribed as regards the arbitration agreement. This means, *inter alia*, that *oral* arbitration agreements are also valid and accepted.[2] Some commentators have suggested that the conditions for an arbitration agreement to have been concluded, in one way or another, are rigid compared to entering into agreements in

---

[1] It follows from section 6 of the SAA that this distinction is, however, made with respect to certain categories of disputes involving consumers.

[2] See para 3.05.

general.[3] In their view, a fairly high contractual threshold is upheld with respect to arbitration agreements.[4] The rationale for such an approach is that an arbitration clause is an important term of the contract and, more importantly, that a party by entering into an arbitration agreement waives its right to go to court to have disputes settled.[5] On the other hand, there is no express support in case law for the proposition that stricter requirements apply with respect to arbitration agreements.[6]

3.2.2 Requisites of a valid arbitration agreement

In order for an arbitration agreement to be valid under Swedish law[7] the following **3.05** five requirements must be satisfied:[8]

(i) *Capacity*. The parties must be legally qualified to conclude the agreement. A corporation must be properly constituted and validly represented. Parties and their agents must have authority to act.[9]

(ii) *Form*. As mentioned above, no particular form is prescribed as regards the arbitration agreement. Accordingly the arbitration agreement may be oral, or even established by the parties' conduct, although in practice such agreements are rare, see para 3.14.[10] The only matter that need be observed in this connection is the fact that in certain circumstances an arbitration clause contained in the general provisions of an 'adhesion contract' may be disregarded by the courts if such clause was not properly brought to the notice of both parties.[11]

---

[3] Hassler and Cars, *Skiljeförfarande* (2nd edn, 1989) 34; Lindskog, *Skiljeförfarande, En kommentar* (2005) 103–105; Adlercreutz, *Avtalsrätt II* (5th edn, 2001) 67. See also *Luftteknik Mellin & Selling AB v Allingsås kommun* (RH 102:82) and *Taisto L v R E Wahlgren Ingenjörsbyrå Aktiebolag* (RH1989:1).

[4] Lindskog, *Skiljeförfarande, En kommentar* (2005) 104.

[5] Cf Reldén and Nilsson, 'Incorporation and Passivity: Entering into Arbitration Agreements under Swedish Law' in Hobér, Magnusson, and Öhrström (eds), *Between East and West: Essays in Honour of Ulf Franke* (2010) 433–434; Heuman, *Arbitration Law of Sweden: Practice and Procedure* (2003) 32; Lindskog, *Skiljeförfarande, En kommentar* (2005) 104.

[6] Cf Heuman, *Arbitration Law of Sweden: Practice and Procedure* (2003) 33.

[7] For a discussion of the law applicable to the arbitration agreement, see Chapter 2.

[8] *Arbitration in Sweden* (2nd revised edn, 1984) 29–30.

[9] As far as non-Swedish parties are concerned, questions relating to capacity and representation of legal entities are usually decided by the *lex corporationis,* see Chapter 2.

[10] The question of written form arose when Sweden ratified the New York Convention in 1971. Since Article II of the New York Convention refers to written arbitration agreements, it was questioned whether Swedish law complied with the requirements of the Convention and if it would be necessary to amend Swedish law on this point, ie to introduce a written form requirement. The Swedish legislator took the view, however, that Article II of the New York Convention prevented Member States from introducing stricter requirements than foreseen in the Convention, but that nothing prevented a Member State from having more lenient requirements. This position was confirmed by the Swedish legislator when preparing the SAA, see Govt Bill 1998/99:35, p 67; cf para 3.13.

[11] Cf the Swedish Supreme Court case *Tureberg-Sollentuna Lastbilcentral ekonomisk förening v Byggnadsfirman Rudolf Asplund* (NJA 1980 p 46) where the Supreme Court concluded that a simple reference to the general provisions containing an arbitration clause is sufficient to make the parties bound by the clause. See also Bernitz, *Standardavtalsrätt* (7th edn, 2008) 59.

(iii) *No Vitiating Element.* The arbitration agreement must not be tainted by duress, fraud, undue influence, mistake, etc, or any other circumstance which may make the arbitration agreement void according to the ordinary rules of contract law. In addition, the circumstances must not be such that enforcement of the arbitration agreement is unreasonable pursuant to Article 36 of the Swedish Contracts Act. In accordance with article 36 of the Swedish Contracts Act, there are certain, very rare, circumstances, which give rise to a possibility for arbitrators (or a court) to set aside or amend an agreement in a commercial transaction, see para 3.37.

(iv) *Contents of Agreement.* Although no particular form is required for the arbitration agreement, it must be clear that the parties have agreed on arbitration, and not on any other kind of dispute resolution, eg by specifying a matter and stating that such matter is to be referred to arbitrators for decision.[12]

As mentioned above, the arbitration agreement may relate to an existing dispute, but the usual form of agreement refers to arbitration of future disputes. The agreement looking to the future generally takes the form of a provision in a contract, usually in the form of an arbitration clause. Section 1 of the Swedish Arbitration Act (SAA) states that an arbitration agreement concerning future disputes must relate to 'a particular legal relationship specified in the agreement'. A reference to the agreement in question is sufficient.

A provision of the following tenor satisfies the requirements indicated above: 'Any dispute in connection with this agreement shall be referred to arbitration'. Such a clause is sufficient to constitute a valid and workable arbitration agreement. Many details of the arbitration may, however, be varied by the parties. The arbitration agreement can accordingly be more or less elaborate,[13] see para 3.183.

(v) *Arbitrability.* The subject matter of the dispute must, in the words of the New York Convention, be 'capable of settlement by arbitration' under the laws of Sweden. This requirement is treated in greater detail in para 3.78 below.

---

[12] See *Alingsås Kommun v Luftteknik Mellin & Selling* (RH 1982:102).

[13] Cf the model clause recommended by the SCC Institute which has the following wording (<http:// www.sccinstitute.se >):

Any dispute, controversy or claim arising out of or in connection with this contract, or the breach, termination or invalidity thereof, shall be finally settled by arbitration in accordance with the Arbitration Rules of the Arbitration Institute of the Stockholm Chamber of Commerce.

The SCC Institute also advises the parties to make the following additions to the arbitration clause, as required:

(i) The arbitral tribunal shall be composed of [. . .] arbitrators (a sole arbitrator).
(ii) The seat of arbitration shall be [. . .].
(iii) The language to be used in the arbitral proceedings shall be [. . .].
(iv) The substantive law of [. . .] shall be applied.

3.3 Concluding the Arbitration Agreement

3.3.1 Arbitration agreement in writing

Most arbitral proceedings are based on an arbitration agreement in writing. Such **3.06**
agreement may be entered into when the dispute has already arisen or may relate to
future disputes. In the latter case the arbitration agreement commonly takes the
form of a specific arbitration clause of the main contract. Pursuant to section 1(1),
second sentence, of the SAA, the arbitration clause must concern a particular legal
relationship, which must be identified.[14] In order for the arbitration agreement to
be binding, the legal relationship must have arisen at the time when the arbitration
agreement is entered into.[15]

An arbitration clause may also be part of a standard contract attached to the main **3.07**
contract. There is no requirement that the main agreement contain a provision
referring to the arbitration clause in the standard contract attached to the main agreement.[16] The Supreme Court has found that a confirmation note which referred to
a standard agreement with an arbitration clause was sufficient for the parties to be
bound by an arbitration agreement.[17]

In addition, the parties may be bound by an arbitration clause included in general **3.08**
terms of contract through a so-called reference clause.[18] A reference clause is a
provision in the main agreement to the effect that certain standard conditions are
to apply, without it being specifically indicated whether those conditions include
an arbitration clause.[19] The generally held view is that the clause is valid if the party
had the opportunity, without any difficulty, to study the conditions before the main
agreement was entered into.[20] In *Tureberg-Sollentuna Lastbilcentral ekonomisk förening
v Byggnadsfirman Rudolf Asplund* (NJA 1980 p 46), the Supreme Court found that
a simple reference to the standard contract with an arbitration clause was sufficient
to make the parties bound by the clause.[21]

The New York Convention, Article II(1), stipulates that an arbitration agree- **3.09**
ment 'in writing' shall be recognized. The term 'agreement in writing' includes an
arbitration clause in a contract or an arbitration agreement, signed by the parties or

---

[14] SOU 1994:81, p 256 *et seq* and Govt Bill 1998/99:35, p 212.

[15] Lindskog, *Skiljeförfarande, En kommentar* (2005) 260 *et seq.*

[16] Heuman, *Arbitration Law of Sweden: Practice and Procedure* (2003) 33.

[17] See *Tureberg-Sollentuna Lastbilcentral ekonomisk förening v Byggnadsfirman Rudolf Asplund*
(NJA 1980 p 46) and *DHL Express AB v Nordic Logistic Service Oy's bankruptcy estate* (NJA 2005
note 8).

[18] Bernitz, *Standardavtalsrätt* (7th edn, 2008) 59; and Ramberg and Ramberg, *Allmän avtalsrätt*
(8th edn, 2010) 141 *et seq.*

[19] Heuman, *Arbitration Law of Sweden: Practice and Procedure* (2003) 34.

[20] Bernitz, *Standardavtalsrätt* (7th edn, 2008) 59.

[21] This approach has subsequently been confirmed by the Supreme Court in *DHL Express AB v
Nordic Logistic Service Oy's bankruptcy estate* (NJA 2005 note 8).

contained in an exchange of letters and telegrams. The New York Convention was adopted in 1958.

3.10 Since then, modern communication technology has developed significantly. This was one aspect addressed during the revision of the UNCITRAL Model Law. The revision resulted in a recommendation regarding the interpretation of Article II of the New York Convention as well as in amendments to article 7 of the Model Law dealing with the arbitration agreement.[22] Article 7 now has two optional wordings. Option I reads as follows:[23]

(1) 'Arbitration agreement' is an agreement by the parties to submit to arbitration all or certain disputes which have arisen or which may arise between them in respect of a defined legal relationship, whether contractual or not. An arbitration agreement may be in the form of an arbitration clause in a contract or in the form of a separate agreement.

(2) The arbitration agreement shall be in writing.

(3) An arbitration agreement is in writing if its content is recorded in any form, whether or not the arbitration agreement or contract has been concluded orally, by conduct, or by other means.

(4) The requirement that an arbitration agreement be in writing is met by an electronic communication if the information contained therein is accessible so as to be useable for subsequent reference; 'electronic communication' means any communication that the parties make by means of data messages; 'data message' means information generated, sent, received or stored by electronic, magnetic, optical or similar means, including, but not limited to, electronic data interchange (EDI), electronic mail, telegram, telex or telecopy.

(5) Furthermore, an arbitration agreement is in writing if it is contained in an exchange of statements of claim and defence in which the existence of an agreement is alleged by one party and not denied by the other.

(6) The reference in a contract to any document containing an arbitration clause constitutes an arbitration agreement in writing, provided that the reference is such as to make that clause part of the contract.

---

[22] Cf 2006 Recommendation regarding the interpretation of Article II (2) and Article VII (1) of the Convention on the Recognition and Enforcement of Foreign Arbitral Awards (New York, 1958), adopted by UNCITRAL on 7 July 2006. The Recommendation was drafted in recognition of the widening use of electronic commerce and enactments of domestic legislation as well as case law, which are more favourable than the New York Convention in respect of the form requirement governing arbitration agreements, arbitration proceedings, and the enforcement of arbitral awards. The Recommendation encourages States to apply Article II(2) of the New York Convention 'recognizing that the circumstances described therein are not exhaustive'. In addition, the Recommendation encourages States to adopt the revised Article 7 of the UNCITRAL Model Law. Both options of the revised Article 7 establish a more favourable regime for the recognition and enforcement of arbitral awards than that provided under the New York Convention. By virtue of the 'more favourable law provision' contained in Article VII(1) of the New York Convention, the Recommendation clarifies that 'any interested party' should be allowed 'to avail itself of rights it may have, under the law or treaties of the country where an arbitration agreement is sought to be relied upon, to seek recognition of the validity of such an arbitration agreement'.

[23] The revised provision of Article 7 was adopted by the Commission at its thirty-ninth session, in 2006.

Option II accepts oral arbitration agreements. It reads as follows: "'Arbitration agreement" is an agreement by the parties to submit to arbitration all or certain disputes which have arisen or which may arise between them in respect of a defined legal relationship, whether contractual or not'.

As reflected in the revised Article 7 of the UNCITRAL Model Law, most modern **3.11** arbitration laws define the written form requirement in a flexible way, and as widely as possible.

3.3.2 Oral arbitration agreement

Swedish law accepts oral arbitration agreements.[24] Thus, with respect to the formation **3.12** of a binding agreement under Swedish law, an arbitration agreement is not distinguished from other agreements. In practice oral arbitration agreements are very unusual. In certain situations, however, oral agreements may become relevant. For example, it may be that subsequent to the commencement of arbitration proceedings the parties agree during a meeting or hearing that claims falling outside the scope of the original arbitration agreement also are to be decided by the arbitrators. This is sometimes done before the arbitrators. A party asserting that such an oral agreement has been made has the burden of proof in this respect. Therefore it is important for the party in question to ensure that the agreement is recorded in the minutes, or included in a procedural order, and for the arbitrators to make clear to the parties that their jurisdiction has been extended to cover the new claims.[25]

The requirement in Article II of the New York Convention that the arbitration **3.13** agreement be in writing may, at first sight, seem to cause a problem in respect of oral arbitration agreements or oral supplements to agreements in writing. In the view of the Swedish legislator, however, provisions of the New York Convention are to be understood only as a minimum regulation imposing no requirements additional to the written form.[26] Moreover, in accordance with Article V(1)(a) of the New York Convention, the recognition and enforcement of an award may only be refused if the arbitration agreement 'is not valid under the law to which the parties have subjected it, or, failing any indication thereon, under the law of the country where the award was made'. This means that, although there is a requirement for the arbitration agreement to be in writing, an award based on an oral arbitration agreement could still be recognized and enforced under the New York Convention if the parties have agreed that the arbitration agreement is governed by Swedish law or, without such agreement, if the award was made in Sweden.[27]

---

[24] Cf para 3.05.
[25] Heuman, *Arbitration Law of Sweden: Practice and Procedure* (2003) 42, referring to *Åsbacka Trävaruaktiebolag v E. Hedberg* (NJA 1924 p 569) and *Boliden Chemtrade Services AB v Western Tankers AB* (RH 1986:162).
[26] See the *travaux préparatoires* to Sweden's accession to the New York Convention (NJA II 1971 p 570 *et seq*).
[27] Recognition and enforcement of arbitral awards are discussed at para 9.02 *et seq*.

3.3.3 Arbitration agreement by conduct

3.14 Arbitration agreements —just like commercial contracts in general— may also be validly 'entered' into by conduct.[28] The primary example of such agreement is a party who participates in arbitration proceedings without objecting thereto. Similarly, if a party during the arbitration proceedings submits a claim not covered by the arbitration agreement, without the opposing party objecting thereto, the arbitration agreement is deemed to have been extended also to cover the new claim. This also means that the opposing party, by his conduct (or inactivity), is deemed to have waived the possibility to challenge the jurisdiction of the arbitrators on the basis that there was no valid arbitration agreement between the parties.[29]

3.15 That an arbitration agreement may be concluded by conduct is accepted in many jurisdictions. Article 7(5) of the revised UNCITRAL Model Law specifically provides that an arbitration agreement is 'in writing' and thus valid if 'the arbitration agreement is 'contained in an exchange of statement of claim and defence in which the existence of an agreement is alleged by one party and not denied by another'.[30]

3.16 Other conduct by a party may also result in a binding arbitration agreement.[31] For example, if a party (non-signatory) is directly involved in the performance of the contract, which includes an arbitration clause, or if the party has otherwise been involved in the negotiation or termination of such contract, the party may, under certain circumstances, be deemed to have accepted or entered into a binding arbitration agreement.[32] The conclusion of an arbitration agreement by conduct is closely linked to the extension of arbitration agreements to third parties, eg in respect of guarantee agreements or within a group of companies, see para 3.131 *et seq.* In fact, in many cases it is difficult, if not impossible, to distinguish between, on the one hand, cases where the effect of an existing arbitration agreement has been extended to a third party (non-signatory) and, on the other hand, cases where the

---

[28] See *Björklund et al v Lundqvist* (NJA 1955 p 500), cf Nerep, 'Till frågan om skiljeavtalets särställning i svensk avtalsrätt', in *Festskrift till Sveriges Advokatsamfund* (1987) 412 *et seq.*

[29] Cf section 34(2) of the SAA and Govt Bill 1998/99:35, pp 142 and 149.

[30] Cf Article 2.1.11 of the UNIDROIT Principles of International Commercial Contracts (2004) (UNIDROIT Principles)—'(1) A reply to an offer which purports to be an acceptance but contains additions, limitations or other modifications is a rejection of the offer and constitutes a counter-offer. (2) However, a reply to an offer which purports to be an acceptance but contains additional or different terms which do not materially alter the terms of the offer constitutes an acceptance, unless the offeror, without undue delay, objects to the discrepancy. If the offeror does not object, the terms of the contract are the terms of the offer with the modifications contained in the acceptance'.

[31] Cf Article 2.1.1 of the UNIDROIT Principles—'A contract may be concluded either by the acceptance of an offer or by conduct of the parties that is sufficient to show agreement'.

[32] Cf Gaillard and Savage (eds), *Fouchard, Gaillard, Goldman On International Commercial Arbitration* (1999) 281 *et seq*, where the following extract from a ruling of the Paris Court of Appeal dated 7 December 1994 in case *V 2000* is to be found: 'In international arbitration law, the effects of the arbitration clause extend to parties directly involved in the performance of the contract, provided that their respective situations and activities raise the presumption that they were aware of the existence and scope of the arbitration clause, so that the arbitrator can consider all economic and legal aspects of the dispute'.

non-signatory has 'entered' into an arbitration agreement by its conduct. In such situations, it is mostly a question of terminology.

With respect to contracts in general, two Supreme Court cases illustrate rather **3.17** typical situations where courts have accepted that agreements have been concluded by conduct. First, in *Rockwool AB and Gullfiber AB v Byggma Syd AB's bankruptcy estate* (NJA 1982 p 244) the question was whether a parent company was bound by orders made by its subsidiaries concerning the supply of goods. The plaintiffs claimed that Byggma Syd AB, by its express undertakings, by its conduct, and by its inactivity had become liable for the costs relating to the supply of goods to the subsidiaries. The plaintiffs argued that they regarded Byggma Syd AB as the actual buyer of the goods and the party closest to the liability for the payment of the goods supplied. The Supreme Court called attention to the fact that Byggma Syd AB had amended its procedure for invoicing to the effect that all invoices were to be sent to Byggma Syd AB, irrespective of which of its subsidiaries had made the purchase of the goods. In accordance with this amended procedure, the plaintiffs sent their invoices to Byggma Syd AB. In addition, the invoices referred to Byggma Syd AB as the purchaser, with however an indication of which of its subsidiaries had actually made the purchase of goods. Byggma Syd AB paid the invoices, in total, hundreds of them, in its own name and through its own bank. It was not until its bankruptcy that Byggma Syd AB objected to its liability to pay.

The Supreme Court found that the way in which Byggma Syd AB acted had given **3.18** the plaintiffs reason to regard Byggma Syd AB as liable for the payment of the goods supplied. The Supreme Court further found that Byggma Syd AB must have understood that the plaintiffs believed that Byggma Syd AB was responsible. Therefore, the Supreme Court found Byggma Syd AB liable for the payment of the goods supplied to its subsidiary.

Secondly, in *Aktiebolaget H v Grästorps kommun* (NJA 1961 p 658), a company had **3.19** delivered white goods to a municipality without an agreement in place before the delivery. The company, however, assumed that such agreement existed, which the municipality must have realized due to the fact that the goods were delivered to and invoiced to the municipality. Since the municipality had signed for the goods, the Supreme Court found that an agreement had been entered into as a result of the conduct by the parties, and that under the agreement the municipality could not avoid liability to pay for the goods delivered.

There is yet another Supreme Court case which is of relevance in this context: **3.20** *Saab-Scania AB v Edgard B* (NJA 1977 p 92). In that case the Swedish company had negotiated with B about representing the Swedish company in Syria. The Supreme Court first tried the question of whether an agreement had been concluded as a result of the negotiations between the company and B, and if not, whether an agreement had subsequently been entered into as a consequence of the conduct of the company. The Court found that no agreement had been reached as a result of the negotiations. The Court concluded, however, that the company had given B confirmation than an agreement had been reached. The Court explained that the company had acted in a manner which had created the impression that it was of the view that it had contractual obligations in relation to B. It was added by the Court that, in any event, the conduct of the company must have been likely to reinforce B's impression that the company viewed itself as having become bound by the agreement.[33]

3.21 There are many examples of arbitral tribunals having accepted that an arbitration agreement has been entered into as a result of the conduct of the parties. The following case, an arbitration between Claimant X (United States) and Respondent Z (Russian Federation), is an illustrative example.[34] In that case the conduct of a parent company (Respondent Z) was considered to constitute acceptance of the entire contract—which was governed by Swedish law—between one of Z's subsidiaries (Y) and Claimant X, including the agreement to arbitrate any dispute with Claimant X. The place of arbitration was Sweden. The majority[35] of the arbitrators reasoned as follows:

> The principles of contracting through conduct (conclusive conduct, '*konkludent handlande*') are, however, well recognised and developed over many decades of Swedish court practice and legal writing. Swedish law takes in fact a liberal view of the forms and mechanism through which contracts may be concluded . . .

> . . . Swedish contract law is based upon the 'theory of trust' *i.e.* the decisive element in forming a contract is not what the party intends but what intention he conveys to the other party. In other words, the other party shall be able to 'trust' the contractual behaviour of the first party. That principle has its legislative support for instance in Section 6.2 of the [Swedish Contracts Act]. The underlying principle is that a party will be bound by the impression that he has created with another party, who is in good faith, regarding an obligation, unless he corrects that impression . . .

> . . . the arbitrators conclude that [Z] held itself out as the party managing and implementing the Contract on the buyers' side, renegotiating it and making payments thereunder. [X] was given the impression that Z acted as contracting party and X, being in good faith, was entitled to rely upon or 'trust' that impression . . .

> . . . The arbitrators thus hold that [Z] has, through its conduct, entered as a party into the Contract with [X] . . .

> . . . The conduct of [Z] must be considered to constitute acceptance of the full contract with all [Y's] obligations including the obligation to arbitrate any dispute with [X]. There is no ground for excluding any specific parts of the contract obligations . . .

---

[33] *Saab-Scania AB v Edgard B* (NJA 1977 p 92) 110–111. It is noteworthy that the Supreme Court did not require that B establish that he de facto viewed the company as bound by the agreement. Rather the Court looked at the conduct of the company and concluded that it objectively 'must have likely reinforced' B's impression in this respect.

[34] SCC Arbitration 108/1997. The case is reported in SAR 2001:1, pp 57–72. The award was challenged and set aside by the then court of first instance; eventually, however, the parties reached an agreed settlement.

[35] One of the arbitrators expressed a dissenting opinion and held that the circumstances of the case were not such as to create a contractual relationship between [X] and [Z] under Swedish law.

... The agreement to arbitrate disputes may be looked upon as a right or an obligation. It is an integral part of the substantive rights and obligations that a new party to the Contract assumes. There is today good support in a Swedish Supreme Court case for the position that an arbitral agreement follows the substantive rights and obligations of a contract (the *Emja*, NJA 1997 p 866), the specific facts of which refer, however, to the transfer of contract) ...

... The arbitrators thus conclude that they are competent to try the claim by [X] against [Z].[36]

The arbitrators' conclusion in the abovementioned case must not be mistaken for a **3.22** finding that the parent company is liable for its subsidiary's obligations under the theory of piercing the corporate veil, or the group of companies theory, see further under para 3.155 below. Liability for a parent company under either of these theories generally requires elements of reproachable or flagrantly reproachable conduct on the part of the parent company. Examples of such elements include the absence of independent commercial objective, the absence of independent management and administration, or under-capitalization of the subsidiary. In the above mentioned case the arbitrators held that 'such causes of action are so different from liability under a contract and require the trial of so many factors outside the contractual relationship that they cannot be considered to be covered by an arbitration clause of the contract'.[37]

3.3.3.1 Arbitration agreement as a result of party usage

An arbitration agreement may also result from the practices established between the **3.23** parties in question (party usage).[38] An express rule to this effect is found in the Swedish Sale of Goods Act, section 3 with respect to contracts in general.[39] This provision can be applied by analogy with respect to agreements other than contracts of sale.[40] If a specific contract does not refer to standard conditions, including an arbitration clause, but the parties have made reference to them previously in several contracts of similar nature, party usage may exist.[41] This was confirmed by the Supreme Court in *Société Planavergne SA v KB i Stockholm AB* (NJA 2003 p 379).[42] The circumstances were the following.

---

[36] Note 34 at 61–64.

[37] Ibid.

[38] Cf Article 1.9(1) of the UNIDROIT Principles (2004)—'The parties are bound by any usage to which they have agreed and by any practices which they have established between themselves'. Party usage must be distinguished from trade usage. As a rule trade usage, without anything more, is not sufficient to constitute an arbitral agreement, even if the trade usage *per se* is well established, cf *Svenska Pontohamnar AB v Precon AB* (RH 1989:51) and *Connection SA Aktiebolag v Exsped Transport Aktiebolag* (RH 1990:7).

[39] Section 3 of the Swedish Sale of Goods Act has the following wording: 'The provisions of this Act shall not apply to the extent that they are contrary to the contract, to practices which the parties have established between themselves or to commercial usage or other customs which must be regarded as binding on the parties'.

[40] Heuman, *Arbitration Law of Sweden: Practice and Procedure* (2003) 35; and Bernitz, *Standardavtalsrätt* (7th edn, 2008) 41 *et seq*, 54 *et seq*; and Ramberg, *Köplagen* (1995) 161.

[41] Heuman, *Arbitration Law of Sweden: Practice and Procedure* (2003) 35.

[42] See observations by Edlund in Jarvin and Magnusson (eds), *International Arbitration Court Decisions* (2nd edn, 2008) 1131 *et seq*.

3.24   The Chambre Arbitrale Internationale pour les Fruits et Légumes in Strasbourg (Tribunal) rendered an award on 1 July 2007 in which KB i Stockholm AB ('KB') was ordered to pay to S.A. Planavergne SA. ('Planavergne') an amount corresponding to the remainder of the purchase price for a shipment of fruit delivered from Planavergne to KB, together with damages and costs.

3.25   There was no signed agreement referring to arbitration. The Tribunal dealt with the issue of jurisdiction under a separate section of the award. The Tribunal concluded, *inter alia*, that the parties had previously had a business relationship and that previous agreements, as well as the agreement in dispute, were entered into under the COFREUROP conditions,[43] which included an arbitration clause. Moreover, KB had never expressed any objection to the application of these conditions. The Tribunal found that it had jurisdiction to determine the dispute.

3.26   In its objection to the recognition and enforcement of the award, KB challenged the jurisdiction of the Tribunal arguing that KB had never entered into an agreement indicating the Tribunal as the forum for a potential dispute. Planavergne claimed that an arbitration agreement had been entered into as a result of party usage which meant that the general conditions COFREUROP, including the arbitration clause, had become part of the parties' agreement.

3.27   The issue before the Supreme Court essentially concerned the burden of proof in an enforcement action. In this respect the Supreme Court concluded that the Tribunal was in a better place to determine the issue of jurisdiction and that KB had not fulfilled its burden of proof as to the alleged lack of jurisdiction of the Tribunal. The Supreme Court therefore found that there was no impediment to enforcement of the award. It thus rejected KB's appeal.

3.3.3.2 Arbitration agreement by 'inactivity'

3.28   A further possible category of arbitration agreements entered into by conduct is based on the concept of 'inactivity', or passivity, under section 6(2) of the Swedish Contracts Act.[44] Under this provision a party who has made an offer (the offeror)

---

[43] Code of practice for fresh edible fruit and vegetables in national and international trade.

[44] Section 6 of the Swedish Contracts Act reads as follows: 6(1) 'A reply which contains an acceptance but which, by reason of any addition, restriction or reservation does not conform with the offer, shall be deemed to constitute a rejection in conjunction with a new offer'. 6(2) 'The aforementioned provisions shall not apply where the offeree believes it to correspond to the offer, and where this fact must have been realised by the offeror. In such circumstances the offeror shall, should he wish to repudiate the acceptance, so inform the offeree without unreasonable delay. Should he fail to do so, a contract shall be deemed to have been concluded through, and in accordance with, the acceptance'; see also section 4(2) of the Swedish Contracts Act, where a party's omission to object to a belated acceptance of an offer is deemed to constitute a binding agreement based on the acceptance; and section 9 of the Swedish Contracts Act which reads 'Where a statement which would otherwise be deemed to constitute an offer includes the words "not binding" or "without obligation", or suchlike expression, such statement shall be deemed to constitute an invitation to tender an offer on the basis of the contents of the statement. Where such an offer is forthcoming within a reasonable period of time thereafter from a party thus invited, and where the recipient must realise that the offer has been

may be bound as a result of inactivity after having received a qualified acceptance of the offer from the other party (the offeree). In certain circumstances, the offeror must, should he wish to repudiate the acceptance, so inform the offeree without unreasonable delay, failing which a contract shall be deemed to have been concluded through, and in accordance with, the acceptance.[45]

It has been argued that the principles of section 6(2) of the Swedish Contracts Act **3.29** cannot be automatically extended to arbitration clauses.[46] However, in *Tureberg-Sollentuna Lastbilscentral v Byggnadsfirman Rudolf Asplund AB* (NJA 1980 p 46) the Supreme Court concluded that a letter which had been sent to a party meant that the party must have understood that the other party considered itself bound only after receiving the letter and on the conditions stated therein, including an arbitration clause in certain standard terms as referred to in the letter. Since the party had not raised any objection to the letter and had begun the work, the Supreme Court found that an agreement had been concluded on the terms indicated by the letter.[47]

It is possible that parties can become bound in accordance with the principles **3.30** expressed in the above-mentioned case, even if the recipient of the reply was unaware of the content of the standard conditions to which the other party referred in his reply or in an order confirmation.[48] Such principles should probably be made subject to certain qualifications. In order to be bound by standard conditions, eg an arbitration clause, without being aware of the contents thereof, it would seem reasonable to require that the standard conditions should have been made available to the party and that he had the opportunity, without any difficulty, to review the conditions

---

occasioned by his invitation, the recipient shall, should he not wish to accept the offer, so inform the offeror without unreasonable delay. Should he fail to do so, he shall be deemed to have accepted the offer'; cf Article 2.1.11 of the UNIDROIT Principles—'(1) A reply to an offer which purports to be an acceptance but contains additions, limitations or other modifications is a rejection of the offer and constitutes a counter-offer. (2) However, a reply to an offer which purports to be an acceptance but contains additional or different terms which do not materially alter the terms of the offer constitutes an acceptance, unless the offeror, without undue delay, objects to the discrepancy. If the offeror does not object, the terms of the contract are the terms of the offer with the modifications contained in the acceptance'.

[45] Cf *Saab-Scania AB v Edgard B* (NJA 1977 p 92).

[46] Heuman, *Swedish Arbitration Law: Practice and Procedure* (2003) 39; cf Dennemark, *Om svensk domstols behörighet i internationellt förmögenhetsrättsliga mål* (1961) 258, where the argument is that prorogation clauses in letters of confirmation and such similar documents transmitted to a party after an agreement has been concluded cannot be considered operative, since the recipient's attention may have been concentrated mostly on other questions.

[47] See also Reldén and Nilsson, *Incorporation and Passivity: Entering into Arbitration Agreements under Swedish Law* in Hobér, Magnusson, and Öhrström (eds), *Between East and West: Essays in Honour of Ulf Franke* (2010) 439–440, where reference is made to an unpublished case from the Svea Court of Appeal, judgment dated 17 December 2007 (Case No T 3108-06), *State of Ukraine v Norsk Hydro ASA*, in which the Svea Court of Appeal held that it could be argued that the party not signing a contract, in principle agreed upon and sent to him, had an obligation to inform the other party when he decided not to sign the contract.

[48] See eg Heuman, *Swedish Arbitration Law: Practice and Procedure* (2003) 40; cf *Tore Johansson med firma Svenska Maskinagentur v Handelsbolaget Maskinfirma Hafo* (NJA 1949 p 609).

before the main agreement was entered into,[49] or that the standard conditions have become part of the parties' dealings through party usage, or as a result of trade usage.[50]

3.4 Interpretation of Arbitration Agreement

3.31 The interpretation of an arbitration agreement is based on the same principles that apply to agreements in general. The common intention of the parties, or the parties' meeting of their minds, is often used to describe the true contents of an agreement. Although this is always the ultimate objective under Swedish law, it is not always very helpful in practice in trying to interpret an agreement between parties in dispute.[51] Instead, the interpretation must be based on certain rules and methods. Under Swedish law there is not one universal rule or method for the interpretation of agreements. To the contrary, several rules and methods may be used depending on the circumstances of the case. Although the so-called language-oriented (*språkinriktad*) method, ie the analysis of the wording of the agreement, is an obvious starting point for any interpretation of agreements, other rules and methods may be used in addition thereto and in combination with the language-oriented method. Examples of rules and methods used in the interpretation of agreements include the norm-oriented (*norminriktad*) method, the purpose-oriented (*ändamålsinriktad*) method, the system-oriented (*systeminriktad*) method, the disloyalty analysis (*illojalitetsanalys*), the equity-oriented (*skälighetsinriktad*) method, the so-called rule of obscurities (*oklarhetsregeln*), as well as consideration of circumstances prior to and after the conclusion of the agreement.[52] In a Supreme Court case the combination of rules and methods used is illustrated as follows:

> In the case it has not been invoked that the parties, in relation to the origin of the agreement ... discussed the closer import of the clauses of the agreement in question. Nor are there any other circumstances present besides the actual wording of the agreement which may contribute to the demonstration of how the parties, at this point in time, interpreted these clauses. Decisive for the determination is therefore, besides the wording of the clauses, their legal background and their general purpose, as well as the circumstance in which these occur.[53]

3.32 It has sometimes been suggested that arbitration agreements should be interpreted in a restrictive fashion, in the sense that the scope of application should be as narrow as possible. It is submitted that this is an outdated approach as far as international commercial arbitration is concerned. The practice—and certainly the trend—today is rather the opposite. When an arbitration clause must be interpreted, the approach

---

[49] Bernitz, *Standardavtalsrätt* (7th edn, 2008) 59.

[50] Cf *Sydkraft v Skandia* (NJA 1998 p 448), where the Supreme Court found that certain standard conditions had become part of trade usage and could thus be applied when interpreting alleged restrictions of a party's liability.

[51] Ramberg and Ramberg, *Allmän avtalsrätt* (8th edn, 2010) 174.

[52] Ibid, 147–174.

[53] *Kontorscenter Ynglingagatan Aktiebolag v R G Kungshuset Aktiebolag* (NJA 1991 p 319).

is usually to do so in an extensive manner, based on the assumption that this corresponds to the intention of the parties.

Arbitrators are often called upon to interpret the arbitration agreement with a   **3.33** view to determining whether a particular claim is covered by it at all, and if therefore the arbitrators have the authority to try it. With respect to this particular situation, the so-called doctrine of assertion[54] may become relevant under Swedish arbitration law.

In short the doctrine of assertion means that the arbitrators are entitled to try their   **3.34** own jurisdiction—ie is the claim covered by the arbitration agreement?—based on the legal grounds relied on by the requesting party. There is no need for the requesting party to prove that he is right on the merits for the arbitrators to have jurisdiction. It is sufficient for the requesting party to base his claim on a contract with an arbitration clause.

In accordance with the doctrine of assertion the arbitrators must not determine the   **3.35** existence of the legal facts asserted by the claimant to be covered by the arbitration agreement. Rather, the arbitrators should assume that the legal facts in question are correct, provided that the claim is not manifestly unfounded,[55] which could be the case if the respondent is in fact a non-signatory to the agreement.[56] In applying the doctrine of assertion, the arbitrators may also find that part of the dispute is contractual, and thus covered by the arbitration agreement, whereas other parts are non-contractual, and thus should be tried by a court of law.[57]

It is, submitted however, that a *sine qua non* for the application of the doctrine of   **3.36** assertion is that there is indeed a valid arbitration agreement. The doctrine of assertion can thus not be used to *create* an arbitration agreement not already existing between the parties.[58] If, for example, arbitration is successfully commenced, this does not exclude the possibility for an alleged party to the agreement to challenge the award

---

[54] The doctrine of assertion has been developed by Welamson in his review of Bolding's book, *Skiljedom*, published in Svensk Juristtidning (1964) 278 *et seq*. See also Heuman, *op cit*, at 75 *et seq*.

[55] See *Petrobart Limited v the Republic of Kirgizistan* (NJA 2008 p 406); Lindskog, *Skiljeförfarande, En kommentar* (2005) 199 *et seq*; Heuman, *Vilken beviskravsbetydelse har separabilitetsprincipen, påståendedoktrinen och anknytningsdoktrinen för bedömningen av behörighetsfrågor inom skiljedomsrätten?*, Juridisk Tidskrift (2009/2010) 335; and Welamson in *Svensk Juristtidning* (1964) 278 *et seq*. See also *Nykvarns Skyltaktiebolag v Esselte Dymo AB* (NJA 1982 p 738), where the Supreme Court endorsed the doctrine of assertion in the form advocated by Welamson, and *Forsman v Inovius* (NJA 1973 p 480).

[56] Cf *Björklund et al v Lundqvist* (NJA 1955 p 500). The binding effect of arbitration agreements on third parties is further discussed in para 3.131 *et seq*.

[57] Welamson in *Svensk Juristtidning* (1964) 278 *et seq*, and Heuman, *Arbitration Law of Sweden: Practice and Procedure* (2003) 56 *et seq*. See also *Nykvarns Skyltaktiebolag v Esselte Dymo AB* (NJA 1982 p 738) and *Icon AB v Göran W and Björn H.* (RH 1991:16).

[58] Lindskog, *Skiljeförfarande, En kommentar* (2005) 199 *et seq*; cf, however, *Petrobart Limited v the Republic of Kirgizistan* (NJA 2008 p 406), where the Supreme Court found that the claimant's assertion that there was an investment should have been accepted by the arbitral tribunal, applying the doctrine of assertion.

on the basis that he was never a party to the arbitration agreement. Moreover, the fact that the claimant asserts a binding arbitration agreement between the parties does not mean that the arbitrators, in determining their jurisdiction, must accept the assertion.[59] It is submitted that the arbitrators must determine the binding effect of the arbitration agreement with the same carefulness as if the opposing party had argued that there was no valid arbitration agreement at all, and not only that the party was not bound by the existing arbitration agreement.[60] Similarly, the legal relationship which the claimant asserts is covered by the arbitration agreement, must either be undisputed or confirmed in due course during the arbitration.

3.5 Unenforceability of Arbitration Agreements due to the Swedish Contracts Act

3.37 An arbitration agreement, although fully valid from a formal point of view, can be declared unenforceable in accordance with section 36 of the Swedish Contracts Act.[61] This provision stipulates that, under certain, quite rare—and for international transactions, unusual —circumstances, eg when one party is a natural person and deemed to be in a 'weaker position', than for instance a company, the agreement may be set aside or modified by the court or the arbitrators. However, it is important to understand that in practice section 36 of the Swedish Contracts Act plays a very limited role in international commercial arbitration in Sweden.

3.38 With respect to arbitration agreements, section 36 of the Swedish Contracts Act has been applied to the effect that the courts have considered that it would be

---

[59] When the respondent raises objections against the jurisdiction of the arbitrators, it is not unusual that facts and legal arguments relied on by the respondent in this context could also be of relevance to the merits of the dispute. In such a situation it is generally accepted that the arbitrators have the authority—at least at the request of one of the parties—to merge the jurisdictional objections to the merits phase of the arbitration. In this sense it could be said that the arbitrators have provisionally accepted jurisdiction. This does not mean, however, that the arbitrators are prevented from dismissing the case for lack of jurisdiction, should they come to this conclusion when trying the facts and the legal arguments.

[60] Lindskog, *Skiljeförfarande, En kommentar* (2005) 199, footnote 366.

[61] Section 36 of the Swedish Contracts Act reads as follows:

A contract term or condition may be modified or set aside if such term or condition is unconscionable having regard to the contents of the agreement, the circumstances prevailing at the time the agreement was entered into, subsequent circumstances, and circumstances in general. Where a term is of such significance for the agreement that it would be unreasonable to demand the continued enforceability of the remainder of the agreement with its terms unchanged, the agreement may be modified in other respects, or may or may be set aside in its entirety.

Upon determination of the applicability of the provisions of the first paragraph, particular attention should be paid to the need to protect those parties who, in their capacity as consumers or otherwise, hold an inferior bargaining position in the contractual relationship.

The provisions of the first and second paragraphs shall apply *mutatis mutandis* to questions relating to the terms of legal acts other than contracts.

The provisions of section 11 of the Consumer Contracts Act shall also apply to the modification of contractual terms relating to consumers.

unreasonable to uphold arbitration agreements. This has the same practical effect as a complete termination of the agreement and lifts the bar to court proceedings.[62]

Swedish case law is relatively comprehensive. The typical example in many of these cases is a contract between a businessman and a consumer.[63] However, these cases have largely lost their importance in practice following the enactment of section 6 of the SAA, in which significant restrictions have been introduced with respect to arbitration agreements in a businessman–consumer relationship. It is noteworthy, however, that the employer–employee relationship falls outside the scope of section 6 of the SAA, which means that case law on this issue remains relevant.[64] In addition, there are cases where the arbitration agreement has been set aside or modified despite both parties being business enterprises.[65] **3.39**

The rationale behind the application of section 36 of the Swedish Contracts Act to arbitration agreements is to safeguard the equality of arms between the parties to a dispute. The fact that the arbitrators are paid by the parties has been held to be a drawback for a financially weaker party to have a dispute tried in arbitration. It is true that the costs for the arbitrators may be substantial. On the other hand, arbitration is a one instance procedure. In addition, arbitration proceedings are often handled in a speedier manner than court proceedings. Both of these circumstances save time and costs for the parties. **3.40**

Where the parties' equal right to appoint the arbitrators is infringed,[66] or where a condition in the arbitration agreement excessively disrupts the balance between the parties,[67] the arbitration agreement may also be set aside or modified in accordance with section 36 of the Swedish Contracts Act. As mentioned above, however, this provision is seldom applied in international commercial arbitrations in Sweden. **3.41**

---

[62] Termination of the the arbitration agreement is discussed at para 3.169 *et seq.*

[63] See eg *Carleric Göranzon v Skandinaviska Aluminiumprofiler AB* (NJA 1979 p 666); *Ragne U v Kvissberg & Backström Byggnads AB* (NJA 1981 p 711); *Stig F v Rohman & Söner Byggnads AB* (NJA 1982 p 800); cf *Nils M v Södra Skogsägarna Aktiebolag* (NJA 1986 p 388) and *Bäckman v Platzer Bygg Aktiebolag* (NJA 1976 p 706).

[64] See eg *Christer J v Svenska Kommunalarbetarförbundet* (NJA 1982 p 853); *Dan D v Småföretagarnas Arbetsgivarorganisation* (AD 120/1994); *Svensk Ekonomibyrå AB v Lena E* (AD 135/1995); *Aktiebolaget Sandviken Steel v Peter H* (AD 43/1997); *Stockholm stad v Knut T* (AD 104/1997). Cf *CD Distribution Sverige Aktiebolag v Niclas H J* (AD 165/1987); *Conny H v Extraversion Aktiebolag* (AD 95/1988); *Lars E v Hem Films Scandinavia Aktiebolag* (AD 181/1988); *Civilekonomernas Riksförbund v Bankinstitutens Arbetsgivareorganisation et al* (AD 28/1994); *Bengt J v Telia Aktiebolag* (AD 111/1994); *Sven v Z v ABV Rock Group Kommanditbolag* (AD 34/1995); and *Ken W v Luleå Basketklubb* (AD 61/1996).

[65] See eg *Tureberg-Sollentuna Lastbilcentral ekonomisk förening v Byggnadsfirman Rudolf Asplund* (NJA 1980 p 46); *Ulla L v Österlen-Hus AB* (NJA 1987 p 639); and *Lars L v Acard Sverige AB* (NJA 1992 p 290).

[66] See *Rita Urhelyi v Arbetsmarknadens försäkringsaktiebolag* (NJA 1974 p 573); *Christer J et al v Svenska kommunalarbetareförbundet* (NJA 1982 p 853); and *Bostadsrättsföreningen Mossviolen 1 v Folkhem Försäljnings AB* (NJA 1992 p 143).

[67] SOU 1995:65, p 207 and Heuman, *Arbitration Law of Sweden: Practice and Procedure* (2003) 114. Cf Lindskog, *Skiljeförfarande, En kommentar* (2005) 137, footnote 160 where Lindskog challenges Heuman's position.

3.6 The Doctrine of Separability

3.6.1 Introduction

3.42   The jurisdiction of an arbitral tribunal depends on the existence of a valid arbitration agreement. When parties enter into a commercial agreement they often include an arbitration clause in it. When a subsequent dispute is referred to arbitration the question frequently arises as to what effect the alleged invalidity of the agreement containing the arbitration clause will have on the arbitration clause itself. If the main agreement is invalid, does that *ipso facto* entail the invalidity of the arbitration clause? Such a jurisdictional plea is sometimes made by the respondent in arbitration proceedings. By virtue of the *doctrine of separability* the arbitrators have obtained an effective tool to resolve this issue. [68]

3.43   The doctrine of separability has developed into a main principle of international arbitration. Today there is no question that the efficiency and integrity of arbitration proceedings are secured and protected by the doctrine of separability.

3.44   In Sweden, the doctrine of separability was cemented in case law before it found its statutory confirmation in section 3 of the SAA, see para 3.51.

3.45   The doctrine of separability means—in a nutshell—that an arbitration clause incorporated in an agreement is regarded as a separate agreement distinguished from the main agreement. This means that when parties enter into a commercial agreement with an arbitration clause, they are not only entering into one, but two agreements: the commercial agreement and the agreement to arbitrate. Accordingly, the fact that the commercial agreement is allegedly invalid—implying lack of jurisdiction of the arbitrators—does not automatically mean that the arbitration agreement is invalid, and does not prevent the arbitrators from deciding the validity issue.[69]

3.46   The doctrine of separability is closely linked to the doctrine of *compétence de la compétence*. The latter, which was also developed in case law before being included in section 2 of the SAA,[70] allows the arbitrators to rule on their own jurisdiction whenever the existence or validity of the arbitration agreement is challenged. The issue of the validity of an agreement containing an arbitration clause may

---

[68] Hobér, 'The Doctrine of Separability under Swedish Arbitration Law, Including Comments on the Position of American and Soviet Law', *Svensk Juristtidning* (1983) 257–271, and Hobér and Magnusson, 'The Special Status of Agreements to Arbitrate: The Separability Doctrine; Mandatory Stay of Litigation' 2 *Dispute Resolution International* (1 May 2008).

[69] Hobér, 'The Doctrine of Separability under Swedish Arbitration Law, Including Comments on the Position of American and Soviet Law', *Svensk Juristtidning* (1983) 259.

[70] Section 2(1) of the SAA reads: 'The arbitrators may rule on their own jurisdiction to decide the dispute. The aforesaid shall not prevent a court from determining such a question at the request of a party. The arbitrators may continue the arbitration proceedings pending the determination by the court'.

thus be submitted to arbitration. A decision by the arbitrators on their jurisdiction is, however, not finally binding. The arbitrators may thus reconsider this issue. The arbitration agreement may also be challenged by the parties before a court of law. This can be done in a parallel proceeding,[71] in an ensuing challenge proceeding,[72] or at the enforcement stage.[73]

Today the doctrine of separability and the doctrine of *compétence de la compétence* are two **3.47** fundamental principles of international arbitration law.[74] These two principles together ensure the efficient and timely commencement of international arbitrations.

3.6.2 Application of doctrine of separability

The application of the doctrine of separability comes into play when the arbitration **3.48** agreement forms part of the main agreement, eg in the form of a particular clause thereof. If the doctrine of separability were not to be applied in a case where the validity of the main agreement is challenged, it would be too easy for a party to evade his obligations under an arbitration agreement. Under the doctrine of separability therefore an arbitration clause constitutes an independent agreement, even if it is an integral part of a contract.

In two early judgments regarding invalidity of arbitration agreements the Supreme **3.49** Court recognized the doctrine of separability. In *Norrköpings Trikåfabrik v Persson* (NJA 1936 p 521), the claimant argued that a contract of sale was invalid due to fraudulent inducement, and that it was not bound by the arbitration clause in the contract. The Supreme Court upheld the arbitration clause, ruling that, in order for the arbitration agreement to be declared invalid, claims to this effect should relate specifically to the agreement, and cannot be tried as part of a general challenge of the main contract as a whole. This conclusion was later confirmed in *Hermanson v Asfaltsbeläggningar* (NJA 1976 p 125), where the Supreme Court held that the issue of the alleged invalidity of a lease agreement must be decided under the arbitration clause included in the lease agreement.[75]

In 1999, the doctrine of separability found its statutory confirmation in section 3(1) **3.51** of the SAA:

> Where the validity of an agreement which constitutes a part of another agreement must be determined in conjunction with a determination of the jurisdiction of the arbitrators, the arbitration agreement shall be deemed to constitute a separate agreement.

---

[71] Ibid, section 2. See discussion at para 5.21.
[72] Section 34(2) of the SAA and Article 34 of the Model Law. See discussion at para 8.57.
[73] Sections 52–60 of the SAA, Article V of the New York Convention, and Article 36 of the Model Law. See discussion at para 9.07.
[74] Section 2 of the SAA and Article 16(1) of the UNCITRAL Model Law.
[75] Both cases are commented by Hobér, 'The Doctrine of Separability under Swedish Arbitration Law, Including Comments on the Position of American and Soviet Law', *Svensk Juristtidning* (1983) 260–261.

3.51 The rationale underlying the principle is twofold. First, it recognizes that an agreement to arbitrate is binding. Secondly, the doctrine of separability serves to protect the integrity and effectiveness of the arbitral process. A party should not be able to avoid its binding obligation to arbitrate, and remove the jurisdiction of the arbitral tribunal, or substantially delay the proceedings, simply by claiming that the contract as a whole is invalid. The doctrine of separability thus provides an effective means to protect the integrity of the arbitral process, especially at the initial stages. Another argument in favour of the doctrine focuses on the situation where an arbitral award is challenged in a court of law. If the court were allowed to set aside the award on the grounds that the arbitration agreement is invalid because the main contract is invalid, this would enable the court to review substantive issues, ie the validity of the main contract.[76] This would be contrary to the fundamental principle of Swedish arbitration law, viz, that the courts' competence in challenge proceedings is restricted to procedural errors in the arbitration proceedings and does not cover the merits of the dispute.

3.52 Another consequence of the doctrine of separability is that the main contract and the arbitration agreement may be governed by different legal systems.[77]

3.6.3 Should the application of the doctrine of separability be limited?

3.53 As a result of the doctrine of separability, the invalidity of the commercial agreement does not automatically result in the invalidity of the arbitration agreement. The type of invalidity claimed, and whether or not it strikes at the arbitration agreement directly, is crucial for the validity of the arbitration agreement and thus for the arbitrators' jurisdiction. The arbitrators' jurisdiction is affected only where the invalidity strikes directly at the arbitration agreement. As such, it could affect (i) the arbitration agreement only, or (ii) both the principal contract and the arbitration agreement, when for example, a party lacks the capacity to perform legally binding actions.[78] The same holds true when duress, coercion, or similar grounds are relied on to invalidate not only the principal contract but also the arbitration clause contained therein. It needs to be shown that the alleged duress has also been exerted in relation to the arbitration agreement as such.[79]

3.54 The most frequently raised challenges to the validity of the arbitration agreement based on arguments relating to the commercial contract fall into the following two main categories:[80]

    (i)   there was never an agreement in the first place, ie no meeting of the minds;

---

[76] Cf eg Heuman, *Arbitration Law of Sweden: Practice and Procedure* (2003) 44–45.

[77] See para 2.201 *et seq.*

[78] *Arbitration in Sweden* (2nd revised edn, 1984) 29.

[79] It should be noted that the principal contract and the arbitration agreement in some cases may be governed by different substantive laws and also that the grounds invoked to invalidate the agreements, respectively, may differ.

[80] Hobér and Magnusson, 'The Special Status of Agreements to Arbitrate: The Separability Doctrine; Mandatory Stay of Litigation', 2(1) *Dispute Resolution International* (May 2008) 56–74 at 61.

(ii) there was an agreement, but it was defective at the outset in such a way that the entire agreement is void *ab initio*; or, the agreement is voidable or should be/has been declared invalid.

3.6.3.1 No agreement in the first place

When interpreting an agreement or the validity thereof there is, as a matter of **3.55** principle, no major difference between a commercial agreement and an arbitration agreement. However, one must bear in mind that the respective agreements have different objectives. A commercial agreement regulates the commercial terms and conditions. An arbitration agreement, on the other hand, is an agreement with respect to the dispute settlement mechanism that the parties wish to use in case of a future dispute. Consequently, if there is a meeting of minds to the effect that arbitration is to be resorted to for resolving disputes based on the commercial agreement, the parties have entered into an arbitration agreement, even if no agreement has been reached with respect to commercial terms.

The important distinction between challenges to the continued validity of an agree- **3.56** ment as opposed to a challenge to its very existence is illustrated by the facts in the *Will-Drill Resources* case.[81] The dispute arose from a proposed agreement for the purchase of properties between Will-Drill Resources, Inc, acting on its own behalf and as agent for over forty sellers, and Samson Resources Co, as buyer. The proposed sales agreement contained an arbitration clause. The agreement was signed by the buyer and had a separate signature block for each seller to sign. However, eight of the sellers included on the signature pages decided not to sell their property, whereas the buyer withdrew from the agreement. The sellers who had signed the agreement subsequently sought to invoke the arbitration clause of the proposed sales agreement. The buyer argued that there was no contract at all between the parties since the sales agreement was an offer to buy *all* of the properties, not only some of them. On appeal, the Fifth Circuit found that 'where the very existence of any agreement to arbitrate is at issue, it is for the courts to decide based on state-law contract formation principles'.[82] The doctrine of separability, the Fifth Circuit continued, rests on the assumption that there is an underlying principal agreement. Where a binding arbitration agreement has been established, a claim that the principal agreement is void must be decided by the arbitrators. The fact that the *enforceability* of the principal agreement is disputed does not change the fact that the parties de facto at some point in time agreed to arbitrate disputes arising out of that agreement. 'Even if the arbitrator concludes that the agreement was void, and the parties are returned to their pre-agreement positions *as if* [emphasis in the original document] the agreement never existed, the agreement existed long enough to give the arbitrator the power to decide the dispute'.[83] In the *Will-Drill Resources* case, however, the defendant

---

[81] *Will-Drill Resources, Inc v Samson Resources Co*, 2003, WL 22809197, 5th Cir, 26 November 2003.
[82] Ibid, 2.
[83] Ibid, section B, 3rd paragraph.

was attacking the *existence* of the principal agreement, as opposed to its continued validity. Assessing the facts, the Fifth Circuit concluded that no principal agreement existed between the parties *and* that the parties never reached an agreement to arbitrate. Consequently, the order of the District Court compelling arbitration was dismissed.

3.57 As the *Will-Drill Resources* case illustrates, a practical example of a dispute on whether an arbitration agreement has come into existence *at all*, or not, is where the parties disagree on whether contractual negotiations have resulted in a binding agreement or not.[84] A Swedish equivalent is *Profura AB v Stig Blomgren*.[85] In this case, the claimant commenced arbitration proceedings under a share purchase agreement which included an arbitration clause. The respondent challenged the jurisdiction of the arbitrators. The respondent argued that, since the principal 'agreement' never went further than negotiations, and thus never came into existence, nor did the arbitration clause. Consequently, there was no meeting of the minds as far as an agreement was concerned. It should be noted that the draft agreements in dispute were not signed by the parties. Nor was the respondent indicated as one of the parties in the draft agreements. Notwithstanding this, the claimant alleged that the parties had discussed the draft share purchase agreement at a meeting between the parties and that they had decided all outstanding issues and reached a final agreement on the terms and conditions of the agreement. After a separate hearing on the issue of jurisdiction, the arbitrators found that it had not been established that both parties intended the last meeting to constitute a binding agreement between the parties. Consequently, the arbitrators concluded that no arbitration agreement had been concluded. The arbitrators therefore dismissed the case for lack of jurisdiction.

3.58 The arbitrators' decision in this case was, however, reversed by the Court of Appeal. The Court held that, even though several outstanding issues were yet to be resolved, a binding share purchase agreement had been concluded orally as a consequence of the parties' agreement with respect to the price for the shares. Moreover, the Court found that there was a binding arbitration agreement between the parties. The Court reasoned as follows:[86]

> In each and all of the agreements drafted by Profura AB an arbitration clause was included and in all but one agreement it was indicated that the Swedish Arbitration Act was to be applied.

---

[84] Hobér and Magnusson, 'The Special Status of Agreements to Arbitrate: The Separability Doctrine; Mandatory Stay of Litigation', 2(1) *Dispute Resolution International* (May 2008) 56–74, at 63–64.

[85] Court of Appeal for Western Sweden's judgment of 19 March 2008 in Case T 2863-07. In that case the arbitral award had been appealed against in accordance with section 36 of the SAA, under which an award whereby the arbitrators dismiss the arbitration for lack of jurisdiction may be appealed. For a discussion of section 36 of the SAA, see para 8.205 *et seq.*

[86] Court of Appeal for Western Sweden's judgment of 19 March 2008 in Case T 2863-07, p 7.

The final and central agreement for the parties was the one which implied that Profura AB became the owner of the shares in Delencia AB, which in accordance with the structure subsequently was to acquire shares in Arema. In this agreement Atial SA and Profura AB are indicated as parties and the arbitration clause of the agreement indicates the SAA as the governing law and that arbitration shall take place in Gothenburg. This is the agreement that Stig Blomgren reviewed during the meeting with Mårten Hulterström on 1 November 2005 and which Stig Blomgren commented on. As far as appeared on the record, Stig Blomgren never presented any objections to this arbitration clause, nor to the similar clause in the other agreements provided to him. Consequently, and even though the arbitration clause was never subject to discussion, it is applicable as between the parties.

It is true that Stig Blomgren is not personally indicated as one of the parties to the now mentioned agreement, but it was contemplated that he should have had acquired Atial SA in accordance with the Luxemburg structure at the time when the agreement was to be signed. Hence, there is such connection between the action against Stig Blomgren and the agreement, which would involve selling the shares in Arema to Profura AB, that the arbitration clause in the agreement must be considered to include the dispute in this case.

Another illustration of the fact that an arbitration agreement can be concluded, **3.59** even though no commercial agreement has come about, is the judgment from the Svea Court of Appeal in the case of *Ukraine v Norsk Hydro ASA*.[87] In this case, the Court of Appeal found that, although a power of attorney held by a signatory prevented him from concluding the main agreement, he was still authorized to sign the arbitration agreement contained therein. Relying on the doctrine of separability, the Court of Appeal stated that the mere fact that the signatory lacked authority to bind the claimant in respect of the substantive obligations of the main agreement did not constitute a ground to conclude that the arbitrators lacked jurisdiction.

3.6.3.2 The principal agreement is void ab initio, voidable, or has been declared invalid

If a principal agreement between the parties can be established, and this agreement **3.60** includes an arbitration clause, any dispute relating to the continued validity of the agreement is to be decided based on the arbitration agreement. The ground for potential invalidity does not affect the arbitrators' jurisdiction unless it strikes directly at the arbitration agreement, a conclusion firmly supported by case law in most jurisdictions with modern arbitration legislation.

For example, in England, the claimant in *Harbour v Kansa*[88] argued that the principal **3.61** agreement, a retrocession agreement between an English insurance and reinsurance company and six Finnish insurance and reinsurance companies, was null and void by reason of the claimed illegality of the underlying insurance and reinsurance contracts.

---

[87] Case T 3108-06, Judgment of 17 December 2007.
[88] *Harbour Assurance Co (UK) Ltd v Kansa General International Insurance Co Ltd* [1993] 1 Lloyds Law Report 455.

The plaintiff argued that disputes as to the initial invalidity or illegality of a contract were never arbitrable, notwithstanding the arbitration clause.[89] The House of Lords was of a different opinion. It held that the initial illegality of the contract can be referred to arbitration provided that the ground for invalidity does not impeach the arbitration agreement itself.

3.62 The ratio of the doctrine of separability was emphasized by Lord Leggatt who held that strong policy reasons speak in favour of an arbitration clause being capable of surviving the initial invalidity of the contract: 'Otherwise it would put in the power of one contracting party to prevent arbitration from taking place simply by alleging that the contract was void for initial illegality'.[90]

3.63 *Harbour v Kansa* was referred to as 'a major evolutionary step' in the case of *Fiona Trust v Privalov*[91] in which the English Court of Appeal concluded that a dispute as to whether a contract could be set aside for alleged bribery fell within the arbitration clause. The Court pointed out that this should be differentiated from a dispute as to whether there was ever a contract at all. The finding of the Court of Appeal was later confirmed by the House of Lords, which unanimously dismissed the appeal against the Court of Appeal's decision.[92]

3.64 As mentioned above, the Swedish position in this respect is clear from section 3(1) of the SAA, which codified the long since prevailing position in Swedish case law.[93] Hence, Swedish arbitration law is in line with the generally accepted understanding of the doctrine of separability.[94]

3.65 Irrespective of whether initial or subsequent invalidity is claimed, the alleged defect must strike directly at the arbitration agreement, in order to quash the jurisdiction of the arbitral tribunal.[95]

---

[89] The plaintiff essentially argued *ex nihil nit fit*—nothing can come out of nothing, ibid, at 457.

[90] See note 84, at 463–464.

[91] *Fiona Trust & Holding Corporation & ors v Yuri Privalov & ors* [2006] EWHC 2583 (Comm).

[92] *Premium Nafta Products Ltd v Fili Shipping Company Ltd* [2007] UKHL 40. (Both parties had subsequently changed names after the Court of Appeal's decision.) See also *El Nasharty v J Sainsbury plc* [2007] EWHC 2618 (Comm). For similar reasoning in Australian case law, see *Commandante Marine Corp v Pan Australia Shipping Corp* [2006] FCAFC 192 and *Walter Rau Neusser Oel und Fett AGv v (1) Cross Pacific Trading Ltd (2) Orbis Commodities Pty Limited* [2005] FCA 955. See also the US Supreme Court cases *Prima Paint Co v Flood Conklin Manufacturing Corp*, 388 US 395 (1967), and *Buckeye Check Cashing Inc v John Cardegna et al*, 546 US (2006) No 04-1264.

[93] See eg Govt Bill 1998/99:35 pp 76 and 215; Hobér, 'The Doctrine of Separability under Swedish Arbitration Law, Including Comments on the Position of American and Soviet Law', *Svensk Juristtidning* (1983) 266–267; *Norrköpings Trikåfabrik v Persson* (NJA 1936 p 521) and *Hermanson v Asfaltsbeläggningar* (NJA 1976 p 125), see para 3.50.

[94] Cf eg Blackaby and Partasides with Redfern and Hunter, *Redfern and Hunter on International Arbitration* (5th edn, 2009) 118–119; and Gaillard and Savage (eds), *Fouchard Gaillard Goldman on International Commercial Arbitration* (1999) para 392 *et seq*.

[95] Hobér and Magnusson, 'The Special Status of Agreements to Arbitrate: The Separability Doctrine; Mandatory Stay of Litigation' 2(1) *Dispute Resolution International* (May 2008) 56–74, at 69.

A related question in this respect is whether the fact that an agreement has been **3.66**
declared invalid through a sovereign act or in a court decision in a country other
than the seat of arbitration can or should affect the applicability of the doctrine of
separability and the jurisdiction of an arbitral tribunal. It is submitted that the
answer is in the negative. The question of validity of the arbitration agreement, for
example, after nationalization affecting a contract with an arbitration clause, does
not present any principal challenge to the doctrine of separability.[96]

In *BP v Libya*,[97] BP initiated arbitration against Libya subsequent to Libya's **3.67**
nationalization of BP's rights under a concession agreement for the exploration and
production of oil. According to the law on nationalization, all properties and assets
relating to the operation of the concession were transferred to the State. BP alleged
that Libya's action constituted a breach of the concession agreement and that the
agreement remained valid. BP requested, *inter alia*, a declaratory award to the effect
that BP was entitled to be restored to the full enjoyment of its rights under the
agreement. In his conclusions, Judge Lagergren, acting as sole arbitrator, did not
find that the concession was still valid, which in his view prevented BP from
seeking specific performance by Libya under the contract. However, this did not
affect the validity of the agreement to arbitrate: 'The BP Concession can be said to
remain in force and effect as a contractual instrument only in the sense that it forms
the basis of the jurisdiction of the Tribunal and of the right of the Claimant to claim
damages from the Respondent before the Tribunal'.[98]

Similarly, the sole arbitrator in *LIAMCO v Libya*[99] concluded that LIAMCO could **3.68**
continue to rely on the arbitration clause in a concession agreement after the nationalization of the concession by the Libyan State.

The arbitrator held that a State is bound by the arbitration clause in a contract with **3.69**
a private party notwithstanding arguments to the effect that the contract has been
terminated or come to an end. No party, be it a State or an investor, may withdraw
its consent to arbitration unilaterally, a fact confirmed by Article 25 of the
Washington Convention.[100]

As far as the doctrine of separability is concerned, the situation is no different if a **3.70**
contract with an arbitration clause is declared invalid by a court in another country

---

[96] Ibid.
[97] *British Petroleum Company (Libya) Ltd v The Government of the Libyan Arab Republic*, Award 19
October 1973, published in *Yearbook Commercial Arbitration*, V (1980) 143–157.
[98] Ibid, 155.
[99] *Libyan American Oil Company (LIAMCO) v Government of the Libyan Arab Republic*, Award 12
April 1977.
[100] Convention of 1965 on the Settlement of Investment Disputes between States and Nationals of
other States, available at <http://.icsid.worldbank.org>. See also *Elf Aquitaine Iran (France) v National
Iranian Company*, Award 14 June 1982, published in *Yearbook Commercial Arbitration*, XI (1986)
97–104, and *Philips Petroleum Co v The Islamic Republic of Iran*, Iran-US Claims Tribunal, 29 June
1989, 21 Iran-US CTR 79.

than the seat of the arbitration without specific mention of the arbitration agreement. In other words, unless the invalidity specifically relates to the arbitration agreement, it remains valid.[101]

3.71 The doctrine of separability is best described as a pragmatic manner in which to handle the interests of parties having opted for efficient dispute resolution through arbitration. In the words of the Australian Federal Court in *Commandante v Pan Australia*:

> . . . the doctrine of separability is not so much a fiction as an approach by the law to accommodating commercial practicality and common sense to the operation of legal rules. Commercial law and honest, practical common sense should never be far apart.[102]

3.72 By requiring that a binding agreement to arbitrate be set aside only for reasons directly attributable to that very agreement, the doctrine of separability plays a very important role in protecting the integrity of the arbitral procedure. Furthermore, in combination with the principle of *compétence de la compétence*, it effectively prevents any possibility of frustrating the commencement of arbitration proceedings simply by alleging invalidity of the main agreement.

3.73 In the end these two fundamental principles of international arbitration law protect not only the integrity of the arbitral procedure, but, more importantly, the interest of its end users.

3.7 Invalidity of the Arbitration Agreement

3.74 As a matter of principle, the general rules on invalidity of contracts under Swedish law—fraud, duress etc—apply also to arbitration agreements. In practice, however, these general rules seem to play a very limited role with respect to arbitration agreements. In fact, there are no reported cases where such invalidity grounds have been relied on in relation to arbitration agreements.

3.75 Prior to the adoption of the SAA, section 36 of the Swedish Contracts Act was applied from time to time to arbitration agreements.[103] This provision makes it possible to have a particular contract term set aside, or modified, if it is found to be unreasonable with respect to the contents of the contract, or the circumstances existing at the time of the conclusion of the contract. The primary objective of this statutory provision is to protect consumers and persons who are otherwise deemed

---

[101] Cf the situation where a court's judgment specifically relates to the arbitration agreement. In such a case the question arises to what extent, if at all, the arbitrators should or must accept the judgment by a court in a country other than the seat of arbitration. This issue, however, is not related to the doctrine of separability. See discussion at para 5.37.

[102] *Commandante Marine Corp v Pan Australia Shipping Corp* [2006] FCAFC 192, at 228.

[103] See discussion at para 3.37 *et seq.*

to be the weaker party in a contractual relationship. As far as international commercial arbitration is concerned, the role of section 36 is indeed very limited. When the provision has been applied to arbitration agreements, both parties have been Swedish; typically one party has been an enterprise and the other a consumer.[104]

By virtue of section 6 of the SAA, most of these cases have, however, lost their **3.76** relevance. This provision generally prohibits arbitration agreements between a business enterprise and a consumer prior to the dispute.

3.8 Arbitrability

As mentioned above, arbitrability is one of the requirements for a valid arbitration **3.77** agreement. Generally speaking, arbitrability is the concept by which it is determined which disputes belong exclusively to the courts. As far as arbitrations in Sweden are concerned, arbitrability is governed by Swedish law even if foreign law is applicable to the arbitration agreement.[105] This follows from section 49 of the SAA, according to which the effects of the arbitration agreement laid down in section 4 of the SAA[106] do not apply if the dispute is non-arbitrable under Swedish law. Arbitrability is a fundamental and important concept. Since arbitration is a private dispute settlement method—albeit with important public consequences, such as finality and enforceability—it is important to determine what kind of disputes are exclusively reserved for national courts and thus fall outside the domain of arbitration.

Section 1 of the SAA stipulates: **3.78**

> Disputes concerning matters in respect of which the parties may reach a settlement may, by agreement, be referred to one or several arbitrators for resolution. Such an agreement may relate to future disputes pertaining to a legal relationship specified in the agreement. The dispute may concern the existence of a particular fact.
>
> In addition to interpreting agreements, the filling of gaps in contracts can also be referred to arbitrators.
>
> Arbitrators may rule on the civil law effects of competition law as between the parties.

Only if an issue is arbitrable can it be referred to arbitration. It follows from section **3.79** 1(1) of the SAA that in order for a matter to be arbitrable, the parties must be able to reach a settlement on the subject matter of the dispute. Matters which cannot be settled out of court are non-arbitrable. Except for the arbitrators' explicit right to fill gaps in contracts (section 1(2) of the SAA) and to rule on the civil law effects of

---

[104] See eg *Carleric Göranzon v Skandinaviska Aluminiumprofiler AB* (NJA 1979 p 666); *Ragne U v Kvissberg & Backström Byggnads AB* (NJA 1981 p 711); *Stig F v Rohman & Söner Byggnads AB* (NJA 1982 p 800); cf *Nils M v Södra Skogsägarna Aktiebolag* (NJA 1986 p 388) and *Bäckman v Platzer Bygg Aktiebolag* (NJA 1976 p 706).
[105] See para 2.201 for a discussion of the law applicable to the arbitration agreement.
[106] See para 3.113 *et seq.*

competition law as between the parties (section 1(3) of the SAA), the SAA does not have any general definition of which disputes are arbitrable.[107] The answer is to be found in the substantive provisions of Swedish law. It is generally accepted , for example, that disputes concerning the registration and validity of patents and trademarks are non-arbitrable. Disputes based on patent and trademark licence agreements are, however, arbitrable and are frequently referred to arbitration. Under Swedish law copyright protection is not dependent on any form of registration. Most aspects of copyright disputes are therefore arbitrable.

3.80 Examples of other matters which *cannot* be settled by arbitration, in addition to the registration and validity of patents and trademarks, are questions of punishment, forfeiture, and other consequences (except damages) of a finding of criminal guilt. The limitation to so-called dispositive civil matters—ie matters with respect to which the parties can reach a settlement—also excludes most questions of family law, such as divorce proceedings, and questions concerning adoption or guardianship.

3.8.1 Disputes capable of settlement

3.81 As already indicated, only issues with respect to which the parties can reach out-of-court settlements may be referred to arbitration. This is logical as the foundation of arbitration proceedings is the arbitration agreement entered into by the parties.

3.82 The fact that there may be provisions of a mandatory nature in a certain area of the law does not disqualify all disputes in the relevant area from being brought to arbitration. For instance, Chapter 3 of the Swedish Contracts Act has a number of provisions on invalidity which are mandatory in the sense that a party cannot with binding effect refrain from invoking them before a dispute has arisen. The same is true for provisions protecting consumers. However, once a dispute has arisen, a party is free to argue his case such that the 'mandatory' provisions do not become applicable. Disputes which include the application of such provisions are nevertheless arbitrable under the main rule.[108] What is relevant is whether the parties are at liberty to reach an out-of-court settlement in the matter.

3.83 The limitation to matters which can be settled by the parties also means that the legal effects of an arbitral award are limited as far as rights *in rem* are concerned and that in some aspects such matters cannot be tried by arbitrators.[109] However, all

---

[107] SOU 1994:81, pp 79 and 256.

[108] Govt Bill 1998/99:35, p 49.

[109] See *Norsa v Baggå AB* (NJA 1925 p 557 (I and II)) and *REW v Byggfirman Oscarsson & Söderberg* (NJA 1931 p 647). The Supreme Court's findings in these early cases have been confirmed in more recent cases, see eg *Five Seasons Fritidsaktiebolags konkursbo (bankruptcy estate) v Five Seasons. Försäljningsaktiebolag* (NJA 1993 s 641) and *Svenska Kreditförsäkringsaktiebolagets konkursbo (bankruptcy estate) v [41 reinsurance companies]* (NJA 2003 p 3). See also Lindskog, *Skiljeförfarande, En kommentar* (2005) 236 *et seq*, who argues that once a dispute with respect to a right *in rem* has arisen, there should be no obstacle to try such disputes in arbitration, insofar as the parties can reach a settlement with respect to the dispute.

affected parties can agree that a question concerning rights *in rem* be referred to arbitration, for instance in the case where a seller has sold the same object to more than one party.

Other issues which are not arbitrable, include injunctions under the 1990 Trade **3.84** Secrets Act,[110] as well as bankruptcy matters. With respect to bankruptcies, the more important issue is whether a bankruptcy estate is bound by an arbitration agreement in a contract entered into by the debtor prior to the bankruptcy. The predominant view is that the bankruptcy estate is indeed bound by such an arbitration clause.[111]

Another issue which is sometimes discussed in the context of arbitrability is corrup- **3.85** tion. In a well-known arbitration from 1963, Judge Gunnar Lagergren concluded that claims based on a contract which contemplated payments to Argentine officials were non-arbitrable.[112] The more modern approach is that an allegation of bribery and corruption does not deprive an arbitral tribunal of jurisdiction because the issue is non-arbitrable. Rather, arbitral tribunals today generally try such claims on the merits.[113]

3.8.2 The existence of factual circumstances

It follows from section 1(1), third sentence, that it is not necessary that the dispute **3.86** concern a purely legal issue. It can also concern the mere existence, or nature, of a particular fact and can thus lead to a declaratory award.

It is generally accepted that the powers of arbitrators in this sense are wider than **3.87** those of courts.[114] The powers of a court to try requests for declaratory judgments are limited to questions of 'whether or not a certain legal relationship exists if uncertainty exists as to the legal relationship, and the uncertainty exposes the plaintiff to a detriment'.[115] In contrast, an arbitral tribunal can render a final and binding award not only on legal relationships but also on *factual circumstances*.

To be arbitrable the fact in question does not need to be related to any specific legal **3.88** consequences, even though this would typically be the situation in practice. The fact in question must, however, be covered by the arbitration agreement.

---

[110] In *TV3 Broadcasting Group Ltd v Kanal 5* (NJA 2000 p 435) the Supreme Court concluded that parties could not reach a settlement with respect to such issues.

[111] See para 3.139.

[112] See Wetter, 'Issues of Corruption before International Tribunals: The authentic Text and True Meaning of Judge Gunnar Lagregren's Award in ICC Case No. 1110', *Arbitration International* (1994) 277.

[113] See Kreindler, Aspects of illegality in the formation and performance of contracts, 16th ICCA Congress, London, May 2002; El Kosheri and Philippe Leboulanger, 'L'arbitrage face a la corruption et aux trafics d'influence', 3 *Revue de l'Arbitrage* (1984).

[114] Govt Bill 1998/99:35, p 60.

[115] Chapter 13, section 2 of the Procedural Code.

3.89 Section 1(1), third sentence, removes the uncertainty which existed under the old Arbitration Act in this respect. The previous uncertainty notwithstanding, arbitrators did pronounce upon the existence or qualification of certain factual circumstances. For example, in *Wall v Försäkringsaktiebolaget Fylgia* (NJA 1918 p 478) arbitrators tried whether a person died as an immediate consequence of an accident. In *Åkesson v Nordiska ömsesidiga olycksfallsförsäkringsföreningen Bore* (NJA 1905 p 23), the degree of disability of a person injured in an accident was the issue. In *Nylund v Sveriges Verkstadsförening and Gylling* (AD 1960 No 27) the question was whether an employee was to be classified as a specialist worker.

3.90 Arbitrators also have the authority to decide how a certain fact is to be legally qualified, for instance whether certain proven facts constitute *force majeure*,[116] or whether goods delivered are defective.[117]

3.91 An award declaring the existence or non-existence of a particular fact has the same legal effect as any other arbitral award.[118]

3.8.3 Filling gaps

3.92 Under Swedish law, contract interpretation includes the filling of gaps to a certain extent.[119] The interpretation of arbitration agreements does not, as a matter of principle, differ from the interpretation of contracts in general. In section 1(2) of the SAA the arbitrators are given the express authority to interpret and to fill gaps in contracts. The intention behind this provision is to bestow arbitrators with wider powers than those of courts in this respect.[120] However, the practical relevance of these wider powers for arbitrators is not entirely clear. It should be pointed out in this connection that while arbitrators have the right to fill gaps in contracts, they can exercise such a right only within the limits set by the parties, particularly in their arbitration agreement and subsequently during the course of the proceedings. Consequently, the arbitrators may not, for example, rule *ultra petita*.[121]

3.93 In practice, filling gaps in contracts would be relevant mostly in relation to long-term contracts, eg concerning industrial cooperation and supply of natural resources, such as oil and gas, and raw materials.

3.94 Arbitrators are thus entitled to determine contract terms and conditions, including the price. Gap filling also means that arbitrators have the right to address and supplement lacunae in a contract put before them.

---

[116] Govt Bill 1998/99:35, p 62.

[117] Ibid, p 212.

[118] Ibid, p 61. The legal effect of arbitral awards is discussed in para 7.91 *et seq*.

[119] Ramberg and Ramberg, *Allmän avtalsrätt* (8th edn, 2010) 147–148, in particular the references in footnote 6 and Govt Bill 1998/99:35 p 62.

[120] Govt Bill 1998/99:35, pp 62–63.

[121] Hobér, 'Arbitration Reform in Sweden', 17(4) *Arbitration International* (2001) 357, and Govt Bill 1998/99:35, p 63.

3.8.4 Consumer and labour disputes

It follows from section 6 of the SAA that arbitration agreements cannot be entered **3.95** into with respect to future consumer disputes. Any such agreement is void. However, once a dispute has arisen, it is possible to enter into an arbitration agreement. Thus, consumer disputes are in fact arbitrable, which means that an arbitral tribunal is only required to dismiss such a dispute upon the demand of the consumer. In contrast, a dispute which is non-arbitrable must be dismissed *ex officio* by the arbitral tribunal.[122]

With respect to labour disputes, it is stipulated in section 1(3) of the Labour Dispute **3.96** Act (1974:371) that it is not possible to enter into arbitration agreements for certain types of future labour disputes.

Finally, there are disputes which are in themselves dispositive but which have **3.97** expressly been excluded from arbitrability.[123]

3.8.5 Civil law effects of competition law

Competition law includes rules of both private law and public law. Public law issues **3.98** of competition law are by their nature not amenable to agreement between the parties. A claim under competition law is not merely a private matter. Violations of competition law can affect many thousands of individuals and entire sectors of the economy. Therefore, from the legislator's point of view it is not acceptable that two parties agree that a certain form of cooperation between them is not in conflict with competition law, or that the jurisdiction of the relevant competition authorities should be restricted. The relevant competition authorities retain exclusive jurisdiction over competition issues which are not *inter partes*, but which involve the public interest. The competition authorities thus retain the exclusive jurisdiction to impose public law sanctions, grant exemptions from prohibitions against cooperation in restraint of trade etc.

It is possible, however, for parties to agree, *inter partes*, on private law aspects of **3.99** competition law issues. The 1929 Swedish Arbitration Act was silent on the issue. A degree of uncertainty prevailed as to whether or not competition law issues were arbitrable, and if so, to what extent they were arbitrable.

In the well-known *Mitsubishi* case (*Mitsubishi Motors Corp v Soler Chryster Playmonth* **3.100** *Inc*, 473 US 614, 105 SCt 3346 (1985)) the US Supreme Court took a bold step in deciding that antitrust issues arising out of international contracts were arbitrable. The Court stated that:

> . . . concerns of international comity, respect for the capacities of foreign and international tribunals and sensitivity to the need of the international commercial system for

---

[122] Heuman, *Arbitration Law of Sweden: Practice and Procedure* (2003) 140.
[123] For instance, according to section 1(3) of the Labour Dispute Act (1974:371), it is not possible to refer to arbitration questions of discharge based on collective bargaining agreements.

predictability in the resolution of disputes require that we enforce the parties' agreement, even assuming that a contrary result would be forthcoming in a domestic court.[124]

3.101 Subsequently, the arbitrability of competition law issues was explicitly accepted also in other jurisdictions, for example, in France[125] and in Switzerland.[126]

3.102 Given the uncertainty prevailing under Swedish law, when preparing the SAA, the legislator decided to include a specific provision addressing this issue.[127] Section 1, paragraph 3 of the SAA thus authorizes arbitrators to rule on the civil law effects of competition law as between the parties. This provision empowers arbitrators to try, for instance, whether or not a contract provision is void under competition law[128] and issues of damages.[129]

3.103 The consideration by arbitrators of any issue generally requires that the issue be raised by the parties. The arbitrators may thus not try issues *ex officio*. This may put the arbitrators in a dilemma with respect to issues of competition law. On the one hand, the arbitrators may not go beyond the submissions of the parties, thereby risking a ruling *ultra petita* which could lead to the setting aside of the resulting award based on section 34 of the SAA.[130] On the other hand, from this it follows that an award could be issued in conflict with peremptory competition regulations, if none of the parties has raised the issue in question. As a consequence, the award may be in danger of being declared invalid on the basis of section 33 of the SAA.[131] The arbitrators thus face the risk of having the award annulled due to a violation of public policy (*ordre public*), should they not observe national rules of public policy, which may include competition law regulations.[132] According to the *travaux préparatoires*, the arbitrators should in such a situation be entitled to terminate the proceedings rather than being obliged to issue an invalid award.[133]

3.104 As far as Member States of the European Union are concerned, the European Court of Justice addressed the interrelationship between arbitration and competition law

---

[124] 473 US 614, 105 SCt 3346 (1985), at 628.

[125] See the French case Mors/Labinal, Cour d'appel de Paris, decision of 19 May 1993, and reaffirmed by the Cour de Cassation in its decision of 5 January 1999, where the arbitrability of competition law issues was acknowledged.

[126] In Switzerland, the arbitrability of EU competition law was recognized by a decision of the Federal Tribunal in 1992, in which case the Court found that: '[n]either Article 85 of the [EU] Treaty nor regulation 17 on its application forbid a national court or an arbitral tribunal to examine the validity of that contract'. (Decision of the Tribunal Fédéral of 28 April 1992, [1992] ASA Bull 368. The same court reaffirmed this position in its decision of 13 November 1998, [1999] ASA Bull 529 and 455.

[127] Govt Bill 1998/99:35, p 57 *et seq*.

[128] Cf Chapter 2, section 6 of the Swedish Competition Act (SFS 2008:579).

[129] Cf ibid, Chapter 3, section 25.

[130] See Chapter 8.

[131] See ibid.

[132] Cf the US Supreme Court case *Mitsubishi Motors v Soler Chrysler-Plymouth, Inc*, 473 US 614 (1985), where the Court stated: 'Having permitted the arbitration to go forward, the national courts of the United States will have the opportunity at the award enforcement stage to ensure that the legitimate interest in the enforcement of the anti-trust laws has been addressed. The [New York Convention] reserves to each signatory country the right to refuse enforcement of an award where the 'recognition or enforcement of the award would be contrary to a public policy of that country'. Ibid, at 628.

[133] Govt Bill 1998/99:35, p 59.

in its landmark decision in *ECO Swiss China Time Ltd v Benetton International NV.*[134] Even though the practical effects of the case remain debatable and unclear, it illustrates the dilemma for arbitrators created by the inherent conflict between, on the one hand, the boundaries of the arbitrators' jurisdiction and powers, established by the arbitration agreement and, on the other hand, the perceived duty of the arbitrators to render awards enforceable at law. The *Eco-Swiss Case* concerned a licensing agreement for a term of eight years entered into in 1986 between Benetton International NV ('Benetton') and Eco-Swiss China Time Ltd ('Eco Swiss') and Bulova Watch Company Inc ('Bulova'). The parties were located in Amsterdam, Hong Kong, and New York, respectively. Under the agreement, Benetton and Bulova granted Eco Swiss the right to manufacture and market watches and clocks bearing the words 'Benetton by Bulova'.

The agreement had an arbitration clause providing that all disputes arising from the   **3.105** agreement were to be settled by arbitration in conformity with the rules of the Nederlands Arbitrage Instituut. The agreement was governed by Dutch law.

In 1991, ie three years before the end of its eight-year term, Benetton unilaterally   **3.106** terminated the agreement. Arbitration proceedings were subsequently commenced in which Eco Swiss and Bulova claimed that Benetton should be held liable for the unlawful termination of the agreement. The arbitral tribunal rendered two awards: first, a partial final award in which it held that Benetton was liable to Eco Swiss and Bulova for the damages they had suffered as a result of the early termination; secondly, a final award ordering Benetton to pay a certain amount in damages to Eco Swiss and Bulova by way of compensation for the damages suffered by them.

In 1995, Benetton brought an action in the Dutch courts for annulment of the two   **3.107** awards. Benetton claimed, *inter alia*, that the awards were contrary to public policy because the licensing agreement was incompatible with Article 81 (ex Article 85)[135] of the EC Treaty. It must be noted in this respect that during the arbitration proceedings, neither the parties nor the arbitrators raised the question whether the agreement was compatible with Community competition law, in particular Article 81 (ex Article 85) of the Treaty. The case travelled through the Dutch judicial system to the highest court of the Netherlands (the Hoge Raad). The Hoge Raad stayed the proceedings and referred, *inter alia*, the following questions to the European Court:

(a) Does the Dutch rule, that neither arbitrators nor judges may *sua sponte* raise issues beyond the ambit of those presented by the parties, apply in proceedings to annul an arbitral award?

(b) Could a Dutch court annul the awards in view of the fact that (i) under Dutch law there are limited grounds for annulment, including violation of public policy (*ordre public*) and (ii) under Dutch law the competition laws of the Netherlands are not viewed as matters of *ordre public*?

---

[134] Case C-126/97, *Eco Swiss China Time Ltd v Benetton International NV* (1999) ECR I-3055.
[135] By virtue of the Treaty of Lisbon, which entered into force on 1 December 2009, Article 81 (ex Article 85) is renumbered as Article 101. The wording of the Article remains, however, unchanged.

3.108 The European Court answered the second question by ruling as follows.

> ... [a] national court to which an application is made for annulment of an arbitration award must grant that application if it considers that the award in question is in fact contrary to Article 81 (ex Article 85) of the Treaty, where its domestic rules of procedure require it to grant an application for annulment founded on failure to observe national rules of public policy.[136]

3.109 The *Eco-Swiss* decision in effect seems to hold not only that matters of competition law are arbitrable but also that, even if not raised by the parties, or considered by the arbitrators, non-compliance with Community competition law constitutes a ground for annulment of the award, if these issues are raised in challenges to arbitral awards in national courts of members of the EU and on the assumption that competition law issues arising out of Article 81 form part of the public policy of the Member State where the award was rendered.[137] Read in this way, the *Eco Swiss* decision could be said to extend the findings in the *Mitsubishi* case, by holding that claims arising out of competition laws must be dealt with in the arbitration and that, if they are not, any award is subject to challenge, presumably not only in an action to set aside the award under domestic law but also in an action to enforce the award under the New York Convention.[138] It must be noted, however, that the European Court did not explicitly rule on whether arbitrators have a duty to apply Article 81 *ex officio*, if the parties have not raised it.

3.110 The *Mitsubishi* and the *Eco-Swiss* cases seem to settle the question whether parties may submit questions of competition law involving public policy concerns to arbitration. It follows that arbitrators should hear and determine such issues and that, in doing so, they should enforce the remedy required by the controlling law. However, the inherent conflict of this perceived obligation and the arbitrators' jurisdiction, and powers, as determined by the parties' arbitration agreement, becomes evident in cases like *Eco-Swiss*, where the parties did not raise the issue of competition law. It appears that the *Eco-Swiss* holding would require arbitrators to raise *sua sponte* questions of competition law that are present in the matter before them in order to be able to render a valid and enforceable award. However, raising questions *sua sponte* is questionable in relation to the principle of party autonomy and the jurisdiction of the arbitrators limited as it is by the arbitration agreement and the claims pursued by the parties. According to the *travaux préparatoires* to the SAA, it should be possible for the arbitrators to raise the question as part of their general duty of substantive case management.[139] Although this may be a practical solution, there is still a risk of exceeding the arbitrator's mandate if the question is

---

[136] Case C-126/97, *Eco Swiss China Time Ltd v Benetton International NV* (1999) ECR I-3055, para 41, and item 1 of the Court's ruling.

[137] See also Case C 168/05, *Mostaza Claro v Centro Móvil Milenium SL* (2006).

[138] von Mehren, 'The Eco-Swiss Case and International Arbitration', 19(4) *Arbitration International* (2003) 468.

[139] Govt Bill 1998/99:35, p 59. See further para 8.165.

raised *sua sponte*, or even in direct conflict with an express exclusion of competition law issues in the arbitration agreement.[140] Perhaps this flaw in the arbitration system must be accepted and also that the arbitrators' handling of this matter should not result in the setting aside of the award as long as the matter is handled in a manner that ensures due process to the parties. It must also be kept in mind that the competition authorities retain their exclusive jurisdiction to impose public law sanctions.

3.9 Effects of Arbitration Agreement

An arbitration agreement which meets the requirements set forth in para 3.05 *et seq* **3.111** above, have the following effects:

3.9.1 Bar to court proceedings

One of the cornerstones of modern arbitration legislation is that a valid arbitration **3.112** agreement constitutes a bar to court proceedings. Section 4 of the SAA codifies this general and basic principle of Swedish arbitration law.

Even where there is a valid arbitration agreement between the parties, one of **3.113** the parties may try to commence court proceedings with respect to the subject matter covered by the arbitration agreement. In such a case, the other party to the arbitration agreement must object to the jurisdiction of the court promptly, ie the first time he pleads to the court, either orally, at a pre-trial hearing, or in writing.[141] Very often the pre-hearing procedure is written, in which case the objection must be made in the statement of defence, or before the expiry of the deadline for submitting it. Failure in this respect results in that party having forfeited its right to object to the court's jurisdiction or, put differently: the party has waived the arbitration agreement with respect to the dispute in question.

The party objecting to the court's jurisdiction may move for either a stay or a **3.114** dismissal of the court proceedings. It should be noted that when the existence of a valid arbitration agreement is raised as an objection to jurisdiction the court must grant such motion, on the assumption that the arbitration agreement is indeed valid and that it covers the dispute in question. If the validity, or applicability, of the arbitration agreement is questioned, the court must invite both parties to argue this issue, and, if need be, to call witnesses.

It is important to note that a dismissal by a court of the dispute is not dependent on **3.115** an arbitration being commenced at the same time, or having been commenced

---

[140] Cf von Mehren, 'The Eco-Swiss Case and International Arbitration' 19(4) *Arbitration International* (2003) 469 and Govt Bill 1998/99:35, p 59.

[141] See Chapter 34, section 2 of the Procedural Code. Cf section 4(2) of the SAA.

prior to the court proceeding.[142] It should also be noted that if a court of law—in Sweden or outside Sweden—is in the process of reviewing the validity of an arbitration agreement, this does not prevent the commencement, or continuation, of an arbitration.[143]

3.116 As mentioned above, the jurisdictional objection must be raised the first time when the party pleads to the court, unless the party had a legal excuse not to do so and invoked the excuse as soon as it ceased to exist. Pursuant to Chapter 32, section 8 of the Swedish Procedural Code, a legal excuse exists when a person is prevented from doing what he is expected to do as a consequence of a general breakdown of communications, illness, or other circumstances that he had no reason to anticipate, or which the court otherwise finds to constitute a valid excuse.

3.117 There are certain circumstances, however, in which a court will generally deny a motion for a stay or dismissal despite the existence of a valid arbitration agreement. Such circumstances include the following situations.

3.9.1.1 Respondent has failed to cooperate in arbitration

3.118 Pursuant to section 5 of the SAA, a party forfeits its right to invoke the arbitration agreement as a bar to court proceedings where the party (i) has previously opposed a request for arbitration, (ii) has failed to appoint an arbitrator in due time, or (iii) has failed in due time to provide his share of the requested security for compensation to the arbitrators (or advance on costs).

3.119 With respect to a party's objection to a request for arbitration, it relates to the issue of jurisdiction of the arbitrators and must be distinguished from a rejection of the claim on the merits brought by the claimant.

3.120 If a claimant is faced with a respondent's failure to cooperate in arbitration proceedings in any of the ways provided for under section 5 of the SAA, he is not compelled to go to court. He may instead choose to proceed with the arbitration and ask the court to facilitate the arbitration proceedings. For instance, the court may assist in appointing any missing arbitrator[144] and the arbitrators may proceed without the participation of one of the parties.[145]

3.9.1.2 Respondent has disregarded the agreement in previous court proceedings

3.121 A court will generally deny a motion for a stay or dismissal based on the lack of jurisdiction of the court because of an arbitration agreement, if the respondent has implicitly waived his right to arbitration in prior court proceedings, either (i) by

---

[142] *Nykvarns skyltaktiebolag v Esselte Dimo* (NJA 1982 p 738); *Halotron Inc v Jan A. and AB Bejaro Product* (RH 1995:123).

[143] For a further discussion of the interplay between court proceedings and arbitration proceedings in this respect, see para 5.01 *et seq.*

[144] See section 15 of the SAA.

[145] See ibid, section 24(3).

having commenced court proceedings himself despite the existence of an arbitration agreement, or (ii) by having failed to raise a jurisdictional plea in a previous court action in which he was the respondent.[146]

In these cases and in those mentioned above,[147] it would appear that the arbitration **3.122** agreement is no longer in effect. However, this appearance must be qualified. The abovementioned cases could also be characterized as breaches of the arbitration agreement, sufficiently serious to allow the other party to treat the agreement as terminated.[148] When the claimant initiates the second action he may therefore choose arbitration, but if he prefers to commence court proceedings, the respondent cannot rely on the arbitration agreement as a bar to court proceedings.

3.9.1.3 *The subject matter of the dispute is non-arbitrable*

As discussed above[149] the arbitration agreement may be governed by a law other **3.123** than Swedish arbitration law. Arbitrability, however, is to be determined on the basis of Swedish law. Consequently, if the arbitration agreement is governed by a non-Swedish law, but the subject matter is non-arbitrable under Swedish law, a Swedish court of law will not accept the arbitration agreement as a bar to court proceedings in Sweden.

This follows from section 49 of the SAA which stipulates: **3.124**

> Where foreign law is applicable to the arbitration agreement, Section 4 [dealing with the arbitration agreement as a bar to court proceedings] shall apply to issues which are covered by the agreement, except when:
>
> - in accordance with the applicable law, the agreement is invalid, inoperative, or incapable of being performed; or
> - in accordance with Swedish law, the dispute may not be determined by arbitrators.
>
> That a court has jurisdiction to issue such decisions regarding security measures as the court is authorized to issue in accordance with law, notwithstanding the arbitration agreement, is set forth in Section 4, third paragraph.

A Swedish court will thus accept jurisdiction over the dispute in question, on the **3.125** assumption that all other requirements for the jurisdiction of Swedish courts are fulfilled.[150]

3.9.2 Assistance by courts

As discussed below a party is entitled to the assistance of the courts to enforce the **3.126** arbitration agreement if need be.[151] Such assistance includes the appointment of

---

[146] *Arbitration in Sweden* (2nd revised edn, 1984) 34.
[147] See para 3.118.
[148] Hobér, 'Arbitration Reform in Sweden' 17(4) *Arbitration International* (2001) 359.
[149] See para 3.113.
[150] See discussion at para 5.01 *et seq.*
[151] See Chapters 4 and 5.

arbitrators, the removal of unsatisfactory arbitrators, security measures, issuance of orders for production of documents, and hearing witnesses under oath.

3.9.3 Rules of organization and procedure

3.127 The SAA has a number of provisions which are discussed in greater detail below[152] regulating the constitution of tribunals and the appointment of arbitrators as well as the arbitration proceedings. These rules become operative as a result of the arbitration agreement. These provisions may be amended or excluded by agreement of the parties eg by reference to institutional rules such as the SCC Rules, the UNCITRAL Rules, or the ICC Rules.

3.9.4 Authority of arbitrators

3.128 A valid arbitration agreement gives duly appointed arbitrators the authority, among other things, to render an award having the following characteristics:

(i) *Final and Binding on the Merits.* The award is challengeable on narrowly defined procedural grounds only and solely in accordance with the provisions of the SAA which, *inter alia*, establish a three-month period within which the challenge must be filed; section 34(3) of the SAA. It is not possible to challenge the award on the merits. In exceptional cases, however, the award is void.[153]

(ii) *Res Judicata.* The award constitutes *res judicata*. Accordingly, the award is final and binding on the parties in relation to the subject matter arbitrated. The award can thus be pleaded in bar of other proceedings—judicial or arbitral—regarding the same matter between the same parties. This is the negative effect of the award in subsequent proceedings. But there is also a positive aspect: if the question decided by the award is a preliminary issue in a subsequent case, then a party may in appropriate circumstances refer to the award, the operative part of which must be accepted in the new proceedings. See further discussion in para 7.104 *et seq.*

(iii) *Directly Enforceable.* A Swedish award is enforceable in Sweden after a summary check by the execution authority, without the need for obtaining a court order acknowledging the award. With respect to foreign awards, ie where the award has been rendered elsewhere than in Sweden,[154] such award is enforceable after leave has been granted by the Svea Court of Appeal.[155]

3.129 In addition, pursuant to section 25(4) of the SAA, the arbitrators have the authority to render decisions on interim measures, see para 6.209.

---

[152] See Chapter 4.
[153] See para 8.26 *et seq.*
[154] See section 52 of the SAA.
[155] See ibid, section 59 and para 9.07 *et seq.*

3.9.5 Effect of arbitration agreement on third parties

In general, an arbitration agreement is binding only on the parties to it: two parties **3.130** cannot impose obligations on a third party and third parties cannot invoke the arbitration agreement for their own benefit or interfere with arbitration proceedings between the parties.[156] In certain situations, however, arbitration agreements may bind third parties, viz:[157]

(i) upon substitution of the parties by way of singular or universal succession, see para 3.132;

(ii) as a consequence of arbitration clauses being extended to guarantee (surety) agreements, see para 3.143;

(iii) as a result of conduct by third parties, including application of the so-called 'group of companies' doctrine, see para 3.155;

(iv) with respect to third-party beneficiary agreements (see para 3.105).

3.9.5.1 Party substitution

Questions concerning party substitution in arbitration proceedings are largely **3.131** unregulated. There is no provision in the SAA addressing this issue. The silence in this respect is not to be interpreted as a general prohibition on party substitution under Swedish law.[158] It is generally agreed that the principle of party autonomy means that party substitution is accepted, if the parties agree to it. It is more uncertain whether an arbitral tribunal may accept party substitution against the objection of the other party.

A party to a dispute may be substituted either by way of *universal succession* (eg **3.132** death, bankruptcy, reorganization, merger or demerger, etc) or by way of *singular succession*. Upon universal succession in the legal relationship to which the arbitration agreement refers the successor assumes all the rights and obligations of the party which he is succeeding, whereas upon singular succession the successor only assumes the rights and obligations specifically succeeded.

The debate with respect to party substitution in Swedish arbitration law has primarily **3.133** focused on whether the successor, in case of singular succession, is bound by an arbitration agreement between the original parties to such agreement. The vast majority of writers believe this to be the case, at least where successor party was aware of, or

---

[156] Heuman, *Arbitration Law of Sweden: Practice and Procedure* (2003) 77.

[157] It could perhaps be argued that multi-party arbitration in some cases extends the arbitration agreement to third parties, eg by virtue of consolidation of disputes with several different persons involved, when this is possible. Under Swedish arbitration law, as well as under the arbitration legislation of most other jurisdictions, consolidation is possible only with the consent of the parties. Without such consent, any extension of the arbitration agreement to an original non-party would fall in one of the categories discussed below. See para 4.13 *et seq* and para 4.28 *et seq* for a discussion of multi-party arbitrations.

[158] See eg the Supreme Court case *David H v Trygg-Hansa AB* (NJA 2000 p 202).

ought to have been aware of, the arbitration agreement.[159] If the arbitration agreement forms an integral part of the contract (which would normally be the case in a commercial relationship), it seems difficult to envisage a situation in which a reasonably diligent successor would have been unaware of the arbitration clause. Under Swedish law there are no provisions explicitly prohibiting party substitution. It is within the discretion of the arbitrators to decide whether or not party substitution should be granted against the objection of the other party, taking all circumstances of the particular case into account.

3.135 **Singular succession** With respect to cases of *singular* succession the Government has pointed out in the *travaux préparatoires* to the SAA that there is much to be said in favour of considering an arbitration agreement *mutually binding*.[160] This is also what the Supreme Court concluded in the only Supreme Court case dealing with this issue, viz the *Emja* case.[161] In short, the facts were as follows.

> In a shipbuilding contract a Dutch Shipyard, Scheepswerf Ferus Smit BV (Ferus), undertook to build a ship, which was later called MS Emja. Subsequently, a German shipping company, Emja, acquired the rights and obligations in relation to Ferus under the shipbuilding contract. Ferus retained another shipyard, Scheepswerf Bijlsma BV (Bijlsma), as subcontractor to build the ship. In a written contract with Bijlsma Wärtsilä undertook to deliver a diesel engine to MS Emja. This contract referred partly to the standard agreement ECE 188, including a supplement entitled 'Marine Equipment Addendum 1987', and partly, with regard to technical personnel, to the standard agreement TP 73 E. Both ECE 188 and TP 73 E contained arbitration clauses. Both clauses stipulated that Swedish law was to be applied.

> Subsequent to delivery of MS Emja to the shipping company, there were problems with the diesel engine. To make it possible for Emja to commence proceedings against Wärtsilä, Ferus and Bijlsma transferred the title to the engine to Emja. On the basis of this transfer agreement, Emja commenced an action against Wärtsilä in a local court concerning the defective engine. The issue before the Swedish Supreme Court was whether the arbitration clauses in ECE 188 and TP 73 F, which constituted part of the agreement between Bijlsma and Wärtsilä, were binding on Emja.

3.135 The Supreme Court, as well as the lower courts, accepted Wärtsilä's jurisdictional objection and concluded that Emja—as well as the original party—was bound by the arbitration clause. The Supreme Court also discussed, albeit *obiter dicta*, whether the remaining party continues to be bound by the arbitration clause in case of singular succession on the other side. The Court concluded that on balance the arguments

---

[159] Govt Bill 1998/99:35, pp 64–66. See also Dillén, *Bidrag till läran om skiljeavtalet* (1933) 245 *et seq*; Edlund in *Svensk Juristtidning* (1993) 905 *et seq*; Hassler-Cars, *Skiljeförfarande* (2nd edn, 1989) 45 *et seq*; Hobér in *Swedish and International Arbitration* (1983) 43 *et seq*; Heuman in *Festskrift till Sveriges Advokatsamfund* (1987) 229 *et seq*; Heuman, *Current Issues in Swedish Arbitration* (1990) *et seq*.

[160] Govt Bill 1998/99:35, p 64 *et seq*; Olsson and Kvart, *Lagen om skiljeförfarande, En kommentar* (2000) 140; cf Lindskog, *Skiljeförfarande, En kommentar* (2005) 166 *et seq*, who argues against the proposition that an arbitration agreement may be transferred with a mutually binding effect on the parties by way of singular succession.

[161] MS 'Emja' Braack Schiffahrts v Wärtsilä Diesel AB (NJA 1997 p 866).

in favour of letting the remaining party continue to be bound, dominate. It added, however, that the conclusion may be different when 'special circumstances' apply. Such special circumstances may include a situation where an assignment could be detrimental to the remaining party, eg because the new party lacks financial means. Arguably, the original party to the arbitration agreement, on his own motion, should not be able to divest himself of the obligations under the arbitration agreement by way of a singular succession. The assignment of a contract which is the subject of arbitration proceedings should therefore reasonably be subject to some form of control by the remaining party, eg by requiring his consent.[162] However, were it to be in the discretion of the remaining party, but not of the successor, to choose between arbitration and court proceedings, this would—so the Supreme Court held—result in an imperfect binding effect since it gives the remaining party the possibility to speculate in the choice of procedure. This speaks in favour of the position that the remaining party should be bound by the arbitration agreement in the absence of special circumstances.

It is generally accepted that the *Emja* case stands for the proposition that an arbitration **3.136** agreement may be transferred with binding effect *also in case of singular succession,* and that it is for the arbitrators in their discretion to decide whether the advantages of a requested party substitution outweigh the disadvantages.

The successor will join the proceedings on the same terms as his predecessor. Hence, **3.137** any admissions or agreements made in the course of the proceedings will continue to bind the party in accordance with general procedural principles, and an award will be binding on the successor. As a procedural matter it will be necessary, however, for the prayers for relief to be amended to the effect that they explicitly relate to the successor rather than to the original party and that the succession is included among the circumstances alleged in support of the prayers for relief. As explained in para 3.43, the doctrine of separability means that the arbitration agreement is to be treated as a separate agreement, at least in certain respects. This raises the question of whether a separate transfer—of the arbitration agreement—is required in cases of singular succession of the rights and obligations under a commercial contract. It is submitted that there is a presumption that the rights and obligations under an arbitration agreement are automatically transferred together with the rights and obligations of the commercial contract. As a matter of principle the presumption can be rebutted, for example if special circumstances indicate that this was not the intention or will of the parties concerned at the time when the singular succession took place.

Universal succession   The relatively small number of cases and limited legal **3.139** writings in this area have focused on universal succession in the context of

---

[162] That such consent may be required would seem to follow from the general principles of Swedish contract law, in particular from the rule stipulating that a debtor may not assign a debt without the consent of a creditor.

bankruptcy proceedings. As will be mentioned below, issues of universal succession may also arise with respect to mergers, demergers, and other forms of corporate re-organizations, eg corporatization within the framework of privatization.

3.139 Upon being declared bankrupt, the debtor loses the capacity to deal with property which legally forms part of the bankruptcy estate. The estate, represented by the trustee, is the proper party to all post-bankruptcy proceedings. With respect to arbitration agreements concluded by the debtor prior to the initiation of bankruptcy proceedings and relating to the property which may legally form part of the bankruptcy estate—ie arbitration agreements which may be of importance in disputes between the debtor and third parties (non-creditors)—the rule is that such arbitration agreements are binding on the bankruptcy estate.[163] It is not required to obtain the consent of a contracting party in case of universal succession. In other words, universal succession is an exception to the main rule that an arbitration clause cannot bind third parties.[164] This principle has been confirmed by the Supreme Court in the case of *Five Seasons Fritidsaktiebolags konkursbo (bankruptcy estate) v Five Seasons Försäljningsaktiebolag* (NJA 1993 p 641).[165] In this case the bankruptcy estate commenced court proceedings against the respondent based on an agreement signed before bankruptcy was declared. The agreement contained an arbitration agreement. The respondent referred to the arbitration agreement and asked for dismissal of the claim before the Court. The Supreme Court held that:

> [a]s a general rule an arbitration agreement is binding only between the parties to the agreement and not on third parties. An exception exists with respect to bankruptcy and other cases of universal succession. This exception, however, is not exhaustive. It seems to be the predominant opinion that a bankruptcy estate is bound by an arbitration clause in a contract which the debtor and his joint party has entered into before the initiation of the bankruptcy proceedings when the dispute relates to a subject matter which the debtor has had the right freely to plead, with binding effect in a subsequent bankruptcy, but that the bankruptcy estate is not, however, bound by an arbitration clause when the dispute relates to an issue to which the debtor lacks such power, eg whether or not a right *in rem* is at hand. Moreover, such an arbitration clause is not binding upon the bankruptcy estate when the trustee in bankruptcy seeks to bring a claim for recovery on behalf of the estate. On the other hand, a trustee in bankruptcy is entitled to enter into arbitration

---

[163] See eg *Byggnadsaktiebolaget Holger Preislers v H Palén* (NJA 1913 s 191), REW *Hagalunds v Byggnadsfirman Oscarsson & Söderberg* (NJA 1931 s 647) and *Svenska Kreditförsäkringsaktiebolagets konkursbo (bankruptcy estate) v [41 reinsurance companies]* (NJA 2003 p 3); Dillén, *Bidrag till läran om skiljeavtalet* (1933) 245 *et seq*; Welamson, *Konkursrätt* (1961) 297 *et seq*, 309 *et seq*, and 317; and *Konkurs* (8th edn, 1988) 97 and 99; Hassler-Cars, *Skiljeförfarande* (2nd edn, 1989) 45 *et seq*; Heuman in *Festskrift till Sveriges advokatsamfund* (1987) 229 and 231 *et seq*; Håstad in *Process och exekution, Vänbok till Boman* (1990) 177 *et seq*.

[164] Dillén, *Bidrag till läran om skiljeavtalet* (1933) 245 *et seq*.

[165] See also *Svenska Kreditförsäkringsaktiebolagets konkursbo (bankruptcy estate) v [41 reinsurance companies]* (NJA 2003 p 3). The Supreme Court's conclusion in this case has been heavily criticized in Lindskog, *Skiljeförfarande, En kommentar* (2005) 174–179, where many issues relating to bankruptcy and arbitration agreements are thoroughly discussed.

agreements in disputes which have arisen in the bankruptcy proceedings in the same manner as he may settle disputes which have occurred prior to the initiation of bankruptcy proceedings, eg with respect to claims for recovery.[166]

Hence, an arbitration agreement succeeded by way of universal succession is bind- **3.140**
ing and must be accepted by the other party to that agreement, except where rights *in rem* are concerned.

While the rule of universal succession is thus relatively straightforward *per se*, the **3.141**
more complicated issue is often to determine whether or not universal succession has taken place as a matter of law. As far as various forms of corporate re-organizations are concerned, this issue is usually decided by the *lex corporationis*,[167] ie the personal law of the legal entity in question. For example, Russian law must be applied to determine whether corporatization within the framework of the privatization programme constitutes universal succession in relation to the State-owned enterprise and the newly formed joint stock company, and whether such universal succession has taken place de facto and de jure. The legal effects of universal succession insofar as the arbitration agreement is concerned, will, however, be determined by Swedish law on the assumption that Swedish law governs the arbitration agreement.

3.9.5.2 Guarantee agreements

The argument could be made that an arbitration clause in a main contract should, **3.142**
at least in certain situations, also bind the guarantor of any of the parties to the main contract.[168] It could perhaps also be argued that earlier Supreme Court cases support such a position.[169] This issue was discussed by the committee of experts preparing the SAA[170] and in the Government Bill presented to parliament.[171] The committee proposed a provision concerning guarantees and guarantors. The pro-posal was not accepted by the Government and was therefore not included in the Government Bill. The SAA is consequently silent on the issue. The question thus remains open, insofar as statutory provisions are concerned. The absence of statu-tory provisions does not mean *ipso facto* that earlier case law is to be taken as the norm, *inter alia,* because the Government explained that the question should be

---

[166] *Five Seasons Fritidsaktiebolags konkursbo (bankruptcy estate) v Five Seasons Försäljningsaktiebolag* (NJA 1993 p 641) at 644.

[167] See discussion at para 2.174.

[168] See Dillén, *Bidrag till läran om skiljeavtal* (1933) 258–259; Hassler-Cars, *Skiljeförfarande* (2nd edn, 1989) 45–46; Hobér, *Svensk domstolspraxis i skiljedomsrätt 1984–1986,* in *Svensk och internationell skiljedom* (1986). Cf Heuman, *Current Issues in Swedish Arbitration* (1990) 47–48 and *Arbitration in Sweden* (2nd revised edn, 1984) 40.

[169] *Orsjö Församling v Gustafsson* (NJA 1896 p 136); *Medicinalstyrelsen v Jonson* (NJA 1916 p 100); and *Kronan v Lindroth* (NJA 1922 p 135). It should be noted that all three cases address only the situation when the guarantor relies on the arbitration clause as a bar to court proceedings, which the guarantor successfully did in all three cases. They thus do not address the situation where the guaran-tor relies on an arbitration in the principal contract with a view to initiating arbitration.

[170] SOU 1984:81, p 94.

[171] Govt Bill 1998/99:35, pp 63–66.

left for case law to decide.[172] The reason for the Government's position was that guarantees can take many different forms and that therefore, it was virtually impossible to draft provisions which would adequately cover all the various situations.[173]

3.143 From a contractual point of view, it is probably justified that a guarantor be bound by an arbitration agreement if the guarantee forms an integral part of the principal contract, or if the guarantor was aware, or ought to have been aware, of the arbitration clause in the principal contract covered by the guarantee.[174] At least if it can be established from other circumstances that the parties' true intention in drawing up the guarantee was that the guarantor—often a parent company—was to be a party to the arbitration agreement.[175] On the other hand, a guarantor could be prevented from relying on an arbitration agreement where the arbitration clause in the principal contract materialized only after the guarantee undertaking had been made.[176] The foregoing illustrates that it would be difficult to apply a general rule with respect to guarantees. Instead, one must resolve this issue on a case-by-case basis applying general rules of contract law.

3.144 Whether the arbitration clause in the principal contract is deemed to extend to the relationship between the creditor and the guarantor, or if the two are deemed to have concluded a separate arbitration agreement between themselves by being aware of and accepting the clause in the principal contract is perhaps primarily a question of terminology. At the end of the day, the question is whether the arbitration clause is to apply to someone who was not originally a party to it.

3.145 In two SCC cases,[177] the arbitral tribunal made a distinction between, on the one hand, guarantees of payment where the debtor's and the guarantor's undertakings were identical and, on the other hand, where the guarantee was of a different and much less stringent nature. In the first case, the arbitral tribunal found that the arbitration agreement was binding also on the guarantor. The reason stated by the arbitral tribunal was that the undertakings were similar, which meant, *inter alia*, that any defences which could be relied on by the debtor could also be relied on by the guarantor. Because of the close link between the undertakings, the tribunal found that it could normally be assumed that in such cases the guarantor would be prepared to accept that the dispute settlement mechanism provided for in the principal contract would also be applied with respect to him. In the second case, however, the tribunal found that such an assumption could not be justified

---

[172] Ibid, pp 66–67.

[173] Ibid.

[174] See Svea Court of Appeal cases *Lönnström Oy v Convexa AB* (RH 1985:137) and *Östgöta Enskilda Bank v Folksam* (RH 1994:103).

[175] Cf Gaillard and Savage (eds), *Fouchard Gaillard Goldman on International Commercial Arbitration,* (1999) para 498.

[176] Cf Svea Court of Appeal case *Kjell Pettersson v Förvaltningsbolaget Gamlestaden* (Ö 4497/94).

[177] *Eisenberg Export Company, Ltd et al v The Republic of Kazakhstan* (SCC cases 38/1997 and 39/1997). The cases are discussed in detail in SAR 2003:1, pp 273–307.

because the legal position of the guarantor differed in important respects from that of the debtor. In the second case, the guarantor did not guarantee that the debtor under the supply contract in dispute would perform its obligations, but merely that the guarantor would assist the debtor in raising the amounts necessary to pay the amount due. Accordingly, the duty of the guarantor was not the same as that of the debtor and, more particularly, the guarantor had not undertaken to pay the debts of the creditor. Consequently, the arbitral tribunal held that the guarantor was not bound by the arbitration agreement between the creditor and the debtor. The award in which the arbitral tribunal accepted jurisdiction over the guarantor was challenged. The District Court[178] and the Court of Appeal[179] upheld the arbitral tribunal's award. The Supreme Court did not grant leave to appeal.

3.9.5.3 *Conduct by third parties, including the 'group of companies' doctrine*

Even though an arbitration agreement is binding only on the parties to it, it is clear **3.146** that others, apart from the original parties, may be bound by the arbitration agreement. As discussed above[180] under Swedish law there is no written form requirement for arbitration agreements. Although rare in practice, they may be entered into orally. Swedish arbitration law also accepts that arbitration agreements are entered into by conduct.[181] This way of concluding an arbitration agreement is closely linked to the idea that an arbitration agreement may also bind third parties.

Strictly speaking this would seem to be a question of terminology. Rather than **3.147** being bound by an arbitration agreement as a third party, that party could be viewed as a new party to the agreement—by virtue of his conduct—and thus no longer an 'outsider' to whom the arbitration clause is extended.

In international arbitration practice, one method of trying to extend an arbitration **3.148** clause to third parties has been described as the 'group of companies' doctrine. Under most legal systems, separation of liability between different, separate, legal entities is recognized. This means, *inter alia*, that a parent company is not liable for the performance of agreements entered into by its subsidiaries. It has, however, been suggested that an arbitration agreement concluded by a company may be binding on its group affiliates, or even a natural person who is the group's ultimate controlling shareholder.[182] Such attempts to pierce the corporate veil are often motivated by the stated aim to find the 'true' party in interest, and, of greater practical importance, to target a more creditworthy member of the relevant group of companies.[183]

---

[178] Stockholm District Court, Case no T 1510-99.

[179] *Eisenberg Export Company Asia House Ltd v Republic of Kazakhstan* (RH 2003:61).

[180] See para 3.05.

[181] See para 3.14.

[182] See generally: Derains, *L'extension de la clause d'arbitrage aux non-signatories—la doctrine des groupes de sociétés*, ASA Special Series No 8 (1994) 241; Sandrock, 'Arbitration Agreements and Groups of Companies', in *Etudes Pierre Lalive* (1993) 625.

[183] Redfern and Hunter, *Law and Practice of International Commercial Arbitration* (4th edn, 2004) 148.

3.149   The leading international authority on the 'group of companies' doctrine is the *Dow Chemical* case,[184] in which a claim was brought before an ICC tribunal not only by the companies that had signed the relevant agreements but also by their parent company, a US corporation, as well as by a French subsidiary in the same group. The French distributor argued that the tribunal's jurisdiction only allowed it to render awards in favour of the two Dow Chemical companies with which it had a direct contract. The arbitrators found that the parent company, Dow Chemical Company (USA), exercised 'absolute control over its subsidiaries having either signed the relevant contracts or, like Dow Chemical France, effectively and individually participated in their conclusion, their performance, and their termination'. Moreover, the arbitrators held that the arbitration clause signed by two of the companies was also intended by the parties to be available to other companies in the group, commenting that:

> . . . irrespective of the distinct juridical identity of each of its members, a group of companies constitutes one and the same economic reality (*une réalité économique unique*) of which the arbitral tribunal should take account when it rules on its own jurisdiction subject to Article 13 (1955 version) or Article 8 (1975 version) of the ICC Rules.[185]

3.150   Hence, the tribunal found that it had jurisdiction over all of the named parties.

3.151   The Paris Court of Appeal subsequently refused to set aside the interim award on jurisdiction, holding that:

> . . . following an autonomous interpretation of the agreements and the documents exchanged at the time of their negotiation and termination, the arbitrators have, for pertinent and non-contradictory reasons, decided, in accordance with the intention common to all companies involved, that Dow Chemical France and The Dow Chemical Company (USA) have been parties to these agreements although they did not actually sign them, and that therefore the arbitration clause was also applicable to them.[186]

3.152   Arbitration case law in this area[187] is succinctly summarized by an award made in Geneva, in 1990, in ICC Case No 5721. The arbitral tribunal stated that:

> [t]he mere fact that two companies belong to the same group, or that they are dominated by a single shareholder, will not automatically justify lifting the corporate veil. However, where a company or individual appears to be the pivot of the contractual relations in a particular matter, one should carefully examine whether the parties' legal independence ought not, exceptionally, be disregarded in the interest of making a global decision. This exception is acceptable in the case of confusion deliberately maintained by the group or by the majority shareholder.

---

[184]   ICC 4131/1982 (Interim Award) in *Dow Chemical France et al v Société Isover-Saint-Gobain* (1983) 110 JDI 899, note Derains, 9 *Yearbook Commercial Arbitration* (1984) 131.

[185]   Ibid at 904. Cf SCC Arbitration 108/1997, discussed in para 3.20 where the Swedish concept of conduct and the 'theory of trust' were applied in a similar fashion.

[186]   CA Paris, 22 October 1983, *Société Isover-Saint-Gobain v Dow Chemical France et al* [1984] Rev Arb 98 at 100–101.

[187]   See eg Gaillard and Savage (eds), *Fouchard Gaillard Goldman on International Commercial Arbitration* (1999) para 501, footnotes 192 and 193.

Although the 'group of companies' doctrine has found expression in the decisions **3.153** of tribunals and national courts in a variety of jurisdictions,[188] there are doubts as to the existence and the parameters of the doctrine. Commentators also differ as to whether the 'group of companies' doctrine is distinct from the existing principles allowing the corporate veil to be pierced. Gaillard and Savage, for instance, treat both together,[189] whereas Born distinguishes the 'group of companies' doctrine from 'alter ego' claims in which a company or individual is deliberately contracting in such a way as to evade legitimate responsibilities. This would typically require an element of fraud to be established.[190]

Under Swedish law, the approach is generally sceptical towards the 'group of com- **3.154** panies' doctrine and the possibility to pierce the corporate veil is very limited.[191] Arbitrators and courts would rather seek to establish a 'new' arbitration agreement based on such party's conduct, see para 3.14.

In a recent case,[192] the Svea Court of Appeal dismissed a claim against a parent **3.155** company with reference to an arbitration agreement entered into by its subsidiary. The Court of Appeal found that the non-signatory parent company could also rely on the arbitration agreement and thus prevent the dispute from being tried in court proceedings. It is not clear from the reasons of the Court of Appeal if the court has applied the 'group of companies' doctrine or simply found that there was a mutual understanding between the parties, including the parent company, that disputes were to be resolved in arbitration, notwithstanding the fact that the parent company was a non-signatory to the agreement with the relevant arbitration clause.

Third-party beneficiary agreements Another situation where it could perhaps be **3.156** argued that an arbitration agreement is binding on a third party relates to so-called third-party beneficiary agreements.

A contract between two parties may, in certain circumstances, entitle a third party **3.157** to claim benefits under that contract as a so-called third-party beneficiary. This is

---

[188] Cf France, where the group of companies doctrine was accepted by the Paris Court of Appeal in *KIS France SA v SA Société Générale (France)* (Cour d'Appel, Paris, 31 October 1989), cf England, where the group of companies doctrine has been rejected by the courts in eg *Caparo Group Ltd v Fagor Arrastate Sociedad Cooperative* (Commercial Court, QBD, 7 August 1998), see LEXIS, and *Peterson Farms, Inc v C&M Farming Limited* [2004] EWHC 121 (Comm).

[189] Gaillard and Savage (eds), *Fouchard Gaillard Goldman on International Commercial Arbitration* (1999) paras 500–506.

[190] Born, *International Commercial Arbitration* (2001) 653–700.

[191] Cf Lindskog, *Skiljeförfarande, En kommentar* (2005) 196–197, and Heuman, *Arbitration Law of Sweden: Practice and Procedure* (2003) 81–82. Cf the Court of Appeal cases *Swedish Marin Equipment AB v Bo J.* (RH 1985:90) and *Icon AB v Göran W and Björn H.* (RH 1991:16), which both dealt with the question of piercing the corporate veil in order to have the director and the members of the board of directors bound by the arbitration agreement included in agreements between the company and another company which was the contracting party. In the latter case the Court concluded that the members of the Board were bound by the arbitration clause.

[192] *Xcaret Confectionery Sales AB v Concorp Scandinavia AB*, Svea Court of Appeal's decision on 4 November 2009 in case Ö 1634-09. The decision has been appealed to the Supreme Court, which has yet to grant leave to appeal.

the case, for instance, where the parties have expressly stipulated rights of such third party in the contract, or where such intention is implicit in the terms of the contract.[193]

3.158 The contract from which a third party derives beneficial rights may contain an arbitration agreement. In the event of a dispute occurring between one of the contracting parties and the third-party beneficiary, the question arises to what extent the third-party beneficiary is bound by the arbitration clause in relation to either of the contracting parties, and vice versa.

3.159 Since case law on this issue is very limited in Sweden, one has to be careful in drawing conclusions of a general nature. However, one aspect of this question came before the Swedish Labour Court in *Göran H v Fritidsbolaget MCB AB* (AD 1976 No 54). In this case, the Labour Court was called upon to determine whether a dispute between A and B was governed by an arbitration clause incorporated in a contract between A and C. A and C had concluded a contract pursuant to which C was to acquire all the shares in B. As part of the contract, A was to perform certain work for B, the terms of which were regulated by the contract. In consideration for the work performed, B was to pay remuneration to A, which was also regulated by the contract. A dispute arose between A and B concerning payment of parts of the remuneration, and the question for the Court was whether A's claim for such remuneration was covered by the arbitration clause in the contract between A and C.

3.160 The Labour Court held that the arbitration agreement covered the dispute between A and B. The Court found that both A and B, as of the date set forth in the contract, had begun to perform their obligations in accordance with the terms of the contract. Consequently, the Court found that a separate legal relationship based on the terms of the contract between A and C had been established also between A and B. Considering in particular the close connection between A's sale of the shares in B and his undertaking to perform certain work as a part of this sale, together with the joint interest that must have existed between B and C in having the work performed, the Court concluded that the arbitration clause must have become part of the legal relationship that arose between A and B. The court action brought by A was therefore dismissed due to the existence of a valid arbitration agreement between A and B.

3.161 With reference to this decision, commentators have argued that in situations where a third-party beneficiary has made use of its rights under the contract, such third party must also have accepted to be bound by the arbitration clause in the contract with regard to disputes concerning such rights or the corresponding obligations of the contracting parties under the contract. In other words, by claiming the benefits

---

[193] See eg UNIDROIT Principles of International Commercial Contracts Article 5.2.1 as well as the comments to Article 5.2.1 where examples of such implied intention are given.

intended for him in accordance with the main contract, the third party must be presumed to have subjected himself to being bound by the arbitration clause in the main contract.[194]

Whether the same would apply in the reverse situation, ie where the third-party **3.162** beneficiary brings a claim against one of the contracting parties, has not been addressed by Swedish courts.[195]

The case discussed above seems to be the only case which has served as the basis for **3.163** the theory underlying the effect of third-party beneficiary agreements. It should be noted, however, that the conclusion of the Labour Court in that case can also be explained by arguing that a new arbitration agreement had been created as a consequence of the conduct of A and B.

3.9.6 Confidentiality

The confidentiality of arbitration proceedings is often said to be one of the impor- **3.164** tant advantages of arbitration. Unlike court proceedings, where the press and public are generally entitled to be present, arbitration proceedings as a rule take place *in camera*. Previously, this was sometimes taken as proof of the confidentiality, in a general sense, of arbitration proceedings. It is noteworthy that the SAA, as well as the 1929 Act, lacks provisions dealing with confidentiality. The current trend, starting around the mid 1990s, in international arbitration is to distinguish between the unquestionable privacy of the hearing, ie hearings *in camera* and the confidentiality of the arbitration proceedings as such.[196]

Sweden has followed this trend. In the *Bulbank* case of 2000[197] the Swedish Supreme **3.165** Court concluded that a party to an arbitration is not bound by confidentiality, unless the parties have explicitly agreed thereto. In the *Bulbank* case one of the parties (AIT) had published a separate award rendered in the course of the arbitration proceedings.[198] Bulbank sought to terminate the arbitration agreement and

---

[194] Lindskog, *Skiljeförfarande, En kommentar* (2005) 196.

[195] Lindskog has argued that the contracting parties, in principle, should also be bound in relation to the third-party beneficiary. Arguably, if B is entitled to invoke the benefits of the main contract, he should also be entitled to invoke the benefits of the arbitration clause incorporated in the main contract. *Op cit.*

[196] See eg *Esso Australia Resources Ltd and others v The Honourable Sidney James Plowman and others* (1995) 183 CLR 10. The case is also discussed in (1995) 11(3) *Arbitration International* 235, and *Commonwealth of Australia v Cockatoo Dockyard Pty Ltd* [1995] 26 NSWLR 662; cf the previously accepted principle of confidentiality set forth in, *inter alia*, the English Court of Appeal case *Ali Shipping Corporation v Shipyard Trogir* [1998] 1 Lloyd's Rep 643, 651. For a brief and helpful article containing the development of the confidentiality issues prior to the Bulbank decision, including citations to articles and cases, see Fortier, 'The Occasionally Unwarranted Assumption of Confidentiality' 15(2) *Arbitration International* (1999) 131–139; see also Sikirić, 'Confidentiality in Arbitral Proceedings', (2006) 13 *Croatian Arbitration Yearbook* 131–166.

[197] *Bulgarian Foreign Trade Bank Ltd (Bulbank) v A.I. Trade Finance Inc (AIT)* (NJA 2000 p 538).

[198] The decision was published in Mealey's International Arbitration Report in 1997.

subsequently tried to have the final award declared void or set aside, *inter alia*, on the basis that AIT had breached the fundamental principle of confidentiality in arbitration and thereby the arbitration agreement, by publishing the separate award. The Supreme Court rejected Bulbank's claim in its entirety. The Supreme Court found that there is no unambiguous position in this respect in legal writings, nor in case law, domestic or international. Against this background, the Supreme Court found that the starting point must be the paramount and general principle of party autonomy in arbitration proceedings. If the parties wish to keep the arbitration proceedings confidential, they must so agree either from the outset in the arbitration agreement, or separately in connection with the arbitration proceedings.[199] Thus, under Swedish law, confidentiality is not an implied term of an arbitration agreement.

3.166 The Supreme Court's conclusion in the *Bulbank* case must not be mistaken for a general relief available to counsel, arbitrators, and the relevant arbitration institute, if applicable. These participants in the arbitral process are still bound by confidentiality, corresponding to their respective roles in the process, unless expressly relieved thereof by the parties.[200] With respect to arbitrators, there is also a general view that, in any event, they must exercise reticence in relation to the arbitration proceedings.[201] In addition, the protection for business secrets in accordance with the Swedish Trade Secrets Act[202] must be upheld by all participants in the arbitral process.

3.167 Noteworthy in this respect is the fact that, unless there are express contractual provisions on confidentiality, sanctions against violations thereof are not laid down in Swedish law. In the *Bulbank* case the District Court found that a violation of confidentiality constituted a material breach of the agreement, including the arbitration agreement, and that Bulbank was therefore entitled to terminate the agreement, which the Court further found affected the validity of the arbitration agreement. The decision was overturned by the Court of Appeal and subsequently by the Supreme Court. If the violation is not deemed to be a material breach, the parties would be left with monetary sanctions to remedy a violation of a contractual provision on confidentiality. However, monetary sanctions by way of damages are often a blunt measure since it would be difficult for the affected party to prove the damages suffered. In case the parties wish to accomplish an effective sanction for the violation of a confidentiality provision, the best remedy is probably to provide for this in their agreement, eg by way of a conventional penalty.

---

[199] Guidelines for the drafting of confidentiality clauses in arbitrations can be found in Magnusson, 'Avtal om sekretess i skiljeförfarande', *Juridisk Tidsskrift* (2002/03), p 161

[200] See eg Article 46 of the SCC Rules, Article 30 of the LCIA Rules, and Article 6 of Appendix I and Article 1 of Appendix II to the ICC Rules. With respect to counsel who is member of the Swedish Bar Association, see section 2.2 of the Ethical Rules for Bar Members.

[201] Cf *Bulgarian Foreign Trade Bank Ltd (Bulbank) v AI Trade Finance Inc (AIT)* (NJA 2000 p 538) and SOU 1995:65, p 165.

[202] SFS 1990:409.

3.10 Termination of Arbitration Agreement

3.10.1 Introduction

The parties to an arbitration agreement are free to terminate and/or alter the agreed **3.168** upon dispute resolution clause at any time. The arbitration agreement may terminate with respect to an existing dispute only, and yet remain in force with respect to any future disputes.

The effects upon termination are generally speaking the following: **3.169**

(i) The ability to plead the arbitration agreement in bar if the jurisdiction of the courts comes to an end.
(ii) The courts will not intervene in aid of the arbitration proceedings by appointing or removing arbitrators.
(iii) The authority of the arbitrators comes to an end; the arbitrators become *functus officio*.

All these consequences do not necessarily occur in all cases of termination, or at the **3.170** same time. The consequences may arise at different times. Modifications, particularly with respect to the ending of the arbitrators' authority, may vary from one case of termination to another.

3.10.2 Termination with respect to existing dispute

3.10.2.1 By understanding

The arbitration agreement may terminate with respect to a particular existing **3.171** dispute as a result of a new agreement reached by the parties. Such understanding may take the form of a settlement of the dispute in question, an agreement not to apply the arbitration agreement to such dispute, or the negotiation of a new arbitration agreement to replace the existing one.

3.10.2.2 Events during proceedings

The Arbitration Act of 1929 provided for the termination of an arbitration agree- **3.172** ment with respect to an existing dispute as a result of various events which could occur in the course of arbitration proceedings. Thus, the arbitration agreement was terminated when a third party had been designated to appoint an arbitrator but had failed to do so;[203] when an arbitrator appointed by the arbitration agreement itself 'resigned, or became disqualified or was prevented for any other reason from performing his functions';[204] or when the arbitrators were unable to reach a decision on a question referred to them.[205] In order to prevent obstruction of the arbitration

---

[203] Ibid, section 8(2).
[204] Ibid, section 9(1).
[205] Ibid, section 16.

proceedings, the SAA provides for certain remedies in these situations rather than termination of the arbitration agreement. For example, section 16 of the SAA stipulates that the District Court shall, upon request of a party, appoint a new arbitrator where the original arbitrator resigns or is discharged. Contrary to the Arbitration Act of 1929, the SAA also deals with the situation where the arbitrators are unable to reach a decision on a question referred to them (sections 30 and 31 of the SAA).[206]

3.10.2.3 *Judgment*

3.173 If an existing dispute is brought to court in spite of the existence of a valid arbitration agreement and carried through to a judgment, the arbitration agreement is considered terminated with respect to that dispute. This situation often arises when a respondent fails to move for a dismissal based on a valid arbitration agreement. As described above,[207] such an objection must be raised in the very first response to the claim, otherwise the respondent is deemed to have waived its right to rely on the arbitration agreement.

3.174 A judgment constitutes *res judicata* with respect to the dispute in question. There is therefore no longer any dispute to be settled by arbitration. If court proceedings are terminated prior to a final judgment on the merits, eg due to voluntary withdrawal of the claim, or because of dismissal, the arbitration agreement is not terminated. Either party may therefore commence arbitration with respect to the dispute.

3.10.2.4 *Expiration of award period*

3.175 The Arbitration Act of 1929 laid down a time limit for rendering the arbitral award. If this time limit was not met the arbitration agreement terminated. Under the SAA, no such time limit applies. However, the parties may agree on a certain period of time within which the award must be rendered, see para 7.52. The SCC Rules stipulate that the award must be rendered within six months from the date when the arbitration was referred to the arbitrators, unless the award period is prolonged by the SCC Institute, or by the parties.[208] If the award period agreed between the parties expires, the termination of the arbitration agreement is not absolute. If the arbitrators render an award after the expiration of the award period, the award is not void but merely voidable. The arbitrators thus retain authority to render an award, albeit a vulnerable one.[209]

3.10.2.5 *Award*

3.176 Probably the most common way in which an arbitration agreement is terminated with respect to an existing dispute is by rendering a valid award. It should

---

[206] See para 7.10.
[207] See para 3.113.
[208] Article 37 of the SCC Rules.
[209] *Arbitration in Sweden* (2nd revised edn, 1984) 43.

be pointed out that the typical consequences of termination (ie no bar to court proceedings, no assistance by the courts, and the end of arbitrators' authority) occur at different times and in varying degrees depending on the character of the award as valid or defective. For example, the arbitrators retain certain authority even after the award has been rendered, since section 32 of the SAA provides for the possibility to correct the award if the award contains any obvious inaccuracy as a consequence of typographical, computational, or other similar mistake by the arbitrators or any other person. The award may also be supplemented if the arbitrators by oversight have failed to decide an issue which should have been dealt with in the award. Such correction or supplementation must be made within thirty days of the announcement of the award. The arbitrators may also correct or supplement an award, or interpret the decision in an award, where any of the parties so requests within thirty days of receipt of the award by this party.[210]

It must also be noted that, in certain circumstances, a court may stay proceedings **3.177** concerning the invalidity or setting aside of an award in order to provide the arbitrators with an opportunity to resume the arbitration proceedings, or to take some other measure which will eliminate the grounds for the invalidity or the setting aside of the award (section 35 of the SAA).[211] In this way, the arbitration agreement may thus become effective again, although with the limited purpose of trying to avoid the setting aside of the award.

3.10.3 Complete termination

There are several ways in which an arbitration agreement may be completely termi- **3.178** nated, ie not only with respect to an existing dispute but with respect to all future disputes. Complete termination may occur under the general rules of contract law, eg through frustration of the agreement, but such situations are rare. Generally, termination will occur as a result of the provisions in the agreement itself, provisions which may be express or implied. Thus, a time limit or a condition may terminate the agreement. Also, the agreement may always be completely terminated through an understanding between the parties.

In addition, there are probably circumstances in which a party may avoid the arbi- **3.179** tration agreement.[212] Under general contract law, a party is entitled to avoid an agreement if the other party has committed a material breach thereof. Bearing in mind the doctrine of separability, however, in order to give the aggrieved party the right to avoid the arbitration agreement, there must be a material breach in relation to the arbitration agreement.[213]

---

[210] See para 7.137 *et seq.*
[211] See further para 8.192 *et seq.*
[212] Lindskog, *Skiljeförfarande, En kommentar* (2005) 152 *et seq.*
[213] See discussion at para 3.43 *et seq.*

3.180   In the *Bulbank* case,[214] one of the questions was whether a breach of the alleged confidentiality obligation entitled the aggrieved party to avoid the arbitration agreement. This question was not ultimately ruled on since the Supreme Court found that there was no valid confidentiality obligation in the first place. The Court of Appeal, however, elaborated on this question and found that also an arbitration agreement may be avoided on the basis of a material breach thereof, but that the right to avoid the agreement must be very limited because of the far-reaching consequences that such action might result in.[215]

3.181   When determining whether or not a right to avoid is available, the interest of one of the parties in having the arbitration agreement avoided must be balanced against the other party's interest in upholding the agreement.[216] Only by such balancing, could the public interest of having arbitration agreements enjoy stability be safeguarded. The timing of the avoidance may also be of some relevance in this respect. Parties generally invest considerable resources in terms of time and money in arbitration proceedings. The balancing of interests between the parties suggests that the later into the proceedings a party seeks to avoid the arbitration agreement, the more severe must the breach of the agreement be.

3.11 Drafting of Arbitration Clauses

3.182   Arbitration can only take place if there is an arbitration agreement between the parties. It goes without saying that the wording of the arbitration clause is important. A poorly drafted arbitration clause can cause a large number of problems for the parties, some of which are usually impossible to solve once a dispute has arisen. In particular, a poorly drafted arbitration clause will usually give an unwilling respondent a number of opportunities to try to delay, or even derail, the arbitration. These simple facts notwithstanding, arbitration clauses are still being neglected by contract negotiators. They are often saved until the end of the negotiations which explains why they are sometimes referred to as 'midnight clauses'. Considerable amounts of time and money will be saved if proper attention is paid to the arbitration clause. At the same time, it must be said that it is a futile exercise to look for the 'miracle clause' which addresses and solves every problem that may arise in an arbitration.[217] Such clauses do not exist. Every arbitration clause must be negotiated and agreed against the background of the circumstances of each contract. There are, however, some considerations of a general nature which should be taken into account.

---

[214]   *Bulgarian Foreign Trade Bank Ltd (Bulbank) v AI Trade Finance Inc (AIT)* (NJA 2000 p 538).
[215]   Ibid, 547.
[216]   Cf Bengtsson, *Hävningsrätt och uppsägningsrätt vid kontraktsbrott* (1967) 205 *et seq.*
[217]   See the discussion in Bond, 'How to Draft an Arbitration Clause', 1 *ICC Int'l Ct Arb Bull* 14 (1990); see also Friedland, *Arbitration Clauses for International Contracts* (2nd edn, 2007).

There are several choices facing parties drafting an arbitration clause. The first **3.183** choice is whether to opt for institutional or *ad hoc* arbitration. In many instances, the prudent course of action is to select institutional arbitration.[218] The services provided by the arbitral institution are often valuable, especially to parties with little experience in international dispute resolution. If the parties choose institutional arbitration, they should seek a reputable institution with an established track record of administering international cases. The major arbitral institutions can administer arbitrations around the world and the arbitration proceedings do not need to take place where the institution is headquartered.[219]

The second choice to be made by the parties is the selection of a set of arbitration **3.184** rules, providing the procedural framework for the arbitration proceedings. When the parties have opted for institutional arbitration, the choice of arbitration rules coincides with that of the arbitral institution. When the parties have opted for *ad hoc* arbitration, the parties may select arbitration rules developed for non-institutional arbitration, eg the UNCITRAL Arbitration Rules. If so, the parties should consider designating an arbitral institution as the appointing authority for the appointment of arbitrators, including the chairman of the tribunal.

Typically it is to be recommended that parties use the model clause recommended **3.185** by the arbitral institution in question. However, even model clauses of arbitral institutions differ. For example, the SCC Institute offers Model Clauses with several variations[220] to suit the parties' wishes; clauses referring to the Arbitration Rules, or the Rules for Expedited Arbitrations, as well as various combination clauses giving greater flexibility when the size and character of dispute is more difficult to predict. The general Model Clause for arbitration at the SCC has the following wording:

> Any dispute, controversy or claim arising out of or in connection with this contract, or the breach, termination or invalidity thereof, shall be finally settled by arbitration in accordance with the Arbitration Rules of the Arbitration Institute of the Stockholm Chamber of Commerce.

The SCC Institute further recommends the following additions to the Model **3.186** Clause:[221]

- The arbitral tribunal shall be composed of three arbitrators/a sole arbitrator.

---

[218] Reisman, Craig, Park, and Paulsson, *International Commercial Arbitration, Cases, Material and Notes on the Resolution of International Business Disputes* (1997) 153.

[219] Cf the IBA Guidelines for Drafting International Arbitration Clauses, see <http://www.ibanet.org>.

[220] The SCC Model Clauses are: Full-scale arbitration (a flexible procedure for all claims), Expedited arbitration (a fast-track procedure for smaller and medium sized claims), Arbitration under the Insurance Arbitration Rules, Expedited arbitration or full-scale arbitration depending on the circumstances, Expedited arbitration or full-scale arbitration depending on the amount in dispute, Mediation first hand, arbitration when the parties cannot agree on mediation or mediation is unsuccessful, see <http://www.sccinstitute.se>.

[221] See <http://www.sccinstitute.se>.

- The seat of arbitration shall be [. . .].
- The language of the arbitration shall be [. . .].
- The substantive law of [. . .] shall be applied.

3.187 Generally speaking, it is advisable to use the model, or standard, clauses developed by the leading arbitration institutions of the world. They usually include all essential components of an efficient arbitration.

3.188 The parties may also agree to include in the arbitration clause a *multi-tier* provision,[222] a confidentiality undertaking, or a waiver of the right to challenge the award, a provision on the arbitrators' authority with respect to provisional or conservatory measures, a provision with respect to document production, time limits, etc.

3.189 An arbitration agreement, even if 'tailor made', should not, however, be too complex. A clause which is too complex increases the risk of ambiguity and could result in an invalid and unenforceable, or at least ineffective, arbitration agreement. Moreover, the scope of the arbitration agreement should, typically, be as broad as possible in order to avoid arguments about whether a given dispute between the parties is subject to arbitration.[223] For example, the Model Clause of the SCC Institute covers 'any dispute, controversy or claim *arising out of or in connection with* this contract, or the breach, termination or invalidity thereof'.

3.190 In multi-party or multi-contract situations, the drafting of an arbitration clause may be particularly difficult. In addition to the issue of appointment of arbitrators, issues of intervention, joinder and/or consolidation may raise a number of very complex questions. Some arbitral institutions have included in their rules certain provisions in order to facilitate the handling of multi-party or multi-contract situations.[224] Although these provisions are not necessarily comprehensive in their scope, it is recommended to opt for institutional arbitration, using one of the arbitral institutions, which has such provisions in their rules, covering multi-party or multi-contract disputes.[225]

---

[222] For example, a provision requiring negotiation or mediation as a condition precedent to arbitration, or provisions with respect to a dispute resolution board, which is common in major construction contracts; such a board would typically try claims before they can be submitted to arbitrators.

[223] Cf the IBA Guidelines for Drafting International Arbitration Clauses, para 13, where it is argued that there may be certain circumstances in which the parties have good reasons to exclude some disputes from the scope of the arbitration agreement, see <http://www.ibanet.org>.

[224] See eg Articles 11 and 13(4) of the SCC Rules.

[225] For further guidance and examples of clauses, see the proposed new IBA Guidelines for Drafting International Arbitration Clauses, paras 92–108, see <http://www.ibanet.org>.

4

THE ARBITRATORS

4.1 Appointment of Arbitrators	4.01	**4.4 Relation of Arbitrators**	
4.1.1 Introduction	4.01	**to the Parties**	4.52
4.1.2 Appointment of arbitrators		**4.5 Challenge and Replacement of**	
under the SAA	4.04	**Arbitrators**	4.62
4.1.2.1 Arbitrators not specifically		4.5.1 The SAA	4.62
named in agreement	4.06	4.5.1.1 Grounds for challenge.	
4.1.2.2 Arbitrators specifically		Disclosure	4.62
named in agreement	4.11	4.5.1.2 Procedure	4.85
4.1.2.3 Arbitrators in multi-party		4.5.1.3 Replacing arbitrators	4.87
arbitrations	4.13	4.5.2 Rules	4.91
4.1.3 Rules	4.18	**4.6 Compensation of Arbitrators**	4.103
4.1.3.1 SCC	4.18	4.6.1 Fees and expenses	4.103
4.1.3.2 Other rules	4.36	4.6.2 Value added tax (VAT) on	
4.2 Qualifications of Arbitrators	4.39	arbitrators' compensation	4.126
4.3 Powers and Duties of Arbitrators	4.46	4.6.3 Rules	4.130

4.1 Appointment of Arbitrators

4.1.1 Introduction

Once the decision to start an arbitration has been taken, and the appropriate form of **4.01** notice or request for arbitration has been made, the next step is to establish the arbitral tribunal. Needless to say, it is important for the parties carefully to exercise this right and to choose the best suited arbitrators for the specific dispute in question.[1] The right in arbitration proceedings to 'choose one's judge' is one of the more obvious differences between arbitration and litigation before ordinary courts and is one of the more important advantages of arbitration. The parties are given a great deal of freedom with respect to the appointment of arbitrators. The statutory framework is to a large extent non-mandatory. It can therefore be modified or replaced by referencing an established set of rules, or otherwise, in order to conform to the desires of the parties.

---

[1] For a comprehensive review of the complex criteria involved in the selection of arbitrators, see Lalive, 'Requirements of International Arbitration, The selection of Arbitrators', and 'On The Neutrality of Arbitrators and The Place of Arbitration', in *Swiss Essays on International Arbitration* (1984) 22–33.

4.02 There are several possible methods of appointing an arbitral tribunal. The most commonly used methods are the following:

- by agreement of the parties;
- by an arbitral institution;
- through a list system;
- the chair by existing co-arbitrators;
- by an appointing authority agreed by the parties;
- by a national court.

4.03 Below there follows a discussion, first of the provisions of the Swedish Arbitration Act (SAA) and then of the SCC Rules, as well as of other rules.

4.1.2 Appointment of arbitrators under the SAA

4.04 The establishment of an arbitral tribunal involves many considerations. The first question is the number of arbitrators. Section 1 of the SAA provides that disputes may be referred to 'one or several arbitrators' for resolution. Sole arbitrators are therefore fully recognized irrespective of the subsequent statutory references to 'arbitrators', ie in the plural, eg in section 10(1) of the SAA.

4.05 The SAA does not explicitly distinguish between arbitration agreements in which the parties have expressly appointed specific individuals as arbitrators, on the one hand, and arbitration agreements in which the parties have not made such appointments, on the other hand, although naturally, some of the provisions of the SAA are only applicable to the latter form of arbitration agreements (except for when a party shall appoint a new arbitrator, see below). With respect to agreements where no specific individuals have been designated as arbitrators, which is by far the most common type of arbitration agreement, the SAA includes provisions concerning the number of arbitrators (section 13), the procedure for carrying out the appointment (section 14(1)), the consequences if appointments are not made (section 5(2), 14(2), and 15)) and the resignation, death, removal, and replacement of arbitrators (section 16). With respect to arbitration agreements naming an individual, which is unusual, the composition of the tribunal and the appointment of the arbitrators have obviously already been agreed by the parties. However, section 16, which refers to sections 14 and 15, applies also where the arbitrator who resigns or is removed was appointed in the arbitration agreement.

4.1.2.1 Arbitrators not specifically named in agreement

4.06 **Number of arbitrators and procedure for appointment**   Under section 12 of the SAA, the parties may determine the number of arbitrators and the manner in which they are to be appointed. In the absence of any agreement of the parties, section 13 of the SAA stipulates that the arbitral tribunal shall consist of three arbitrators, of which each party shall appoint one arbitrator and the arbitrators so appointed shall appoint the third. Although many arbitral tribunals consist of a sole arbitrator, the typical tribunal in arbitrations involving large or complex transactions consists of three arbitrators appointed in the above-described manner.

In situations where each party is entitled to appoint an arbitrator, the first party **4.07** shall notify the opposing party of his choice of arbitrator in the request for arbitration, which must be in writing.[2] Under section 14(1) of the SAA, the receipt of such notice triggers an obligation of the opposing party to, within 30 days thereof, notify the first party in writing in respect of his choice of arbitrator. Pursuant to section 14(3) of the SAA, the District Court[3] shall appoint an arbitrator upon request by the first party if the opposing party fails in this regard. This provision is designed to expedite the proceedings and to prevent obstruction. The effect of this provision is reinforced by the inability of a party to revoke his choice of arbitrator once notification thereof has been given to the other party in writing, unless the other party consents thereto, in accordance with section 14(2) of the SAA.

The SAA has no provision concerning the manner in which the two arbitrators **4.08** selected by the respective parties are to select a third arbitrator. In practice, the party requesting arbitration will normally notify his appointee of the choice made by the other party. Such appointee will then contact the other appointee and attempt to reach agreement on the third arbitrator. It would appear that the party-appointed arbitrators must be unanimous in their selection of the final arbitrator, even in those fairly unusual situations in which there are more than two party-appointed arbitrators. Once the third arbitrator has been appointed he continues to hold office, even if either or both of the arbitrators who have chosen him are replaced by a person, or persons, who would not have agreed to his appointment.

Failure to appoint   The SAA has specific provisions dealing with the failure of a **4.09** party, or appointing authority, to select an arbitrator within the prescribed time period. Typically, the party requesting arbitration notifies the other party of his choice of arbitrator through the request for arbitration itself, as described above. If the other party does not provide written notice of his choice of arbitrator within 30 days of receipt of the abovementioned notice, three options are available to the first party:

(i) The first party may apply to the District Court to make the appointment (section 14(3)). This is the option most frequently pursued. The procedure before the District Court upon such an application is of a summary character only. The District Court may reject a request to appoint an arbitrator on the

---

[2] Section 19 of the SAA. See para 6.35.
[3] Pursuant to section 44 of the SAA, the competent court with respect to an application for the appointment of an arbitrator is the District Court at the place where one of the parties is domiciled or the District Court at the place of arbitration. The application may also be submitted to the Stockholm District Court.

grounds that the arbitration manifestly is not legally permissible, eg because of defects related to the arbitration agreement (section 18). It must be noted, however, that the District Court's decision in such a matter with respect to the application of the arbitration agreement is not final and binding. If the party desires a final and binding judgment on the applicability of the arbitration agreement he must request a declaratory judgment in addition to the request to appoint an arbitrator,[4] or proceed as outlined under (ii) below.

(ii)   Alternatively, the first party may commence a court action and request that the other party be ordered to select an arbitrator, at least in cases where such other party has denied the applicability of the arbitration agreement. Although rarely pursued, this option may be the most attractive if there is some doubt as to the validity or applicability of the arbitration agreement and if time pressure is not a factor.

(iii) The third option permits the first party to abandon arbitration and bring the dispute before a court of law (section 5(2)). As discussed in para 3.112 above, a valid arbitration agreement is normally a bar to the jurisdiction of courts as regards any dispute covered by the arbitration agreement. This bar is lifted, however, if the opposing party fails to appoint an arbitrator.

4.10 If the party-appointed arbitrators fail to appoint a third arbitrator within 30 days from the date on which the last arbitrator was appointed, any party (but not an arbitrator) may apply to the District Court to make the appointment (section 15(1)). The same rule applies if the arbitrator is to be appointed by someone other than a party, or the arbitrators, for example, by an appointing authority under the UNCITRAL Arbitration Rules, or by the Board of the SCC Institute. In these cases, however, the 30-day period commences when the party desiring the appointment of an arbitrator requests that the person responsible therefore makes such appointment (section 15(2)).

4.1.2.2 *Arbitrators specifically named in agreement*

4.11 No statutory provisions are necessary with respect to the composition of the tribunal or the appointment of arbitrators when the arbitration agreement itself specifically names an arbitrator or arbitrators. If such an arbitrator resigns or is removed, the new arbitrator is to be appointed in the same manner as if the arbitration agreement did not specifically name arbitrators.

4.12 In practice, it is unusual to see arbitrators specifically named in the agreement. One of the reasons is certainly that it is difficult to choose a suitable arbitrator (or arbitrators) for a dispute which has not yet arisen. In addition, it is very difficult to predict the

---

[4] See Govt Bill 1998/99:35, pp 96–97, where it is stated that the appointment of an arbitrator is a matter that must be handled in a speedy manner. Should the court be forced to do a comprehensive review of the validity of the arbitration agreement this may delay the procedure for quite some time. In any event, the decision of the court in relation to the validity of the arbitration agreement is not final and binding.

arbitrator's future potential conflict of interest in relation to the dispute or the parties, or his or her health condition. It is, however, not unusual to designate eg an accounting firm as an expert in order to decide a particular issue identified in advance, either in the form of a preliminary decision, or in a final and binding decision with respect to the particular issue.

4.1.2.3 Arbitrators in multi-party arbitrations

When more than two parties are involved in a dispute, it is usually considered **4.13** desirable that all issues be dealt with in the same proceeding rather than in a series of separate proceedings. In general terms, this saves time and money.[5] More importantly, it avoids the possibility of conflicting decisions on the same issues of law and fact, since all issues would be determined by the same arbitrators at the same time.

Over the years contracts have become increasingly complex, with a growth in the **4.14** number of parties involved and in the number of ancillary contracts. This, in turn, has resulted in debates and publications concerning the problems encountered in multi-party arbitrations.[6] Unlike in national courts, where it is generally possible to join additional parties, or to consolidate separate sets of proceedings,[7] in arbitration this may be difficult, or even impossible, to achieve. This is so because arbitration has a contractual basis, ie the effect of the arbitration agreement is, as a matter of principle, limited to the contracting parties.[8] It is thus only the common will of the contracting parties which gives the arbitrators the power (or mandate) to join additional parties, or to consolidate separate sets of proceedings. Many attempts have been made over the years, by scholars, practitioners, and arbitral institutions alike, to find the magic formula to resolve the problems resulting from multi-party arbitration. Despite heroic efforts, they have generally not been crowned with success. The reason is simply that multi-party arbitrations can take very many different forms and, almost without exception, create complicated legal situations.

Multi-party situations may occur where the parties to a contract consist of several **4.15** individuals or entities, for example, several entities in the same group of companies, or where there are several independent parties which are bound by the same arbitration agreement, for example, a joint venture, a consortium agreement, a shareholders' agreement, or in case of a guarantee undertaking. In the former case, it is unlikely that there exists any conflicting interest between the companies on the 'same side'

---

[5] Redfern and Hunter, *Law and Practice of International Commercial Arbitration* (4th edn, 2004) 168.

[6] See eg Hanotiau, *Complex Arbitrations, Multiparty, Multicontract, Multi-issue and Class Actions* (2005) and 'Problems Raised by Complex Arbitrations Involving Multiple Contracts-parties-Issues—An Analysis' 18(3) *Journal of International Arbitration* (2001) 253–360.

[7] Cf Chapter 14 of the Swedish Procedural Code.

[8] See para 3.130 for a discussion of the extent to which an arbitration agreement is binding on third parties.

of the dispute. Problems associated with multi-party disputes therefore rarely arise in these situations. The latter situation, however, which involves several independent parties, represents a true multi-party situation generating practical difficulties, such as the number and appointment of arbitrators, the relation to third parties, etc. To the true multi-party situations should also be added more complex arbitrations arising among parties working together based on a series of related contracts, where there is no single contract, or single arbitration clause, linking all parties together, which is the case with large construction contracts.

4.16 Since the typical arbitration involves two parties, the application of a typical arbitration clause in a multi-party context raises problems with respect to the appointment of arbitrators. Where possible, the general approach is to separate the parties into two groups in relation to each issue. Then, in the manner described above, each group appoints one arbitrator and the two arbitrators so appointed select a third. It would appear that the several parties in each group must be unanimous in their choice of an arbitrator (or arbitrators). If unanimity cannot be attained, no valid appointment can be made and the rules under which a substitute appointment is to be made become applicable. The SAA has no specific provision concerning the appointment of arbitrators in these circumstances, since the legislator's view was that it should be the responsibility of the parties to agree on these issues. However, pursuant to section 12(3), the District Court has a general duty to appoint arbitrators where the parties have so agreed and any of the parties so requests.

4.17 Most national arbitration laws do not provide for a mechanism governing multi-party arbitration proceedings. Moreover, they do not generally provide for consolidation, joinder, or any other practical solutions which may assist in disputes involving more than two parties. The SAA is no exception. The provisions of the Swedish Procedural Code on consolidation of separate but related court proceedings, or joinder of related claims, are not applicable to arbitrations. Any solution in this respect must thus be sought on the basis of the fundamental principle of arbitration, ie freedom of contract, the will of the parties, or put differently: the initiative, or at least the final say, must always rest with the parties. In practice consolidation and/or joinder may, however, be the only preferable and logical way forward to avoid conflicting decisions and also increased costs in arbitration proceedings. Accordingly, in a multi-party situation parties are often well-advised to agree to have the dispute resolved in accordance with any of the institutional rules that provide guidance and practical assistance in relation to multi party situations. For example, the SCC Rules include both rules with respect to appointment of arbitrators in multi-party disputes and rules on consolidation of related cases.[9]

---

[9] See also eg Article 10 of the ICC Rules and Article 8 of the LCIA Rules.

4.1.3 Rules

4.1.3.1 SCC

While the SCC Rules do not differ substantially from the SAA in terms of the **4.18** composition of the tribunal and the appointment of arbitrators, some variations do exist. Essentially, under the SCC Rules, the Board has the same role and function as the District Court has under the SAA. Absent any agreement to the contrary,[10] the arbitral tribunal shall consist of three members (Article 12 of the SCC Rules), of which the parties choose one each. Instead of the two party-appointed arbitrators appointing the third, however, it is the responsibility of the Board of the SCC Institute to make that appointment (Article 13(2) of the SCC Rules). The SCC Rules further prescribe, as a general rule, that if the parties are of different nationalities, the sole arbitrator or the chairman of the arbitral tribunal shall be of a different nationality than the parties (Article 13(5) of the SCC Rules).

The SCC Institute does not have a list of arbitrators. When appointing arbitrators, **4.19** the SCC Board seeks to appoint the individual who is the arbitrator best suited for the arbitration in question. In so doing, the SCC Board takes into account a number of considerations, including experience in general, experience of the particular kind of dispute, language skills, familiarity with the applicable law, availability etc. Although there is no specific provision in the SCC Rules as regards language skills, the SCC Board always tries to appoint an arbitrator who is conversant in the language of arbitration.

There are three special features of the SCC Rules that are noteworthy in this respect, **4.20** viz, the Rules for Expedited Arbitration, the Rules for Emergency Arbitrations, and the provisions concerning multi-party arbitrations.

Rules for expedited arbitration The parties may agree to resolve a dispute in **4.21** accordance with the SCC Rules for Expedited Arbitration (Expedited Rules). The Expedited Rules were primarily developed for minor disputes regarding less complex issues and involving a smaller amount in dispute. The parties may, however, agree to use them with respect to any kind of dispute. The Expedited Rules offer a speedy and cost-efficient dispute resolution, so-called 'fast track arbitration', and have become very popular in recent years.[11] Today the SCC administers both domestic and international arbitration cases under the Expedited Rules.

It is up to the parties to decide whether to use the Expedited Rules or the ordinary **4.22** SCC Rules. They can so decide in the arbitration agreement, or once the dispute has

---

[10] Contrary to the UNCITRAL Arbitration Rules and the ICC Rules, the SCC Rules thus permit the arbitral tribunal to consist of more than three arbitrators.

[11] Statistics show that of 215 new cases registered at the SCC Institute in 2009, 60 (or 28 per cent) were cases applying the Expedited Rules, see SCC Statistical Report 2009 at <http://www.sccinstitute.se>. It must, however, be noted that only eight of these cases were international, with parties primarily from Scandinavia; the Expenses Rules are reproduced in Appendix 2.

arisen. Another option is to leave it to the SCC to determine which set of rules should be applied, taking into account the complexity of the matter, the amount in dispute, and other relevant circumstances.

4.23 One key feature of the Expedited Rules is that the arbitral tribunal always consists of a sole arbitrator (Article 12) who is always appointed by the SCC Board. In making such appointments the Board usually regards extensive arbitration experience as important.

4.24 **Rules for Emergency Arbitrators** In some disputes it may be important for a party to be able to secure that assets or important documents are preserved. One way of accomplishing this is to order interim measures. Examples of interim measures are orders to maintain or restore the status quo, orders to take action, or to refrain from taking action, and orders to preserve evidence pending determination of the dispute.

4.25 Under the 2007 SCC Rules, and under previous versions of the SCC Rules, a party to an arbitration agreement could not request interim measures until the case had been referred to the arbitrators, which may take up to two to three months in international arbitrations.

4.26 The 2010 SCC Rules give the parties the option of requesting the appointment of an Emergency Arbitrator with the authority to order interim measures before the case is referred to an arbitral tribunal or to a sole arbitrator. The rules entered into force on 1 January 2010 and are set out in Appendix II to the SCC Rules.[12] The rules apply to every arbitration commenced on or after 2 January 2010. Consequently, it is possible to appoint an Emergency Arbitrator also with respect to arbitration agreements entered into prior to 1 January 2010.

4.27 At the application of a party, the Board of the SCC Institute will seek to appoint an Emergency Arbitrator within 24 hours (Article 4(1)). The parties undertake to comply with any emergency decisions without delay (Article 9(3)). The emergency decision ceases to be binding, *inter alia*, if the Emergency Arbitrator or an arbitral tribunal so decides, or if arbitration is not commenced within 30 days from the date of the emergency decision (Article 9(4)(i) and (iii)). In any event, the emergency decision is replaced by the final award (Article 9(4)(ii)). It is important to note that the Emergency Arbitrator cannot act as an arbitrator in any future arbitration relating to the dispute, unless the parties agree otherwise (Article 4(4)).

---

[12] The first case under the rules for Emergency Arbitrators was decided in April 2010. For comments on the Emergency Rules, see eg Shaughnessy, 'The New SCC Emergency Arbitrator Rules', in Hobér, Magnusson, and Öhrström (eds), *Between East and West: Essays in Honour of Ulf Franke* (2010) 459; Brower-Meyerstein-Schill, 'The Power and Effectiveness of Pre-arbitral Provisional Relief: The SCC Emergency Arbitrator in Investor—State Disputes', in Hobér, Magnusson, and Öhrström (eds), *op cit* at 61.

Multi-party arbitration   In contrast to the SAA, the SCC Rules do have provisions   **4.28**
addressing some of the difficulties in relation to multi-party arbitrations.[13] Article
13(4) of the SCC Rules, dealing with the appointment of arbitrators, reads as
follows:

> Where there are multiple Claimants or Respondents and the Arbitral Tribunal is to
> consist of more than one arbitrator, the multiple Claimants, jointly, and the multiple
> Respondents, jointly, shall appoint an equal number of arbitrators. If either side fails to
> make such joint appointment, the Board shall appoint the entire Arbitral Tribunal.[14]

Article 11 of the SCC Rules addressing consolidation has the following wording: **4.29**

> If arbitration is commenced concerning a legal relationship in respect of which an
> arbitration between the same parties is already pending under these Rules, the Board
> may, at the request of a party, decide to consolidate the new claims with the pending
> proceedings. Such decision may only be made after consulting the parties and the
> Arbitral Tribunal.

The provision in Article 13(4) of the SCC Rules, to the effect that the Board shall   **4.30**
appoint the entire arbitral tribunal if the multiple parties on either side do not agree
on a joint appointment of an arbitrator, is in line with the decision in the so-called
Dutco case.[15] In this case, a dispute arose out of a consortium contract for the
construction of a cement plant in Oman. One of the members of the consortium,
Dutco, brought an arbitration against the other two members, Siemens and BKMI.
Its claims against its partners were separate and quite dissimilar. In accordance with
the then applicable ICC Rules, the respondents had to agree on a joint arbitrator,
failing which the ICC Court would select an arbitrator for them both. Siemens and
BKMI protested and maintained that they wanted the same opportunity as the
claimant to appoint their own arbitrator.

Challenged in court, the ICC practice was upheld by the Paris Court of Appeal, but   **4.31**
the Cour de Cassation (the Supreme Court) held that the ICC practice violated the
principle of 'equality of the parties', which the Court held to be a matter of non-
waivable *ordre public* under French law. Moreover, the Court found that this
inequality of treatment violated the French new code of civil procedure,[16] which
provides for the setting aside of an award in cases where the arbitral tribunal was
irregularly constituted.

---

[13] Cf para 4.13 *et seq.*

[14] Cf eg Article 10 of the ICC Rules which stipulates that where there are multiple parties on either
side, the claimants, jointly, and the respondents, jointly, shall nominate an arbitrator for confirmation if the dispute is to be decided by three arbitrators. In the absence of such a joint nomination and
where all parties are unable to agree to a method for the constitution of the arbitral tribunal, the ICC
Court may appoint each member of the arbitral tribunal and shall designate one of them to act as
chairman.

[15] *Siemens AG and BKMI Industrianlagen GmbH v Dutco Consortium Construction Co*, Cour de
Cassation, Première chambre civile, 7 January 1992, France, 1992 Rev Arb 470. See also Craig, Park,
and Paulsson, *International Chamber of Commerce Arbitration* (3rd edn, 2000) 198–202.

[16] Article 1502(2) of the *Nouveau code de procédure civile*.

4.32   The SCC Rules thus adopts the French interpretation of the principle of 'equality of the parties' by providing for appointment of the entire arbitral tribunal by the SCC Board. From a Swedish law perspective, however, such interpretation could be called into question. For example, why should a party who has successfully appointed its arbitrator be 'punished' because opposing parties fail to agree on a joint arbitrator, in some instances only by way of obstruction? In this respect it should be noted that, in contrast to the SCC Rules, under the ICC Rules, the ICC Court retains the discretion to permit one party to nominate its arbitrator while itself making the appointment on behalf of the defaulting joint parties.[17] In practice, this option is reserved only for unusual cases, eg where it is obvious that there is obstruction.

4.33   With respect to the appointment of arbitrators, it should also be noted that section 12(3) of the SAA includes a provision that may be applied in a multi-party situation. In accordance with this provision the relevant District Court shall appoint arbitrators, at the request of one of the parties, provided that the parties have so agreed, also in other situations than where the court may step in and appoint an arbitrator for a party, or where two party-appointed arbitrators fail to agree on a chairman.[18] Pursuant to sections 14–17 of the SAA, based on an agreement to this effect, the parties may thus also leave it to the District Court to appoint arbitrators in a multi-party dispute under the SAA.

4.34   Article 11 of the SCC Rules deals with consolidation of arbitration proceedings. The SAA does not have any provisions dealing with consolidation. The explanation is simple: it is up to the parties to agree on consolidation. It is clear from the wording of Article 11 that its scope of application is limited. The provision does not deal at all with the question of appointment of arbitrators. Presumably, this must be one of the issues to be dealt with during the consultations with the parties and the arbitral tribunal, in the already pending arbitration.

4.35   Whereas institutional rules may thus resolve some of the difficulties in multi-party situations, there are other various specific problems which still need to be overcome. These problems include the language of the arbitration (in case of consolidation of disputes with different languages applied), procedure (for example conflicting procedural rules), disclosure of documents to all parties in consolidated proceedings, the right for all parties to cross-examine all witnesses in consolidated proceedings, and enforcement.[19]

---

   [17] Cf Article 10(2) of the ICC Rules which stipulates that 'in the absence of such a joint nomination and where all parties are unable to agree to a method for the constitution of the Arbitral Tribunal, the Court may appoint each member of the Arbitral Tribunal and shall designate one of them to act as chairman' (emphasis added). See Craig, Park, and Paulsson, *International Chamber of Commerce Arbitration* (3rd edn, 2000) 201.
   [18] See para 4.09 *et seq.*
   [19] See para 4.13 *et seq.*

4.1.3.2 Other rules

UNCITRAL   The 1976 UNCITRAL Arbitration Rules have provisions concerning the composition of the tribunal (Article 5)—under which three-arbitrator tribunals are the main rule—the appointment of arbitrators (Articles 6–8), the replacement of arbitrators (Article 13), and the repetition of hearings upon such replacement (Article 14).   **4.36**

One practically important aspect of the UNCITRAL Rules is the role played by the so-called appointing authority. By and large it fulfils the function of an arbitration institution when it comes to the appointment and replacement of arbitrators. If the parties have not agreed on an appointing authority, the Secretary-General of the Permanent Court of Arbitration in The Hague will, at the request of one of the parties, designate an appointing authority.   **4.37**

ICC   Like the 1976 UNCITRAL Arbitration Rules, the ICC Rules provide for either a sole arbitrator or a three-arbitrator tribunal (Article 8(1)). Where the dispute is to be referred to three arbitrators, each party nominates one arbitrator for confirmation by the ICC Court of Arbitration (the Court) (Article 8(4)).[20] The third arbitrator, who will act as chairman of the arbitral tribunal, is appointed by the Court, unless the parties have agreed upon another procedure for such appointment, in which case the nomination will be subject to confirmation by the Court (Article 8(4)). A sole arbitrator or the chairman of the arbitral tribunal shall, as a general rule, be of a nationality other than those of the parties (Article 9(5)). Where there are multiple parties on either side, Article 10(1) provides that the claimants, jointly, and the respondents, jointly, nominate an arbitrator for confirmation if the dispute is to be decided by three arbitrators. In the absence of such a joint nomination and where all parties are unable to agree on a method for the constitution of the arbitral tribunal, the Court may appoint each member of the arbitral tribunal and shall designate one of them to act as chairman (Article 10(2)).[21]   **4.38**

4.2 Qualifications of Arbitrators

Section 7 of the SAA stipulates that any person who enjoys full legal capacity in regard to his actions and his property may act as an arbitrator under the SAA.   **4.39**

---

[20] The confirmation procedure in relation to the party-nominated arbitrators does not have its counterpart under the SCC Rules. In confirming or appointing arbitrators, the Court shall consider the prospective arbitrator's nationality, residence, and other relationships with the countries of which the parties or the other arbitrators are nationals and the prospective arbitrator's availability and ability to conduct the arbitration in accordance with the ICC Rules. In practice the Court's actions are focused on the assurance of consistency in the qualification of the chairmen and sole arbitrators it appoints, whereas its function in confirming party-nominated arbitrators is quite limited. See Craig, Park, and Paulsson, *International Chamber of Commerce Arbitration* (3rd edn, 2000) 194 *et seq.*

[21] See para 4.30. Cf Article 13(4) of the SCC Rules.

An arbitrator must thus be of full age and cannot have a trustee or be bankrupt.[22] This requirement is considered to be 'absolute' in the sense that it applies irrespective of who the parties are and what the nature of the dispute is,[23] whereas section 8 lists grounds which disqualify a person from acting as an arbitrator with respect to a particular dispute.[24] As will be discussed below,[25] pursuant to section 9, a person who is asked to accept an appointment as arbitrator is obliged immediately to disclose all circumstances which might prevent him from serving in this capacity.

4.40 Sections 7, 8, and 9 of the SAA illustrate the balance between two opposite interests: on the one hand the principle of party autonomy, ie a party's right freely to choose an arbitrator, and on the other hand, a party's right to timely and exhaustive information in order to be able to make well-informed and independent decisions on whether certain circumstances are sufficient to try to have an arbitrator replaced.[26]

4.41 The parties are free to add any further criteria which must be met by the arbitrators. Similarly, it would seem that the parties are at liberty to agree in advance on a waiver of specific grounds of disqualification so long as this agreement is made with full knowledge of all relevant circumstances. Such a waiver may, however, not be so broad and general as to encompass section 34 of the SAA in its entirety.[27] An exception in this respect is made where none of the parties is domiciled or has its place of business in Sweden. In such cases the parties in a commercial relationship may exclude or limit the application of the grounds in section 34 for setting aside an award through an agreement in writing, a so-called exclusion agreement.[28]

4.42 It follows from the foregoing that under Swedish law, arbitrators need not be lawyers. In practice, however, the overwhelming majority of arbitrators sitting in Sweden are lawyers. On the other hand, in construction disputes it is not unusual to find engineers as arbitrators. Auditors and accountants also sit as arbitrators from time to time in disputes concerning the valuation of shares and businesses. Even in such disputes, however, the presiding arbitrator is normally a lawyer. Also, if the dispute is to be heard before a sole arbitrator, the generally accepted practice is to appoint a lawyer. Even if the dispute is relatively small and simple, as far as the merits are concerned, it may give rise to complicated procedural issues which are typically better addressed by a lawyer.

---

[22] The participation in the arbitral tribunal of a person who does not enjoy full legal capacity does not render an arbitral award *invalid*. A party must thus *challenge* the award in order to have it set aside on this basis (see section 34(5) of the SAA).

[23] Govt Bill 1998/99:35, p 82.

[24] For a discussion of section 8, see para 4.62 *et seq*.

[25] See para 4.70.

[26] See Hobér, 'Intressekonflikter och skiljeförfaranden—Vägmärken och trafiksignaler från IBA', in Nord and Thorell, *Intressekonflikter och Finansiella marknader* (2006) 228.

[27] Govt Bill 1998/99:35, pp 156–159.

[28] Cf section 51 of the SAA, discussed in para 8.187.

As mentioned above, it is possible for the parties to agree on specific qualifications **4.43** for the arbitrators. The parties may, for example, require experience of a particular business or sector of the economy. This seems to be relatively common in the commodity trades, in the insurance and re-insurance industries and in shipping. While the parties are free to include such, or similar, qualifications, experience shows that they often create more problems for the parties: unless defined in detail, they often invite different interpretations which in turn have the potential of delaying the arbitration, or otherwise creating problems. In most cases, it is wiser to decide which qualifications the arbitrator should have once the dispute has arisen, but not before.

As far as professional qualifications, in general, of arbitrators are concerned, it is for **4.44** the parties to take the decision. It will depend on the character and complexity of the individual dispute and on the strategy decided by the party with respect to the dispute in question. Generally speaking, however, an arbitrator must have an adequate knowledge of the language of the arbitration, at least such that he or she can review briefs and documentation and understand oral argument. Another general requirement, in the view of most parties, is that the person in question has some previous experience of international commercial arbitration, either in general, or of a particular category of disputes.

During the last 15–20 years, it has become increasingly common for prospective **4.45** arbitrators to be asked to participate in interviews conducted by the party—usually its counsel—who is contemplating an appointment of the person in question. There is nothing in the SAA, nor otherwise in Swedish law, prohibiting such interviews. It is up to the prospective arbitrator in question to decide if, and to what extent, he is willing to participate in such interviews. As will be discussed below,[29] under Swedish arbitration law all arbitrators—ie not only the chairperson—must be and remain impartial and independent. This rule is therefore the ultimate borderline beyond which interviews with prospective arbitrators cannot go. Any discussion during an interview of the case in question, or of potential legal issues in the case, will risk putting the impartiality and independence of the prospective arbitrator in jeopardy.

4.3 Powers and Duties of Arbitrators

The powers and duties of arbitrators are closely linked with the question of their **4.46** jurisdiction and the difficult question of determining the validity of the arbitration agreement. The powers of the arbitrators arise when the tribunal is constituted.[30] Unless an arbitrator resigns or otherwise ceases to be a member of the tribunal

---

[29] See para 4.62.
[30] See, however, the powers of an Emergency Arbitrator as discussed in para 4.24.

during the proceedings, his authority lasts, in principle, until the arbitration agreement terminates with respect to the dispute which the tribunal was constituted to hear.[31] Normally, this coincides with the rendering of the final award, see section 27(4) of the SAA.[32] However, under section 32 of the SAA, an arbitrator retains the power—and has a residual duty—to correct obvious defects or errors (such as miscalculations) in the award, as well as to interpret the operative part of an award.[33] Further, pursuant to section 35 of the SAA, a court of law may provide the arbitrators with an opportunity to resume the arbitration proceedings by staying challenge proceedings concerning an award for a certain period of time. This option is available if the arbitrators believe that the ground for the invalidity or setting aside may thereby be eliminated.[34] Section 35 further requires either that the court is of the opinion that the challenge will be successful and one of the parties requests such a stay, or that both parties agree to resume the arbitration proceedings. The termination of the arbitrator's authority, or his becoming *functus officio*, is but one aspect of the termination of the arbitration agreement.[35]

4.47 The powers of an arbitral tribunal are those conferred upon it by the parties within the limits allowed by the applicable law.[36] In general terms, the arbitrators enjoy broad powers to determine the appropriate procedure, however, subject to observing the requirements of due process, ie equality of treatment and an opportunity to be heard.[37]

4.48 The starting point for determining the arbitral tribunal's powers is the arbitration agreement and the *lex arbitri*, including powers with respect to the conduct of the arbitration proceedings. Such powers are likely to include the power to order production of documents, to appoint experts, to hold hearings, to require the presence of witnesses, to receive evidence, etc. Particular powers may also be conferred by the parties' reference to institutional rules of arbitration, which set out the powers of the tribunal. As mentioned, the powers of the arbitral tribunal also follow from the *lex arbitri*. For example, under section 22 of the SAA, the arbitrators have the power to determine the place of arbitration, should the parties not have agreed thereon, and also to decide to hold hearings and other meetings elsewhere in Sweden or abroad, unless otherwise agreed by the parties.

4.49 As explained above, the basic philosophy underlying Swedish arbitration law is that the arbitrators derive their authority from the parties, by virtue of the arbitration

---

[31] See para 3.168 *et seq* for a discussion of when the arbitration agreement terminates.
[32] See para 7.84.
[33] See para 7.137 *et seq*.
[34] See para 8.01 *et seq*, where the challenge proceedings are discussed in detail.
[35] See discussion in Chapter 3.
[36] So far as the arbitrators' *powers* are concerned, the applicable law is usually the proper law of the arbitration agreement, often in combination with the law of the place of arbitration, ie the *lex arbitri*; for discussion of applicable law generally, see Chapter 2.
[37] See para 6.64 *et seq* for a discussion of the conduct of the arbitration, including due process.

agreement. This is confirmed and enshrined in the SAA, ie in a statute, but does not change the consensual nature of the origin of the arbitrator's powers. This origin explains why arbitrators are not empowered to exercise any governmental authority. For example, they have no subpoena powers, and therefore cannot compel parties or witnesses to appear, or to do, or not do, certain things. The contractual nature of the powers of the arbitrators also explains why arbitrators cannot administer oaths under Swedish law. This is expressly stipulated in section 25(3) of the SAA.

In the same manner as the powers of arbitrators, duties may be imposed on them **4.50** by the parties or by the applicable law. In addition, duties of arbitrators may be imposed by ethical rules, eg rules of a national bar association.[38] The duties imposed by the parties are either initial, ie duties which follow the acceptance of an appointment as arbitrator, or duties imposed on the arbitrators during the course of the proceedings. Duties imposed by law include, for example, that the arbitrators shall handle the dispute in an impartial and speedy manner,[39] that the arbitrators shall afford the parties an opportunity to present their respective cases, and that the award must be in writing.[40]

Stated in general terms, the duty of the arbitrators—while observing the aforemen- **4.51** tioned fundamental principles—is to decide the dispute before them on the basis of the facts, arguments, and evidence presented by the parties. The duty cannot be to find out the 'truth', or to take 'the right decision'. It is for the parties, not the arbitrators, to determine the scope and complexity of their dispute.[41] Needless to say, every arbitrator has the desire and ambition to take 'the right decision', but it is not a duty in the legal sense of the word.

4.4 Relation of Arbitrators to the Parties

The legal nature of an arbitrator's mandate is a much debated issue.[42] The question of **4.52** practical importance in this respect is whether or not an arbitrator may be held liable for malpractice and, if so, what the remedy is. Or, do the arbitrators enjoy immunity?

---

[38] It may be noted that the IBA adopted its 'Rules of Ethics for International Arbitrators' in 1987. This is a set of principles designed to assist international arbitrators as to how the required arbitrator qualities of impartiality, competence, diligence, and discretion might be applied in practice in order to ensure a degree of harmonization in the approach of arbitrators to these ethical issues. The 1987 Rules of Ethics have partially been replaced by the IBA Guidelines on the Conflict of Interest in International Arbitration, adopted in 2004.

[39] See section 21 of the SAA.

[40] See ibid, section 31.

[41] This approach raises a number of other issues, many of them linked to the concept of *iura novit curia*, see discussion at para 6.69 *et seq*.

[42] Heuman, *Skiljemannarätt* (1999) 216 *et seq*; Schöldström, *The Arbitrator's Mandate* (1998) 139 *et seq*; Lindskog, *op cit*, 410 *et seq*. See also Schöldström, 'Contractual Relations in Institutional Arbitration', in Hobér, Magnusson, and Öhrström, *op cit*, at 451 *et seq*; Söderlund, 'The Parties' Contract with the Arbitration Institution', ibid, at 487 *et seq*.

4.53 At the outset, it is important to note that there is no provision in the SAA addressing this issue, nor are there any reported cases where parties have tried—let alone successfully—to hold arbitrators liable in damages for their professional activities as arbitrators.

4.54 There are two principal views with respect to the legal nature of the arbitrator's mandate, viz, the contract theory and the status theory.[43] In addition, and as mentioned above, arbitrators may also be bound by certain ethical rules.

4.55 Under the *contract theory*, which used to be the prevailing view in Swedish arbitration doctrine,[44] the mandate of an arbitrator is viewed as a specific type of trusteeship agreement. Under the *status theory*, however, the arbitrator's authority and obligations are fundamentally derived from statutory provisions. Each theory raises questions. For instance, it could be argued that the contract theory fails to explain how a party-appointed arbitrator has received a mandate from the other party as well. As to the status theory, it does not set out the extent to which the arbitrator's powers and obligations could be modified by way of agreement. It therefore appears reasonable to make the assumption that the relationship between the arbitrator and the parties combines elements of both theories.[45] It is more helpful to regard and treat it as a *sui generis* legal relationship, which does not need a specific label. In addition to duties of an arbitrator imposed by the parties under the contract theory and the duties imposed by law under the status theory, ethical duties may, as stated above, also apply. For example, a Swedish lawyer who is a member of the Swedish Bar Association must always observe the Code of Conduct of the Swedish Bar Association.[46]

4.56 As mentioned, the liability of arbitrators is not addressed in the SAA, nor is there any case law on this issue. In this sense, it is thus an open issue under Swedish law. On the other hand, it would seem clear that arbitrators do not enjoy immunity, at least, it is submitted, not absolute immunity. This would have required explicit statutory provisions, of which there are none. At the same time it is telling that there are no reported cases where arbitrators have been held liable for their activities as arbitrators. While it is generally accepted that the relationship between the parties and the arbitrators is contractual and that its nature is that of a trusteeship, it would not be reasonable to apply the rules regarding trusteeships lock, stock, and

---

[43] It could be argued that there is also a mixed or hybrid theory, which includes a mixture of the contract and the status theories. Commentators who support it believe that the reality lies somewhere between the contractual and status theories, since the arbitrator's duty is to adjudicate, to decide the dispute, but the power to do so is conferred on him by the agreement of the parties.

[44] Schöldström, *The Arbitrator's Mandate* (1998) 138–142; Lindskog, *Skiljeförfarande, En kommentar* (2005) 410; and *Arbitration in Sweden* (2nd revised edn, 1984) 78, footnote 26.

[45] Heuman, *Skiljemannarätt* (1999) 219–220.

[46] The Code of Conduct provides a framework for the professional and ethical standards to be observed in lawyers' professional activities. It contains rules on running a law firm, on fees, on relations to the opposite party and to the court, and on conflicts of interest, see <http://www.advokatsamfundet.se>.

barrel without taking into account the special character of the relationship between arbitrators and parties, which makes it a *sui generis* relationship.

To hold an arbitrator liable for his adjudication activities—eg alleged misapplication **4.57** of law, or alleged inadequate analysis of facts and evidence—would seem inappropriate and would run counter to the philosophy and principles underlying challenges of arbitral awards, ie that they can never be retried on the merits. Arbitral awards cannot be set aside on the basis of the aforementioned grounds. If arbitrators could be held liable in this situation, the same result would be achieved, albeit indirectly. Such a state of affairs would undermine the independence and integrity of the arbitrator as decision-maker. Ultimately this is a policy decision. It is submitted that it has never been the policy of the Swedish legislator to accept that arbitrators could be subject to reprisals by disgruntled parties.

At the same time, there are certain situations where arbitrators could, and probably **4.58** would, be held liable. For example, if the arbitrator has committed a crime under Swedish law—eg acceptance of a bribe—damages are available. If an arbitrator has committed gross violations of due process, which have resulted in significant damage to one of the parties, this may also be a situation where the arbitrator may be liable in damages. Another situation might be if an award is set aside based on circumstances which the arbitrator had a duty to disclose, but did not, having a bearing on his impartiality and independence. It is possible that liability could also result if an arbitrator resigns without a valid reason.

It thus seems clear that there is a theoretical basis for holding arbitrators liable in **4.59** damages in certain circumstances. As a practical matter, however, given the absence of mandatory provisions as well as reported cases, Swedish arbitration law remains agnostic with respect to this issue.

In this context it is important to note Article 48 of the SCC Rules which excludes the **4.60** liability of the SCC and arbitrators acting under the SCC Rules. The provision reads:

> Neither the SCC nor the arbitrator(s) are liable to any party for any act or omission in connection with the arbitration rules unless such act or omission constitutes wilful misconduct or gross negligence.

Similar provisions are found in the ICC Rules and in the LCIA Rules. **4.61**

4.5 Challenge and Replacement of Arbitrators

4.5.1 The SAA

4.5.1.1 Grounds for challenge. Disclosure

The fundamental principle that an arbitrator, whether party-appointed or not, **4.62** must be impartial is enshrined in section 8 of the SAA. Thus, the concept of 'non-neutral' arbitrators is unknown to Swedish law. In addition, most arbitration institutions set forth the requirement of independence in their rules.[47] The concept of 'independence' is concerned exclusively with the relationship between an arbitrator and one of the parties, whether financial or otherwise. By contrast, the concept of 'impartiality' is concerned with the bias of an arbitrator, either in favour of one of the parties, or in relation to the subject matter of the dispute. Although the SAA does not specifically provide for independence, this is deemed to be implied in the requirement of impartiality.

4.63 At the request of one of the parties, an arbitrator shall be disqualified if there exists any circumstance which may diminish confidence in the arbitrator's impartiality. Whereas the arbitration laws of some countries simply refer to the national rules concerning impartiality of judges, the drafters of the SAA considered such a solution unsatisfactory. Taking into account that non-lawyers may serve as arbitrators and that foreign arbitrators must be able to apply the provisions, it was deemed more appropriate to include specific guidance in the SAA itself.[48] Section 8 therefore lists four situations in which such a circumstance shall always be deemed to exist:

   (1) Where the arbitrator, or a person closely associated with him, is a party, or otherwise may expect considerable benefit, or detriment, as a result of the outcome of the dispute;
   (2) Where the arbitrator, or a person closely associated with him, is the director of a company or any other association which is a party, or otherwise representing a party or any other person who may expect considerable benefit, or detriment, as a result of the outcome of the dispute;
   (3) Where the arbitrator has taken a position in the dispute, as an expert or otherwise, or has assisted a party in the preparation or conduct of his case in the dispute; or
   (4) Where the arbitrator has received or demanded compensation in violation of section 39, second paragraph.

4.64 It should be noted that the list is merely illustrative. The situations listed are thus not meant to exclude other situations in which an arbitrator may fail to satisfy the requirement of impartiality.[49]

4.65 The first two situations mentioned in section 8, and to some extent the third, address not only lack of impartiality, but also doubts as to the arbitrator's independence. Thus, the scope of impartiality (and independence) under the SAA is no different from the scope of impartiality and independence under the UNCITRAL Model Law.[50]

4.66 More specifically, sections 8(1) and (2) of the SAA set out grounds for disqualification based on *interest* in the subject matter of the dispute and *bias* towards one of

---

[47] See, *inter alia*, Article 14(1) of the SCC Rules, Article 7(1) of the ICC Rules, and Article 5.2 of the LCIA Rules.

[48] Govt Bill 1998/99:35, p 83.

[49] The rule laid down in section 8 of the SAA corresponds to Article 12 of the UNCITRAL Model Law.

[50] Hobér, 'Arbitration Reform in Sweden' 17(4) *Arbitration International* (2001) 362.

the parties. Such interest may be either direct or indirect. Examples of the latter include when a person, closely associated with the arbitrator, is a party or when the arbitrator or a person closely associated with him is the director of a company or any other association which is a party to the dispute. In addition, any interest—direct or through a person closely associated with him—in the outcome of the dispute, whether beneficial or detrimental, would disqualify the arbitrator. Moreover, a biased arbitrator would certainly be disqualified, although bias is usually very difficult to establish.

Pursuant to section 8(3) of the SAA, an arbitrator may be disqualified where he has **4.67** taken a position with respect to the dispute in question, as an expert or otherwise, or where he has assisted a party in the preparation or conduct of his case in the dispute. This does not include, however, situations where, eg a scholar has written a book or an article in which he has taken a position *in abstracto* with respect to a legal or technical question which is relevant to the dispute.

The arbitrator is also disqualified in accordance with section 8(4) of the SAA if he **4.68** has received or demanded compensation privately from one of the parties.[51]

In this respect it should also be mentioned that, pursuant to section 17 of the SAA, **4.69** an arbitrator may also be discharged if he delays the proceedings. In such cases, the District Court shall, upon request by a party, discharge the arbitrator and appoint a replacement. The parties may decide that such a request shall, instead, finally be determined by an arbitration institute. The arbitrator may be discharged even if he has not intentionally attempted to obstruct the proceedings or been negligent.[52]

Section 9 of the SAA imposes a disclosure obligation on the arbitrators. A person **4.70** who is asked to accept an appointment as arbitrator is required to disclose immediately all circumstances which might cause him to be regarded as incapacitated or not impartial. He must inform the parties of such circumstances, as well as the other arbitrators, when all arbitrators have been appointed. The obligation to disclose such circumstances is continuing throughout the arbitration proceedings. This means that the arbitrator must disclose any new circumstance in this respect as soon as he learns of it.

In *AJ v Ericsson* (NJA 2007 p 841), the Swedish Supreme Court addressed several **4.71** questions concerning the impartiality of arbitrators. In a dispute involving Ericsson, the chairman of the tribunal, appointed by the two party-appointed arbitrators, was employed on a part-time basis with a law firm whose client Ericsson was. The law firm in question was not involved in the dispute in question, but was retained from time to time by Ericsson in various legal matters. Ericsson was deemed to be an important client of the firm by the Supreme Court. The major issue in the case was whether the part-time consultancy of the chairman was sufficient to raise

---

[51] Such an arrangement would also be void in accordance with section 39(2) of the SAA.
[52] Govt Bill 1998/99, p 223.

justifiable doubts as to his impartiality. The court thus had to address the general and overarching rule in section 8, not one of the enumerated specific situations in the provision. The Svea Court of Appeal found that the circumstances were such so as to give rise to justifiable doubts. It therefore set aside the award.[53] In affirming this decision, the Supreme Court made several interesting comments. First, it explained that the determination of whether or not the circumstances give rise to justifiable doubts must be made on the basis of objective grounds and not on the basis of a risk assessment in the specific case. In order to make this determination, the Court therefore discussed in detail the nature as well as the practical arrangements of the contract that the chairman had with the law firm. Secondly, on the basis thereof, the Court concluded that there was no reason to treat the chairman differently than other employees, eg. associates, of the law firm. A third interesting observation is that in its reasons the Court referred to the IBA Guidelines on Conflicts of Interest in International Arbitration.[54] The Court did not strictly speaking apply the Guidelines, but apparently found support for its conclusions in the Guidelines.

4.72 The claimant in the case also argued that the chairman had failed to disclose the circumstances in question and that such failure in and of itself, or combined with the other circumstances of the case, gave rise to justifiable doubts as to his impartiality. In its reasons, however, the Supreme Court did not address this aspect of the case. This aspect was, however, dealt with by the Supreme Court in its most recent case on the impartiality of arbitrators, *Korsnäs Aktiebolag v AB Fortum Värme* decided on 9 June 2010.[55] The main issue in this case was whether the impartiality of an arbitrator could be put in question on the basis that he had been appointed by the same law firm on several occasions. During a ten-year period—1995–2005—the arbitrator in question had been appointed arbitrator in 112 disputes. In twelve of those disputes he had been appointed by the law firm in question. Between 2002 and 2005, he sat as arbitrator in four cases where the law firm in question was involved as counsel. In two of those cases he was chairman and in the remaining two he was appointed by the law firm in question. The Supreme Court concluded that these facts were not sufficient to raise doubts as to the impartiality of the arbitrator. The Court noted, *inter alia*, that the majority of appointments of the arbitrator came from other law firms.

4.73 The claimant in the case also argued that the arbitrator had failed to disclose his previous appointments by the law firm in question and that this failure gave rise to justifiable doubts as to his impartiality. The Supreme Court did not agree. The Court explained, referring to a statement in the Government Bill,[56] that the failure

---

[53] As discussed at para 8.114, lack of impartiality is a ground to have an arbitral award set aside on the basis of section 34 of the SAA.

[54] See para 4.75 *et seq.*

[55] Docket no: T156-09.

[56] Govt Bill 1998/99:35, p 219.

to disclose relevant circumstances may be a factor to take into account, but only in borderline situations. In the view of the Court this case was not such a borderline situation.

It is worth noting that in both cases discussed above, the Supreme Court has made **4.74** reference to the IBA Guidelines on Conflicts of Interest in International Arbitration. Even though the Guidelines have not been applied *strictu senso*, it is a prudent approach to seek guidance from them since questions relating to the impartiality and independence of arbitrators are often difficult and complex. In addition there is, generally speaking, a lack of case law in this area, as well as a lack of reasoned decisions from arbitration institutions. It would therefore seem reasonable to assume that the Guidelines will continue to play an important role in this respect.

IBA Guidelines on Conflict of Interest in International Arbitration The IBA **4.75** Guidelines[57] are the result of two years of work in a working group of nineteen arbitration experts from common law and civil law countries. The objective of the working group was to draw up several General Standards with respect to conflicts of interest to be applied by practitioners who participate in (i) the appointment of arbitrators, (ii) the disqualification of arbitrators, and (iii) the determination of arbitrators' duty of disclosure. The working group identified seven such General Standards based on, *inter alia*, the legal practice from the countries represented in the working group as well as the practice at several arbitration institutions. In addition to the General Standards, the IBA Guidelines include so-called Application Lists. The General Standards and the Application Lists are summarized below.

As an initial remark, it must be stressed that the IBA Guidelines are not binding, **4.76** unless the parties so agree. Applicable law and the parties' agreements in relation to these issues thus take precedence over the IBA Guidelines. The working group emphasized that the IBA Guidelines must be applied with a good portion of common sense and without a formalistic approach. Although not binding on a practical level in recent years, the IBA Guidelines have to a large extent served as a benchmark for arbitrators, counsel, and institutions in international commercial arbitration.

General Standards The IBA Guidelines include seven General Standards with **4.77** explanations.

The first General Standard stipulates that: **4.78**

> [e]very arbitrator shall be impartial and independent of the parties at the time of accepting an appointment to serve and shall remain so during the entire arbitration proceeding until the final award has been rendered or the proceeding has otherwise finally terminated.

---

[57] The IBA Guidelines were approved by the Council of the International Bar Association on 22 May 2004.

4.79 This standard reflects universally accepted premises in the international arbitration community.

4.80 The second General Standard deals with the issue of conflict of interest. In short, the principle states that an arbitrator should not accept an appointment if there is any doubt with respect to his ability to act independently and impartially.[58] The third General Standard relates to the arbitrator's duty of disclosure,[59] see below. The fourth General Standard describes a party's waiver in respect of grounds for disqualification. The fifth General Standard sets the scope of application of the General Standards. The sixth General Standard deals with the situation where the arbitrator is a lawyer in a large law firm.[60] The seventh General Standard deals with the duty of disclosure of a party and the duty of the arbitrator to make reasonable enquiries to investigate any potential conflict of interest.

4.81 **Application Lists** The IBA Guidelines also include a classification of certain criteria in respect of the concepts of impartiality and independence in four Application Lists, viz, (i) a non-waivable Red List, (ii) a waivable Red List, (iii) an Orange List, and (iv) a Green List. The two Red Lists constitute a non-exhaustive enumeration of specific situations which, depending on the facts of a given case, give rise to justifiable doubts as to the arbitrator's impartiality and independence.[61] In these circumstances an objective conflict of interest exists from the point of view of a reasonable third party having knowledge of the relevant facts. The non-waivable Red List includes situations based on the overriding principle that no person can be his or her own judge. Therefore, disclosure of such a situation cannot cure the conflict. The waivable Red List includes situations which are serious but not severe. Because of their seriousness, unlike circumstances described in the Orange List, these situations should be considered waivable only if and when the parties, being aware of the conflict of interest, nevertheless *expressly* state their willingness to have such a person act as arbitrator.

4.82 The Orange List is a non-exhaustive enumeration of specific situations which (depending on the facts of a given case) in the eyes of the parties may give rise to justifiable doubts as to the arbitrator's impartiality or independence. The Orange List thus reflects situations where the arbitrator has a duty to disclose them. In all these situations, the parties are *deemed* to have accepted the arbitrator if, after disclosure, no timely objection is made.

---

[58] See Hobér, 'Intressekonflikter och skiljeförfaranden—Vägmärken och trafiksignaler från IBA', in Nord and Thorell, *Intressekonflikter och Finansiella marknader* (2006) 229. It should be noted that the benchmark is an *objective* standard, also found in Article 12.2 of the UNCITRAL Model Law.

[59] The benchmark in this respect is a *subjective* standard, similar to the principles set forth in Article 7(2) of the ICC Rules.

[60] If one of the parties is a client of the arbitrator's law firm this will not *automatically* disqualify the arbitrator or give rise to a duty of disclosure. Such a situation must be assessed by applying the other General Standards on a case-by-case basis.

[61] Altogether, the two Red Lists include eighteen different situations where the arbitrator's independence or impartiality may be challenged.

The Green List constitutes a non-exhaustive enumeration of specific situations **4.83** where no appearance of, and no actual, conflict of interest exists from the relevant objective point of view. Thus, the arbitrator has no duty to disclose situations falling within the Green List.

One issue frequently discussed is how many appointments as arbitrator by one of **4.84** the parties, or even by the party's counsel (or law firm), in other unrelated disputes, are acceptable without raising justifiable doubts as to the arbitrator's impartiality or independence. The fact that an arbitrator has within the past three years been appointed as arbitrator on two or more occasions by one of the parties, or an affiliate of one the parties, is listed in the Orange List of the IBA Guidelines (Part II, item 3.1.3). The Orange List also includes the situation where an arbitrator has within the past three years been appointed by the same counsel, or the same law firm on more than three occasions.[62]

4.5.1.2 Procedure Pursuant to section 10 of the SAA, a party must present a **4.85** challenge in relation to an arbitrator based on a circumstance set forth in section 8 within fifteen days from the date on which the party became aware both of the appointment of the arbitrator and of the existence of the circumstance in question. The challenge shall be tried by the arbitrators (including the arbitrator whose participation is challenged), unless the parties have decided that it is to be determined by someone else, for example an arbitral institution. Section 11 of the SAA allows the parties to agree that an arbitration institution is conclusively to determine such issues. This option may be useful if the parties prefer to avoid publicity. A decision to disqualify an arbitrator cannot be appealed. By contrast, section 10(3) of the SAA provides that if a motion to disqualify an arbitrator is denied, or dismissed on the grounds that the motion was not filed in a timely fashion, the challenging party may file an application with the District Court that the arbitrator be removed. Needless to say, this remedy is not available if the parties have agreed to submit requests to disqualify an arbitrator for conclusive determination by an arbitration institution. An application to the District Court must be submitted within thirty days from the date when the party received the decision. Failure to object within

---

[62] See *Korsnäs Aktiebolag v AB Fortum Värme* , discussed at para 4.72; cf SCC Institute's decision in Case 14/2004 where an arbitrator was removed on the ground that during the past two years before his appointment in the case in question he had been appointed by a lawyer at the same law firm representing the claimant in this case in eight different arbitration proceedings, five of which had not been terminated at the time of the last appointment. During the same period of time, the arbitrator had also been appointed by companies in the same group of companies as the claimant in six different arbitration proceedings. The case is discussed in SIAR 2004:2, p 70 *et seq*; cf Svea Court of Appeal's judgment on 10 December 2008 in Case no T 10321-06, where the Court concluded that ten appointments as arbitrator from the same law firm within the past ten years (two of them within the past three years) did not constitute, in this case, a valid ground for disqualification of the arbitrator. Another example is the ruling of the Stockholm District Court on 21 June 2004 in Case no Ä 7145-04, where the Court found that five appointments as arbitrator from the same law firm within the past eight years did not disqualify the arbitrator from serving in the dispute. The fact that he had also, on eight occasions during the past seven years, acted as an arbitrator in disputes to which the same company was a party was not deemed to make any difference in this regard (he was appointed by the company on five of these occasions).

the prescribed time period prevents a party from challenging the award on the basis of arbitrator bias. Similarly, a decision of the District Court not to disqualify the arbitrator is binding in a future challenge proceeding. It follows from section 44(3) of the SAA that the decision of the District Court cannot be appealed. Consequently, the ground for challenging an award laid down in section 34(5) of the SAA is only applicable if the challenging party became aware of the relevant circumstances after the decision of the District Court.

4.86 It is up to the arbitrators to decide whether to stay or to continue the proceedings pending the decision of the District Court. The latter alternative may include the rendering of a final award. The rationale underlying this possibility to continue, and even to conclude, the arbitration is to deter parties from attempting to obstruct or delay the proceedings.[63] The risk of delay is further reduced by the fact that the decision of the District Court may not be appealed.

4.87 **4.5.1.3 Replacing arbitrators**   If an arbitrator resigns or is removed, a new arbitrator will be appointed unless the parties have agreed otherwise. Under section 16 of the SAA, the form and method of appointment depend on whether the circumstance due to which the arbitrator cannot fulfil his duties arose before or after his appointment. In the former case, the District Court shall, upon a party's request, appoint a new arbitrator, whereas, in the latter case, the party who originally was required to make the appointment shall appoint a new arbitrator.[64] It follows from this provision that if a party-appointed arbitrator dies or falls seriously ill, the party who appointed him is entitled to appoint a new arbitrator.[65] It should be noted that the arbitration agreement does not terminate even if the arbitrator who resigns or is removed was named in the arbitration agreement and thus appointed.[66] Absent an agreement between the parties indicating otherwise, the appointment of a new arbitrator by a party is governed by the procedure set out in sections 14 and 15 of the SAA, ie the procedure for appointing the original arbitrator.

4.88 The SAA does not set out the extent to which proceedings must be repeated when an arbitrator is replaced. Proceeding on the basis of party autonomy, it is primarily up to the parties to decide this issue, see section 21 of the SAA. If the parties are not in agreement, however, the arbitrators, ie the newly composed tribunal, will make the decision.

4.89 If the oral hearings have not begun when the vacancy arises, a general rule would seem to be that it should not be necessary for either the newly constituted arbitral

---

[63] Govt Bill 1999:35, p 88.

[64] The provision seeks to prevent a party from deliberately appointing an arbitrator who may be subject to disqualification. The SAA differs from several other Arbitration Acts in this regard. For instance, Article 15 of the Model Law provides that where the mandate of an arbitrator terminates, irrespective of the reason for this, a substitute arbitrator shall be appointed according to the rules that were applicable to the appointment of the arbitrator being replaced.

[65] SOU 1994:81, p 126.

[66] Govt Bill 1999:35, pp 95–96. Again, the parties are at liberty to agree otherwise.

tribunal or the parties themselves to go back over previous submissions. However, the replacement arbitrator must be given time to review the pleadings and other documents exchanged between the parties, as well as to consider any procedural orders given by the former arbitral tribunal, and to signify his assent to them. Although no particular form for this assent is required, in practice, the assent should be recorded in writing. If the vacancy arises after the oral hearings have begun, however, it will be necessary either to bring them to a close for a period of time, or to continue the proceedings before a truncated tribunal.

When the replacement arbitrator has been appointed, the question arises as to **4.90** whether or not the oral hearings must be commenced once again from the very beginning and be repeated or if it is sufficient for the replacement arbitrator to 'catch up' with the proceedings. To avoid unnecessary loss of time and increased costs related thereto, it should be in the interest of both parties, as far as possible, to avoid repetition of the hearing. Where a transcript is available, it should be sufficient for the replacement arbitrator to read the transcript and so come up to date with the proceedings. If required by the replacement arbitrator, the parties should agree to recall a particular witness or to have the opportunity to explain a particular argument in more detail. Where there is no transcript of the oral hearing, the parties and the arbitrators must discuss the situation and try to resolve this by mutual understanding.

4.5.2 Rules

Just like the SAA, the SCC Rules, in Article 14, require that every arbitrator must **4.91** be impartial and independent. Article 14 of the SCC Rules also requires any person who is asked to be an arbitrator to disclose any circumstances which may give rise to justifiable doubts as to his impartiality and independence. If a person is appointed arbitrator he must submit to the secretariat of the SCC Institute a signed statement of impartiality and independence disclosing any circumstances which may give rise to justifiable doubts in this respect.[67] This disclosure obligation continues throughout the arbitration (Article 14(3) of the SCC Rules).

The SCC Rules establish a special procedure for dealing with objections alleging **4.92** that an arbitrator is disqualified.[68] A party may challenge any arbitrator if circumstances exist which may give rise to justifiable doubts as to the arbitrator's impartiality or independence, or if he does not possess qualifications agreed upon

---

[67] Corresponding statements are required by the ICC Rules (Article 7(2)) and the LCIA Rules (Article 5.3).

[68] See the survey by Magnusson and Larsson, *Recent Practice of the Arbitration Institute of the Stockholm Chamber of Commerce Prima Facie Decisions on Jurisdiction and Challenges of Arbitrators*, in SIAR 2004:2, pp 47–84. See also Johansson in SAR 1999:2, pp 175–196, Öhrström in SAR 2002:1, pp 35–56, and Jung in SIAR 2008:1, pp 1–18. Decisions by the SCC Institute with respect to challenges of arbitrators do not have reasons. Notwithstanding this, useful guidance may be had from the aforementioned surveys.

by the parties.[69] A party may challenge an arbitrator whom it has appointed or in whose appointment it has participated, only for reasons of which it becomes aware after the appointment was made. This provision is intended to prevent obstruction. It is thus more far-reaching than section 16 of the SAA, which provides that the District Court shall appoint a new arbitrator in such cases upon request by a party.

4.93 A challenge of an arbitrator must be made in writing to the secretariat of the SCC Institute (the Secretariat) within fifteen days from when the circumstances giving rise to the challenge became known to the party (Article 15(2) of the SCC Rules). In conformity with the SAA, failure to challenge an arbitrator within the stipulated period of time constitutes a waiver of the right to make the challenge. Pursuant to Article 15(3) of the SCC Rules, the Secretariat shall notify the parties and the arbitrators of the challenge and give them an opportunity to submit comments thereon. The decision is taken on the basis of the written comments, which means that no hearings are held before the Board of the SCC Institute. If the other party agrees to the challenge, the arbitrator shall resign, whereas in all other cases the Board of the SCC Institute makes the final decision on the challenge (Article 15(4) of the SCC Rules).

4.94 Cases relating to challenges of arbitrators before the SCC Board are, generally speaking, few. The number of cases where the arbitrator is discharged is even fewer.[70] Between January 2005 and December 2007, there were 411 arbitration proceedings initiated at the SCC Institute. In those proceedings, there was a total of twenty-two challenges of arbitrators. Ten of the challenges led to the removal of an arbitrator.[71] In 2008 there were two challenges. Both were denied. In 2009 there were four challenges, two of which were denied, and two granted.

4.95 Circumstances which have led to the removal of arbitrators include the following:

(a) The arbitrator, or his law firm, has within the past three years served as counsel for one of the parties.[72] For example, in a case where the chairperson's law firm had previously acted as counsel for one of the parties, although the chairperson had not been involved himself, the SCC Board sustained the challenge and removed the chairperson.[73]

(b) The arbitrator was retained as legal expert by one of the parties in another arbitration.[74]

---

[69] Article 15(1) of the SCC Rules.

[70] See Johansson in SAR 1999:2, p 175 *et seq*, Öhrström in SAR 2002:1, p 35 *et seq*, Magnusson and Larsson in SAR 2004:2, p 47 *et seq*, and Jung in SIAR 2008:1, p 1 *et seq*.

[71] See Jung in SIAR 2008:1, p 1. It should be noted that the number of challenges does not seem to follow the number of initiated arbitration proceedings, ibid, p 2.

[72] Cf the Orange List, sections 3.1.1 and 3.1.4, of the IBA Guidelines on Conflict of Interest in International Arbitration, discussed in para 4.81.

[73] SCC case V (053/2005). See also SCC case (60/1999) and SCC case (60/2001).

[74] SCC case V (046/2007); cf, however, SCC case V (081/2007) and the Orange List, section 3.1.1, of the IBA Guidelines on Conflict of Interest in International Arbitration, discussed in para 4.81.

(c) The arbitrator had been appointed on several occasions by the law firm representing one of the parties.[75] In one case the arbitrator had, during the past two years, been appointed by a lawyer at the same firm, now representing one of the parties, in eight different arbitration proceedings, five of which had not yet been terminated.[76]

Circumstances which have not led to the removal of an arbitrator include the following:

(a) The arbitrator had been a partner of the law firm where counsel of one of the parties worked.[77] In this case the arbitrator argued that, at the time he left the law firm, counsel for the party in question did not yet work at the firm.
(b) The arbitrator worked for a company that on several occasions had performed work for one of the parties.[78]
(c) The arbitrator was the chief judge of the District Court in the city where one of the parties had its registered office.[79]
(d) The arbitrator's cousin was a Board member of the parent company to one of the parties.[80]
(e) The arbitrator had been a client of the law firm representing one of the parties.[81]
(f) The arbitrator had acted as arbitrator in other disputes related to the arbitration in question.[82]

From these few cases it is not possible to identify a consistent and firm practice of **4.97** the SCC Board. In this respect it is noteworthy that the decisions of the SCC Board are not reasoned. However, with respect to the most commonly used ground for a challenge, viz, that the arbitrator's law firm has had previous contact with one of the parties, the decisions by the SCC Board reflect a rather strict view, clearly influenced by the standards in the IBA Guidelines. If an arbitrator or the arbitrator's law firm has had previous contacts with one of the parties within the past three years and the arbitrator is challenged, the SCC Board tends to sustain the challenge and dismiss the arbitrator, even when no actual bias has been shown.[83]

---

[75] Cf the Orange List, section 3.3.6, of the IBA Guidelines on Conflict of Interest in International Arbitration, discussed in para 4.81.

[76] SCC case (14/2004). It should also be noted that on 21 June 2004, the Stockholm District Court decided to dismiss a challenge on similar grounds in an *ad hoc* arbitration (case Ä 7145). For a comparative analysis of the Stockholm District Court case and case (14/2004), cf Wallin, *Skiljemannajäv grundat på flera uppdrag från samma part eller advokatbyrå*, JT 2004-05, p 449 *et seq*. Cf the SCC cases (10/2000) and V (002/2006) and the Orange List, sections 3.3.6 and 3.3.7, of the IBA Guidelines on Conflict of Interest in International Arbitration, discussed in para 4.81.

[77] SCC case V (002/2006). Cf the Orange List, section 3.3.3, of the IBA Guidelines on Conflict of Interest in International Arbitration, discussed in para 4.81.

[78] SCC case V (019/2006).

[79] SCC case (60/1999).

[80] SCC case (87/2000).

[81] SCC case (72/2003).

[82] SCC case (148/2003).

[83] See Jung in SIAR 2008:1, p 18.

4.98 The SCC Board is responsible for the removal of an arbitrator if he resigns or if a challenge against him is sustained pursuant to Article 16(1) of the SCC Rules. Under the same provision, the SCC Board is authorized to remove an arbitrator if he is prevented from fulfilling his duties, or if he fails to perform his functions in an adequate manner. Although not explicitly stated in the SCC Rules, the Board may always remove an arbitrator upon a request from both parties.

4.99 Should the Board decide to remove the arbitrator (or where an arbitrator has died), the Board shall appoint another arbitrator, replacing the person being discharged (Article 17(1) of the SCC Rules). However, if the arbitrator who is being replaced was appointed by a party, that party shall appoint the new arbitrator, unless otherwise deemed appropriate by the Board. In this respect, the SCC Rules differ from the SAA but correspond to the UNCITRAL Model Law.[84] It is, however, possible for the Board to decide that the remaining arbitrators may proceed with the arbitration (a so-called *truncated tribunal*) (Article 17(2)). A prerequisite, however, is that the tribunal consists of three or more arbitrators. In making its decision, the Board shall take into account the stage of the arbitration and other relevant circumstances. The parties and the arbitrators must be given an opportunity to submit comments. The option to let the remaining arbitrators proceed without appointing a new arbitrator is not used very often.[85]

4.100 The 1976 UNCITRAL Arbitration Rules, in Articles 9–12 (Challenge of Arbitrators) set forth provisions on the disqualification of arbitrators. Only one very broad ground for disqualification of an arbitrator is mentioned—'justifiable doubts as to his impartiality or independence'. A contested challenge is tried by the appointing authority.

4.101 The ICC Rules, which do not set forth any specific grounds for disqualification other than 'lack of independence' (Article 11(1)), state that the ICC Court of Arbitration in Paris is the sole and final judge of challenges (Article 11(3)).

4.102 As mentioned above, section 11 of the SAA provides that the parties may agree that the decision of an arbitration institution[86] regarding the disqualification of an arbitrator shall be conclusive. Thus, such a decision cannot be subject to review by the District Court upon application by a party. However, the decision may still be reviewed in the course of challenge proceedings, with respect to the final award, primarily based on formal deficiencies but, under certain exceptional circumstances, perhaps also on severe substantive errors.[87] In order to be binding, it must

---

[84] Article 15 of the UNCITRAL Model Law.

[85] Öhrström, Stockholms Handelskammares Skiljedomsinstitut—*En handbok och regelkommentar för skiljeförfaranden* (2009) p 170.

[86] The term is not defined in the SAA. One criterion, however, is that the institution must be governed by an established set of rules, see Govt Bill 1998/99:35, p 221.

[87] Lindskog, *Skiljeförfarande, En kommentar* (2005) 494–495. Lindskog discusses the unusual situation where the arbitration institution does not dismiss an arbitrator who evidently is biased. In such a case, it is perhaps possible that the challenge to the award may also be based on such substantive error.

be clearly stated in the parties' agreement, or in the arbitration rules to which the agreement refers, that recourse to judicial proceedings is excluded. If the wording is ambiguous, it is presumed that the decision of the arbitration institute is not final and binding.[88] Under the SCC Rules, by virtue of the standard arbitration clause, it is generally held that decisions of the SCC Board on challenges of arbitrators are final and cannot be brought to the competent District Court. Under the UNCITRAL Arbitration Rules, however, there is no language indicating that decisions by the appointing authority are final. The parties are of course free to agree on such (additional) language. Otherwise, it would seem possible to appeal a decision of the appointing authority to the competent District Court, pursuant to section 10(3) of the SAA, ie if the challenge has been denied or dismissed.

4.6 Compensation of Arbitrators

4.6.1 Fees and expenses

The most important right of an arbitrator is his right to compensation. The amount **4.103** of compensation to which an arbitrator is entitled is fixed either by the agreement between the parties or pursuant to the provisions of the SAA. An agreement may cover compensation either expressly or implicitly through the inclusion in the arbitration agreement—expressly or by reference to the rules of a particular organization—of compensation provisions (section 39 of the SAA). In the absence of any agreement, the arbitrators may fix their own compensation in the final award (section 37(2) of the SAA). They are entitled to reasonable remuneration for their services and to reimbursement for reasonable expenses properly incurred, eg for travel, lodging, meals, conference facilities, secretarial and clerical assistance etc (section 37(1) of the SAA). In Sweden, the predominant method of assessing the fees of the arbitrators in *ad hoc* arbitrations is the time spent.

Even though it is thus possible to agree with arbitrators with respect to their fees, **4.104** such agreements must be entered into jointly between all the parties and all the arbitrators. If not, such agreements are void pursuant to section 39(2) of the SAA. This means that in practice it is virtually impossible to enter into such agreements prior to commencement of the arbitration, which would typically have been desirable for the parties with a view to predicting—and limiting—the cost of the arbitration. It is also very unusual that such discussions and negotiations take place once the tribunal has been constituted. In addition, it is not without problems for the parties to conduct such negotiations with the arbitrators.

An arbitrator who has stipulated for or received compensation from only one of **4.105** the parties is disqualified under section 8(4) of the SAA. The statutory provision,

---

[88] Govt Bill 1998/99:35, pp 90 and 220.

section 39(2) of the SAA, merely prohibits prior *agreements* concerning unequal payment of compensation. There are several situations when payment of compensation is in fact divided unevenly. For example, the joint and severable nature of the duty to compensate arbitrators may result in the more cooperative (or solvent) party paying more than his share. Such party would of course have a right of recovery from the other party, such that in theory the compensation eventually will be shared equally. In addition, if the parties have not otherwise provided and if either party so requests, the arbitrators may determine how the costs of the arbitral proceedings (including the compensation of the arbitrators) are to be divided as between the parties (section 42 of the SAA).[89] In relation to the arbitrators, however, the parties remain jointly and severally liable.

4.106 Finally, it should be mentioned that an arbitrator who has been obliged to resign because of disqualification will generally be entitled to compensation for the work that he has done, provided that he made full disclosure of the ground for disqualification.

4.107 When determining 'reasonable compensation' a number of factors will be taken into account. In *NEMU Mitt i Sverige AB v JH et al* (NJA 1998 p 574), which concerned an *ad hoc* arbitration, the Supreme Court made an important statement of principle to the effect that fees of arbitrators are to be determined on the basis of going market rates. For example, when the parties appoint practising commercial attorneys as arbitrators, they are entitled to fees commensurate with their ordinary fees. In practice this means that the number of hours spent by the arbitrators in hearing and deciding the case will be of decisive importance. The number of hours will in turn depend on the complexity of the case from a legal and factual point of view, the amount of documentary evidence, and the number of witnesses and experts. If the complexity of the case has increased as a result of how the parties have conducted their respective cases, this fact should not reflect negatively on the fees of the arbitrators. In the aforementioned case, the Supreme Court did not explicitly say that the disputed amount is to be taken into account when determining arbitrators' fees. On the other hand, a general statement is made to the effect that the arbitrators should try to ensure that the costs of the arbitration are reasonably proportionate to the disputed amount.

4.108 In most arbitrations, the chairperson typically spends more time on the case than his co-arbitrators. The chairperson normally has the duty to manage and administer the arbitration and to prepare the first draft of the award. It is therefore normal practice that the fees of the chairperson are higher than the fees of the co-arbitrators.

4.109 It follows from section 32(1) of the SAA that the expenses incurred by the arbitrators must also be reasonable. Typical costs incurred during the course of an arbitration include travel and accommodation costs for the arbitrators. In international arbitrations costs for interpreters, translators, and court reporters are common, as well as

---

[89] See discussion in Chapter 7.

costs of premises for hearings. In practice the arbitrators will usually consult and agree with the parties with respect to interpreters, translators, and hearing premises.

As discussed in para 6.150 below, the arbitrators may on their own initiative retain **4.110** experts to give evidence before the arbitrators. All fees and other costs associated with such evidence are regarded as expenses to the extent that they have been paid by the arbitrators.

In large or complex cases, it is common practice that the chairperson appoints a **4.111** secretary for handling some of his tasks in the proceedings. The fees of the secretary are not covered by section 37(2) of the SAA which means that the arbitrators may not impose an obligation on the parties with respect to the secretary's fees. Rather, the fees of the secretary are usually considered as an expense of the arbitrators, or primarily of the chairperson.[90]

It follows from section 37(2) that the arbitrators are entitled to interest on their fees, **4.112** such interest to start running one month following the date of the rendering of the final award. The interest rate is not specified in the SAA. As far as domestic arbitrations are concerned, it is likely that the interest rate will be that specified in the Procedural Code. In international arbitrations, however, it may be reasonable to determine other interest rates.[91]

There is no statutory, nor any generally accepted definition of 'reasonableness' in **4.113** relation to arbitration costs. It is inevitable that the arbitrators must exercise their discretion in determining what is reasonable and what is not. It is submitted that the following statement in a separate opinion by Judge Howard Holtzmann in the Iran-US Claims Tribunal provides helpful guidelines in this respect:

> A test of reasonableness is not, however, an invitation to mere subjectivity. Objective tests of reasonableness of lawyers' fees are well-known. Such tests typically assign weight primarily to the time spent and complexity of the case. In modern practice, the amount of time required to be spent is often a gauge of the extent of the complexities involved. Where the Tribunal is presented with copies of bills for services, or other appropriate evidence, indicating the time spent, the hourly billing rate, and a general description of the professional services rendered, its task need be neither onerous nor mysterious. The range of typical hourly billing rates is generally known and, as evidence before the Tribunal in various cases including this one indicates, it does not greatly differ between the United States and countries of Western Europe, where both claimants and respondents before the Tribunal typically hire their outside counsel. Just how much time any lawyer reasonably needs to accomplish a task can be measured by the number of issues involved in a case and the amount of evidence requiring analysis and presentation. While legal fees are not to be calculated on the basis of the pounds of paper involved, the Tribunal by the end of a case is able to have a fair idea, on the basis

---

[90] Lindskog, *Skiljeförfarande, En kommentar* (2005) 1042–1043. Cf *NEMU Mitt i Sverige AB v J.H. et al* (NJA 1998 p 574), where the Supreme Court held that the appointment of a secretary normally should reduce the fees of the chairman since he is relieved of some of his work in the arbitration.

[91] Govt Bill 1998/99:35, p 239.

of the submissions made by both sides, of the approximate extent of the effort that was reasonably required.

Nor should the Tribunal neglect to consider the reality that legal bills are usually first submitted to businessmen. The pragmatic fact that a businessman has agreed to pay a bill, not knowing whether or not the Tribunal would reimburse the expenses, is a strong indication that the amount billed was considered reasonable by a reasonable man spending his own money, or the money of the corporation he serves. That is a classic test of reasonableness.[92]

4.114 As mentioned above, under Swedish law the arbitrators themselves are entitled to determine their own compensation. Section 37(2), last sentence, stipulates that this is to be done separately for each arbitrator, and it is to be done in the final award. As a consequence of the fees being determined only in the final award, arbitrators are not allowed to be paid during the course of the arbitration, unless the parties have so agreed. This follows indirectly from section 38(2) of the SAA which stipulates that the arbitrators may, during the proceedings, use advance deposits made by the parties, or other security, to cover *expenses*, ie not fees.

4.115 Section 40 of the SAA stipulates that arbitrators may not withhold the arbitral award pending the payment of compensation due to them. The philosophy underlying this provision is that the arbitrators should not be able to put the parties under any form of pressure with respect to their fees at this stage of the proceedings.[93] The right of the arbitrators to request security for their compensation laid down in section 38 of the SAA is deemed to constitute sufficient protection for the arbitrators. It must be noted, however, that this provision is not mandatory, which means that the parties can reach agreement on the issue for example by referring to institutional rules which allow the withholding of the award.[94] Also, there is nothing preventing the arbitrators from asking for additional security at a late stage of the proceedings. In practice, therefore, this is largely a terminological question.

4.116 In most international commercial arbitrations the parties are asked to provide security for the compensation of the arbitrators. This follows from section 38 of the SAA which codifies earlier, longstanding practice. Security for costs is usually provided in the form of advance deposits made by the parties. In practice the chairperson would arrange for deposits to be made on an interest-bearing bank account. The arbitrators would typically ask for deposits to be made at the very beginning of the arbitration, but may do so throughout the course of the arbitration. Section 38(1), last sentence, explicitly states that if the requested security is not provided, the arbitrators may terminate the proceedings, in whole or in part.

4.117 Section 38(1) of the SAA also codifies the commonly accepted practice that if one of the parties fails to provide its share of the requested security, the other party may

---

[92] 8 Iran–US Claims Tribunal Reports, 332–333, as quoted from Redfern-Hunter, *Law and Practice of International Commercial Arbitration* (4th edn, 2004) 399.
[93] Govt Bill 1998/99:35, p 164.
[94] Ibid, p 241.

provide the entire amount. Even though it is not stated in section 38 of the SAA, it is premised on the idea that the parties will be asked to pay 50 per cent each of the requested deposits, or other security. The request from the tribunal should be addressed to both parties, even if the tribunal suspects that one of the parties may have financial problems and may thus not be able to pay his share of the security. If one of the parties does not pay his share of the security, the other party may, instead of paying the share of that party, decide to go to court based on section 5 of the SAA.[95]

It follows from section 37(1) that the parties are jointly and severally liable for the compensation to the arbitrators. There is one exception, however, to this rule. When the arbitrators reject a claim for lack of jurisdiction, the respondent is not liable for any part of the arbitrators' compensation, unless 'special circumstances so require'. Generally speaking it is not reasonable to require the respondent to pay any share of the compensation to the arbitrators when the claimant has caused all the costs. The specific circumstances referred to in the exception include situations where the dispute is non-arbitrable, or if the respondent has caused the costs of the arbitration to rise unreasonably.[96]   **4.118**

A party who is dissatisfied with the decision of the arbitrators as to their compensation has the right to bring an action in the District Court and ask for a reduction of the compensation. Such action must be brought within three months from the date when the parties received the award. The decision of the arbitrators on their compensation forms part of the arbitral award and is thus enforceable as an award. At the same time, however, that decision may be 'appealed' separately on the basis of section 41 of the SAA. It is important to note that the decision of the arbitrators to order the parties to pay their compensation, pursuant to section 37(2) of the SAA, must be included in the *final* arbitral award.[97] If not, the decision will not be enforceable. Consequently, a decision of this kind included in a partial award is not enforceable. If the arbitrators terminate the proceedings due to lack of jurisdiction, that is done in an award.[98] This means that a decision as to the compensation of the arbitrators, included therein, is enforceable.   **4.119**

Since the arbitrators are allowed to determine their own compensation, it is not surprising that the parties have the right to challenge such a decision and seek to have the compensation reduced. Section 41 of the SAA stipulates that the arbitral award shall contain clear instructions as to what must be done by a party who wishes to bring an action against the award in so far as the compensation of the arbitrators is concerned. It should be noted, however, that should the award not have such instructions, the lack thereof cannot lead to the setting aside of the award. It is also   **4.120**

---

[95] See discussion at para 3.118 *et seq.*
[96] Govt Bill 1998/99:35, pp 163, 239.
[97] Ibid, p 241.
[98] See discussion at para 3.45.

important to understand that the review by the court of the arbitrators' decision is *not* limited to procedural aspects, but is a review of the 'merits' of the decision.

4.121 Section 41(2) of the SAA stipulates that if the review by the court results in the reduction of the compensation to the arbitrators, the judgment of the court applies also for the benefit of the party who did not bring the action.

4.122 The decision of the arbitrators on their own compensation need only be a majority decision. It is thus possible also for an arbitrator to challenge the decision on compensation. It follows from section 41(1) that he must do so within three months after the rendering of the award.

4.123 The possibility to challenge the decision of the arbitrators in court relates only to their own compensation, ie their fees and expenses. If a party is unhappy with the decision of the arbitrators insofar as it concerns the distribution as between the parties of the liability for the arbitrators' compensation,[99] the only possibility is to raise this issue as part of a challenge of the award, which would thus presuppose that a procedural error has been committed by the arbitrators.

4.124 In *Soyak v WM et al* (NJA 2008 p 1118) the Supreme Court took the view that section 41 is applicable also when the compensation of the arbitrators has been decided by an arbitral institution—in this case the SCC Institute—pursuant to the agreement of the parties. The decision is controversial,[100] *inter alia,* because it challenges the *travaux préparatoires* where it is stated that when the decision on the arbitrators' compensation has been taken by someone other than the arbitrators themselves, such decision is not covered by section 41 of the SAA.[101]

4.125 The SAA is silent on cancellation fees, ie compensation for time reserved, but not used for the arbitration in question. Generally speaking, cancellation fees are very unusual in arbitrations in Sweden. If arbitrators wish to have cancellation fees this matter should be raised and agreed with the parties at the time when the arbitral tribunal is being constituted.

4.6.2 Value Added Tax (VAT) on arbitrators' compensation

4.126 Pursuant to section 37(2) of the SAA the compensation to the arbitrators must be stated separately for each arbitrator. A much debated question nowadays is whether, and if so to what extent, value added tax (VAT) shall be levied on arbitrators' compensation in international arbitrations. Previously, the position in Sweden was

---

[99] See discussion at para 7.78 *et seq.*

[100] For a discussion and criticism of the case see eg Ramberg and Lazareff, 'Challenging Arbitrators' Fees Determined by Arbitration Institutions', in Hobér, Magnusson, and Öhrström, *op cit,* at 417 *et seq.* In their conclusion, at p. 428, the authors say, *inter alia,* the following: 'Our view is that when an institution administers the case, its decision on fees should not be reviewed by state courts. Thus, we suggest that the decision of the Supreme Court of Sweden should be narrowly construed and not interpreted as allowing any recourse anywhere against any institution . . .'

[101] Govt Bill 1998/99:35, p 241.

that arbitrators, irrespective of their nationality, were under no obligation to account for Swedish VAT in relation to services performed to foreign parties, because the services performed were not deemed to be supplied in Sweden.[102]

The European Court of Justice, in *von Hoffman v Trier*,[103] brought about a change. **4.127** In that case the Court found that a German arbitrator, acting in an ICC case in France, was obliged to add German VAT to his fees. The judgment of the European Court of Justice complicated the situation in most EU Member States. The rather controversial effect of the judgment was that VAT was to be charged in the jurisdiction where the arbitrator was located, since the supply of the services was deemed to take place there.

With effect from 1 January 2010, the Swedish VAT Act has been amended based on **4.128** an updated version of the relevant EU VAT Directive.[104] Since the amendment the situation for a Swedish arbitrator[105] may be summarized as follows:[106]

(i) If both the arbitrator and the party ultimately paying the arbitrator's fees are based in Sweden, the arbitrator should charge Swedish VAT at a rate of 25 per cent on the fees. Consequently, it is the arbitrator who should account for the VAT to the Swedish Tax Agency.[107]

(ii) If the party ultimately paying the arbitrator's fees is based in another EU Member State, the services are not deemed to have been supplied in Sweden and thus no Swedish VAT should be charged on the fees. Instead, the party ultimately paying the fees should account for VAT in relation to the fees in the EU Member State in which the party is based.[108]

(iii) If the party ultimately paying the arbitrator's fees is based outside the EU, the services are not deemed to have been supplied in Sweden and thus no Swedish VAT is to be charged on the fees. Whether or not any VAT is payable in the jurisdiction where the party is based depends on the legislation in that jurisdiction.[109]

---

[102] Cf Edlund in *Juridisk Tidskrift* 1998–99, p 1039.

[103] ECJ's judgment on 16 September 1997 in Case C-145/96.

[104] Council Directive 2008/8/EG amending Directive 2006/112/EG as regards the place of supply of services.

[105] It is assumed that the arbitrator performs the services as part of business activities based in Sweden or carried out through a fixed establishment in Sweden. If this is not the case, no VAT should generally be charged. Instead social security contributions may be imposed on the compensation. It is further assumed that the party paying the compensation is a taxable person for VAT purposes. If this is not the case, the jurisdiction in which VAT is to be accounted for may be different than described below.

[106] The summary describes the position in Sweden but is not an exhaustive description of all potential VAT implications and the situation may partly depend on the circumstances in each individual case.

[107] Chapter 5, section 5, Swedish VAT Act.

[108] However, the Swedish arbitrator should include a reference on the invoice explaining that no VAT has been charged as VAT should be accounted for by the recipient under the reverse charge system: Chapter 5, section 5, Swedish VAT Act.

[109] Chapter 5, section 5, Swedish VAT Act.

Since the Swedish VAT Act is based on the Sixth VAT Directive, the position in other EU Member States can be expected to correspond to that in Sweden. Thus, if the services are provided by a *non-Swedish EU arbitrator*,[110] the VAT treatment in the State from which the arbitrator carries out his business should correspond to that in Sweden. However, it cannot be ruled out that there may be domestic deviations depending on how the Sixth VAT Directive has been implemented in the relevant Member State.

4.129 The situation for a *non-EU arbitrator*[111] may be summarized as follows:

(i)   If the party ultimately paying the arbitrator's fees is based in Sweden, Swedish VAT at a rate of 25 per cent is payable on the fees. It is, however, not the arbitrator but the party that should account for the VAT to the Swedish Tax Agency.[112]

(ii) If the party ultimately paying the arbitrator's fees is based outside Sweden, the services are not deemed to have been supplied in Sweden and thus no Swedish VAT is to be charged on the fees. Whether or not any VAT is payable in the jurisdiction where the party is based depends on the legislation in that jurisdiction.[113]

4.6.3 Rules

4.130 Under the SCC Rules the costs of the arbitration consist of:[114]

(i)   the fees of the arbitral tribunal;
(ii)   the administrative fee of the SCC; and
(iii) the expenses of the arbitral tribunal and the SCC.

4.131 Before making the final award, the arbitral tribunal must request the SCC Board to determine the costs of the arbitration. The Board determines the costs of the arbitration in accordance with the Schedule of Costs[115] in force on the date of commencement of the arbitration. The Schedule of Costs is based on the amount in dispute, but provides for a range between the minimum and maximum for each amount.[116]

4.132 The calculation of the amount in dispute includes the value of all claims, counterclaims, and set-off claims, but excludes claims for interest. When the amount in dispute is not evident, for example if the claimant is requesting a declaratory award, the SCC

---

[110] It is assumed that the arbitrator performs the services as part of business activities based in an EU State other than Sweden, or carried out through a fixed establishment in that country or an EU State other than Sweden. It is further assumed that the party paying the compensation is a taxable person for VAT purposes. If this is not the case, the jurisdiction in which VAT should be accounted for may be different than described below.

[111] It is assumed that the arbitrator performs the services as part of business activities based in a non-EU Member State, or carried out through a fixed establishment in that country or another non-EU Member State.

[112] Chapter 1, section 2, paragraph 1(2) and Chapter 5, section 5, Swedish VAT Act.

[113] Chapter 5, section 5, Swedish VAT Act.

[114] Article 43 of the SCC Rules. See Öhrström, Stockholms Handelskammares Skiljedomsinstitut— *En handbok och regelkommentar för skiljeförfaranden* (2009) 233 *et seq.*

[115] The Schedule on Costs is attached as Appendix III to the SCC Rules.

[116] In exceptional circumstances, the Board may deviate from the amounts set out in the table (Article 3 of Appendix III to the SCC Rules).

Institute determines the value of the dispute based on its own assessment. In making this determination, the SCC Institute will ask the parties to provide relevant information in this respect.

Based on the Schedule of Costs, the SCC Board determines the fees of the chairperson or a sole arbitrator. Each co-arbitrator will receive 60 per cent of the total fee paid to the chairperson. **4.133**

Under the SCC Rules, the parties are required to pay an amount equal to the estimated cost of the proceedings, including the arbitrators' fees, as an advance on costs (Articles 9 and 45 of the SCC Rules, cf Article 43 of the SCC Rules). The general rule is that each party shall pay half of the advance on costs. If a party fails to make a required payment, the Secretariat shall give the other party an opportunity to make that payment within a specified period of time. If the required payment is not made, the Board shall dismiss the case in whole or in part (Articles 10 and 45 of the SCC Rules). However, pursuant to Article 45(4) of the SCC Rules, the arbitrators may, at the request of the party who has made the required additional payment, issue a separate award for reimbursement of the payment.[117] In a decision in 2009, the Svea Court of Appeal found that a separate award on the advance on costs pursuant to Article 45(4) of the SCC Rules was enforceable.[118] **4.134**

When the parties submit counterclaims or set-off claims, the SCC Board may decide that each party is to pay separate advances on costs corresponding to its respective claim (Article 43(3) of the SCC Rules). This may be done provided it is possible to separate the claims. Separate advances are requested primarily in situations when the requested amounts differ significantly and it would be unreasonable for the parties to pay 50 per cent each of the advance on costs.[119] **4.135**

The arbitrators are required to state in the award the amounts of compensation due to the SCC Institute as well as to the arbitrators. The parties are jointly and severally liable with respect to both amounts (Article 43 of the SCC Rules). **4.136**

The 1976 UNCITRAL Arbitration Rules deal with deposits, costs, and arbitrators' compensation in Articles 38–41. The ICC Rules treat the same subjects in Articles 30 and 31. It may be noted that the UNCITRAL Model Law does not contain any provisions in this regard. **4.137**

---

[117] This provision entered into force with the 2007 amendments to the SCC Rules. The amendment was a consequence of the outcome in *3S Swedish Special Supplier AB v Sky Park AB* (NJA 2000 p 773) where the Supreme Court took the view that such repayment required that the parties had specifically agreed thereon, see Öhrström, Stockholms Handelskammares Skiljedominstitut—*En handbok och regelkommentar för skiljeförfaranden* (2009) 224 and 250–251. The first separate award on the advance on costs under the SCC Rules was rendered at the beginning of 2008: see Söderlund in SIAR 2008:1, p 137 *et seq*.

[118] Svea Court of Appeal judgment on 11 March 2009 in case Ö 280-09. For a further discussion on enforceability, see Chapter 9.

[119] Öhrström, Stockholms Handelskammares, *En handbok och regelkommentar för skiljeförfaranden* (2009) 249.

5

JURISDICTION OF THE ARBITRAL TRIBUNAL

5.1 Introduction   5.01

5.2 Issues Affecting the Jurisdiction of the Arbitrators   5.07

5.3 The Arbitrators' Determination of their Jurisdiction   5.13

5.4 Court Review of the Arbitrators' Jurisdiction   5.19

  5.4.1 Situations in which a court may consider a declaratory action with respect to the jurisdiction of the arbitrators   5.21

5.4.1.1 Jurisdiction of the Swedish courts   5.21

5.4.1.2 Requirements with respect to declaratory judgements   5.34

  5.4.2 Potential effects of a declaratory action with respect to the jurisdiction of the arbitrators   5.36

5.5 Anti-suit Injunctions   5.38

5.6 Rules   5.43

5.1 Introduction

As discussed in Chapter 3, a valid arbitration agreement is a *sine qua non* for any **5.01** arbitration. No party can be compelled to participate in arbitration unless he has agreed to do so. The arbitration agreement is also the basis for the authority of the arbitrators. Without a valid arbitration agreement they have no authority to rule on any issue. The validity and the scope of application of the arbitration agreement determine the procedural framework of the dispute between the parties.

The arbitrators cannot go beyond the arbitration agreement of the parties. If they do, **5.02** they exceed their mandate and the resulting award may be set aside on that ground.[1]

Needless to say, a party's right to 'attack' the arbitration proceedings by challenging **5.03** the jurisdiction of the arbitrators serves as a legal safeguard to ensure that a party is not forced to participate in arbitration proceedings, which are not covered by a valid and applicable arbitration agreement. At the same time challenges of the jurisdiction of the arbitrators are frequently used by parties (usually the respondent) to obstruct, delay, or complicate the proceedings.

---

[1] See p 8.72 *et seq.*

5.04   Faced with a challenge to the jurisdiction of the arbitrators, the claimant may abandon the arbitration proceedings, and commence court proceedings with respect to the subject matter of the dispute. If the claimant chooses to commence court proceedings, the respondent may not—due to its prior challenge of the jurisdiction of the arbitrators—rely on the arbitration agreement as a bar to court jurisdiction.[2] However, to commence court proceedings is normally not a viable alternative in an international context. Claimants would therefore normally request that the arbitration proceedings continue despite the respondent's challenge to the jurisdiction of the arbitrators. In such cases, the respondent may try to attack the arbitration proceedings by requesting the *arbitrators* to dismiss the case for want of jurisdiction and/or by challenging the jurisdiction of the arbitrators *before the courts* of Sweden. The latter action may be brought in parallel with the jurisdictional objection in the arbitration proceedings. With respect to such parallel court proceedings, it must be emphasized, however, that the court hearing the challenge cannot stay, or otherwise interfere with, the arbitration proceedings and that the arbitrators may continue the arbitration proceedings pending the determination by the court. This follows from section 2 of the Swedish Arbitration Act (SAA).

5.05   It is important to understand that in Swedish legal terminology no distinction is made between admissibility and jurisdiction when it comes to the delineation of the competence of an arbitral tribunal. The decision to be taken by arbitral tribunals is an 'either or' decision. This means that if the arbitral tribunal has jurisdiction, it will as a matter of principle, try all the issues on their merits. The tribunal will not accept jurisdiction and then refrain from ruling on an issue on the merits, referring to the inadmissibility of the issue.

5.06   Consequently, the following discussion refers only to the jurisdiction of arbitrators.

5.2 Issues Affecting the Jurisdiction of the Arbitrators

5.07   There are a number of issues, which may have the unwanted effect of rendering the award eventually given either invalid or subject to the risk of being set aside, if the arbitral proceedings result in an award.[3] Such issues may exist already prior to the commencement of the arbitration proceedings, or may arise during the course of the proceedings, or in connection with the issuing of the award.

5.08   Some of these issues are so serious that the arbitrators should dismiss the proceedings on their own motion, regardless of whether any request for dismissal is made.

---

[2] See section 5 of the SAA.
[3] The grounds for invalidity of an award are set out in section 33 of the SAA, whereas the grounds for setting aside awards are set out in section 34 of the SAA; see Chapter 8.

Such mandatory, non-waivable, bars to the arbitration proceedings would render an eventual award invalid under section 33 of the SAA, if the proceedings were to proceed to an award. These issues are the following:

(a) The matter submitted to the arbitration is non-arbitrable under Swedish law. The requirement of arbitrability is a matter of public policy and cannot be waived.[4]

(b) The matter submitted to arbitration is clearly incompatible with the basic principles of the Swedish legal system, ie the matter is contrary to Swedish public policy/ *ordre public*.[5] This is also a non-waivable requirement.

5.09 There are also issues that do not constitute absolute bars to the jurisdiction of the arbitrators, but which could lead to the setting aside of the award under section 34 of the SAA. These issues should not be raised by the arbitrators themselves, but must be pleaded by either of the parties if it so desires. If not, such party may otherwise be deemed to have waived such issue pursuant to section 34(2) of the SAA. These issues include, *inter alia*, the following:

(a) The arbitration proceedings should not take place in Sweden.
(b) The arbitration agreement is invalid or terminated.
(c) The matter submitted to arbitration is not covered by the arbitration agreement.
(d) The matter submitted to the arbitral tribunal is *res judicata*.
(e) The arbitral tribunal was not properly constituted.

5.10 With respect to arbitration proceedings brought against a respondent who is not domiciled in Sweden, such proceedings may take place in Sweden, if Sweden is indicated in the arbitration agreement as the place of arbitration, if the arbitrators or an arbitration institution have determined that the proceedings shall take place in Sweden, or if the respondent otherwise consents thereto.[6]

5.11 In case the arbitration agreement is invalid,[7] or the matters submitted to arbitration are not covered by the arbitration agreement, the opposing party may nevertheless accept that such matters are determined through arbitration. Such acceptance may either be expressed explicitly, or implicitly by participating in the arbitration without raising any objections. The same applies to situations where the arbitral tribunal was not properly constituted.

5.12 In relation to *res judicata*,[8] the parties may agree to limit the scope of a previous award or judgment, thus giving the arbitrators jurisdiction to reassess issues otherwise covered by the previous award or judgment.

---

[4] See para 3.77 *et seq* for a discussion of arbitrability.
[5] For a discussion of public policy and *ordre public,* see para 8.57.
[6] Section 47 of the SAA.
[7] See para 3.74.
[8] See para 7.104.

5.3 The Arbitrators' Determination of their Jurisdiction

5.13 As mentioned above, one way for a party to attack the arbitration proceedings is to make an objection to the effect that the arbitrators do not have jurisdiction.[9] Under the SAA, there is no provision explicitly regulating the timing of such jurisdictional objections. However, a party that does not raise at an early stage of the arbitration proceedings a jurisdictional objection of which it was aware, or should have been aware, will according to section 34(2) of the SAA be precluded from invoking such objection in later court proceedings for the setting aside of the arbitral award.[10] Furthermore, it has been suggested that this provision should be applied by the arbitral tribunal by way of analogy where a party has failed to present such objection without undue delay.[11] It is believed that in practice most arbitral tribunals follow this recommendation.

5.14 When it comes to ruling on the jurisdiction of the arbitrators there are two important rules to keep in mind. First, the doctrine of separability which is codified in section 3 of the SAA.[12] This doctrine ensures that an allegation to the effect that the contract is invalid, or void, does not automatically invalidate the arbitration agreement. Second, the principle of *kompetenz-kompetenz,* or *compétence de la com-pétence,* which authorizes the arbitrators' to rule on their own jurisdiction. This principle is laid down in section 2 of the SAA which simply states that 'arbitrators may rule on their own jurisdiction to decide the dispute'. As will be explained in the following, the ultimate decision with respect to the jurisdiction of the arbitrators will always, as a matter of principle, be taken by the courts.[13]

5.15 Objections to the jurisdiction of the tribunal must be handled by the arbitrators as any other disputed issue in the arbitration. This implies, *inter alia,* that the arbitrators must afford the parties, to the extent necessary, an opportunity to present their respective cases in writing, or orally. Evidence, also in the form of witness statements and expert opinions, may be presented and, where required, a separate hearing on jurisdiction be held.

5.16 It is within the discretion of the arbitrators to decide whether to rule on an objection to jurisdiction as a preliminary question or in the award on the merits.[14] In case of a separate ruling on jurisdiction, a positive finding of jurisdiction by the

---

[9] See Sekolec and Eliasson, 'The UNCITRAL Model Law and the Swedish Arbitration Act', in Heuman and Jarvin,(eds.)*Swedish Arbitration Act of 1999—Five Years On* (2006)195–197.

[10] SOU 1994:81, p 292.

[11] Heuman, *Arbitration Law of Sweden,* 271–272; Cars, *Lagen om skiljeförfarande,* 52.

[12] See discussion at para 3.42 *et seq.*

[13] Parties may under certain conditions enter into so-called exclusion agreements provided for in section 51 of the SAA, which limit the jurisdiction of courts in this respect; see discussion at para 8.186.

[14] See discussion at para 6.184.

arbitrators must be in the form of a *decision*.[15] According to section 2(2) of the SAA, such a decision is *not* binding.[16] This implies both that a court that subsequently may be called upon to determine the jurisdiction of the arbitrators may make a *de novo* review of the arbitrators' jurisdiction. It also means that the arbitrators may revisit its ruling on jurisdiction later during the proceedings, or in the final award, upon the request of a party. This does not mean that the arbitrators may arbitrarily change their mind, but if new circumstances reveal that the arbitrators do not have jurisdiction they would be free to issue a new decision.[17]

Moreover, the fact that a positive ruling on jurisdiction by the arbitrators is not **5.17** binding means that such decision, regardless of how it is labelled (decision, order, or award), is not separately challengeable under the SAA during the arbitration proceedings. A dissatisfied party must therefore either request the arbitrators to revisit their conclusion, or await the final award before challenge proceedings may be commenced. A third option, however, is to commence a separate court action asking the court to declare that the arbitration agreement is invalid or inapplicable (see 5.4 below).

Should the arbitrators conclude that they lack jurisdiction to resolve the dispute, **5.18** such decision must be made in the form of an award.[18] In accordance with section 36 of the SAA, such an award may be appealed by the dissatisfied party to the Court of Appeal. Unlike challenge proceedings, the court has the power to replace the arbitrators' negative ruling on jurisdiction with a binding judgment confirming the jurisdiction of the arbitrators.[19]

5.4 Court Review of the Arbitrators' Jurisdiction

As mentioned in the previous section, in accordance with section 2 of the SAA, the **5.19** power of the arbitrators to rule on their own jurisdiction does not prevent a party from bringing a court action in order to obtain a declaratory judgment on the jurisdiction of the arbitrators. Such an action is brought as a regular declaratory action in civil and commercial matters pursuant to the Procedural Code. It is thus independent of the arbitral proceedings, and can, as a matter of principle, be brought at any time, ie before any arbitral proceedings are pending, in parallel with the tribunal's determination of its jurisdiction, or after the tribunal has found that it has jurisdiction. However, as will be further explained below, the right to bring such action is subject to the courts of Sweden having jurisdiction, and, if they have

---

[15] Section 2 of the SAA.
[16] It should be noted, however, that if a party fails to protest against such a decision he might be considered to have waived the objection pursuant to section 34(2) of the Arbitration Act.
[17] Cars, *Lagen om skiljeförfarande*, 53.
[18] For a discussion of the difference between awards and decisions, see para 7.22.
[19] See discussion at para 8.204.

jurisdiction, that the action meets the requirements laid down in the Procedural Code for a declaratory judgment.

5.20 It must also be emphasized that a declaratory action before the Swedish courts on the jurisdiction of the tribunal is independent from the arbitral proceedings also in the sense that the courts are not allowed to stay the arbitral proceedings while the declaratory action is pending, or otherwise interfere with the arbitral proceedings. Section 2(2) expressly authorizes the arbitral tribunal to continue the proceedings pending a determination by the courts, if they so deem appropriate.

5.4.1 Situations in which a court may consider a declaratory action with respect to the jurisdiction of the arbitrators

5.4.1.1 Jurisdiction of the Swedish courts

5.21 A party who wishes to attack arbitration proceedings through a declaratory action before the Swedish courts must first satisfy the court that it has jurisdiction. Whereas sections 43 and 44 of the SAA have provisions designating the proper forum for the setting aside, or invalidity, of awards under sections 33 and 34, appeals of negative rulings on jurisdiction under section 36, challenges of the compensation of the arbitrators, applications to appoint and remove an arbitrator, and applications for the taking of evidence in aid of arbitration, the SAA does not have any provisions regarding the proper forum for declaratory actions regarding the jurisdiction of the arbitrators. To establish the proper forum for such an action, as well as for the determination whether the courts of Sweden have jurisdiction where the arbitration or the arbitration agreement has an international connection, it is therefore necessary to rely on the general principles for determining when Swedish courts have jurisdiction with respect to such issues.

5.22 In the absence of specific statutory provisions providing for such jurisdiction, the basic and overarching requirement for Swedish courts to have jurisdiction is that the Swedish legal order has an interest in resolving the matter. This is often formulated such that the *dispute* or the *parties* must have a sufficiently strong connection to Sweden for there to be a Swedish interest in the administration of justice, with respect to the issue in question. Needless to say, the jurisdiction of the Swedish courts may also be based on international conventions, treaties, or EU legislation.[20]

5.23 Frequently, the determination of whether the matter has a sufficiently close connection to Sweden is made by reference to the provisions in the Procedural Code governing the local competence of Swedish courts in domestic matters.

---

[20] See for example Council Regulation (EC) No 44/2001 of 22 December 2000 on Jurisdiction and the Recognition and Enforcement of Judgments in Civil and Commercial Matters (the Brussels I Regulation) and the Brussels (1968) and Lugano (1988) Conventions.

The theory is that if there is a competent Swedish forum according to the domestic **5.24** rules, it is normally, although not automatically, presumed that the matter also has a sufficiently strong connection to Sweden for Swedish courts to exercise jurisdiction.

The rules of competence relevant to civil and commercial cases in domestic **5.25** proceedings are set forth in Chapter 10 of the Procedural Code.

The competent court for civil cases in general is the District Court at the place **5.26** where the respondent resides.[21] A corporation, partnership, cooperative, association or similar society, foundation, or institution is considered to reside at the place where the Board has its seat or, if the Board has no permanent seat, or there is no Board, at the place from which the administration is carried out. This rule also applies to municipalities and similar public authorities.[22] By analogy, a Swedish interest in the administration of justice, and, thus, jurisdiction of Swedish courts, is generally deemed to exist if the respondent resides in Sweden.

There are, however, several exceptions to the general rule that it is the court at the **5.27** place where the respondent resides that is the proper internal forum. These exceptions may, by analogy, be of relevance for the jurisdiction of Swedish courts. For instance, a Swedish interest in the administration of justice, and thus, Swedish jurisdiction, is generally deemed to exist where the respondent does not reside in Sweden, but if the respondent has assets in Sweden,[23] if the contract under which the dispute arose was entered into in Sweden,[24] or in case of torts, if the tortious act occurred in Sweden, or the injury or damage occurred in Sweden.[25]

On a practical level, Chapter 10, section 18 of the Procedural Code may also be **5.28** of importance. This rule provides that, subject to certain exceptions, actions which have been brought in a court which is not competent are nonetheless deemed to have been brought in the competent court unless the respondent has pleaded lack of competence in a timely fashion, or if he has failed to appear in court at the first hearing or omitted to submit a response in writing. In such cases the respondent is deemed to have waived any objection to jurisdiction. Accordingly, in such cases, the claimant's position as to the circumstances making the court competent shall be accepted, unless there is reason to believe that it is incorrect.

With respect to disputes coming within the scope of the Brussels I Regulation, or **5.29** the Lugano Convention, the general rule is similar to the rules under the Procedural Code, viz, that the general forum is the court where the respondent resides.[26]

---

[21] Chapter 10, section 1 of the Procedural Code
[22] Chapter 10, section 1 of the Procedural Code.
[23] Chapter 10, section 3 of the Procedural Code.
[24] Chapter 10, section 4 of the Procedural Code.
[25] Chapter 10, section 8 of the Procedural Code.
[26] See Chapter 1, Article 2(1) of the Brussels I Regulation, and Chapter 2, Article 2 of the Lugano Convention.

There are, however, several exceptions to this general rule and a proper forum may be found in different places depending on the circumstances of the particular case.

If the respondent in a declaratory action regarding the jurisdiction of the arbitrators resides in Sweden, Swedish courts would have no difficulty in finding that they have jurisdiction to hear such an action. However, in many international arbitrations taking place in Sweden, none of the parties resides in Sweden. Nor do the parties, typically, have any assets in Sweden. Also, the contract in dispute is normally concluded elsewhere. In such a case the only factor connecting the declaratory action to Sweden is that the arbitration agreement designates Sweden as the seat of arbitration, or that there is an ongoing arbitration having its seat in Sweden. Due to the fact that parties rarely bring this type of declaratory action, the Supreme Court has not until recently had the opportunity to rule on whether an arbitration agreement providing for arbitration in Sweden or an arbitration having its seat in Sweden is sufficient to establish Swedish jurisdiction for this type of action.

5.30 In *Russian Federation v RosInvestCo UK Ltd*,[27] the Supreme Court found that the courts of Sweden have jurisdiction to hear an action to obtain a declaratory judgment on the jurisdiction of the arbitrators in arbitral proceedings governed by the SAA.[28] In reaching this conclusion the Court emphasised that pursuant to Section 2 of the SAA, a ruling by the arbitrators on their jurisdiction does not prevent a court, at the request of a party during the arbitral proceedings, from ruling on the jurisdiction of the arbitrators and that the issue of the jurisdiction of the arbitrators may also come under review in a challenge against the award. Since RosInvestCo and the Russian Federation had agreed that the place of arbitration was in Sweden, and since the SAA therefore was applicable to the arbitration, the Supreme Court found that the arbitrators' jurisdiction could be reviewed by the Swedish courts. Consequently, there was sufficient connection to the Swedish legal system to rule on the Russian Federation's request for declaratory relief.[29] Another question, which was also put to the Supreme Court in the abovementioned case, is whether jurisdiction of the Swedish courts could be excluded by the Brussels I Regulation. Pursuant to Article 2.1 of the Brussels I Regulation, persons domiciled in a Member State shall, irrespective of their nationality, be sued in the courts of that Member State. The rules in the Brussels I Regulation are mandatory for the courts of the Member States. In the absence of any express basis in Articles 2–7 of Chapter II of the Regulation, a claim may not be brought in a forum other than the forum of the domicile. Thus, the question arises whether the Brussels I

---

[27] *Russian Federation v RosInvestCo UK Ltd*, Case No. Ö 2301-09, Decision of the Supreme Court of 12 November 2010.

[28] *Russian Federation v RosInvestCo UK Ltd*, Case No. Ö 2301-09, Decision of the Supreme Court of 12 November 2010, para 6.

[29] *Russian Federation v RosInvestCo UK Ltd*, Case No. Ö 2301-09, Decision of the Supreme Court of 12 November 2010, paras 5–7.

Regulation would preclude a party from bringing a declaratory action before the Swedish courts regarding the jurisdiction of an arbitral tribunal having its seat in Sweden, when the respondent in such proceedings is not domiciled in Sweden, and none of the other grounds for jurisdiction in Articles 2–7 are applicable, or whether such an action comes within the 'arbitration exception' in Article 1(2)(d).

Article 1.2(d) of the Brussels I Regulation provides that 'the Regulation shall not **5.31** apply to [. . .] *arbitration*' (author's emphasis). The exact scope of this exception is somewhat unclear. The European Court of Justice addressed the interpretation of Article 1.2(d) in its decision in *Marc Rich*,[30] which related to a preliminary ruling at the request of an English court. In *Marc Rich*, the European Court of Justice held that a case regarding the appointment of an arbitrator is covered by the exception in Article 1.2(d). The European Court of Justice also held that the issue of the scope or validity of an arbitration agreement is covered by the exception in Article 1.2(d), provided that this issue only constitutes a preliminary issue, eg within the scope of an action regarding the appointment of an arbitrator.[31] However, the ruling in *Marc Rich* did not address the question whether a declaratory claim, where the validity or scope of an arbitration agreement constitutes the *main issue*, is covered by the exception in Article 1.2(d). The European Court of Justice had the possibility to decide also upon this issue, since it was covered by the question that was referred to the European Court of Justice by the English court, but it chose not to do so.

Thus, the question whether a declaratory action regarding the scope or validity of **5.32** an arbitration agreement comes within the 'arbitration exception' in Article 1.2(d) has not yet been resolved by the European Court of Justice. On the one hand, it could be argued that such an action is associated with pending or future arbitration proceedings, since the court's ruling on the scope or validity of the arbitration agreement will be binding upon the arbitrators, and therefore should come within the 'arbitration exception'. On the other hand, it could be argued that such a declaratory action, unlike appointment of arbitrators, challenge of arbitrators, challenge of arbitral awards etc, which actions are directly linked to a pending or concluded arbitration, does not have a sufficiently strong connection to arbitration proceedings to justify an application of the 'arbitration exception' in Article 1(2)(d) of the Brussels I Regulation. Such a declaratory action may be pursued entirely independently of pending arbitration proceedings, and it does not constitute an action which is necessary for the efficient conduct of the arbitration proceedings. It could also be argued that such an action does not constitute a necessary part of the supervision of arbitration exercised by the courts in the jurisdiction where the arbitral tribunal has its seat, since such supervision may be carried out within the scope of a challenge of the award. It should also be noted that the exception in Article 1.2(d)

---

[30] C-190/89 *Marc Rich & CoAG v Società Italiana Impianti SpA* [1991] ECR 1-3855.
[31] C-190/89 *Marc Rich*, paras 26–27.

of the Brussels I Regulation, according to its wording, relates to disputes concerning 'arbitration', not to disputes concerning 'arbitration agreements'.

5.33   Despite the fact that the 'arbitration exception' in Article 1.2(d) of the Brussels I Regulation is open to different interpretations, in *Russian Federation v RosInvest Co*, the Supreme Court did not grant leave to appeal with respect to the question whether a declaratory action concerning the jurisdiction of the arbitrators comes within the scope of the 'arbitration exception'. Nor did the Supreme Court request a preliminary ruling from the European Court of Justice. The Supreme Court simply stated that 'it is evident that the exception mentioned above is also applicable to a claim for a declaratory judgment on the jurisdiction of an arbitral tribunal in an ongoing dispute. Thus, there is no reason to request any preliminary ruling'.[32]

5.4.1.2 Requirements with respect to declaratory judgements

5.34   Assuming that the courts of Sweden have jurisdiction, the second obstacle to overcome for the court to accept a declaratory action with respect to the jurisdiction of the arbitral tribunal is set out in Chapter 13, section 2 of the Procedural Code. This provision stipulates that '[a]n action for a declaration of whether or not a certain legal relationship exists may be entertained on the merits if uncertainty exists as to the legal relationship and the uncertainty exposes the plaintiff to a detriment'. The legal relationship relevant in this context is the existence of a valid and applicable arbitration agreement. In other words, the acceptance of such action is within the court's discretion. It could perhaps be argued that, in cases where the arbitration is already underway, the objective interest for a concurrent action in court is less than in a case where the arbitration is yet to commence. Moreover, the objective interest for a concurrent action may further be reduced by the arbitrators' own decision on the issue of jurisdiction during the course of the arbitration proceedings. In addition, the timing of the court action may be crucial, since it is difficult—it could be argued—to find valid arguments for a concurrent action in court proceedings when the arbitration is soon to be finalized in an award. The simple reason is that a party challenging the jurisdiction is entitled to do so also in proceedings challenging the final award on the basis that the arbitrators lacked jurisdiction (section 34(1) of the SAA). If a concurrent action is accepted by the court at a late stage of the arbitration proceedings, this may result in parallel proceedings in Swedish courts, viz, the declaratory action, tried by the District Court, as the court of first instance, and the challenge proceedings, tried by the Court of Appeal as the court of first instance. This raises questions of *lis pendens* and *res judicata*, which might be difficult to manage and resolve in a practical and meaningful manner.

5.35   The question whether the courts pursuant to Chapter 13, Section 2 of the Procedural Code should accept a concurrent court action regarding the

---

[32] *Russian Federation v RosInvestCo UK Ltd*, Case No. Ö 2301-09, Decision of the Supreme Court of 12 November 2010, para 16.

jurisdiction of the arbitrators despite the fact that the arbitral award in all likelihood will be issued before the court action can be concluded was also addressed in *Russian Federation v RosInvestCo*. In its decision, the Supreme Court acknowledged that 'it can be questioned whether an action concerning lack of jurisdiction in a particular dispute under Section 2 of the SAA is appropriate and admissible, if the action cannot be expected to be finally adjudicated within such time that it will result in significant cost savings in the arbitral proceedings'.[33] That notwithstanding, the Supreme Court found that according to the *travaux préparatoires* to the SAA, it is a basic principle that an action concerning lack of jurisdiction is admissible even if the arbitration proceedings will continue and the award will be rendered prior to the final resolution of the issue on jurisdiction. The Supreme Court therefore held that a party should be entitled to initiate an action concerning the arbitrators' jurisdiction prior to the issuance of an arbitral award, at least in situations where the award may not reasonably be expected in the near future.[34]

5.4.2 Potential effects of a declaratory action with respect to the jurisdiction of the arbitrators

As mentioned above, in case of a declaratory action with respect to the jurisdiction of the arbitrators, the arbitration proceedings may continue pending the court proceedings.[35] The arbitrators are entitled to stay the arbitration at the request of a party, but in practice this would only be done in exceptional circumstances. In fact, arbitrators are usually reluctant to stay the arbitration in these cases, *inter alia*, because of their duty under section 21 of the SAA to 'handle the dispute in an impartial, practical, and speedy manner'.[36] Moreover, in case of an arbitration under the SCC Rules, there is a time limit of six months for the arbitrators to render an award set forth in Article 37 of the SCC Rules. Although this time limit may be extended by the Board of the SCC Institute upon a reasoned request from the arbitrators, this time limit would typically speak against a stay of the arbitration proceedings. **5.36**

However, the court's final declaratory judgment on the jurisdiction of the arbitrators is binding on the arbitrators and on other courts. Accordingly, should the court determine that the arbitrators lack jurisdiction, the arbitration proceedings must be terminated. Should the court find that the arbitrators partially lack jurisdiction, such judgment prevents the arbitrators from adjudicating claims which are outside **5.37**

---

[33] *Russian Federation v RosInvestCo UK Ltd*, Case No. Ö 2301-09, Decision of the Supreme Court of 12 November 2010, para 10.

[34] *Russian Federation v RosInvestCo UK Ltd*, Case No. Ö 2301-09, Decision of the Supreme Court of 12 November 2010, paras 11–12.

[35] Section 2(1) of the SAA.

[36] Cf Article 19 (2) of the SCC Rules—'In all cases, the Arbitral Tribunal shall conduct the arbitration in an impartial, practical and expeditious manner . . .'

their mandate. Failure to comply with the court's judgment makes the award challengeable in accordance with section 34(1) and (2) of the SAA.[37]

5.5 Anti-suit Injunctions

5.38 Attempts to attack arbitration proceedings taking place in Sweden may also be undertaken by requesting a foreign court to issue an injunction forbidding such proceedings with respect to a dispute. This tool, a so-called anti-suit injunction, is frequently used in common law jurisdictions. An anti-suit injunction may be directed against actual or potential claimants in arbitration proceedings. In common law jurisdictions, non-compliance with an anti-suit injunction constitutes contempt of court, for which penalties can be imposed, including imprisonment or seizure of assets.[38]

5.39 Anti-suit injunctions are directed against one party, or sometimes against both parties, to the arbitration. The injunctions are thus made *in personam*, ordering the parties not to proceed with the arbitration. However, they may also be directed against the arbitrators, which can put the arbitrators in a difficult position. An anti-suit injunction may also be directed against an arbitration institution.

5.40 In respect of arbitration proceedings in Sweden, however, an anti-suit injunction by a foreign court would have no direct effect on the arbitrators' determination of whether they have jurisdiction to hear the dispute. This follows from the fundamental fact that the arbitrators' authority is based on the parties' agreement to arbitrate and the general principle of *compétence de la compétence*, ie that the arbitrators are competent to rule on their own jurisdiction. It must be noted, however, that although an anti-suit injunction does not directly affect the arbitrators' authority in Sweden to rule on its jurisdiction, such an injunction may, if directed at the arbitrators, nevertheless cause legal and practical problems for the arbitrators, in particular if they are domiciled in the country where the order was made.[39]

5.41 The argument could perhaps be made that Sweden's entry into the European Union and the ratification of the Brussels I Regulation (and the Brussels and Lugano Conventions) have extended the scope of the powers of a court of another Member State to interfere with Swedish court proceedings and arbitration proceedings in Sweden. This is so, it could be argued, because such court judgments, and also decisions with respect to interim measures, should, as a matter of principle, be recognized

---

[37] In any case, the arbitrator's failure to comply with the court's judgment would be a procedural error in handling the case which would render the award voidable under section 34(6) of the SAA, should it be proved that the outcome of the dispute was likely to have been affected by the arbitrators' action.

[38] See the Advocate General's opinion, point 14, in ECJ Case C-185/07; *Allianz SpA et al v West Tankers Inc.*

[39] Schwebel, *International Arbitration: Three Salient Problems* (1987) 144 *et seq* and the *Himpurna California Energy v Indonesia* case, discussed in Int'l Arb Rep 39 (2000).

and enforced in Sweden.[40] With respect to anti-suit injunctions, however, in the *West Tankers Case*,[41] the European Court of Justice (ECJ) concluded that 'it is incompatible with Council Regulation (EC) No 44/2001 of 22 December 2000 on jurisdiction and the recognition and enforcement of judgments in civil and commercial matters for a court of a Member State to make an order to restrain a person from commencing or continuing proceedings before the courts of another Member State on the ground that such proceedings would be contrary to an arbitration agreement'. Effectively, the ECJ thus seems to have removed the ability of the courts within the jurisdiction of the Brussels I Regulation to take pre-emptive strikes against satellite litigation.

It is still unclear, however, to what extent the *West Tankers* case, which concerned **5.42** the relationship between two national courts, limits the authority of national courts to issue anti-suit injunctions directed at an arbitration proceeding with its seat in another EU Member State.

5.6 Rules

Article 10(1) of the SCC Rules stipulates that the Board shall dismiss a case in **5.43** whole or in part if the SCC 'manifestly lacks jurisdiction over the dispute'.

It should be emphasized that the issue here is the jurisdiction of the SCC Institute, **5.44** not of the arbitrators. This means that if the SCC Institute accepts jurisdiction—ie it decides that it does not manifestly lack jurisdiction—the respondent may still raise the jurisdictional issue before the arbitrators.

As the language of Article 10(1) indicates, the threshold—'manifestly lacks juris- **5.45** diction'—is very low. It must be obvious that the SCC Institute lacks jurisdiction. The decision taken by the SCC Board is of a *prima facie* nature. Decisions are taken on the basis of documents only. No oral hearings are held before the SCC Board. This means that the SCC Board is not in a position to resolve any complicated jurisdictional issues. These are for the arbitrators to decide.

The low threshold means that in practice it is sufficient that the SCC Institute is **5.46** mentioned, one way or the other, in the arbitration agreement.[42] Even if the name is mentioned incorrectly, this is usually sufficient. Situations where the SCC Institute manifestly lacks jurisdiction include a clear reference to another arbitration institution, and language clearly showing that the parties have intended *ad hoc* arbitration.

---

[40] Chapter III of the Brussels I Regulation; cf Article 31 thereof.
[41] ECJ Case C-185/07; *Allianz SpA et al v West Tankers Inc.*
[42] For a review of decisions by the SCC Board, see Magnusson, in Swedish Arbitration Report 2002:2, 171 *et seq*; Magnusson and Larsson, in Stockholm International Arbitration Report 2004:2, 47 *et seq.*

5.47 Jurisdictional issues are tried by the SCC Board at the request of a party, ie the respondent, and not at the initiative of the SCC Board. The explanation is that the parties may of course agree at any time with respect to the validity and scope of the arbitration agreement. One situation where the SCC Institute may consider reviewing the jurisdictional issues *ex officio* is if the respondent has not been in contact with the SCC Institute at all.[43] Another such situation is if the request for arbitration concerns a non-arbitrable issue.[44]

---

[43] See Öhrström, *op cit*, at 139.
[44] See para 3.77 *et seq* concerning arbitrability.

6

THE PROCEDURE BEFORE
THE ARBITRAL TRIBUNAL

6.1 Introduction	6.01	
6.2 General Principles of Swedish Judicial Procedure	6.16	
6.3 Basic Principles of Arbitration Procedure	6.29	
6.3.1 Party autonomy	6.30	
6.3.2 Impartiality, practicality, speed	6.31	
6.3.3 *Audi alteram partem*	6.32	
6.4 Commencing the Arbitration Proceedings	6.35	
6.4.1 Request for arbitration	6.35	
6.4.1.1 SCC Rules	6.42	
6.4.2 Service of the request for arbitration, the award and other documents	6.44	
6.4.2.1 Proof of notification and methods of service	6.48	
6.4.2.2 'Notices' clauses	6.52	
6.4.2.3 Persons authorized to accept service	6.54	
6.4.2.4 Particular rules for service of documents outside Sweden	6.57	
6.4.2.5 SCC Rules	6.58	
6.5 Conduct of the Arbitration	6.64	
6.5.1 General	6.64	
6.5.2 Written submissions	6.71	

6.5.2.1 Prayers for relief	6.73
6.5.2.2 Legal grounds	6.76
6.5.2.3 Facts and circumstances	6.77
6.5.3 Post-hearing briefs	6.87
6.5.4 Evidence	6.89
6.5.4.1 Introduction	6.89
6.5.4.2 Powers of the arbitrators	6.97
6.5.4.3 Admissibility of evidence	6.101
6.5.5 Documentary evidence and production of documents	6.109
6.5.5.1 Documentary evidence	6.109
6.5.5.2 Production of documents	6.112
6.5.6 Witnesses and experts	6.122
6.5.6.1 Hearing of witnesses	6.122
6.5.6.2 Written witness statements	6.145
6.5.6.3 Experts	6.150
6.5.6.4 Inspection of the subject matter of the dispute	6.160
6.5.6.5 Evaluation of evidence	6.162
6.5.7 Evidence taken with court assistance	6.170
6.5.8 Hearings	6.184
6.5.8.1 Introduction	6.184
6.5.8.2 The main hearing	6.218

6.1 Introduction

After years of preparation, the Swedish Arbitration Act of 1929 and the Act **6.01** Concerning Foreign Arbitration Agreements and Awards of 1929 were replaced by the Swedish Arbitration Act (SAA). The SAA takes account of developments in international arbitration, notably the UNCITRAL Model Law on International Commercial Arbitration. The SAA applies equally to domestic and international arbitrations, but nevertheless conforms closely to the Model Law. The SCC Rules have been prepared on the basis of, and taking into account, the SAA. The 2010 SCC Rules have also taken into account recent developments on the international arena of commercial arbitration proceedings. The SAA and the SCC Rules together constitute an efficient and comprehensive collection of arbitration provisions and rules relating to arbitrations in Sweden.

6.02 The SAA is based on and recognizes the fundamental principle of party autonomy. Thus, the SAA has remarkably few rules of procedure, mainly those set forth in sections 19–26. The general, and overarching, rule of procedure is set forth in section 21 of the SAA, which reads as follows:

Section 21

The arbitrators shall handle the dispute in an impartial, practical, and speedy manner. In doing so, they shall act in accordance with the decisions of the parties insofar as there is no impediment to do.

6.03 Attractively simple as the procedural scheme thus outlined in the SAA may appear, it is clearly too simplistic to constitute a satisfactory framework for arbitration proceedings even in uncomplicated disputes. Additional rules and practices inevitably must play an important role.

6.04 In contrast to the SAA, the Swedish Procedural Code has numerous detailed provisions with respect to the procedure in Swedish courts. It is generally accepted that the SAA must be applied autonomously, ie without recourse to the Procedural Code.[1] This is particularly important if the arbitrators, the parties, or their counsel come from other jurisdictions. The principles of orality, concentration, and immediacy,[2] which are the predominant rules of judicial procedure under the Procedural Code, do not automatically apply to arbitration proceedings. For example, it is clear that the arbitrators must consider all materials presented in the arbitration, including pleadings and documents submitted by the parties to the arbitrators before the main hearing.

6.05 This being said, however, the arbitrators are free to look to the Procedural Code for guidance where the SAA is silent and the parties have not reached agreement with respect to the conduct of the arbitration. For example, the Swedish Supreme Court has ruled that principles of civil procedure with respect to *res judicata* apply, by analogy, to arbitration, unless there are special reasons to the contrary.[3] The possibility of looking to the Procedural Code for guidance must not be mistaken for a general acceptance of applying the Procedural Code in arbitrations, not even in purely domestic arbitrations, ie where both parties are Swedish. Instead, the overriding principle of party autonomy must always be kept in mind when dealing with arbitration.

---

[1] See eg Govt Bill 1998/99:35, p 46.
[2] See para 6.16 *et seq*.
[3] *Esselte AB v Allmänna Pensionsfonden* (NJA 1998 p 189).

Under Swedish law, there is no requirement that Swedish lawyers participate in **6.06** international arbitrations. There is no requirement by law or practice to use Swedish citizens either as arbitrators or counsel. For all practical purposes, however, Swedish lawyers play important roles in international arbitrations in Sweden, as counsel, arbitrators, and in other capacities. The legal education, training, attitudes, and traditions of Swedish lawyers[4] therefore influence the conduct of international arbitrations in Sweden. Needless to say, this is particularly true when the chairperson of the tribunal is a Swedish lawyer and when Swedish attorneys act as lead counsel.

The different arbitration cultures which exist today are converging more and more, **6.07** such that it is perhaps even possible to speak of a culture of international commercial arbitration. There is an ever-growing number of lawyers who take part in international arbitrations as counsel and as arbitrators. A common approach to the conduct of international arbitrations is gradually developing. Differences do, however, remain.

As far as international commercial arbitration in Sweden is concerned, it is, by **6.08** virtue of the role played by Swedish lawyers, to a large extent permeated by the philosophy and the cardinal rules underlying the Swedish Procedural Code. As noted in the foregoing, it is important to understand that the Procedural Code is, however, not applicable to arbitrations in Sweden, not even by analogy; clearly, arbitration and court litigation are two different methods of resolving disputes, a fact which is recognized by the Swedish legislator. This notwithstanding, most Swedish lawyers practising today are imbued with the legal culture developed on the basis of, and around, the Procedural Code. Hence its importance for arbitrations, domestic as well as international.

The Swedish Procedural Code was introduced in 1948, and brought about a major **6.09** reform in Swedish court procedure. The Procedural Code largely did away with written procedure and introduced an oral procedure, including oral preparatory meetings—subsequent to the submission of written briefs—geared towards preparing the case so as to facilitate one single, concentrated main hearing during which all evidence—both documentary evidence and witnesses—is presented and during which all arguments, factual as well as legal, are presented.

Much of the discussion today about different approaches to international arbitration **6.10** goes back to the differences between the adversarial and inquisitorial approaches to adjudication. The adversarial system is intimately linked with the common law system and is used in common law jurisdictions. The inquisitorial system, with its foundation in Roman law, is used in the civil law jurisdictions of continental Europe, such as France, Germany, and Italy.

Without going in to any details, and by way of simplification, the adversarial system **6.11** leaves the conduct of the litigation to the parties and the function of the judge is to

---

[4] See para 1.22 and 1.23.

sit and listen and determine the issues raised by the parties. His role is thus not to conduct an investigation, or examination, in pursuit of a public interest, or on behalf of one of the parties. In short, the proceedings are essentially controlled by the parties to the dispute.

6.12 Under the inquisitorial system, however, the judge, or the court, is much more active, even pro-active and inquisitive. This means, *inter alia*, that counsel play a far lesser role in the trial process. Generally speaking, there is more emphasis on written submissions than on oral advocacy. It is not unusual for there to be no cross-examination at all of witnesses.

6.13 As will be described below,[5] Swedish court procedure represents a merger between the adversarial and inquisitorial systems in that it combines written and oral procedure. As far as the oral procedure is concerned, however, in commercial cases it is clearly adversarial in nature, and thus to a large extent resembles the Anglo-American system.

6.14 When it comes to the conduct of arbitrations in Sweden, the starting point for Swedish lawyers is the consensual nature of arbitration, which in turn is an outflow of party autonomy. Every arbitration is based—and must be based—on the agreement of the parties. The arbitrators derive their authority from the agreement of the parties. Put differently: the arbitrators sit there because the parties have put them there. Most Swedish arbitrators therefore regard the parties as the masters of the procedure. The parties control the arbitration. Consequently, if both parties agree on how to conduct the arbitration, the arbitrators must follow the agreement of the parties. It follows from the foregoing that arbitrations in Sweden are adversarial in nature, rather than inquisitorial. Swedish arbitrators thus expect the parties to present their cases—the facts and the law—and to determine which evidence, documentary as well as oral, they wish to rely on. This also means that the typical Swedish arbitrator would be hesitant to become actively involved in attempts to settle the dispute—unless the parties ask him to—for fear of undermining his impartiality. The fear of appearing to favour one side will also cause most Swedish arbitrators to be very cautious in putting questions—at least sensitive questions—to the parties. Usually, questions, save for clarification purposes, will be put only after counsel for both sides have had the opportunity to present their respective cases.

6.15 It has been pointed out that accepting party autonomy and the adversarial approach—as these concepts have been explained above—will increase the risk of an arbitral tribunal reaching the 'wrong' conclusion and taking the 'wrong' decision from a substantive law point of view. This is so, it is argued, because the arbitrators may lack essential information, or because all relevant documents have not been submitted to them. The task of the arbitrators, however, it is submitted, is to decide the case on the basis of the facts, arguments, and evidence submitted to them; and

---

[5] See para 6.16 *et seq.*

not—to put it in dramatic terms—to find out the truth. After all it is the parties' dispute. They must be allowed to determine the scope and complexity of the arbitration.

6.2 General Principles of Swedish Judicial Procedure

When the Procedural Code was introduced in 1948, it constituted a radical **6.16** departure from practices which had become entrenched over a period of a century and a half and which took the form of an inquisitorial and largely written procedure. The three cardinal principles of the new judicial process were *orality, immediacy,* and *concentration*. The first among the cardinal principles simply means that all materials on which judgments are to be based must be presented orally. The second principle means that such presentation must be made directly to the court and the third that the main hearing is to be arranged without interruption. To permit, and prepare for, a main hearing without interruption, the Procedural Code provides for a pre-trial stage of the proceedings, which may be oral or written, or both, divided into any number of sessions and stretched over a period of time. In complex cases written pleadings may become voluminous and delays between the various stages of the pre-trial proceedings may become substantial. A commercial action in a Swedish court is commenced by the filing, by the plaintiff, with the court of a so-called summons application. The requirements of the Procedural Code with respect to such summons applications highlight three fundamental aspects of Swedish judicial procedure.

First, the summons applications will be dismissed by the court if the plaintiff does **6.17** not specify the relief sought, ie the prayers for relief. Similarly, the respondent must respond directly in this regard and specify any relief which may be sought by him. These provisions relating to summons applications have a corollary in section 3 of Chapter 17 of the Procedural Code which provides that the judgment may not grant different, or more extensive, relief than has been properly demanded by a party. In other words, the parties' prayers for relief have a preclusive effect. This rule of Swedish procedural law may be quite different from the law and practice of many other countries where a similar requirement of specificity is not imposed.

Secondly, the plaintiff must clearly identify the factual circumstances which, by **6.18** virtue of the relevant provisions of the applicable law, in his view result in granting the prayers for relief.

Thirdly, both parties are required to state clearly all evidence on which they wish to **6.19** rely and what they intend to prove by each specified item of oral testimony and/or documentary evidence. Needless to say, at this early stage of the proceedings such a statement of evidence will be of a preliminary nature and the parties will be given the opportunity to submit a final statement of evidence closer to the main hearing.

6.20 The relief normally sought from a Swedish court of law is performance, either in terms of specific affirmative action or the payment of monies. Declaratory judgments may also be rendered within the limits provided by relevant provisions of the Procedural Code.[6]

6.21 As mentioned above, the procedure laid down in the Procedural Code is geared towards preparing the case for the main hearing. The main hearing is usually divided into four stages, viz:

(i)   statement of the relief requested by each of the parties, which in most cases is simply a confirmation—sometimes with minor amendments and/or refinements—of the prayers for relief specified in the summons application;

(ii) presentation of the facts of the dispute, including the facts which are immediately relevant for granting the relief sought;

(iii) presentation of the evidence, both oral and documentary; all documentary evidence must be submitted, and all witnesses identified, well in advance of the main hearing; and

(iv) closing arguments, the purpose of which is to weave together arguments of fact and law, due account taken of the evidence presented during the main hearing.

6.22 The entire main hearing is oral and in principle adversarial, rather than inquisitorial, in character. The Procedural Code sets forth a number of rules designed to satisfy the requirement of concentration and to avoid interruptions during the main hearing. The main hearing may thus continue for a number of days, or indeed weeks and even months, depending on the complexity and size of the case.

6.23 It should be noted that no new evidence may, as a matter of principle, be introduced during the main hearing.

6.24 As far as evidence is concerned, Swedish law is very liberal in the sense that there are few formal rules of evidence. Generally speaking, the concepts of relevance and admissibility are co-extensive. A Swedish court may freely evaluate all events in the course of the proceeding, matters formally relied on as proof by one side or the other and the demeanour of witnesses, as well as the general behaviour of the parties, their obedience to court orders, and claims of privilege with respect to testimony or documentary proof. However, even though a court of law may evaluate almost everything, it is expected to identify in its judgment each of the factors relevant to its ultimate determination.

6.25 With regard to witnesses, the general practice is that they are examined under oath by counsel for the parties. Another important aspect of oral testimony in Swedish courts is that the witness is both permitted and expected to relate its entire story, without interruption, and in particular without being prompted by direct questions from bench or bar. In practice, however, witnesses are often questioned by counsel,

---

[6] Cf discussion at para 5.34.

similar to the Anglo-American way. After the examination in chief, cross-examination by opposing counsel will usually follow. As a rule a witness is not allowed to attend the hearing before being examined.

As far as discovery is concerned, it must be mentioned that the scope of a request **6.26** for production of documentary evidence is restricted by provisions of the Procedural Code to the effect that a court would not permit discovery of facts which are immaterial, or if proof can be adduced by different means at lesser cost and inconvenience. Documents may be withheld by virtue of the privileges generally corresponding to those relating to testimony, such as attorney–client privilege, for example.[7]

In appropriate cases, the possessor of a document—even if not a party to the dispute— **6.27** may be directed to produce, in lieu of the document, certified relevant excerpts therefrom. Again, the obligation of the possessor may be limited to permitting a designated person, or persons, to study the document.

Before issuing a subpoena, the court must afford the alleged possessor the opportu- **6.28** nity to present any objections he may wish to advance. For example, a person to whom the request is addressed may deny possession, assert a privilege, or dispute the importance of the document as proof. It is thus important to note that as a matter of principle discovery may be had only with respect to documents which can be assumed to be of importance as evidence in a particular case. Consequently, under Swedish law it is not possible to embark on so-called fishing expeditions which are sometimes said to be the result of American and English rules on discovery. It also follows from the foregoing that production of documents is not possible if the documents requested are intended merely to supplement and/or support the case of the requesting party. Generally speaking, either party is expected to analyse the facts and the legal position on the basis of available documents and other available information prior to submitting the summons application.

6.3 Basic Principles of Arbitration Procedure

Swedish arbitration procedure is governed by the following basic principles. Violation **6.29** of these basic principles may lead to the setting aside of the arbitral award.[8]

6.3.1 Party autonomy

The arbitration procedure is to a large extent governed by the agreement of the **6.30** parties, subject, however, to some, but in fact very few, statutory requirements. In practice the party autonomy is often exercised by referring to the rules of arbitration institutions, such as the SCC or the ICC. Pursuant to section 21, second sentence

---

[7] See discussion at para 6.109.
[8] See Chapter 8.

of the SAA, the arbitrators shall 'act in accordance with the decisions of the parties insofar as there is no impediment to do so'.[9] Depending on the parties and their interest in taking an active role with respect to the procedure, and also their ability to reach agreement on the procedure, the arbitrators' procedural freedom may vary from case to case. It must also be noted, however, that the arbitrators' procedural freedom may be restricted not only by the parties' agreement but also by mandatory rules and public policy requirements of the law at the place of arbitration. In addition, the arbitrators are also expected take into account those provisions of international conventions on arbitration, for instance the New York Convention, that aim to ensure that the arbitration proceedings are conducted fairly.[10]

6.3.2 Impartiality, practicality, speed

6.31 As mentioned above, section 21 of the SAA provides that the arbitrators shall 'handle the dispute in an impartial, practical, and speedy manner'.[11] Although the impartiality rule finds its main application in the principle *audi alteram partem* discussed in para 6.32, it also has wider implications. For example, an arbitrator should never in the course of the proceedings meet either of the parties alone. This should not, however, prevent the chairperson from contacting either party by telephone in order to discuss or clarify practical matters with respect to the procedure. In such a case the chairperson should communicate any substantive information to the other party without delay. In addition, the arbitrators should take the necessary steps to ensure that any submission received from one party is without delay communicated to the other party, if need be by the arbitrators themselves.

6.3.3 *Audi alteram partem*

6.32 A basic principle of Swedish arbitration procedure is that the arbitrators shall afford the parties 'an opportunity to present their respective cases' (section 24 of the SAA).[12] This rule is based on the universally recognized principles of arbitral due process and equality in the treatment of the parties enshrined in the SAA. The provision in section 24 of the SAA includes the right to review all documents and all other material pertaining to the dispute which are supplied to the arbitrators by the opposing party or another person. A party is also entitled to an oral hearing prior to the determination of an issue referred to the arbitrators, unless otherwise agreed between the parties. The arbitrators' duty to give both parties an opportunity to present their respective cases does not prevent the arbitrators from acting against an

---

[9] Cf Article 19(1) of the SCC Rules.

[10] Redfern and Hunter, *Law and Practice of International Commercial Arbitration* (4th edn, 2004) 264.

[11] Cf Article 19(2) of the SCC Rules.

[12] Cf Article 19(2) of the SCC Rules which states that the arbitrators shall give 'each party an equal and reasonable opportunity to present its case'. This principle is qualified in the UNCITRAL Model Law by the words 'each party shall be given a *full* opportunity of presenting his case' (Article 18).

obstructing party. Section 24(3) of the SAA stipulates that '[w]here one of the parties, without a valid cause, fails to appear at a hearing or otherwise fails to comply with an order of the arbitrators, such failure shall not prevent a continuation of the proceedings and a resolution of the dispute on the basis of the existing materials'.[13]

The arbitrators are thus authorized to proceed *ex parte* if a party fails without justi- **6.33** fication to appear or to plead his case. They are not, however, entitled to render a 'default judgment', but must base their award on the available material.[14] The respondent's failure to appear or to plead may be given evidentiary weight in this connection. Under the SCC Rules this is expressly set forth in section 30(3) where the arbitrators are entitled to 'draw such interferences as [they] consider [. . .] appropriate', most likely negative ones. Although not specifically set forth in the SAA, this is a generally applicable rule.[15] The arbitrators are required to reach a decision, however—since a reluctant respondent could otherwise frustrate the proceedings without sanction—and the award may therefore in fact closely resemble a default judgment.

Unless the parties have agreed to a particular 'cut-off date' with respect to documentary **6.34** evidence (and statements of facts, if applicable) it would be difficult for arbitrators to dismiss or disregard such evidence and statements, even if presented at a late stage of the proceedings, in some cases as late as after the main hearing. Although the arbitrators are certainly entitled to refuse to admit evidence if such refusal is justified having regard to the time at which the evidence is offered,[16] in practice arbitrators are often reluctant to dismiss evidence or statements because it could result in the award being challenged by the aggrieved party. Instead, the arbitrators often apply the principle of *audi alteram partem* and allow the other party to comment on the new documents and occasionally to submit rebuttal documents.

6.4 Commencing the Arbitration Proceedings

6.4.1 Request for arbitration

Unless the parties have agreed otherwise, arbitration proceedings are initiated when **6.35** a party receives a 'request for arbitration'.[17] The requirements as to form and content of the request for arbitration are set out in section 19(2) of the SAA. However, the parties may agree on other ways of initiating arbitration proceedings, for example, by referring to a set of arbitration rules in the arbitration agreement.[18]

---

[13] Cf Article 30 of the SCC Rules.
[14] See discussion at para 7.22 *et seq.*
[15] See discussion at para 6.101 *et seq.*
[16] See section 25(2) of the SAA. Cf Article 26(1) of the SCC Rules.
[17] Section 19 of the SAA.
[18] Govt Bill 1998/99, p 224.

6.36 According to section 19(2) of the SAA, a request for arbitration must be made in writing and include an express and unconditional request for arbitration. A proposal to arbitrate or an expression of an intention to initiate arbitration does not constitute an express and unconditional request. If, for instance, a party notifies the other party that it will request arbitration if payment is not received by a certain date, such notice does *not* constitute an express and unconditional request for arbitration pursuant to section 19(2) of the SAA.

6.37 The second requirement according to section 19(2) of the SAA is that the request for arbitration must include a statement of the issue, covered by the arbitration agreement, and which is to be resolved by the arbitrators. It should be noted that the SAA does not require that the claim or the facts relied on in support of the claim be set in the request for arbitration. Rather, the claimant must set out its claim and supportive facts within the time fixed by the arbitrators.[19] However, the request for arbitration must, nevertheless, identify the issue or issues to be resolved with sufficient specificity to give the respondent enough information about the dispute so as to be able to decide whom to appoint as arbitrator.

6.38 It should also be noted that the description of the issues to be resolved in the arbitration does not once and for all fix the scope of the arbitration, since the SAA provides a possibility for the claimant subsequently to introduce new claims, as well as for the respondent to present counterclaims.[20]

6.39 Unless otherwise agreed, the claimant must also make his choice of arbitrator in the request for arbitration. Failure to do so means that the claimant has not made a 'request for arbitration' within the meaning of the SAA.[21]

6.40 A request for arbitration that does not fulfil all of the above-described requirements will not constitute a 'request for arbitration' pursuant to the SAA. Consequently, the arbitration proceedings will not be deemed to have commenced as a result of a defective request for arbitration.

6.41 However, there is always a possibility that the other party, nevertheless, accepts a defective request by appointing its arbitrator in accordance with section 14 of the SAA, or otherwise responds to the request for arbitration in a manner that implies acceptance of the commencement of the arbitration.[22] In such a case, the arbitration proceedings will be deemed to have commenced despite the defectiveness. If such a defective request for arbitration is *not* accepted by the respondent, the proceedings will not commence until the respondent receives such supplementary information that makes the request for arbitration complete.

---

[19] Section 23 of the SAA.
[20] Govt Bill 1998/99:35, p 106; see para 6.81.
[21] Govt Bill 1998/99:35, p 102.
[22] SOU 1994:81, p 274.

6.4.1.1 SCC Rules

Under the SCC Rules the arbitration proceedings are deemed to have commenced **6.42** when the request for arbitration is received by the SCC Institute (Article 4). In accordance with Article 2 of the SCC Rules, the request for arbitration shall include (i) details of the parties and their counsel, (ii) a summary of the dispute, (iii) a preliminary statement of the relief sought by the claimant, (iv) a copy or description of the arbitration agreement or clause under which the dispute is to be settled, (v) any comments on the number of arbitrators and the seat of arbitration, and (vi) if applicable, details of the arbitrator appointed by the claimant.

Upon filing the request for arbitration the claimant shall pay the registration fee **6.43** (Article 3).[23] If the claimant fails to pay the registration fee after receiving a reminder from the SCC Institute, the request for arbitration shall be dismissed. The SCC Institute will send a copy of the request for arbitration and the documents attached thereto to the respondent. In so doing, the SCC Institute will decide on a time limit for the respondent to submit an answer (Article 5).

6.4.2 Service of the request for arbitration, the award, and other documents

Under the SAA, service of the request for arbitration must, in principle, be effected **6.44** personally.[24] It is therefore of outmost importance for the claimant to make sure that the other party actually receives the request for arbitration, and to secure proof thereof.

According to section 19 of the SAA, the arbitration commences at the time when **6.45** the respondent receives the request for arbitration. The date of receipt of the request for arbitration is important for several reasons, eg in respect of statutory limitation periods, contractual cut-off dates, and *lis pendens*.

Similarly, service of the award must also be effected personally. This is important, **6.46** since receipt of the award by a party marks the beginning of the period during which he may challenge the award under section 34 of the SAA, appeal a negative ruling on jurisdiction under section 36, or challenge the arbitrators' decision as to their own compensation under section 41.

Documents in the arbitration other than the request for arbitration and the award do not **6.47** have to be served personally on the recipient, but can be distributed in any way agreed upon between the parties and the tribunal, or as otherwise directed by the tribunal.

6.4.2.1 Proof of notification and methods of service

As mentioned above, as a general rule, service of the request for arbitration and the **6.48** award must be effected personally, ie by actual receipt of the document by a person

---

[23] In accordance with Appendix II to the SCC Rules, the fee amounts to €1,500.

[24] Section 19 provides that: 'unless otherwise agreed by the parties, the arbitral proceedings are initiated *when a party receives* a request for arbitration' (author's emphasis).

duly authorized to receive it on behalf of the recipient. The burden of proof in this respect is with the sender.

6.49 Personal service can take place by courier services with acknowledgement of receipt. Notification can also take place via letter or telefax provided that the sender ensures that he receives confirmation that the document was in fact received by an authorized representative of the recipient. The Supreme Court has ruled that a normal fax report is insufficient proof of personal service of documents.[25] Therefore, the sender must always request confirmation that the request for arbitration or other relevant document was in fact received. Such confirmation should be made by an authorized representative of the recipient.

6.50 It is uncertain how a document sent by email with acknowledgement of service sent to an authorized representative of the other party should be treated. The technical improvement of email services renders it possible not only to obtain an acknowledgement of service but also an acknowledgement *of reading* in respect of emails. However, contrary to a signature in writing of the recipient, as in the case of courier services, emails can be received and read by other persons authorized by the email addressee. It is possible that such an acknowledgement would not suffice to prove that service of process has been effected.

6.51 The requirement that the request for arbitration must have been received by a person authorized to receive it on behalf of the recipient has been upheld also in connection with the enforcement of foreign awards in Sweden. Section 54(1)(2) of the SAA provides that: 'a foreign award shall not be recognised and enforced in Sweden where the party against whom the award is invoked proves: that the party against whom the award is invoked was not given *proper notice* of the appointment of the arbitrator or of the arbitration proceedings, or was otherwise unable to present his case' (author's emphasis).[26] In *Lenmorniiproekt OAO v Arne Larsson & Partner Leasing AB* (Supreme Court Case No Ö 13-09), decided on 16 April 2010, the Supreme Court held that although the wording 'proper notice' in the SAA and the New York Convention did not provide any clear guidance regarding the way in which such notice had to be submitted, the respect for due process required that the request for arbitration must in fact reach the respondent. The Supreme Court refused to enforce the award, since the request for arbitration had not been delivered to an authorized representative of the company, nor had the company otherwise been notified of the proceedings.

6.4.2.2 'Notices' clauses

6.52 A 'notices' clause in a contract stipulates to whom notice may validly be made under the agreement, or the way in which notice is to be made, eg by email, letter, or fax.

---

[25] *Kenneth O v Motor Union Assuransfirma AB* (NJA 1993 p 308).
[26] Section 54(1)(2) corresponds to Article V(1)(b) of the New York Convention.

A 'notices' clause may also regulate when notice will be deemed to have been made under the agreement. It is uncertain under Swedish law whether service of the request for arbitration in accordance with the terms of such a provision will be considered valid and effective in the absence of proof of actual receipt by an authorized representative of the recipient.[27]

In *Lenmorniiproekt OAO v Arne Larsson & Partner Leasing AB* (Supreme Court   **6.53** Case No Ö 13-09),[28] referred to above, the Supreme Court refused to enforce a Russian arbitral award despite the fact that the request for arbitration had been sent to an address, which was specified as respondent's address in the arbitration agreement. However, respondent had changed its address, officially registered its new address with the Swedish Companies Registration Office, and moved offices before the arbitration proceedings started. Moreover, the respondent had not participated in any stage of the arbitration proceedings. Representatives of the respondent testified in the enforcement proceedings that they had not been aware of the fact that any arbitration proceedings had taken place until they were notified of the application to enforce the arbitral award. Although the Supreme Court in *Lenmorniiproekt OAO v Arne Larsson & Partner Leasing AB* did not make any general and principled statements regarding the effectiveness of notice clauses, it is reasonable to assume that the Supreme Court would also in other situations require that the claimant—even if notification takes place in accordance with a 'notices' clause—in the absence of a confirmation of actual receipt of the request for arbitration by the respondent, at the very least check public records to verify that the address provided in the agreement is still valid.

6.4.2.3 *Persons authorized to accept service*

Where the party to be notified is a Swedish corporation, the Swedish Service of   **6.54** Documents Act has provisions specifying the persons who are competent to receive notification. Although the Supreme Court has ruled that the Service of Documents Act is not applicable to arbitration proceedings,[29] the rules specifying the persons who are entitled to accept service on behalf of a Swedish corporation can probably provide some guidance also with respect to arbitration proceedings. For instance, in a Swedish joint stock company, any member of the Board of directors or any other person with so-called signatory powers (even if he is only entitled to sign in conjunction with some other person) is individually authorized to receive service on behalf of such corporation. It is therefore sufficient to notify any one of them.

Attorneys are sometimes authorized to accept service on behalf of their clients.   **6.55** In Swedish court litigation, if no limitation with regard to acceptance of service has been made, an attorney appointed to represent the client in proceedings generally

---

[27] Cf Lindskog, *Skiljeförfarande, En kommentar* (2005) 88.
[28] See para 6.51.
[29] *Christine L och Sven A* (NJA 1999 p 300).

is authorized to accept service. Although the SAA does not have any corresponding provisions, similar principles would probably be applicable to acceptance of service in arbitration proceedings. This was the approach taken by the Supreme Court in *Christine L och Sven A* (NJA 1999 p 300). It applied provisions of the Swedish Service of Documents Act by analogy to find that an arbitral award had been served on a party, when the award had physically been received by a messenger on the basis of an acknowledgement of receipt signed by the party, but when the party had not de facto had the opportunity to review the award.

6.56   Since it might sometimes be difficult to ascertain whether an attorney has been authorized to accept service, parties sometimes regulate this matter by including provisions in the contract, requiring particular 'process agents', authorized to accept service, to be appointed.

6.4.2.4 *Particular rules for service of documents outside Sweden*

6.57   In principle, the SAA maintains the same requirements for service of the request of arbitration and other documents on parties domiciled or incorporated outside Sweden as it does for service on Swedish parties, ie proof that the document in fact was received by the party in question or an authorized representative of the party.[30] It is uncertain whether the party serving the request for arbitration or other documents may rely on provisions not requiring service to be effected personally that may be applicable in the jurisdiction where the recipient is domiciled or incorporated.

6.4.2.5 *SCC Rules*

6.58   The SCC Rules do not have any specific rule regarding service of documents. However, as mentioned above, according to Article 4 of the SCC Rules, the arbitration is commenced on the date when the SCC receives the request for arbitration. This is a significant advantage compared to *ad hoc* arbitration under the SAA, since it avoids the uncertainty in establishing the exact point in time when the request for arbitration was received by the respondent, which may be of utmost importance if the proceedings are commenced close to the expiry of statutory or contractual time limits.

6.59   Moreover, once the request for arbitration has been received and accepted by the SCC, the SCC assumes responsibility for serving the request for arbitration on the respondent.

6.60   The SCC Rules do not have any provisions regarding service of the award other than that the 'Arbitral Tribunal shall deliver a copy of the award to each of the parties and to the SCC without delay'.[31] Thus, it is the responsibility of the arbitral tribunal to serve the award on the parties. According to the SCC Arbitrator's

---

[30] The question of who is authorized to represent a legal entity, and to accept service of documents on behalf of the legal entity, is governed by the *lex corporationis*; see para 2.174.

[31] Article 36(4) of the SCC Rules.

Guidelines,[32] the arbitral tribunal shall without delay distribute the award to the parties and is recommended to request a proof of the receipt from the parties.

Article 8 of the SCC Rules deals with notifications under the Rules. Section 1 stipulates **6.61** that any notice or communication from the Secretariat and the Board shall be sent to the last known address of the addressee.

Section 2 of Article 8 explains that notices may be sent by any means of communi- **6.62** cation which provides a record of the sending thereof, including facsimile transmissions and emails.

Section 3 of Article 8 stipulates that a notice 'shall be deemed to have been received **6.63** by the addressee on the date it would normally have been received given the chosen means of communication'. This provision is primarily intended to deal with the situation when the respondent is trying to frustrate the arbitration by not communicating at all. It means that the SCC Rules do not require actual receipt of a document. This provision of the SCC Rules is similar to a corresponding provision in the rules of the International Commercial Arbitration Court at the Chamber of Commerce and Industry of the Russian Federation which was the arbitration court that rendered the arbitral award in *Lenmorniiproekt OAO v Arne Larsson & Partner Leasing AB* (Supreme Court Case No Ö 13-09) discussed above.[33] It cannot be ruled out that the Supreme Court would take a similar approach with respect to Article 8 of the SCC Rules were it to be tried by the court.

6.5 Conduct of the Arbitration

6.5.1 General

As we shall see in the following, the general, yet very fundamental, principles of **6.64** Swedish Court procedure referred to in the foregoing[34] influence the conduct of arbitrations in Sweden. However, as mentioned above, ultimately the control of the conduct of the arbitration lies with the parties. Consequently, if the parties agree on a certain procedure, eg with respect to the submission of briefs or the examination of witnesses, that is the procedure which the arbitrators must follow.

Unless the parties have agreed otherwise, an arbitration in Sweden would typically **6.65** go through the following stages, listed in chronological order:

(i) The claimant serves a *request for arbitration* in writing on the respondent, or with an arbitration institution, as the case may be. The request must include

---

[32] Arbitration Institute of the Stockholm Chamber of Commerce, Arbitrator's Guidelines (2010) p 17

[33] See para 6.53.

[34] See para 6.16.

(i) an express and unconditional request for arbitration, (ii) a statement of the issue which is covered by the arbitration agreement and which is to be resolved by the arbitrators, and (iii) claimants' appointment of an arbitrator (section 19 of the SAA).[35]

(ii) The respondent serves its *reply to the request for arbitration*, in which he also appoints an arbitrator.[36]

(iii) The two arbitrators select a *third arbitrator* (who is generally appointed chairperson) (section 20 of the SAA).[37]

(iv) The claimant submits his *statement of claim* (once the arbitral tribunal has been duly constituted) in respect of the issues stated in the request for arbitration, including the circumstances relied on by him in support of his claim(s) (section 23 of the SAA).[38]

(v) The respondent submits his *statement of defence* in relation to the claims and the circumstances relied on by the respondent in support of this case, as well as any counterclaim (Section 23 of the SAA).[39]

(vi) The initial stage of the proceedings is usually followed by further submissions from both parties, respectively (section 24 of the SAA) ie *reply to the statement of defence* and *rejoinder*.[40] At this stage it may also be necessary for the arbitrators to decide upon various procedural issues, such as jurisdiction, production of documents, amended claims, as well as the question of applicable law. In this respect, the arbitrators may conduct preparatory conferences and/or separate hearings to hear the parties' arguments in respect of a particular procedural issue.

(vii) In arbitrations in Sweden the parties are sometimes requested to submit their respective *statements of evidence*, indicating the witnesses and the documentary evidence they wish to rely on together with an explanation as to what they intend to prove with each witness and document.

(viii) A *main hearing* is conducted, at which witnesses are heard and factual as well as legal argument is presented (section 24 of the SAA).[41]

(ix) In some cases the parties submit *post-hearing briefs*. Generally, Swedish arbitrators would seem reluctant to admit post-hearing briefs since they typically expect all the evidence and arguments to be presented at the main hearing.

(x) The *award* is rendered in writing (sections 27 and 31 of the SAA).[42]

6.66 It follows from what has been said above that the general principles of Swedish judicial procedure have a significant impact on the way counsel prepare their briefs

---

[35] Cf Article 2 of the SCC Rules, which describes the request for arbitration in more detail. See para 6.35.

[36] Cf ibid, Article 5.

[37] Cf ibid, Article 13.

[38] Cf ibid, Article 24(1).

[39] Cf ibid, Article 24(2).

[40] Cf ibid, Article 24(3).

[41] Cf ibid Article 27(1).

[42] Cf ibid, Article 36(1).

and other submissions and how they prepare for the oral hearing, as well as on how arbitrators administer and conduct the arbitration in question. It is worthwhile to emphasize in particular three aspects which will typically influence counsel and arbitrators alike.

First, in the typical arbitration conducted in Sweden there is no room for discovery, **6.67** as such a concept is understood in the Anglo-American system. Parties and counsel must thus initiate an arbitration and file briefs—arguing both facts and law—without having the benefit of the results of a discovery procedure. Parties are expected to obtain, themselves, and analyse, the documents and other information they deem necessary for their respective cases.

Secondly, there are very few rules of evidence in Swedish arbitration law, which **6.68** means, *inter alia*, that it is unusual for arbitrators to reject evidence on the ground that it is inadmissible. Generally speaking, in practice a party will be allowed to rely on almost anything as long as it states that the document in question is important evidence for its case. The fact that a document is admitted in evidence does not mean, however, that its contents are automatically accepted. The arbitrators have the right, and the duty, freely to evaluate all the evidence presented by the parties. The free evaluation of evidence by the arbitrators is thus the remedy against the very liberal approach taken with respect to admissibility of evidence. The reason why arbitral tribunals are reluctant to reject evidence is of course the desire to avoid that the party in question will challenge the award arguing that it has not been able to present its case.

Thirdly, the principle of *iura novit curia* is a concept unknown to the Anglo-American **6.69** system, but is generally accepted in Swedish court procedure. Literally, this doctrine means that the court knows the law and that—strictly speaking—it is not necessary for the parties to argue the law since the judge is the ultimate high priest of the law. In other words, under this principle party control does not extend to the law to be applied. One consequence of a strict application of the *iura novit curia* principle might be that a court decides a dispute on the basis of statutory provisions and/or legal principles which have not been argued by any of the parties. The outcome of the case may thus come as a complete surprise to both parties. Such consequences would be difficult to reconcile with the fundamental principle that arbitration is consensual in nature, and with the philosophy that the parties are the masters of the procedure. For these reasons it is very doubtful if the principle of *iura novit curia* is applicable in international commercial arbitrations conducted in Sweden. Most arbitrators would be reluctant to apply the principle in an international case.[43]

To avoid the uncertainty with respect to *iura novit curia* most parties and counsel **6.70** would typically try to present their respective cases with as great a specificity as

---

[43] See Calissendorff, 'Jura Novit Curia i Internationella Skiljeförfaranden i Sverige' *Juridisk Tidskrift* (1995/96) 141; Hobér, *Extinctive Prescription and Applicable Law in Interstate Arbitration* (2001) 140–141.

possible, also with respect to applicable statutory provisions and/or legal principles, both in their written and oral submissions.

6.5.2 Written submissions

6.71 In virtually all arbitrations conducted in Sweden the parties exchange some form of written submissions. In practice, few commercial arbitrations will proceed without such documents. Generally speaking, the function of written submissions is initially to define the issues to be determined by the arbitrators and subsequently to elaborate on these issues and the facts and circumstances surrounding them.

6.72 Generally speaking, most Swedish arbitrators would typically expect at least the first written submission following the request for arbitration, and the reply thereto, to be structured in the following three-tier fashion:

(i) Prayers for relief (*yrkanden*);
(ii) Legal basis for prayers for relief (*the 'legal grounds'*) which often includes a short explanation of the facts which are relevant to the legal principle or rule relied on; and
(iii) Facts and circumstances.

The same considerations apply with respect to counterclaims filed by the respondent.

6.5.2.1 Prayers for relief

6.73 The jurisdiction of the arbitrators is limited by the original arbitration agreement, as supplemented by agreements or admissions made by the parties in the course of the proceedings. The prayers for relief (and the respondent's counterclaims, if applicable) also define the limits of the arbitrators' powers and are thus of fundamental importance to the outcome of the proceedings. Accordingly, an award may be set aside, if challenged, if the arbitrators have exceeded their mandate by going beyond the matter submitted to them, and an award outside the scope of the arbitration agreement may constitute such an *ultra vires* action (section 34(2) of the SAA).[44] There is also, however, another aspect of section 34 of the SAA which relates to the written submissions of the parties and particularly to their prayers for relief. This aspect mirrors the rule of the Procedural Code that a court may not grant different or more extensive relief than has been properly claimed by a party: arbitrators cannot rule *ultra petita*. The other side of that coin is that the court must grant such relief to the extent that the opposing party does not object and such relief may lawfully be granted. The preclusive effect of the prayers for relief is as great in Swedish arbitration proceedings as in Swedish judicial proceedings. The prayers for relief thus have decisive implications for the *res judicata* effect of awards and for their *lis pendens* effect.

---

[44] See discussion at para 8.72 *et seq.*

It may be appreciated therefore that the prayers for relief are of vital practical and **6.74** legal importance, since they define the limits of the arbitrator's powers. Consequently, parties are well advised to spend considerable time on analysing and formulating the prayers for relief. The parties must state explicitly and unequivocally what they wish the arbitrators to decide. In Sweden it is virtually unheard of to leave it to the discretion of an arbitral tribunal to order 'appropriate remedies', or to award interest which is 'reasonable and just'.

One consequence of the importance of the prayers for relief is that they must, as **6.75** mentioned above, state explicitly and unequivocally what the parties wish the arbitrators to decide. Put differently, the prayers for relief are expected to be specified to such a degree that there is no doubt with respect to the award requested. Unlike the Procedural Code,[45] the SAA does not have provisions requiring the claims to be specified in detail. In practice, however, a high degree of specification is expected. In addition, the arbitrators must always bear in mind that the lack of specification could result in an award *ultra petita* rendering the award voidable, see para 8.72 *et seq*. In addition, the arbitrators have an obligation to clarify the claims submitted by a party within the framework of their case management duties. Failure in this respect may also render the award voidable, see para 8.165.

6.5.2.2 Legal grounds

Another important aspect is that the parties are expected to indicate and explain the **6.76** legal basis for each prayer for relief. This is usually done by reference to the legal concept, or notion, as well as the statutory provision—if relevant—on which the prayer is based, for example, breach of guarantee clause in contract, defective goods, invalidity of contract, infringement of contractual rights etc, and describing the facts and circumstances constituting the legal basis.

6.5.2.3 Facts and circumstances

It should be recognized that the form and content of the written submissions vary **6.77** depending on the nature and scope of the dispute and the parties involved. Some written submissions may be quite voluminous, containing full arguments of both law and fact, whereas in other cases the written submissions may be characterized as a merely preliminary to the oral hearing.

Generally speaking, however, the first brief submitted by each party in an arbitra- **6.78** tion—ie the Statement of Claim and the Statement of Defence, respectively—is typically expected to set forth in detail the factual as well as legal arguments relied on by the party. All briefs submitted to the tribunal would cover both factual and legal issues. The philosophy underlying this approach is that the parties

---

[45] Chapter 42, section 2 of the Procedural Code.

themselves should, and are expected to, narrow down the issues successively as they submit their briefs. Needless to say, this does not always happen. Parties may have a number of reasons—both good and bad—for not addressing directly factual and legal arguments presented by their counterparties. This is where the preparatory/preliminary hearing comes into the picture.[46] At this hearing the arbitral tribunal will seek further clarification of the parties' positions and ask them to address—either at the hearing, or in an additional brief—issues raised by the other party. All this is done with a view to preparing the case for the main hearing.

6.79 In addition, in their first briefs, the parties would be expected to indicate, albeit in a preliminary fashion at this stage, the evidence, both documentary and oral, that they wish to rely on. Moreover, a Swedish arbitrator would typically focus on the legal issues involved from the very outset of the proceedings. This explains why the prayers for relief play such a crucial role in arbitrations in Sweden. It is thus necessary for the parties to review and analyse the facts—and in particular their relevance to the legal issues involved—prior to submitting their briefs, such that they are able to present to the tribunal those facts which are relevant to the legal issues involved.

6.80 As a practical matter, it is noteworthy that the parties are expected to submit supporting documentation together with their briefs. Indeed they are expected to refer to such documents and to explain the relevance of the documents to the arbitrators. In most cases the majority of such documents would then be listed as evidence in the statement of evidence which the parties will often be asked to submit prior to the main hearing.[47]

6.81 **New claims, amendments of claims, and set-off claims** The respondent may raise a counterclaim or set-off claim, provided that such claim falls within the scope of the arbitration agreement.[48] The counterclaim or set-off claim may be raised in the statement of defence (section 23(2) of the SAA).[49] A counterclaim or set-off claim should be allowed in the arbitration proceedings if the arbitrators do not consider it inappropriate to adjudicate such claims. It is thus within the discretion of the arbitrators, taking into consideration the time at which the counterclaim or set-off claim is submitted, and other circumstances, to decide whether or not the counterclaim or set-off claim should be allowed. The *travaux préparatoires* state that the presumption is that arbitrators should be generous in allowing any new claim,

---

[46] See discussion at para 6.198.
[47] See Hobér in Bishop (ed), *The Art of Advocacy in International Arbitration* (2004) 182.
[48] Cf Articles 24(2) and 25 of the SCC Rules.
[49] Cf ibid, Article 24(2) which provides that a counterclaim or set-off claim *shall* be included in the Statement of Defence. However, in accordance with Article 25 of the SCC Rules, the claims, including counterclaims and set-off claims may be amended or supplemented at any time prior to the close of the proceedings pursuant to Article 34 of the said rules, unless the arbitrators consider it inappropriate.

for instance counterclaims and set-off claims, as long as these claims fall within the scope of the arbitration agreement.[50] However, the timing of such claim is of fundamental importance since it is particularly vital to prevent obstruction of the proceedings.

Similar to what has been discussed above with respect to counterclaims and set-off **6.82** claims, both parties are, as a matter of principle, entitled to amend or supplement their respective claim (section 23(2) of the SAA).[51] One peculiarity in Swedish arbitration should be noted in this respect, viz, that the parties may enter into a valid arbitration agreement orally or by conduct, including by an omission to object.[52] This implies that in case a party articulates a claim that goes beyond the original arbitration agreement, and is therefore not covered by it, that claim may, nevertheless, be allowed should the opposing party fail to raise an objection thereto.[53] In such a situation the original arbitration agreement is deemed to have been extended to cover also the new claim.

In the case of an amendment of, or supplement to, a claim being allowed, where the **6.83** timing of the amendment or supplement causes a delay in the proceedings, this may have an impact on the allocation of costs among the parties.[54]

In disputes involving more than two parties, the issue of so-called cross-claims **6.84** arises from time to time. For example, in a dispute under a shareholders' agreement a respondent shareholder may wish to raise claims against a shareholder other than the claimant. If this eventuality is foreseen in the shareholders' agreement, this is of course possible. If the parties have not agreed on the possibility of filing cross-claims, it would not seem to be possible. The SAA is silent on the issue. The SCC Rules also do not envisage this possibility. In fact, most institutional rules are silent with respect to cross-claims. To the extent that cross-claims are allowed, they are based on the agreement of the parties concerned.

Occasionally parties in an arbitration submit claims for payment to a third party, **6.85** ie an entity or individual who is not a party to the arbitration agreement and therefore not to the arbitration either. For example, a parent company might file a claim for payment to a subsidiary, or vice versa. The Supreme Court has concluded that such claims could be made in court proceedings, but only in 'clearly exceptional circumstances'.[55] In the case in question, the Court found that no such circumstances existed. Despite several attempts, no case is know where such a claim has been successful in an arbitration. The explanation is simply that the rights and

---

[50] Govt Bill 1998/99:35, p 226.
[51] Cf Article 25 of the SCC Rules, Article 23.2 of the UNCITRAL Model Law, and Article 20 of the UNCITRAL Arbitration Rules.
[52] See discussion at paras 3.12 and 3.14.
[53] Govt Bill 1998/99:35, p 226.
[54] Cf section 42 of the SAA.
[55] *Karl Gustaf G v Nils S* (NJA 1984 p 215).

obligations following from an arbitration agreement are, as a matter of principle, limited to the parties.[56]

6.86 **Withdrawal of arbitration request and claim** Where a party withdraws a claim, the arbitrators shall dismiss that part of the dispute, unless the opposing party requests that the arbitrators rule on the claim (section 28 of the SAA). This provision unconditionally entitles the opposing party to obtain a final settlement of the dispute.[57] It may, however, be difficult to distinguish between a withdrawal and a limitation of a claim. The right to have the arbitrators' ruling on a claim, in this respect, only applies to the former situation. This question is closely related to the doctrine of *res judicata*.[58] If the party were allowed to present the withdrawn claim in a new dispute, then there is a withdrawal of the claim. If, on the other hand, the withdrawn claim, eg, an alternative claim, could not be examined in a new arbitration dispute, then there is a limitation of the claim.[59] The purpose of section 28 of the SAA is to prevent the opposing party from initiating new arbitration proceedings concerning the same claim.[60] If the claim is withdrawn in its entirety, the arbitration proceedings shall be terminated by issuing an award in accordance with section 27 of the SAA.[61] The SAA, however, does not regulate whether a partial withdrawal or limitation of the claim should be decided in an award or in an order. The difference is significant, *inter alia*, in respect of the possibility to appeal against the decision. An award terminating the arbitration proceedings may be appealed against and reviewed by the Court of Appeal within three months from the receipt of the award (section 36 of the SAA). By contrast, it is not possible to appeal separately against an order in the course of the arbitration proceedings.[62]

6.5.3 Post-hearing briefs

6.87 Although the oral hearing usually concludes the submission of arguments and evidence by the parties, the parties may agree to further briefing by way of so-called post-hearing briefs. Sometimes post-hearing briefs may substitute the oral closing arguments, giving the parties a possibility to summarize their respective legal arguments and to comment on the oral testimonies of witnesses and experts taken

---

[56] As discussed at para 3.130 *et seq* the arbitration agreement may, however, in certain situations also have effect in relation to third parties.

[57] If the claimant withdraws his claim in its entirety before the arbitral tribunal is constituted or before the statement of claim has been submitted, eg before the respondent has incurred any substantial costs, it could perhaps be argued that the respondent has no unconditional right to obtain an award, see Heuman, *Arbitration Law of Sweden: Practice and Procedure* (2003) 418.

[58] See para 7.104.

[59] Heuman, *Arbitration Law of Sweden: Practice and Procedure* (2003) 418.

[60] Govt Bill 1998/99:35, p 129.

[61] The first paragraph of section 27 reads: 'The issues which have been referred to the arbitrators shall be decided in an arbitral award. Where the arbitrators terminate the arbitral proceedings without deciding such issues, this shall also be done in an arbitral award'. See para 7.22 for a discussion of different kinds of awards and decisions.

[62] Govt Bill 1998/99:35, p 231.

at the hearing. In some situations, the arbitrators may also ask the parties to comment on a particular issue which has arisen at the hearing or a particular argument or piece of evidence presented (and accepted) at a late stage of the proceedings, or even during the hearing. Post-hearing briefs can also be used to limit the duration of the hearing or when the time allocated for the hearing turns out to be insufficient to permit the parties to present their cases.

The parties should be prevented from submitting new unsolicited material after the **6.88**
hearing. Indeed, it is good practice for arbitrators to declare the evidentiary record closed at the end of the hearing.[63] However, arbitrators should have the discretionary power, in exceptionally compelling cases, to admit materials presented even after the record has been declared closed at the hearing.[64] This may, of course, lead to further submissions and even to an additional hearing. Needless to say, it is usually desirable to restrict the scope of post-hearing briefs in order to avoid the dispute turning into something completely different including new arguments and evidence. In practice, in addition to restricting the scope of the post-hearing briefs, they may be limited to a specific number of pages. It is a frequently adopted practice that post-hearing briefs are submitted simultaneously in order not to encourage the parties to comment further on each other's briefs.[65]

6.5.4 Evidence

6.5.4.1 Introduction

The purpose of presenting evidence is to assist the arbitrators to determine issues of **6.89**
fact and disputed issues of *opinion* presented by 'experts'. Needless to say, the presentation of evidence is of great importance to the outcome of almost every dispute.

Generally speaking, the presentation of evidence in Swedish arbitrations does not **6.90**
create problems. To the extent the parties wish to hear witnesses, the witnesses attend, generally on a voluntary basis, and the parties submit to the arbitrators the documentary evidence they wish to rely on.

The Procedural Code foresees four basic methods of presenting evidence, viz: **6.91**

(i) production of documents

---

[63] Cf Redfern and Hunter, *Law and Practice of International Commercial Arbitration* (4th edn, 2004) 325.

[64] Cf Heuman, *Arbitration Law of Sweden: Practice and Procedure* (2003) 402–403, and Redfern and Hunter, *Law and Practice of International Commercial Arbitration* (4th edn, 2004) 326; cf Article 34 of the SCC Rules and Chapter 43, section 14 of the Procedural Code.

[65] In some instances it may be necessary to have more than one round of post-hearing submissions. Moreover, in large international arbitrations it is sometimes suggested that the arbitrators should hold a very limited oral hearing after the submission of post-hearing briefs in order to clarify that it is satisfied that the parties have had a reasonable opportunity to present their cases and that all issues are correctly understood by the arbitrators.

(ii) hearing of witnesses

(iii) hearing of experts

(iv) inspection of the subject matter of the dispute.

6.92 In Swedish arbitrations the same methods of presenting evidence are available and may be used in a number of different ways by the parties in trying to prove their respective cases. It is important to recognize, however, that each arbitral tribunal may take a different approach as to how and when evidence is to be presented. The tribunal will usually seek to reach a consensus with the parties on such matters, unless the parties have already agreed thereon.

6.93 Under the SAA the initiative with respect to evidence is exclusively in the hands of the parties.[66] Section 25(1) of the SAA stipulates that 'the parties shall supply the evidence'. This includes documentary evidence, witnesses, experts and, if applicable, site inspections. However, the arbitrators may on their own motion appoint experts, unless both parties are opposed thereto.[67]

6.94 The dividing line between 'fact' and 'opinion' mentioned above is not always clear. One example is whether the contents and application of 'foreign' law must be established as matters of fact or whether it is a question of law. As far as international commercial arbitrations in Sweden are concerned, foreign law is usually treated as a matter of fact. As a consequence, the parties submit documentation establishing the contents and interpretation of the applicable law(s). The contents of foreign law may be established by extracts from statutes or cases. However, it is the application of law that is often the crux of the matter. In this respect, the parties may wish to rely on expert opinions and/or on the writings of legal authorities.

6.95 The parties may certainly agree, and are often asked to agree on particular rules for the presentation of the evidence, eg the use of written witness statements, see para 6.415. In arbitrations in Sweden chaired by a Swedish lawyer, the parties are sometimes asked to submit their respective statements of evidence, indicating the witnesses and the documentary evidence they wish to rely on.

6.96 Although not applicable to arbitration proceedings in Sweden, unless the parties so agree, the IBA Rules on the Taking of Evidence in International Commercial Arbitration ('IBA Rules')[68] may play a role in such proceedings as guidelines in respect of issues of evidence. The IBA Rules may serve as a resource for parties and arbitrators in order to enable them to conduct the evidence phase of international arbitration proceedings in an efficient and economical manner.[69] The IBA Rules

---

[66] Govt Bill 1998/99:35, p 115.

[67] Ibid, p 116; see para 6.150.

[68] International Bar Association's 2nd edition 1999 of its Rules adopted by a resolution of the IBA Council on 29 May 2010.

[69] See Foreword to the IBA Rules by David W Rivkin in the 2nd edition of the 1999 Rules adopted on 1 June 1999.

provide mechanisms for the presentation of documents, witnesses of fact, expert witnesses and inspections, as well as for the conduct of evidentiary hearings. The IBA Rules are designed to be used in conjunction with, and adopted together with, institutional or *ad hoc* rules or procedures governing international commercial arbitrations. In practice, the parties seldom agree to apply the IBA Rules *strictu senso*, but rather agree to use them as guidelines.

6.5.4.2 *Powers of the arbitrators*

The principle of party autonomy applies also with respect to evidence, save for some limited powers of the arbitrators to dismiss evidence manifestly irrelevant or untimely presented, see para 6.101. As mentioned above, section 25(1) of the SAA stipulates that the parties 'shall supply the evidence'. This means that the parties are in charge of the evidence, including witnesses, that they wish to rely on and the way the evidence will be presented to the arbitrators. Thus, the parties cannot rely on assistance from the arbitrators to find out and present the facts. Notwithstanding this, parties may benefit from the arbitrators' case management activities in this respect, at least in the sense that the arbitrators may indicate which facts they deem relevant. On the other hand, any case management activity must be carefully balanced so as not to jeopardize the impartiality of the arbitrators. **6.97**

For the parties, the presentation of evidence is crucial. If irrelevant and insufficient evidence has been presented and caused the party to lose the dispute, there is no second chance to present additional evidence. Also, if the tribunal has evaluated evidence in a way not anticipated by the party, this cannot serve as a ground to have the award set aside. Not even if new important evidence were to come to light only after the award has been rendered, is it possible to have the award set aside.[70] The foregoing underlines the crucial importance for the parties properly to prepare and present evidence to the arbitrators. The arbitral award can only be based on facts and evidence presented to the tribunal by the parties. The private knowledge of the arbitrators can thus not serve as the basis for their decision. **6.98**

In the majority of cases, the parties are usually able to reach an agreement with respect to evidentiary matters and their respective witnesses will voluntarily attend the main hearing, at the request of the party relying on them. If they do not, the arbitrators' powers are restricted. The arbitrators have no subpoena powers and cannot compel a witness or an expert to appear at the hearing. In addition, the arbitrators have no power to administer oaths and truth affirmations. The criminal sanction of perjury is therefore not available if a witness fails to speak the truth. Ultimately, a party must rely on the possibility to seek court assistance in this respect,[71] see para 6.169. **6.99**

---

[70] See SOU 1994:81, p 184.
[71] Govt Bill 1998/99:35, pp 117–118.

6.100 In spite of the restrictions described above, the discovery of reliable evidence is assisted by two factors. First, the arbitrators are entitled to allocate evidentiary weight, in light of all the circumstances, to a person's (and especially a party's) refusal to be examined, to answer specific questions, or to produce documents. Second, an intensive cross-examination may be a more powerful instrument in extracting the truth than any oath or truth affirmation.[72] In addition, the practice in international commercial arbitration shows that very often reliance on documentary evidence is favoured by international arbitral tribunals and that the role of the witness is often reduced to comment on such documentary evidence.[73]

6.5.4.3 Admissibility of evidence

6.101 Generally speaking, the Swedish law of evidence allows the parties to rely on virtually all kinds of documents, statements, and occurrences to prove their case. The arbitrators in their discretion may freely evaluate the evidence presented by the parties, as well as all occurrences during the proceedings, for example, compliance with the arbitrators' orders.[74] It is important for lawyers coming from common law countries to appreciate this freedom from restrictions with respect to the admissibility of evidence. Consequently, reliance cannot successfully be placed on any technical rules concerning admissibility of evidence.

6.102 Rather, most arbitrators would be reluctant to accept any restrictive rules of evidence that prevent them from establishing the facts they deem necessary for deciding the dispute. Even though the arbitrators have the power to reject evidence as irrelevant, this is relatively seldom done in practice. Given the fact that it is difficult to determine before the hearing what is irrelevant, and considering that no second hearing on the merits may take place, most arbitrators tend to take a rather liberal approach in this respect. Under the Swedish law of evidence there are no restrictions against submitting evidence which the opposing party alleges is forged, or has been stolen from him. Such documents would not be rejected as inadmissible *per se*. Likewise, there is no prohibition against hearsay evidence. It will be for the arbitral tribunal to take account of such factors when evaluating the evidence in question.

6.103 Evidence may be rejected if it is presented too late in the arbitration or if it is manifestly irrelevant. This follows from section 25(2) of the SAA. The SAA does not, however, set forth any time limits for the presentation of evidence. As a rule the parties state their evidence well in advance of the final hearing in their respective statement of evidence and/or submit it together with their respective briefs. Nevertheless, it may happen that one of the parties wishes to introduce new evidence

---

[72] *Arbitration in Sweden* (2nd revised edn, 1984) 118.

[73] Cf Redfern and Hunter, *Law and Practice of International Commercial Arbitration* (4th edn, 2004) 298.

[74] The principle of free evaluation of evidence is generally accepted in international arbitration; see, for example, Article 25(6) of the 1976 UNCITRAL Arbitration Rules.

immediately prior to or sometimes even during the final hearing. In such situations the arbitrators have the power to reject the evidence, at least if it can be assumed that the new evidence is presented in bad faith, eg with a view to delaying the arbitration or to surprising the opponent. As mentioned above, arbitrators are generally rather reluctant to reject evidence. The reason is of course that the rejection may be relied on as a ground to challenge the award arguing that the party in question has not been given the opportunity to present its case.[75] If, however, the arbitrators are minded to reject evidence, a decision to this effect should be taken without delay, and certainly well in advance of the main hearing. If evidence is rejected because it is deemed to be manifestly irrelevant, the party in question may want to submit other documentary evidence and must thus be given sufficient time to do so. A decision by the arbitral tribunal to reject evidence cannot be appealed during the course of the arbitration. In this sense such a decision is final and binding. The decision can, however, be relied on by the party in question in an attempt to challenge the resulting award.

Occasionally the arbitrators may accept new evidence, even if offered during the main hearing, typically because it is deemed to be of potentially vital importance. In such situations, the arbitrators will offer the other party the opportunity to submit rebuttal evidence after the hearing and/or to submit a post-hearing brief commenting on the evidence in question. Unless otherwise agreed by the parties, Swedish arbitrators are, however, usually reluctant to allow post-hearing briefs.[76] As mentioned above, the underlying philosophy is that the main hearing should be the final step in the arbitration, save for the rendering of the award. **6.104**

With respect to the admissibility of evidence, the paramount principle of party autonomy must also be borne in mind. Hence, the parties are free to agree on issues of evidence, *inter alia*, with respect to formal requirements, certain restrictions with respect to the right to offer evidence, eg number of witnesses or experts on particular issues, and also exclusivity, eg a valuation report provided by an expert which the parties agree to accept beforehand.[77] **6.105**

The SAA, as well as most Arbitration Acts in other jurisdictions, does not require documents to be produced in the original, unless the other party challenges the authenticity thereof. The practice in international arbitrations in Sweden, is that a document drawn up in another language than the language of the proceedings is submitted in the original language with a translation into the language of the proceedings attached to it. **6.106**

As mentioned above the IBA Rules are often used as a guideline for the determination of admissibility of evidence in arbitration proceedings. The IBA Rules provide for **6.107**

---

[75] See discussion at para 8.118.
[76] Cf discussion at para 6.86.
[77] Cf Lindskog, *Skiljeförfarande, En kommentar* (2005) 735–738.

an 'international standard' of admissibility of evidence. Article 9(2) of the IBA Rules stipulates:

> The Arbitral Tribunal shall, at the request of a Party or on its own motion, exclude from evidence or production any document, statement, oral testimony or inspection for any of the following reasons:
>
> (a) lack of sufficient relevance or materiality;
> (b) legal impediment or privilege under the legal or ethical rules determined by the Arbitral Tribunal to be applicable;
> (c) unreasonable burden to produce the requested evidence;
> (d) loss or destruction of the document that has been reasonably shown to have occurred;
> (e) grounds of commercial or technical confidentiality that the Arbitral Tribunal determines to be compelling;
> (f) grounds of special political or institutional sensitivity (including evidence that has been classified as secret by a government or a public international institution) that the Arbitral Tribunal determines to be compelling; or
> (g) considerations of fairness or equality of the Parties that the Arbitral Tribunal determines to be compelling.

6.108 This very much corresponds to the approach taken by arbitral tribunals in international commercial cases sitting in Sweden. One important difference must be noted, however: arbitrators sitting in Sweden would *not* exclude evidence on their own motion. The adversarial nature of arbitration and the principle of party autonomy require them to act only at the request of one of the parties.

6.5.5 Documentary evidence and production of documents

6.5.5.1 Documentary evidence

6.109 In international arbitration, documentary evidence will often be of decisive importance to the outcome of the case. There are no provisions in the SAA defining documentary evidence. Generally, the lack of a definition is of less importance, since Swedish law allows the parties to rely on virtually all kinds of evidence. However, with respect to production of documents the distinction between documentary evidence and other evidence may be important. Today there are many categories of information which do not exist in written form, eg computerized information. In this respect, guidance could perhaps be sought from the Procedural Code.

6.110 Pursuant to Chapter 38, section 2 of the Procedural Code dealing with the production of documents, a party is entitled to obtain *written* documents only. However, the Procedural Code was adopted more than sixty years ago. Therefore this restriction has been interpreted by the courts. The Swedish Supreme Court has, for example, ruled that a court may order a party to submit computer printouts of information available only by computer. The decision illustrates that a request for disclosure of this kind of information can also be granted.[78] Accordingly, as long as the information is stored in a retrievable form, eg computerized, film, magnetic tape etc, it will probably be subject to production.

As far as the presentation of documentary evidence is concerned this is usually **6.111** agreed between the parties and the arbitral tribunal. As a rule the parties will submit documentary evidence together with their respective briefs. In many arbitrations the tribunal will, in consultation with the parties, determine a cut-off date after which no new documents can be submitted. The purpose is of course to prevent surprises and to afford the parties an equal opportunity to present their respective cases. Sometimes the arbitrators will ask the parties to submit so-called statements of evidence, which is the accepted practice in Swedish court proceedings. Such statements cover documentary as well as oral evidence. With respect to documentary evidence, the statement of evidence is expected to identify all documents that the party wishes to rely on and to explain, with respect to each document, what fact(s) the document is intended to prove. Needless to say, such statements of evidence are very helpful both for the arbitrators and the opposing party.

6.5.5.2 Production of documents

In contrast to the Procedural Code[79] and the SCC Rules,[80] the SAA does not have **6.112** provisions concerning production of documents. Notwithstanding this, in practice it is accepted that arbitrators, at the request of a party, may order the opposing party to produce documents in its possession. This authority is based on section 25 of the SAA. The arbitrators have no authority to order production of documents which are in the possession of third parties.

Normally the production of documents does not present problems: the parties **6.113** submit the documents they wish to rely on. However, if one party is in possession of documents which are unfavourable to his case and the other party wishes to rely on them, problems may arise. It may well be that the tribunal—at the request of one party—orders the other party to produce such documents. It is important to note, however, that the tribunal has no subpoena powers. There is consequently no way of enforcing such an order. The arbitrators may, however, attach evidentiary weight to the fact that a party refuses to abide by such an order.[81] On the other hand, it is possible to obtain evidence with the assistance of Swedish courts, including production of documents, subject to the approval of the arbitral tribunal.[82] This

---

[78] *Rolf Gummesson AB v Securitas Teknik AB* (NJA 1998 p 829). See also Heuman, *Arbitration Law of Sweden, Practice and Procedure* (2003) 453–455.

[79] See Chapter 38, section 2 of the Procedural Code.

[80] See Article 26(3) of the SCC Rules.

[81] See para 6.164.

[82] See discussion at para 6.170.

possibility is, however, seldom used in practice. Moreover, even if this means that discovery is thus available, this procedure is quite different from discovery procedures practised in common law countries.[83]

6.114 It is not unusual that the parties agree, at least in principle, to discovery, in the sense that they agree to provide the opposing party with identified documents requested by him. Acting on requests for discovery by the parties, Swedish arbitrators will typically follow the rules and principles of discovery contained in the Procedural Code, unless the parties have agreed on specific rules to be applied with respect to discovery. This means, *inter alia*, that discovery will not be permitted as regards immaterial documents, or if proof can be obtained by different means and at lesser cost. For a tribunal to determine whether a document is immaterial or not the document must be identified, or at least be characterized by category.

6.115 This very much corresponds to the approach taken in the IBA Rules. It is not unusual for parties to agree to use the IBA Rules as guidelines with respect to production of documents. Article 3(3) of the Rules stipulates:

> A Request to produce documents shall contain:
>
> (a) (i) a description of each requested document sufficient to identify it; or
>
>   (ii) a description in sufficient details (including subject matters) of a narrow and specific requested category of documents that are reasonably believed to exist; in the case of documents maintained in electronic form, the requesting party may, or the Arbitral Tribunal may order that it shall be required to identify specific files, search terms, individuals or other means of searching for such documents in an efficient and economic manner;
>
> (b) a statement as to how the Documents requested are relevant to the case and material to its outcome; and
>
> (c) (i) a statement that the Documents requested are not in possession, custody or control of the requesting party or a statement of the reasons why it would be unreasonably burdensome for the requesting Party to produce such Documents; and
>
>   (ii) a statement of the reasons why the requesting Party assumes that the Documents requested are in the possession, custody or control of another Party.

6.116 As a consequence of the foregoing, under Swedish law parties cannot be ordered to produce lists of documents which are, or may have been, in their possession and which might be of *general relevance* in the dispute. As a matter of principle, parties can be ordered to produce documents, only if they may constitute *evidence* in the dispute. As mentioned above, this means that so-called fishing expeditions are not possible under Swedish law, save, of course, for the unlikely event that the parties would so agree. It should also be noted that the obligation to produce documents

---

[83] For details, see Brocker, *Discovery in International Arbitration—the Swedish Approach*, SAR 2001:2, p 19.

in a Swedish court proceeding is limited in the same way as the obligation to give oral testimony. This means, for example, that documents falling under the attorney–client privilege may not be produced to a court, nor to an arbitral tribunal, unless the party in question agrees thereto.

Even though there are no provisions in the SAA to this effect, the generally held view **6.117** seems to be that the privileges laid down in the Swedish Procedural Code[84] should as

---

[84] The relevant provisions in the Swedish Procedural Code are the following:

Chapter 36, Section 5

Persons who may not provide information pursuant to either the Public Access to Information and Secrecy Act (2009:400), Chapter 15, Section 1 or 2, Chapter 16, Section 1 or Chapter 18, Section 5, 6 or 7 or any provision referred to in any of these statutory provisions, may not be heard as a witness concerning that information without the permission by the authority in the activity of which the information has been obtained.

Attorneys, physicians, dentists, midwives, trained nurses, psychologists, psychotherapists, officers at family guidance, officers under the Social Services Act (2001:453) and their counsel, and authorised patent attorneys and their counsel in relation to matters of patent law under section 2 of the [lagen (2010:000) om auktorisation av patentombud] may not testify concerning matters entrusted to, or found out by, them in their professional capacity unless the examination is authorized by law or is consented to by person for whose benefit the duty of secrecy is imposed. A person who pursuant to the Public Access to Information and Secrecy Act (2009:400), Chapter 24, Section 8, may not provide the information therein referred to, may be heard as a witness concerning that information only if authorised by law or the person for whose benefit the duty of secrecy is imposed consents thereto.

Attorneys, counsel or defence counsel may be heard as a witness concerning matters entrusted to them in the performance of their assignment only if the party gives consent.

Notwithstanding the provisions in the second and third paragraphs, there is an obligation to give evidence for

1. attorneys and their counsel, except for public defenders, in criminal cases where the minimum penalty is at least 2 years' imprisonment.

2. persons other than defence counsel in cases concerning offences referred to in Public Access to Information and Secrecy Act (2009:400), Chapter 10, Section 21 or 23.

3. persons obliged to provide information under Chapter 14, Section 1 of the Social Services Act (2001:453) on cases under Chapter 5, Section 2 or Chapter 6, Section 6,13 or 14 of the same Act or under the Special Provisions for the Care of Young Persons Act (1990:52).

Ministers of a congregation other than the Church of Sweden or those having a corresponding standing in such a congregation may not be heard as a witness concerning matters about which they have been informed at a secret confession or else during conversations for pastoral care.

Anyone who is bound by duty to observe secrecy pursuant to the Freedom of Press Act, Chapter 3, Section 3, or the Fundamental Law on the Freedom on the Freedom of Expression, Chapter 2, Section 3, may be heard as a witness concerning the circumstances to which the secrecy duty relates only to the extent prescribed by the said sections.

If pursuant to what is stated in this section a person may not be heard as a witness concerning a particular circumstance, nor may a witness examination occur with the person who, bound by duty of secrecy, has assisted with interpretation or translation.

a matter of principle apply by analogy in arbitrations.[85] If the person in whose possession the relevant document is, has his domicile outside Sweden, the rules of privilege applicable at his domicile may also be applicable. Article 9(3) of the IBA Rules sets forth recommendations for how an arbitral tribunal can deal with issues of privilege.

6.118 On the practical level, arbitrators usually try to reach a consensus with the parties on such matters as authenticity and translation of documents, number of copies to be submitted etc.

6.119 In order to manage requests for production of documents efficiently, parties and arbitrators often agree to use the so-called 'Redfern Schedule'. The Redfern Schedule is a chart containing the following four columns:

> *First Column*: identification of the document(s) or categories of documents that have been requested;
> *Second Column*: short description of the reasons for each request;
> *Third Column*: summary of the objections by the other party to the production of the document(s) or categories of documents requested; and
> *Fourth Column*: the decision of the arbitral tribunal on each request.

6.120 The chart is exchanged between the parties, and if need be submitted to the arbitral tribunal for decision.

Chapter 36, Section 6

A witness may decline to testify concerning a circumstance that should reveal that he, or a person related to him as stated in Section 3, has committed a criminal or dishonourable act.

Further, a witness may refuse to give testimony that should involve disclosure of a trade secret. A witness may also refuse to disclose personal information about a private individual under Chapter 35, Section II of the Public Access to Information and Secrecy Act (2009:400).

Paragraph 2 does not apply if there is extraordinary reason for examining the witness on the matter.

Chapter 38, Section 2

Anybody holding a written document that can be assumed to be of importance as evidence is obliged to produce it; in criminal cases, however, such a obligation is not imposed upon the suspect or any person related to him as stated in Chapter 36, Section 3.

Neither a party, nor any person related to him as stated above, is obliged to produce written communication between party and such a related person or between such related persons. Neither a public official nor any other person referred to in Chapter 36, Section 5, may produce a written document if it can be assumed that its contents are such that he may not be heard as a witness thereto; when the document is held by the party for those who benefit an obligation of confidentiality is imposed, the party is not obliged to produce the document. The provision in Chapter 36, Section 6, as to the privilege of a witness to refuse to testify shall correspondingly apply to the holder of a written document if the contents of the document are such as referred to in the said Section.

The obligation to produce written documents does not extend to jottings or any other personal notes exclusively for one's private use unless extraordinary reason exists for their production.

[85] Cf Govt Bill 1998/99:35, 116–117.

In many cases the arbitrators will instruct the parties to request documents from **6.121** each other before they seek the assistance of the arbitrators, and suggest that correspondence and documents exchanged in the course of this process should not be sent to the arbitrators. This is usually an efficient practice which avoids unnecessary work for the arbitrators and therefore saves money for the parties.[86]

6.5.6 Witnesses and experts

6.5.6.1 Hearing of witnesses

In the Swedish Procedural Code a distinction is made between witnesses and **6.122** party representatives. A witness testifies under oath, whereas a party representative testifies under a so-called truth affirmation. No such distinction is made in the SAA. As mentioned above, in arbitrations no national rules of evidence apply, unless the parties so agree. As a consequence any person can testify in an arbitration. Needless to say, when evaluating oral evidence the arbitrators will take into account whether testimony has been given by a party representative or by a witness in the strict sense of the word, ie by a person who is not related to the party in question. In the following reference will be made to 'witnesses' irrespective of whether they are party representatives or witnesses in the narrower sense. In one situation, however, tribunals tend to maintain the difference. As a rule, witnesses are not allowed to be present prior to their own testimony, unless otherwise agreed by the parties. Party representatives may, however, participate in the hearings from the very beginning. The SAA does not deal with this situation, but Swedish arbitrators tend to follow the provisions of the Procedural Code in this respect.

As mentioned above, it is the responsibility of the parties to provide the evidence to **6.123** be reviewed by the tribunal. This includes the responsibility to make sure that witnesses are present. Each party is responsible for witnesses called by it. In most cases the parties will have agreed, in consultation with the arbitrators, on a timetable for the hearing, which means that the presence of witnesses does not usually present a problem. If, such an agreement notwithstanding, a witness fails to appear at the hearing, the party having called the witness will usually have to bear any negative consequences of such failure. Only in rare situations would the arbitrators postpone the hearing. This could happen, for example, if the party in question can show a valid cause for the failure of the witness to appear, eg serious illness, breakdown in communications etc, and if the witness is crucial for that party. Rather than postponing the hearing, the arbitrators would probably try to arrange for the witness to testify via videolink or telephone. Another possibility would be to schedule a subsequent, separate session for examination of that witness.

---

[86] Hanotiau, *Document Production in International Arbitration*—2006 Special Supplement, ICC International Court of Arbitration Bulletin, p 118.

6.124 In arbitrations in Sweden it is generally accepted that witnesses may be interviewed and prepared before they testify orally. The same approach is taken by the IBA Rules, Article 4(3) of which stipulates:

> It shall not be improper for a Party, its officers, employees, legal advisors or other representatives to interview its witnesses and to discuss their prospective testimony with them.

6.125 It goes without saying that there are limits in this respect. Experienced arbitrators are usually good at detecting 'over prepared' witnesses, in which case the effect is usually counter-productive. It must always be kept in mind that the ultimate purpose of witness testimony is to convince the arbitrators, not the client and not the opposing party.

6.126 As previously mentioned, arbitrators have no power with respect to witnesses and thus cannot compel a person to appear as a witness. Also, pursuant to section 25(3), arbitrators are not entitled to administer oaths, which means that witnesses cannot testify under oath before an arbitral tribunal.[87]

6.127 There are several different methods of taking evidence by hearing and examining witnesses. In international commercial arbitrations today it is common practice that the parties submit written statements of the witnesses on whose testimony they wish to rely.[88] Sometimes such statements are referred to as affidavits, which typically means that they are submitted under oath.[89] More often, however, they are simply signed by the witness. By using written witnesses statements the arbitration can be conducted in a more speedy and efficient manner. In such cases, the witness statement will usually stand in lieu of the direct examination of the witness, which usually means that the hearing can be shortened dramatically, by starting with cross-examination of the witness, followed by re-direct examination. Usually the arbitrators try to reach agreement with the parties as regards the use of written witness statements. When it comes to the hearing of witnesses, it should be recalled that it is for the parties themselves to decide what witnesses they wish to rely on.

6.128 In most arbitrations the parties try to agree on the order in which witnesses are to be heard. If the parties cannot agree, the arbitral tribunal will determine the order, but usually with some degree of cooperation from the parties. The traditional approach is to examine all the witnesses called by the claimant first and then all the witnesses called by the respondent. Needless to say, there may be variations of this approach depending on the circumstances in the individual case and on the agreement of the parties.

---

[87] It is possible, however, to hear witnesses under oath before the competent District Court, subject to the consent of the arbitral tribunal; section 26(1) of the SAA; see discussion at para 6.169.

[88] See discussion at para 6.144.

[89] Hobér in Bishop (ed), *The Art of Advocacy in International Arbitration* (2004) 187.

Generally speaking, witnesses would be expected to be called with a view to **6.129** proving disputed facts. Most Swedish arbitrators would not look favourably on witnesses who 'plead', or explain, the case of the party who has called them. This is for counsel to do in the written submissions and during oral argument. Furthermore, there is no need to have witnesses 'confirm' the contents of documents which have been submitted as evidence. It is sufficient for counsel to refer to such documents in the written submissions and during the opening and/or closing statement at the main hearing. During closing arguments counsel is expected to draw factual and legal conclusions from, and build arguments on the basis of, such documents.

The examination of witnesses usually proceeds in three stages, viz, (a) direct exami- **6.130** nation, (b) cross-examination, and (c) re-direct examination.

In arbitrations in Sweden, the examination of witnesses is done by counsel, unless **6.131** the parties have otherwise agreed. Needless to say, the arbitrators have the right to put questions as well. Traditionally, however, it is deemed appropriate for the arbitrators to wait with their questions until counsel have finished their examination of the witness. Sometimes all the questions from the arbitrators are channelled through the chairperson. This is not necessary, however, since the party-appointed arbitrators too should have the possibility to put questions. Generally speaking, arbitrators are expected to tread very carefully, if at all, in areas which have not been addressed during examination by counsel, lest the impartiality of the arbitrators be questioned.

Direct examination   In cases where written witness statements are used, no direct **6.132** examination will, as a rule, take place, save possibly for a few introductory questions. The witness will thereafter be handed over for cross-examination.

The general purpose of the direct examination is for the witness to prove disputed **6.133** facts which are relevant to the case, but not, as mentioned above, to 'plead', or explain, the case of the party who has called him.

In arbitrations where no written witness statements are used, the arbitrators would **6.134** usually ask the parties to submit statements of evidence. As far as witnesses are concerned the statements indicate the circumstances with respect to which the witness will testify as well as what fact the witness will prove. The primary purpose of these statements is to inform the opposing party so as to facilitate the preparation of his case and evidence, and to avoid surprises at the main hearing. As a matter of principle the witness cannot go beyond the theme indicated in the statement of evidence. Opposing counsel usually make sure that the other party is not taken by surprise as a result of statements going beyond the theme indicated in the statement of evidence. If such statements are made anyway, experienced arbitrators are usually good at finding practical solutions to such a problem, rather than postponing the hearing to allow the other party time to consider rebuttal evidence.

6.135 During direct examination counsel is not allowed to put leading questions, ie questions which invite a certain answer by the witness.[90] Although witnesses are often 'prepared' by counsel[91] before the main hearing it may be difficult to uphold the objective of having the witness testify in a comprehensive and coherent way without interruption. In practice, therefore, counsel will usually assist the witness by putting questions to it from the very outset of the examination.[92]

6.136 It is sometimes said that from a tactical point of view it may be prudent to use the direct examination as a way to 'defuse' potentially difficult and vulnerable questions and areas of inquiry. The underlying philosophy is simply that this will be less damaging than if the witness were to answer such questions during cross-examination.[93]

6.137 **Cross-examination** The purpose of cross-examination in arbitrations, just as in court litigation, is generally to weaken the case for the side that has called the witness—typically by trying to undermine the credibility of the witness—and to strengthen your own case by trying to establish facts which are favourable to you. This being said, however, in most cases it is very difficult entirely to ruin the credibility of the other party's witness or to reveal him as a liar through cross-examination. Rather, it is usually more efficient to point to a few flaws in the witness testimony—the cross-examination should be 'a stiletto, not a sledge hammer attack'.[94] A different approach is to use cross-examination as a way to argue your case through the testimony of the other party's witnesses. Generally speaking, it is believed that most arbitrators would find such an approach unhelpful. In discussing the methods to employ when cross-examining a witness it is crucial to answer the following questions: Has the witness testified to anything that is material against us? Has his testimony injured our side of the case? Has he made an impression with the arbitrators against us? Is it necessary for us to cross-examine him at all?[95] Only if the three first questions are answered in the affirmative should the last question be answered in the same way.

6.138 Needless to say, thorough preparation of the cross-examination is essential. One complicating factor in this respect is that the cross-examiner in international arbitration will usually not know what the witness will answer, because the witness will not have given any depositions, unless the parties have agreed thereto.[96]

---

[90] The SAA is silent in this respect but this principle is set forth in Chapter 36, section 17(1) and (5) of the Procedural Code. There is general agreement that the same rules should also apply to arbitration proceedings in Sweden.

[91] As mentioned above in para 6.123, under Swedish law it is not improper to interview and to prepare witnesses prior to the main hearing; see Article 4(3) of the IBA Rules on the Taking of Evidence in Commercial Arbitration.

[92] Hobér in Bishop (ed), *The Art of Advocacy in International Arbitration* (2004) 189.

[93] Ibid, 189–190.

[94] Neubauer, 'Mastering the Blind Cross-Examination' 35(2) *Litigation* (2009).

[95] Wellman, *The Art of Cross-Examination* (2nd edn, 1903), republished by the American Bar Association in 2009, p 8.

[96] Cf Neubauer, 'Mastering the Blind Cross-Examination'.

On the other hand, preparation of the cross-examination is facilitated when written witness statements are being used. There is always a risk, however, that the witness cannot, or will refuse to, answer questions because he does not remember, or because he claims that he has not had the opportunity to refresh his memory.

There are some ways to overcome, or at least diminish, the aforementioned diffi- **6.139** culties. First and foremost, a detailed knowledge of the case and all documents related thereto gives the cross-examiner an advantage and an opportunity to reveal weaknesses in the witness's answers. Secondly, during cross-examination counsel may put leading questions to the witness.[97] In fact, all, or most, questions should ideally be leading. Thirdly, the use of documents as the starting-point, or as the basis, for questions often strengthens the position of the cross-examiner and leaves less room for the witness to argue.

The techniques of cross-examination are many and varied.[98] Some prefer short and **6.140** quick questions so as to keep the witness under control throughout the cross-examination. That is, at least, the hope. Others would prefer questions which are woven in into a dialogue with the witness, the underlying philosophy being that it is better to have the cooperation of the witness than being confrontational. The style and technique of cross-examination will of course vary with the character and personality of the witness—and of counsel—as well as with the circumstances of the individual case.

While cross-examination by Swedish counsel and/or under the chairpersonship **6.141** of a Swedish arbitrator is usually less combative than in the traditional Anglo-American setting, it may occasionally be both combative and heated.

It goes without saying that if cross-examination is too combative, it will often be **6.142** counterproductive. First, it may be very difficult to have the witness answer any question without making reservations and/or asking for clarifications. Secondly, the credibility of the witness may indeed increase, at least in the eyes of the arbitrators, which is clearly undesirable. After all it is the tribunal which needs to be convinced.

During cross-examination counsel will often refer to documents as the starting- **6.143** point, or as the basis, for his questions. This is accepted practice, certainly if the documents have already been submitted well in advance of the main hearing. Problems may arise if new documents are presented during cross-examination. If a new document is produced as evidence, the document may well be rejected on the ground that it is too late.[99] It is possible, however, that a document in the

---

[97] Cf Chapter 36, section 17(2) and (5) of the Procedural Code.
[98] For a general discussion, see Cremades and Cairns, 'Cross-examination and International Arbitrations', in Hobér, Magnusson, and Öhrström (eds), *Between East and West: Essays in Honor of Ulf Franke* (2010) 91 *et seq.*
[99] See discussion at para 6.102.

cross-examiner's possession which proves that the witness has been lying during direct examination—which typically cannot be foreseen and thus there was no need to submit the document prior to the hearing—would be accepted as proof with respect to the credibility, or rather the lack thereof, of the witness. If a new document were to be produced, not as evidence but for illustration purposes during cross-examination—sometimes referred to as a reliance document—such a document may sometimes be accepted. The problem here, however, is that such a document may, and usually does, come as a surprise for the other party and for the witness. It would also deprive the other party of the possibility to prepare that particular aspect of a cross-examination.

6.144 **Re-direct examination.** As mentioned above, the last phase of the examination of witnesses is the re-direct examination. This affords the witness an opportunity to supplement and/or clarify answers given during cross-examination. The questions put during cross-examination thus constitute the framework for the re-direct examination. Leading questions are not allowed during this phase of the examination.

6.5.6.2 Written witness statements

6.145 As mentioned above, the use of written witness statements, or affidavits, is common practice nowadays in international arbitration proceedings.[100] Even though affidavits are typically submitted under oath, arbitrators generally do not seem to attach more evidentiary weight to such affidavits than to written statements simply signed by the witness.

6.146 The benefit of using written statements, be they affidavits or not, is that the arbitration can be conducted in a more speedy and efficient manner. The normal practice is that a witness who has submitted an affidavit appears at the hearing and subjects him/herself to cross-examination by counsel for the other party. The right to cross-examine the other parties' witnesses follows from the general and fundamental notion of due process in arbitration proceedings.[101] In such case no direct examination of the witness will usually take place, save perhaps for a few introductory questions with a view to giving the witness the opportunity to confirm his statement, or to make minor amendments to it.

6.147 It is not uncommon for counsel for the parties in fact to draft the statements for the witnesses. From a practical point of view, this is efficient for the purpose of focusing the statements only on issues of direct relevance for the dispute. On the other hand, such practice does tend to erode the evidentiary weight of the statement.

---

[100] See Article 28(2) of the SCC Rules and Article 4 of the IBA Rules on the Taking of Evidence in Commercial Arbitration (2nd edn, 1999); cf the general practice in Swedish domestic arbitration proceedings where the use of written witness statements is still unusual.

[101] Cf section 24 of the SAA and Article 28(3) of the SCC Rules.

As mentioned above, written witness statements are now generally accepted in **6.148** international arbitrations. This is also reflected in Article 4 of the IBA Rules. Pursuant to section 5 of Article 4, a witness statement shall contain:

(a) the full name and address of the witness, a statement regarding his or her present and past relationship (if any) with any of the Parties, and a description of his or her background, qualifications, training and experience, if such description may be relevant to the dispute or to the contents of the statement;

(b) a full and detailed description of the facts, and the source of the witness's information as to those facts, sufficient to serve as that witness's evidence in the matter dispute. Documents on which the witness relies that have not already been submitted shall be provided;

(c) a statement as to the language in which the Witness Statement was originally prepared and the language in which the witness anticipates giving testimony at the Evidentiary Hearing;

(d) an affirmation of the facts of the Witness Statement; and

(e) the signature of the witness and its date and place.

Historically, in domestic arbitrations, ie those between Swedish parties before **6.149** Swedish arbitrators, the use of written witness statements was restricted due to the Swedish legal tradition prohibiting such statements in judicial proceedings. However, this practice is about to shift, *inter alia*, as a result of recent amendments to the Procedural Code which now accepts written statements[102] and also through the influence from international arbitration practice.

6.5.6.3 Experts

In most international commercial arbitrations conducted in Sweden, the arbitrators **6.150** are lawyers. This means that when complicated technical issues are involved they may need the assistance of experts to resolve the dispute. This may be the case in construction disputes and also in arbitrations were the quantification of a claim is complicated. This may be done either by experts appointed by the parties—in which case they are more correctly characterized as witnesses with expert knowledge—or by experts appointed by the tribunal. When the parties appoint their own experts the testimony of these tends to differ, thus leaving the arbitrators with the difficult task of evaluating the expert evidence, sometimes after having appointed their own expert.

Usually the arbitrators are given the express power by the parties to appoint experts **6.151** at the expense of the parties. Under Swedish arbitration law the arbitrators may appoint their own expert, unless both parties object thereto, although this is rarely done in practice.[103]

---

[102] See Chapter 35, section 14(2) of the Procedural Code, which provides for an exception to the general prohibition against affidavits in judicial procedure if both parties so agree and the court does not consider this to be manifestly inappropriate.

[103] See section 25, first paragraph of the Arbitration Act; cf Article 29 of the SCC Rules.

6.152   The reason for this exception from the main rule—ie that the parties themselves must supply the evidence, oral as well as documentary—is simply that there may be issues with respect to which the arbitrators lack the necessary expertise.[104] If the arbitrators come to the conclusion that they need the assistance of an expert, they should—and it is common practice—raise this issue with the parties and ask for their comments. Likewise it is common practice for the arbitrators to discuss with the parties the terms of reference for any expert appointed by the tribunal. It is important in this context to emphasize that the arbitrators cannot delegate their duty to determine the dispute to their experts; the arbitrators cannot abdicate from their role as decision-makers. Rather, the arbitrators are expected to take the views of the expert into account, as one of several factors, when deciding the dispute.

6.153   As long as it is clear that the arbitrators are merely taking advice that forms part of the material on which they base their decision, it is generally accepted that they appoint an expert. If the tribunal needs assistance to understand complicated technical matters it is difficult to see any objection to the appointment of an expert by the tribunal, even if one of the parties objects.

6.154   If the arbitrators appoint an expert, his report will be delivered to the parties and in most cases the expert will attend the final hearing and be prepared to answer questions from the parties.

6.155   When experts are appointed by the parties, it is important to keep in mind that the SAA does not set forth any requirements or qualifications with respect to such experts. Consequently, it is not possible to challenge an expert, for example due to alleged lack of impartiality or expertise, and have him removed. The opposing party can, however, point out facts and circumstances which in its view undermine the credibility of the expert and ask the tribunal to take that into account when evaluating the evidentiary weight of the expert's testimony.

6.156   As far as the admissibility of expert evidence is concerned, the same principles apply as with respect to other forms of evidence.[105]

6.157   Expert evidence is almost without exception presented by way of expert reports. At the hearing, experts are usually subjected to cross-examination, unless otherwise agreed by the parties, or when the opposing party refrains from cross-examination. Articles 5 and 6 of the IBA Rules set forth some practical and helpful suggestions with respect to party-appointed experts and tribunal-appointed experts, respectively.

6.158   In addition to the traditional way of examining experts appointed by the parties—ie primarily cross-examination—there are a number of alternative methods of presenting expert evidence, including so-called witness conferencing.

---

[104] Govt Bill 1998/1999:35, p 116.
[105] See discussion at para 6.100.

Such conferencing means that experts appointed by both parties are heard at the **6.159**
same time, usually with questions asked by the chairperson. There are, however,
several variations of this approach, all of which should be agreed with the parties.

6.5.6.4 Inspection of the subject matter of the dispute

This method of presenting evidence is usually in the form of a site inspection and is **6.160**
mainly used in construction disputes and disputes related to turn-key deliveries
of plants and equipment belonging thereto. It would seem that this way of presenting evidence is relatively seldom used in practice. The reason is usually the cost
and time involved, especially as compared to the added benefit. Very often the
same purpose can be fulfilled by using photographs, drawings, maps and
models, and sometimes video films. Arbitrators would normally not make an
inspection without counsel of both parties being present and would not put
questions to personnel at the site directly related to the dispute, unless counsel
are given the opportunity to put additional questions.

As a practical matter, it is submitted that it is good practice not to allow any impromptu **6.161**
witness testimonies, or even informal discussions with site personnel unless this has
been planned, or at least agreed, beforehand. Furthermore, it is important to agree
on how the site visit and observations made during it are to be recorded.

6.5.6.5 Evaluation of evidence

As stated above arbitrators may *freely* evaluate all evidence presented during the **6.162**
proceedings. Furthermore, they may freely evaluate all occurrences during the
proceedings, for example, compliance with orders issued by the tribunal. Thus, if a
party refuses to answer questions, or to produce a certain document requested by
the tribunal, the arbitrators are free to allocate such evidentiary weight to this
fact as they deem appropriate in light of all circumstances. Consequently, there are
no rules under Swedish arbitration law which regulate the evaluation of evidence, a
fact which is in stark contrast to the relatively strict application of the 'law of evidence' in common law countries, at least as far as court litigation is concerned.
Indeed, the principle of free evaluation of evidence is a hallmark of Swedish judicial
and arbitral procedure.

It follows from the foregoing that it is difficult, if not impossible, to provide guide- **6.163**
lines concerning evaluation of evidence in arbitrations. Generally speaking,
however, arbitrators tend to give more weight to testimony if it is corroborated
by documentary evidence. Also, testimony of a truly independent witness is typically
given more evidentiary weight than that of a witness, or representative of either
party, with a clear interest in the outcome of the case.

As mentioned above, one factor that arbitrators may come to take into account **6.164**
when evaluating the evidence in a dispute is a party's compliance—or rather non-
compliance—with orders issued by the tribunal. The most practical situation is
probably when a party has failed, sometimes refused, to produce a document ordered

by the tribunal to be produced to it and to the other party.[106] It is often said that the arbitrators may draw negative, adverse, inferences from such a fact. For example, the IBA Rules stipulates in Article 9(5):

> If a Party fails without satisfactory explanation to produce any Document requested in a Request to Produce to which it has not objected in due time or fails to produce any Document ordered to be produced by the Arbitral Tribunal, the Arbitral Tribunal may infer that such documents would be adverse to the interests of that Party.

6.165 A similar provision is found in Article 30(3) of the SCC Rules, where it is stated:

> If a party without good cause fails to comply with any provision of, or requirement under, these Rules or any procedural order given by the Arbitral Tribunal, the Arbitral Tribunal may draw such inferences as it considers appropriate.

6.166 While the right to draw negative inferences is generally acknowledged,[107] it is submitted that the practical importance of this right is limited. Few arbitrators would in all likelihood be prepared to decide a case solely on the basis of a negative inference. It may, however, be included among other factors to be evaluated and assessed by the arbitrators.

6.167 Evaluation of evidence is generally viewed as a *procedural* matter which is governed by the *lex arbitri*. Under Swedish arbitration law an error in the evaluation of evidence is not a ground on which an award can successfully be challenged; it forms part of the arbitrators' analysis of the merits of the dispute.

6.168 Intertwined with the question of evidentiary weight is the question of the burden of proof. Neither the Procedural Code nor the SAA has any rules as regards the burden of proof. These issues are very intricate and present problems of great philosophical nicety. As regards Swedish court procedure they remain largely unresolved in the sense that no hard and fast rules seem to have developed. With respect to international commercial arbitrations in Sweden the practice seems to be to require each party to prove the facts on which he is relying, at least as the starting point. This approach is recognized in the 1976 UNCITRAL Arbitration Rules, Article 24. Depending on the facts and circumstances of the individual case, however, as well as the arguments relied on by the parties, the burden of proof may shift. This practice would seem to be accepted by most international arbitral tribunals. Under Article 14 of the 1980 Rome Convention, the burden of proof is a matter which is governed by the law applicable to the *substance* of the contract, ie the *lex contractus*. This makes sense since the burden of proof, and the way it may shift, will depend to

---

[106] For comments in general on this situation, see Sharpe, 'Drawing Adverse Interferences from Non-Production of Evidence' 22(4) *Arbitration International* (2006) 549–571; van Houtte, 'Adverse Interferences in International Arbitration', in Giovannini and Moure, *Written Evidence and Discovery in International Arbitrations—New Issues and Tendencies*, ICC Dossiers (2009) 195.

[107] See Nilsson, 'Negative Inferences: An Arbitral Tribunal's Power to Draw Adverse Conclusions from a Party's Failure to Comply with the Tribunal's Orders', in Hobér, Magnusson, and Öhrström (eds), *op cit*, 351 *et seq*.

a large extent on the nature of the legal relationship in question. The burden of proof being determined, there remains the question of the *standard of proof* which is required of a party to *fulfil* the burden of proof. The processes involved in determining the required level of proof would seem to elude meaningful description, although arbitrators—like judges—presumably consider a spectrum of probabilities in reaching their decisions in this respect.

It should also be mentioned that when witness testimony is contradictory, arbitrators are under no obligation to base their conclusions on non-contradictory testimony which seems more probable than other evidence. In such a situation it is reasonable to assume that the arbitrators will base their decision(s) on their own analysis of testimony and facts which have been established otherwise. **6.169**

6.5.7 Evidence taken with court assistance

As mentioned above,[108] arbitrators are not entitled to administer oaths. Pursuant to section 26 of the SAA, however, a party wishing a witness or an expert to testify under oath, or a party to be examined under truth affirmation, may submit an application to such effect to the District Court. First, however, the party must obtain the approval of the arbitrators. The same applies also with respect to requests for production of documents assuming that a party wants to have a court order to this effect, since such order is enforceable, also in relation to third parties. **6.170**

The arbitrators must give their consent to such an application if they consider that the measure is justified, having regard to the evidence in the case. Cases where the arbitrators may refuse their consent could be if, for example, they believe that sufficient evidence has already been produced on the issue, the issue is irrelevant, the costs involved would be exorbitant, or the application has been made solely for some extraneous reason, such as a desire to obtain publicity or to obstruct or delay the arbitration proceedings. **6.171**

If the party against whom measures foreseen in section 26 is a non-Swedish party, two questions arise, viz, (i) do Swedish courts have jurisdiction with respect to such issues, and (ii) is an order by a Swedish court enforceable in the country where the requested document is and/or where the witness is domiciled? If the answer to the second question is negative, most parties would probably not be interested in spending the time and money required to obtain an order from a Swedish court. This is probably an important reason why applications based on section 26 of the SAA are seldom made in international arbitrations in Sweden. Most of the documents and witnesses in such cases are located outside Sweden. **6.172**

The question of whether Swedish courts have jurisdiction is not directly addressed in the SAA. Section 44(2) of the SAA stipulates that applications in accordance **6.173**

---

[108] See para 6.98.

with section 26 of the SAA are to be submitted to the District Court determined by the arbitrators, and that the Stockholm District Court shall hear such applications in the absence of a decision by the arbitrators. It is important to understand that this provision deals with the allocation of jurisdiction as between Swedish courts, ie available fora in Sweden. The provision does not automatically mean that Swedish courts have jurisdiction in relation to a non-Swedish party.[109] As discussed above,[110] the international jurisdiction of Swedish courts is dependent on whether there is a Swedish interest in the administration of justice with respect to the issue in question.

6.174 This is still an open issue which has so far not been addressed by the Swedish Supreme Court. For example, in a situation where none of the parties is Swedish and the document requested to be produced is not located in Sweden, it is not self-evident that there is a Swedish interest in the administration of justice to order the production of such a document. The fact that the Stockholm District Court is identified as a default forum in section 44(3) does not mean that there is necessarily a Swedish interest in the administration of justice with respect to such cases. For such an interest to be present, it is usually required that the dispute or the parties have some connection to Sweden.[111] In a decision from 1994 (*Sveriges Pälsdjursuppfödares Riksförbund och AB Nordiska Skinnauktioner mot Dansk Pelsdyravlerforening* NJA 1994 C48), the Supreme Court concluded that the mere fact that an arbitration was pending in Sweden was not a sufficient connection to Sweden for Swedish courts to have jurisdiction in relation to a non-Swedish respondent with respect to an application for interim measures, despite the fact that the respondent was said to have property in Sweden.

6.175 As mentioned above, applications pursuant to section 26 of the SAA require the prior approval of the arbitral tribunal. This approval must be submitted to the court together with the application. Section 26 stipulates that the arbitrators 'shall approve' a request for approval if they consider 'that the measure is justified having regard to the evidence in the case'. What does this mean? First of all, it should be mentioned that in taking this decision, the arbitrators must also comply with their obligation under section 21 of the SAA to handle the dispute in an impartial, practical, and speedy manner. Involving courts in the taking of evidence will undoubtedly delay the arbitration proceedings, which may be a significant problem if the parties have agreed on an award period but are unable to agree on an extension thereof. In the *travaux préparatoires* it is stated that the measure requested must be of significance as evidence,[112] which means that it must be capable of affecting the outcome of the case. Insofar as requests for production of documents are concerned, this

---

[109] Bogdan, *Svensk internationell privat- och processrätt* (7th edn, 2008) 117.
[110] See para 5.21.
[111] Bogdan, *Svensk internationell privat- och processrätt* (7th edn, 2008) 114.
[112] Govt Bill 1999/98:35, p 229.

probably means that they must be as detailed as any other request for documents submitted to the arbitral tribunal.[113] In fact the request must be detailed enough for the District Court to issue an order based thereon, should it decide to rule in favour of the applicant. It is only on the basis of such a detailed request that the arbitrators can determine whether the document in question may be of relevance as evidence. Another factor that arbitrators take into account when determining whether the measure is justified, is the extent to which their right freely to evaluate the evidence may be sufficient to address the situation. This may be particularly relevant in relation to the timing aspect.

When the requested measure is the examination under oath of a witness, the applicant must be able to give a plausible explanation as to why this is deemed necessary. One such explanation could perhaps be the credibility of the witness and the argument that it is better tested under oath. **6.176**

It is important to note that, pursuant to section 26(1) of the SAA, the District Court 'shall grant the application' where the requested measure may lawfully be taken, on the assumption that the tribunal has given its approval. This means that the District Court cannot review and retry the approval of the arbitral tribunal. This approach does seem to presuppose, however, that the arbitral tribunal has in fact made the detailed analysis described above. If this is not the case, it would seem inevitable that this analysis must be made by the District Court. **6.177**

One situation where it is possible that the measure may not be 'lawfully taken' is if it would involve the disclosure of trade secrets—as defined in the Swedish Trade Secrets Act—either by producing certain documents or as a result of testimony. The general rule under the Procedural Code is that a party is under an obligation to disclose trade secrets only if there are special reasons for doing so. **6.178**

If an application for the examination of witnesses or experts is granted by the District Court, the arbitrators shall be called to the hearing in court and be afforded the opportunity to put questions. Presumably, however, examination of the witness will be carried out by counsel, subsequent to the administration of the oath by the presiding judge. **6.179**

In practice, hearing witnesses and experts under oath before a District Court rarely occurs. With respect to disclosure, however, a court action is the only possible way to have documents disclosed by third parties, if these are not voluntarily cooperating. Moreover, since arbitrators' orders for production of documents, contrary to court orders of this kind, are not enforceable, a court action may be the last resort to obtain documents in the possession of the other party. **6.180**

SCC Rules   The SCC Rules have three provisions which deal with questions of evidence, viz, Article 26, Article 28, and Article 29. **6.181**

---

[113] See discussion at para 6.112.

6.182 Article 26 sets forth general provisions on the admissibility and presentation of evidence. Section 2 incorporates the philosophy underlying statements of evidence,[114] in that it entitles the arbitrators to ask a party to identify the circumstances intended to be proved by the evidence. Corresponding language is found in Article 28(1) dealing with witnesses.

6.183 Article 29 deals with experts appointed by the tribunal which in practice is a rare occurrence. Section 1 of Article 29 mirrors section 25 of the SAA in that the arbitrators may at their own initiative appoint experts. It is explicitly stated in section 1 of Article 29 that the parties must be consulted prior to such appointment.

6.5.8 Hearings

6.5.8.1 Introduction

6.184 In most, but not all, arbitrations there will usually be an oral hearing, at which witnesses and experts are presented and examined. This kind of hearing is usually called a main, or, final hearing. Sometimes it is referred to as the evidentiary hearing. As will be discussed below, there may also be other kinds of hearings, for example, for the purposes of preparing the case for the main hearing, or separate hearings dealing with specific issues.

6.185 Even though the place of arbitration, or the seat of the arbitration, is Sweden, this does not automatically mean that all hearings or meetings in the case must, or will, take place in Sweden. Subject to any agreement of the parties to the contrary, the arbitral tribunal is usually deemed to have the right to hold meetings and hearings in any other place or country.

6.186 This approach, which corresponds to international practice, is reflected in the SCC Rules. Article 20(1) of the SCC Rules stipulates that the seat of arbitration is decided by the Board, unless the parties have agreed on it. Section 2 of Article 20 then goes on to say:

> The Arbitral Tribunal may, after consultation with the parties, conduct hearings at any place which it considers appropriate. The Arbitral Tribunal may meet and deliberate at any place which it considers appropriate. If any hearing, meeting, or deliberation is held elsewhere than at the seat of arbitration, the arbitration shall be deemed to have taken place at the seat of arbitration.

6.187 Section 3 of Article 20 of the SCC Rules provides that the award shall be deemed to have been made at the seat of arbitration.[115]

---

[114] See para 6.134.

[115] It is submitted that Article 20 of the SCC Rules correctly reflects the position of Swedish arbitration law despite the 2005 decision by the Svea Court of Appeal, *Alcatel CITSA v The Titan Corporation* (RH 2005:1), where the Court refused to accept jurisdiction to hear a challenge of an award which identified Stockholm as the place of arbitration and which was based on an arbitration agreement identifying Stockholm as the place of arbitration, but where the hearings took place in London.

It follows from the foregoing that parties and arbitrators have a large degree of flexibility when it comes to determining the place of the hearings. In practice, however, at last one meeting or hearing session usually takes place in Sweden, when the place of arbitration is Sweden. **6.188**

The distinction discussed above between the place of *arbitration* and the place of the *hearings* is confirmed in section 22 of the SAA, the second paragraph of which provides that hearings may be held 'elsewhere in Sweden or abroad, unless otherwise determined by the parties'. Elsewhere in this context means at a place other than the place of arbitration.[116] **6.189**

When the place of arbitration is Sweden, the SAA applies. This is laid down in section 46 of the SAA. As previously discussed,[117] this means that Swedish arbitration law is the *lex arbitri*, ie the law governing the arbitration. Since Swedish arbitration law is based on the principle of party autonomy, this means that the form and procedure with respect to hearings will to a large extent depend on the agreement of the parties. **6.190**

Organization of work; appointment and functions of chairperson If there are two or more arbitrators, one of them must be appointed chairperson (section 20 of the SAA).[118] The parties are entitled to appoint the chairperson, failing which the chairperson shall be the arbitrator appointed by the other arbitrators or by the District Court, in their stead (section 20 of the SAA).[119] The task of the chairperson is to take charge of the deliberations of the arbitral tribunal and of the organization and conduct of meetings and hearings. Moreover, although not specifically regulated in the SAA, the chairperson is deemed to have special powers with respect to the management and administration of the proceedings. A large part of the chairperson's role relates to case management. He has the key responsibility for ensuring that the arbitral tribunal's general duties of fairness and impartiality in the treatment of the parties and avoidance of unnecessary delay or expense are upheld.[120] According to the *travaux préparatoires*, the chairperson should, *inter alia*, be entitled to draw up a schedule for the proceedings and arrange the venue for the hearings, and other practical matters.[121] If the chairperson is to be given more extensive powers, this should be expressly agreed between the parties and the arbitrators.[122] **6.191**

---

[116] Cf Govt Bill 1998/99:35, pp 113–114 and 225.

[117] See para 2.05.

[118] If the parties have not agreed on the number of arbitrators, there shall be three by default, see section 13 of the SAA.

[119] Cf Article 13(3) of the SCC Rules where it is stated that 'the Chairperson shall be appointed by the Board', ie the Board of the SCC Institute.

[120] See Briner, 'The Role of the Chairperson', in Newman and Hill (eds), *The Leading Arbitrators' Guide To International Arbitration* (2nd edn, 2008) 66.

[121] See Govt Bill 1998/99:35, p 110.

[122] Ibid, p 111 where it is said that delegation of authority 'ought to' rest on an agreement between the arbitrators and the parties. However, as long as it is a question purely of case management it is doubtful that there is a need for the parties' consent. Cf Article 35(2) of the SCC Rules which entitles the arbitral tribunal to decide that the chairperson alone may make procedural rulings.

6.192 The case management duties of the arbitrators thus include several elements of the procedure of the arbitration. These duties also extend to the substantive aspects of the dispute. As mentioned above,[123] the prayers for relief and the legal grounds relied upon by the parties play an important role in arbitrations in Sweden. It is the duty of the arbitrators to make sure that they properly understand the positions of the parties in these respects. This is important because the prayers for relief and the legal grounds constitute the mandate for the arbitrators. If the arbitrators rule *ultra petita* or *infra petita,* the resulting award may be set aside. If there is a need to clarify the positions of the parties, such clarification should take place as early as possible. Clarifications are important not only for the arbitrators but also for the other party. It is entitled to know what case it has to meet. In seeking clarifications from the parties it is essential for the arbitrators to maintain their impartiality, which means that any questions or comments from the arbitrators, either in writing, or orally, must be made in a balanced way.

6.193 Needless to say, the arbitrators cannot help one of the parties to improve its case, nor could they be seen by the other party to do so. The arbitrators should limit themselves to trying to understand the respective cases of the parties. Even if the arbitrators believe that they can balance assistance to one party, by also assisting the other party, this is not to be recommended. The explanation is simply that it is almost impossible to predict the consequences of such assistance. For example, if the assistance to one party causes him to amend his prayers for relief, or the legal grounds, and if these amendments turn out to be decisive for the outcome of the case, there is a significant risk that the resulting award may be set aside.

6.194 In international arbitrations, parties and counsel come from different jurisdictions with different legal traditions and approaches. Active case management is therefore important to avoid misunderstandings and mistakes and to ensure that the parties are treated in an equal manner and that they are given the opportunity to present their respective cases. It is clear from the foregoing that active case management is a difficult balancing act. If the chairperson is too explicit in his questions and/or comments, this may be perceived as lack of impartiality by one of the parties, or both of them. On the other hand, if the chairperson is too general and too vague, there is a risk that the parties do not understand what the chairperson is getting at.

6.195 As previously mentioned,[124] it is submitted that the principle of *iura novit curia* does not, and should not, apply in international commercial arbitrations. Rather the arbitrators have an obligation to decide the case based on the facts, arguments, and evidence presented by the parties. The arbitrators have no obligation, in the legal meaning of the word, to find the 'correct' solution, to make the 'right' decision from a substantive law point of view, even though this is naturally the ambition of every arbitrator. In a way, it is helpful to regard the case management duty of the arbitrators as the remedy against, or at least a counterweight to, the lack of the principle

---

[123] See para 6.72.
[124] See para 6.69.

of *iura novit curia*. Active case management will assist the arbitrators in their ambition to find the 'correct' solution. The case management duty does not, however, extend to a duty to issue a 'correct' award from a substantive law point of view.

In practice, the chairperson prepares the first draft of the award when the arbitrators **6.196** have decided the relevant issues and, if applicable, the recitals of the award prior to the hearing, see para 7.57 *et seq*. The chairperson may appoint an attorney or junior judge to serve as secretary to the tribunal, but only after having consulted the parties. In international arbitration, it has become increasingly common with verbatim records of hearings created with the assistance of court reporters.[125] Since this is an additional cost of the arbitration, the chairperson cannot decide to use such services without the parties' consent. Whether minutes or some other form of record should be kept may, however, be decided by the chairperson in his discretion.

Unlike, for example, the SCC Rules, where the arbitrators have the express power **6.197** to determine the language of the arbitration when there is no agreement between the parties, the SAA is silent in this respect. However, should the parties be unable to agree on the language of the arbitration, the arbitrators must decide this issue at the initial stages of the arbitration taking into account, *inter alia*, the nationalities of the parties and their counsel, the language of the contract, and other documentation, and the language used in any correspondence between the parties.

Preliminary hearings and meetings   In most international arbitrations today the **6.198** tribunal will try to arrange some form of preliminary meeting between the parties and the tribunal, or at least with the chairperson of the tribunal. Such a preliminary meeting will often be in person, but may also be in the form of a telephone conference or video link meeting. The purpose of these preliminary meetings is to try to agree on a timetable for the arbitration, including deadlines for the submission of briefs and dates for the final hearing. Another purpose is to try to agree on various practical aspects of the conduct and management of the arbitration.[126]

In 1996 UNCITRAL adopted the Notes on Organizing Arbitral Proceedings (the **6.199** 'Notes').[127] The Notes provide a checklist of matters which the arbitral tribunal may wish to address when organizing arbitral proceedings. The list, while not exhaustive, covers a broad range of situations that may arise in an arbitration. In many arbitrations, however, only a limited number of the matters mentioned in the list need to be considered. It also depends on the circumstances of the individual case at which stage or stages of the proceedings it would be useful to consider matters—if at all—concerning the organization of the proceedings. Generally, in order not to

---

[125] In addition to verbatim recording of the hearing, real-time reporting (or live notes) is efficient, in particular in respect of cross-examination of witnesses. Real-time reporting instantly displays the transcribed text on the laptop computer as the reporter is recording what is being said.

[126] Cf Göthlin and Bexelius, 'Voluntary Solutions to Procedural Problems', in Hobér, Magnusson, and Öhrström, *op cit*, 175 *et seq*.

[127] The text of the Notes is found at <http://www.uncitral.org>.

create opportunities for unnecessary discussions and delay, it is advisable not to raise a matter prematurely, ie before it is clear that a decision is needed.

6.200 The list in the Notes includes the following matters for possible consideration in organizing arbitral proceedings:

　　(i) Set of arbitration rules.
　　(ii) Language of proceedings.
　　(iii) Place of arbitration:
　　　　(a) Determination of the place of arbitration, if not already agreed upon by the parties.
　　　　(b) Possibility of meetings outside the place of arbitration.
　　(iv) Administrative services that may be needed for the arbitral tribunal to carry out its functions.
　　(v) Deposits in respect of costs; amounts and management thereof.
　　(vi) Confidentiality of information relating to the arbitration; possible agreement thereon.
　　(vii) Distribution of written communications among the parties and the arbitrators.
　　(viii) Telefax and electronic means of sending documents.
　　(ix) Arrangements for the exchange of written submissions; sequence and deadlines.
　　(x) Practical details concerning written submissions and evidence (eg method of submission, copies, numbering, references).
　　(xi) Defining points at issue; order of deciding issues; defining relief or remedy sought.
　　(xii) Possible settlement negotiations and their effect on scheduling proceedings.
　　(xiii) Documentary evidence; scheduling; sequence; production of documents.
　　(xiv) Physical evidence other than documents.
　　(xv) Witnesses; manner and order of testimony.
　　(xvi) Experts and expert witnesses.
　　(xvii) Hearings; dates; length of hearings.

6.201 **Other preliminary matters** In addition to administrative and practical issues, there are typically four preliminary matters that a tribunal may have to deal with at the initial stage of the arbitration, viz, (i) a jurisdiction, (ii) applicable law, (iii) questions of bifurcation, and (iv) interim measures. With the exception of interim measures, there are no provisions in the SAA addressing these issues. The practical handling of them is resolved based on discussions and consultations between the parties and the arbitrators.

6.202 When the respondent in an arbitration challenges the jurisdiction of the tribunal,[128] it can either deal with the issue as a separate and preliminary matter, or join the jurisdictional issue to the merits of the dispute.

---

[128] See para 5.13.

The latter option is often sensible when the jurisdictional issues—factual, and **6.203** sometimes legal as well—are intertwined with the merits of the case to such a degree that it may be difficult to rule on jurisdiction without, at the same time, at least indirectly, ruling on the merits of the case. The disadvantage of not ruling on jurisdiction separately is of course that the parties may have spent time and money on the case only to discover in the final award that the tribunal has no jurisdiction.

If the tribunal decides, or if the parties agree, to hear the jurisdictional issue sepa- **6.204** rately, it is not unusual to have a separate hearing on jurisdiction. Even though there are exceptions, jurisdictional hearings seldom last longer than a couple of days. Sometimes jurisdictional objections are decided without an oral hearing, ie based on documents only.

Another typical preliminary issue is that of applicable law.[129] When this issue arises, it **6.205** is usually the law applicable to the merits of the case that the parties want the tribunal to rule on. Needless to say, the law applicable to the merits of the case may often be of decisive importance to the outcome of the dispute.[130] In situations where one can assume that the applicable law may be decisive, it also makes sense, from a practical point of view, to resolve the issue as a preliminary matter. Otherwise the parties may have to argue their respective case on the basis of two, or perhaps even more, legal systems. This adds cost and complexity to most arbitrations. When applicable law issues are decided as separate and preliminary issues, this is often done without an oral hearing. It is not unheard of, however, that one of the parties, and sometimes both parties, want to have an oral hearing, perhaps to hear legal experts and sometimes fact witnesses testifying about facts which may be of relevance in the choice of law context.

Bifurcation of the proceedings—apart from jurisdictional issues—is another pre- **6.206** liminary issue which arises from time to time, mostly concerning whether or not issues of liability and quantum should be dealt with separately. If such bifurcation takes place, there will usually be separate hearings, starting with a hearing devoted to the liability issue. Such a separate hearing will usually result in a separate award on liability.[131] Depending on the outcome of the liability issue, a second hearing may follow on quantum. In many international arbitrations today, the quantification of claims involves a significant amount of work. This is often the case in major construction disputes and other disputes where loss of future profits is claimed. In such situations it may make sense both for the parties and for the tribunal to decide issues of liability first. In this way, the parties avoid spending time and money on preparing documentation and calculations on quantum that may turn out to be unnecessary.

Ultimately, the question of bifurcation is always for the parties to decide; that is to **6.207** say, if they agree, the tribunal must follow their agreement. If the parties do not agree, the tribunal must rule on the issue.

---

[129] See Chapter 2.
[130] See ibid.
[131] See para 7.27.

6.208 Yet another situation where there may be preliminary hearings is with respect to interim measures. As will be discussed below,[132] under section 25 of the SAA, the tribunal has the authority to order interim measures. Depending on the nature of the interim relief requested, and on the facts and circumstances of the individual case, it may well be that the parties, or one of them, or the tribunal, wishes to hear the parties and/or examine witnesses.

6.209 Sometimes parties find it necessary to ask the arbitrators or a court of law to issue orders intended to protect or preserve assets, to preserve evidence or to take, or refrain from taking measures, with a view to preserving the *status quo* pending the outcome of the case. Measures covered by such orders are usually referred to as *interim measures.* Section 25(4) of the SAA explicitly authorizes arbitrators to issue such orders. The relevant provision reads:

> Unless the parties have agreed otherwise, the arbitrators may, at the request of a party, decide that, during the proceedings, the other party must undertake a certain interim measure to secure the claim, which is to be tried by the tribunal.

6.210 For a party in need of an interim measure the problem, is however, that speed is typically of critical importance. That is why in practice many parties submit their applications for interim measures to national courts, on the assumption that they have jurisdiction. A valid arbitration agreement does not constitute a bar to such court proceedings.[133] In arbitrations in Sweden between two non-Swedish parties, it is usually not meaningful to seek such orders from a Swedish court, since as a rule the assets and/or evidence in question are typically not located in Sweden. The ultimate effectiveness of such an order would thus depend on the extent to which the order is enforceable where the asset/evidence is. On the other hand, if the party against whom the measure is sought is domiciled in Sweden, or has assets in Sweden, it may make sense to seek the assistance of Swedish courts.[134]

6.211 The fact that it takes time to establish a tribunal may thus create problems for the party seeking interim measures. With a view to addressing this problem, the SCC Institute has adopted a set of rules for so-called emergency arbitrations[135] which make it possible to issue orders for interim measures before the establishment of an arbitral tribunal.

---

[132] See para 6.209 *et seq*.

[133] See section 4(3) of the SAA.

[134] See para 5.21 *et seq* for a discussion of the jurisdiction of Swedish courts. A request for security measures may be made in parallel with the arbitration proceedings or even prior to the commencement of such proceedings. In the latter case the claimant must commence arbitration proceedings within one month from the date of the decision of the court, failing which the security measure must immediately be reversed (Chapter 15, section 7 of the Procedural Code). In contrast to interim awards on security measures rendered by the arbitrators, the decision of a Swedish court is enforceable in Sweden (Chapter 16, sections 11–16 of the Swedish Enforcement Code). In addition, the court could impose a fine on the opposing party with a view to having that party comply with the security measure (Chapter 15, section 3 of the Procedural Code).

[135] See para 6.233 *et seq*.

Based on the consensual and contractual nature of arbitration, it is clear that the **6.212** powers of the arbitrators to order interim measures is limited to the parties to the arbitration. An order directed to a third party—eg a bank or other financial institution—would not be binding on, nor enforceable against, such a third person.

Another limitation on the effectiveness of orders issued by an arbitral tribunal is the **6.213** fact that in most legal systems, including Sweden, such orders are not enforceable.[136] The explanation is that interim orders, as the name clearly indicates, are not intended to, and do not, finally resolve the dispute. As far as Swedish law is concerned, an interim order is unenforceable even if it is called an 'award'. Such new nomenclature does not make it enforceable.

Since time is typically of critical importance, it may sometimes be necessary to issue **6.214** an interim order *ex parte,* ie without giving the other party the opportunity to comment on the application. It seems to be accepted in most legal systems, including Sweden, that courts may issue such orders on an *ex parte* basis. It is more doubtful whether arbitral tribunals have this authority. The SAA does not address this issue, nor is it discussed in the *travaux préparatoires.* Lacking explicit statutory support, and without the agreement of the parties, most arbitrators would be reluctant to issue *ex parte* orders of this nature. What arbitrators may do, however, is to ask the party against whom an order is sought not to take certain measures pending a decision with respect to the interim measures.

Section 25(4) of the SAA does not address the requirements which the applicant **6.215** must satisfy for the tribunal to order interim relief. There are, it is submitted, at least two requirements that the applicant must meet. First, he has to establish that he has a *prima facie* case, ie that he has a reasonable chance of winning the case. Second, he must establish that there is a relatively high degree of urgency, for example, that there is a risk that the respondent will transfer money from a bank account, or otherwise dispose of assets, or destroy documents. Guidance can also be found from the revised Article 17 of the UNCITRAL Model Law, which provides in relevant part:

> Article 17A. Conditions for granting interim measures
> (1) The party requesting an interim measure under article 17(2)(a), (b) and (c) shall satisfy the arbitral tribunal that:
>   (a) Harm not adequately reparable by an award of damages is likely to result if the measure is not ordered, and such harm substantially outweighs the harm that is likely to result to the party against whom the measure is directed if the measure is granted; and
>   (b) There is a reasonable possibility that the requesting party will succeed on the merits of the claim. The determination on this possibility shall not

---

[136] It should be noted however that the amended version of Article 17 of the UNCITRAL Model Law provides for a system under which an order for interim measures is binding and enforceable under certain conditions.

affect the discretion of the arbitral tribunal in making any subsequent determination.

(2) With regard to a request for an interim measure under article 17(2)(d), the requirements in paragraphs (1)(a) and (b) of this article shall apply only extent the arbitral tribunal considers appropriate.

6.216 When issuing an order for interim measures, it is important that the decision of the arbitrators do not pre-empt a full and fair trial of the merits of the dispute. For example, a party should not be ordered provisionally to pay a certain amount pending the final outcome, but it should be possible to order a party to pay an amount to an escrow account with a bank, or other financial institution.

6.217 The interests of the party against whom the order is sought are to a certain extent protected by the right of the arbitrators pursuant to section 25(4) of the SAA to order the party requesting the measure to provide reasonable security for the damage which might be incurred as a result of the measure.[137]

6.5.8.2 The main hearing

6.218 Prior to the determination of an issue referred to the arbitrators for resolution, a hearing shall be held where a party so requests (section 24(1) of the SAA).[138] The right to an oral hearing is absolute, ie the arbitrators have no discretion to reject a party's request. This absolute right, however, is only applicable in respect of the *issue referred to the arbitrators* for resolution, ie the main issues.[139] Consequently, the arbitrators are not under any obligation to hold an oral hearing to determine an issue concerning the administration and management of the case, unless both parties so request.

6.219 In respect of the importance of the oral hearing, Swedish law takes the common law approach and not the traditional approach of several civil law countries, where the oral proceedings do not take on the same importance.[140] In accordance with the principle of party autonomy the parties may, of course, agree to limit the scope of the main hearing, for example, to cover only legal argument or witness examination.

6.220 The principle of immediacy applicable in judicial proceedings is not applicable in arbitration.[141] Hence, all the material submitted to the arbitrators, including arguments and documents, must be considered by the arbitrators.[142]

---

[137] Similar provisions on interim measures are found in Article 32 of the SCC Rules.

[138] Cf Article 27(1) of the SCC Rules.

[139] Lindskog, *Skiljeförfarande, En kommentar* (2005) 701–702.

[140] Heuman, *Arbitration Law of Sweden: Practice and Procedure* (2003) 475, who refers, *inter alia*, to Mustill and Boyd, *Commercial Arbitration* (1989) 312.

[141] As a result of recent amendments to the Procedural Code, the principle of immediacy is not emphasized as much as it used to be in judicial procedure. However, in judicial procedure the parties must still refer the court to the documents it wishes to rely on, but the documents must not be reviewed during the hearing.

[142] Cf, however, *Systembolaget AB v V & S Vin & Sprit Aktiebolag* (Svea Court of Appeal Case No T 4548-08), summarized in para x.xxx.

One of the difficulties in complex arbitrations is to find hearing dates which are **6.221**
convenient for everyone concerned. The goal is typically to conduct the hearing for
a continuous period of time without any prolonged intermissions. If the main
hearing, however, is expected to continue for several weeks, this may not be possible. The hearing may then have to be scheduled for different periods of time with
intermissions. As mentioned above, the main hearing may also be split into two or
more separate hearings on separate issues, eg, liability, quantum etc.[143]

The typical final oral hearing is divided into three stages. First, the parties present **6.222**
their opening statements. These are usually relatively short, since they are presented
on the assumption that the arbitrators have a full knowledge of the documents that
have been submitted. Unless otherwise agreed by the parties, the claimant will start
with his opening statement. Secondly, witnesses and experts will be examined and
cross-examined. This is the most time consuming part of the main hearing. In many,
if not most, international arbitrations today there is no direct examination of
witnesses and experts, since they will typically have submitted affidavits or written
witness statements.[144] This means that oral testimony at the main hearing will consist
of cross-examination and re-direct examination of witnesses and experts. Notwithstanding this, witnesses and experts are usually given a shorter period of time to
correct and/or amend their witness statements. The third, and final, stage of the main
hearing is the presentation of the closing arguments of the parties. In the closing
arguments the parties are expected to argue their respective cases in a summarized
fashion, taking account of the evidence presented at the hearing, as well as documents
previously submitted. The parties are expected to address both legal and factual aspects
of the case and to refer to, and discuss, the legal authorities on which they rely.

It goes without saying that in complex cases where the main hearing may have lasted **6.223**
several weeks, it will be difficult for the parties to present their closing arguments at
the end of the hearing. Very often in such cases, the closing arguments are presented
in writing. This approach gives the parties the possibility to analyse the evidence
presented at the hearing and to review the transcripts from the hearing. In most
major arbitrations today, court reporters are used to take down everything that is
said by witnesses and experts during the hearing. This facilitates the preparations of
focused and structured post-hearing briefs. Such transcripts are also very helpful for
the tribunal when drafting the award. It is not uncommon for the parties to agree
on various aspects of the submission of post-hearing briefs with the tribunal well in
advance of the hearing.[145] At the very latest, such issues will be discussed and agreed
during the final hearing.

Unless otherwise agreed by the parties, the presentation of the closing arguments— **6.224**
oral or written—marks the end of the hearings.

---

[143] See para 6.205.
[144] Cf para 6.126.
[145] See para 6.86 with respect to post-hearing briefs.

6.225 ***Ex parte* proceedings** Should one of the parties (usually the respondent) refuse, or fail, to appear at the hearing, or in the arbitration at all, the arbitral tribunal may, and in most cases should, proceed with the arbitration. The right to proceed *ex parte* is codified in section 24(3) of the SAA. The provision stipulates that failure to appear without valid cause 'should not prevent the proceedings from continuing, nor a resolution of the dispute on the basis of existing materials'.

6.226 The starting point here is the fact that each party should be given the opportunity to present their respective cases, as stipulated in section 24(1). If a party decides not to avail itself of this opportunity, that party must bear the consequences thereof. It is not possible to stop or delay an arbitration simply by not participating. It is important to note, however, that section 24 presupposes that the party in question has been duly notified of the arbitration and of the hearing or meeting.[146] If that is not the case, it is possible that the resulting award may be set aside[147] or refused enforcement under the New York Convention.[148]

6.227 Another important aspect of section 24(3) is that the award in an *ex parte* proceeding must be based on 'the existing materials'. This means that there is no room for 'default awards', ie awards which are based exclusively on the failure of a party to appear, or to participate in the arbitration. If the respondent has failed or refused to participate at all in the arbitration, the only materials available to the arbitrators would be the briefs and documents submitted by the claimant. In such a situation the resulting award would in most cases come very close to a 'default award' in favour of the claimant.

6.228 A party who relies on a 'valid cause' has the burden of proof therefor. It is difficult to envisage situations which constitute 'a valid cause' for a party, or its duly authorized representatives, not to participate. Accordingly there are no reported cases dealing with this situation. As a matter of principle, failure or refusal by the arbitrators to stay or postpone a hearing when a party does have a valid cause could lead to the setting aside of the award.

6.229 As mentioned above, the arbitrators cannot issue 'default awards', but must try the merits of claimant's case. The arbitrators have no duty to—and should not—act as counsel or representative of the party who has chosen not to participate. Notwithstanding this, the arbitrators must satisfy themselves that the claims are well-founded in fact and in law.

6.230 **Expedited and emergency arbitrations** Many leading international arbitration institutions have introduced various forms of expedited, or fast-track, arbitrations. Such arbitrations are usually governed by a separate set of arbitration rules adopted

---

[146] See para 6.44.
[147] See Chapter 8.
[148] See Chapter 9.

by the institution in question. For such rules to be applicable the parties must have agreed to them either by inserting the relevant arbitration clause in their contract, or by agreeing to use such rules once a dispute has arisen.

The SCC has adopted rules for expedited arbitrations,[149] the characteristic features of which are the following: **6.231**

(a) the arbitral tribunal always consists of one arbitrator;
(b) in addition to the statement of claim and the statement of defence, each party can submit only one brief, including the statement of evidence;
(c) deadlines for submitting briefs may as a rule not exceed ten days;
(d) a hearing will be held only if requested by a party and deemed necessary by the arbitrator;
(e) the award must be rendered within three months after the file has been transferred to the arbitrator;
(f) reasons for the award will be provided, if requested by one of the parties.

Needless to say, the actual conduct of the arbitration will be significantly different if the parties have agreed on expedited arbitration. **6.232**

One problem that commonly arises in commercial arbitration today is that one party needs emergency relief due to a dispute that has arisen, but the party has no initial recourse because the arbitral tribunal is not yet constituted to grant the relief.[150] To remedy this situation, some arbitration institutions provide a mechanism in the form of so-called *emergency interim measures*, which are issued *before* an arbitral tribunal has been constituted. This procedure provides an efficient protection at a very early stage, avoiding the possibly lengthy phase of filing a request for arbitration and constituting an arbitral tribunal. **6.233**

The SCC has adopted emergency arbitration provisions allowing parties to request interim measures where the arbitral tribunal has *not* yet been constituted.[151] The emergency provisions allow a party to apply for the appointment of an Emergency Arbitrator until the case has been referred to the arbitral tribunal pursuant to Article 18 of the SCC Rules. The emergency rules are included in the Arbitration Rules and in the Expedited Rules by a reference in Article 32. **6.234**

The distinctive features of the emergency rules include the following: **6.235**

• 'The Board shall seek to appoint an Emergency Arbitrator within 24 hours of receipt of the application for the appointment of an Emergency Arbitrator. An Emergency Arbitrator shall not be appointed if the SCC manifestly lacks jurisdiction'.

---

[149] See Appendix 2.
[150] See discussion at para 6.207.
[151] See Appendix 2.

- 'Article 15 of the SCC Rules applies except that a challenge must be made within 24 hours from when the circumstances giving rise to the challenge of an Emergency Arbitrator became known to the party'.
- 'An Emergency Arbitrator may *not* act as an arbitrator in any future arbitration relating to the dispute, unless otherwise agreed by the parties'.
- Pursuant to Article 8, any emergency decision on interim measures should be made no later than five days from the date on which the application was referred to the Emergency Arbitrator, should be made in writing, and should state the reasons upon which the decision is based. The emergency provisions are included in the Arbitration Rules and applicable to all arbitrations commenced after 1 January 2010. Therefore, it is important to note that parties must 'opt-out' of the emergency procedure for them to be non-binding.

6.236   In addition to the SCC, the AAA/ICDR Arbitration Rules also include provisions for emergency arbitrations. Pursuant to Article 37 of the AAA/ICDR Arbitration Rules, '[t]he emergency arbitrator shall have the power to order or award any interim or conservancy measure the emergency arbitrator deems necessary . . . '[152] Further, 'the one-person tribunal [should be] constituted within one business day of the notice being received and for a very tight timetable'.[153]

6.237   Also, the International Chamber of Commerce ('ICC') allows parties to obtain a 'referee' for urgent provisional measures in relation to a dispute.[154] Unlike the SCC emergency arbitration provisions, the ICC's Rules for a Pre-Arbitral Referee require the parties to 'opt-in'.[155]

---

[152] See eg Besson, *Arbitrage internationale et mesures provisoires* (1998) 43–33. A study carried out by the AAA indicated that the number of requests for interim measures in international commercial arbitrations was nearly double the number of such requests in domestic arbitration.

[153] See Hilary Heilbron, *A Practical Guide to International Arbitration in London* (2008) 42.

[154] International Chamber of Commerce Pre-Arbitral Referee Rules; available at <http://www.iccwbo.org/court/arbitration/id5002/index.html>.

[155] See Ali Yesilirmak, 'Provisional Measures', in Mistelis and Lew, *Pervasive Problems in International Arbitration* (2006) 194. See also section 1(6) of the Arbitration Rules 1995 of the International Commercial Arbitration Court at the Chamber of Commerce and Industry of the Russian Federation, Articles 2 and 8 of the Rules for International Arbitration 1994 of the Italian Association for Arbitration, and Article 13 of the Arbitration Rules of the French Arbitration Association. Article 26 of the Swiss Rules of International Arbitration stipulates that the tribunal may, at the request of a party, order interim measures.

7

THE AWARD

7.1 **Introduction**	7.01	7.9.1 Execution	7.93
7.2 **Principles of Decision**	7.02	7.9.2 Time starts running	7.94
7.2.1 Decision according to law	7.04	7.9.3 Termination of arbitration	
7.2.2 Keeping within authority	7.08	agreement	7.96
7.2.3 Dealing with all matters	7.09	7.9.4 *Res judicata*	7.104
7.3 **Deliberations and Voting**	7.10	7.9.4.1 Application of the	
7.4 **Different Kinds of Awards and**		principles of *lis*	
Decisions	7.22	*pendens* and *res*	
7.4.1 Award or decision?	7.22	*judicata* in Swedish	
7.4.2 Separate awards	7.27	arbitration law	7.108
7.4.3 Interim awards	7.36	7.9.4.2 *Res judicata* and *lis*	
7.4.4 Consent awards	7.38	*pendens* in international	
7.4.5 Default awards	7.42	arbitration	7.120
7.5 **Formalities**	7.43	7.10 **Correction and Interpretation**	
7.6 **Reasons and Dissenting Opinions**	7.57	**of the Award**	7.137
7.7 **Interest and Costs**	7.71	7.10.1 General	7.137
7.7.1 Interest	7.71	7.10.2 Correction of arbitral awards	7.140
7.7.2 Costs	7.78	7.10.3 Amendment of arbitral	
7.8 **Rendering the Award**	7.84	awards	7.146
7.9 **Effects of the Award**	7.92	7.10.4 Interpretation of arbitral	
		awards	7.149
		7.10.5 SCC Rules	7.152

7.1 Introduction

The intended final product of the arbitral process is the arbitral award which is **7.01** usually the resolution by the arbitrators of the dispute on the merits. The award is final and binding on the parties. As will be discussed in what follows, a number of important legal consequences result from the award. One such consequence is the enforceability of the award. Even though the hope is that the losing party will comply with the award voluntarily, this is not always the case. It is therefore crucial for the winning party that the arbitrators render an enforceable award. Ensuring the enforceability of the award—in Sweden, as well as internationally—is one purpose of the provisions in the Swedish Arbitration Act (SAA) dealing with the arbitral award. These provisions are found in sections 27–32 of the SAA. Even though the provisions are relatively detailed, they mostly address the formal side of rendering the arbitral award. They do not address the decision-making process as such, nor the rules and principles on the basis of which the tribunal reaches its decision.

7.2 Principles of Decision

7.02 In rendering their decision the arbitrators typically act like members of any other judicial body—they assess evidence, analyse and apply rules, etc. The arbitrators may also draw adverse inferences from the silence of a party or the failure to comply with a reasonable request from the arbitrators for the production of documentary or witness evidence.[1]

7.03 In addition, arbitrators must give consideration to the following general principles.

7.2.1 Decision according to law

7.04 In accordance with the general principle of party autonomy, under Swedish law, the parties may agree that the arbitrators may decide the matter *ex aequo et bono* or act as *amiables compositeurs*. Without such express powers given, however, arbitrators must base their decision on the applicable law.[2] In this respect it must be noted that arguments of fairness and reasonableness may come into play under Swedish law— and most other legal systems—anyway, without expanding into equity. For example, under section 36 of the Swedish Contracts Act, an agreement, or a term, or condition thereof, may be modified or set aside if it is unconscionable having regard to the contents of the agreement, the circumstances prevailing at the time the agreement was entered into, subsequent circumstances, and circumstances in general. In international commercial transactions, however, it is highly unlikely that this provision will be applied.[3]

7.05 The main reason behind the general approach that the award must be based on the applicable law is predictability. The parties would normally expect, and have the right to assume, that their dispute is to be resolved in this fashion. This allows the parties to structure their actions to achieve a certain result. Moreover, a decision which is supposedly based on law has the greatest chance of being accepted as the 'correct' solution.[4]

7.06 This being said, it should be noted, however, that there is no practical way to scrutinize whether or not the arbitrators have properly based their decision on the applicable law, since the award may not be appealed or challenged on the merits.

---

[1] See discussion at para 6.163 *et seq.*
[2] Govt Bill 1998/99:35, p 123. See Chapter 2 for a discussion of how the applicable law is determined.
[3] See para 3.37 *et seq.*
[4] *Arbitration in Sweden* (2nd revised edn, 1984) 126.

In respect of the arbitrators' duty to base their decision on the applicable law the **7.07** principle of *iura novit curia* must also be mentioned. In Swedish court proceedings, the courts are not bound by the *legal arguments* presented by the parties, but only by the facts and circumstances relied on. This is the case since, in accordance with the principle of *iura novit curia,* the court supposedly knows the law, at least the domestic law.[5] It may be called into question whether the principle of *iura novit curia* is applicable to arbitrations. Arguably, this is not the case, at least not where the parties, or at least one of them, are foreign, see para 6.69 below.

7.2.2 Keeping within authority

In deciding the dispute the arbitrators must keep within the confines of the matter **7.08** referred to them.[6] This means that the claim must be covered by the arbitration agreement and that the arbitrators cannot go beyond the prayers for relief of the parties: the arbitrators cannot rule *ultra petita.* Moreover, the arbitrators must not base their decision on any facts other than those relied on by the parties in support of their respective position. Should the arbitrators exceed their mandate in these respects, the award is challengeable in accordance with section 34(1) and (2) of the SAA.[7]

7.2.3 Dealing with all matters

The arbitrators must consider all claims submitted to them. If they fail to deal **7.09** with a claim, the award will be valid *pro tanto,* but they then have only a limited time under section 32 of the SAA (or until the expiration of the award period, if applicable) to supplement the award. Moreover, a ruling *infra petita* may constitute a procedural error which could make the award challengeable under section 34 of the SAA.

7.3 Deliberations and Voting

Section 30(2) of the SAA sets forth that, unless the parties have agreed otherwise, **7.10** the opinion agreed upon by the majority of the arbitrators participating in the determination shall prevail.[8] If no majority is attained for any opinion, the opinion of the chairman shall prevail. The SAA thus provides for an efficient procedure in respect of taking decisions. The voting procedure under the SAA has been framed such that the dispute may always be determined.[9] For instance, the arbitration

---

[5] See Chapter 35, section 2 of the Procedural Code. Note, however, that with respect to foreign law, the court may ask the parties to provide evidence of the contents of such law.
[6] *Arbitration in Sweden* (2nd revised edn, 1984) 127.
[7] See discussion in Chapter 8.
[8] Cf Article 36(3) of the SCC Rules.
[9] Govt Bill 1998/99:35, p 127 *et seq.*

proceedings may not be hung by a divided arbitral tribunal or by an arbitrator not participating in the determination of an issue (section 30(1) of the SAA).

7.11 The SAA is silent with respect to the voting procedure. This is left to the discretion of the arbitrators.[10] If there is disagreement on the procedure, the arbitrators may vote on that matter.[11] In practice this is, however, very unusual. Also in such a situation the majority or, as a last resort, the chairperson decides the voting procedure. The rationale for leaving the question of voting procedure unregulated in the SAA is to avoid challenge proceedings based on alleged irregularities during the voting.

7.12 With respect to the voting it is only the vote itself, not the arbitrator's reasons for it, which is important. Thus, a valid decision may be reached on an issue even though the arbitrators have widely differing opinions concerning the reasons justifying the decision.[12]

7.13 One particular issue in relation to the voting procedure may arise where the arbitrators have rendered a separate award.[13] A separate award is final and binding. The arbitrators are thus bound by the dispositive, or operative, part of a separate award. If one of the arbitrators has expressed a dissenting opinion in the separate award, he would nevertheless be bound by the majority's decision in the further proceedings. Moreover, the dissenting arbitrator must participate in the adjudication of the remaining questions and must do so in a loyal manner, so as to ensure that the proceedings can be brought to an end.[14] For example, if the majority of the arbitrators has determined that a party is liable for damages in a separate award, the dissenting arbitrator must assess the remaining questions without consideration of his previous dissenting opinion. Put differently, in conjunction with the later determination, the arbitrators must treat the dissenting opinion in the separate award as non-existent. If this were not the case, there would be procedural chaos and injustice. The parties would not be able to trust that a separate award was final. Nor would the parties know if and when the facts and evidence might be re-tried by the arbitrators. In addition, the arbitrators would be free, without notifying the parties, to revisit old issues, re-assess old evidence, and issue a new ruling.

7.14 There is no provision in the SAA dealing directly with the deliberations of the arbitrators.[15] Logically, deliberations precede, or should precede, voting. In practice it is very rare that arbitrators cast formal votes. Rather, deliberations and voting go hand in hand: once the deliberations are over, the outcome of the case is usually clear.

---

[10] Ibid, pp 128 and 232.

[11] Ibid, p 129.

[12] *Arbitration in Sweden* (2nd revised edn, 1984) 130.

[13] For a discussion of separate awards, see para 7.27.

[14] See, *inter alia*, Heuman, *Arbitration Law of Sweden: Practice and Procedure* (2003) 494 *et seq.* and the references made therein. See also Lindskog, *Skiljeförfarande, En kommentar* (2005) 839.

[15] The term 'deliberations' is used to describe the internal debates and discussions between the arbitrators preceding the rendering of the award.

Section 30 of the SAA provides a useful starting point in trying to understand the **7.15** role and importance of the deliberations. The provision stipulates that an arbitrator who fails 'without valid cause' to participate in the deliberations cannot thereby prevent the other arbitrators from deciding the case. This raises two important aspects. First, all arbitrators must be given the opportunity to participate in the deliberations. In practice this is usually not a problem. The chairperson, who is normally organizing the discussions, will typically contact and agree with his co-arbitrators well in advance on how and when to hold deliberations. This may be done in person, via telephone, or via videolink. The SAA does not have any provision in this respect. The normal practice[16] is for the arbitrators to have a first, albeit short, sitting immediately after the close of the oral hearing, at least if no substantial post-hearing briefs are forthcoming. At this meeting the arbitrators will usually agree on how to proceed with their deliberations. The method of proceeding depends very much on the individual case, the preferences and workloads of the arbitrators. If the dispute is relatively uncomplicated, and if the arbitrators seem to reach a consensus already at the first meeting, the chairman will usually prepare a first draft of the award and send it to his co-arbitrators for their comments. If the dispute is large and complicated and/or there is no consensus after the first meeting, or if the positions are unclear, the deliberations will usually continue, as agreed by the arbitrators.

Secondly, if an arbitrator does have a valid cause, the other two arbitrators cannot **7.16** proceed to decide the case.[17] If they do, such conduct could lead to the setting aside of the award on the basis of section 34 of the SAA. It goes without saying that an arbitrator cannot be excluded from the deliberations. Such conduct may also lead to the setting aside of the award. Complicated issues may arise in situations where it is clear—perhaps at an early stage—that one of the arbitrators will dissent. To what extent are the other two arbitrators under an obligation to include the dissenting arbitrator in their further discussions? The answer to that question may vary depending on the circumstances of the individual case, including the number, character and complexity of the issues with respect to which the arbitrator in question dissents. This situation arose in the challenge proceedings relating to the award in *Czech Republic v CME Czech Republic BV* (RH 2003:55) which was heard by the Svea Court of Appeal.[18] One of the arbitrators stated in his dissenting opinion that he had been deliberately excluded by his co-arbitrators from the deliberations. In addressing this aspect of the case, the court stated that:

> ... when two arbitrators have agreed on the outcome of the dispute, the third arbitrator cannot prolong the deliberations by demanding continued discussions in an attempt to convince the others of the correctness of his view. The dissenting arbitrator is thus not given any opportunity to delay the drafting of the award.[19]

---

[16] For a general discussion of deliberations, see Fortier, 'The Tribunal's Deliberations', in *The Leading Arbitrators' Guide to International Arbitration* (2004) 393.

[17] Govt Bill 1998/99:35, p 231.

[18] A summary in English of the case is provided in SAR 2003:2, pp 167–195.

[19] Ibid, 180.

7.17 Needless to say, all arbitrators must be treated equally during the deliberations. It is incumbent on the chairperson to make sure that equality between the two party-appointed arbitrators is maintained. He should, for example, avoid meeting with the party-appointed arbitrators separately; they should be given the same amount of time to review drafts and provide comments thereon.

7.18 As discussed above,[20] under Swedish arbitration law all arbitrators, including party-appointed arbitrators, must be impartial and independent. This obligation continues throughout the deliberations. It goes without saying that a party-appointed arbitrator cannot hold discussions with the party who nominated him about the substance of the case during the arbitration. At the same time, however, it is generally accepted, or at least not viewed as improper, that a party-appointed arbitrator tries to ensure that the tribunal properly understands the arguments put forward by that party. In doing so the arbitrator must take care to consider carefully the merits of both sides' arguments. A party-appointed arbitrator who is too partisan will very quickly lose the attention of the other arbitrators. Since parties tend to select arbitrators with views similar, or at least sympathetic, to their own, it is not surprising that such arbitrators tend to view the facts and law in a similar fashion.

7.19 In most international commercial arbitrations, at least of any magnitude, there will be three arbitrators. It is submitted that the ambition of most tribunals is to render a unanimous award. That is probably also what most parties wish to have. A unanimous award is a clear and authoritative resolution of the dispute. It is not always possible, however, to achieve a unanimous result. The next best thing is to have a majority award, but even that is sometimes not possible, although this is unusual in practice. In such a situation, the view of the chairperson shall prevail. This is a practical and efficient way of ensuring that there will be a resolution of the dispute.[21] There may be cases where it is impossible to achieve a majority which might lead to endless deliberations in the hope of finding some sort of compromise. When a number of different issues are raised in an arbitration, it is theoretically possible for the arbitrators to disagree on some issues and to be unanimous on other issues. The voting rules described above—ie a majority, with a casting vote for the chairperson as the default option—would seem to avoid the rather complicated voting issues which could otherwise arise.

7.20 The deliberations of the arbitrators are confidential. This means, *inter alia,* that parties and their representatives are not allowed to be present during the deliberations nor may an arbitrator disclose to any of the parties what is being discussed during deliberations. This also applies subsequent to the rendering of the award.[22]

---

[20] See para 4.39 *et seq.*
[21] See Govt Bill 1998/99:35, p 127 *et seq.*
[22] It should be noted, however, that under the Procedural Code arbitrators may be called as witnesses in challenge proceedings and may then be asked questions about the deliberations.

With respect to the voting, it must be noted that it concerns the dispositive part **7.21** of the award and not the reasons for it, at least as a rule. A valid decision may thus be reached even if the arbitrators rely on different reasons for the decision.[23]

7.4 Different Kinds of Awards and Decisions

7.4.1 Award or decision?

Section 27 of the SAA defines the concepts of, and distinguishes between, 'awards' **7.22** and 'decisions'. The first paragraph of the provision stipulates that the issues which have been referred to the arbitrators—ie essentially the merits of the dispute—shall be decided in an award. It goes on to say that when the arbitrators terminate the proceedings without deciding such issues such a ruling is also called an award.

This means that if the arbitrators find that they do not have jurisdiction—and thus **7.23** terminate the proceedings—that determination must be done in the form of an award. This award thus becomes *res judicata* unless it is appealed to the Court of Appeal within whose district the arbitral proceedings were held. That such an appeal is possible follows from section 36 of the SAA.[24] The philosophy underlying this provision is that a party must always have the possibility to have the jurisdiction of the arbitrators tried by a court of law.

If, on the other hand, the arbitrators find that they have jurisdiction, such a ruling takes **7.24** the form of a decision which cannot be reviewed by a court of law unless and until the final arbitral award is challenged.[25] Such decisions are not final and binding.[26]

All determinations and rulings of the arbitrators which are not 'awards' constitute **7.25** 'decisions'.

It should be noted that rulings by which the arbitrators partially reject the claims of **7.26** a party must be issued in the form of decisions. The right of a party to appeal a ruling on the basis of section 36 is available only with respect to a complete termination of the proceedings; otherwise the dissatisfied party must wait until he can challenge the final award.[27]

---

[23] Cf *Arbitration in Sweden* (2nd edn, 2004) 130.

[24] See discussion at para 8.204.

[25] It should be noted that it is also possible for a party to institute separate court proceedings with a view to obtaining a declaratory judgment concerning the jurisdiction of the arbitrators; see discussion at para 5.19 *et seq.*

[26] Govt Bill 1998/99:35, pp 77 and 124. See *Joint Stock Company Acron v Yara International ASA*, Svea Court of Appeal judgment dated 7 April 2009 in Case T 7200-08. The Court of Appeal reasoned that 'irrespective of how the ruling has been characterized, the arbitrators have rendered such a decision in the course of the arbitration proceedings which pursuant to Section 2(2) of the SAA is not binding upon the arbitrators. Hence, the decision may not be challenged by a party through an action in accordance with Sections 34 or 36 of the SAA'.

[27] Govt Bill 1998/99:35, p 238.

7.4.2 Separate awards

7.27   The arbitrators are entitled to render *separate awards* in certain circumstances, unless both parties object thereto (section 29 of the SAA). Consequently, one of the parties may not prevent the arbitrators from rendering a separate award if deemed efficient.[28] If both parties so request, a separate award should be rendered. Notably, however, a separate award may not be made on questions of procedure but can only deal with the substance of the dispute.[29]

7.28   In contrast to the Procedural Code, the SAA does not distinguish between different kinds of separate awards. Notwithstanding this, from a practical point of view, it may be helpful to make a distinction between partial awards and interlocutory awards.

7.29   It must be emphasized that all separate awards are final and binding and may be challenged in the same way as any other arbitral award. The time period within which the separate award must be challenged starts to run as of receipt of the separate award.[30] The dissatisfied party thus cannot wait until the final award has been rendered, which almost invariably is subsequent to the expiration of the time period in question. The arbitrators are under no obligation to stay the proceedings based on the fact that a separate award has been challenged. It is in the discretion of the arbitrators to stay, or not to stay, the proceedings. This underscores the rationale behind separate awards, ie to be used with a view to facilitating a smooth and speedy resolution of the dispute. It is up to the arbitrators to take the appropriate decisions at the relevant time.

7.30   **Partial awards**   In a separate award, in the sense of a *partial* award, one of several claims, or part of one claim, is determined. Section 29 of the SAA sets forth one example of a case where a partial award may be rendered, viz, where a party has admitted a claim, in whole or in part. In such a situation, the claimant may wish to obtain an enforceable award sooner rather than later. It must be noted, however, that a claim invoked as defence by way of set-off must be adjudicated in the same award as the main claim.

7.31   A partial award is possible also with respect to claims which have not been admitted, but which are uncomplicated and/or do not require much evidence to be presented and evaluated. The ultimate purpose, again, is to enable the claimant to obtain an enforceable award.

7.32   Separate awards in the form of partial awards seem to be rather unusual in practice. The explanation is probably that many international commercial arbitrations are relatively complicated, and claims are often intertwined. This means that it is difficult to see what is to be gained by issuing a partial award.

---

[28] Ibid, p 132.
[29] Ibid, p 124.
[30] Ibid, p 236.

Interlocutory awards   A separate award in the form of an *interlocutory* award **7.33**
typically determines one specific issue but leaves other issues dependent on the first
for later determination. For example, issues of liability may be separated from those
of *quantum*.[31] If the determination of a particular issue of liability may make it
unnecessary for the arbitrators to investigate questions of quantum, it is often worth
disentangling that issue from the issue of quantum. Moreover, a decision by the
arbitrators on certain issues of principle may well encourage the parties to reach a
settlement on quantum. Another question which is sometimes decided in an
interlocutory award is the law applicable to the merits of the case. If this issue is
resolved at an early stage of the arbitration proceedings a situation where the parties
must argue the case with reference to two alternatively applicable laws may be
avoided, thereby saving time and money for the parties. A further example of a
question with respect to which an interlocutory award may be suitable is the statute
of limitations.[32] If the claim is time-barred, there is no need to let the arbitration
proceedings continue.

The rationale of interlocutory awards is to make the proceedings efficient and less **7.34**
expensive. The flip side of the coin is, however, that the process of rendering an
interlocutory award can itself be a time-consuming and expensive one. The effect of
the interlocutory award may also be difficult to predict, *inter alia*, because the parties
may amend and change their respective cases during the course of the arbitration
proceedings.

As mentioned above, interlocutory awards are final and binding, and have *res judicata* **7.35**
effect. When the arbitration proceedings continue, the arbitrators are thus bound
by the operative part of the award. A consequence of the binding nature of the
interlocutory award is that the final award must not deviate from the operative part
of the interlocutory award but may rely on different reasons.[33]

7.4.3 Interim awards

Interim awards refer almost exclusively to rulings by an arbitral tribunal with respect **7.36**
to security measures, such as a prevention order or an injunction. In accordance
with section 25(4) the arbitrators may, at the request of a party, decide that, during
the arbitration proceedings, the opposing party must undertake a certain interim
measure to secure the claim which is to be adjudicated by the arbitrators.[34] The
scope of the arbitrators' powers is relatively wide. The arbitrators may thus take
decisions directly related to the securing of a subsequent enforcement of a final
award, as well as decisions on a party's obligation to preserve certain evidence.[35]

---

[31] Ibid, p 131.
[32] Ibid.
[33] Heuman, *Arbitration Law of Sweden: Practice and Procedure* (2003) 533.
[34] Cf Article 32 of the SCC Rules and Chapter 15, section 3, of the Procedural Code.
[35] Govt Bill 1998/99:35, p 229.

On the other hand, however, an interim award with respect to security measures is not enforceable and the arbitrators have no powers to impose a fine in relation to an interim award.[36] Strictly speaking, such rulings should not be called 'awards' but rather 'decisions' pursuant to the terminology of the SAA.[37] The non-enforceability may limit the application and practical effect of this provision, eg in respect of sequestration of assets of the opposing party or similar.[38]

7.37 In order to reduce the opportunities for a respondent to obstruct the arbitration proceedings, the SCC Institute has enacted in Article 45(4) of the SCC Rules a provision which empowers the arbitrators, at the request of the party which has paid the entire advance on costs, to make a separate (interim) award for reimbursement of the payment made for the other party.[39] The Svea Court of Appeal has found that an interim award on the advance on costs is enforceable and may form the basis for an application for bankruptcy.[40] It is an open question whether such an interim award may also be recognized and enforced abroad under the New York Convention.[41]

7.4.4 Consent awards

7.38 Section 27(2) of the SAA confirms that the arbitrators may at the request of the parties confirm in an award a settlement reached by the parties.[42] Such awards are commonly referred to as *consent awards*. Such an award has the same legal effect and consequences as any other award and the same formal requirements apply to it.

7.39 There are no restrictions as to when parties can reach a settlement and ask for a consent award. They can do this at any stage of the proceedings, indeed even after the conclusion of the proceedings, but before the award is issued by the arbitrators. Parties may have several and varied reasons for asking for a consent award. First, the award is a final and binding resolution of the dispute and thus constitutes *res judicata*. Another reason, particularly where the payment of monies is involved, is that a

---

[36] Ibid, pp 73–74; cf Chapter 15, section 3(2) of the Procedural Code.

[37] See para 7.22 *et seq.*

[38] See discussion at para 6.208 *et seq.*

[39] Cf *3S Swedish Special Supplier AB v Sky Park AB* (NJA 2000 p 773) where the Supreme Court held that an interim award on the advance on costs was conditional on the parties agreement to this effect. The judgment has been commented in Tao, Vincent, and Polkinghorne, *International Arbitration Court Decisions*, 867 *et seq.* Separate awards to this effect have been a relatively regular feature in the ICC arbitral practice, see Söderlund in SIAR 2008:1, p 142; cf Article 23(1) of the ICC Rules which provides that '. . . the Arbitral Tribunal may, at the request of a party, order any interim or conservatory measure it deems appropriate'. This power has been interpreted to include a power to award security for costs as an interim measure.

[40] *Consafe IT AB v Auto Connect Sweden AB*, Svea Court of Appeal judgment 11 March 2009 in Ö 280-09. The first interim award on the advance on costs under the SCC Rules was rendered at the beginning of 2008 and has been commented on by Söderlund in SIAR 2008:1, p 137 *et seq.*

[41] Cf Govt Bill 1998/99:35, p 124.

[42] Such request must be made by both parties which of course presupposes that they are in agreement as to the contents and meaning of the settlement; cf Govt Bill 1998/99:35, p 230.

consent award is enforceable just like any other award. A third reason might be that the signatures of the arbitrators on the settlement, ie the consent award, somehow enhance the status of the settlement and increase the chances of its being fulfilled.

As mentioned above, section 27(2) of the SAA says that the arbitrators *may* render **7.40** a consent award. They are thus under no obligation to do so,[43] but the situations in which they can refuse to issue a consent award are said to be limited.[44] Arbitrators do have the right, however, to refuse to issue a consent award if the award in question would violate public policy or if it deals with an issue which is non-arbitrable.[45]

A situation which occurs from time to time is that the arbitral tribunal is asked to **7.41** confirm—in the form of a consent award—an entirely new agreement between the parties, which may include issues which have never been disputed between the parties. As long as the parties are in agreement, such a consent award should not create any problems under Swedish arbitration law. As explained in Chapter 3, arbitrators have the authority both to fill gaps in agreements and to confirm the existence of factual circumstances.[46]

7.4.5 Default awards

As mentioned above,[47] default awards do not exist in arbitration, in the sense of an **7.42** award which is based exclusively on the non-appearance or non-participation of a party, in practice always the respondent. The fact that a party, without valid cause, fails to participate in the arbitration, does not prevent the proceedings from continuing, nor does it prevent the arbitrators from rendering an award. As stipulated in section 24(3) of the SAA such an award must be based on the materials submitted to the arbitrators.[48] In rendering a default award it is crucial for the arbitrators to ensure that the non-active party has been given an opportunity to present his case. This is also in the interest of the claimant who presumably wants an award which is effective and enforceable. It is often advisable for the arbitrators to explain in the reasons of a default award the measures which have been taken with a view to giving the respondent the opportunity to present his case.

7.5 Formalities

The fundamental principle of party autonomy in arbitration proceedings is important **7.43** also with respect to the formalities and contents of the award.[49] Accordingly, the

---

[43] Govt Bill 1998/99:35, p 132.
[44] Ibid, p 133.
[45] Ibid, pp 133 and 230.
[46] See para 3.86 *et seq.*
[47] See para 6.224.
[48] See discussion at para 6.224.
[49] Govt Bill 1998/99:35, p 134.

form and contents of the award will to a large extent depend on the parties' agreement in this respect. However, this freedom of the parties is restricted in relation to some minimum requirements which have been set out in order to render the award enforceable.[50]

7.44 Generally speaking the SAA has very few formal requirements with respect to an arbitral award. They are set forth in section 31 of the SAA:

    (i) the award must be made in writing;
    (ii) the award must be signed by the arbitrators; it is sufficient that a majority of the tribunal signs the award, provided that the reason why not all arbitrators have signed the award is noted in the award;
    (iii) the place of arbitration must be stated in the award; and
    (iv) the date when the award is made must be stated in the award.

7.45 The two first requirements are mandatory in the sense that their non-observance leads to the invalidity of the arbitral award pursuant to section 33 of the SAA.[51] These two requirements are purely formal. They do not in any way guarantee the quality of the award, nor even that all the arbitrators have de facto reviewed and approved the award. The signature requirement relates to the last page of the award. There is no need for the arbitrators to initial or sign each page of the award, nor must the award be signed at the place of arbitration.[52]

7.46 Failure to observe the other two requirements does not render the award invalid. Also, it is unlikely that the award can be successfully challenged based on such failure.

7.47 If the place of arbitration is not stated in the award, this fact does not automatically exclude the jurisdiction of Swedish courts when it comes to challenge proceedings. In the *travaux préparatoires*, for example, it is suggested that challenge proceedings may be initiated at the Court of Appeal in the place which ought to have been stated in the award, or if no such place can be determined, with the Svea Court of Appeal.[53]

7.48 Although not explicitly stated in the SAA, the award must of course identify the parties to the dispute, as well as the dispute itself. The award must also contain a clear and definitive decision, ie the operative part of the award.[54]

7.49 It should be noted that there is no statutory requirement that the arbitrators state their reasons in the award.[55] However, the predominant position among Swedish

---

[50] Ibid.
[51] See discussion at para 8.26 *et seq.*
[52] Govt Bill 1998/99:35, p 242.
[53] Ibid, p 242.
[54] *Arbitration in Sweden* (2nd edn, 1984) 133.
[55] Govt Bill 1998/99:35, pp 134–135, where it is discussed whether or not it should be required that the arbitrators state their reasons in the award. On the one hand, it is said that the Model Law and several other foreign arbitration laws set forth such a requirement. The reasons may also be

lawyers is that arbitrators should give reasons for their award. In practice this is almost invariably done.[56] The articulation of reasons in the award increases the likelihood that the arbitrators will reach the 'correct' solution.[57] This will require the arbitrators to analyse the different issues in the dispute. A well reasoned award will also greatly increase the parties' confidence, particularly that of the losing party, in the award and thus in arbitration in general. A reasoned award may thus serve as a guarantee of legal certainty and predictability.

In *Soyak International Construction & Investment Inc v Hochtief AG* (NJA 2009 p 128) **7.50** the Supreme Court discussed, *inter alia,* what the requirements are with respect to the reasons in an award when, as in that case, it follows from the arbitration agreement that the award shall be reasoned.[58] The Supreme Court held that the requirement for reasons must be balanced against the interest in the finality of the award. Since challenge proceedings only concern procedural irregularities, an adjudication with respect to the reasons of the award would give rise to considerable difficulties in distinguishing between such irregularities and the merits of the case. Consequently, the Supreme Court concluded that only a total lack of reasons, or reasons so poor that they must be deemed equivalent to non-existing, could constitute a successful ground for the challenge of an award. The Court found, however, that the arbitrators had accounted for their reasons for the award on the basis of the evidence presented and of what had occurred during the arbitration proceedings. The challenge was thus rejected.

The award ends with the signatures of the arbitrators. **7.51**

Most national laws on arbitration provide for a speedy resolution of disputes, either **7.52** explicitly[59] or implicitly. There are, however, different ways to monitor fulfilment of this requirement. Some legal systems empower the courts to issue an order directing arbitrators to render their award within a specified time period. Other legal systems include such a specific period of time in their arbitration laws. The latter was the case in the 1929 Swedish Arbitration Act, with respect to domestic arbitrations.

---

important for the interpretation of the ultimate decision and the scope of the legal effect of the award. It is assumed that the parties would also be interested in the grounds for the decision. On the other hand, however, the lack of reasons may be a valid ground to challenge the award should this be a statutory requirement. In this respect, it would be difficult to assess whether poorly stated reasons should be deemed to fulfil the requirement or not. In order to protect the finality of an arbitral award and to avoid challenges, the Government concluded that reasons in the award should not be a statutory requirement, but this should be left to the discretion of the parties and the arbitrators. The Government took note of the practice in domestic arbitration proceedings, where reasoned awards are predominant, and thus found that, in practice, this issue was of limited interest. Cf *Soyak International Construction & Investment Inc v Hochtief AG* (NJA 2009 p 128), discussed at para 7.50.

[56] Cf Article 36(1) of the SCC Rules which explicitly provide that the award must be reasoned, and eg Article 31.2 of the UNCITRAL Model Law.

[57] *Arbitration in Sweden* (2nd revised edn, 1984) 134.

[58] The arbitration agreement in the *Soyak* case referred to the SCC Rules, which provide for reasoned awards (Article 36(1)).

[59] See, for example, section 21 of the SAA.

Whereas most countries, including Sweden, have nowadays abandoned a specified time period for the rendering of the award,[60] it is still common that there is a time limit for rendering awards in most institutional arbitral rules.[61]

7.53 In accordance with the principle of party autonomy, the parties themselves may agree on a time limit for rendering the award (the 'award period'). The parties may also agree on when the award period begins, eg upon receipt of the request for arbitration, or when the arbitral tribunal is constituted or, in some instances, from the closing of the final hearing. In arbitrations under the SCC Rules, the six-month award period begins on the date when the arbitration is referred to the arbitral tribunal (Article 37 of the SCC Rules).[62]

7.54 It must be noted that there is no *automatic* extension of the award period. In the case of an arbitration under the SCC Rules, the Board of the SCC Institute may extend the award period upon a reasoned request from the arbitral tribunal, or if otherwise deemed necessary. The SCC Institute monitors the award period and reminds the arbitrators well in advance of the approaching expiry of such period.

7.55 It is submitted that in general it is preferable that no time limit be prescribed for the making of the award in an arbitration clause or submission agreement.[63] This might enable one of the parties to frustrate the arbitration. However, if the parties consider it desirable to agree on an award period, or if it is necessary to do so under the applicable law, the award period should, if possible, be related to the closure of the hearings and not to the appointment of the arbitral tribunal, or to some other earlier stage in the arbitration proceedings at which the respondent will have opportunities to create delay.[64]

7.56 If the award is not rendered within the award period (including any extension thereof) the arbitration agreement terminates with respect to the dispute in question. The arbitrators thus become *functus officio*, see para 7.102. An award rendered after the expiration of the award period is not invalid, but challengeable pursuant to section 34(2) of the SAA. If no challenge proceedings are commenced within the three-month period stipulated in the SAA, the award is valid and enforceable. It should be noted that termination of the arbitration agreement does not occur if

---

[60] Cf for example, Article 31 of the Model Law, which has no time limit for rendering the award.

[61] See, for example, Article 37 of the SCC Rules (six months), Article 24(1) of the ICC Rules (six months); cf Chapter VI, Rule 46 of the ICSID Rules that stipulates that the award must be drawn up and signed within sixty days from the closure of the proceedings; cf the LCIA Rules, which provide for no time limit.

[62] Statistics from the SCC Institute show that the average length of time for arbitrations under the SCC Rules, from the commencement of arbitration until the rendering of an award, is 14 months. In domestic cases, the average time is even shorter; with only nine months for a final award, see SCC Newsletter 2/2010, <http://www.sccinstitute.se>.

[63] See the discussion on pros and cons in Govt Bill 1998/99:35, pp 124–126.

[64] Redfern and Hunter, *Law and Practice of International Commercial Arbitration*, (4th edn, 2004) 384 and 385.

the proceedings themselves are terminated prior to the expiration of the award period. In such a case new arbitration proceedings may be commenced at a later date.[65]

7.6 Reasons and Dissenting Opinions

As mentioned above, there is no statutory requirement that the arbitrators provide reasons for their award. In practice, however, it is very unusual that the arbitrators do not give reasons, unless the parties have agreed thereon. **7.57**

The structure and style of the reasons vary with the nature and complexity of the dispute, as well as with the background and training of counsel and arbitrators. Consequently, there is no 'right' or 'wrong' way of drafting the reasons in an award. It is submitted, however, that in many international commercial arbitrations the award would typically be structured in the following, or similar, way: **7.58**

   (i)   procedural background;
   (ii) the recitals;
  (iii) the reasons for the outcome of the case; and
  (iv) the operative part of the award.

In most arbitrations it is a good rule of thumb to describe the *procedural background*. This section would include the identification of the parties and of the dispute. A short summary of the disputed contract is usually helpful. In addition most arbitrators prefer to reproduce the arbitration agreement together with an explanation that they have jurisdiction and why. It is also common practice nowadays to describe the chronology of the proceedings, starting with the request for arbitration and ending with the final oral hearing, and/or post-hearing briefs, as the case may be. Such a chronology is helpful when determining whether a party has been given the opportunity to present his case. **7.59**

The following section in the award, *the recitals,* attempts to describe the positions taken, and the arguments relied on, by the parties. The level of detail will vary and very much depend on the circumstances of the individual case. There are typically three aspects that the arbitrators would seek to cover in this section. First, the exact prayers for relief of the parties should be identified and reproduced. Second, most arbitrators would like to identify the specific legal grounds relied on by the parties in support of their respective prayers for relief. Third, a summary of the facts and circumstances relied on by the parties. This summary usually includes references to the evidence presented by the parties. Assessment and evaluation of the evidence, however, are carried out in the following section of the award. **7.60**

---

[65] See *Arbitration in Sweden* (2nd revised edn, 1984) 123, where reference is made to *Jansson v Reprotype* AB (NJA 1975 p 536).

7.61 The reason for including recitals in the award is twofold. First, it is a good way for the arbitrators to make sure that they have properly understood the parties and their arguments. Experience shows that trying to reduce this understanding to writing in a summarized form is an excellent test in this respect. Second, most arbitrators view it as an obligation, or at least a courtesy, to the parties that they demonstrate that they have understood them.

7.62 Needless to say, the length and structure of the recital will vary with the nature and complexity of each case.

7.63 The legal analysis of the arbitrators is found in the third section of the award—the *reasons* for the outcome of the award. Again, the structure and style of the reasons will vary depending on the dispute in question, as well as on counsel and arbitrators. The general idea is that the arbitrators discuss and analyse the legal and factual arguments put forward by the parties. This is also where the arbitrators assess and evaluate the evidence presented by the parties. In many cases, a sensible approach is to have an introductory section where the arbitrators outline the various issues which will be discussed in detail in the remainder of the reasons.

7.64 One question that troubles arbitrators from time to time is whether they should, or must, discuss or analyse *every* argument put forward by a party—even if the argument is hopeless in the view of the arbitrators. It is submitted that there is no general answer to this question. Often it makes sense for the arbitrators at least to address, however briefly, all arguments put forward. In other cases, it would seem unnecessary.

7.65 The final, and in many ways the most important, section of the award is the *operative part*. This is where the legal and practical implementations of the arbitrators' conclusions are set forth. This is the arbitrators' ultimate response to the prayers for relief of the parties. The operative part will typically enumerate a number of 'conclusions', for example:

    (i) The Contract is hereby terminated.
    (ii) The respondent is hereby ordered to pay damages to the claimant in the amount of X, plus interest at an annual rate of Y per cent, from (date) until full payment is made.

7.66 The operative part of the award is of critical importance in several respects. For the winning party enforcement is usually essential. The operative part must therefore be clear and succinct so as not to create problems at the enforcement stage. To the extent that prayers for relief are found by the arbitrators to be unclear and imprecise, such issues must be sorted out well in advance of the rendering of the award. The arbitrators cannot themselves change, amend, or refine the prayers for relief. If they do, they exceed their mandate, as a result of which the award may be set aside.

The operative part is also decisive for the *res judicata* effect of the award. As will be **7.67** discussed,[66] usually it is only the operative part of an award which has *res judicata* effect, not the reasons.

As far as Swedish arbitration law is concerned, there are few procedural limitations **7.68** as far as available remedies are concerned. It is probably correct that most international commercial arbitrations concern payments of sums of money. Consequently, the operative part would provide for payment of sums, or reject such claims. Awards may also provide for specific performance, restitution, declaratory relief, adaptation of contracts, and the filling of gaps in contracts.

There are no provisions in the SAA dealing with dissenting opinions. It is generally **7.69** held, however, that an arbitrator is entitled to attach a dissenting opinion to the award.[67] If an arbitrator dissents he is expected fully to state the reasons for his dissenting opinion. Often the dissenting arbitrator will sign the award together with the other arbitrators, but indicate next to his signature that his dissenting opinion is attached to the award. On the other hand, sometimes the dissenting arbitrator will not sign the award, but will simply indicate that he is attaching a dissenting opinion.

The normal practice in Sweden is that dissenting opinions are sent to both parties **7.70** at the same time as the award. Even though dissenting opinions are thus accepted under Swedish law, they do not seem to be very frequent. When they do occur there is usually no drama about it. There are, needless to say, many different ways to draft dissenting opinions. The dissenting arbitrator is generally expected to explain the reasons for his position, rather than to criticize the majority, thereby perhaps undermining it.

7.7 Interest and Costs

7.7.1 Interest

Arbitrators have the general power to order payment of interest. They may, how- **7.71** ever, not go beyond the relief claimed by either party. Consequently, interest may not be awarded unless a party has so requested and not more interest than has been asked for. This follows from the general prohibition against ruling *ultra petita*.

According to Swedish classification rules (see para 2.198) questions concerning **7.72** interest are regarded as matters of substantive law.[68] The rate of interest and whether interest is to be simple or compound, as well as the period of time during which

---

[66] See discussion at para 7.104 *et seq.*
[67] *Arbitration in Sweden* (2nd edn ,1984) 133.
[68] *Arbitration in Sweden* (2nd revised edn, 1984) 135; see discussion at para 2.198.

interest will accrue, are all issues which are thus determined by the law applicable to the merits of the case.

7.73 As far as Swedish substantive law is concerned, absent an agreement by the parties, these matters are regulated by the Interest Act. The Interest Act generally provides for an interest rate equal to the official reference rate of the Bank of Sweden, as determined from time to time, plus a stated number of percentage points. In case of late payments, for example, the interest rate amounts to the official reference rate plus eight percentage points.[69]

---

[69] The relevant provisions of the Interest Act read as follows:

Section 3

Where payment on a debt, the due date of which has been established in advance, is not made during the period for payment, interest shall accrue on the debt commencing on the due date.

Interest on debts which are based upon the obligation of a custodian or other person to provide an accounting for funds which he has received from the principal, or a third party, shall accrue from the day of the accounting or, where such accounting is not presented in due time, from the day on which an accounting should have been presented.

Section 4

In circumstances other than those set forth in section 3, interest shall accrue on any debt which is due and payable and for which payment has not been made during the period for payment, commencing on the day which occurs thirty days following dispatch by the creditor of an invoice or some other form of demand for payment of a specified sum, indicating that failure to make payment shall subject the debtor to liability for interest. The debtor shall not be liable, however, to make payment of interest in respect of the period of time prior to his receipt of the invoice or demand for payment.

In the creditor–debtor relationship between traders in their professional activities, interest shall be payable in accordance with the first paragraph without a requirement, when the claim is made, to state that failure to pay will result in a liability to pay interest. The aforesaid shall apply where a trader, in his professional activities, has a claim against a public authority or other public body in respect of payment for goods or services.

Where the debt relates to damages or other similar compensation, the amount of which cannot be determined without separate evidence, interest shall be payable on any sums due and payable commencing on the day which occurs thirty days following the day on which the creditor demands compensation and presents such evidence which, based upon the circumstances, can reasonably be required. The debtor shall not be liable, however, to make payment of interest in respect of the period of time prior to his receipt of the demand for payment and the evidence.

Notwithstanding the provisions set forth in paragraphs one, two, and three above, interest on any debt which is due and payable shall be payable not later than the day on which service of process is made in respect of an application for summary collection proceedings or a writ in proceedings seeking payment of the debt.

Notwithstanding the provisions set forth in paragraphs three and four above, interest on any debt for damages which are payable as a consequence of an intentional criminal act and which shall not be paid in the form of an annuity, shall accrue from the day on which the damage was sustained.

Section 6

In the circumstances specified in sections 3 or 4, interest shall be calculated per annum according to a rate of interest equivalent to the reference rate of interest in accordance with

From the perspective of Swedish arbitration law, questions concerning interest are **7.74** thus governed by the law applicable to the disputed contract, the *lex contractus*. Such law will consequently determine whether simple or compound interest is to be, or should be, awarded to the winning side.[70]

When interest is awarded, the normal practice in Sweden is to include language to the **7.75** following effect in the operative part of the award: '[T]he respondent is ordered to pay interest at an annual rate of X per cent from [date] until full payment is made'.

This means that interest will continue to run also after the award has been rendered. **7.76** In some jurisdictions this may create problems at the enforcement stage since there is no specific interest amount indicated in the operative part of the award. With a view to avoiding this problem parties sometimes prefer to calculate interest as per a specific date as close as possible to the expected date of the award. Under this approach any interest in addition to that amount would not be enforceable as part of the award.

Section 42, last sentence, of the SAA authorizes the arbitrators to order interest to **7.77** be paid also on the compensation for arbitration costs which the losing party is sometimes ordered to pay. Such an order for interest presupposes that interest has been requested.

7.7.2 Costs

Unless otherwise agreed by the parties, the arbitrators may, upon request by a party, **7.78** order the opposing party to pay compensation for the party's costs (section 42 of the SAA).[71] In addition, upon request of a party, the arbitrators may determine the manner in which the compensation to the arbitrators shall be finally allocated as

---

section 9 as applicable from time to time, plus eight percentage points. Where, however, in the determination of damages as a consequence of personal injury, deduction shall be made for benefits to which the injured party is entitled pursuant to Chapter 5, section 3, subsection 1 of the Tort Liability Act, the supplement to the reference rate of interest for the period until the benefits are finally determined shall be only two percentage points.

Section 9

The reference rate of interest pursuant to this Act shall be determined each calendar half year through a special decision taken by the Central Bank of Sweden. The reference rate of interest shall correspond to the rate of interest applied by the Central Bank of Sweden in the principal refinancing transactions carried out immediately prior to the calendar half year during which the rate of interest is to apply, rounded up to the nearest half percentage point.

---

[70] Under the Swedish Interest Act, for example, compound interest is not available unless the parties have agreed thereto.

[71] Cf Article 44 of the SCC Rules. The SCC Rules provide that the costs available for reimbursement must be reasonable. This corresponds to the provisions under Chapter 18 of the Procedural Code.

between the parties.[72] As discussed above,[73] in relation to the arbitrators, the parties are jointly and severally liable for paying the compensation to the arbitrators. A party's request for costs must be submitted in connection with the closing arguments at a final hearing or, if the parties so agree, at a subsequent date ordered by the arbitrators. In complex matters, the latter would usually be the case since it would be difficult to assess all costs in relation to the hearing, including costs for witnesses and expenses in connection with the hearing, before the hearing has been concluded.

7.79 With respect to the apportionment of arbitration costs, the arbitrators will give effect to any agreements of the parties. If no such agreements have been made, the general opinion in Sweden is that the arbitrators may seek guidance in the rules set out in Chapter 18 of the Procedural Code, ie those applied by the courts of general jurisdiction.[74] The general rule is that the losing party is liable for his own expenses as well as those of his adversary.

7.80 Exceptions to this general rule apply in certain situations, eg when the winning party has negligently brought an unnecessary action or either party by negligence has caused the other party to incur costs.[75] The arbitrators may also be more sophisticated in their approach, taking into account, for instance, how different issues have been decided and how the amount of work has been distributed with respect to the various issues. It may also be the case that a party is not fully successful, for example, in respect of the amount of damages claimed. The arbitrators may then allocate the costs *pro rata* to the initial claim.[76]

7.81 The recoverable costs of the successful party would usually include the following:[77]

(a) The party's share of the compensation payable to the arbitrators (discussed in para 4.103 *et seq* above);
(b) If applicable, the party's share of the charges of an arbitration institution under whose auspices the arbitration has taken place;[78]
(c) Costs relating to evidence presented by the party (such as compensation to witnesses and experts, etc);
(d) The reasonable fees and expenses of the party's counsel; and
(e) Compensation to the party himself for work done and time spent on the case, including loss of salary or other remuneration.[79]

---

[72] Cf Article 43 of the SCC Rules.

[73] See discussion at para 4.103 *et seq.*

[74] Govt Bill 1998/99:35, p 166; cf Articles 43 and 44 of the SCC Rules; Article 31(3) of the ICC Rules; and Article 28 of the LCIA Rules.

[75] Cf Chapter 18, section 6 of the Procedural Code.

[76] Cf Article 28.4 of the LCIA Rules.

[77] *Arbitration in Sweden* (2nd revised edn, 1984) 136; cf Articles 43 and 44 of the SCC Rules.

[78] Govt Bill 1998/99:35, pp 166 and 241 *et seq.*

[79] Ibid, p 241.

The list reflects the philosophy that a winning party, who has not been at fault, **7.82** should not suffer any loss in asserting or defending his rights.

The parties must be given the opportunity to comment on each other's statements **7.83** of costs. If the parties accept each other's statements of costs, the arbitrators must also accept them, pursuant to the overriding principle of party autonomy. If a party does not accept the other party's statement of costs, or if he leaves it to the tribunal to decide, the arbitrators must assess the costs claimed by the parties. The ultimate focus is usually on the reasonableness of the amounts claimed. The SAA is silent on how to determine whether incurred costs are reasonable or not. It is submitted that the following statement, reproduced in para 4.113, by Judge Howard Holtzmann provides a helpful guideline in this respect:

> A test of reasonableness is not, however, an invitation to mere subjectivity. Objective tests of reasonableness of lawyers' fees are well-known. Such tests typically assign weight primarily to the time spent and complexity of the case. In modern practice, the amount of time required to be spent is often a gauge of the extent of the complexities involved. Where the Tribunal is presented with copies of bills for services, or other appropriate evidence, indicating the time spent, the hourly billing rate, and a general description of the professional services rendered, its task need be neither onerous nor mysterious. The range of typical hourly billing rates is generally known and, as evidence before the Tribunal in various cases including this one indicates, it does not greatly differ between the United States and countries of Western Europe, where both claimants and respondents before the Tribunal typically hire their outside counsel. Just how much time any lawyer reasonably needs to accomplish a task can be measured by the number of issues involved in a case and the amount of evidence requiring analysis and presentation. While legal fees are not to be calculated on the basis of the pounds of paper involved, the Tribunal by the end of a case is able to have a fair idea, on the basis of the submissions made by both sides, of the approximate extent of the effort that was reasonably required.
>
> Nor should the Tribunal neglect to consider the reality that legal bills are usually first submitted to businessmen. The pragmatic fact that a businessman has agreed to pay a bill, not knowing whether or not the Tribunal would reimburse the expenses, is a strong indication that the amount billed was considered reasonable by a reasonable man spending his own money, or the money of the corporation he serves. That is a classic test of reasonableness.[80]

7.8 Rendering the Award

Various steps must be taken by the arbitrators in connection with the making of the **7.84** award. Some of these steps should be reflected in the award itself.

Usually, the chairman drafts the award. The other arbitrators comment on the **7.85** draft(s) and then give their final approval to the award. The fact that the award has

---

[80] 8 Iran–US Claims Tribunal Reports 329, 332–333 as quoted in Redfern and Hunter, *Law and Practice of International Commercial Arbitration* (4th edn, 2004) 399.

received the arbitrators' final approval, however, does not mean that it has been rendered. The award is not considered rendered until it is made available to the parties.[81]

7.86 The date when the award is rendered is important with respect to any award period that may have been agreed by the parties, either directly, or by reference to a set of institutional rules. The date is also important in respect of several time periods for actions in connection with the award, eg the arbitrators' right to correct and/or supplement the award (section 32 of the SAA)[82] and the arbitrators' action against the award regarding the payment of compensation to the arbitrators (section 41 of the SAA).[83]

7.87 Reference is made in section 31 of the SAA to when the award is made. There is, however, no explanation or definition of when the award is deemed to have been made. At the earliest an award can be deemed to have been made when the last signature of an arbitrator has been provided, sufficient to constitute a majority. The generally held view is that the award is deemed to have been made within the meaning of section 31 of the SAA when it has been made available to the parties.[84] Actual receipt by the parties is thus not required for an award to be deemed to have been made. Section 31 of the SAA also prescribes, however, that the award shall be delivered to the parties immediately. Also, time limits affecting the parties start to run as of actual receipt of the award.

7.88 The place of the arbitration, which must be stated in the award,[85] is important. It determines which Swedish court is competent with respect to actions against the award regarding invalidity (section 33 of the SAA), challenges (section 34 of the SAA), decisions terminating the proceedings (section 36 of the SAA), and compensation to the arbitrators (section 41 of the SAA)—see section 43 of the SAA.

7.89 In accordance with section 31(3) of the SAA, the award shall be delivered to the parties immediately after it has been rendered. The arbitrators may not refuse to render, or withhold, the award for the purpose of pressuring the parties to pay the compensation to the arbitrators (section 40 of the SAA). The three-month period for a challenge of the award in section 34 of the SAA, and for a party to bring an action against the award regarding the payment of compensation to the arbitrators, as well as the thirty-day period for correcting or supplementing the award in section 32 of the SAA, are also dependent on the day when the party *received* the award.

7.90 The various duties of the arbitrators in connection with the rendering of the award may be discharged in a convenient manner by sending each party a signed copy of

---

[81] Cf section 31 of the SAA.
[82] See para 7.137.
[83] See para 4.122.
[84] Heuman, *Skiljemannarätt* (1999) 523; Lindskog, *Skiljeförfarande. En kommentar* (2005) 800–801.
[85] Section 31(2) of the SAA.

the award by regular mail.[86] However, when proof of receipt is deemed necessary the award should be sent by registered mail with a Post Office receipt or by courier service, also with receipt.[87] The signed acknowledgment of receipt, in combination with testimony as to the contents of the package, will in most cases constitute sufficient evidence of transmission.[88]

Swedish law does not require that the award be filed or registered with any court or other authority. **7.91**

7.9 Effects of the Award

The award has a number of effects. These effects usually arise when the award is rendered, ie when the complete and signed award is made available to the parties. However, some effects arise only after the award has been received by the party in question. The following discussion generally applies to valid awards only, but invalid or defective awards also may have important consequences. **7.92**

7.9.1 Execution

The award, unless it is purely declaratory in character, becomes enforceable when rendered. There is no need to await the expiry of the time period for challenging awards. The special, summary execution procedure which is available in Sweden is discussed in para 9.02. **7.93**

7.9.2 Time starts running

The award marks the beginning of several important time periods, viz, (i) the thirty-day period for correcting or supplementing the award under section 32 of the SAA, (ii) the three-month period for challenging the award under section 34 of the SAA, (iii) the three-month period for an action against the award regarding the payment of compensation to the arbitrators under section 41 of the SAA. **7.94**

The periods described in (i), (ii), and (iii) commence on the date the party in question actually receives the award. The SAA does not require the arbitrators to arrange formal service of the award; delivery by regular mail is sufficient.[89] In order to determine the commencement of time periods, it may however, be necessary to prove the day of service, see para 7.90. With respect to the time periods in (i) and (iii) in relation to the arbitrators' own actions, these periods commence on the date the award is rendered. **7.95**

---

[86] Govt Bill 1998/99:35, pp 240–241.
[87] *Arbitration in Sweden* (2nd revised edn, 1984) 131.
[88] Ibid.
[89] Govt Bill 1998/99:35, pp 240–241; see also *EO et al v ICA Handlarnas AB* (NJA 2001 p 855).

7.9.3 Termination of arbitration agreement

7.96 The award normally results in the termination of the arbitration agreement with respect to the subject matter in dispute. The typical consequences of termination discussed in para 3.168 (ie bar to court proceedings lifted, no official assistance, end of arbitrators' authority etc) do not, however, always follow immediately and without reservations. It is necessary in this respect to distinguish between various types of awards.

7.97 *Valid awards* Subject to the three reservations with respect to the authority of the arbitrators, described below, a valid award results in the termination of the arbitration agreement with respect to the specific dispute. This follows from section 27(4) of the SAA which reads:

> The mandate of the arbitrators shall be deemed to be completed when they have rendered a final award, unless otherwise provided in Sections 32 and 35.

7.98 Although court proceedings would no longer be barred by the arbitration agreement, they would be barred by the fact that the award constitutes *res judicata*.

7.99 Despite the termination, the arbitrators retain authority with respect to the following:

(a) The arbitrators may correct any obvious inaccuracy as a consequence of a typographical, computational, or other similar mistake by the arbitrators or any another person (section 32 of the SAA).[90]

(b) The arbitrators may also interpret the decision in the award at the request of any of the parties (section 32 of the SAA).[91]

(c) The arbitrators retain their powers for purposes of so-called remissions proceedings under section 35, ie proceedings aimed at trying to avoid the setting aside of an award.[92]

7.100 *Incomplete awards* If the arbitrators render a separate or interlocutory award they of course retain the authority to make a further and final award dealing with the remaining issues. Pursuant to section 32 of the SAA the arbitrators may amend or supplement the award.[93] Such amendment or supplement requires that the arbitrators by oversight have failed to decide an issue which should have been dealt with in the award.

7.101 *Void awards* In accordance with section 33 of the SAA, awards are void (or invalid) in a very limited number of cases. The invalidity may also apply to a certain part of the award. A void (or invalid) award, even though considered final by the arbitrators, does not result in the termination of the arbitration agreement *per se*. The arbitrators therefore retain the authority to render a new award in the dispute,

---

[90] Cf Article 41 of the SCC Rules.
[91] Cf ibid.
[92] See discussion at para 8.193.
[93] See discussion at para 7.146. Cf Article 42 of the SCC Rules.

provided new proceedings have commenced. However, with respect to the grounds for invalidity in section 33(1) and (2), ie non-arbitrable issues and awards clearly incompatible with the basic principles of the Swedish legal system, it is difficult, but maybe not impossible, to see how the arbitrators could bypass these grounds and render a new valid award on the subject matter in dispute.

Challengeable awards If the arbitrators render an award which is challengeable **7.102** on some ground the arbitration agreement seems to be, at least temporarily, terminated. This means that the arbitrators become *functus officio*, ie they have no authority to render a new award pending the challenge proceedings, save for the exceptional case described in section 35 of the SAA.[94] However, if the award is finally set aside the arbitration agreement becomes effective again. Consequently, a new dispute between the parties should be tried by a new arbitral tribunal.

In this respect, it is noteworthy that the award retains its binding force until it has **7.103** been set aside in a final judgment.[95]

7.9.4 *Res judicata*

A valid arbitral award constitutes *res judicata*. Sweden has not codified the appli- **7.104** cation of the principles of *lis pendens* and *res judicata* for the purpose of arbitral proceedings and awards. However, case law has confirmed that the principles of *res judicata* and *lis pendens*, as expressed in the Procedural Code, are generally also applicable in arbitration.[96] This means that the *res judicata* effect of an arbitral award must be recognized both by courts and other arbitral tribunals. Thus, if a dispute has already been determined in an arbitral award, a court or arbitral tribunal subsequently seized with the same dispute between the same parties shall dismiss the dispute on grounds of *res judicata*.[97] Furthermore, if a certain issue has already been ruled on in an arbitral award, such previous determination is binding between the same parties in subsequent arbitral or court proceedings where such issue constitutes a preliminary issue.[98] It should be noted, however, that the latter, 'positive' *res judicata* effect of arbitral awards has not yet been confirmed in case law. However, the Supreme Court has, as mentioned, stated that as a rule the same *res judicata* principles apply in arbitration as in court proceedings and that compelling reasons are required to depart from these principles.

As to *lis pendens*, it is generally considered that an arbitral tribunal or a court must **7.105** dismiss a dispute, if the same matter is already pending before another arbitral tribunal, and an arbitral tribunal shall dismiss a dispute if the same matter is already

---

[94] See discussion at para 8.192.
[95] Heuman, *Arbitration Law of Sweden: Practice and Procedure* (2003) 648.
[96] *Aktiebolaget Skånska Cementgjuteriet v Motoraktiebolaget I Karlstad*, (NJA 1953 s 751) and *Esselte AB v Allmänna Pensionsfonden*, (NJA 1998 s 189).
[97] Ibid.
[98] Cf L Heuman, *Arbitration Law of Sweden: Practice and Procedure* (2003) 357.

pending before a court.[99] According to the *travaux préparatoires* to the SAA, problems with respect to the application of the principle of *lis pendens* in arbitration should be resolved through case law.[100] It should be emphasized, however, that issues of *lis pendens* rarely seem to occur between courts and arbitral tribunals. Parallel proceedings before courts and arbitral tribunals are usually resolved through enforcement of the arbitration agreement rather than through the application of the principle of *lis pendens*. In case the arbitration agreement is valid and applicable to the dispute, the court should dismiss the dispute on the ground that the arbitration agreement constitutes a bar to court proceedings and if the arbitration agreement is invalid or not applicable, the arbitral tribunal should dismiss the dispute since it lacks jurisdiction.

7.106 It is important to remember, however, that an arbitral tribunal—unlike a court— may only dismiss a dispute on the grounds of *lis pendens* or *res judicata*, if so requested by one of the parties. In Swedish arbitration law *lis pendens* and *res judicata* are not deemed to form part of public policy and can consequently be waived by a party.[101] If an arbitral tribunal fails to dismiss a claim, after a request by one of the parties for dismissal of a dispute on the basis of *lis pendens* or *res judicata*, the subsequent award is not invalid under section 33 of the SAA, but may be set aside in accordance with section 34 of the SAA upon the timely application by one of the parties.[102]

7.107 In line with the principles applicable in court proceedings, it has been argued that foreign arbitral proceedings and arbitral awards have *lis pendens* and *res judicata* effect in Sweden to the extent they are recognized in Sweden.[103] Under the SAA foreign arbitral awards are recognized in Sweden irrespective of where they have been made, subject only to the grounds for refusing recognition and enforcement pursuant to sections 54 and 55 of the SAA, which correspond to the grounds set out in Article V of the New York Convention.[104] This means that a Swedish court or an arbitral tribunal in Sweden must recognize the *lis pendens* and *res judicata* effect of foreign arbitral proceedings and awards.

7.9.4.1 Application of the principles of lis pendens *and* res judicata *in Swedish arbitration law*

7.108 As mentioned above, the Swedish Supreme Court has ruled that in Swedish arbitration law the principles of *lis pendens* and *res judicata* shall be applied in the same manner as in court proceedings, unless there are compelling reasons for departing

---

[99] Ibid, 356 and 707.

[100] SOU 1994:81, p 137.

[101] See RH 2003:55 Judgment of Svea Court of Appeal, Stockholm, in *Czech Republic v CME Czech Republic BV*, Case 8735-01, SAR 2003:2, p 187.

[102] Judgment of the Supreme Court, *Aktiebolaget Skånska Cementgjuteriet v Motoraktiebolaget i Karlstad*, NJA 1953 s 751 and *Esselte AB v Allmänna Pensionsfonden*, NJA 1998 s 189.

[103] Heuman, *Arbitration Law of Sweden: Practice and Procedure* (2003) 706–707.

[104] See Chapter 9.

from these principles.[105] Thus, the same requirements with respect to identity of parties and identity of subject matter apply before Swedish courts and in arbitrations.

In Swedish court proceedings, the requirement of *party identity* is strictly applied **7.109** and the *res judicata* effect of a judgment may only extend to third parties in certain narrowly defined situations.[106] For example, it is generally considered that the *res judicata* effect of a judgment extends to a third party if such third party would be bound by a party's civil law dispositions over the legal relationship under dispute. For instance, partners in a partnership are bound by a judgment between the partnership and a third party, since such partners, according to Swedish substantive law, are jointly liable for the obligations of the partnership.[107] Under Swedish law there is no equivalent to the common law concept of '*privies*'.

As regards the requirement with respect to *identity of subject matter*, the elements **7.110** that need to be satisfied in order to establish such identity do not easily translate into a simple formula.

The determination of the subject matter is closely related to the provision in **7.111** Chapter 13 section 3 of the Procedural Code, according to which the parties can amend their claims by relying on new circumstances in a proceeding, provided that it concerns the same subject matter. Insofar as a claimant can rely on new circumstances in a proceeding, the *res judicata* effect of the judgment will include these new circumstances. However, case law indicates that the subject matter also includes certain claims that may not de facto have been made.

Accordingly, preclusion affects alternative and economically equivalent legal grounds **7.112** and objections. In principle, a dispute regarding liability to pay for a product or a service is indivisible in respect of its legal effect. In *Kurt Wilhelm M v Aktiebolaget Ragnar J* (NJA 1965 p 94) a purchaser, who had been ordered by a court to pay the remainder of the purchase price, was then prevented by *res judicata* from claiming damages from the seller in a subsequent proceeding on the grounds that the goods were defective. The Supreme Court stated that the issue of liability to pay had already been decided and could not be tried again. An exception to this rule concerns issues that could not have been raised in the previous proceedings. Such issues constitute *facta supervenientia* and are not affected by the *res judicata* effect of the judgment. For instance, if future damages are specified by the claimant and the respondent causes new losses, clearly falling outside what was anticipated by the parties, this new, independent breach of contract may constitute a *factum superveniens*.

The scope of *res judicata* is entirely dependent on the legal effect of the judgment.[108] **7.113** As previously stated, all circumstances that the plaintiff could have invoked are

---

[105] *Esselte AB v Allmänna Pensionsfonden*, (NJA 1998 s 189).
[106] Ibid, pp 145–154.
[107] Ibid.
[108] Ekelöf, Bylund, and Edelstam, *Rättegång III* (7th edn, 2006) 191 *et seq*.

covered by the legal effect of the judgment. Thus, claims where the legal consequences differ qualitatively from a legal consequence already tried, should be tried without Chapter 17, section 11, of the Procedural Code preventing this. However, new claims differing only quantitatively from an earlier claim should be dismissed due to *res judicata*.[109]

7.114 A performance claim will have the same effect in respect of *res judicata* as a claim for declaratory judgment. Accordingly, a claim for declaratory judgment following a performance claim regarding the same subject matter should be dismissed.

7.115 A difficult question in this respect may arise in the clash between the positive effects of an award, ie the preclusion of alternative and economically equivalent grounds and objections, on the one hand, and the power of the arbitrators under section 32 of the SAA to supplement the award under certain circumstances.[110] If, in error, a question has not been tried in the award, such question may be tried in a subsequent decision, notwithstanding any *res judicata* effect of the award *provided* this is deemed to be a supplement to the award in accordance with section 32 of the SAA.[111]

7.116 Different theories on the delimitation of the *res judicata* effect have been developed in doctrinal writings, and case law is ambiguous.[112] However, it is generally considered that the subject matter of a judgment (and thus the *res judicata* effect) includes, first, the claim that has been adjudicated through the judgment in question (or more precisely the legal consequence of such claim as expressed in the *operative part* of the judgment) and, secondly, claims that are alternative to and, at the same time, financially equivalent to the original claim, and which it would have been reasonable to require the claimant to present together with the original claim. Furthermore, in addition to such claims that are covered by the *res judicata* effect of a judgment, any grounds or objections (whether invoked or not) which could have been invoked in support of (or in defence of) the above-defined claims are covered by the *res judicata* effect.[113]

7.117 Reasons in an award, or in a judgment, do not have *res judicata* effect. Very often, however, the reasons play a critical role in properly understanding the operative part of an award or a judgment.

---

[109] Fitger, *Kommentar till rättegångsbalken*, 17:47

[110] See discussion at para 7.146.

[111] Cf the Svea Court of Appeal's judgment on 24 March 1999 in *Government of the Federative Socialist Soviet Republic of Russia v Compagnie NOGA d'Importation et d'Exportation* (Switzerland) (Case No T 925-98-80). The case is summarized in Jarvin and Magnusson (eds), *International Arbitration Court Decisions* (2nd edn, 2008) 1168–1175, with observations by Schöldström, 1177 *et seq*.

[112] See eg Fitger, Rättegångsbalken. *En kommentar, Norstedts Juridiska Databaser*, section 17:11, pp 4–6.

[113] Ibid, section 17:11, pp 5–6.

Although the principles of *res judicata* and *lis pendens* in arbitration, as described   **7.118**
above, are generally applied in the same manner as in Swedish court proceedings, it
must be noted that the Supreme Court has left some room for courts and tribunals
to adapt the application of the principles of *lis pendens* and *res judicata* to the distinctive characteristics of arbitral proceedings, provided that such adaptation is justified
by compelling reasons.[114] This has been confirmed also in the *travaux préparatoires*
to the SAA, which indicate that problems of application of the said principles
should be resolved through case law.[115]

Furthermore, the abovementioned Supreme Court case[116] concerned domestic   **7.119**
arbitration. The interest of upholding domestic Swedish principles of *lis pendens*
and *res judicata* would appear to be less compelling in international arbitrations.
Thus, it could perhaps be argued that courts and tribunals should have wider discretion
to deviate from the civil procedure principles of *lis pendens* and *res judicata* in international arbitration, when justified by the particular characteristics of international
arbitration.

7.9.4.2 Res judicata *and* lis pendens *in international arbitration*

The application of the principles of *lis pendens* and *res judicata* in international   **7.120**
arbitration was addressed by the Svea Court of Appeal in *Czech Republic v CME
Czech Republic BV*.[117]

This case concerned the challenge of the partial award on liability in an investment   **7.121**
treaty arbitration, *CME Czech Republic BV v Czech Republic*.[118] In this case, the Czech
Republic argued, *inter alia*, that the award should be set aside because the tribunal
had failed to acknowledge that the liability of the Czech Republic had already been
determined in a parallel arbitration, *Lauder v Czech Republic*,[119] and, thus, was *res
judicata*.

The *CME/Lauder* arbitrations, and the ensuing challenge proceedings, triggered a   **7.122**
discussion about alleged abuse by investors of the right to arbitration in investment
treaties, in general, and whether the principles of *lis pendens* and *res judicata*, in their
traditional application, are sufficient to avoid conflicting proceedings and awards
in international arbitrations, in particular.

In the *Lauder* case the ultimate controlling shareholder in the group of companies   **7.123**
holding the investment in the Czech Republic initiated arbitration under one
investment protection treaty. Subsequently, in the *CME* case, the group subsidiary

---

[114]   *Esselte AB v Allmänna Pensionsfonden*, (NJA 1998 s 189).
[115]   SOU 1994:81, p 137.
[116]   *Esselte AB v Allmänna Pensionsfonden*, (NJA 1998 s 189).
[117]   See note 101.
[118]   *CME Czech Republic BV v Czech Republic*, Partial Award and Separate Opinion, signed on 13
September 2001.
[119]   *Lauder v Czech Republic*, Final Award, signed on 3 September 2001.

directly holding the shares in the local company initiated separate arbitration proceedings under another investment protection treaty regarding exactly the same investment and based on exactly the same alleged acts and omissions of the Czech Republic. None of the arbitral tribunals declined jurisdiction in favour of the other tribunal. The two arbitrations resulted in completely contradictory findings as to whether there had been a violation of the host State's obligations under international law. The award in the *CME* case, which was the later of the two awards, held the Czech Republic liable for breaches of its obligations under international law, while the award in the *Lauder* case held that no such breaches had occurred.[120]

7.124 One of the questions raised in these cases, and subsequently in the challenge proceedings before the Svea Court of Appeal, was whether the *res judicata* effect of an arbitral award regarding alleged violations of a an investment protection treaty could extend to a company belonging to the same group as the entity or individual bringing the first claim, but which was not a party to the first proceedings, in situations where the two entities are relying on the protection of different treaties, but in relation to the same alleged acts and omissions of the host State and in relation to the same investment.

7.125 These types of conflicting proceedings and awards are not likely to occur in a domestic context, since, under the municipal company law of most jurisdictions, a shareholder is not allowed (except for narrowly defined exceptions) to bring a claim on behalf of the company in which he owns shares. Thus, such conflicting proceedings involve circumstances that are unique to international arbitration, or more particularly to investment treaty arbitration where investment protection treaties frequently extend the right to bring a claim not only to the entity directly suffering the loss or damage, but also to shareholders of such company suffering indirect loss or damage. It could therefore be argued, and it was indeed argued by the Czech Republic in its challenge of the award in the *CME* case, that the particular circumstances of the conflicting proceedings in the *Lauder* and *CME* arbitrations merited such a deviation from the traditional application of the principles of *res judicata* and *lis pendens*, which the Supreme Court endorsed in *Esselte AB v Allmänna Pensionsfonden* (NJA 1998 s 189).

7.126 The Svea Court of Appeal, however, did not make use of this opportunity.[121] It took a rather formalistic and restrictive approach to the application of *res judicata* in international arbitration involving parallel claims under investment protection treaties. As to the question whether there can be *lis pendens* or *res judicata* at all between two different arbitral tribunals under two different treaties, the Court of Appeal stated that:

---

[120] See further Hobér, 'Parallel Arbitration Proceedings—Duties of the Arbitrators: Some Reflections and Ideas', in *Parallel State and Arbitral Procedures in International Arbitration*, ICC Publication No 692, (2005).

[121] See note. An unofficial translation into English of the judgment is published in SAR 2003:2, p 167 *et seq.*

[t]he mere fact that the issue is whether proceedings were demanded based on different investment protection treaties which were entered into between different states, the Czech Republic and the Netherlands in the one treaty and the Czech Republic and the United States in the other, militates against these legal principles [*lis pendens* and *res judicata*] being applicable at all. However, a couple of arbitration awards have been invoked from which it is evident, in any event, that the actual dispute appears in practice to be the same in arbitration proceedings which were brought pursuant to two different treaties. Since, in any event, it cannot be ruled out entirely that the principles of *lis pendens* and *res judicata* may become applicable in the relations between two different international arbitration proceedings, the Court of Appeal will proceed with its assessment.[122]

However, with regard to the requirement of identity of parties, the Court found that: **7.127**

According to Swedish law, one of the fundamental conditions for *lis pendens* and *res judicata* is that the same parties are involved in both cases. As far as is known, the same condition applies in other legal systems which recognise the principles in question. Identity between a minority shareholder, albeit a controlling one, and the actual company cannot, in the Court of Appeal's opinion, be deemed to exist in a case such as the instant one. This assessment would apply even if one were to allow a broad determination of the concept of identity.[123]

Thus, the Court of Appeal, found that the award in the *Lauder* case did not have any **7.128** *res judicata* effect in relation to the award in the *CME* case, since the parties were different. The Court of Appeal did not further consider whether the specific characteristics of the underlying investment protection regime in the *CME* and *Lauder* cases merited a deviation from the traditional civil procedure approach to *lis pendens* and *res judicata*. Leave for appeal to the Supreme Court was not granted.

Thus, under Swedish arbitration law as it stands today, the application of the principles **7.129** of *lis pendens* and *res judicata* in international arbitration still seems to follow more or less the same pattern as in domestic arbitration and court procedure.

The abovementioned criteria with respect to *res judicata* and *lis pendens* are inter- **7.130** preted differently in different jurisdictions. Whereas some legal systems will give *res judicata* effect to an award as of the day when it was rendered, other jurisdictions will consider it to be binding only once the challenge process has been completed, or relevant time periods have expired.[124] Also other criteria vary between different jurisdictions.[125] In general, common law jurisdictions afford arbitral awards broader preclusive effect than civil law countries.[126]

---

[122] SAR 2003:2, p 186 (unofficial translation).
[123] SAR 2003:2, p 189 (unofficial translation).
[124] 2004 Interim ILA Report 'Res Judicata and Arbitration', p 6 and Söderlund, 'Lis pendens, Res judicata and the Issue of Parallel Judicial Proceedings' 22(4) *Journal of International Arbitration*, August 2005, p 302.
[125] In Switzerland and Sweden only the operative part will have *res judicata* effect whereas in France it may be possible to take the reasons into account. See ILA 2004 Report on *Res Judicata*, p 26. Although generalizations are difficult, French law would in this respect seem to resemble the more extensive approach adopted in common law countries, see Born, II *International Commercial Arbitration* 2882–2887.
[126] Born, II *International Commercial Arbitration* 2889.

7.131 One possible approach to address this disparity between national laws could be to launch a transnational—a *sui generis*—approach to *res judicata* in international commercial arbitration.

7.132 The question of establishing a transnational approach to *res judicata* has been the focus of the International Law Association (ILA) and its Committee on International Commercial Arbitration. The ILA initiative resulted in a recommendation that was published in its 2004 and 2006 Reports '*Res judicata* and Arbitration'.[127] In short, the ILA recommendation proposed that arbitrators take an approach that reflects the transnational nature of international arbitration. However, the ILA recommendation also observes that some issues cannot be solved by a transnational approach simply because the differences between the legal systems are too significant and because there is no internationally accepted conflict of laws rule in this respect.

7.133 Several of the approaches suggested with respect to an international *res judicata* standard are based on a contractual starting point. Instead of viewing *res judicata* as a procedural rule, the question of *res judicata* is seen as one of many rights derived from the parties' arbitration agreement. From this perspective the agreement to arbitrate normally gives rise to expectations of finality and efficiency which must be given effect by appropriate rules on *res judicata*. If the parties in the arbitration agreement have agreed to apply institutional arbitration rules, these rules could be used to create an appropriate *res judicata* effect on a contractual basis. If the first award is rendered under the ICC Rules, for example, it would imply that the parties had agreed that the first award would be binding (Article 28(6) of the ICC Rules) and therefore at the same time had agreed not to re-litigate the same dispute. It has also been suggested that since an ICC award must include the arbitrators' reason for its decision (Article 25(2) of the ICC Rules), the reasons must be binding on the parties and have *res judicata* effect.[128]

7.134 Although one can question the appropriateness of exclusively applying national rules on *res judicata* in international arbitration this has been, at least historically, the favoured approach taken by arbitrators when faced with the task of interpreting the preclusive effect of a prior award. In assessing the *res judicata* effect of an arbitral award, guidance will therefore still be needed from appropriate choice of law rules identifying which national law to apply.[129] In determining what the applicable law

---

[127] See ILA, Berlin Conference (2004), International Commercial Arbitration, Interim Report on '*Res judicata* and Arbitration' and ILA, Toronto Conference (2006), International Commercial Arbitration, Final Report on '*Res Judicata* and Arbitration'.

[128] Sheppard, *Res Judicata and Estoppel in Parallel State and Arbitration Procedures in International Arbitration* ICC Publication No 692 (2005) 230.

[129] The ILA recommendation was not intended to cover all aspects of *res judicata* and consequently it also made references to appropriate conflict rules in relation to issues where the committee perceived that the development of transnational rules was premature and therefore refrained from formulating transnational rules. See also Born, II *International Commercial Arbitration*, 2909–2913.

is, the following laws are normally applied: (i) the law of the State of the prior award, and/or (ii) the law of the seat of the second arbitration.

Of these alternatives the seat of the second arbitration seems to be the one most **7.135** favoured by arbitrators.[130] The reason for this is probably that *res judicata*, at least in civil law jurisdictions, is characterized as a procedural issue which according to *lex arbitri* is governed by the procedural law of the seat of the arbitration.[131] A further reason to apply the law of the second forum is that the *res judicata* issue will arise in the second arbitration. Thus, it will fall on the second tribunal to deal with any cost and inefficiencies caused by the duplication of proceedings.

Although there is general acceptance of the overall principles of *res judicata* and *lis* **7.136** *pendens* in international arbitration there is little agreement on the precise contents of these principles and on the choice of law rules to be applied in determining *res judicata* and *lis pendens* issues. Traditionally arbitrators have in general applied the law of the seat of the second arbitration. There may be a trend, however, to avoid strict application of preclusion rules from one particular legal system. Instead a pragmatic approach may be emerging where the arbitrators try to avoid applying municipal law preclusion rules in a restrictive and technical manner. It is possible that over time we will see a more *sui generis* approach to *res judicata* issues in international arbitration. Meanwhile, however, municipal law rules will continue to play an important role.

7.10 Correction and Interpretation of the Award

7.10.1 General

As mentioned in the foregoing, an arbitral award is final and binding on the merits **7.137** when rendered. It cannot be appealed. It cannot be changed. Under certain circumstances an arbitral award may be challenged and set aside. In certain situations there is a need, however, to make minor adjustments to an award without changing the outcome of the case and without setting the award aside. Such situations are dealt with in section 32 of the SAA. This provision deals with the correction, amendment, and interpretation of arbitral awards.

It follows from section 27(4) of the SAA that the arbitrators' mandate terminates **7.138** when they have rendered the final award, save for situations provided for, eg in section 32 of the SAA. The mandate of the arbitrators thus covers corrections, amendments, and interpretations of arbitral awards. It must be noted, however that the arbitrators have no *obligation* to correct, amend, or interpret awards. It is in their discretion to do so, or not to do so. This raises the question as to what parties can do

---

[130] Born, II *International Commercial Arbitration* 2910 and 2917; see also Sheppard, note 128.
[131] Born, II *International Commercial Arbitration* 2910.

in the unlikely event that the arbitrators refuse to correct, amend, or interpret an award. Under Swedish law there is no other body which could perform this task. The courts are not authorized to do so, nor the Enforcement Authority. It would seem that the only possibility for the party in question is to request the competent District Court, or the relevant arbitration institution, to replace the arbitrator(s) so that the new arbitrator(s) will perform this task.

7.139 Neither section 32 of the SAA nor any other provision in the Act explicitly addresses the issue of whether arbitrators are entitled to additional compensation for work done when correcting, amending, or interpreting an award. Decisions by the arbitrators to correct, amend, or interpret an award constitute a part of the final award.[132] There is no need to issue an additional award, even though for practical reasons a new document is usually prepared, signed, and issued. The explanation is that it is often difficult to obtain the original awards from the parties with a view to making the correction etc on the original. The arbitrators are entitled to make decisions as to the costs of the parties in the final award, as well as decisions with respect to their own compensation. To the extent that the arbitrators request additional compensation, it should therefore, as a matter of principle, be possible to deal with such compensation in the same way as in the final award. From a practical point of view, however, the amount of work required in this respect will often be insignificant. On the other hand, a request to interpret an award may sometimes require substantial amounts of work by the arbitrators. If the additional work, however, is a consequence of errors and mistakes made by the arbitrators, it would not seem reasonable that they should be entitled to additional compensation.

7.10.2 Correction of arbitral awards

7.140 Corrections of arbitral awards under section 32 of the SAA are limited to obvious inaccuracies which are the 'consequences' of a typographical error, error in computation, or other similar error by arbitrators, or any other person.

7.141 It is clear from the language of the provision that errors in law and logical errors are excluded.[133] Sometimes it may be difficult to determine if a miscalculation is just that, or if it is a result of a misapplication of the law or misunderstanding of evidence. This distinction can only be made based on the facts of the individual case.

7.142 The reference in section 32 of the SAA to an 'obvious inaccuracy' means that the rule must be applied in a restrictive fashion. The restrictive application is not connected with the amounts *per se*. Small amounts as well as large amounts may be corrected.

7.143 It is noteworthy that errors warranting a correction may stem not only from the arbitrators, but from 'another person', eg a party representative or counsel. Amounts

---

[132] Govt Bill 1998/99:35, p 233.
[133] Ibid, p 136.

included in briefs, witness statements, or expert reports may have been miscalculated, but the mistake was not discovered during the proceedings, or when drafting the award. It could perhaps be argued that parties who make mistakes of this kind should themselves bear the consequences thereof. Since the statutory text refers to obvious mistakes, the objective here, however, is to prevent a flagrantly unjust and unreasonable result.

Any correction of an arbitral award initiated by the arbitrators themselves must **7.144** be made within thirty days of the date of the award. A party wishing to correct the award must file his request with the arbitrators within thirty days of receipt of the award by that party. The arbitrators must then correct the award within thirty days of receipt of the request by the party.

Pursuant to section 32(3) of the SAA the arbitrators should afford the other party **7.145** the opportunity to comment on the request to correct the award. Even though the arbitrators thus have no obligation to invite the other party, most arbitrators would view it as good and prudent practice to do so, even in situations when the nature of the requested measure does not warrant it.[134]

7.10.3 Amendment of arbitral awards

If the arbitrators have failed to decide 'an issue' which should have been dealt with **7.146** in the award, section 32(1) authorizes the arbitrators to rule on such issue by amending the award.[135] The reference to 'an issue' does not only cover prayers for relief, but also legal grounds relied on by the parties. The typical example is when the arbitrators have simply forgotten to address and to rule on one of several prayers for relief. If the arbitrators have forgotten to rule on a counterclaim, or set-off claim, an amendment may lead to a reduction of the amount which the party has been ordered to pay. Needless to say, the right to amend the award does not entitle the arbitrators otherwise to change the award, for example by excluding certain parts of the award, or reducing the amounts.

The right to amend the award is based on the idea that the incomplete award is **7.147** the result of an 'oversight' by the arbitrators. This means that if the arbitrators have taken a conscious—but in the view of one of the parties, a wrong—decision, the award cannot be amended. The party in question may, however, be able successfully to challenge the award.

If the arbitrators amend the award on their own initiative they must do so within **7.148** thirty days of the date of the award. If an amendment is requested by one of the parties—which must be done within thirty days of receipt of the award by the party—the arbitrators have sixty days to amend the award, if they so decide.

---

[134] Govt Bill 1998/99:35, p 233.
[135] As discussed in para 8.72, this situation may also under certain circumstances entitle a party to challenge the award and have it set aside.

7.10.4 Interpretation of arbitral awards

7.149 Section 32 of the SAA entitles parties to ask for an interpretation of the award. It is important to note that the provision refers to an interpretation of the operative part of the award. Consequently, the reasoning of the arbitrators leading to the operative part cannot be interpreted. This limitation is necessary to prevent the parties from trying to re-argue their case. It also means that the fact that the reasons may be unclear and vague does not entitle a party to obtain an interpretation or clarification of them.[136]

7.150 Generally speaking, most arbitrators seem to be reluctant to become involved in post-award debates about the meaning of the award, and for good reasons. An exchange of views on various aspects of the award could easily lead to statements being made by arbitrators which parties misunderstand, or choose to misunderstand. An important safeguard in this respect is that under section 32 of the SAA only the operative part of the award can be interpreted. Another safeguard is the fact that the requesting party must specify in which respect he wants an interpretation of the award. This is not explicitly stated in the statutory text but is clearly stated in the *travaux préparatoires*.[137] This is of importance not only for the arbitrators, but also for the other party. When interpretation of the award is requested, most arbitrators would invite the other party to comment on the request. It is then vital for that party to understand what he has to comment on.

7.151 If the arbitrators decide to interpret the award, it must be done within thirty days after having received the request from one of the parties.

7.10.5 SCC Rules

7.152 In the SCC Rules, Articles 41 and 42 deal with the correction, amendment, and interpretation of arbitral awards. The provisions build on the corresponding sections in the SAA and are very similar.[138] There are some differences, however.

7.153 Article 41 of the SCC Rules deals with the correction and interpretation of the award. Whereas section 32 of the SAA leaves it to the discretion of the arbitrators, pursuant to Article 41(1) of the SCC Rules the arbitral tribunal 'shall' correct or interpret the award as the case may be, provided that the arbitrators find the request well-founded. Under Article 41(1) of the SCC Rules the requesting party must always inform the other party of his request.

---

[136] Govt Bill 1998/99:35, pp 137 and 233.

[137] Ibid, p 137.

[138] Article 29 of the ICC Rules has provisions on correction and interpretation of arbitral awards. There is nothing, however, in the ICC Rules about amendment of an award. In the LCIA Rules Article 27 deals with correction and amendment of awards. The LCIA Rules do not, however, address interpretation of awards. The 1976 UNCITRAL Arbitration Rules deal with correction in Article 35 and with interpretation in Article 36.

When the arbitrators correct or interpret the award on their own initiative, Article **7.154** 41(2) does not require them to invite comments from the parties. In practice, however, this is almost always done. The arbitrators must correct the award within thirty days of the date of the award, or within thirty days from receipt by them of the request from one of the parties.

The SCC Rules, like the SAA, do not allow the arbitrators to interpret the award on **7.155** their own initiative. This can only be done at the request of a party. In contrast to the SAA, however, Article 42 of the SCC Rules allows the arbitrators to issue an amendment to the award, only at the request of a party. The other party must always be advised of the request.

If the arbitrators find that the request for an amendment is well-founded, they shall **7.156** issue an amended award. This is to be done within sixty days of receipt of the request. It should be noted that the SCC Board may grant extensions of this time period.

It should be noted that, unlike section 32 of the SAA, Article 42 of the SCC Rules **7.157** does not limit the interpretation of an arbitral award to the operative part. Rather, Article 42 of the SCC Rules refers to a 'specific point or part of the award'.

8

SETTING ASIDE ARBITRAL AWARDS

8.1 **Invalid and Challengeable Awards** 8.01
  8.1.1 General remarks 8.01
  8.1.2 Principle of *in dubio
    pro validitate* 8.09
  8.1.3 Burden of proof 8.12
  8.1.4 Other means of recourse 8.15
  8.1.5 Jurisdiction of Swedish
    courts 8.19
8.2 **Invalid Arbitral Awards** 8.26
  8.2.1 Grounds for invalidity 8.27
    8.2.1.1 Non-arbitrability 8.29
    8.2.1.2 Violation of public policy 8.33
    8.2.1.3 Formal requirements of
      the arbitral award 8.47
  8.2.2 Non-statutory grounds
    for invalidity 8.50
    8.2.2.1 Situations where an 'award'
      may not be characterized
      as an arbitral award 8.51
    8.2.2.2 The party against whom the
      award was made was not a
      party to the arbitration
      proceedings 8.53
    8.2.2.3 An award too obscure
      to enforce 8.56
  8.2.3 Invalidity of part of the award 8.57
8.3 **Challenge of Arbitral Awards** 8.58
  8.3.1 Grounds for challenging
    an award 8.58
  8.3.2 No arbitration agreement 8.63
  8.3.3 Excess of mandate 8.65

8.3.3.1 Award after the expiration
  of a time limit for
  rendering of the award 8.66
8.3.3.2 Excess of mandate 8.69
  8.3.4 The arbitration should not have
    taken place in Sweden 8.109
  8.3.5 Improper appointment
    of arbitrators 8.112
  8.3.6 One of the arbitrators should
    have been disqualified 8.114
  8.3.7 Other procedural
    irregularities 8.118
    8.3.7.1 The irregularities to
      which the general clause
      applies 8.118
    8.3.7.2 Probable influence on the
      outcome of the dispute 8.176
    8.3.7.3 The procedural irregularity
      must not have been caused
      by the fault of the
      challenging party 8.182
8.4 **Waiver of Right to Challenge** 8.184
  8.4.1 Implied waiver 8.185
  8.4.2 Exclusion agreements 8.187
8.5 **Remission of Arbitral Awards** 8.193
8.6 **Review of Jurisdictional Awards** 8.205
  8.6.1 Introduction 8.205
  8.6.2 Scope of application 8.209
  8.6.3 Scope of the review 8.211
  8.6.4 Application of section 36 of
    the SAA in practice 8.215

8.1 Invalid and Challengeable Awards

8.1.1 General remarks

As mentioned above, an arbitral award is intended to be a final and binding resolu- **8.01**
tion of a dispute. Under Swedish law, an arbitral award is final and binding on the

merits as of the moment when it is rendered by the arbitrators. This fact notwithstanding, most legal systems seek to exercise some degree of control over arbitrations conducted in their territories. This control focuses on procedural aspects of the arbitration with a view to ensuring a minimum standard of objectivity, fairness, and justice. Control is usually exercised by means of a challenge procedure.

8.02 The Swedish Arbitration Act (SAA) distinguishes between *invalid* awards (section 33) and *challengeable* awards (section 34). Awards falling under section 33 are invalid *ipso facto* and *ab initio*. Legally such awards do not exist. Consequently, there is, in theory, no need to go to court to have such awards declared invalid, since they are invalid *ipso facto*. In practice, however, it is often necessary to request a court of law to declare such an award invalid, or rather confirm that it is invalid. Otherwise the winning party could still try to have the award recognized and enforced under the New York Convention. Since invalid awards are invalid *ab initio*, no time limit applies with respect to court actions for the declaration that an award is invalid.

8.03 Challengeable awards, on the other hand, must be challenged within the stipulated period of time, ie three months from the date upon which the party received the award (section 34(3)).[1] If not challenged, the award will remain final and binding despite the fact that a procedural error may have occurred.

8.04 When the SAA was being prepared, the issue was raised whether it was meaningful to maintain the distinction between invalid and challengeable awards, particularly against the background that the UNCITRAL Model Law does not explicitly make any such distinction.[2] It was finally decided to maintain this distinction. The reason was to emphasize the difference between circumstances which are under the control of the parties, ie the grounds for challenging awards under section 34 of the SAA, on the one hand, and circumstances beyond the control of the parties, ie section 33 of the SAA, on the other.[3] The latter provision thus covers situations where the public interest, in the opinion of the legislator, requires that awards are invalid. It largely corresponds to the grounds in Article 34(2)(b) of the UNCITRAL Model Law, which are subject to *ex officio* court scrutiny.[4] The list of grounds of invalidity in section 33 is intended to be exhaustive.

8.05 When discussing the Swedish rules with respect to challenges of arbitral awards, it is important to remember that the rules of the SAA are not optional, but rather

---

[1] In case the award has been corrected, supplemented, or interpreted pursuant to section 32 of the SAA, the award must be challenged within three months from the date when the party received the award in its final wording.

[2] Secolec and Eliasson, 'The UNCITRAL Model Law on Arbitration and the Swedish Arbitration Act: A Comparison', in Heuman and Jarvin (eds), *The Swedish Arbitration Act of 1999, Five Years On: A Critical Review of Strengths and Weaknesses* (2006) 236–239.

[3] Govt Bill 1998/99:35, pp 138–140.

[4] Secolec and Eliasson, 'The UNCITRAL Model Law on Arbitration and the Swedish Arbitration Act: A Comparison', in Heuman and Jarvin (eds), *The Swedish Arbitration Act of 1999, Five Years On: A Critical Review of Strengths and Weaknesses* (2006) 236.

mandatory in the sense that it is not in the discretion of a court to set aside, or not to set aside, an award if all the conditions for setting aside the award have in fact been met.[5] In this respect the SAA thus differs from the UNCITRAL Model Law. On the other hand, it should be borne in mind that the provisions of the law must not be applied in an overly formalistic fashion by the courts such that the practice of courts limits the possibilities of arbitrators to handle arbitration in a flexible manner. In reviewing the issue of whether or not an arbitral tribunal has committed a procedural error, for example, the perspective must be that of arbitrators, rather than that of a court of law. In other words, courts of law must and should accept that arbitrators, generally speaking, have fairly wide discretion in deciding and administering procedural issues, much more so than courts of law typically have.

Pursuant to section 43 of the SAA, an action against an allegedly invalid or challenge- **8.06** able award shall be determined by the appellate court within the jurisdiction of which the arbitral proceedings were held.[6] If the place of arbitration has not been stated in the award, the action may be brought before the Svea Court of Appeal. The main rule is that the judgment of the Court of Appeal may not be appealed. However, the Court of Appeal may grant leave to appeal to the Supreme Court where it is of importance as a matter of precedent that the appeal be considered by the Supreme Court. Even if the Court of Appeal allows such an appeal, the Supreme Court can still decide not to hear the case.

It should be emphasized that, under Swedish law, an arbitral award is final and **8.07** binding until it has been set aside by a final and binding judgment of a court of law having jurisdiction to determine challenges to the arbitral award. This means, for example, that a request to have an award set aside cannot be combined with requests which seek to have the dispute retried on the merits. In one case decided by the Supreme Court, the respondent in the arbitration had voluntarily complied with the arbitral award but nevertheless asked the court, when challenging the award, not only to set aside the award but also to order the other party to repay what he had paid under the arbitral award.[7] The conclusion of the Supreme Court was that there could be no question of repayment until the issue of setting aside the arbitral award had been finally decided. On that basis the Supreme Court dismissed the action for repayment since there was, at that point in time, nothing to be repaid. Such action could only be brought after a successful challenge of the award.

By the same token, a party who is seeking to set aside an arbitral award pursuant **8.08** either to section 33 or 34 of the SAA cannot substitute such challenge proceedings with a claim for damages based on the claims made during the arbitration proceeding. Such actions must be dismissed without being tried on the merits since

---

[5] Ibid, 235.
[6] This means that if the arbitral proceedings were held in Stockholm, an action against the award will be tried by the Svea Court of Appeal.
[7] *Esselte AB v Allmänna Pensionsfonden* (NJA 1998 p 189).

they cannot, by definition, be granted until and unless an arbitral award has been set aside and such decision has become final and binding. Moreover, such a substantive claim in court would also likely be precluded by the arbitration agreement, the validity of which remains unaffected.[8]

8.1.2 Principle of *in dubio pro validitate*

8.09 As mentioned above, the generally accepted approach in Sweden, and in most other jurisdictions today, is that an arbitral award once rendered is final and binding on the merits. This general approach is also reflected in the general attitude of courts when hearing challenges to arbitral awards. It is sometimes said that courts should apply the principle of *in dubio pro validitate*. In other words, in uncertain situations, the decision of a court of law should be in favour of upholding an arbitral award. This general approach has at least partially been confirmed by the Supreme Court, which has confirmed that only serious procedural errors or mistakes may serve as the basis for a request to challenge an award on procedural grounds. It is only in situations where a procedural rule has been violated in a significant manner that a party should have the possibility to set aside an award.[9] This does not mean, however, that only *gross* violations of procedural rules can serve as a basis for having the award set aside. Rather, there has to be a certain level of seriousness in the procedural mistake or error for such an error to serve as a basis for having the award set aside. Only procedural mistakes and errors which are of certain significance should be able to serve as a basis for setting aside the award. In other words: not every minor violation of every minor procedural rule can lead to this result.

8.10 Another reflection of the general approach to upholding arbitral awards in cases of doubt is the willingness of Swedish courts to interpret arbitral awards and alleged procedural errors in a benevolent way, ie in a way which would support the validity of the arbitral award. Courts seem to be prepared to give unclear language in the arbitral award the benefit of doubt in the sense that the presumption should be that the intention of the parties as well as the arbitrators is to create a valid arbitral award.

8.11 Statistics on invalidity and challenge proceedings confirm the very limited prospects of succeeding in having an award declared invalid or set aside.[10]

8.1.3 Burden of proof

8.12 The SAA does not address questions relating to the burden of proof in respect of invalidity or challenge proceedings. Under the UNCITRAL Model Law, however, Article 34(2) places the burden of proof on the party who has initiated the challenge.

---

[8] See discussion at para 3.112.

[9] *Jansson v Retrotype AB* (NJA 1975 p 536).

[10] Appendix 7 lists all cases that have tried under sections 33 and 34 of the SAA and which have become final binding as of 1 November 2010. This means that there are additional cases still pending. Appendix 7 makes clear that there are very few cases where an arbitral award has been set aside.

Generally speaking, the same rule with respect to the burden of proof should, and does, apply under Swedish law. There is a complication, however, insofar as the SAA makes a distinction between invalid awards and challengeable awards. Under the UNCITRAL Model Law, the plaintiff does not have the burden of proof for two grounds which under the SAA constitute grounds for invalidity, viz, violation of public policy and non-arbitrability. The UNCITRAL Model Law is based on the assumption that a court of law will adjudicate such issues *ex officio*.[11]

While, in general terms, insofar as the grounds for invalidity are concerned, it is up to the court to establish such facts *ex officio*, issues of burden of proof may nevertheless arise. If that does indeed happen, the only reasonable starting point must be that the burden of proof is borne by the plaintiff. For example, if the plaintiff is alleging that the arbitral award is invalid because one of the arbitrators has been bribed (if true, such a situation would typically violate Swedish public policy), but the plaintiff has not been able to establish all the relevant facts, it would be reasonable to say that the plaintiff must carry the burden of not having proven its case, rather than imposing a far-reaching inquisitorial duty on the court. **8.13**

With respect to challenges to an arbitral award based on section 34 of the SAA, a reasonable starting point, must again be that the plaintiff carries the burden of proof. Such an approach follows generally accepted rules of evidence under Swedish law, ie that the party who alleges a fact carries the burden of proof for that fact.[12] There are, however, situations where the burden of proof may shift depending on the arguments presented by the parties. This may also result in a situation where, with respect to certain facts, the respondent does carry the burden of proof. **8.14**

8.1.4 Other means of recourse

As described in the foregoing, the result of a successful challenge of an arbitral award is that the award is set aside. Since a court of law is not authorized to 'replace' the award with other decisions on the merits, the parties must initiate a new arbitration, if they still wish to have the dispute resolved.[13] In many situations the setting aside of the award is a rather dramatic consequence for the parties. The SAA therefore also offers a possibility to 'heal the defect' in the award, and thereby prevent it from being set aside. Pursuant to section 35 of the SAA, a court of law that hears a challenge may, under certain circumstances, remit the award to the arbitrators with the request that they heal the defect in the award.[14] **8.15**

---

[11] Secolec and Eliasson, 'The UNCITRAL Model Law on Arbitration and the Swedish Arbitration Act: A Comparison', in Heuman and Jarvin (eds), *The Swedish Arbitration Act of 1999, Five Years On: A Critical Review of Strengths and Weaknesses* (2006) 236.

[12] See discussion at para 6.168.

[13] The arbitration agreement remains valid and thus still constitutes a bar to court proceedings; see para 796.

[14] This provision, which is inspired by Article 34 of the Model Law, is discussed at para 8.193 *et seq.*

8.16   Another provision of the SAA which must be mentioned in this context is section 36. In situations where an arbitral tribunal has declined jurisdiction, a decision which shall be made in the form of an award, this provision entitles parties to have the jurisdictional issue retried by a court of law.[15] Such cases are tried at the appellate court level, and involve a complete *de novo* trial of the jurisdictional issue decided by the arbitral tribunal.[16] Moreover, unlike challenge proceedings, if the Court of Appeal finds that the tribunal was wrong in deciding that it did not have jurisdiction, the court may revise the award. Such a judgment by the court will constitute a final and binding determination of the validity or applicability of the arbitration agreement.

8.17   A final aspect which must be addressed is the extent to which—if any—extraordinary means of recourse are available in arbitration. The Procedural Code entitles the Supreme Court to exercise the extraordinary remedy of granting relief for substantive defects in a *judgment* even after such judgment has become final and binding.[17] Grounds permitting such remedy include criminal conduct or misconduct by a public official with respect to the court proceeding in question which can be assumed to have affected the outcome of the case; forged evidence or false testimony which might have affected the outcome of the case; and newly asserted facts or evidence which 'probably would have led to a different outcome'.

8.18   The SAA does not provide for similar extraordinary means of recourse. The underlying philosophy is that sections 33 and 34 provide sufficient protection for the parties. The generally held view is that the extraordinary means of recourse in the Procedural Code are not available with respect to arbitral awards.[18]

8.1.5 Jurisdiction of Swedish courts

8.19   The Brussels I Regulation,[19] to which Sweden is a party, does not apply to arbitration proceedings.[20] The exact scope of the so-called 'arbitration exception' in the

---

[15] See discussion at para 8.205 *et seq.*

[16] As explained in the foregoing (para 5.19 *et seq*) it follows from section 2(2) of the SAA that a party can also go to court while the arbitration is pending and ask the court to rule on the jurisdiction of arbitrators.

[17] Chapter 58, section 1 of the Procedural Code.

[18] See eg *Arbitration in Sweden* (2nd revised edn, 1984) 145–146; See also NJA 1986 p 620 where the Supreme Court states that as a general rule it must be assumed that an arbitral award cannot be subject to extraordinary means of recourse: one commentator, Lindskog, suggests that the judgment of the Supreme Court should be understood so as not to exclude the possibility of resorting to extraordinary means of recourse in exceptional circumstances, see Lindskog, *Skiljeförfarande, En kommentar* (2005) 891, footnote 13. From a practical point of view, however, most, if not all situations where this issue could arise are covered by the public policy provision in section 33; see para 8.33 *et seq.*

[19] The Brussels and Lugano Conventions contain identical provisions to the Brussels I Regulation in this regard.

[20] Article 1.2(d) of the Brussels I Regulation provides that 'the Regulation shall not apply to [. . .] arbitration'.

Brussels I Regulation and the Lugano Convention is unclear.[21] It is generally held, however, that this exception excludes from the application of the Regulation certain court proceedings concerning arbitration, eg appointment of arbitrators and challenge proceedings.[22] This means that the Brussels I Regulation defers to the domestic law of the individual Member States to regulate the extent to which their courts are to exercise jurisdiction over challenges to arbitral awards.

Under Swedish law, the SAA itself does not explicitly regulate the international **8.20** jurisdiction of Swedish courts in relation to proceedings for the invalidity and challenge of arbitral awards.[23] However, in the so-called *Uganda* case[24] of 1989 the Supreme Court held that Swedish courts are competent to hear claims for the invalidity or challenge of arbitral awards rendered in Sweden even if none of the parties has any connection to Sweden. The *Uganda* case made clear that all parties arbitrating in Sweden require a single competent forum for challenges to arbitral awards issued in Sweden. In the arbitration in the *Uganda* case, the claimants were Israeli contractors and the respondents were the Republic of Uganda and the National Housing and Construction Corporation of Uganda. The parties had concluded a construction contract that called for arbitration pursuant to the 1955 Rules of the Court of Arbitration of the International Chamber of Commerce. It was this institution that eventually named a Swedish engineer as arbitrator. The *travaux préparatoires* of the SAA also endorse the *Uganda* case, by stating that the scope of Swedish jurisdiction in challenge cases as expressed in this case is well founded and should be preserved.[25] There should therefore be no doubt that Swedish courts always have jurisdiction in relation to challenges to arbitral awards issued in Sweden.

Having said that the appeal court decision in *Titan Corporation v Alcatel CIT S.A.*[26] **8.21** must be addressed. In this case, the Titan Corporation requested that the arbitral award between the parties be set aside. The arbitral award in question indicated that Stockholm was the place of arbitration and that the English sole arbitrator had held a meeting for the taking of evidence in Paris. Although the parties and the arbitrator had acknowledged that Stockholm was the place of arbitration and that Swedish arbitration law was the law applicable to the proceedings, ie the *lex arbitri*, the Svea

---

[21] See also para 5.30 *et seq.*

[22] Cf C-190/89 *Marc Rich v Società Italiana Impianti* [1991] ECR 1-3855.

[23] For a discussion of the international jurisdiction of Swedish courts with respect to arbitration, see para 5.21 *et seq.* As explained there, the fact that Section 43 of the SAA identifies a Swedish court for purposes of challenge proceedings, does not automatically mean that such Swedish court has international jurisdiction.

[24] *National Housing and Construction Corporation of Uganda v Solel Boneh International Ltd* (NJA 1989 p 143). For a discussion of this case see Hobér, *Ogiltighet och klander i internationella skiljeförfaranden* in 1989 *Yearbook of the Arbitration Institute of the Stockholm Chamber of Commerce* (1989), 9.

[25] Govt Bill 1998/99:35, p 187.

[26] Svea Court of Appeal, Case No T 1038-05. For a more detailed discussion of the case see Shaughnessy, *Decision by the Svea Court of Appeal in Sweden Rendered in 2005 in Case no T 1038-05,* SIAR 2005:2.

Court of Appeal found that the dispute did not have a sufficiently strong connection to Swedish for there to be Swedish jurisdiction in relation to the challenge proceedings.

8.22 The decision of the Court of Appeal in the *Titan* case has been heavily criticized, and rightly so.[27] In essence, the court based its decision on language included in the *travaux préparatoires* to the effect that 'the arbitration shall in some way have a connection to the place of arbitration'.[28] This language is perhaps a bit confusing. It must be noted, however, that the *travaux préparatoires* first explain that 'it is primarily up to the parties to decide upon the place for the arbitration'.[29] The court seems to have ignored the basic principle of party autonomy expressly endorsed by Swedish arbitration law, including the right of the parties freely to agree on the place (or seat) of arbitration. In addition, pursuant to section 22(2) of the SAA, the arbitrators may hold hearings and other meetings elsewhere in Sweden, *or abroad*, unless otherwise agreed by the parties. The 'connection' mentioned in the *travaux préparatoires* must, if applicable at all, be deemed to have been fulfilled already by the parties' choice of Sweden as the place (or seat) of arbitration and their acceptance of Swedish law as the *lex arbitri*.

8.23 In fact, the parties and the sole arbitrator applied Swedish law to the proceedings, which raises questions in the hypothetical case that a non-Swedish court were to review the award. Would that court then have to apply Swedish arbitration law or would it apply its domestic arbitration law even though the arbitration was conducted under Swedish law?[30]

8.24 This case is best forgotten. The Court of Appeal must have known that its decision was controversial and therefore granted leave to appeal to the Supreme Court, something which the Court of Appeal seldom does. Since the parties settled the case no appeal was ever submitted. It is suggested that it is likely that the Supreme Court would have overturned the Court of Appeal's decision.

8.25 This has also—at least indirectly in an *obiter dicta*—subsequently been confirmed by the Supreme Court in *Russian Federation v RosInvestCo UK Ltd*.[31] Although this decision concerned a different question, the Supreme Court made some general

---

[27] See eg Bagner, 'Olycksfall i arbetet, ICC-skiljedom avvisad av Svea hovrätt', in *ICC-Nytt* 2005:3, p. 6; Jarvin and Dorgan, 'Are Foreign Parties Still Welcome in Stockholm?—The Svea Court's Decision in Titan Corporation v Alcatel CIT S.A. Raises Doubts', in MEALEY's International Arbitration Report, Vol 20, #7, July 2005, pp 42–48.

[28] Govt Bill 1998/99:35, pp 113–114 and 225.

[29] Govt Bill 1998/99:35, p 113.

[30] Shaughnessy, *Decision by the Svea Court of Appeal in Sweden Rendered in 2005 in Case No T 1038-05*, SIAR 2005:2, p 269.

[31] *Russian Federation v RosInvestCo UK Ltd*, Case No Ö 2301-09, Decision of the Supreme Court of 12 November 2010.

remarks as part of its reasoning which effectively rejects the conclusion of the Court of Appeal in the *Titan* case. The Supreme Court held that:

> [...] According to Section 22 of the SAA, the place of arbitration is determined by the parties and otherwise by the arbitrators. It is additionally provided that the arbitrators may hold hearings in other locations in Sweden or abroad, unless the parties have agreed otherwise.
>
> Thus, it follows that where the parties have agreed that the proceedings shall take place in Sweden, it is irrelevant whether the parties or the arbitrators have decided to hold hearings in other countries, whether the arbitrators are not from Sweden, whether their duties have been carried out in another country or if the dispute concerns a contract which otherwise has no connection to Sweden [...][32]

8.2 Invalid Arbitral Awards

The grounds for invalidity of arbitral awards set forth in section 33 of the SAA are **8.26** based on the philosophy that an award is invalid *only* if the interests of third parties, ie individuals, or legal entities, other than the parties to the arbitration, are affected by the award. Put differently: the grounds for invalidity are *beyond* the control of the parties to the dispute. By contrast, the grounds for setting aside an arbitral award are *within* the control of the parties and are dealt with in section 34 of the SAA as grounds for challenging an arbitral award.

8.2.1 Grounds for invalidity

Section 33 of the SAA sets out three grounds for the invalidity of an arbitral award. **8.27** These grounds are:

(a) the arbitral award decides an issue which is non-arbitrable under Swedish law;
(b) the award or the manner in which the award has been rendered violates Swedish public policy; and
(c) the award has not been made in writing and it has not been signed by the arbitrators.

This enumeration in the SAA is exhaustive. The general view is that these rules **8.28** are to be interpreted and applied restrictively.[33] It should be noted at the outset that there is no time limit for a claim of invalidity. This is logical, since if an award is invalid, it is invalid *ipso facto* and *ab initio*.

---

[32] *Russian Federation v RosInvestCo UK Ltd*, Case No Ö 2301-09, Decision of the Supreme Court of 12 November 2010, paras 3–4.
[33] Govt Bill 1998/99:35 pp 142–143; Heuman, *Arbitration Law of Sweden: Practice and Procedure* (2003) 584.

8.2.1.1 *Non-arbitrability*

8.29 The first ground for invalidity is non-arbitrability. The concept of arbitrability is strictly speaking a public policy limitation on arbitration as a dispute settlement method. Notwithstanding this, and given the importance of this limitation, arbitrability is addressed separately in section 33 of the SAA. It is for each State allowing arbitration to take place in its territory to determine the limitation, if any, to be imposed on arbitration. Most legal systems use the concept of arbitrability to determine the outer limits of arbitration. While the same concept is thus used, it is important to keep in mind that the contents of it may vary. In addition, several national systems of law may be involved in determining whether or not a particular dispute is arbitrable.

8.30 As explicitly stated in section 33(1), the issue of non-arbitrability is decided on the basis of Swedish law.[34] Hence, the fact that a matter is non-arbitrable under foreign law does not lead to invalidity under section 33 of the SAA, even if such foreign law is applicable to the arbitration agreement, or to the substance of the dispute. This does not exclude, however, the application of another law to other aspects of the concept of arbitrability. Let us assume that the arbitration agreement is governed by German law[35] and that under German law the dispute is *not* arbitrable. The dispute would still be arbitrable under Swedish law, but the award could be challenged on the basis of section 34, item 1 of the SAA since the arbitration agreement is invalid under German law.[36] Lack of arbitrability under foreign law would typically also lead to enforcement difficulties.[37]

8.31 Issues of arbitrability may also arise at the enforcement stage, primarily by virtue of Article V.2(a) of the New York Convention.[38] This will be for the enforcing court to decide. One question in this respect which arises from time to time is if the arbitrators should, or perhaps must, take into account the arbitrability concept in the country of enforcement. One complication is of course that there may be several—at least potential—countries of enforcement. Must the arbitrators take all of them into account? What if they differ in their respective definitions of arbitrability? A further question is what it means to 'take into account'. Let us assume that a dispute is arbitrable under Swedish law but not under the law of the country where enforcement is likely to take place. In such a situation, it is not possible for arbitrators sitting in Sweden to dismiss the dispute on the ground that it is nonarbitrable in the country of enforcement. On the contrary, the award will be valid under Swedish law. It is thus up to the claimant and not the arbitrators to decide whether he is prepared to take the risk of obtaining an award that may not be enforceable.

---

[34] For an account of arbitrability under Swedish law, see para 3.81 *et seq.*
[35] If the parties have chosen German law to be applied to the arbitration agreement, it follows from section 48 of the Act that such choice of law must be respected; see discussion at para 2.201.
[36] For a discussion of section 34, item 1 of the Act, see para 8.63.
[37] This follows from Article V(2)(a) of the New York Convention; see discussion at para 9.52.
[38] See para 9.52.

A risk which might be worth taking, in particular if the respondent also has assets in countries other than in the jurisdiction in question.

As mentioned above, issues of arbitrability in fact form part of public policy. It is there- **8.32** fore difficult to draw the line between arbitrability and public policy. The distinction is of little practical relevance as far as invalidity of arbitral awards is concerned.[39]

8.2.1.2 Violation of public policy

Item 2 of section 33 of the SAA stipulates that an arbitral award is invalid if the **8.33** award, or the way in which it was achieved, is manifestly incompatible with the fundamental principles of Swedish law. This is the definition of public policy (or *ordre public*) under Swedish law. The concept of public policy is seldom applied as part of Swedish private international law. The generally accepted view is that this concept represents a very high threshold. Indeed, in international commercial transactions it is virtually unheard of for public policy to come into play. Put differently, it is only if a transaction, or in our case an arbitral award, violates the most basic rules of fairness and justice that a transaction or arbitral award can be invalidated as a result of violation of public policy. Accordingly, the generally held view is that public policy is to be applied in a very restrictive manner.[40] In fact, no arbitral award has ever been declared invalid on this ground under the SAA.

It should also be noted that many elements must be considered when deciding if an **8.34** award violates public policy; for example, if the award concerns an international matter, this could lead to a more restrictive interpretation of the public policy principle. If the party defending the award, on the other hand, is found to have caused the circumstance which is giving rise to the public policy violation, it could possibly be argued that a less restrictive interpretation of the public policy principle should be applied.[41]

The public policy concept falls into two categories, viz, (i) violation of procedural **8.35** public policy, and (ii) violation of substantive public policy.

Violation of procedural public policy There is a narrow distinction between **8.36** invalidity due to violation of procedural public policy (section 33 of the SAA) and the setting aside of an award as a result of challenge proceedings on the basis of violation of due process (section 34(1), item 6, of the SAA). The latter is in fact the more common situation. An award would be invalid under section 33 of the SAA only if there has been a *gross* violation of due process which challenges law and order.[42] An example of

---

[39] Bribery and corruption, for example, raise questions of arbitrability as well as of public policy. In Swedish arbitration law such issues are usually treated as part of public policy; see para 8.36 and para 8.40.

[40] Govt Bill 1998/99:35, pp 142 and 234.

[41] Lindskog, *Skiljeförfarande, En kommentar* (2005) 903.

[42] Lindskog, *Skiljeförfarande, En kommentar* (2005) 906; Heuman, *Arbitration Law of Sweden: Practice and Procedure* (2003) 590; and Gaillard and Savage (eds), *Fouchard, Gaillard, Goldman On International Commercial Arbitration* (1999) 947 *et seq.*

such gross violation of procedural public policy is if one of the parties has influenced one or several arbitrators through criminal conduct, eg by threatening or bribing the arbitrator(s) and this may be presumed to have affected the outcome of the case.[43]

8.37 Another situation which would violate Swedish procedural public policy is when an award is based on forged evidence, ie one of the parties has introduced evidence which is forged and which is decisive for the outcome of the case.[44] The public policy principle probably applies only to evidence which has been wilfully forged by one of the parties or with the knowledge of one of the parties where it is clear that a document is decisive to the outcome of the case. Thus, the fact that a witness presented false, or misleading, testimony does not in itself cause the award to be invalid. The distinction between wilfully forged evidence and other situations involving questionable evidence is drawn to avoid the parties' disagreement as to the truthfulness or authenticity of the evidence leading to the invalidity of the award on public policy grounds.[45] In practice, the right and duty of the arbitrators freely to evaluate evidence presented by the parties usually resolve most problems concerning allegedly forged evidence.[46]

8.38 A third situation where an award may be invalid due to violation of procedural public policy is where a party has not been allowed to present its case or present evidence.[47] However, it would only be possible to have an award declared invalid with reference to public policy in cases of gross infringement of the principles of due process.[48]

8.39 The fact that one party has appointed all arbitrators could also constitute a violation of procedural public policy.[49] Such violation exists even if the appointment of arbitrators by one party is stipulated in the arbitration agreement.[50] However, it is open to discussion whether this constitutes a violation of public policy or whether it is a non-statutory ground for invalidity, see para 8.50.[51] In any event, such classification is typically of little practical relevance.

8.40 **Violation of substantive public policy**   It has been explained in the foregoing that under Swedish law an arbitral award is final and binding on the merits when rendered and that it can never be retried as far as the merits are concerned. Notwithstanding this, the public policy provision of section 33 of the SAA enables a court of law to review the merits of an arbitral award, but only for purposes of determining whether or not the award is invalid. It goes without saying that this review is very limited and that an award can be declared invalid only in very exceptional circumstances.

---

[43] Govt Bill 1998/99:35 pp 142, 150–151 and 234.
[44] Govt Bill 1998/99:35 pp 150–152.
[45] Heuman, *Arbitration Law of Sweden: Practice and Procedure* (2003) 588.
[46] See discussion at para 6.162 *et seq.*
[47] See para 6.32 *et seq.*
[48] Heuman, *Arbitration Law of Sweden: Practice and Procedure* (2003) 590.
[49] *Rita Urhelyi v Arbetsmarknadens Försäkringsaktiebolag* (NJA 1974 s 573).
[50] Lindskog, *Skiljeförfarande, En kommentar* (2005) 906.
[51] Heuman, *Arbitration Law of Sweden: Practice and Procedure* (2003) 585.

An example of when an award might be found to violate Swedish substantive public **8.41** policy is when the award orders either party, or both parties, to engage in a contract which is illegal under Swedish law, a so-called *pactum turpe*.[52] Consequently, an award that violates the law on cartels in Sweden or the competition laws of the European Union may be deemed to be invalid. This seems to have been the position taken by the ECJ in *Eco Swiss China Time Ltd v Benetton International NV* (C-126/97).[53] In that judgment, the ECJ concluded that a national court to which application is made for invalidity of an arbitral award must grant such application if it considers that the award in question is in fact contrary to Article 81 EC[54] and where the Member State's domestic rules of procedure require it to set aside an award which fails to observe national rules of public policy.

The view that national courts must declare arbitral awards violating EC rules invalid **8.42** if the Member State's domestic laws provide that arbitral awards violating national rules of public policy are invalid, was reiterated by the ECJ in *Mostaza Claro v Centro Móvil* (C-168/05). In that case, a Spanish court referred the following question to the ECJ for a preliminary ruling:

> May the protection of consumers under Council Directive 93/13/EEC . . . require the court hearing an action for annulment of an arbitration award to determine whether the arbitration agreement is void and to annul the award if it finds that that arbitration agreement contains an unfair term to the consumer's detriment, when that issue is raised in the action for annulment but was not raised by the consumer in the arbitration proceedings?

The ECJ referred to the nature and importance of the public interest underlying the **8.43** Directive and found that even though the consumer had not pleaded invalidity in the course of the arbitration proceedings, but only in the action for annulment, the Directive must be interpreted to mean that a national court that is to rule on the action for annulment must first determine whether the arbitration agreement is void and, if the agreement contains an unfair term, then it must annul the arbitral award.[55]

Another example of awards violating Swedish substantive public policy is when the **8.44** contract in dispute is a result of corruption, particularly bribery.[56]

The protection against corrupt contracts is also expressed in the so-called 'Unclean **8.45** Hands Doctrine' which stands for the principle that 'he who comes to equity for relief must come with clean hands'.[57] Under the Unclean Hands Doctrine, an arbitral tribunal

---

[52] Govt Bill 1998/99:35, p 141.

[53] The *Eco Swiss* case is discussed in para 2.75 *et seq*.

[54] The regulation in question can now be found in Article 101 EC.

[55] *Mostaza Claro v Centro Móvil* (C-168/05) paras 38–39.

[56] Govt Bill 1998/99:35 p 141; Hobér, *Enforcement of Arbitral Awards*, Stockholm Arbitration Report, 1999:1, p 69; cf Gaillard and Savage (eds), *Fouchard, Gaillard, Goldman On International Commercial Arbitration* (1999) 960–962. Bribing of arbitrators constitutes a violation of procedural public policy, see para 8.36.

[57] Kreindler, 'Corruption in International Investment Arbitration: Jurisdiction and the Unclean Hands Doctrine', in Hobér, Magnusson, and Öhrström (eds), *Between East and West: Essays in Honour of Ulf Franke* (2010) 309 *et seq*.

can and should deny relief to a claimant 'whose conduct in regard to the subject matter of the litigation has been improper'.[58] Likewise, an arbitral tribunal should 'refuse to aid a complainant in protecting any right acquired or retained by inequitable conduct'.[59] Although the Unclean Hands Doctrine has been developed in common law, it is closely related to several Roman law concepts and Latin maxims expressing the same idea:[60]

- *Ex delicto non oritor action* ('an unlawful act cannot serve as the basis of an action in law');
- *Nemo ex suo delicto meliorem suam conditionem facit* ('no one can put himself in a better legal position by means of a delict');
- *Ex turpi causa non oritur* ('an action cannot arise from a dishonourable cause');
- *Inadimplenti non est adimplendum* ('one has no need to respect one's obligation if the counter-party has not respected its own'); and
- *Nullus commodum capere potest de injuria sua propria* ('no one can be allowed to take advantage of his own wrong').

8.46 Further, an award may also be of such punitive character that it cannot be deemed acceptable and therefore violates public policy.[61] Moreover, an award where the arbitrators have failed to observe a rule which is mandatory for the protection of a third party interest or a public interest, may, in very exceptional cases, be considered violating public policy.[62]

8.2.1.3 Formal requirements of the arbitral award

8.47 Under item 3 of the first paragraph of section 33 of the SAA, an arbitral award may also be declared invalid in its entirety if it does not fulfil the formal requirements set out in section 31 of the SAA. The elementary requirements are that the award must be in writing and that it must be signed by the arbitrators. Oral arbitral awards are thus not valid. It suffices that a majority of the arbitrators has signed the award as long as the reason why all of the arbitrators have not signed the award is noted in the award. The parties may also agree that only the chairman needs to sign the award.[63] In *Wirgin Advokatbyrå Handelsbolag v If Skadeförsäkring AB*,[64] the award

---

[58] *S&E Contractors, Inc v United States*, 92 S Ct 1411, 1419 (US Supreme Court 1972), individual opinion of Judge Hudson.

[59] *International News Service v The Associated Press*, 248 US 215 (US Supreme Court 1918).

[60] Kreindler, 'Corruption in International Investment Arbitration: Jurisdiction and the Unclean Hands Doctrine', in Hobér, Magnusson, and Öhrström (eds), *Between East and West: Essays in Honour of Ulf Franke* (2010) 317 318, and the references therein.

[61] Govt Bill 1998/99:35, p 141; Heuman, *Arbitration Law of Sweden: Practice and Procedure* (2003) 590; Hobér, *Enforcement of Arbitral Awards*, Stockholm Arbitration Report, 1999:1, p 70.

[62] Govt Bill 1998/99:35, pp 141–142; Hobér, *Enforcement of Arbitral Awards*, Stockholm Arbitration Report, 1999:1, p 70; and Heuman, *Arbitration Law of Sweden: Practice and Procedure* (2003) 590–591.

[63] If an award is only signed by one person, it is assumed that it is the chairman's signature and that the parties have agreed that only the chairman needs to sign the award, Kvart and Olsson, Lagen om skiljeförfarande-en kommentar (2000), 137.

[64] Svea Court of Appeal, judgment of 12 September 2005 in Case No T 4390-04.

had been corrected in accordance with section 32 of the SAA.[65] However, the correction was only signed by the chairman and no agreement between the parties to the effect that this was sufficient was forthcoming. Accordingly, *the correction of the award did not meet the formal requirements under the SAA*. The correction was thus declared invalid. This did not affect the validity of the award itself, which remained valid and in force.

The fact that the parties can agree on exceptions to the formal requirements has **8.48** raised the question as to whether the formal requirements in item 3 of section 33 should really constitute grounds for invalidity. It has been argued that it would be more appropriate to deal with such formal requirements as part of the grounds for setting aside under section 34, ie being subject to waiver and the three-month time limit on initiating the challenge.[66] In addition, an application for invalidity on this ground is usually a fruitless endeavour for the losing party, since an award may be amended to fulfil the requirements, as follows from section 35 of the SAA.[67]

The fact that an award is not dated correctly, or that the seat of arbitration is not stated **8.49** in the award, does not constitute a ground for invalidity under section 33 of the SAA.[68]

8.2.2 Non-statutory grounds for invalidity

The grounds listed in section 33 of the SAA are the only statutory grounds on which **8.50** an award may be rendered invalid. In addition to those grounds there are also three other situations where an arbitral award will not have legal effect. These situations cannot strictly speaking be characterized as cases of invalidity, but are simply situations where an award will have no legal effect.

8.2.2.1 Situations where an 'award' may not be characterized as an arbitral award

The first such situation is the case where an award has been rendered in such a way **8.51** and under such circumstances that it cannot, from a legal point of view and on the basis of the SAA, be characterized as an arbitral award. The standard example is where one of the parties to the dispute was also the arbitrator deciding the dispute, for example where the charter of an association stipulates that disputes between a member and the association are to be decided by a body of the association. Such 'self-judgment' would not be characterized as an arbitral award under the SAA.[69]

However, if a representative of a legal entity is appointed as arbitrator in a dispute **8.52** to which the legal entity he is representing is a party, this is not considered 'self-judgment'. However, the award could be challenged on the ground that the

---

[65] For a discussion of correction of arbitral awards, see para 7.137 *et seq.*
[66] Lindskog, *Skiljeförfarande, En kommentar* (2005) 908.
[67] See para 8.193.
[68] Govt Bill 1998/99:35, p 142.
[69] Govt Bill 1998/99:35, p 64.

arbitrator was not independent and impartial provided that the other party did not accept such an appointment in the first place.[70]

8.2.2.2 *The party against whom the award was made was not a party to the arbitration proceedings*

8.53 The second situation referred to above includes arbitral awards which are directed against parties who were not in fact, nor in law, parties to the arbitration proceedings. This is perhaps to restate the obvious, ie that an arbitral award cannot bind a party who is not a party to the arbitration clause and thus not properly a party to the arbitration proceedings.[71] It goes without saying that an arbitral award rendered in a dispute between parties A and B and containing an order directed at C will not bind C. On the other hand, such an award is not automatically invalid as between parties A and B.

8.54 In *AB Hans Osterman v Stockholms Automobilhandlarförening and AB Autostandard* (NJA 1943 p 527), the Supreme Court found that the arbitral award, which was based on an arbitration clause in the charter of an association and concerned the expulsion of members from the association, did not bind an affected member of the association since the award concerned membership in the association and the member had not been a party to the arbitration.

8.55 A somewhat similar situation occurs when a respondent, who has been ordered to comply with a request for specific performance or to pay a certain sum in an arbitral award, is able to prove that the arbitration proceedings were conducted without him being advised of it. One could argue that he has not then been a party to the arbitration *proceedings* even though he may have been a party to the arbitration *agreement*. This situation, however, is probably not to be characterized as a case where the arbitration award is not binding on the party in question, but rather a case where the arbitral award may be successfully challenged under section 34 of the SAA on the basis that the respondent did not have an opportunity to present its case.[72]

8.2.2.3 *An award too obscure to enforce*

8.56 The third situation where an arbitral award may lack legal force, even though it is not to be characterized as invalid, is the situation when the award in question is deemed to be so obscure so as to make enforcement of it impossible. In the Arbitration Act of 1929 a specific provision addressed this situation, viz, section 22. In accordance with this provision such an award was not characterized as invalid but the award was simply not enforceable. In addition, the existence of such an award

---

[70] *Altinel v Sudoimport* (RH 1991:15); and Heuman, *Arbitration Law of Sweden: Practice and Procedure* (2003) 226.

[71] Govt Bill 1998/99:35, p 142. The effect of arbitral awards is discussed at para 7.92 *et seq*. This situation is closely linked to the question of the extent to which an arbitration agreement is binding on third parties, see para 3.130 *et seq*.

[72] See para 8.118.

did not prevent a party from commencing an action in court concerning the question decided by the arbitrators. Under the SAA this provision has been deleted, *inter alia*, because it was a provision that was unknown to other jurisdictions and because of its very limited practical relevance in Sweden.[73] Notwithstanding this, the fact remains that should an award be so obscure as to prevent enforcement of it, it will in all likelihood be deemed to lack legal force even though it is not formally invalid.[74]

8.2.3 Invalidity of part of the award

The invalidity of an award may apply only to a certain part of the award in accordance with section 33(2) of the SAA. For example, if the arbitrators have determined an issue that is non-arbitrable together with other issues which are arbitrable, only the part of the award that relates to the non-arbitrable issue is invalid. Naturally, this presupposes that the non-arbitrable issue is distinguishable from the other issues dealt with in the award. Likewise, the enforceability of the award also depends on whether the invalid part of an award is distinguishable from the rest of the award.[75]   **8.57**

8.3 Challenge of Arbitral Awards

8.3.1 Grounds for challenging an award

Pursuant to section 34(1) of the SAA, an arbitral award will be wholly or partially   **8.58**
set aside on the request of a party:

1. if it is not covered by a valid arbitration agreement between the parties;
2. if the arbitrators have rendered the award after the expiration of the period decided on by the parties, or where the arbitrators have otherwise exceeded their mandate;
3. if arbitral proceedings, according to section 47, should not have taken place in Sweden;
4. if an arbitrator has been appointed contrary to the agreement between the parties or the SAA;
5. if an arbitrator was unauthorized due to any circumstance set out in sections 7 or 8 of the SAA; or
6. if, without fault of the party, there otherwise occurred an irregularity in the course of the proceedings which probably influenced the outcome of the case.

---

[73] Govt Bill 1998/99: 35, p 141.
[74] In such a situation a party might be entitled to have the dispute retried by an arbitral tribunal, possibly on the basis of section 35 of the SAA. For a discussion of section 35 of the SAA, see para 8.193.
[75] Govt Bill 1998/99:35, p 234.

8.59   As mentioned above,[76] it is not in the discretion of the court to decide on whether or not to set aside an award if all the conditions for setting aside the award have in fact been met. If a party has requested such action and the conditions are met, the court *shall* set aside the award. Although, the court, subject to the fulfilment of certain requirements, may also give the arbitrators the opportunity to rectify defects in the award.[77] Furthermore, the entire arbitral award need not be set aside. If, for instance, a procedural mistake has only affected a certain part of an award, it may be sufficient to set aside only that part of the award.

8.60   A party challenging an award must bring such action within three months from the date when the party received the award. The period begins when the party in question received the award in its entirety.[78] If after the rendering of the award the arbitrators have corrected, supplemented, or interpreted the operative part of the award pursuant to section 32 of the SAA, the challenge must be brought within a period of three months from the date when the party received the award in its final wording.

8.61   Expiry of the three-month period without a challenge precludes any subsequent attempts to have an award set aside. It is important to note that it is not sufficient to file a blank challenge within the three-month period. The party challenging the award must also within the three-month period specify the legal grounds upon which the challenge rests.[79] No extension of time may be granted to the challenging party.[80] However, in order for the grounds to be precluded the respondent must also make an objection to this effect the first time that the respondent answers to the court.[81] Accordingly, the court will not *ex officio* try whether or not the challenge has been made within the three-month period. Moreover, following the expiry of the time limit, a party may not invoke a new legal ground in support of his claim.

8.62   The term 'ground' in this context does not refer to the grounds enumerated in section 34, but rather to the more legal-technical concept of a 'legal ground' under Swedish procedural law. This means, for example, that if a party has challenged an award by arguing that one of the arbitrators was not qualified to act as arbitrator, it

---

[76] See para 8.05

[77] See para 8.193.

[78] See *AB Akron-Maskiner v N–GG* (NJA 2002 p 377).

[79] Govt Bill 1998/99:35, p 149; *Restaurangprodukter i Tyresö AB v KF/Procordia International AB* (NJA 1996 s 751) and *Bostadsrättsföreningen Korpen v Byggnads AB Åke Sundvall*, Svea Court of Appeal, judgment of 16 February 2007 in Case No T 1649-04.

[80] In the case of *Fastigheten Preppen v Carlsberg* (RH 2009:91) the challenging party Fastigheten Preppen submitted its challenge on 12 November 2008 (within the three-month period) but the challenge did not include any grounds. The court did, however, grant Fastigheten Preppen an extension of time to supplement its challenge, until 5 December 2008 at the latest. On 9 December 2008, Fastigheten Preppen finally submitted the grounds for its challenge. Carlsberg requested that the challenge be dismissed since the grounds had not been identified until after the three-month period. The court concluded that the grounds had been submitted too late and that Carlsberg had duly made an objection as to this fact. The court therefore declared the grounds presented by Fastigheten Preppen to be precluded and dismissed the challenge in its entirety.

[81] Ibid.

could not, after the expiration of the three-month period, argue that another arbitrator was not qualified to act. On the other hand, a party would not be prevented from adjusting certain sets of *facts* which come within the scope of the same legal ground. For example, if a party has argued that an arbitrator should be prevented from acting as arbitrator because he is the nephew of the other party, that party could argue, even after the expiration of the three-month period, that the same arbitrator is actually the son of the other party.[82]

8.3.2 No arbitration agreement

8.63 The first ground in section 34 of the SAA for challenging an award is lack of a valid arbitration agreement covering the dispute. It follows from the consensual nature of arbitration that arbitration proceedings cannot be based on an arbitration agreement which is invalid or no longer in effect. An award may therefore be challenged and set aside if the arbitration agreement was void *ab initio* or, though originally valid, was terminated prior to or in the course of the proceedings.[83] If the arbitrators have ruled in a dispute which is not covered by a valid arbitration agreement, the arbitral award must be set aside on the basis of this provision. It may sometimes be difficult, however, to distinguish between this provision and item 2 of section 34 of the SAA which deals with the arbitrators having exceeded their mandate. On the other hand, it matters little from a practical point of view if the award is set aside on the basis of item 1 or on the basis of item 2.

8.64 As mentioned above, as a main rule, an arbitration agreement is, with a few exceptions, binding only on the parties to such an agreement.[84] Consequently, if a third party has become involved in the arbitration proceeding against its will, such party may subsequently challenge the award on the basis that the award was not covered by a valid arbitration agreement binding upon him. It is also noteworthy that non-arbitrability on the basis of an applicable foreign law does not mean that the resulting award is void, but rather that the arbitration agreement is invalid and that therefore the resulting award may be challenged on the basis that there was no valid arbitration agreement.[85] In practice, however, this situation is very unusual, since Swedish law would be applicable to the arbitration agreement in most arbitration in Sweden by virtue of section 48 of the SAA.[86]

8.3.3 Excess of mandate

8.65 The second challenge ground mentioned in section 34 of the SAA is various situations where the arbitrators have exceeded their mandate. In paragraph 2 reference is first made to an award rendered after the expiry of the award period, if any.

---

[82] Hobér, 'Arbitration Reform in Sweden', *Arbitration International* (2001) para 383.
[83] See paras 3.168 *et seq* and 3.77 *et seq.*
[84] Cf para 3.130 *et seq*, with respect to the effect of an arbitration agreement on third parties.
[85] See para 8.30.
[86] See para 2.201.

Then reference is made to other situations where the arbitrators have exceeded their mandate.

8.3.3.1 *Award after the expiration of a time limit for rendering of the award*

8.66   The SAA does not provide for any time limit for the rendering of the award. However, the parties may in the arbitration agreement, or during the course of the proceedings, agree on such a time limit. If the parties have agreed on a time limit for the rendering of the award, an award rendered after the expiration of such time limit shall be set aside pursuant to item 2 of section 34 of the SAA. There is no express exception to this rule in the SAA, not even for the situation where the party challenging the award has caused the rendering of the award to be delayed by misconduct during the proceedings. It could perhaps be argued that such an exception ought to apply in some cases.[87] However, since the SAA does not provide for any express exception and/or possibility for the arbitrators to grant such an extension of time, parties are advised not to agree on any unconditional time limits for the rendering of the award.

8.67   The dispute in question may still be terminated in the form of an award after the expiration of the award period. This is so because the rules with respect to challenges of awards do not apply to awards where the proceedings have been terminated without a ruling on the merits.[88] Moreover, if the arbitrators have merely corrected or supplemented an award after the expiration of the award period, such action is in general not deemed to constitute a ground for challenge.[89]

8.68   It should be noted that the SCC Arbitration Rules have a time limit for the rendering of the award. However, the SCC Board has the power to extend such time limit upon request from the arbitral tribunal or on its own initiative.[90]

8.3.3.2 *Excess of mandate*

8.69   Item 2 of section 34 of the SAA further stipulates that an award may be set aside if the arbitrators have '*otherwise exceeded their mandate*'. It is thus important to determine the mandate of the arbitrators.

8.70   **Establishing the scope of the arbitrators' mandate**   In analysing the mandate of the arbitrators, the starting point must be the arbitration agreement. The arbitration agreement may define in specific terms the mandate given to the arbitrators. If, for example, the arbitrators in the arbitration agreement, or during the course of the proceedings, have been instructed by the parties to decide the dispute on the basis of a particular foreign law this would be an instruction which is binding on the arbitrators. Consequently, if they do not apply the law identified as the applicable

---

[87] Lindskog, *Skiljeförfarande En kommentar* (2005) 928.
[88] See para 7.24.
[89] Govt Bill 1998/99:35, p 233.
[90] The SCC Arbitration Rules, Article 37.

law this is deemed to constitute excess of the mandate given to them by the parties. Likewise, the parties may have agreed either in the arbitration clause, or separately, that the arbitrators are to rule on limited aspects of the dispute only. For example, they may have been asked to rule on whether or not a particular statutory provision is applicable to the dispute, how such provision should be applied to a particular set of facts, or to determine the existence of a particular fact.[91] If the arbitrators then go beyond the issues submitted to them and determine other issues, the determination of such other issues would also be characterized as excess of mandate, and may, thus, result in a challenge to the award.

In *If Skadeförsäkring AB v Securitas AB et al*,[92] the Court of Appeal found that the **8.71** arbitrators had gone beyond their mandate by rejecting a claim of the respondent with reference to circumstances (relating to the scope of the re-insurance cover), which the respondent had explicitly asked the arbitrators not to take into account since these circumstances had yet to be established. The arbitral award was partly set aside.[93]

Arbitration clauses may also include specific procedural instructions to the arbitrators **8.72** as to the conduct of the actual procedure. It follows from the foregoing that to the extent that arbitrators deviate from such procedural instructions from the parties, the deviation is to be characterized as going beyond the mandate given to them by the parties. Such an award may thus be challenged and set aside on this ground.

It must be emphasized, however, that the mandate of the arbitrators is not only **8.73** defined by the arbitration agreement itself, but also by subsequent agreements and/ or arrangements, understandings, instructions, or conduct by the parties during the course of the arbitration. This is explicitly confirmed by section 21 of the SAA. It goes without saying that such agreements, understandings, arrangements, or instructions must be accepted by both parties. Thus, a unilateral position taken by one of the parties cannot change or amend the mandate of the arbitrators as defined in the arbitration agreement.

Award *ultra petita* and award *infra petita* Another example of excess of mandate **8.74** is where the arbitrators have awarded the parties, or one of the parties, more than that party has asked for. In other words, an award *ultra petita* is beyond the submission and may thus result in the award being set aside.

A related issue is whether or not an award *infra petita* is to be characterized as an **8.75** 'excess' of mandate. This is clearly not the case where the arbitrators have awarded

---

[91] Section 1 of the SAA.
[92] Svea Court of Appeal, judgment of 3 November 2005 in Case No T 8016-04.
[93] In this case the Court of Appeal also discussed whether or not to set aside the award in its entirety or only partially. With reference to the *travaux préparatoires* (Govt Bill 1998/99:35 p 43) the court concluded that, in order to promote the finality of an arbitral award, the setting aside of the award should be limited only to the parts directly affected by the excess of the arbitrators' mandate.

damages in the amount of for example 100,000 euros when one of the parties has asked for 150,000. This is simply the result of the decision-making process involved in the resolution of the dispute and can not result in the award being set aside. However, the situation may be different if, for example, the arbitrators have granted the claimant a certain amount without determining a counterclaim or set-off claim by the respondent. If such a claim or objection has been raised by the respondent, it is difficult to see that the arbitrator is not under an obligation to determine such an objection or claim. Put differently: the mandate of the arbitrators is to rule on the dispute in its entirety, ie the claimant's claim, as well as the objections and counterclaims raised by the respondent, provided that such objections or counterclaims are covered by the arbitration agreement. Failure to do so implies that the arbitrators have gone beyond, or rather not fulfilled, the mandate given to them by the parties. The foregoing does not mean, of course, that the arbitrators must accept the set-off claims and/or objections submitted by the respondent, but simply that the award must show that the arbitrators have also ruled on that issue. It is thus possible that, in cases where the arbitrators have failed to deal with all claims and objections, such failure may be characterized as excess of mandate, while, in fact, the arbitrators have not carried out their mandate to the full extent.

8.76 Another similar situation is where the arbitrators have not addressed a particular prayer for relief raised by one of the parties. This is probably a situation which occurs very seldom in practice. In international arbitration nowadays most arbitrators are fully aware of the fact that they are being asked to address specifically all the prayers for relief raised by the parties. If the arbitrators, at any stage, believe that the issues underlying the prayers for relief are complicated and require more information and/or argument, they will make the parties aware of this fact.[94] The parties will usually then provide the arbitrators with all necessary information so as to be able properly to address the prayers for relief.

8.77 The obligation of the arbitrators to act in accordance with the agreement of the parties is fundamental. However, the situation differs when the parties have given instructions concerning how the proceedings are to be conducted within the framework of the arbitration agreement, the presentation of prayers for relief, the facts, and the evidence. Should the arbitrators not follow such procedural instructions, the situation would normally not be regarded as going beyond their mandate, but would instead be regarded as a procedural irregularity that could be challenged under section 34, item 6.

8.78 The situation becomes a bit more complicated if the focus is shifted from prayers for relief to legal grounds and/or circumstances relied upon by the parties.

---

[94] This is in fact part of the case management duty of the arbitrators; see discussion at para 8.166.

As mentioned in the foregoing,[95] one part of the pleadings submitted by the parties **8.79** which is important from a Swedish perspective, are the so-called legal grounds relied upon by the parties in the arbitration. Generally speaking, it is accepted that arbitrators may not go beyond such facts and/or grounds when determining a case. If they do, they risk the award being set aside on the basis that the arbitrators have exceeded their mandate. The theory underlying this approach is again based on the consensual nature of arbitration. As pointed out above, the parties are the masters of the proceedings.[96] One consequence of this is that the parties must be allowed to determine the complexity and the scope of their dispute. The scope of the arbitration, and the mandate of the arbitrators, are thus set by the parties' oral and written submissions. If the arbitrators base their decision on facts or grounds which have not been raised by the parties, they thus enlarge the dispute in a way which may, and often will, come as a surprise to both parties when they receive the award. Consequently, if the arbitrators have decided a case relying on a legal ground which has not been raised by either party it would seem natural to characterize this situation as an excess of the mandate given to the arbitrators.

This approach was confirmed by the Svea Court of Appeal in its decision from 2009 **8.80** in *Systembolaget AB v V & S Vin & Sprit Aktiebolag*.[97] According to the Court of Appeal, the arbitrators had based their reasoning in the challenged arbitral award on facts that had not been relied on by the claimant. The award was therefore set aside.

Although the court was correct in principle to say that the arbitrators may not base **8.81** their award on facts or grounds that have not been invoked by the parties, the application of such principle by the Court of the Appeal in *Systembolaget v Vin & Sprit* raises questions. In particular, the Court of Appeal's view on how arguments and facts must be presented by the parties in order to be properly invoked before the arbitral tribunal is, it is submitted, problematic. In the arbitration, the arbitrators had prepared a summary (recitals) of the parties' submissions. It is common practice in Swedish domestic arbitration to prepare such recitals which set out the essential facts and evidence presented by the parties. The recitals are usually prepared by the chairman of the tribunal once all the parties' submissions have been submitted. It is then used by the arbitrators for ease of reference during the final hearing and during the arbitrators' subsequent deliberations. The recitals could be said to ensure forseeability, since the parties are made aware of how the tribunal has understood all facts presented by the parties up to the hearing. Since the parties are invited to submit comments on the draft recitals it would be difficult for a party to argue in challenge proceedings that the arbitrators have failed to consider facts or arguments presented by it unless such party during the course of the arbitration brought to the attention of the arbitral tribunal that such facts or arguments were not included in the draft

---

[95] See discussion at para 6.76.
[96] See para 8.73.
[97] Svea Court of Appeal, judgment of 1 December 2009 in Case No T 4548-08.

recitals. Such a claim would likely be considered to have been waived pursuant to section 34(2) of the SAA.[98]

8.82 The Court of Appeal in this case, however, seems to have applied such a principle *e contrario*. The parties had been allowed to review the summary beforehand and had approved it. The Court of Appeal stated that it could be presumed that the ultimate facts relied on by the parties should also be reflected in the summary which they have approved. If a particular fact was not included in the summary, it would not be considered to have been properly relied on, even if such fact actually had been relied on by one of the parties in its written submissions. In reviewing the summary, the Court of Appeal found that one of the facts on which the arbitrators based their decision had not been relied on by the winning party, *Vin & Sprit*. According to the Court of Appeal, the arbitrators had therefore gone beyond the submission of the parties and, thus, exceeded their mandate. *Vin & Sprit* had, for its part, argued that there was no basis for the suggestion that the parties' actual submissions in the arbitration should not be considered part of the proceedings, and that they had been replaced by the summary. Even though not explicitly stated by the Court of Appeal, the judgment could be interpreted to suggest that the use of an approved summary means that the parties' actual submissions are excluded and replaced by the summary.[99] It could possibly be argued that this far-reaching effect promotes forseeability, but it would reduce the practical benefit of using such a summary, since the parties—in order to safeguard their positions—would have to request the tribunal to include in such summary each and every fact and argument advanced during the course of the proceedings.

8.83 The practical consequence resulting from this case therefore seems to be to object to the use of summaries and otherwise to exercise extreme caution before approving any such summary. It should be noted that both parties in the case were Swedish. If the arbitration had been of an international nature it is possible, perhaps even likely, that the court would not have taken such a strict view. That said, however, the decision of the Court of Appeal raises questions also in a purely domestic arbitration context.

8.84 **Award based on legal rules that have not been relied on by the parties** An issue related to the principle that the arbitrators may not rely on other legal grounds than those invoked by the parties is whether or not the arbitrators are also bound by the legal *arguments* presented by the parties. In Swedish court proceedings this is not the case, since the principle of *jura novit curia* applies, ie the parties are not required to establish the content of Swedish law since the court supposedly knows the law. It is up to the court to assess freely the facts and evidence presented and to arrive at the

---

[98] Lindskog, *Skiljeförfarande, En kommentar* (2005) 660.
[99] Cf *NCC Aktiebolag v Dykab i Luleå Aktiebolag*, Svea Court of Appeal, judgment of 20 June 2002 in Case No T 3863-01, where similar language with respect to the effect of a summary (recitals) has been used.

correct legal determination of the dispute. This means that in Swedish litigation, the court is permitted to apply legal rules and provisions even if they have not been discussed or identified as relevant by the parties during the proceedings.

In arbitration the situation is more complicated.[100] In a case from 2000, the Svea **8.85** Court of Appeal held that the fact that the arbitrators, in a Swedish domestic arbitration, had applied legal rules that had not been relied upon by the parties should not lead to the award being set aside.[101] It has yet to be addressed by a court of law whether the same holds true in international arbitration. The *travaux préparatoires* to the SAA clearly state that the fact that the parties in an international arbitration may hail from jurisdictions where the principle of *jura novit curia* does not apply should be taken into consideration when determining the mandate of the arbitrators.[102] It is submitted that it is unlikely that the courts would allow an award in an international arbitration to stand, if the arbitrators have decided the case by applying rules of law, or legal arguments, which had not been relied upon by the parties. In all likelihood such an award would be challengeable under item 2 of section 34 of the SAA on the basis that the arbitrators exceeded their mandate. At any rate, as will be described below, to base the award on rules of law not relied upon by the parties would probably also constitute a procedural error pursuant to item 6 of section 34 of the SAA.

The proper way for the arbitrators to deal with the situation when they become **8.86** aware of a rule of law which they think could be of relevance, but which has not been referred to by the parties, or if it is not entirely clear whether such rule has been referred to by the parties, is to resolve these issues with the parties during the hearings at the latest, and preferably before the hearings. The *travaux préparatoires*[103] to the SAA stress the importance of the arbitrators' proactive case management in this regard. Arbitrators should ascertain that the parties are properly informed of how and which laws and legal principles might be applied by the arbitrators in order to avoid surprises once the award is rendered.[104]

Procedural instructions to the arbitrators Arbitration clauses may also include **8.87** specific procedural instructions to the arbitrators as to the conduct of the arbitral procedure. If the arbitrators deviate from such procedural instructions by the parties, the deviation may be characterized as excess of mandate. Such an award

---

[100] For a discussion of the *iura novit curia* principle, see para 6.69.
[101] *Gustafson v Länsförsäkringar*, Svea Court of Appeal, Case No T 8090-99. In the case in question, the District Court's award, which was not altered by the Svea Court of Appeal, stated that the arbitrators' construction of the law, built on the interpretation of an earlier Supreme Court decision, could not be regarded as a surprise for the parties. It should be noted, however, that the Supreme Court decision had been commented upon by the parties at the final hearing. See observations by Wallin in Jarvin and Magnusson (eds), *International Arbitration Court Decisions* (2nd edn, 2008) 1143 *et seq.*
[102] Govt Bill 1998/99:35, p 145.
[103] Ibid, p 146.
[104] See para 8.166 where the case management duties of the arbitrators are discussed.

may thus be challenged and set aside on this ground. However, failure of the arbitrators to follow normal instructions by the parties concerning the conduct of the proceedings would normally not be regarded as excess of mandate, but would rather be regarded as a procedural irregularity that could be challenged only under section 34, item 6. The distinction is important, since an award may only be set aside due to procedural irregularities, if it is established that such procedural irregularity is likely to have influenced the outcome of the case. This is not a requirement, at least not explicitly, with regard to excess of mandate.[105]

8.88 In *Soyak v Hochtief AG* (NJA 2009 p 128)[106] the Supreme Court dealt with the issue of whether lack of reasons in an arbitral award is to be characterized as an excess of mandate, or a procedural irregularity. The claimant argued that the arbitral award in question did not contain reasons and that the arbitrators had therefore exceeded their mandate. However, the Supreme Court concluded that if the arbitrators have not complied with the instructions of the parties to include reasons in the arbitral award, that is to be characterized as a *procedural irregularity*, rather than as an *excess of mandate*. Also, only a complete lack of reasons, or reasons that are so incomplete as to be tantamount to a lack of reasons, may be regarded as a procedural irregularity. The Supreme Court concluded that the arbitrators in question had, on every contested issue, accounted for what they had found to be established in the case. The Supreme Court, therefore, denied the claimant's application to have the award set aside.

8.89 *Res judicata* Another situation where arbitrators have been deemed to exceed their mandate is where they disregard the *res judicata* effect of an earlier award. Previously, the commonly adopted interpretation of a case decided by the Supreme Court in 1953 was that failure to recognize that issues before the arbitrators have already been finally settled by previous judgment or award, and, thus, become *res judicata*, constituted excess of the arbitrators' mandate.[107] However, this view has

---

[105] See discussion at para 8.106.

[106] See also para 8.3.8.1.

[107] *AB Skånska Cementgjuteriet v Motoraktiebolaget i Karlstad* (NJA 1953 p 751). Skånska Cementgjuteriet (Skånska) had constructed a building for Motoraktiebolaget i Karlstad (M). Arbitration was requested concerning certain alleged breaches of warranty. An award rendered in 1947 included, *inter alia*, the text of a settlement whereby Skånska was relieved, subject to minor exceptions, from all liability in connection with the construction project. The settlement was further confirmed by a statement in the conclusions of the actual award to the effect that 'Skånska by virtue of this award shall be relieved of all liability in connection with the construction project'. The award rendered in 1947 was never challenged. In 1948, certain building materials came down and M again claimed compensation in new arbitration proceedings. Skånska rejected the claim but the arbitrators rendered an award in 1950 awarding M compensation. Skånska challenged the award. The district court held that the award in 1950 was void as a result of *res judicata* and cited sub-paragraph 3 of the first paragraph of section 20 of the 1929 Arbitration Act. On appeal, the Court of Appeal concluded that the 1950 award was valid, explaining that the statement in the 1947 award relieving Skånska of liability did not have the character of an award, since the arbitrators had not 'entered into a substantive consideration' of the question whether Skånska should be relieved of liability. The Supreme Court by a vote of three to two decided that the 1947 award must be taken for what it purported to be, ie a final decision that Skånska was to be relieved of liability. The 1950 award had therefore dealt

subsequently changed as a result of the ruling of the Supreme Court in *Esselte AB v Allmänna Pensionsfonden* (NJA 1998 p 189). A failure to recognize that a claim is *res judicata* is now characterized as a procedural irregularity rather than as an excess of the arbitrators' mandate.[108]

The arbitrators' duty freely to evaluate all evidence   When discussing the mandate   **8.90** of the arbitrators it is important to remember that not all measures and steps of a procedural nature taken by the parties, nor arguments made by them, bind the arbitrators in this respect. This may become particularly relevant when dealing with the evaluation of the evidence presented to the arbitrators. Parties and their representatives will invariably take different approaches with respect to the relevance, importance, and interpretation of certain documents. For example, nothing prevents the arbitrators from drawing different conclusions from a particular document or witness testimony than those suggested by either party. It is the duty of the arbitrators to evaluate all evidence presented to them. Under Swedish arbitration law, and indeed under Swedish procedural law, arbitrators and judges are to engage in the free evaluation of evidence.[109] Free evaluation of evidence cannot result in an excess of the mandate given to the arbitrators by the parties. The grounds for setting aside an arbitral award are based on the idea that only procedural mistakes made by the arbitrators may serve such purposes. By contrast, a mistake made by arbitrators as to the substantive aspects of the dispute, cannot serve as a ground to set aside an arbitral award. It therefore becomes important to draw the distinction between an excess of the mandate and mistakes as to the substance of the dispute.

A similar situation occurs when arbitrators find that certain evidence presented to   **8.91** them is irrelevant, but they do not say so explicitly in the award. If, for example, a party has introduced, or rather relied on, evidence in support of a statement which the arbitrators find irrelevant, the fact that this is not explicitly stated in the award does not, under Swedish arbitration law, constitute excess of the mandate given to the arbitrators.

The distinction between contractual provisions imposing limitations on the arbitrators' mandate and contractual limitations that form part of the merits of the case   It is possible, although not very common, that arbitration clauses set forth   **8.92** specific limitations on the authority of the arbitrators. For example, the parties may have agreed to submit only certain issues to the arbitrators. In such cases, the

---

with a question which was already decided. That award was accordingly set aside by the Supreme Court which expressly referred to section 21 of the 1929 Arbitration Act, ie dealing with challenges to arbitral awards. One of the dissenting Supreme Court justices also considered section 21 of the 1929 Arbitration Act to be applicable, but took the view that Skånska by its conduct had waived its right to rely on such section. The other dissenting Supreme Court justice found the 1950 award void on the basis of sub-paragraph 3 of the first paragraph of section 20 of the 1929 Arbitration Act. Cf Arbitration in Sweden, (2nd edn 1984), at 153–154.

[108] For a discussion of *res judicata*, see para 7.104 *et seq.*
[109] See discussion at para 6.162 *et seq.*

arbitrators may not, needless to say, rule on other issues than those submitted by the parties. Rather than having such limitations on the authority of arbitrators included in an arbitration clause, such limitations will usually be discussed and agreed upon once the dispute has arisen, or even in the course of the arbitral proceedings,[110] for example to submit certain issues to be resolved in a separate award, eg the issue of liability. The arbitrators may then not also address issues of quantum in the separate award, which would constitute an excess of the mandate given to the arbitrators.

8.93 Commercial contracts may also include limitations on the authority of the arbitrators, which are not necessarily characterized as procedural limitations. In such situations it may be difficult to draw the distinction between procedural mistakes and substantive mistakes. It is not unusual, for example, for contracts to stipulate that parties are entitled only to a certain kind of damages, for example, excluding so-called indirect losses such as lost profits. If the losing party challenges the award and alleges that the arbitrators have ordered him to pay such damages, that situation would not be characterized as a procedural mistake by the arbitrators, but rather as a substantive mistake by them. If the losing party is right, the arbitrators have misunderstood or misapplied the substantive aspects of the contract, something which may not lead to the setting aside of the arbitral award.

8.94 Another type of contractual provisions which may cause particular problems in this regard are contractual time limits or cut-off dates within which claims must be raised. Such provisions are often, at least from linguistic point of view, characterized as *procedural*. Typically, such contractual provisions stipulate that unless a claim is raised within a certain period of time, the claiming party loses the right to raise the claim. Such a time period is thus deemed to have a preclusive effect. While the wording used in such clauses would normally lead to the conclusion that they are procedural in nature, it is clear that under Swedish law such provisions are to be characterized as substantive provisions.[111] Accordingly, under Swedish law a claim which has been filed after the expiration of such a time period can only be denied on the merits and not rejected on procedural grounds. This in turn means that if arbitrators have mistakenly accepted to determine such a claim submitted after the expiry of the time limit, the arbitrators have not exceeded their mandate, nor made a procedural mistake, but rather a substantive mistake. Consequently, an arbitral award cannot be challenged on this ground since the situation described would not under Swedish law constitute an excess of the mandate given to the arbitrators.

8.95 It has already been mentioned in the foregoing that the arbitrators are bound by the choice of law agreed upon by the parties. In other words, the arbitrators must apply the law chosen by the parties. If they fail to do so, or refuse to do so, such failure or refusal by the arbitrators would constitute an excess of their mandate. Needless to

---

[110] Cf *If Skadeförsäkring AB v Securitas AB et al*, Svea Court of Appeal, judgment of 3 November 2005 in Case No T 8016-04.

[111] Lindskog, *Preskription* (2002) 614–615

say, however, it may sometimes be very difficult, if not impossible, to determine whether or not the arbitrators have *failed* to apply the substantive law chosen by the parties, or if they have simply *misapplied* the law chosen by the parties.[112] In the latter case an award would not be challengeable, since an arbitral award may not be reviewed on the merits. While the general rule is thus relatively easy to formulate, in practice it may be quite difficult to draw the line between non-application and mis-application of the applicable law.[113] Few arbitral awards have language to the effect that the arbitrators have refused to apply a law specifically chosen by the parties. This means that a court of law must interpret the reasons given by the arbitrators in the award to be able to determine whether or not they have failed, or refused, to apply a substantive law, or simply misapplied it. Moreover, it could also be argued that where the choice of law is expressed in a clause separate from the arbitration agreement, such choice of law does not become part of the mandate of the arbitrators, which would imply that failure to apply the law agreed upon by the parties is a substantive error rather than an excess of mandate.

It is often difficult to determine whether the arbitrators have failed to apply the law **8.96** chosen by the parties, or if they have misapplied the law. When the parties have made a clear choice of law, it is virtually unheard of that arbitrators fail or refuse to follow the instructions of the parties, unless one of the limitations on party auton-omy is applicable in so far as the choice of law is concerned.[114] If they do, such an award would in most cases be challengeable. The situation becomes more compli-cated when the choice of law clause is unclear and/or difficult to apply. Such a case was tried by the Svea Court of Appeal in *JSC Aeroflot Russian Airlines v Russo International Venture Inc* and *MGM Productions Group Inc* (T 1164-03) and decided in 2005. The parties had signed an agreement concerning the leasing of commercial aircraft. The contract provided for arbitration in Stockholm. The choice of law clause—item 15 of the agreement—read as follows: 'This Agreement is governed by the regulations and shall be construed by the laws of Russian Federation and the State of New York (USA)'.

The arbitral tribunal found the choice of law clause 'somewhat confusing'. It went **8.97** on to say: 'Thus the conflict of laws provisions of the respective jurisdictions must be analyzed to determine which law shall be applied'. One critical issue was whether Russian or New York statutes of limitations were to be applied. With respect to one of the substantive issues, the tribunal concluded that in the end it did not need to go into 'the question whether Russian or New York law is applicable'. The reason in the view of the tribunal was that the claimant in the arbitration had de facto taken measures which pre-empted the application of any time bar, even under Russian law.

---

[112] Govt Bill 1998/99:35 p 123; Lindskog, *Skiljeförfarande, En kommentar* (2005) 933 *et seq* and 946 *et seq*.

[113] See, however, Hobér, *Extinctive Prescription and Applicable Law in International Arbitration* (2001) 101 *et seq*, where a 'formula' is presented to facilitate the determination of this issue.

[114] See para 2.51 *et seq*.

With respect to another disputed issue, the tribunal concluded that the application of Russian conflict of laws rules would lead to the same result as the application of the conflict of laws rules of the State of New York, ie that the statute of limitations in the State of New York was to be applied.

8.98 Aeroflot challenged the award and argued that the arbitrators had exceeded their mandate and/or committed a procedural error by not applying the law agreed by the parties. Aeroflot argued that the choice of law clause was very clear. The parties had agreed to apply Russian law *and* the law of the State of New York, to wit, the *substantive* law of the respective country. The parties had *not* agreed to apply the conflict of laws rules of Russia and the State of New York, respectively. This was, however, argued Aeroflot, what the arbitrators explicitly acknowledged that they had done. Consequently, in Aeroflot's view, the arbitrators had refused to follow the instructions of the parties. Even if a clear choice of law provision is difficult to apply, Aeroflot argued, the arbitrators are not entitled to deviate from such clear instructions from the parties.

8.99 The Svea Court of Appeal did not agree with Aeroflot. In its reasons the court said, *inter alia,* the following:

> The choice of law clause indicates substantive rules in two different jurisdictions without any order of priority. If the substantive rules are contradictory, the arbitral tribunal must therefore decide which rules are to apply. To do so does not constitute excess of the mandate; on the contrary it must be deemed to form part of the mandate. There is excess of mandate, if the arbitral tribunal knowingly disregards a choice of law provision. An erroneous interpretation, by contrast, forms part of the evaluation of the substance.

8.100 It is noteworthy that the court did not address the generally held view that a choice of law clause excludes the conflict of laws rules of the chosen legal system, an argument raised by Aeroflot. In Aeroflot's view the arbitrators had applied a set of rules—conflict of laws rules—not agreed by the parties. The court seems to have characterized the activity of the arbitral tribunal in this respect as an interpretation of the choice of law clause, which is a substantive, rather than procedural, aspect of a dispute and therefore not challengeable. In this respect, the court said the following:

> This [the application of conflict of law rules by the tribunal] cannot in the view of the Court of Appeal be understood such that the arbitral tribunal has made a completely new choice of law and thereby disregarded the fundamental—but incomplete—choice of law by the parties pursuant to the provision in item 15. Rather, it must be seen as a way of dealing—by way of interpretation—with the difficulty built in into the clause by virtue of the fact that it indicates contradictory substantive rules.

8.101 Questions concerning applicable law were also discussed in *Czech Republic v CME Czech Republic BV* (Case 8735-01)[115] where a partial award on liability in *CME*

---

[115] Judgment of Svea Court of Appeal, Stockholm, *Czech Republic v CME Czech Republic BV*, Case No T 8735-01. An unofficial translation into English of the judgment is published in Stockholm Arbitration Report 2003:2, p 167 *et seq.*

Czech Republic BV v Czech Republic[116] was challenged before the Svea Court of Appeal. The Czech Republic argued that the arbitral tribunal had gone beyond the scope of its mandate by failing to apply the law specified in the arbitration clause in the bilateral investment protection treaty, in this case Czech law and international law. Instead, the arbitral tribunal had based the arbitral award on a general assessment of fairness.

The Court of Appeal commenced its review of the arbitral award by stating that **8.102** Swedish law adopts a very restrictive approach to the possibility of setting aside arbitral awards.

The Court of Appeal acknowledged, however, that, as a matter of principle, it is **8.103** possible for the parties to agree that the law according to which the dispute is to be decided shall be part of the mandate of the arbitral tribunal. The Court emphasized, however, that in order to safeguard the principle that there can be no review of the merits of an arbitral award (including the application of the law applicable to the dispute), Swedish law seeks to limit the possibility to set aside an arbitral award on the ground that the arbitrators have applied the wrong law. With reference thereto, the Court found that the arbitrators exceed their mandate by failing to apply the law agreed by the parties, only where they have more or less deliberately disregarded the designated law. The Court further found that there is no excess of mandate where the arbitrators have applied the designated law incorrectly. There can hardly be any question of excess of mandate, in the view of the Court, where the arbitrators have been required to interpret the parties' designation of applicable law and, in so doing, have interpreted the designation incorrectly.

The Court found that the wording of the choice of law provision in the arbitra- **8.104** tion clause of the Dutch-Czech bilateral investment treaty (BIT) gave the impression that the contracting States had intended to let the arbitrators determine, on a case-by-case basis, which of the several sources of law, enumerated in the arbitration clause, it should apply. The Court concluded that the arbitral tribunal in its determination of the dispute had applied the choice of law clause in the arbitration clause of the Dutch-Czech BIT, and based its decision on the sources enumerated in that clause, in particular the BIT itself and international law. The Court also concluded that the arbitral tribunal had not based its decision on a general assessment of fairness. The arbitral tribunal had, therefore, not exceeded its mandate by failing to apply the applicable law.

As mentioned above, arbitrators are bound by the prayers for relief submitted by **8.105** the parties and by the legal grounds relied upon by the parties in support thereof. This means that arbitrators are not allowed to embark on a discussion of other solutions than those suggested by the parties during the arbitration. The arbitrators

---

[116] *CME Czech Republic BV v Czech Republic*, Partial Award and Separate Opinion, Ad hoc—UNCITRAL Arbitration Rules, signed 13 September 2001.

could, for example, take the view that a more reasonable and just resolution of the dispute would result if the arbitrators were allowed to deviate from the prayers for relief and/or legal grounds relied upon by the parties, or even to act as *amiables compositeurs,* or decide *ex aequo et bono.* If arbitrators do so, even if their ambition is to create a better solution, such a decision by the arbitrators would constitute an excess of the mandate and would thus result in a challengeable award.[117]

8.106 **Does the SAA require that an excess of mandate influenced the outcome of the dispute?** Unlike the general clause regarding procedural irregularities in item 6 of section 34, item 2 does not set forth any causal requirement, ie the challenging party is not required to establish that the arbitrators' excess of mandate is likely to have influenced the outcome of the dispute. It has been suggested that the primary objective of the grounds for challenge is to safeguard the observance of due process. Therefore, the mere fact that uncertainty exists as to whether or not an excess of mandate influenced the outcome of a dispute is sufficient to find that the interest of due process has been affected. For that reason, it is appropriate that no causal requirement has been stipulated for this ground.[118] However, if it is obvious to everyone that the excess of mandate did not influence the outcome, then a causal requirement would seem to be warranted.

8.107 On the other hand, it has been argued that an implicit causal requirement also exists with respect to excess of mandate.[119] The fact that an award may be set aside 'wholly or partially' and that the *travaux préparatoires*[120] state that it may be sufficient to set aside only such part of an award as is affected by a procedural irregularity are relied upon in support of this argument. Consequently, parts of an award that are unaffected by an excess of mandate should not be set aside.

8.108 In *Systembolaget AB v V & S Vin & Sprit Aktiebolag*[121] the court seems to have accepted that some form of causal requirement does exist. The Svea Court of Appeal stated that an award should not be set aside if it is possible to conclude that the outcome would not have been affected by the excess of mandate of the arbitrators. In the circumstances of the case, however, the Court of Appeal found that it could not be ruled out that the excess of mandate had not affected the outcome of the dispute. The arbitral award was therefore set aside. As applied by the Court of Appeal in *Systembolaget AB v V & S Vin & Sprit Aktiebolag,* however, the threshold for such a

---

[117] Cf *Venantius AB v Innovativ Informationsteknologi i Sverige Aktiebolag,* Svea Court of Appeal, judgment of 21 April 2004 in Case No T 7483-02. In this case, it was argued that the arbitrators' application by analogy of Chapter 35, section 5 of the Procedural Code in the determination of damages suffered by the claimant, in fact amounted to a determination *ex aequo et bono.* The court, however, found that the provision of the Procedural Code is rather a general rule of relaxation of the burden of proof, which arbitrators may apply without the prior consent of the parties.

[118] Lindskog, *Skiljeförfarande, En kommentar* (2005) 937.

[119] Heuman, *Arbitration Law of Sweden: Practice and Procedure* (2003) 596–602.

[120] Govt Bill 1998/99:35, p 235.

[121] Svea Court of Appeal Case No T 4548-08. See also para 8.78.

causal requirement appears to have been considerably lower than under item 6 of section 34. The causal requirement under section 34(6) is that the procedural irregularity 'likely influenced the outcome of the case', whereas the Court of Appeal in *Systembolaget AB v V & S Vin & Sprit Aktiebolag* concluded that 'it could not be ruled out that the excess of mandate had not affected the outcome of the dispute'.

8.3.4 The arbitration should not have taken place in Sweden

Item 3 of section 34 of the SAA stipulates that an arbitral award shall be set aside if **8.109** the arbitration should not have taken place in Sweden. The provision refers to section 47, which allows arbitrations to be commenced in Sweden only if (i) the arbitration agreement provides that the proceedings shall take place in Sweden, (ii) the arbitrators or an arbitration institute have determined pursuant to the arbitration agreement that the proceedings shall take place in Sweden, or (iii) the respondent otherwise agrees to the arbitration taking place in Sweden. Arbitration may also be initiated in Sweden if the respondent is domiciled in Sweden or is otherwise subject to the jurisdiction of the Swedish courts with regard to the matter in dispute, unless the arbitration agreement provides that the proceedings shall take place abroad.[122]

In other situations than those enumerated in section 47, arbitral proceedings may **8.110** not take place in Sweden under the SAA. This means that if an arbitration clause provides for a foreign seat of arbitration, but the arbitrators, despite an objection by one of the parties, decide that the arbitration, nevertheless, is to be conducted in Sweden pursuant to the SAA, the award may be set aside under item 3 of section 34. However, such a decision by the arbitrators would also constitute excess of mandate and the resulting award would be challengeable under item 2 of section 34. The specific regulation in item 3 of section 34 follows from the basic principle that a Swedish court, or other public authority, should not contribute to an arbitration taking place in Sweden which lacks the consent of a party who otherwise would not have to answer in Swedish courts.[123]

It must be emphasized, however, that the fact that arbitrations may only take place **8.111** in Sweden under the SAA in the situations enumerated in section 47 does not preclude arbitral tribunals in arbitrations having their seat of arbitration outside Sweden to conduct hearings in Sweden, or meet in Sweden for deliberations. The sole purpose of section 47 is to regulate when arbitrations may be conducted under the SAA.

---

[122] It must be noted that the respondent's domicile is not determinative with respect to the place for arbitration proceedings and does not establishes a place for arbitration *per se*. The domicile of the respondent may, however, serve as factor for assisting the arbitrators in their interpretation of an arbitration agreement which is silent in this respect.

[123] Govt Bill 1998/99:35, p189.

8.3.5 Improper appointment of arbitrators

8.112 An arbitral award may also be set aside if an arbitrator has been appointed contrary to the arbitration agreement or to the SAA. One example is that an arbitrator lacks certain qualifications, which the arbitration agreement requires, for instance that the arbitrator should be a judge or possess particular technical expertise. If the arbitrator did not have the qualifications at the time of appointment, it does not matter whether the arbitrator previously had such qualifications. It is also not possible to 'cure' the lack of qualification or expertise by acquiring it after the arbitration.[124]

8.113 An award may also be set aside on this ground if the arbitrator was appointed after the expiry of the time limit agreed by the parties, or if the arbitrator was appointed by an arbitration institute, district court, or other appointing authority, if the requirements for such appointment were not fulfilled.

8.3.6 One of the arbitrators should have been disqualified

8.114 An award may be challenged on the ground that one of the arbitrators should have been disqualified. Challenges based on this provision are unusual, since challenges of arbitrators would usually have come up and already have been decided during the arbitration.[125] The provision in question, section 34, item 5, of the SAA, refers to the circumstances set forth in sections 7 and 8 of the SAA, ie that an arbitrator must possess full legal capacity and be impartial.[126] The requirements of impartiality ought to be applied in the same way, and the same level of impartiality ought to be maintained, irrespective of whether the issue is determined as part of a challenge to the award or as part of a challenge to the arbitrator during the proceedings.[127] This does not mean, however, that a party can 'gamble' and wait to raise the objection to the impartiality of the arbitrator until the award has been issued. A party which has participated in the proceedings without raising an objection to the impartiality of an arbitrator, based on circumstances of which such party was aware, will be deemed to have waived such objection.[128]

8.115 Section 8 of the SAA enumerates certain circumstances which shall always be deemed to diminish confidence in the arbitrator's impartiality, and thus lead to his or her disqualification. The list is not meant to be exhaustive and is not to be interpreted *e contrario*. Cases that do not fall within any of the listed categories may still put in question the impartiality of the arbitrator, and, thus, constitute grounds for disqualification under the general clause, ie that '. . . *an arbitrator shall be discharged if there exists any circumstance which may diminish confidence in the arbitrator's impartiality*'.[129]

---

[124] Heuman, *Arbitration Law of Sweden: Practice and Procedure* (2003) 616.
[125] For a further discussion regarding the arbitrators' impartiality, see para 4.62 *et seq.*
[126] See discussion at para 4.39.
[127] Heuman, *Arbitration Law of Sweden: Practice and Procedure* (2003) 223.
[128] Section 34, para 2 of the SAA.
[129] Cf the Supreme Court case *Korsnäs Aktiebolag v AB Fortum Värme*, judgment of 9 June 2010 in Case No T 156-09 discussed in para 4.72 *et seq.*

The term *bias*, used in the Procedural Code with regard to judges, is no longer used **8.116** in the SAA. The new wording, which focuses on 'circumstances that may diminish confidence in the arbitrator's impartiality', was chosen to bring the SAA more into line with the UNCITRAL Model Law. The Model Law, Article 12(2), provides that 'an arbitrator may be challenged if circumstances exist that give rise to justifiable doubts as to his impartiality or independence . . .' While the SAA only refers to 'impartiality', and thus not expressly to 'independence', the wording of section 8 of the SAA nevertheless makes it clear that 'independence' is included in the notion of 'impartiality'.[130] The wording 'circumstances that may diminish confidence in the arbitrator's impartiality', also covers the notion of 'independence', ie various types of relationships between the party and the arbitrator.[131]

In *Ingela C v Kommunernas Försäkringsaktiebolag* (NJA 1981 p 1205), which was **8.117** decided under the 1929 Arbitration Act, an arbitrator was deemed biased because a judge in a similar situation would have been deemed biased under the Procedural Code. It follows from the foregoing that the relevance of this case for the application of the SAA is questionable, since the requirement of impartiality under the SAA is meant to be autonomous. Thus, when applying the impartiality test under the SAA, it is more relevant to look at international arbitration practice regarding the application of corresponding requirements in foreign Arbitration Acts or in different arbitration rules than to look at the Swedish Procedural Code. This is emphasized by the fact that the SAA is intended to be applied by foreign and Swedish users alike, irrespective of any knowledge of the Procedural Code.[132]

8.3.7 Other procedural irregularities

8.3.7.1 The irregularities to which the general clause applies

Section 34(1), item 6, provides that an arbitral award may be set aside 'if, without **8.118** fault of the party, there otherwise occurred an irregularity in the course of the proceedings which probably influenced the outcome of the case'. This rule serves as a general clause. Its predecessor was section 21, item 4 of the 1929 Arbitration Act. Except the requirement that such a procedural error must be likely to have influenced the outcome of the case, the new provision is intended to have the same scope as section 21, item 4 of the 1929 Arbitration Act. Thus, case law concerning the old provision still remains relevant.[133]

The term 'other irregularity in the course of the proceedings' would seem to indicate **8.119** that, as a matter of principle, any irregularity in the conduct of the arbitration proceedings could result in the setting aside of the award. The *travaux préparatoires*

---

[130]   See discussion at para 4.39 *et seq.*
[131]   Sekolec and Eliasson, 'The UNCITRAL Model Law and the Swedish Arbitration Act', in Heuman and Jarvin, (eds) *Swedish Arbitration Act of 1999—Five Years On* (2006) 208–209.
[132]   Cf Madsen, *Commercial Arbitration in Sweden* (3rd edn, 2007) 116.
[133]   Govt Bill 1998/99:35, p 148.

confirm that no limitation as to the type of procedural irregularity is intended and that the rule has intentionally been drafted employing general language so as to cover a wide range of 'unacceptable errors'.[134] However, the *travaux préparatoires* also emphasize that the provision should be restrictively applied, and that the requirement that it must be probable that the irregularity has influenced the outcome of the case has been included to ensure such restrictive application. This requirement is further discussed in para 8.176.

8.120 The word *otherwise* suggests that the general clause is subsidiary to the other grounds for challenge. It has been argued, however, that it can be applied also when another of the provisions in section 34 of the SAA apply, at least in some cases.[135] It is unlikely that it would be applied in such a situation, since the challenge is already covered by one of the more specific grounds. A court would typically first determine whether one of the specific grounds for challenge in items 1 to 5 applies which means that the challenging party will not have to establish a probable influence on the outcome.[136]

8.121 However, it may sometimes be difficult to determine whether the general clause or another ground is applicable. For example, views differ as to whether it is to be seen as an excess of mandate or a procedural irregularity, if arbitrators disregard an agreement between the parties regarding the conduct of the proceedings, such as an agreement limiting their rights to produce evidence, or if the arbitrators disregard the parties' agreement on applicable law.[137]

8.122 One example of an error that is commonly seen as a procedural irregularity, but which could also be seen as an excess of mandate, is the arbitrators' deviation from their mandate. For example, a ruling *infra petita* could be both a procedural irregularity and excess of mandate.

8.123 In order to determine whether there has been an irregularity in the course of the proceedings, it is necessary that the acts or omissions of the arbitrators be evaluated against relevant norms for how the arbitrators should have acted. The SAA, applicable arbitration rules (if any), and the parties' instructions serve as primary sources for establishing such norms. Violations of such norms can constitute irregularities in the procedure on the basis of which the award is to be set aside, provided that all other requirements for such setting aside are fulfilled.[138]

---

[134] Ibid, p 148.

[135] Cf Heuman, *Arbitration Law of Sweden: Practice and Procedure* (2003) 623.

[136] However, see the discussion on whether an implicit causal requirement may be deemed to exist as regards excess of mandate, para 8.106.

[137] Cf Heuman, *Arbitration Law of Sweden: Practice and Procedure* (2003) 595 and 598 *et seq*; Lindskog, *Skiljeförfarande, En kommentar*, 929–930 and SOU 1994:81 p 154.

[138] As regards instructions from the parties, see *Soyak v Hochtief* (NJA 2009 p 128), Govt Bill 1998/99:35, p 143, and Lindskog, *Skiljeförfarande, En kommentar* (2005) 929–930.

Some rules will set out clear and unambiguous norms that the arbitrators must **8.124** adhere to, while other rules give the arbitrators a wider discretion, which may require that standards outside the SAA and the parties' agreement must be taken into account when assessing whether there has been any procedural irregularity. For example, section 24(1) of the SAA provides that the parties are to be given the opportunity to present their respective cases in writing or orally 'to the extent necessary' and that the hearing is to be held if requested by a party and provided the parties have not agreed otherwise.[139] While the meaning of this provision with respect to hearings is rather clear, the 'due process' guarantee to the effect that the parties are to be given the opportunity to present their cases in writing, or orally, 'to the extent necessary' may require the court hearing the challenge to establish an appropriate standard against which the actions and/or omissions of the arbitrators are to be judged.

Similarly, when the SAA is silent on an issue, this does not mean that the arbitrators' **8.125** discretion is without limitation. Requirements of due process represent the ultimate standard against which the arbitrators' conduct of the proceedings must be judged. For example, if the parties have legitimate expectations as to the procedural rules that are to be applied in the absence of an agreement, the arbitral tribunal may not deviate from these rules, at least not without advising the parties of its intention.[140]

Section 21 of the SAA provides that the arbitrators must follow the instructions of **8.126** the parties unless there is an impediment to doing so. Under this rule, the arbitrators must take principles of due process into account and may be required to deviate from the parties' instructions, should they for example propose unacceptable restrictions on one of the party's right to plead its case.[141] This provision implies that there may, at least in theory, be a clash between the arbitrators' duty to follow the parties' instructions and the requirements of due process.

Needless to say, an arbitral award can only be set aside with reference to procedural **8.127** irregularities, and not with reference to substantive errors.[142] However, the distinction between the arbitrators' misjudgement of facts or misapplication of substantive law, on the one side, and procedural irregularities on the other, is not always readily made. It is, for example, a substantive and unchallengeable misjudgement if the arbitrators disregard relevant evidence, because the arbitrators after evaluating such evidence erroneously find it irrelevant. It may, however, be a procedural irregularity if the arbitrators without proper reason refuse to accept evidence presented to them or do not consider evidence presented by the parties.[143] Similarly, it may be an

---

[139] See discussion at para 6.32.
[140] This requirement is closely connected with that of substantive case management. See further para 6.191 *et seq.*
[141] Cf Lindskog, *Skiljeförfarande, En kommentar* (2005) 650-651. See para 8.129.
[142] This follows from the wording of section 34. See also, *inter alia*, Govt Bill 1998/99:35, p 147 *et seq.*
[143] Heuman, *Arbitration Law of Sweden: Practice and Procedure* (2003) 641 and 645; and *Gunnar Jansson v The Estate of Oscar Jansson* (NJA 1965 p 384).

unchallengeable error in the arbitrators' assessment of the merits of the case if it misinterprets a choice of law clause in the parties' agreement, but it is a procedural error if they wholly disregard the parties' agreement on applicable law.[144]

8.128 Below there follows a discussion of potential procedural irregularities within the meaning of the general clause in section 34(1), item 6:

8.129 (a) **Violation of due process**   Serious violations of due process typically constitute procedural irregularities. However, it is important to emphasize that, in the interest of the finality of arbitral awards, only apparent violations of due process may lead to the setting aside of the award.[145]

8.130 A fundamental principle of arbitration is that the procedure is adversarial. This means, *inter alia*, that it is for the parties to present their respective cases and that the arbitrators may not base the award on their own inquiries into the matter in dispute, which are out of the parties' control. The parties must also be provided with sufficient time to prepare and present their submissions on various issues that arise in the arbitration.[146]

8.131 Another basic requirement of due process is that each party must be given the opportunity to present its case. This is expressly set out in the section 24(1) of the SAA, under which the parties must be given the opportunity to present their cases in writing or orally to the extent necessary. What this means in practice must be determined on a case by case basis, taking into account eg the particular circumstances of the case, the background and expectations of the parties, the parties' conduct, and the procedure to which the parties have agreed. Should the parties, for example, have agreed to make only a limited number of submissions,[147] a party would typically not be able to challenge the award by claiming that it could not present its case to the extent necessary.

8.132 Another aspect of the right of each party to plead its case relates to the submission of evidence. In this respect, section 25(2) of the SAA provides that the arbitrators may dismiss evidence if it is manifestly irrelevant, or if the point in time at which it is presented so warrants.[148] To the extent that the arbitrators dismiss evidence or decide not to consider such evidence on the basis of it being irrelevant given the arbitrators' assessment of the merits of the case, the decision is not challengeable.[149]

---

[144] See discussion at para 8.95 *et seq*; Lindskog, *Skiljeförfarande, En kommentar* (2005) 945 *et seq* and Govt Official Report (SOU) 1994:81 p 154.

[145] Cf Govt Bill 1998/99:35, p 148.

[146] See discussion at para 6.32.

[147] Cf the SCC Rules for Expedited Arbitration, under which the parties are only allowed two submissions each.

[148] The *travaux préparatoires* indicate that the disregard of evidence offered could be a ground to challenge the award under the general clause: Govt Bill 1998/99:35, p 148. See para 6.89 *et seq* for a discussion of evidence.

[149] Heuman, *Arbitration Law of Sweden: Practice and Procedure* (2003) 629.

If, on the other hand, the evidence is dismissed for some other reasons, for example, that it was presented too late in the proceedings, an erroneous decision could constitute a procedural irregularity.[150]

Whether an award should be set aside because a party has not been given the oppor- **8.133** tunity fully to plead its case and to submit evidence was decided in *Gunnar Jansson v The Estate of Oscar Jansson* (NJA 1965 p 384). In this case, both awards were set aside because the claimant had not been given sufficient opportunity to present its case. Before the hearing leading up to the first award, the claimant had requested that he be heard under oath concerning certain events of relevance in relation to, among other things, an objection by the respondent that the claimant's claims were time-barred. However, the claimant was not heard, and, in the view of the Supreme Court, the claimant was therefore not given the opportunity to give an account of what allegedly took place. In addition to this procedural error, the claimant had not been provided with a copy of one of the respondent's submissions, which included at least one piece of information which had not previously been submitted. These facts were held by the Supreme Court to constitute a procedural irregularity, which justified the setting aside of the award. In rendering the second award, the arbitrators were required to rule on a set-off claim presented by the respondent. However, the set-off claim had only been presented in general terms and did not specify the debts on which it was based. The Supreme Court, therefore, held that the case had not been adequately prepared, since the arbitrators had not ensured that the debts were properly specified in order to afford the claimant an opportunity to comment on the debts. The Supreme Court further found that the claimant had thus not been provided with sufficient possibility to present its case.

The refusal of the arbitrators to request assistance of the courts in taking evidence **8.134** may constitute a procedural irregularity. This may be the case, for instance, if they do not consent to a party's request for court assistance in hearing a witness under oath (in accordance with section 26(1) of the SAA) where such testimony under oath would be required.[151] However, in such cases the arbitrators' decision would often be based on their assessment of the relevance of the proffered evidence with respect to the merits of the case, and thus not be challengeable.[152] It is also very difficult to prove that a witness would have given a different testimony if heard before the court under oath than before the arbitrators. Thus, even if the failure to allow a witness to be heard in court is deemed to constitute a procedural irregularity, it may be difficult to prove that such failure likely affected the outcome of the case.

(b) Mistakes in relation to the position taken by a party If the arbitrators **8.135** misunderstand a party's position on a procedural issue and act according to this

---

[150] Heuman, *Arbitration Law of Sweden: Practice and Procedure* (2003) 633 and 635.
[151] See discussion at para 6.170 *et seq.*
[152] Cf *AB Eletrolux v G Rejving i Stockholm* (NJA 1963 A 23), in which the arbitral tribunal's omission to take action to procure certain documents was not considered a challengeable irregularity.

(mis)understanding, this may constitute a procedural irregularity.[153] In the *travaux préparatoires* it is said that a serious misunderstanding of a party's position on procedural matters may be a ground for challenge, on the theory that it is a procedural irregularity.[154]

8.136 In *Jansson v Reprotype AB* (NJA 1975 p 536), Jansson had requested arbitration with respect to a certain dispute. During the course of the proceedings, Jansson had agreed to an extension of the time limit for the issuing of the award until 31 October 1971.[155] When that date drew near, the arbitrators tried to persuade Jansson to agree to a further extension. On 26 October 1971, the arbitrators issued a decision whereby they terminated the arbitration, alleging that certain statements by Jansson amounted to a withdrawal of his request for arbitration.

8.137 Jansson challenged the decision in the district court,[156] which found that Jansson's statements indicated that he wanted the time limit for the award to expire without an award having been made so that the arbitration agreement would terminate with respect to the specific dispute. Jansson had not intended to withdraw his request for arbitration. The arbitrators had accordingly misconstrued Jansson's statements and committed a procedural error. The decision to terminate the proceedings was, therefore, set aside by the district court.

8.138 The Svea Court of Appeal reversed this judgment on the ground that even if the arbitrators were wrong in interpreting Jansson's actions as amounting to a withdrawal of the request, this interpretation was an erroneous decision as to the substance of the case and thus was not challengeable.

8.139 A unanimous Supreme Court, however, restored the judgment of the district court. After finding that the rules for challenging of awards were applicable by analogy to a decision to terminate the proceedings without ruling on the merits of the dispute, the Supreme Court went on to conclude that 'both an error concerning the actual consideration of the procedural question and the irregular handling of the same' were 'irregularities of procedure' within the meaning of section 21 of the 1929 Arbitration Act.

8.140 *Shipping Partnership for M/S Red Sea v Götaverken Sölvesborg AB* (NJA 1990 p 419) is another case in which an arbitral tribunal's decision to dismiss a case without a ruling on the merits was challenged. The claimant's request for a declaration that it was entitled to cancel the parties' contract was rejected in a partial award.

---

[153] See further, Heuman, *Arbitration Law of Sweden: Practice and Procedure* (2003) 635.

[154] Govt Bill 1998/99:35, p 148.

[155] Section 18 of the 1929 Arbitration Act provided that if the parties had agreed on an award period, the arbitration agreement became inoperative if an award was not rendered within the agreed time.

[156] In accordance with the 1929 Arbitration Act, the proper forum for challenge proceedings was the district court.

Following this ruling, the arbitrators requested further advance payment of their fees. The respondent paid its part of the advance while the claimant wrote to the arbitrators indicating that it lacked the financial resources to plead its case and that it lacked the funds to pay its part of the advance. The respondent informed the arbitrators that it did not request that the dispute be determined by the arbitrators, and that it thus requested that the claim be dismissed. The claimant was ordered to indicate whether it disputed or accepted the respondent's requests and the grounds for its objection, if any.

Since the claimant's next submission included arguments only in relation to the **8.141** responsibility for costs, but did not dispute the respondent's request, the arbitrators explained that it understood the claimant's position to be that it had withdrawn its claim. This caused the claimant to submit that it 'was not presently in a position to raise the financial qualifications necessary to pursue the claim, but that it had not withdrawn its claim, unlike [the respondent]'. The claimant also repeated its claim for compensation for its legal costs. This was followed by one further submission from each party.

The arbitrators found that, against the background of the objective meaning of **8.142** what the claimant had submitted in its briefs, the position of the claimant must be deemed to have been that the arbitration could not go on and that the case must be dismissed. The claimant was ordered to compensate the respondent for its costs for the arbitration and to carry the arbitrators' fees.

An action to set aside the decision to dismiss the case was filed by the claimant, who **8.143** argued, in essence, that it had not withdrawn its claim before the arbitrators and that the arbitrators had therefore not been entitled to dismiss the case. The district court found that the arbitrators had misinterpreted the claimant's position and set aside the decision to dismiss the claim. The Svea Court of Appeal concluded that a withdrawal of the claim must be unambiguous and that the submissions by the claimant gave room for different interpretations. The Court of Appeal, therefore, also found that the arbitrators had not been entitled to dismiss the case.

The Supreme Court, however, concluded that the claimant had not clearly set out **8.144** its position concerning the continuation of the arbitration, and that it was possible to interpret the claimant's position as if the claimant had withdrawn its claim. The arbitrators, who had made several attempts to bring clarity in the matter, were not without reason to understand the claimant's position as a request that the case be terminated, and, thus, as a request for withdrawal. The Supreme Court also added that if the claimant had intended anything else, the misunderstanding must be considered to have been caused by the claimant.

The wording of item 6 of section 34 of the SAA does not indicate that the assess- **8.145** ment of whether there is a procedural irregularity is to be exclusively an objective assessment. However, in the ruling of 1990, the Supreme Court indicated that the arbitrators' understanding was justified. The Supreme Court's reasoning thus seems to suggest that it considered it decisive whether the arbitrators' conduct of the case was satisfactory given the circumstances, not whether the decision made by the arbitral tribunal was correct. The reasoning in eg *Jansson v Reprotype AB* (NJA 1975 p 536) and in *Brigitte H v Skandinaviska Färginstitutet AB* (NJA 2000 p 335)[157] seem, however, to suggest the contrary. It is submitted that the better view is that it should be determined based on objective criteria whether an irregularity has occurred and that the reasons and intentions of the arbitrators should play a very limited role for this determination.[158]

8.146 (c) **Amendment of claims and dismissal of claims** The arbitrators' decision to dismiss an action without ruling on the merits can be appealed under section 36 of the SAA[159] and can thus not be challenged under section 34. When the arbitrators have assumed jurisdiction to rule on the substance of the dispute, its wrongful denial of a request for amendment of a party's claim or of a request to submit new prayers for relief can constitute a procedural irregularity. Under section 23 of the SAA, both parties are entitled to submit new claims covered by the arbitration agreement provided that the arbitrators do not consider it inappropriate, taking into account for example the point in time at which the new claims are presented. However, with the exception of the obvious requirement that the new claims come within the scope of the arbitration agreement, the wording of section 23 suggests that the arbitrators have full discretion to decide on the appropriateness of allowing a request.[160]

8.147 The 1929 Arbitration Act did not include a provision similar to section 23 of the SAA and it was unclear to what extent set-off claims had to be determined by the arbitrators. In its ruling from 2000, *Brigitte H v Skandinaviska Färginstitutet AB* (NJA 2000 p 335), the Supreme Court held that the arbitrators' dismissal of a set-off claim did not constitute a procedural irregularity, because it was unclear under the old Arbitration Act whether such a claim had to be tried.

8.148 (d) *Res judicata* A ruling by an arbitral award can render an issue *res judicata*.[161] An award may thus be relied on as a bar to the arbitral tribunal's jurisdiction if a

---

[157] With respect to *Jansson v Reprotype AB*, see para 8.135 *et seq*. In *Brigitte H v Skandinaviska Färginstitutet AB* (NJA 2000 p 335), Brigitte H's set-off claim had been dismissed and Brigitte H had been ordered to pay a sum to the respondent, which she argued fell below her claim against the respondent. Brigitte H challenged the award arguing that the dismissal of her set-off claim was a procedural irregularity. The two lower courts held, *inter alia*, that whether the set-off claim was to be accepted was a question of opinion and that the arbitrators' decision could not be challenged, regardless of the contents of its decision.

The Supreme Court reasoned along the same lines, holding that no procedural irregularity was at issue since the 1929 Arbitration Act did not contain any rules on the right to introduce set-off claims and that there was no case from which to seek guidance.

[158] Cf, however, Lindskog, *Skiljeförfarande, En kommentar* (2005) 948–951.

[159] See discussion at para 8.205.

[160] See discussion at para 6.81.

[161] See para 7.104 *et seq*.

subsequent claim is covered by the *res judicata* effect of the previous award. Should the second arbitral tribunal try the claim despite the *res judicata* effect of the first award, the subsequent award can be challenged on the ground that there has been a procedural irregularity.

In arbitration, unlike court proceedings, the parties control the *res judicata* effect in **8.149** the sense that they can agree to have the issue re-tried in spite of the previous ruling. In addition, the respondent must raise the defence of *res judicata* in order to bar the second arbitration. If such defence is not raised, the second award cannot be set aside on the ground that the arbitrators failed to consider that the dispute was *res judicata*.

The fact that disregarding *res judicata* is a procedural irregularity covered by the **8.150** general clause (and not excess of mandate) follows from the Supreme Court's ruling in *Esselte AB v Allmänna Pensionsfonden* (NJA 1998 p 189).[162] In this case the Supreme Court found that the claim ruled upon in the award was covered by the *res judicata* effect of a previous award, in which the claim had been asserted as a set-off claim, but been rejected. Before the 1998 case, it was uncertain whether disregard of *res judicata* was to be treated as an excess of mandate or a procedural irregularity. In *AB Skånska Cementgjuteriet v Motoraktiebolaget i Karlstad* (NJA 1953 p 751),[163] a violation of *res judicata* was held to be a ground for setting aside an award. However, in that case, the Supreme Court did not specify the legal ground on which the award was vacated. It has been suggested, however, that the better view was that the award was set aside because the arbitrators had exceeded their mandate, since the court did not address the issue of whether the irregularity had affected the outcome of the case.[164]

Interestingly, this aspect was not addressed in the *Esselte* case of 1998 either, notwith- **8.151** standing the fact that the Supreme Court expressly held that the violation of *res judicata* was a procedural irregularity under section 21, item 4 of the 1929 Arbitration Act.

The application of the principles of *lis pendens* and *res judicata* in international **8.152** arbitration under the SAA, and the willingness of the Swedish courts to deviate from the traditional civil procedure application of such principles, was addressed in *Czech Republic v CME Czech Republic BV* (Case No 8735-01).[165]

This case concerned the challenge before the Svea Court of Appeal of the partial **8.153** award on liability in the famous BIT case, *CME Czech Republic BV v Czech Republic*.[166] In this case, the Czech Republic argued, *inter alia*, that the award should

---

[162] See para 8.89.
[163] See note 107.
[164] Heuman argues that the Supreme Court appears to have applied item 2 of section 34 of the SAA, dealing with excess of mandate. Heuman, *Arbitration Law of Sweden: Practice and Procedure* (2003) 606. See also Lindskog, *Skiljeförfarande, En kommentar* (2005) section 34–5.2.5.
[165] See discussion at para 7.120 *et seq.*
[166] *CME Czech Republic BV v Czech Republic*, Partial Award and Separate Opinion, signed 13 September 2001. This case was tried under the Dutch-Czech bilateral investment protection treaty.

be set aside because the arbitral tribunal had failed to acknowledge that the liability of the Czech Republic had already been determined in the parallel arbitration *Lauder v Czech Republic*,[167] and, thus, was *res judicata*.

8.154 The Court of Appeal found that the award in the *Lauder* case did not have any *res judicata* effect in relation to the award in the CME case, since the parties were different. The Court of Appeal did not further consider whether the specific characteristics of the underlying investment protection regime in the *CME* and *Lauder* cases merited a deviation from the traditional civil procedure application of *lis pendens* and *res judicata*. Leave for appeal to the Supreme Court was not granted.

8.155 Thus, under Swedish arbitration law, as it stands today, the application of the principles of *lis pendens* and *res judicata* in international arbitration still seems to follow more or less the same pattern as in domestic arbitration and civil procedure.

8.156 To the extent that the notion of *lis pendens* is applicable in Swedish arbitration, the misapplication of this principle couldalso constitute a procedural irregularity.[168]

8.157 **(e) Deviation from mandate or instructions**   Arbitrators *exceeding* their mandate is an irregularity covered by item 2 of section 34(1) of the SAA. As indicated above, however, there are instances where it may be uncertain whether an irregularity is to be regarded as an excess of mandate or as a procedural irregularity.[169] The parties' written and oral submissions define the scope of the arbitrators' mandate in the sense that the arbitrators may not rule on claims not submitted by either of the parties, and not base their ruling on facts and/or arguments that were not presented by the parties. The arbitrators exceed their mandate if they go beyond the submissions of the parties when ruling on the dispute, while a violation of the parties' instructions as to the conduct of the proceedings constitutes a procedural irregularity.

8.158 In *Soyak International Construction & Investment Inc v Hochtief AG* (NJA 2009 p 128), a unanimous Supreme Court held that the provision on excess of mandate in section 34(1), item 2 of the SAA addresses the scope of the arbitrators' assessment of the merits of the case. The provision applies, for example, if the arbitrators' ruling was in excess of the party's claim or based on a fact not invoked by the parties. This is in general true also if the parties have restricted the arbitrators' examination so that it concerns the application of a certain rule, or their possibilities to dispose of the proceedings in some other way. However, violations of instructions as to *how* the proceedings are to be conducted within the framework following from the arbitration agreement, the parties' claims, the facts invoked, and evidence submitted, would normally constitute a procedural irregularity under section 34(1), item 6.

---

[167] *Lauder v Czech Republic*, Final Award.
[168] Lindskog, *Skiljeförfarande, En kommentar* (2005) 964–965. See para 7.108 *et seq* as regards the applicability of *lis pendens* in arbitration.
[169] Cf para 8.88.

For instance in a ruling from 1937, *Försäkringsaktiebolaget Fylgia and Brand- och* **8.159**
livförsäkringsaktiebolaget Svea brandförsäkring v AE (NJA 1937 p120), an arbitral tribunal had failed to follow instructions in the parties' contract on how it was to conduct
a valuation of a number of buildings. This was considered a procedural irregularity.

In this case, AE had an insurance policy issued by Fylgia and Svea covering a number **8.160**
of buildings. The policy set out that valuation of damage to the buildings was to be
made in relation to each building, not as an assessment of the total damage. In
proceedings following a claim under the insurance, the arbitrators failed to follow
this instruction and assessed the total damage suffered. AE challenged the award
arguing, *inter alia*, that this omission was a procedural irregularity on the basis of
which the award should be set aside. A majority of the Supreme Court held that the
arbitrators were obliged to follow the instruction in the contract, but that that this
irregularity could not be assumed probably to have affected the outcome of the
case. It could also be argued, perhaps, that, at least if the valuation principles are set
out in the substantive parts of the contract, and not in the arbitration agreement, a
misapplication of such principles would constitute an unchallengeable error on the
merits of the case.

Moreover, a distinction is to be made between agreements on the procedure, being **8.161**
binding under civil law, and procedural acts, which a party is entitled to withdraw
during the proceedings.[170] In *Gunnar Jansson v The Estate of Oscar Jansson* (NJA 1965
p 384), the Supreme Court did not, however, attach any importance to a party's
revocation of its agreement to a partial award being rendered on an issue. The Supreme
Court came to this conclusion despite the fact that the nature of the parties' agreement suggested that it was a procedural act rather than a civil law agreement.[171]

In this case, the rendering of a partial award despite one party's objection was not **8.162**
considered a procedural irregularity. The parties had previously been in agreement
that a partial award was to be rendered on the issue, and instructed the arbitrators
accordingly. This was considered to be an instruction that the arbitrators were
required to follow. The Supreme Court held that under these conditions the arbitrators were entitled to render a partial award and, as a consequence, no procedural
irregularity had occurred.

(f) Failure to provide reasons The SAA does not include any express obligation **8.163**
for the arbitrators to provide reasons for the award (cf section 31 of the SAA).[172]
However, despite the lack of an express obligation to provide reasons, most parties

---

[170] Lindskog, *Skiljeförfarande, En kommentar* (2005) 598.
[171] Lindskog, *Skiljeförfarande, En kommentar* (2005) 651–652.
[172] A stipulation to this effect is discussed in the *travaux préparatoires*, Govt Bill 1998/99:35, p 134
et seq.

expect the arbitral tribunal to issue a reasoned award, and it is common practice in arbitrations in Sweden to provide detailed reasons,[173] see para 7.57 *et seq*.

8.164 The SCC Rules lay down an express obligation for the arbitrators to provide reasons for the award.[174] In *Soyak International Construction &Investment Inc v Hochtief AG* (NJA 2009 p 128), which was conducted under the SCC Rules, Soyak argued that the arbitrators had largely omitted to give reasons or that the reasons provided were incomplete or contradictory. The Supreme Court held that failure to provide reasons was a challengeable procedural irregularity only if there was a complete lack of reasons, or if the reasons were so incomplete that they could be equated with a failure to provide reasons at all, see para 8.88. The Supreme Court did not find this to be the case, since the arbitrators had provided reasons on every disputed point.

8.165 **(g) Arbitrators not participating in the conduct of the proceedings** If one or more arbitrators fail to participate in the deliberations, or if two arbitrators decide issues without allowing the third arbitrator to take part, such failure or exclusion may constitute a procedural error.[175] In *Czech Republic v CME Czech Republic BV*,[176] the Czech Republic argued, *inter alia,* that the award should be set aside since one of the arbitrators had been excluded from the deliberations. When determining this issue, the Court concluded that 'arbitrators shall be treated equally and be provided the same possibilities to participate in the deliberations and attempt to influence the other arbitrators though substantive arguments'. However, in the circumstances of the case, the Court found that the Czech Republic had not demonstrated that one of the arbitrators had been excluded. The award was not set aside.

8.166 **(h) Substantive case management** As has been explained in para 6.192 *et seq*, arbitrators have the obligation to conduct substantive case management for the purpose of avoiding uncertainties in the parties' respective cases, and to avoid unexpected rulings. It has been argued that serious deficiencies in the arbitrators' substantive case management could constitute procedural errors.[177]

8.167 In *TBB Tekniska Byggnadsbyrån v Kronan* (NJA 1973 p 740), a public authority, the National Board of Public Building (the 'Board'), had agreed with a private company to perform certain construction work. The Board made an advance payment. The company went into bankruptcy, and the Board cancelled the original contract and entered into a new contract with the bankruptcy estate. According to this second contract, the estate was to finish the construction work. When the Board and the estate tried to settle their accounts, the Board claimed that it was

---

[173] Govt Bill 1998/99:35, p 135 and Heuman, *Arbitration Law of Sweden: Practice and Procedure* (2003) 497.

[174] Article 36(1) of the SCC Rules.

[175] Heuman, *Arbitration Law of Sweden: Practice and Procedure* (2003) 642.

[176] See note 116.

[177] Nordensson, JT 1993-94 p 218, Heuman, *Arbitration Law of Sweden: Practice and Procedure* (2003) 368 *et seq* and 635, See also Heuman, *Current Issues in Swedish Arbitration* (1990) 172, Lindskog, *Skiljeförfarande, En kommentar* (2005) 967–968.

entitled to set-off against its debts to the estate the advance payment made under the original contract. The estate denied that a set-off was allowed, and the dispute was referred to arbitration.

The arbitrators in their award took note of the fact that the new agreement said **8.168** nothing about the advance payment. They then went on to say that the estate in bankruptcy, 'which evidently drafted the text of the agreement dated 22 December 1966' (the second contract), ought to have seen to it that the agreement made clear how anything performed under the previous contract was to be credited. Since this had not been done, the arbitrators determined that the Board was entitled to claim a set-off in respect of the advance payment.

The estate challenged the award on the ground that the arbitrators had based their **8.169** decision on the assumption that the estate had drafted the contract. This assumption (something which the courts later acknowledged) was incorrect. It was alleged that the arbitrators, by relying on the assumption without ascertaining whether it was correct or not, had committed a procedural error, which had had a decisive influence on the outcome of the case.

A unanimous Supreme Court denied the challenge with reference to the fact that **8.170** there was evidence to the effect that the estate itself had provided the basis for the arbitrators' incorrect assumption as to which party had drafted the contract through one of its submissions to the arbitrators. Thus, the challenging party itself had caused the situation that it now complained of.

However, the Supreme Court also addressed the question of whether an error of **8.171** procedure had been committed at all. The Supreme Court pointed out that it is 'an open question to what extent shortcomings of the arbitrators in its substantive case management may furnish grounds for vacating an award'. However, in the present case, it was clear, the Supreme Court went on, that the arbitrators' statement as to the draftsmanship of the second agreement was part of its evaluation of the evidence on the basis of the available material and accordingly went to the 'very consider-ation of the case'. When analysed in this way, the arbitrators' apparent decision that they had no reason to ascertain the draftsmanship by questioning the parties appeared justified. 'At any rate in these circumstances, what has happened cannot be said to amount to such an irregularity of procedure as is contemplated by sub-paragraph 4 of section 21 of the Arbitration Act [of 1929]'.

The Supreme Court, in other words, considered the actions of the arbitrators to be **8.172** part of the evaluation of evidence and, thus, part of the merits. The Court, accord-ingly, reaffirmed the principle that the arbitrators' decisions on the merits of the case cannot be reviewed by the courts. In an earlier ruling, *Gunnar Jansson v The Estate of Oscar Jansson* (NJA 1965 p 384),[178] the Supreme Court took into account

---

[178] The case is summarized in para 8.161.

that the arbitrators had not taken measures to invite a party to clarify the grounds for its claim to ensure that the case was adequately prepared before the arbitrators made their ruling. The failure by the arbitrators to clarify the facts on which the claim of one of the parties relied before issuing its ruling could be seen as a failure to conduct substantive case management. However , the failure by the arbitrators to conduct active substantive case management was not the only relevant consideration for the Supreme Court in this case. It also emphasized that the other party was not provided with the opportunity to comment on the facts relied onby the other party.

8.173 In a 2002 ruling from the Svea Court of Appeal, *NCC Aktiebolag v Dykab i Luleå Aktiebolag*,[179] tried under the 1929 Arbitration Act, the court found that the arbitrators had not erred in its case management.

8.174 Dykab, argued, *inter alia*, that the arbitrators had neglected to rule on a legal ground relied upon by Dykab, namely that Dykab's responsibility for any damages inflicted upon NCC was limited under the parties' contract to SEK 100,000. NCC argued that this defence was only mentioned in passing during Dykab's closing argument and that it constituted an amendment of Dykab's claim, which had not been previously made in the proceedings. The district court found that the arbitrators, first, ought to have asked Dykab to clarify its position, and whether it was ascertained that Dykab in fact had intended to rely upon the new defence in question, and, secondly, whether Dykab should be allowed to do so, and, if that was the case, thirdly, the arbitrators ought to have ruled on the merits of the new argument. The court found that the negligence of the arbitrators in this regard was a procedural irregularity which may probably be presumed to have influenced the outcome of the case. The district court therefore set aside the arbitral award.

8.175 One aspect that the Svea Court of Appeal took into account was the fact that the parties had been allowed to review the arbitrators' summary of the case (recitals) prior to the final hearing and that the position of Dykab had been set forth as late in the proceedings as during the closing arguments.[180] If Dykab did have the intention to amend its claim, it was up to Dykab clearly to express this intention. Dykab did not do so. The Svea Court of Appeal did not find that the arbitrators should have noted any ambiguitythat ought to have been addressed. The Svea Court of Appeal added that if any procedural irregularity had occurred, the fault rested with Dykab. Also for that reason, the Svea Court of Appeal found that the arbitral award ought not to be set aside and the district court's decision was therefore reversed.

---

[179] Svea Court of Appeal, judgment of 20 June 2002 in Case No T 3863-01.

[180] Regarding the importance of the tribunal's summary, see also *Systembolaget AB v V & S Vin & Sprit Aktiebolag*, Svea Court of Appeal, judgment of 1 December 2009 in Case No T 4548–08. The case is summarized in para 8.80.

Unlike the other grounds for challenge, the general *clause* requires that the irregu- **8.176** larity in question must have 'probably influenced the outcome of the case'. This requirement means that the court will assess whether the *arbitrators*, and not the court itself, would have decided the case differently had the irregularity not taken place.[181] This does not mean that the court is to speculate as to whether the arbitrators would have committed additional mistakes, but that the court accepts the view of the arbitrators on the substance of the case.[182]

The evidentiary requirement 'probably' presents a relatively low threshold for the **8.177** challenging party. However, the threshold was even lower under the 1929 Arbitration Act, according to which it sufficed that it could 'probably be presumed' that the outcome of the case had been affected by the procedural irregularity.[183] When the SAA was prepared, this language was deemed to be too vague and to give the impression that it was enough to show a noteworthy possibility of a different outcome in order to fulfil this requirement.[184] The new wording is, thus, meant to establish a requirement for a more tangible connection between the irregularity and the outcome of the case.[185]

The thoroughness in the application of the test of probable influence may vary. In **8.178** *Fylgia v Svea* (NJA 1937 p 120), which was decided under the old Arbitration Act of 1929, the challenging party did not manage to establish that the irregularity, concerning the method of assessing the damage, probably could be assumed to have affected the outcome.

In *TBB Tekniska Byggnadsbyrån v Kronan* (NJA 1973 p 740), also decided under **8.179** the old Arbitration Act of 1929, the Svea Court of Appeal undertook a rather extensive analysis of the reasoning of the arbitrators to find that the irregularity could probably not have been assumed to have affected the outcome. The contrary conclusion was reached by the Supreme Court in *Gunnar Jansson v The Estate of Oscar Jansson* (NJA 1965 p 384) (old Act), where it was held, without explanation, that the outcome could be assumed probably to have been affected, although reference was made to the value of the evidence that the challenging party was not able to present. Commentators have cited this case in support of the view that influence on the outcome of the case may be presumed where the irregularities are particularly serious.[186]

In two cases where awards were set aside because the subject matter was *res judicata*, **8.180** the Supreme Court did not apply the test at all, at least not explicitly. This was the case both in *Esselte AB v Allmänna Pensionsfonden* (NJA 1998 p 189) and in *AB*

---

[181] Heuman, *Arbitration Law of Sweden: Practice and Procedure* (2003) 624.
[182] Cf Lindskog, *Skiljeförfarande, En kommentar* (2005) 953–957.
[183] Section 21, item 4 of the 1929 Arbitration Act.
[184] Govt Bill 1998/99:35, p 148.
[185] Ibid.
[186] Heuman, *Arbitration Law of Sweden: Practice and Procedure* 625.

Skånska Cementgjuteriet v Motoraktiebolaget i Karlstad (NJA 1953 p 751), although it is uncertain whether the ruling in the latter case was based on the general clause or an excess of mandate.[187]

8.181   In both these cases the arbitrators had rendered awards in favour of the claimant in the second arbitration. The outcome would, thus, evidently have been different if the arbitrators had dismissed the disputes due to *res judicata* without any determination of the merits.

8.3.7.3 *The procedural irregularity must not have been caused by the fault of the challenging party*

8.182   As set out in the *travaux préparatoires*, a party ought not to be able to benefit from an error that it has caused itself.[188] Consequently, the general clause excludes irregularities caused by a party's own fault. A party's behaviour must thus have been negligent in relation to the procedural error and there must be a sufficiently causal connection. A party may, for example, be prevented from challenging a procedural irregularity which is a consequence of such party expressing itself ambiguously. If both parties have been negligent, the challenging party should be barred from having the award set aside only if his negligence was a *sine qua non* for the irregularity.

8.183   In *Shipping Partnership for M/S Red Sea v Götaverken Sölvesborg AB* (NJA 1990 p 419),[189] the arbitrators had interpreted the claimant's submissions as a withdrawal of the claim. The claimant, however, argued in the challenge proceedings that it had not withdrawn its claim. The claimant's submissions, which had been interpreted as a withdrawal of the claim, were contradictory, and the arbitrators had requested clarifications from the claimant. The Supreme Court held that the arbitrators were justified in their understanding, but went on to say that 'if the [claimant] intended anything else, the misunderstanding must be considered to have been caused by the [claimant] itself'. The reasoning of the Supreme Court suggests that the claimant's negligence alone would have sufficed to reject the challenge.[190]

8.4 Waiver of Right to Challenge

8.184   A party may waive its right to challenge an award. Such waiver may be an express declaration set out in an agreement between the parties. A party may also be deemed

---

[187]   See discussion in note 107.
[188]   Govt Bill 1998/99:35, p 148.
[189]   See para 8.140.
[190]   Cf Lindskog, *Skiljeförfarande, En kommentar* (2005) 950–953. Cf *NCC Aktiebolag v Dykab i Luleå Aktiebolag*, Svea Court of Appeal, judgment of 20 June 2002 in Case No T 3863-01, discussed in para 8.173.

to have implicitly waived, or rather forfeited, its right to challenge an award if it has failed to object to an error during the arbitral proceedings.

8.4.1 Implied waiver

Section 34(2) of the *SAA* sets out the rule regarding implicit waiver. While the **8.185** language has been changed from that used in the 1929 Arbitration Act, the new wording is not intended to change the law itself. Under this provision, a party is not entitled to rely on a circumstance which it may be deemed to have waived by taking part in the proceedings without any objection. The fact that a party has appointed an arbitrator, however, does not imply a waiver of the party's right to challenge the jurisdiction of the tribunal in question. This wording of section 34(2) was first introduced in the SAA, but merely codified already existing case law.

Any ground for the setting aside of an award may be waived by a party through **8.186** participation in the proceedings, eg if a valid arbitration agreement has not been in place but the party nevertheless participated in the proceedings. However, a party must have been aware of the circumstance in question to be deemed to have waived it.[191] The *travaux préparatoires* only refer to actual knowledge of the circumstance.[192] Whether or not the challenging party should also be deemed to have lost his right to challenge an award if he *should* have been aware of the circumstance in question is a contested issue. In *Återförsäkringsbolaget Patria v Trygg-Hansa Försäkringsaktiebolag* from 2001,[193] the Svea Court of Appeal declared that waiver only applies to circumstances known to the party, and not to circumstances that the party ought to have known of. However, the court also held that evidence of a party's knowledge does not have to relate directly to what the party knew. Rather, it suffices if it is possible to conclude on the basis of such evidence that a party must have had knowledge. The challenging party, Patria, had argued that one of the arbitrators, an attorney, was partial since he also acted as receiver in bankruptcy and counsel to a party in another arbitration where the facts of that case showed great similarities to the arbitration in question. The Svea Court of Appeal found that the circumstances were such that they diminished confidence in the arbitrator's impartiality. However, the court also concluded that during the course of the arbitral proceedings, Patria had sought and gained information concerning the other arbitration and that the only conclusion one could draw was that Patria must have known of the arbitrator's role in the other arbitration. Since Patria had failed to make an objection during the arbitral proceedings, its challenge was dismissed.

---

[191] Govt Bill 1998/99:35, p 149.

[192] See also the case *Altinel v Sudoimport* (RH 1991:15), where the Svea Court of Appeal found that circumstances diminishing confidence in the arbitrator's impartiality indeed existed but since the challenging party, with knowledge of these circumstances, had appointed the arbitrator and participated in the arbitral proceedings without objecting to his impartiality, the party was precluded from relying on these circumstances as grounds for challenging the award.

[193] Svea Court of Appeal, Case No 677–99.

8.4.2 Exclusion agreements

8.187 The possibility for parties, under certain conditions, to agree to exclude the possibility to challenge the award (exclusion agreements) is based on the reasoning of the Supreme Court in the so-called *Uganda* case.[194] In this case, which was decided under the 1929 Arbitration Act, the respondent in the challenge proceedings, *inter alia*, argued that the challenge should be dismissed, because Article 29 in the ICC Arbitration Rules (1955) must be interpreted such that the parties had agreed not to challenge the arbitral award.

8.188 The Supreme Court held that it must be considered possible for parties without any connection to Sweden to agree beforehand to limit the possibilities to challenge an award. This was the first time the Supreme Court had recognized that it could be possible, under certain conditions, to exclude or limit the possibilities of challenging an arbitral award issued in Sweden. The Court found, however, that the respondent in the challenge proceedings had not demonstrated that the parties, by referring to the 1955 ICC Arbitration Rules in the arbitration clause, had agreed to exclude the possibility of challenging the award.[195] The Supreme Court did not further clarify, however, what would be required for an agreement to exclude or limit the possibility of challenging the award. Nor did the Supreme Court clarify whether it would be possible to exclude all grounds for setting aside or invalidity of the award, or just certain grounds.

8.189 Building on the general principle established in the *Uganda* case, the rationale underlying section 51 of the SAA is further to clarify the extent to which such exclusion agreements validly may be entered into under the SAA.[196]

8.190 Section 51 of the SAA provides that two non-Swedish parties may enter into an exclusion agreement, by which they waive in advance the right under section 34 of the SAA to challenge the arbitral award. This presupposes, however, that the parties in question are commercial parties and that the relationship between them is of a commercial nature. Consequently, section 51 of the SAA stipulates that if neither of the parties in a commercial relationship has its domicile or place of business in Sweden, the parties may, by agreement in writing, exclude or limit the applicability of the grounds for setting aside awards which are listed in section 34 of the SAA. It is important to note that the exclusion agreement must be in *writing* and that it must *specifically* refer to the parties' waiver of the right to challenge an award pursuant to section 34 of the SAA. This means that a standard reference to institutional

---

[194] *Republic of Uganda and National Housing and Construction Corporation of Uganda v Solel Boneh International Ltd and Water Resources Development (International) Ltd*, judgment of the Supreme Court, 18 April 1989 (NJA 1989 s 143). For a discussion of this case, see Hobér, *Ogiltighet och klander i internationella skiljeförfaranden* in *1989 Yearbook of the Arbitratiion Institute of the Stockholm Chamber of Commerce* (1989), 9.

[195] *Republic of Uganda and National Housing and Construction Corporation of Uganda v Solel Boneh International Ltd and Water Resources Development (International) Ltd*, judgment of the Supreme Court, 18 April 1989, (NJA 1989 s 143) p 154.

[196] Govt Bill 1998/99:35, p 156.

rules, for example the ICC Rules, or the SCC Rules which contain wording similar to an exclusion agreement, does not constitute an exclusion agreement under section 51. The parties must explicitly state that they waive their rights pursuant to section 34 of the SAA.

Section 51 of the SAA also implies that it is not possible to waive the invalidity **8.191** grounds set out in section 33 of the SAA. Invalidity is beyond the control of the parties; it is beyond party autonomy. Since the invalidity grounds have been formulated with a view to safeguarding the interest of the general public and/or of third parties, it is only logical that parties cannot waive such grounds.

In accepting exclusion agreements, which seem to be rare in practice, the Swedish **8.192** legislature was acting on the assumption that an award, with respect to which an exclusion agreement has been concluded, could still be scrutinized at the place of enforcement. In other words, it was assumed that an arbitral award, despite the waiver of the right to challenge such award at the seat of arbitration, could still be subject to judicial control at the place of enforcement. Since enforcement of Swedish awards in Sweden is not subject to any court review,[197] to the extent that an award, which is covered by an exclusion agreement is to be enforced in Sweden, section 51 of the SAA sets out that such an award shall for enforcement purposes be considered as a foreign award, and, thus, be recognized and enforced in Sweden on the basis of the requirements and conditions stipulated for foreign arbitral awards.[198] It will in other words be possible for the respondent in enforcement proceedings to object to enforcement of such an award by invoking any of the grounds enumerated in sections 53 to 60 of the SAA. These are the same grounds as those set out in Article V of the New York Convention.[199]

8.5 Remission of Arbitral Awards

Section 35 of the SAA grants the courts of appeal the power, at the request of a party, **8.193** to stay the proceedings for invalidity or setting aside to provide the arbitrators with an opportunity to resume the arbitral proceedings or to take such other action that, in the arbitral tribunal's opinion, will eliminate the grounds for the invalidity or setting aside. The court may stay the proceedings if either (i) the court has found that the action is substantiated, ie that the award is to be set aside, and that either of the parties has requested a stay, or (ii) both parties have requested such a stay.

If only one of the parties requests remission of the case, the court can thus only **8.194** grant the request if it finds that the action to challenge the award is substantiated. In practice, this means that the court in many cases would have to hear all

---

[197] See para 9.02.
[198] See para 9.07.
[199] See para 9.09.

arguments of the parties, including holding the final hearing, before it could decide whether the challenge is substantiated. However, in some cases it may be obvious from the outset that the action is substantiated. The court may then grant a request to remit the award without holding a main hearing. According to the *travaux préparatoires*, it is for the court to determine whether or not a request should be granted without first hearing the arbitrators.[200]

8.195   If both parties request remission the court is not required first to determine whether the challenge is substantiated, but even in this case, it is still within the court's discretion to grant the request.[201] A decision by the court to remit the award to the arbitrators is not subject to appeal.[202]

8.196   Section 35 of the SAA, which is modelled on and inspired by Article 34(4) of the UNCITRAL Model Law, has been introduced to promote efficiency and finality of arbitral proceedings. The purpose of the provision is to give the arbitrators the opportunity to remedy procedural defects, which otherwise could have led to the setting aside of the award, or the award being declared invalid. This would save time and money, since the parties, if the award were set aside, would have to commence new arbitral proceedings.

8.197   A typical example when remission is appropriate might be when one of the arbitrators' signatures on the award is missing. An amendment of the award thus presupposes that the procedural defect is of such nature that it is possible to remedy. If, for example, one of the arbitrators was not impartial, it will be of little use to remit the case to a tribunal of which the arbitrator is a member.

8.198   If the procedural defect is such that it could be remedied, the arbitrators would be expected to take such remedial action. This presupposes, however, that the arbitrators are willing to do so. It is not clear whether the arbitrators have a duty to participate in new arbitral proceedings, the sole objective of which would be to remedy procedural defects. It should be noted in this context that section 27(2) of the SAA stipulates that the arbitrators shall be deemed to have completed their mandate when they have rendered a final award, unless otherwise provided in sections 32 and 35 of the SAA. The mandate—but perhaps not the obligation—of the arbitrators thus covers remission hearings as well as corrections and interpretations of the award pursuant to section 32 of the SAA.

8.199   Section 35 of the SAA may be seen as a deviation from the principle that the arbitrators lack jurisdiction to take measures with respect to the dispute once the award has been rendered.[203] There are no formal constraints as to what measures are

---

[200]   Govt Bill 1998/99:35, p 237.

[201]   Govt Bill 1998/99:35, pp 153 and 237; cf Lindskog, *Skiljeförfarande, En kommentar* (2005) 1000, footnote 14.

[202]   Govt Bill 1998/99:35, p 237.

[203]   See para 3.168 *et seq* and para 7.96 *et seq*.

allowed to be taken to remedy the defects of the arbitral award. Even though the provision thus gives the arbitrators substantial authority, it obviously does not grant the arbitrators jurisdiction to go back and review the award on the merits. The types of defects that may be remedied are defects that concern formal requirements with respect to the award and procedural defects. For example, an award which includes a determination of issues that are outside the mandate of the arbitral tribunal should not be remitted to the arbitrators, since the only way to remedy such defect would be to reduce the substantive scope of the award.[204] Such remedy is just as readily available to the court itself by setting aside the parts of the award that are exceeding the mandate of the arbitral tribunal.

There is a possibility that a remission of the dispute to the arbitrators could lead to **8.200** further review of the merits of the case. For example, if the procedural defect in question is that one of the parties was not allowed to hear a witness, and that witness is heard once the arbitration has been remitted, the arbitrators must assess the impact of that witness's testimony for the evaluation of the evidence that was available when the arbitral award was first rendered.

As follows from the second paragraph of section 35 of the SAA, if the arbitrators do **8.201** render a new award, the party may within such period of time as is determined by the court, and without filing a new action, challenge the new award insofar as such challenge relates to the remitted arbitration proceeding, or to amendments made to the first award. The respondent in the first challenge proceedings may, however, still invoke irregularities that relate to the original arbitral award. The respondent may wish to do so in a situation where he, for example, was not allowed an oral hearing, but with regard to the outcome of the dispute he found no reason to challenge the award. If the award is later amended to his detriment, he ought still to have an opportunity to challenge the award, even if the grounds relate to the original arbitral proceedings.[205]

Remission of the dispute to the arbitrators should in most cases result in a new **8.202** arbitral award, since even if the arbitrators do not change the outcome of the dispute, the renewed arbitral proceedings will most likely result in additional costs for the parties and for the arbitrators.[206] If the measures taken by the arbitrators to remedy the defect cause the challenging party to withdraw its action, the court will write off the case. If the challenge is not withdrawn, the court will have to try the case. The court will then review the arbitral award as it stands after the arbitrators' amendments, if any. If the court had decided to remit the case after having held the final hearing in the challenge case, and the challenge is not withdrawn after the dispute had been remitted to the arbitrators, the court may continue at the point where the case was stayed when it was remitted to the arbitrators.[207]

---

[204] Lindskog, *Skiljeförfarande, En kommentar* (2005) 1002.
[205] Govt Bill 1998/99:35.
[206] Govt Bill 1998/99:35, p 237.
[207] Madsen, *Commercial Arbitration in Sweden* (3rd ed 2007) 298.

8.203 A remission to the arbitrators might be problematic in cases where the parties have agreed on a time limit for the rendering of the arbitral award. According to the *travaux préparatoires*, however, the court ought to be able to give the arbitrators the possibility to remedy the award as long as the original award was rendered within the time limit.[208] However, the court should still make an independent assessment, taking into consideration the purpose and the length of the original time limit agreed upon by the parties and the time that could be expected to remedy the award.

8.204 Even though it is possible to foresee a number of procedural complications in the application of section 35 of the SAA, one must always keep the alternative in mind, ie the setting aside of the award, or having it declared invalid. Section 35 of the SAA means that it may be possible to prevent such dramatic consequences in situations where a procedural defect can be remedied by arbitrators. So far section 35 of the SAA seems to have played a very limited role in practice. No court of law has yet been called upon to apply it.

8.6 Review of Jurisdictional Awards

8.6.1 Introduction

8.205 Section 36 of the SAA provides for the possibility to challenge awards by which the arbitrators have concluded the proceedings without ruling on the issues submitted to them for resolution. Section 36 of the SAA must be understood in relation to section 27 of the SAA. As discussed above,[209] section 27(1) of the SAA provides that where the arbitrators terminate the arbitral proceedings in their entirety without a ruling on the merits, such termination of the proceedings shall be done in the form of an award. Thus, if, for example, the tribunal dismisses the claim in its entirety because the tribunal finds that there is no valid or applicable arbitration agreement, such dismissal must be in the form of an award.

8.206 If none of the parties challenges such an award within three months under section 36 of the SAA, the award will become final and binding. Thus, if the arbitral tribunal, for instance, has dismissed a case for want of jurisdiction, because the arbitration agreement was invalid, or because the arbitral tribunal found that the substantive issue referred to them for resolution was not covered by an otherwise valid arbitration agreement, a party cannot later try to commence new arbitral proceedings with the hope that another tribunal will view the jurisdictional issues differently. If such party did not successfully challenge the jurisdictional ruling pursuant to section 36 of the SAA, a subsequent arbitral tribunal or court must accept the

---

[208] Govt Bill 1998/99:35, p 237.
[209] See para 7.22 *et seq.*

ruling of the first tribunal as a final and binding determination of the validity or scope of the arbitration agreement. Such question is *res judicata*.

Conversely, if a party appeals the jurisdictional ruling of the arbitral tribunal under **8.207** section 36 of the SAA, the relevant court of appeal has the power to revise and change the ruling of the arbitrators, if it finds that the arbitral tribunal was wrong in finding that the arbitration agreement was invalid or inapplicable to the dispute. Such a judgment of the court will constitute a binding determination that the arbitration agreement is valid and applicable to the dispute in question. A subsequent arbitral tribunal seized with the same dispute may, consequently, not reach a contradictory ruling with regard to its own jurisdiction, should the respondent in the new proceedings repeat its previous objections to the jurisdiction of the tribunal.

Section 36 of the SAA also provides that an arbitral award which terminates the **8.208** proceedings without having ruled on the merits must include clear instructions as to what must be done by a party who wishes to challenge the award.

8.6.2 Scope of application

As indicated above, jurisdictional rulings are, from a practical point of view, the **8.209** most important form of rulings that come within the scope of section 36 of the SAA. Section 36, however, applies to all awards that terminate the proceedings without ruling on the merits. Section 36 of the SAA, therefore, also applies where the arbitrators terminate the proceedings, for example, because they find that the issues submitted to them are not arbitrable.

Other examples of awards whereby the arbitration is terminated without a ruling **8.210** on the merits include situations when the arbitrators have *written off* the case, because the claimant has withdrawn his claim, or because the time limit for rendering the award has expired, or because the requested security for the arbitrators' fees has not been provided. If a party considers that the arbitrators wrongly interpreted a statement as a withdrawal of a request for arbitration, the party might thus bring an action under section 36 of the SAA.[210] Section 36 of the SAA does not apply, however, if the arbitrators dismiss part of a claim during the proceedings. Such a decision may only be attacked by challenging the final award.[211]

---

[210] As regards *Jansson v Retrotype AB* (NJA 1975 p 536) and *Shipping Partnership for M/S Red Sea v Götaverken Sölvesborg AB* (NJA 1990 p 419), described in para 8.135, those cases were determined under the Arbitration Act of 1929 which did not have a corresponding provision.

[211] Govt Bill 1998/99:35, p 238.

8.6.3 Scope of the review

8.211 As part of the procedure under section 36 of the SAA the court may review the substantive basis for the decision to terminate the arbitration, as well as the arbitrators' handling of the termination of the proceedings.[212] The court will of course not determine the dispute with respect to the substance, but it will review the merits of the jurisdictional issue (or other procedural issue) that caused the proceedings to be terminated. In that respect the court will hold a *de novo* trial. Should the court find that the arbitrators were wrong in finding that they did not have jurisdiction (or otherwise erred in terminating the proceedings without ruling on the merits), the court will change the decision of the arbitrators. As far as the arbitrators' decision to terminate the proceedings is concerned, this can only be done by setting aside the arbitral award.[213] According to the *travaux préparatoires*, the arbitration proceedings shall not resume if the arbitral award is set aside.[214] A party that still wishes to resolve the dispute must thus request arbitration anew.

8.212 If the Court of Appeal sets aside the award under section 36 of the SAA, the court may also change the arbitral award's *allocation* of the arbitration costs. An action concerning the *reasonableness* of the arbitrators' fees, however, is not governed by this provision. Such an action is brought in the District Court pursuant to Article 41 of the SAA.[215]

8.213 It should also be noted that section 36(2) of the SAA, under certain circumstances, permits a party to challenge only the allocation of the arbitration costs as between the parties, even if such party does not challenge the remainder of the award. This right, however, is limited to the situation where the arbitrators have ruled that they *lack jurisdiction* to determine the dispute. The Court of Appeal is in this situation authorized to review whether the arbitral tribunals' allocation of the arbitration costs was reasonable. This might be the case, for instance, where one of the parties, most likely the respondent, is satisfied with the dismissal of the dispute but unhappy with the arbitrators' decision on the allocation of costs.

8.214 Such an action for review of the cost allocation may not be brought, however, where the arbitration was terminated without a ruling on the merits for other reasons than want of jurisdiction, such as where the arbitration was written off due to the claimant's withdrawal of its claim. The allocation of costs in such a situation may only be challenged and set aside due to procedural errors in accordance with section 34.[216] The reason behind this distinction between situations where the case has been dismissed for want of jurisdiction and other situations where the proceedings

---

[212] Govt Bill 1998/99:35, p 155.
[213] Govt Bill 1998/99:35, p 238.
[214] Govt Bill 1998/99:35, p 231.
[215] See para 4.119.
[216] Govt Bill 1998/99: 35 p 155.

have been terminated without a ruling on the merits is that, as a matter of principle, the arbitrators lack jurisdiction to rule on the issue of allocation of costs and other substantive issues in cases where they have found that there is no valid arbitration agreement. It therefore seems reasonable to allow a court of law to review such allocation.[217] The same does not apply where the proceedings were terminated for other reasons, since, in such situations, a valid arbitration agreement authorizing the arbitrators to rule on the allocation of costs does exist. It is then reasonable to limit the remedies against such cost allocation to those available under sections 33 and 34 of the SAA.

8.6.4 Application of section 36 of the SAA in practice

Section 36 of the SAA should probably be characterized as a Swedish peculiarity. **8.215** This is true, at least in the sense that there is no similar provision in the UNCITRAL Model Law. It is, however, a very arbitration-friendly peculiarity. The possibility of attacking negative jurisdictional rulings is particularly important in international arbitration, where the disputed arbitration forum is often the only forum available to the claimant. Frequently, in these cases, arbitration at a neutral seat is chosen to remove the case from the home jurisdictions of the parties. If, in such a situation, there were to be no remedy available against a negative ruling on jurisdiction at the seat of arbitration, the claimant would often have no other choice than to abandon its claim, since litigation in the respondent's home jurisdiction would typically not be a realistic option. It is therefore not surprising that foreign parties have relatively often challenged negative jurisdictional rulings under section 36 of the SAA. Some of these cases are briefly addressed below.[218] In *Archangelskoe Geologodobychnoe Predpriyatie v Archangel Diamond Corporation*,[219] the Svea Court of Appeal upheld the District Court's decision to set aside the arbitrators' award. The case was tried under the 1929 Arbitration Act, and thus decided by the district court, as opposed to the court of appeal, as the court of first instance. The case is nevertheless interesting, since it is a typical example of a case where the claimant would have been left with no recourse against the respondent had the Swedish courts not set aside the arbitrators' negative jurisdictional ruling.

In this case, the arbitrators applied Russian law in their determination of jurisdic- **8.216** tion and found that they lacked jurisdiction, since the subject matter of the dispute was not arbitrable under Russian law. The claimant, Archangel Diamond Corporation, requested that the arbitral award be set aside. The Court of Appeal concluded that the validity of the arbitration agreement should be determined in

---

[217] Olsson and Kvart, *Lagen om skiljeförfarandeen kommentar* (2000) 157; cf Lindskog, *Skiljeförfarande, En kommentar* (2005) 1019, footnote 24.

[218] Appendix 8 sets forth a list of all cases tried under Section 36 of the SAA and which have become final and binding as per 1 November 2010.

[219] Svea Court of Appeal, judgment of 15 November 2005 in Case No T 2277-04.

accordance with Swedish law, since the place of arbitration was in Stockholm.[220] According to the Court of Appeal, the question of whether the dispute was arbitrable or not should also be determined under the same law as the validity of the arbitration agreement, since such a question has a closer connection to the law governing the arbitration agreement than the law governing the substance of the contract. The fact that the dispute might not be arbitrable under Russian law did not alter this view. The Court of Appeal concluded that there was a valid arbitration agreement under Swedish law and consequently that the issue was arbitrable under Swedish law.

8.217 Some of the cases that have been determined under section 36 of the SAA have been investment arbitration cases. If a tribunal in an investment arbitration case finds that it does not have jurisdiction, that is normally the end of the matter. Without a remedy under the investment protection treaty, or under the applicable foreign investment law, the foreign investor almost invariably has nowhere else to bring its claim.

8.218 One such example is *Nagel v Czech Republic*.[221] The UK-based investor, Mr Nagel, had initiated arbitration proceedings against the Czech Republic alleging that he had been the victim of expropriation as well as discriminatory treatment. The basis for the dispute was that Mr Nagel accused the Czech authorities of failing to honour a commitment to award him a GSM mobile phone licence. The claim was brought under the bilateral investment protection treaty between the UK and the Czech Republic. The proceedings were conducted under the auspices of the Arbitration Institute of the Stockholm Chamber of Commerce.

8.219 The arbitral tribunal dismissed all of Mr Nagel's claims, because it found that Mr Nagel's alleged investment did not qualify as an 'investment' under the UK-Czech bilateral investment treaty. In making this determination the arbitral tribunal stated that the determination as to whether the claimant qualified as an 'investor' that had made an 'investment' under the treaty was an issue concerned with the merits of the case and not a preliminary issue of jurisdiction.

8.220 The tribunal also found that some of Mr Nagel's claims in the arbitration were based on provisions of the treaty which were not covered by the arbitration clause in the treaty.

8.221 Mr Nagel challenged the award before the Svea Court of Appeal. In his application to the Court, Mr Nagel argued, with reference to section 36 of the Swedish Arbitration Act, that the court should change the jurisdictional determination made by the tribunal and confirm that his rights qualified as an 'investment' under

---

[220] The Svea Court of Appeal in this regard also referred to the Supreme Court's assessment in *Bulgarian Foreign Trade Bank v Giro Credit Bank Aktiengesselschaft der Sparkassen* (NJA 2000 p 538). See para 2.201.

[221] Svea Court of Appeal, decision of 30 May 2005 in Case No T 9059-03.

the treaty, and that he therefore was entitled to have his claims determined on the merits by the arbitral tribunal.

The court, however, found that it was clear from the circumstances of the case that **8.222** the arbitral tribunal, when concluding that Mr Nagel's rights did not qualify as an 'investment' under the treaty, had made a final determination of the substance of the claim. To reach this conclusion the court merely referred to the statement made by the arbitral tribunal that the question whether the investor's rights qualified as an 'investment' under the treaty was a matter of substance rather than a matter of jurisdiction.[222] The court did not discuss whether the arbitral tribunal was correct in such a conclusion, nor did it review whether the arbitral tribunal had been correct in concluding that Mr Nagel's rights did not qualify as an 'investment' under the treaty. Since the court found that the dispute had been resolved on the merits, section 36 of the Act was not considered applicable.

Another—but this time successful—challenge of a negative jurisdictional ruling in **8.223** an investment arbitration is *Petrobart Limited v Kyrgyz Republic*. Petrobart entered into a contract with the Kyrgyz State-owned joint stock company KGM regarding the supply of gas condensate. Petrobart delivered five shipments of gas but was only paid for the first two. At the same time as Petrobart turned to domestic courts for recourse, Kyrgyz authorities—as part of a reform of the system for the supply of oil and gas in the Kyrgyz Republic—took certain measures that made it impossible for Petrobart to enforce its rights under the contract. Petrobart then initiated arbitral proceedings against the Kyrgyz Republic under the Law on Foreign Investments of the Kyrgyz Republic.

The arbitral tribunal, however, dismissed Petrobart's claim for want of jurisdiction. **8.224** According to the tribunal, Petrobart had not made an investment in the Kyrgyz Republic that qualified as an 'investment' as defined in the Foreign Investment Law which was the basis, and indeed the only basis, for the claim.[223]

Petrobart challenged the arbitral award before the Svea Court of Appeal **8.225** in Stockholm in accordance with section 36 of the SAA.[224] Parallel to the challenge proceedings, Petrobart commenced new arbitral proceedings under the Energy Chapter Treaty.[225]

In the challenge proceedings, Petrobart claimed that the arbitral tribunal had been **8.226** wrong in finding that it lacked jurisdiction.

---

[222] *Nagel v Czech Republic*, note 222 at p 6.

[223] See further Hobér and Eliasson, 'Review of Investment Treaty Awards by Municipal Courts', in Katia Yannaca-Small (ed) *Arbitration under International Investment Agreements* (2010) 651 *et seq.*

[224] *Petrobart Limited v Kyrgyz Republic*, judgment of the Svea Court of Appeal 13 April 2006, Case No T 3739-03. This case went all the way to the Supreme Court and is reported as NJA 2008 p 406. See para 3.33 *et seq* for a discussion of the case.

[225] See further Hobér and Eliasson, 'Review of Investment Treaty Awards by Municipal Courts', in Katia Tannaca-Small (ed) *Arbitration under International Investment Agreements* (2010)653 *et seq.*

8.227   The Court of Appeal agreed with the arbitral tribunal that the question of whether Petrobart had made an 'investment' in accordance with the Foreign Investment Law was a matter of jurisdiction. It also found that, in order for the tribunal to have jurisdiction, it had to be established that the investor actually had made an 'investment' in accordance with the Foreign Investment Law.

8.228   Petrobart appealed the decision of the Court of Appeal to the Supreme Court. Unlike the Court of Appeal, the Supreme Court found that the arbitral tribunal had been wrong in finding that it did not have jurisdiction.[226] The Supreme Court held that when deciding on its jurisdiction the arbitral tribunal should have assumed that the circumstances referred to by the claimant were correct. If this had been done, the arbitral tribunal would—in the opinion of the Supreme Court—have found that it had jurisdiction.[227]

---

[226] *Petrobart Limited v Kyrgyz Republic*, judgment of the Supreme Court of 28 March 2008, (NJA 2008 p 406).

[227] *Petrobart Limited v Kyrgyz Republic*, judgment of the Supreme Court, (NJA 2008 p 406) pp 411 *et seq.*

9

RECOGNITION AND ENFORCEMENT
OF ARBITRAL AWARDS

9.1 Enforcement of Swedish Awards	9.02		9.2.5.2 Violation of procedural due process	9.26
9.1.1 Enforcement in Sweden	9.02		9.2.5.3 Excess of mandate	9.31
9.1.2 Enforcement abroad	9.06		9.2.5.4 Improper composition of the arbitral tribunal or improper arbitral procedure	9.34
9.2 Enforcement of Foreign Awards	9.07			
9.2.1 Nationality of award	9.08			
9.2.2 Recognition and enforcement	9.09			
9.2.3 The New York Convention v the Swedish Arbitration Act	9.11		9.2.5.5 Arbitral award not binding	9.38
9.2.4 Separate, partial, and interim awards	9.14		9.2.5.6 Non-arbitrability	9.52
9.2.5 Grounds for refusing recognition and enforcement	9.17		9.2.5.7 Public policy	9.53
9.2.5.1 Lack of capacity of the parties and invalidity of arbitration agreement	9.23		9.2.6 Procedures for recognition	9.64

The SAA has, as far as recognition and enforcement are concerned, retained the **9.01** distinction between foreign and Swedish arbitral awards. Recognition and enforcement of foreign awards are dealt with in sections 52–60 of the Swedish Arbitration Act (SAA), whereas enforcement of Swedish awards, ie awards rendered in Sweden, is governed by the Swedish Enforcement Code. This is different from the UNCITRAL Model Law, which deals with all awards rendered in international commercial arbitration in a uniform manner irrespective of where they were made.[1]

---

[1] See eg Sekolec and Eliasson, 'The UNCITRAL Model Law and the Swedish Arbitration Act', in Heuman and Jarvin (eds), *Swedish Arbitration Act of 1999—Five Years On* (2006) 242–245.

9.1 Enforcement of Swedish Awards

9.1.1 Enforcement in Sweden

9.02 The SAA does not have any provisions on recognition and enforcement in Sweden of arbitral awards issued in Sweden. Under the Enforcement Code, Swedish arbitral awards are automatically recognized in Sweden and may be enforced in Sweden based on an application for execution directly to the Swedish Enforcement Authority. Thus, there is no requirement to obtain a declaration of enforceability from a court, or the Enforcement Authority, before applying for actual execution. Unlike Swedish court judgments, however, Swedish arbitral awards are not immediately enforceable, since the Enforcement Authority must make a summary check of the award prior to execution thereof.

9.03 Pursuant to Chapter 3, section 15 of the Enforcement Code, the Enforcement Authority may refuse execution only where (i) the arbitral award does not meet the requirements of written form and signature under section 31(1) of the SAA, or (ii) the arbitration agreement foresees a right to challenge the award on the merits and the time for such challenge has not yet expired.[2]

9.04 Moreover, if the Enforcement Authority believes that the award may be invalid on the grounds that the award decides issues that are not arbitrable under Swedish law, or the award, or the manner in which the award arose, is incompatible with Swedish public policy (*ordre public*), the Enforcement Authority shall direct the party seeking enforcement to initiate, within one month, court proceedings regarding the validity of the award, provided that the respondent has not already initiated proceedings to have the award declared invalid on the same ground (Chapter 3, section 16 of the Enforcement Code). After court proceedings have been initiated it is for the court to decide on the enforcement. If the party does not initiate court proceedings within the time prescribed, the enforcement proceedings shall be cancelled (Chapter 3, section 18(2) of the Enforcement Code).

9.05 It must be noted that the respondent in the enforcement proceedings before the Enforcement Authority cannot prevent enforcement by invoking the grounds for setting aside an award in section 34 of the SAA. These grounds can only be determined in court within the framework of an application for setting aside the award and cannot be addressed in enforcement proceedings.

9.1.2 Enforcement abroad

9.06 Enforcing Swedish arbitral awards abroad is a matter entirely for the laws of the enforcing State. Since Sweden has ratified the New York Convention without any

---

[2] The decision of the Enforcement Authority to enforce, or not to enforce, an award can be appealed in court: Chapter 18, section 2 of the Enforcement Code.

reservation, reciprocity requirements—which are available to members of the New York Convention—should as a rule not bar Swedish awards from being enforced abroad. In addition, if the award is rendered in Sweden the arbitration agreement would generally be regarded as a Swedish arbitration agreement and would be governed by Swedish law. Since Sweden has generous rules regarding the validity of arbitration agreements, an arbitral award rendered on the basis of such an agreement will rarely be refused enforcement by reason of invalidity of the agreement.[3]

9.2 Enforcement of Foreign Awards

As mentioned above, the SAA has retained the distinction between foreign and Swedish arbitral awards. The provisions governing the recognition and enforcement of foreign awards are found in sections 52–60 of the SAA. The grounds in the SAA for refusing recognition and enforcement of foreign arbitral awards (sections 54 and 55) correspond to the New York Convention. It should be noted that Sweden has ratified the New York Convention without exercising the reciprocity reservation or commercial nature reservation. The SAA consequently applies without distinction to any foreign arbitral award.

9.07

9.2.1 Nationality of award

Section 52 of the SAA provides that an arbitral award which has been rendered abroad shall be deemed to be a 'foreign' award and that in applying the SAA an award shall be deemed to have been made in the State where the arbitration took place. Accordingly, under Swedish law a territorial test is applied, which means that all awards rendered in a country other than Sweden are deemed to be foreign and thus enforceable under the New York Convention and the corresponding Swedish legislation, ie sections 53–59 of the SAA.[4]

9.08

9.2.2 Recognition and enforcement

Sections 53–59 of the SAA incorporate the relevant provisions of the New York Convention. Section 53 of the SAA provides that 'unless otherwise stated in sections 54–60, a foreign award which is based on an arbitration agreement shall be recognised and enforced in Sweden'. The circumstances under which a foreign arbitral award will be refused recognition and enforcement are set out in sections 54 and 55

9.09

---

[3] See para 3.04 for a discussion of the validity of arbitration agreements under Swedish law.

[4] As discussed above in para 2.09 *et seq* it has been suggested that some arbitral awards are to be characterized as 'a-national' or 'floating', in the sense that they are detached from all national arbitration laws. This raises the question whether such an 'a-national' award would be enforceable in Sweden. Under Swedish law a territorial test applies with respect to the nationality of an arbitral award. Put differently: every arbitral award that is not rendered in Sweden is a foreign award and therefore enforceable as such according to sections 53–59 of the SAA.

of the SAA. These circumstances refer to form, procedure, and public policy, but not to questions related to the substance of the case.[5]

9.10 The fact that an award is recognized in Sweden has two important consequences for the award: firstly it constitutes *res judicata* and secondly it may be enforced in Sweden (unless it is of a purely declaratory character).

9.2.3 The New York Convention v the Swedish Arbitration Act

9.11 Sweden ratified the New York Convention in 1972 without either the 'reciprocity' reservation or the 'commercial nature' reservation available to the signatories. Accordingly, foreign arbitral awards, wherever rendered and whether of a commercial character or not, are enforceable in Sweden pursuant to the New York Convention. The provisions of the New York Convention have been incorporated into the SAA. Prior to the enactment of the SAA in 1999, rules on recognition and enforcement of foreign arbitral awards were laid down in a special statute, the 1929 Act on Foreign Arbitration Agreements and Arbitral Awards. Since the 1929 Act also was based on Article V of the New York Convention, case law under the 1929 Act may be relevant also under the SAA.

9.12 Since the New York Convention is not incorporated by reference, but transformed into Swedish law through specific statutory provisions, it should be noted that the implementation of Article V of the New York Convention in the Swedish Arbitration Acts demonstrates slight variations from the wording of the New York Convention.[6]

---

[5] Appendix 9 sets forth a list of all enforcement matters handled by Swedish courts since Sweden's ratification of the New York Convention in 1971.

[6] The UNCITRAL has initiated different projects to facilitate enforcement of arbitral awards and to promote uniform application of the New York Convention in all member States.

For instance, at its twenty-eighth session (Vienna, 2–26 May 1995), the Commission decided to undertake a survey with the aim of monitoring the implementation in national laws of the New York Convention and of considering the procedural mechanisms that various States have put in place to make the Convention operative. The Secretariat of UNCITRAL, in cooperation with the Arbitration Committee of the International Bar Association, prepared a questionnaire circulated to States parties to the Convention. The information on the procedural framework in which the Convention operates would enable the Commission to consider any further action it might take to improve the functioning of the Convention and would contribute to increasing awareness of its application. A synthesis in respect of the survey was presented by the Secretariat of UNCITRAL at the forty-first session (New York, 16 June–3 July 2008) of the Commission covering implementation of the New York Convention by States, its interpretation and application, based on replies received from 108 States parties to the New York Convention. (Report on the survey relating to the legislative implementation of the Convention on the Recognition and Enforcement of Foreign Arbitral Awards (New York, 1958), A/CN.9/656 and A/CN.9/656/Add.1.)

Another effort by UNCITRAL to assist in the dissemination of information on the Model Law, as well as the New York Convention, and further promote their uniform interpretation is the creation of an analytic digest of court and arbitral decisions interpreting and applying the various provisions of the Model Law and the New York Convention. Such digests are also intended to help judges, arbitrators, practitioners, academics and government officials use the case law relating to UNCITRAL texts more efficiently. The digest is in preparation.

For example, the provisions on procedural due process in section 54 of the Act may appear stricter than the original version in the New York Convention, as under the Swedish Act recognition and enforcement 'shall' be refused where procedural errors have occurred, as opposed to the Convention's use of 'may' in Article V(1). However, given the pragmatic approach of Swedish courts in relation to arbitration matters, it appears unlikely that enforcement would be refused unless it is sufficiently clear that the procedural error has influenced the outcome of the case.[7] Accordingly, it is safe to assume that parties relying on the rules of Article V for recognition and enforcement of an arbitral award in Sweden can expect the courts to apply foreseeable and internationally established principles on procedural due process, arbitrability, and public policy.

Thus, the generally arbitration-friendly approach of Swedish courts applies also in **9.13** enforcement matters. When requested to decide on the recognition and enforcement of foreign arbitral awards, the Swedish Supreme Court has always stressed the importance of respecting the object and purpose of the New York Convention, and to ensure conformity between the New York Convention and the 1929 Act and/or the SAA. In *Götaverken Arendal AB (Sweden) v General National Maritime Transport Company (Libya)* (NJA 1979 p 527), the Supreme Court referred to 'the overall objective of the New York Convention to facilitate enforcement', and emphasized that certain differences in the wording of one of the provisions of the 1929 Act relied on by the respondent in that case and the corresponding provision of the New York Convention were not intended to produce any substantive difference between the two instruments.[8] Moreover, in *Société Planavergne SA v KB i Stockholm AB* (NJA 2003 p 379),[9] the Supreme Court stated that the Swedish provisions on enforcement of foreign arbitral awards should be interpreted in light of 'the general efforts to facilitate enforcement which [is] the main objective of the [New York] Convention'.

9.2.4 Separate, partial, and interim awards

Sometimes a specific part of the dispute or a certain issue in the dispute is decided **9.14** separately in a *separate* or *partial* award.[10] To the extent that such separate or partial

---

[7] Heuman, *Arbitration Law of Sweden: Practice and Procedure* (2003) 729. This position is also manifested in section 34 of the Act, according to which an award may be set aside if an irregularity has occurred in the course of the proceedings which has 'influenced the outcome of the case'.

[8] *Götaverken Arendal AB (Sweden) v General National Maritime Transport Company (Libya)*, Decision of the Supreme Court, 13 August 1979 (NJA 1979 s 527). An unofficial English translation appears in Paulsson, *The Role of Swedish Courts in Transnational Commercial Arbitration*, 21 *Virginia Journal of International Law* 244–248 (1981) and in VI *Yearbook of Commercial Arbitration* 237–242 (1981). An unofficial French translation appears in *Revue de l'Arbitrage* (1980) 555. For a discussion of the case, see Paulsson, 'Arbitrage et juge en Suède: Exposé général et réflexions sur la délocalisation des sentences arbitrales', *Revue de l'Arbitrage* 441 (1980): Paulsson, 'Arbitrage Unbound: Award Detached From the Law of its Country of Origin', 30 *International and Comparative Law Quarterly* (1981) 358; Park, 'The Lex Loci Arbitri and International Commercial Arbitration', 32 *International and Comparative Law Quarterly* (1983) 21.

[9] *Société Planavergne SA v KB i Stockholm AB*, Decision of the Supreme Court, 30 September 2003, (NJA 2003 p 379).

[10] See discussion at para 7.27 *et seq.*

awards include final and enforceable rulings of parts of the dispute as opposed to purely declaratory awards, there is nothing preventing separate enforcement proceedings of such separate or partial awards under the SAA. This may be the case, for example, where the request for arbitration included a large number of separate claims, which is not unusual in construction disputes, and the arbitrators decide to deal with some of these claims separately.

9.15 Another example would be separate awards for payment of the advance on costs. If the respondent in an arbitration under the SCC Rules fails to pay its share of the advance of costs, and the claimant pays such share of the advance on behalf of the respondent, the claimant may request the arbitrators to issue a separate award for reimbursement of the payment (Article 45(4) of the SCC Rules). The Svea Court of Appeal has found that such an interim award on the advance of costs is enforceable.[11]

9.16 Whereas separate awards and partial awards may include enforceable rulings, *interim awards* on security measures are, as a general rule, not enforceable under Swedish law. The *travaux préparatoires* to the SAA provide that only courts should be able to decide on enforceable security measures.[12]

9.2.5 Grounds for refusing recognition and enforcement

9.17 In the SAA, the grounds for refusing recognition and enforcement in Article V(1) of the New York Convention have been incorporated in section 54, whereas section 55 of the SAA implements Article V(2) of the New York Convention. As is the case under the New York Convention, the grounds set out in section 54 of the SAA should only be considered by the court hearing the application for enforcement and recognition to the extent such grounds are relied on by the respondent in the enforcement proceedings. Such grounds consequently do not form part of any *ex officio* review by the court. Moreover, the party against whom enforcement is sought has the burden of proof to show that recognition and enforcement should be refused under section 54.[13]

9.18 The wording of section 55 of the SAA on the other hand, 'recognition and enforcement of a foreign award shall also be refused *where a court finds* ...', indicates that the grounds enumerated therein—ie non-arbitrability and public policy—are to be applied *ex officio* by the court.[14]

---

[11] See para 7.37.

[12] Govt Bill 1998/99:35, p 73.

[13] In relevant parts section 54 provides: 'A foreign award shall not be recognised and enforced in Sweden where the party against whom the award is invoked proves ...'

[14] In *Sodemaco SA v Gräsås Trävaru AB* (NJA 1986 C 89) the Supreme Court has used language which could perhaps be understood to mean that the court is of the view that the burden of proof rests with the party against whom enforcement is sought also in the case of public policy and non-arbitrability. It is doubtful that the Supreme Court intended to express this view; it simply affirmed the decision of the Court of Appeal without adding any explanation or reasons. At any rate it cannot be right. Leaving the observance and monitoring of public policy and arbitrability to the parties would undermine the *ratio* of these two concepts.

Although not expressly stated in the SAA, the enumeration of grounds for **9.19** refusing recognition and enforcement in sections 54 and 55 of the SAA is exhaustive.[15] It must be noted, however, that neither the New York Convention not the SAA deals with the question of sovereign immunity.[16] The New York Convention—and national legislation based thereon—does not prevent a party from trying to raise the defense of sovereign immunity in enforcement and execution proceedings.

Another important aspect which is not covered by the New York Convention is the **9.20** issue of the statutes of limitation (extinctive prescription) with respect to enforcement proceedings. It is reasonable to assume that an arbitral award will not remain enforceable forever.[17] The answer is usually found in the municipal legislation of the enforcing State. As far as Swedish law is concerned there are no specific time limits with respect to the enforcement of arbitral awards. Rather, the general limitation period of ten years will apply.

Whilst the New York Convention does not allow the enforcing court to introduce **9.21** new defences, Article VII(1) of the Convention does enable the enforcing court to apply more lenient conditions to the extent allowed by the law or the treaties of the enforcing State.

The following individual grounds are enumerated in section 54 of the SAA. **9.22**

9.2.5.1 Lack of capacity of the parties and invalidity of arbitration agreement

Pursuant to section 54, item 1, recognition and enforcement may be refused if the **9.23** party against whom recognition and enforcement are sought proves that the parties to the arbitration agreement, pursuant to the applicable law, lacked capacity to enter into the agreement or were not duly represented, or if the arbitration agreement is invalid under the law to which the parties have subjected it or, failing any indication thereon, under the law of the country where the award was made.

Section 54, item 1, thus, with one exception, corresponds to Article V(1)(a) of the **9.24** New York Convention. Whereas the New York Convention provides that when ruling on the capacity of the parties, the court shall apply 'the law applicable to them', the SAA merely refers to the 'applicable law' without including the words 'to them'. This will probably not lead to any differences in practice, however, since the New York Convention also leaves open the question of *how* the law applicable to a party is to be determined. Under both the SAA and the New York Convention the question must normally be resolved by means of the conflict of laws rules of the law

---

[15] See, for example, *Fløjstrup v Madsen* (NJA 2008 N 32) where the Supreme Court found that the fact that a party was named incorrectly in the award did not constitute a ground for refusing enforcement.

[16] See para 1.52 *et seq.*

[17] See eg Lebedev, 'How Long does a Foreign Award Stay Enforceable?, in Schultsz and van den Berg (eds), *The Art of Arbitration, Lhiber Amicorum Pieter Sanders* (1982) 213.

of the court before which the enforcement of the arbitral award is sought.[18] A Swedish court applying section 54 of the SAA will therefore, when ruling on questions of capacity, normally refer to the personal law of the party in question determined pursuant to Swedish conflict of laws rules.[19]

9.25 The situation is different for questions concerning the invalidity of the arbitration agreement, since both the SAA and the New York Convention provide a complete conflict of laws rule for such questions, ie the law of the country where the award was made unless the parties have agreed on the law applicable to the arbitration agreement.[20] This raises the question about the relationship between Swedish law—which does not require arbitration agreements to be in writing[21]—and Article II of the New York Convention. The language of Article II seems to indicate that the Convention requires that arbitration agreements must be in writing. The position of the Swedish legislator has always been that Article II is a maximum requirement in the sense that no contracting State can impose more demanding requirements than those laid down in Article II, but a contracting State is free to require less.[22] The position of the Swedish legislator is thus that Swedish law fully complies with the New York Convention even though Swedish law does not require arbitration agreements to be in writing. As far as the enforcement of the foreign arbitral awards in Sweden is concerned, this aspect of Article VI(1)(a) of the New York Convention will not create problems since the arbitration in question will by definition have taken place outside Sweden, which means that it is very unlikely that the arbitration agreement would be governed by Swedish law. The situation may be different when it comes to the enforcement abroad of Swedish arbitral awards, depending on how the enforcing court interprets Article II of the New York Convention in relation to the choice of law rules in Article V(1)(a) of the Convention.

9.2.5.2 Violation of procedural due process

9.26 Pursuant to section 54, item 2 of the SAA, a person may also object to the recognition and enforcement of an award on the ground that he was not given proper notice of the arbitration proceedings or of the appointment of the arbitrator, or was otherwise unable to present his case. This provision corresponds to Article V(1)(b) of the New York Convention, and safeguards the fundamental principle of a fair hearing and adversary proceedings, ie due process.

9.27 As is the case under the New York Convention, however, it is not quite clear under which law the standards of due process are to be judged. Similarly to courts in other

---

[18] Albert Jan van den Berg, *The New York Arbitration Convention of 1958: Towards a Uniform Judicial Interpretation* (TMC Asser Institute, 1981) p 276 *et seq.*

[19] See para 2.174.

[20] See para 2.201.

[21] See para 3.04 *et seq.*

[22] This position was taken when the New York Convention was ratified in 1971—see Govt Bill 1971:131, pp 27–28 and again when the SAA was being prepared, Govt Bill 1998/99:35, pp 67–68.

countries applying the New York Convention,[23] a Swedish court applying section 54, item 2, would likely rule on due process objections based on the notions of Swedish law. That would not mean, however, that a Swedish court would measure the due process objection against particular rules of Swedish law. An overall assessment would have to be made to determine whether the action complained of by the party in question falls below the standards of due process that—from a Swedish point of view—must be maintained in international arbitrations.

In *Lenmorniiproekt OAO v Arne Larsson & Partner Leasing AB* (NJA 2010 p 219), the Supreme Court addressed the requirement of 'proper notice of the proceedings' under section 54, item 2.[24] In this case, the respondent in the arbitration (and the enforcement proceedings) claimed that it had not learnt about the arbitration nor the award until the claimant applied for enforcement. The request for arbitration had been sent to an address, which was specified as the respondent's address in the disputed contract. However, the respondent had changed its address, officially registered its new address with the Swedish Companies Registration Office, and moved offices before the arbitration proceedings started. Moreover, the respondent had not participated at any stage of the arbitration proceedings. Representatives of the respondent testified in the enforcement proceedings that they had not been aware of the fact that any arbitration proceedings had taken place until they were notified of the application to enforce the arbitral award. **9.28**

The Supreme Court held that although the wording 'proper notice' in the SAA, and the New York Convention, did not provide any clear guidance regarding the way in which such notice had to be made, respect for due process required that the request for arbitration *must in fact have reached the respondent*. The Supreme Court refused to enforce the award, since the record showed that the request for arbitration had not been delivered to an authorized representative of the company, nor had the company otherwise been notified of the proceedings. The fact that the respondent had not informed the claimant of its change of address was not considered to be of relevance by the Supreme Court in the present situation, where the respondent had not been made aware of the commencement of the arbitral proceedings. **9.29**

Thus, the Supreme Court did not apply, nor seek guidance from any specific rules of Swedish law, but rather made an overall evaluation of what due process requires with respect to notification of the commencement of arbitral proceedings.[25] **9.30**

---

[23] Albert Jan van den Berg, *The New York Arbitration Convention of 1958: Towards a Uniform Judicial Interpretation* (TMC Asser Institute, 1981) para 297 *et seq.*

[24] See para 6.53.

[25] In an earlier case *Richard E v Monimpex* (NJA 1993 C 56), the Supreme Court dismissed the appeal from the Court of Appeal which had ruled that since the arbitral award stated that the respondent in the arbitration had received notice of the arbitration, the respondent had not established that he had not been able to present his case. Under similar circumstances, the same conclusion was reached by the Supreme Court in *Klatzkow Konsult AB v Pevaeche SA* (NJA 1989 C 22).

9.2.5.3 *Excess of mandate*

9.31   Pursuant to section 54, item 3 of the SAA, an arbitral award may not be recognized and may not be enforced to the extent that it deals with a dispute not contemplated by, or not falling within, the terms of the submission to arbitration, or where it contains decisions on matters which are beyond the scope of the arbitration agreement. However, if a decision on a matter which falls within the mandate can be separated from those which fall outside the mandate, the part of the award which contains decisions on matters falling within the mandate shall be recognized and enforced. The provision corresponds to Article V(1)(c) of the New York Convention.

9.32   To determine whether the arbitrators have ruled on matters which are beyond the scope of the arbitration agreement the court must interpret the agreement between the parties. This raises the question of applicable law. Neither the New York Convention nor the SAA indicates which law should govern such interpretation. Relying on the generally accepted principle of party autonomy, it would seem reasonable that the law chosen by the parties should govern this question. If no choice of law has been made, the court could apply either the law of the place where the award was rendered or the *lex fori*. The natural starting point would perhaps be to apply the same choice of law rule that applies to questions concerning the invalidity of the arbitration agreement pursuant to section 54, item 1. Consequently, where it is alleged that the award deals with issues that fall outside of the terms of the submission to arbitration, it would seem natural to apply the *lex arbitri* unless the parties have agreed on the law to be applied to the arbitration agreement.[26]

9.33   In *Götaverken*,[27] an objection based on exceeding the scope of authority was raised by the respondent in the enforcement proceedings. In the arbitral award GNMTC had been ordered to take delivery of three oil tankers from Götaverken against a price reduction for certain minor defects. When resisting enforcement, GNMTC, *inter alia*, claimed that the arbitrators had exceeded their authority, since they had never been asked whether there should be any price reduction. The Svea Court of Appeal held that the arbitrators' mandate was to decide whether GNMTC was obliged to take delivery of the tankers and to pay the reminder of the purchase price. This meant—the Court went on to say—that they had the power to determine that GNMTC should take delivery and pay the remainder of the price with a reduction for minor defects. Thus, the reduction was not an unsolicited award for damages, but rather a price adjustment in connection with the general determination that GNMTC was obliged to pay the remainder of the price. The award was, thus, recognized and enforced in Sweden.

---

[26] See para 2.201.
[27] *Götaverken Arendal AB (Sweden) v General National Maritime Transport Company (GNMTC) (Libya)* (NJA 1979 s 527). See also para 9.13 above.

9.2.5.4 Improper composition of the arbitral tribunal or improper arbitral procedure

Pursuant to section 54, item 4, recognition and enforcement of an award may be **9.34** refused if the respondent can prove that the appointment of the arbitral tribunal, or its composition or the arbitral procedure, was not in accordance with the agreement of the parties or, failing such agreement, was not in accordance with the law of the country where the arbitration took place. This provision corresponds to Article V(1)(d) of the New York Convention.

As set out in section 54, item 4, and Article V(1)(d) of the New York Convention, **9.35** irregularities with regard to the composition of the arbitral tribunal and the procedure shall in the first place be resolved on the basis of the agreement of the parties. This means that to the extent that the parties have made an agreement on these matters, the alleged irregularities are to be judged under that agreement alone. Consequently, the law of the jurisdiction where the arbitration took place, ie the *lex arbitri*, comes into play only if no agreement exists, or to the extent that matters are not covered by the agreement. It also means that if the mandatory provisions of the law of the jurisdiction where the arbitration took place have been violated, such circumstance is not, in itself, a sufficient ground for refusal of recognition of the award under Swedish law. This conclusion does not, however, foreclose the possibility of having the award set aside in its jurisdiction of origin or resist enforcement in Sweden on other grounds, eg because the agreement on the composition of the arbitral tribunal or the arbitral procedure violates due process. If that is the case recognition and enforcement could be refused pursuant to section 54, item 2 or section 55, item 2.

In *Götaverken*,[28] the respondent asserted that the award should be denied recognition **9.36** on the basis that procedural irregularities had occurred so as to make the award ineffective, since one of the two party-appointed arbitrators had not participated in a number of essential decisions made by the tribunal. The Svea Court of Appeal held that those portions of the award which were subject to recognition and enforcement had not been altered after the day on which all three arbitrators had agreed to draft the award and that the respondent had failed to show that the arbitration took place in contravention of French law. The respondent also alleged that the ICC Court of Arbitration had unduly influenced the arbitrators by issuing directives to them, which addressed more than procedural matters and therefore constituted an interference with the substantive consideration of the dispute and violated Article 21 of the ICC Rules (1955).

The Svea Court of Appeal, however, in dismissing this allegation, interpreted the **9.37** ICC Court of Arbitration's instructions as merely a request for confirmation by the arbitrators in the text of the award that all issues submitted to them had been dealt

---

[28] *Götaverken Arendal AB (Sweden) v General National Maritime Transport Company (Libya)* (NJA 1979 s 527). See also para 9.33.

with and not as an impermissible interference with the substantive aspects of the award. On appeal, the Supreme Court stated briefly that it found no reason to depart from the decision of the Svea Court of Appeal as far as this ground was concerned.

9.2.5.5 *Arbitral award not binding*

9.38 Pursuant to section 54, item 5, an award may not be recognized and executed if it has not yet become binding on the parties, or has been set aside or suspended by a competent authority of the country in which, or under the law of which, the arbitral award was rendered. This provision corresponds to Article V(1)(e) of the New York Convention.

9.39 The exact meaning of this provision in the New York Convention, and especially of the word 'binding', is not clear. A similar ground for objection was included in the Geneva Convention, although there the term 'final' was used. The replacement of 'final' in the Geneva Convention by 'binding' in the New York Convention was intended to eliminate the double *exequatur* requirement. But does 'binding' mean anything more? The legislative history of the New York Convention seems to indicate that something more than just the elimination of the double *exequatur* requirement was intended. In discussing the concept of a 'binding' award at the diplomatic conference which preceded the New York Convention, a distinction was proposed between ordinary means of recourse, meaning review of the award on the merits, and extraordinary means of recourse, such as various forms of nullification proceedings. In accordance with this distinction, an award would become 'binding' as soon as it was no longer open to review on the merits, even if it was still open to nullification proceedings. This would in most cases mean that an arbitral award becomes 'binding' immediately when rendered, since the arbitration laws of most jurisdictions prohibit courts from reviewing an arbitral decision on the merits and since most arbitration clauses do not provide for appellate arbitration proceedings. Although the distinction between ordinary and extraordinary means of recourse was not incorporated into the text of the New York Convention, no departure from the proposed distinction seems to have been intended thereby.[29] This concept of 'binding', as used in the New York Convention, was accepted by the Supreme Court in *Götaverken* and in the *travaux préparatoires* of the SAA.[30] The arbitral award in *Götaverken* was rendered in Paris under the ICC Arbitration Rules of 1955. Having lost the arbitration, *General National Maritime Transport Company (Libya)* (GNMTC) challenged the award in Paris by submitting both a so-called 'Declaration d'Appel' and a so-called 'Opposition à Ordonnance d'Exequatur de Sentence Arbitrale'.

9.40 In the Swedish recognition and enforcement proceedings against GNMTC, GNMTC claimed that the commencement of such 'Opposition' had the effect under

---

[29] Van den Berg, *op cit* at 342.
[30] *Götaverken Arendal AB (Sweden) v General National Maritime Transport Company (Libya)* (NJA 1979 s 527) and Govt Bill 1998/99:35, p 200.

French law that enforcement is automatically prohibited and suspended until the Tribunal de Grande Instance de Paris ruled on the validity of the arbitral award. GNMTC further asserted that in France 'Opposition' is the proper way for a party to have the enforcement of the award suspended and that it is not possible to obtain any other form of decision on suspension of the award. With reference thereto GNMTC claimed that the award had not yet become binding and enforceable[31] in France and/or that its enforcement had been suspended by a competent French authority.

In rejecting GNMTC's claim that the award had not become binding, the Supreme **9.41** Court endorsed the views expressed in the legislative history of the 1929 Foreign Arbitration Act to the effect that the fact that an arbitral award may be subject to challenge proceedings does not mean that it is not binding.[32] The Court further held that an award would not be binding, if it is open to review on the merits. In the present case, however, the parties had agreed, both in the arbitration clause and by reference to the ICC Arbitration Rules, that the award would be final and binding. The Supreme Court found that the award had become binding and enforceable within the meaning of the 1929 Foreign Arbitration Act from the moment it was rendered. The fact that GNMTC had thereafter submitted 'Opposition' did not have any effect on the binding nature of the award.[33]

The second part of section 54, item 5, provides that recognition and enforcement of **9.42** an award may be refused if the respondent shows that the award has been set aside or suspended by a competent authority of the jurisdiction in which, or under the law of which, it was rendered. In order to prevent recognition and enforcement, the award must in fact have been set aside; a pending application for setting aside the award will not suffice.[34] Likewise, suspension of an award must have been ordered

---

[31] The reference to 'enforceable' is explained by the fact that the wording of Article 7, paragraph 1, item 5 of the 1929 Foreign Arbitration Act (under which the case was heard) deviated somewhat from Article V(1)(e) of the New York Convention. Rather than providing that enforcement may be refused if the award *'has not yet become binding'*, the 1929 Foreign Arbitration Act provided that enforcement could be refused if the award *'has not become enforceable or otherwise binding'*. However, as confirmed by the Supreme Court in *Götaverken*, the provision was not indented to have a different meaning than Article V(1)(e) of the New York Convention.

[32] *Götaverken Arendal AB (Sweden) v General National Maritime Transport Company (Libya)* (NJA 1979 s 527) p 539.

[33] *Götaverken Arendal AB (Sweden) v General National Maritime Transport Company (Libya)*, (NJA 1979 s527) p 539 *et seq.*

[34] As far as Swedish law is concerned, the position has traditionally been that an award which has been set aside by a competent court at the place of arbitration cannot be enforced in Sweden. This was the view expressed in the *travaux préparatoires* leading to Sweden's adoption of the New York Convention in 1971, see Govt Bill 1971:31, p 74. No other view was expressed in the *travaux préparatoires* of the SAA. The very intensive debate following the *Chromalloy* (*Chromalloy Aero Services v Arab Republic of Egypt*, 939 F Supp 907 (D.O.C 1996)) and *Hilmarton* cases (*Omnium de Traitment et de Valorisation (OIV) v Hilmarton Ltd*, Cass 1e civ, 10 June 1997) is thus largely irrelevant for Swedish arbitration law. For an overview of this debate see eg International Council for Commercial Arbitration Congress Series No 9 (1999) 505 *et seq*; Hobér, 'Sista striden mellan internationalister och territorialister?—Berättelsen om Hilmarton och Chromalloy', in *Essays in Honor of Ulf K Nordenson* (1999) 195 *et seq.*

by a competent authority in the jurisdiction of origin. Automatic suspension of an award by operation of law in the jurisdiction of origin would not seem to be sufficient. This was the position taken by the Supreme Court in *Götaverken*. In *Götaverken*, GNMTC also claimed that recognition and enforcement should be refused, since enforcement of the award had been suspended by a competent French authority. GNMTC asserted that the so-called 'Opposition à Ordonnance d'Exequatur de Sentence Arbitrale', which it had submitted in Paris automatically prohibited and suspended enforcement of the award until the Tribunal de Grande Instance de Paris ruled on the validity of the arbitral award. Under French law it was—according to GNMTC—neither necessary nor possible to obtain any other kind of decision on suspension of the award.

9.43　The Supreme Court, however, held that the wording of the 1929 Foreign Arbitration Act, as well as its legislative history, made it clear that recognition and enforcement of foreign arbitral awards could only be refused where the competent authority of the country in which the award was made, after actual review, decides that the arbitral award shall be set aside or that its enforcement shall be suspended. The automatic suspension asserted by GNMTC in the present case would therefore not suffice.[35]

9.44　In the interest of facilitating enforcement of foreign arbitral awards, Swedish courts adopt a restrictive position on the issue of postponing enforcement for reasons of a challenge procedure pending against the arbitral award.[36] As a general rule, Swedish courts will not stay enforcement proceedings on this ground unless it is shown that the party challenging the award is likely to succeed in its challenge of the award.[37] Section 58(2) of the SAA, which is based on Article VI of the New York Convention, provides that if an application for setting aside or suspension of an award has been made to a competent court of the country in which, or under the law of which, that award was made, the court where recognition or enforcement is sought may adjourn its decision and may also, on the application of the party claiming recognition or enforcement of the award, order the other party to provide appropriate security.

9.45　In *Götaverken*, GNMTC made the alternative claim that if recognition and enforcement was not refused, the Supreme Court should at least adjourn its decision to recognize and enforce the arbitral award until the competent French courts had ruled on its validity.[38] GNMTC argued that an adjournment would be

---

[35] *Götaverken Arendal AB (Sweden) v General National Maritime Transport Company (Libya)*, (NJA 1979 s 527) p 540.

[36] *Götaverken Arendal AB (Sweden) v General National Maritime Transport Company (Libya)*, (NJA 1979 s 527); and *Forenede Cresco AS v Datema AB*, Decision of the Supreme Court, 23 November 1992, (NJA 1992 s 733).

[37] *Datema v Forenede Cresco Finans* (NJA 1992 p 733), Govt Bill 1998/99:35, p 202. See also *Swembalt v Republic of Latvia* (NJA 2002 C 62);, the Court of Appeal decision dated 29 October 2002 is reproduced in SAR 2003:2, p 263 *et seq.*

[38] The request was made on the basis of section 9, paragraph 2 of the 1929 Foreign Arbitration Act, which contained a provision corresponding to section 52, paragraph 2 of the SAA.

appropriate in the present case, since GNMTC had challenged the award by bringing two actions before the French courts (Declaration d'Appel and Opposition à Ordonnance d'Exequatur de Sentence Arbitrale). GNMTC argued that an adjournment would be appropriate also since it had commenced new arbitral proceedings against Götaverken, in which it requested the arbitral tribunal to confirm that it was not obliged to take delivery of the three ships, which the first arbitral tribunal had ordered it to do.

Referring to the overall objective of the New York Convention, and the Swedish imple- **9.46** menting legislation, to facilitate enforcement of foreign arbitral awards, the majority of the Supreme Court stated that the proceedings, which GNMTC had commenced in France, did not constitute such a circumstance that could justify an adjournment of the decision on the recognition and enforcement of the arbitral award.[39]

The Supreme Court took an equally restrictive approach to stay enforcement pro- **9.47** ceedings in *Forenede Cresco AS v Datema AB* (NJA 1992 p 733).

Having lost arbitral proceedings in Norway under a cooperation agreement with **9.48** Forenede Cresco AS, Datema challenged the arbitral award before the competent courts of Norway on the ground that the arbitral tribunal had exceeded its mandate. Datema had also requested that the competent Norwegian court should suspend the award. However, such request for suspension had been dismissed both by the Norwegian first instance court and the Norwegian Court of Appeal without determining the substance of the request. Datema's appeal to the Norwegian Supreme Court on this issue was still pending when the Supreme Court ruled on Forenede Cresco's enforcement application.

In the enforcement proceedings, Datema first argued that recognition and enforce- **9.49** ment should be refused, since the arbitral tribunal had exceeded its authority, and, secondly, that the Supreme Court should adjourn its decision on recognition and enforcement, until the Norwegian courts had ruled on Datema's challenge of the award and/or request to suspend the award.

The majority of the Supreme Court, however, did not adjourn its decision on **9.50** recognition and enforcement of the arbitral award. The Supreme Court noted that the reasons underlying the Norwegian courts' decision not to hear the merits of Datema's request for suspension of the award were based on a questionable interpretation of the New York Convention, and that it therefore could not be excluded that their decisions would be reversed by the Norwegian Supreme Court. The Swedish Supreme Court, however, also noted that even if Datema's request to the competent Norwegian court to suspend the award were to be heard on the merits, it was uncertain whether or not such request would be granted. The Supreme Court

---

[39] *Götaverken Arendal AB (Sweden) v General National Maritime Transport Company (Libya)*, Decision of the Supreme Court, 13 August 1979, (NJA 1979 s 527) p 540.

further emphasized that it could take a long time before Datema's challenge of the award would be finally determined, and that it was uncertain whether Datema would be successful in the challenge proceedings. For those reasons, and in the general interest of facilitating enforcement of arbitral awards, the Supreme Court found that it would not be appropriate to adjourn its decision.[40]

9.51 It is also interesting to note that the pronounced pro-enforcement policy of the Supreme Court was further underlined by the fact that the Supreme Court—when ruling on Datema's objection to enforcement on the grounds of excess of mandate— had found the arbitral tribunal's ruling on its jurisdiction questionable. Despite such conclusion, the Supreme Court decided to recognize and enforce the award, and not to adjourn its decision pending the outcome of the challenge proceedings. One of the Justices of the Supreme Court dissented and found in favour of adjourning the decision on enforcement due to the above-described uncertainties concerning the jurisdiction of the arbitral tribunal and the questionable decision of the Norwegian courts not to hear the merits of Datema's request for suspension of the award.[41]

9.2.5.6 Non-arbitrability

9.52 Pursuant to section 55, item 1, an award should not be recognized and enforced, if the court finds that the arbitral award includes determination of an issue which, in accordance with Swedish law, may not be decided by arbitrators.[42] On this ground a court may refuse enforcement on its own motion (*ex officio*). This provision corresponds to Article V(2)(a) of the New York Convention. There are no reported cases where an arbitral award has been refused recognition and enforcement in Sweden on this ground.

9.2.5.7 Public policy

9.53 Finally, pursuant to section 55, item 2 of the SAA, an award will not be recognized and enforced if the court finds that it would be manifestly incompatible with the fundamental principles of the Swedish legal system to recognize and enforce the arbitral award. Although worded differently than Article V(2)(b) of the New York Convention, its meaning and application are the same, ie that a court may refuse enforcement on its own motion if the enforcement would be contrary to public policy. The wording used in the SAA reflects the customary way of defining *ordre public* or public policy in Swedish statutes.

9.54 Swedish law adopts a restrictive approach to the interpretation of public policy. Examples mentioned in the *travaux préparatoires* to the Act include awards rendered as a result of threats of physical violence or bribes or claims based upon criminal acts

---

[40] *Forenede Cresco AS v Datema AB*, (NJA 1992 s 733) p 739.
[41] *Forenede Cresco AS v Datema AB*, Decision of the Supreme Court, 23 November 1992, (NJA 1992 s 733) p 739 *et seq.*
[42] See discussion at para 3.77 *et seq.*

such as debts emanating from unlawful gambling.[43] Witness statements induced by duress have also been mentioned as a ground for resisting enforcement, always assuming that the high evidentiary burden can be satisfied in the enforcement proceedings.[44]

There is only one case reported where the Supreme Court has refused to recognize and enforce a foreign arbitral award for reasons of public policy.[45] In 2002, the Court denied enforcement in *Robert G v Johnny L* (NJA 2002 C 45), concluding that 'the circumstances in connection with the arbitral award and its origin are such that it must be deemed manifestly incompatible with the fundamental principles of the Swedish legal system to enforce the award'. Since the Court's reasoning is somewhat brief (the case not being reported in full by the Supreme Court), additional background information may be sought in the reasons of the Svea Court of Appeal, which also denied enforcement.[46] *Robert G v Johnny L* is the only case ever where the Supreme Court has refused to recognize and enforce a foreign arbitral award for reasons of public policy.

9.55

According to the applicant seeking enforcement of the arbitral award, the facts were as follows. A commission agency contract was entered into in Slovenia by Johnny and Robert, who were brothers, concerning the procurement of a car, two mobile phones, a digital camera, and a floor-heating device. Johnny was to procure these items as a commission agent on behalf of Robert.

9.56

An arbitral award was issued on 16 August 2001, in Ljubljana, Slovenia, with Robert as claimant and Johnny as respondent. The award covered the car, the mobile phones, and the camera. The award also stated that Johnny was liable for rent (€38,160) for the hire of certain premises owned by Robert, as well as damages (€50,000) for breach of the rental contract.

9.57

Robert applied to the Svea Court of Appeal to have the award declared enforceable. The Svea Court of Appeal, however, refused to recognize and enforce the award on

9.58

---

[43] Govt Bill 1998/99:35, pp 141, 150.

[44] Heuman, *Arbitration Law of Sweden: Practice and Procedure* (2003) p 734.

[45] Two more cases should be mentioned where the Supreme Court has tried the public policy defence. It was rejected in both cases. In the first case, *Kvarnabo Timber v Cordes GmbH & Co* (NJA 1986 C 26), the Court found that the appointment of an arbitrator for the respondent in the arbitration—ie Kvarnabo—by the German Verein Deutscher Holzeinfuhrhäuser eV was not manifestly incompatible with the fundamental principles of Swedish law in a situation where Kvarnabo had been repeatedly requested—but had failed—to appoint an arbitrator. In the second case, *SwemBalt AB v Republic of Latvia* (NJA 2002 C 62), the Republic of Latvia argued that the award, rendered in Denmark, violated the principle of *lis pendens* since the dispute was already pending before another arbitral tribunal. The tribunal sitting in Denmark had concluded that there was no *lis pendens*. The Court of Appeal found that a violation of the principle of *lis pendens* does not qualify as a public policy circumstance. The decision of the Court of Appeal was affirmed by the Supreme Court without further reasons.

[46] See also Heuman and Millqvist, 'Swedish Supreme Court Refuses to Enforce an Arbitral Award Pursuant to the Public Policy Provision of the New York Convention', 20 *J Int'l Arb* 500–01 (2003).

public policy grounds. The decision of the Court of Appeal was upheld by the Swedish Supreme Court on appeal. The facts and circumstances of relevance for the decision to refuse recognition and enforcement were as follows.

9.59 In April 2001, Johnny had been sentenced to prison in Sweden for bank fraud and forgery. In connection with his arrest, goods allegedly covered by a title-transfer security transaction were seized to satisfy the claims of Johnny's creditors. Johnny objected to the seizure and claimed that he and Robert had made a title-transfer security transaction under German law concerning the goods, with Robert as buyer. The Swedish Enforcement Authority as well as the District Court, however, rejected Johnny's assertions that the property was pledged to Robert. The District Court found it more than likely that the goods in question had been acquired by Johnny with money he had gained through his criminal activities.

9.60 Moreover, in September 2001, about one month after the arbitral award was issued, Johnny was declared bankrupt. This was prior to the District Court's decision in the execution proceedings. The application for the enforcement of the arbitral award was filed by Robert in the spring of 2002.

9.61 The Svea Court of Appeal refused to recognize and enforce the award due to the fact that the Court found reason to question whether the award *reflected a true legal relationship*.[47] The Court, *inter alia*, referred to the fact that the parties were brothers. No explanation seems to have been given in the enforcement proceedings as to why a dispute arose between the brothers or how it led to arbitration proceedings. The Court also referred to the fact that the goods in question were subject to another legal proceeding in Sweden where it had been alleged that a security transfer had taken place, whereas the arbitral award was based on a commission agency contract without any reference to the alleged security transfer. The Court also pointed to the fact that two awards had been presented with different dates.

9.62 Recognition and enforcement appear to have been denied because the Court of Appeal had reason to believe that the award constituted a fictitious document created to deceive the bankruptcy estate of the respondent.

9.63 The decision not to grant recognition and enforcement was upheld by the Supreme Court, which simply held that the circumstances in connection with the arbitral award were deemed to be of such a nature that it would be contrary to Swedish public policy to enforce the award.

9.2.6 Procedures for recognition

9.64 In order to have a foreign award recognized and enforced in Sweden, an application for recognition (consisting of the original or a certified copy of the award and a Swedish translation thereof) shall be submitted to the Svea Court of Appeal in

---

[47] The Svea Court of Appeal, Decision 31 May 2002, case Ö 3221-02.

Stockholm, which has been given exclusive jurisdiction in this respect (section 56 of the SAA). The court will notify the party against whom enforcement is sought, who is then given an opportunity to raise any objection he may have (section 57 of the SAA). The court may request a further exchange of written statements and may arrange a hearing. Unlike Article IV of the New York Convention, a party applying for recognition and enforcement does not need to supply the original arbitration agreement or a duly certified copy thereof (section 56 of the SAA). The reason why the arbitration agreement does not need to be submitted is that oral arbitration agreements are recognized in Sweden. However, if the other party makes an objection as to the existence of an arbitration agreement, the party seeking recognition and enforcement will, in case of a written arbitration agreement, have to submit the arbitration agreement in an original or a certified copy, or, in case of an oral agreement 'in some other manner prove that an arbitration agreement was entered into' (section 58 of the SAA).

If the application is granted, execution may be commenced immediately. This is the case even if the decision of the Svea Court of Appeal is appealed against to the Supreme Court. If the Supreme Court reverses the decision of the Svea Court of Appeal the execution will be revoked and any property transferred by virtue thereof will have to be returned. **9.65**

If the Svea Court of Appeal grants the application for recognition, it enters an order to the effect that the arbitral award shall be enforceable 'in the same manner as a final non-appealable judgment of a Swedish court of law' (section 59 of the SAA). This means that the applicant may take the award to the Enforcement Authority and have it executed immediately, without any further review, provided, however, that the Supreme Court on appeal does not order otherwise. **9.66**

APPENDIX 1

The Swedish Arbitration Act

The Arbitration Agreement

SECTION 1

Disputes concerning matters in respect of which the parties may reach a settlement may, by agreement, be referred to one or several arbitrators for resolution. Such an agreement may relate to future disputes pertaining to a legal relationship specified in the agreement. The dispute may concern the existence of a particular fact.

In addition to interpreting agreements, the filling of gaps in contracts can also be referred to arbitrators.

Arbitrators may rule on the civil law effects of competition law as between the parties.

SECTION 2

The arbitrators may rule on their own jurisdiction to decide the dispute. The aforesaid shall not prevent a court from determining such a question at the request of a party. The arbitrators may continue the arbitral proceedings pending the determination by the court.

Notwithstanding that the arbitrators have, in a decision during the proceedings, determined that they possess jurisdiction to resolve the dispute, such decision is not binding. The provisions of sections 34 and 36 shall apply in respect of an action to challenge an arbitration award which entails a decision in respect of jurisdiction.

SECTION 3

Where the validity of an arbitration agreement which constitutes part of another agreement must be determined in conjunction with a determination of the jurisdiction of the arbitrators, the arbitration agreement shall be deemed to constitute a separate agreement.

SECTION 4

A court may not, over an objection of a party, rule on an issue which, pursuant to an arbitration agreement, shall be decided by arbitrators.

A party must invoke an arbitration agreement on the first occasion that a party pleads his case on the merits in the court. The invocation of an arbitration agreement raised on a later occasion shall have no effect unless the party had a legal excuse and invoked such as soon as the excuse ceased to exist. The invocation of an arbitration agreement shall be considered notwithstanding that the party who invoked the agreement has allowed an issue which is covered by the arbitration agreement to be determined by the Debt Enforcement Authority in a case concerning expedited collection procedures.

During the pendency of a dispute before arbitrators or prior thereto, a court may, irrespective of the arbitration agreement, issue such decisions in respect of security measures as the court has jurisdiction to issue.

SECTION 5

A party shall forfeit his right to invoke the arbitration agreement as a bar to court proceedings where the party:

1. has opposed a request for arbitration;
2. failed to appoint an arbitrator in due time; or
3. fails, within due time, to provide his share of the requested security for compensation to the arbitrators.

SECTION 6

Where a dispute between a business enterprise and a consumer concerns goods, services, or any other products supplied principally for private use, an arbitration agreement may not be invoked where such was entered into prior to the dispute. However, such agreements shall apply with respect to rental or lease relationships where, through the agreement, a regional rent tribunal or a regional tenancies tribunal is appointed as an arbitral tribunal and the provisions of Chapter 8, section 28 or Chapter 12, section 66 of the Real Estate Code do not prescribe otherwise.

The first paragraph shall not apply where the dispute concerns an agreement between an insurer and a policy-holder concerning insurance based on a collective agreement or group agreement and handled by representatives of the group. Nor shall the first paragraph apply where Sweden's international obligations provide to the contrary.

The Arbitrators

SECTION 7

Any person who possesses full legal capacity in regard to his actions and his property may act as an arbitrator.

SECTION 8

An arbitrator shall be impartial.

If a party so requests, an arbitrator shall be discharged if there exists any circumstance which may diminish confidence in the arbitrator's impartiality. Such a circumstance shall always be deemed to exist:

1. where the arbitrator or a person closely associated to him is a party, or otherwise may expect benefit or detriment worth attention, as a result of the outcome of the dispute;
2. where the arbitrator or a person closely associated to him is the director of a company or any other association which is a party, or otherwise represents a party or any other person who may expect benefit or detriment worth attention as a result of the outcome of the dispute;
3. where the arbitrator has taken a position in the dispute, as an expert or otherwise, or has assisted a party in the preparation or conduct of his case in the dispute; or
4. where the arbitrator has received or demanded compensation in violation of section 39, second paragraph.

SECTION 9

A person who is asked to accept an appointment as arbitrator shall immediately disclose all circumstances which, pursuant to sections 7 or 8, might be considered to prevent him from serving as arbitrator. An arbitrator shall inform the parties and the other arbitrators of such circumstances as soon as all arbitrators have been appointed and thereafter in the course of the arbitral proceedings as soon as he has learned of any new circumstance.

SECTION 10

A challenge of an arbitrator on account of a circumstance set forth in section 8 shall be presented within fifteen days commencing on the date on which the party became aware both of the appointment of the arbitrator and of the existence of the circumstance. The challenge shall be adjudicated by the arbitrators, unless the parties have decided that it shall be determined by another party.

If the challenge is successful, the decision shall be subject to no appeal.

A party who is dissatisfied with a decision denying a motion or dismissing a motion on the grounds that the motion was not timely filed may file an application with the District Court that the arbitrator be removed from his post. The application must be submitted within thirty days commencing on the date on which the party receives the decision. The arbitrators may continue with the arbitral proceedings pending the determination of the District Court.

SECTION 11

The parties may agree that a motion as referred to in section 10, first paragraph shall be conclusively determined by an arbitration institution.

SECTION 12

The parties may determine the number of arbitrators and the manner in which they shall be appointed.

Sections 13–16 shall apply unless the parties have agreed otherwise.

Where the parties have so agreed, and any of the parties so requests, the District Court shall appoint arbitrators also in situations other than those stated in sections 14–17.

SECTION 13

The arbitrators shall be three in number. Each party shall appoint one arbitrator, and the arbitrators so appointed shall appoint the third.

SECTION 14

Where each party is required to appoint an arbitrator and one party has notified the opposing party of his choice of arbitrator in a request for arbitration pursuant to section 19, the opposing party must, within thirty days of receipt of the notice, notify the first party in writing in respect of his choice of arbitrator.

A party who, in this manner, has notified the opposing party of his choice of arbitrator may not revoke the appointment without the consent of the other party.

If the opposing party fails to appoint an arbitrator within the stipulated time, the District Court shall appoint an arbitrator upon request by the first party.

SECTION 15

Where an arbitrator shall be appointed by other arbitrators, but they fail to do so within thirty days commencing on the date on which the last arbitrator was appointed, the District Court shall appoint the arbitrator upon request by a party.

Where an arbitrator shall be appointed by someone other than a party or arbitrators, but such is not done within thirty days of the date on which a party desiring the appointment of an arbitrator requested that the person responsible for the appointment make such appointment, the District Court shall, upon the request by a party, appoint the arbitrator. The same shall apply where an arbitrator shall be appointed by the parties jointly, but they have failed to agree within thirty days commencing on the date on which the question was raised through receipt by one party of notice from the opposing party.

SECTION 16

Where an arbitrator resigns or is discharged, the District Court shall, upon request by a party, appoint a new arbitrator. Where the arbitrator cannot fulfil his duties due to circumstances which arise after his appointment, the person who originally was required to make the appointment shall, instead, appoint a new arbitrator. Sections 14 and 15 shall apply in conjunction with such an appointment. The period of time within which a new arbitrator shall be appointed, even for the party who requested the arbitration, is thirty days calculated, with respect to all parties, from the date on which the person who shall appoint the arbitrator became aware thereof.

SECTION 17

Where an arbitrator has delayed the proceedings, the District Court shall, upon request by a party, discharge the arbitrator and appoint another arbitrator. The parties may decide that such a request shall, instead, be conclusively determined by an arbitration institution.

SECTION 18

Where a party has requested that the District Court appoint an arbitrator pursuant to section 12, third paragraph or sections 14–17, the Court may reject the request on the grounds that the arbitration is not legally permissible only where such is manifest.

The Proceedings

SECTION 19

Unless otherwise agreed by the parties, the arbitral proceedings are initiated when a party receives a request for arbitration in accordance with the second paragraph hereof.

A request for arbitration must be in writing and include:

1. an express and unconditional request for arbitration;
2. a statement of the issue which is covered by the arbitration agreement and which is to be resolved by the arbitrators; and
3. a statement of the party's choice of arbitrator where the party is required to appoint an arbitrator.

SECTION 20

Where the arbitral tribunal is composed of more than one arbitrator, one of them shall be appointed chairman. Unless the parties or the arbitrators have decided otherwise, the chairman shall be the arbitrator appointed by the other arbitrators or the District Court, in their stead.

SECTION 21

The arbitrators shall handle the dispute in an impartial, practical, and speedy manner. They shall thereupon act in accordance with the decisions of the parties insofar as there is no impediment to so doing.

SECTION 22

The parties shall determine the place of arbitration. Where this is not the case, the arbitrators shall determine the place of arbitration.

The arbitrators may hold hearings and other meetings elsewhere in Sweden, or abroad, unless otherwise agreed by the parties.

SECTION 23

Within the period of time determined by the arbitrators, the claimant shall state his claims in respect of the issue stated in the request for arbitration, as well as the circumstances invoked by the party in support thereof. Thereafter, within the period of time determined by the arbitrators, the respondent shall state his position in relation to the claims, and the circumstances invoked by the respondent in support thereof.

The claimant may submit new claims, and the respondent his own claims, provided that the claims fall within the scope of the arbitration agreement and, taking into consideration the time at which they are submitted or other circumstances, the arbitrators do not consider it inappropriate to adjudicate such claims. Subject to the same conditions, during the proceedings, each party may amend or supplement previously presented claims and may invoke new circumstances in support of his case.

The first and second paragraphs hereof shall not apply where the parties have decided otherwise.

SECTION 24

The arbitrators shall afford the parties, to the extent necessary, an opportunity to present their respective cases in writing or orally. Where a party so requests, and provided that the parties have not otherwise agreed, an oral hearing shall be held prior to the determination of an issue referred to the arbitrators for resolution.

A party shall be given an opportunity to review all documents and all other materials pertaining to the dispute which are supplied to the arbitrators by the opposing party or another person.

Where one of the parties, without valid cause, fails to appear at a hearing or otherwise fails to comply with an order of the arbitrators, such failure shall not prevent a continuation of the proceedings and a resolution of the dispute on the basis of the existing materials.

SECTION 25

The parties shall supply the evidence. However, the arbitrators may appoint experts, unless both parties are opposed thereto.

The arbitrators may refuse to admit evidence which is offered where such evidence is manifestly irrelevant to the case or where such refusal is justified having regard to the time at which the evidence is offered.

The arbitrators may not administer oaths or truth affirmations. Nor may they impose conditional fines or otherwise use compulsory measures in order to obtain requested evidence.

Unless the parties have agreed otherwise, the arbitrators may, at the request of a party, decide that, during the proceedings, the opposing party must undertake a certain interim measure to secure the claim which is to be adjudicated by the arbitrators. The arbitrators may prescribe that the party requesting the interim measure must provide reasonable security for the damage which may be incurred by the opposing party as a result of the interim measure.

SECTION 26

Where a party wishes a witness or an expert to testify under oath, or a party to be examined under truth affirmation, the party may, after obtaining the consent of the arbitrators, submit an application to such effect to the District Court. The aforementioned shall apply where a party wishes that a party or other person be ordered to produce as evidence a document or an object. If the arbitrators consider that the measure is justified having regard to the evidence in the case, they shall approve the request. Where the measure may lawfully be taken, the District Court shall grant the application.

The provisions of the Code of Judicial Procedure shall apply with respect to a measure as referred to in the first paragraph. The arbitrators shall be summoned to hear the testimony of a witness, an expert, or a party, and be afforded the opportunity to ask questions. The absence of an arbitrator from the giving of testimony shall not prevent the hearing from taking place.

The Award

SECTION 27

The issues which have been referred to the arbitrators shall be decided in an award. Where the arbitrators terminate the arbitral proceedings without deciding such issues, such shall also take place through an award.

Where the parties enter into a settlement agreement, the arbitrators may, at the request of the parties, confirm it in an award.

Other determinations, which are not embodied in an award, are designated as decisions. The mandate of the arbitrators shall be deemed to be completed when they have delivered a final award, unless otherwise provided in sections 32 or 35.

SECTION 28

Where a party withdraws a claim, the arbitrators shall dismiss that part of the dispute, unless the opposing party requests that the arbitrators rule on the claim.

SECTION 29

A part of the dispute, or a certain issue which is of significance to the resolution of the dispute, may be decided through a separate award, unless opposed by both parties. However, a claim invoked as a defence by way of set off shall be adjudicated in the same award as the main claim.

Where a party has admitted a claim, in whole or in part, a separate award may be rendered in respect of that which has been admitted.

SECTION 30

Where an arbitrator fails, without valid cause, to participate in the determination of an issue by the arbitral tribunal, such failure will not prevent the other arbitrators from ruling on the matter.

Unless the parties have decided otherwise, the opinion agreed upon by the majority of the arbitrators participating in the determination shall prevail. If no majority is attained for any opinion, the opinion of the chairman shall prevail.

SECTION 31

An award shall be made in writing, signed by the arbitrators. It suffices that the award is signed by a majority of the arbitrators, provided that the reason why all of the arbitrators have not signed the award is noted therein. The parties may decide that the chairman of the arbitral tribunal alone shall sign the award.

The award shall state the place of arbitration and the date when the award is made.

The award shall be delivered to the parties immediately.

SECTION 32

If the arbitrators find that an award contains any obvious inaccuracy as a consequence of a typographical, computational, or other similar mistake by the arbitrators or any nother person, or if the arbitrators by oversight have failed to decide an issue which should have been dealt with in the award, they may, within thirty days of the date of the announcement of the award, decide to correct or supplement the award. They may also correct or supplement an award, or interpret the decision in an award, where any of the parties so requests within thirty days of receipt of the award by that party.

Where, upon request by any of the parties, the arbitrators decide to correct an award or interpret the decision in an award, such shall take place within thirty days from the date of receipt by the arbitrators of the party's request. Where the arbitrators decide to supplement the award, such shall take place within sixty days.

Before any decision is made pursuant to this section, the parties should be afforded an opportunity to express their views with respect to the measure.

Invalidity of Awards and Setting Aside Awards

SECTION 33

An award is invalid:

1. if it includes determination of an issue which, in accordance with Swedish law, may not be decided by arbitrators;
2. if the award, or the manner in which the award arose, is clearly incompatible with the basic principles of the Swedish legal system; or
3. if the award does not fulfil the requirements with regard to the written form and signature in accordance with section 31, first paragraph.

The invalidity may apply to a certain part of the award.

SECTION 34

An award which may not be challenged in accordance with section 36 shall, following an application, be wholly or partially set aside upon motion of a party:

1. if it is not covered by a valid arbitration agreement between the parties;
2. if the arbitrators have made the award after the expiration of the period decided on by the parties, or where the arbitrators have otherwise exceeded their mandate;
3. if arbitral proceedings, according to section 47, should not have taken place in Sweden;
4. if an arbitrator has been appointed contrary to the agreement between the parties or this Act;
5. if an arbitrator was unauthorized due to any circumstance set forth in sections 7 or 8; or
6. if without fault of the party, there otherwise occurred an irregularity in the course of the proceedings which probably influenced the outcome of the case.

A party shall not be entitled to rely upon a circumstance which, through participation in the proceedings without objection, or in any other manner, he may be deemed to have waived. A party shall not be regarded as having accepted the arbitrators' jurisdiction to determine the issue referred to arbitration solely by having appointed an arbitrator. Pursuant to sections 10 and 11, a party may lose the right in accordance with the first paragraph, sub-section 5 to rely upon a circumstance as set forth in section 8.

An action must be brought within three months from the date upon which the party received the award or, where correction, supplementation, or interpretation has taken place pursuant to section 32, within a period of three months from the date when the party received the award in its final wording. Following the expiration of the time limit, a party may not invoke a new ground of objection in support of his claim.

SECTION 35

A court may stay proceedings concerning the invalidity or setting aside of an award for a certain period of time in order to provide the arbitrators with an opportunity to resume the arbitral proceedings or to take some other measure which, in the opinion of the arbitrators, will eliminate the ground for the invalidity or setting aside:

1. provided the court holds that the claim in the case shall be accepted and either of the parties requests a stay; or
2. both parties request a stay.

Where the arbitrators make a new award, a party may, within the period of time determined by the court and without issuing a writ of summons, challenge the award insofar as it was based upon the resumed arbitral proceedings or an amendment to the first award.

Notwithstanding Chapter 43, section 11, second paragraph of the Code of Judicial Procedure, a trial may continue even where the period of the stay exceeds fifteen days.

SECTION 36

An award whereby the arbitrators concluded the proceedings without ruling on the issues submitted to them for resolution may be amended, in whole or in part, upon the application of a party. An action must be brought within three months from the date upon which the party received the award or, where correction, supplementation, or interpretation has taken place in accordance with section 32, within a period of three months from the date upon which the party received the award in its final wording. The award shall contain clear instructions as to what must be done by a party who wishes to challenge the award.

An action in accordance with the first paragraph which only concerns an issue as referred to in section 42 is permissible where the award means that the arbitrators have considered themselves to lack jurisdiction to determine the dispute. Where the award entails another matter, a party who desires to challenge the award may do so in accordance with the provisions of section 34.

Costs of Arbitration

SECTION 37

The parties shall be jointly and severally liable to pay reasonable compensation to the arbitrators for work and expenses. However, where the arbitrators have stated in the award that they lack jurisdiction to determine the dispute, the party that did not request arbitration shall be liable to make payment only insofar as required due to special circumstances.

In a final award, the arbitrators may order the parties to pay compensation to them, together with interest from the date occurring one month following the date of the announcement of the award. The compensation shall be stated separately for each arbitrator.

SECTION 38

The arbitrators may request security for the compensation. They may fix separate security for individual claims. Where a party fails to provide its share of the requested security within the period specified by the arbitrators, the opposing party may provide the entire security. Where the requested security is not provided, the arbitrators may terminate the proceedings, in whole or in part.

During the proceedings, the arbitrators may decide to realise security in order to cover expenses. Following the determination of the arbitrators' compensation in a final award and where the award in that respect has become enforceable, the arbitrators may realise their payment from the security, in the event the parties fail to fulfil their payment obligations in accordance with the award. The right to security also includes income from the property.

SECTION 39

The provisions of sections 37 and 38 shall apply unless otherwise jointly decided by the parties in a manner that is binding upon the arbitrators.

An agreement regarding compensation to the arbitrators that is not entered into with the parties jointly is void. Where one of the parties has provided the entire security, such party may, however, solely consent to the realisation of the security by the arbitrators in order to cover the compensation for work expended.

SECTION 40

The arbitrators may not withhold the award pending the payment of compensation.

SECTION 41

A party or an arbitrator may bring an action in the District Court against the award regarding the payment of compensation to the arbitrators. Such action must be brought within three months from the date upon which the party received the award and, in the case of an arbitrator, within the same period from the announcement of the award. Where correction, supplementation, or interpretation has taken place in accordance with section 32, the action must be brought by a party within three months from the date upon which the party received the award in its final wording and, in the case of an arbitrator, within the same period from the date when the award was announced in its final wording. The award shall contain clear instructions as to what must be done by a party who wishes to bring an action against the award in this respect.

A judgment pursuant to which the compensation to an arbitrator is reduced shall also apply to the party who did not bring the action.

SECTION 42

Unless otherwise agreed by the parties, the arbitrators may, upon request by a party, order the opposing party to pay compensation for the party's costs and determine the manner in which the compensation to the arbitrators shall be finally allocated between the parties. The arbitrators' order may also include interest, if a party has so requested.

Forum and Limitation Periods

SECTION 43

An action against an award pursuant to sections 33, 34, and 36 shall be considered by the Court of Appeal within the jurisdiction where the arbitral proceedings were held. Where the place of arbitration is not stated in the award, the action may be brought before the Svea Court of Appeal.

The determination of the Court of Appeal may not be appealed. However, the Court of Appeal may grant leave to appeal the determination where it is of importance as a matter of precedent that the appeal be considered by the Supreme Court.

An action regarding compensation to an arbitrator shall be considered by the District Court at the place of arbitration. Where the place of arbitration is not stated in the award, the action may be brought before the Stockholm District Court.

SECTION 44

Applications to appoint or discharge an arbitrator shall be considered by the District Court at the place where one of the parties is domiciled or by the District Court at the place of arbitration. The application may also be considered by the Stockholm District Court. Where possible the opposing party shall be afforded the opportunity to express his opinion upon the application before it is granted. Where the application concerns the removal of an arbitrator, the arbitrator should also be heard.

Applications concerning the taking of evidence in accordance with section 26 shall be considered by the District Court determined by the arbitrators. In the absence of such decision, the application shall be considered by the Stockholm District Court.

Where the District Court has granted an application to appoint or remove an arbitrator, such decision may not appealed. Nor may a determination of the District Court in accordance with section 10, third paragraph otherwise be appealed.

SECTION 45

Where, according to law or by agreement, an action by a party must be brought within a certain period, but the action is covered by an arbitration agreement, the party must request arbitration in accordance with section 19 within the stated period.

Where arbitration has been requested in due time but the arbitral proceedings are terminated without a legal determination of the issue which was submitted to the arbitrators, and this is not due to the negligence of the party, the action shall be deemed to have been instituted in due time where a party requests arbitration or institutes court proceedings within thirty days of receipt of the award, or where the award has been set aside or declared invalid or an action against the award in accordance with section 36 has been dismissed, from the time that this decision becomes final.

International Matters

SECTION 46

This Act shall apply to arbitral proceedings which take place in Sweden notwithstanding that the dispute has an international connection.

SECTION 47

Arbitral proceedings in accordance with this Act may be commenced in Sweden, where the arbitration agreement provides that the proceedings shall take place in Sweden, or where the arbitrators or an arbitration institution pursuant to the agreement have determined that the proceedings shall take place in Sweden, or the opposing party otherwise consents thereto.

Arbitral proceedings in accordance with this Act may also be commenced in Sweden against a party which is domiciled in Sweden or is otherwise subject to the jurisdiction of the Swedish courts with regard to the matter in dispute, unless the arbitration agreement provides that the proceedings shall take place abroad.

In other cases, arbitral proceedings in accordance with this Act may not take place in Sweden.

SECTION 48

Where an arbitration agreement has an international connection, the agreement shall be governed by the law agreed upon by the parties. Where the parties have not reached such an agreement, the arbitration agreement shall be governed by the law of the country in which, by virtue of the agreement, the proceedings have taken place or shall take place.

The first paragraph shall not apply to the issue of whether a party was authorised to enter into an arbitration agreement or was duly represented.

SECTION 49

Where foreign law is applicable to the arbitration agreement, section 4 shall apply to issues which are covered by the agreement, except when:

1. in accordance with the applicable law, the agreement is invalid, inoperative, or incapable of being performed; or
2. in accordance with Swedish law, the dispute may not be determined by arbitrators.

The jurisdiction of a court to issue such decisions regarding security measures as the court is entitled to issue in accordance with law, notwithstanding the arbitration agreement, is set forth in section 4, third paragraph.

SECTION 50

The provisions of sections 26 and 44 regarding the taking of evidence during the arbitral proceedings in Sweden shall also apply in respect of arbitral proceedings which take place abroad, where the proceedings are based upon an arbitration agreement and, pursuant to Swedish law, the issues which are referred to the arbitrators may be resolved by arbitrators.

SECTION 51

Where none of the parties is domiciled or has its place of business in Sweden, such parties may in a commercial relationship through an express written agreement exclude or limit the application of the grounds for setting aside an award as are set forth in section 34.

An award which is subject to such an agreement shall be recognised and enforced in Sweden in accordance with the rules applicable to a foreign award.

Recognition and Enforcement of Foreign Awards, etc.

SECTION 52

An award made abroad shall be deemed to be a foreign award.

In conjunction with the application of this Act, an award shall be deemed to have been made in the country in which the place of arbitration is situated.

SECTION 53

Unless otherwise stated in sections 54–60, a foreign award which is based on an arbitration agreement shall be recognised and enforced in Sweden.

SECTION 54

A foreign award shall not be recognised and enforced in Sweden where the party against whom the award is invoked proves:

1. that the parties to the arbitration agreement, pursuant to the law applicable to them, lacked capacity to enter into the agreement or were not properly represented, or that the arbitration agreement was not valid under the law to which the parties have subjected it or, failing any indication thereon, under the law of the country where the award was made;
2. that the party against whom the award is invoked was not given proper notice of the appointment of the arbitrator or of the arbitration proceedings, or was otherwise unable to present his case;
3. that the award deals with a dispute not contemplated by, or not falling within, the terms of the submission to arbitration, or contains decisions on matters which are beyond the scope of the arbitration agreement, provided that, if the decision on a matter which falls within the mandate can be separated from those which fall outside the mandate, that part of the award which contains decisions on matters falling within the mandate may be recognised and enforced;

4. that the composition of the arbitral tribunal, or the arbitral procedure, was not in accordance with the agreement of the parties or, failing such agreement, was not in accordance with the law of the country where the arbitration took place; or

5. that the award has not yet become binding on the parties, or has been set aside or suspended by a competent authority of the country in which, or under the law of which, the award was made.

SECTION 55

Recognition and enforcement of a foreign award shall also be refused where a court finds:

1. that the award includes determination of an issue which, in accordance with Swedish law, may not be decided by arbitrators; or

2. that it would be clearly incompatible with the basic principles of the Swedish legal system to recognise and enforce the award.

SECTION 56

An application for the enforcement of a foreign award shall be lodged with the Svea Court of Appeal.

The original award or a certified copy of the award must be appended to the application. Unless the Court of Appeal decides otherwise, a certified translation into the Swedish language of the entire award must also be submitted.

SECTION 57

An application for enforcement shall not be granted unless the opposing party has been afforded an opportunity to express his opinion upon the application.

SECTION 58

Where the opposing party objects that an arbitration agreement was not entered into, the applicant must submit the arbitration agreement in an original or a certified copy and, unless otherwise decided by the Court of Appeal, must submit a certified translation into the Swedish language, or in some other manner prove that an arbitration agreement was entered into.

Where the opposing party objects that a petition has been lodged to set aside the award or a motion for a stay of execution has been submitted to the competent authority as referred to in section 54, sub-section 5, the Court of Appeal may postpone its decision and, upon request by the applicant, order the opposing party to provide reasonable security in default of which enforcement might otherwise be ordered.

SECTION 59

Where the Court of Appeal grants the application, the award shall be enforced as a final judgment of a Swedish court, unless otherwise determined by the Supreme Court following an appeal of the Court of Appeal's decision.

SECTION 60

Where a security measure has been granted in accordance with Chapter 15 of the Code of Judicial Procedure, in conjunction with the application of section 7 of the same Chapter, a request for arbitration abroad which might result in an award which is recognised and may be enforced in Sweden shall be equated with the commencement of an action.

Where an application for the enforcement of a foreign award has been lodged, the Court of Appeal shall examine a request for a security measure or a request to set aside such decision.

1. This Act shall enter into force on 1 April 1999, at which time the Arbitration Act (SFS 1929:145) and the Foreign Arbitration Agreements and Awards Act (SFS 1929:147) shall be repealed.

2. The previous Act shall apply to arbitral proceedings which have been commenced prior to the entry into force or, with respect to enforcement of a foreign award, when the application for enforcement was lodged prior to the entry into force.

3. Where an arbitration agreement has been concluded prior to the entry into force, the provisions of section 18, second paragraph, section 21, first paragraph, sub-section 1, and section 26, second and third paragraphs of the Arbitration Act (SFS 1929:145) shall apply, with respect to the period within which the award shall be rendered, to proceedings that are commenced within two years from the date of the entry into force of the new Act.

4. In the circumstances set forth in sub-sections 2 and 3, the parties may agree that only the new Act shall apply.

5. References in statutes or other legislation to the Arbitration Act (SFS 1929:145) shall refer instead to the new Act.

APPENDIX 2A

Arbitration Rules of the Arbitration Institute of the Stockholm Chamber of Commerce (2010)

Arbitration Institute of the Stockholm Chamber of Commerce

ARTICLE 1 ABOUT THE SCC

The Arbitration Institute of the Stockholm Chamber of Commerce (the "SCC") is the body responsible for the administration of disputes in accordance with the "SCC Rules"; the Arbitration Rules of the Arbitration Institute of the Stockholm Chamber of Commerce (the "Arbitration Rules") and the Rules for Expedited Arbitrations of the Stockholm Chamber of Commerce (the "Rules for Expedited Arbitrations"), and other procedures or rules agreed upon by the parties. The SCC is composed of a board of directors (the "Board") and a secretariat (the "Secretariat"). Detailed provisions regarding the organisation of the SCC are set out in Appendix I.

Commencement of Proceedings

ARTICLE 2 REQUEST FOR ARBITRATION

A Request for Arbitration shall include:

(i)   a statement of the names, addresses, telephone and facsimile numbers and e-mail addresses of the parties and their counsel;
(ii)   a summary of the dispute;
(iii)   a preliminary statement of the relief sought by the Claimant;
(iv)   a copy or description of the arbitration agreement or clause under which the dispute is to be settled;
(v)   comments on the number of arbitrators and the seat of arbitration; and
(vi)   if applicable, the name, address, telephone number, facsimile number and e-mail address of the arbitrator appointed by the Claimant.

ARTICLE 3 REGISTRATION FEE

(1)   Upon filing the Request for Arbitration, the Claimant shall pay a Registration Fee. The amount of the Registration Fee shall be determined in accordance with the Schedule of Costs (Appendix III) in force on the date when the Request for Arbitration is filed.
(2)   If the Registration Fee is not paid upon filing the Request for Arbitration, the Secretariat shall set a time period within which the Claimant shall pay the Registration Fee. If the Registration Fee is not paid within this time period, the Secretariat shall dismiss the Request for Arbitration.

ARTICLE 4 COMMENCEMENT OF ARBITRATION

Arbitration is commenced on the date when the SCC receives the Request for Arbitration.

ARTICLE 5 ANSWER

(1) The Secretariat shall send a copy of the Request for Arbitration and the documents attached thereto to the Respondent. The Secretariat shall set a time period within which the Respondent shall submit an Answer to the SCC. The Answer shall include:

    (i) any objections concerning the existence, validity or applicability of the arbitration agreement; however, failure to raise any objections shall not preclude the Respondent from subsequently raising such objections at any time up to and including the submission of the Statement of Defence;

    (ii) an admission or denial of the relief sought in the Request for Arbitration;

    (iii) a preliminary statement of any counterclaims or set-offs;

    (iv) comments on the number of arbitrators and the seat of arbitration; and

    (v) if applicable, the name, address, telephone number, facsimile number and e-mail address of the arbitrator appointed by the Respondent.

(2) The Secretariat shall send a copy of the Answer to the Claimant. The Claimant shall be given an opportunity to submit comments on the Answer.

(3) Failure by the Respondent to submit an Answer shall not prevent the arbitration from proceeding.

ARTICLE 6 REQUEST FOR FURTHER DETAILS

The Board may request further details from either party regarding any of their written submissions to the SCC. If the Claimant fails to comply with a request for further details, the Board may dismiss the case. If the Respondent fails to comply with a request for further details regarding its counterclaim or set-off, the Board may dismiss the counterclaim or set-off. Failure by the Respondent to otherwise comply with a request for further details shall not prevent the arbitration from proceeding.

ARTICLE 7 TIME PERIODS

The Board may, on application by either party or on its own motion, extend any time period which has been set for a party to comply with a particular direction.

ARTICLE 8 NOTICES

(1) Any notice or other communication from the Secretariat or the Board shall be delivered to the last known address of the addressee.

2) Any notice or other communication shall be delivered by courier or registered mail, facsimile transmission, e-mail or any other means of communication that provides a record of the sending thereof.

(3) A notice or communication sent in accordance with paragraph (2) shall be deemed to have been received by the addressee on the date it would normally have been received given the chosen means of communication.

ARTICLE 9 DECISIONS BY THE BOARD

When necessary the Board shall:

(i) decide whether the SCC manifestly lacks jurisdiction over the dispute pursuant to Article 10 (i);

(ii) decide whether to consolidate cases pursuant to Article 11;

(iii) decide the number of arbitrators pursuant to Article 12;

(iv) make any appointment of arbitrators pursuant to Article 13;

(v) decide the seat of arbitration pursuant to Article 20; and

ARTICLE 10 DISMISSAL

The Board shall dismiss a case, in whole or in part, if:

(i) the SCC manifestly lacks jurisdiction over the dispute; or

(ii) the Advance on Costs is not paid pursuant to Article 45.

ARTICLE 11 CONSOLIDATION

If arbitration is commenced concerning a legal relationship in respect of which an arbitration between the same parties is already pending under these Rules, the Board may, at the request of a party, decide to consolidate the new claims with the pending proceedings. Such decision may only be made after consulting the parties and the Arbitral Tribunal.

Composition of the Arbitral Tribunal

ARTICLE 12 NUMBER OF ARBITRATORS

The parties may agree on the number of arbitrators. Where the parties have not agreed on the number of arbitrators, the Arbitral Tribunal shall consist of three arbitrators, unless the Board, taking into account the complexity of the case, the amount in dispute or other circumstances, decides that the dispute is to be decided by a sole arbitrator.

ARTICLE 13 APPOINTMENT OF ARBITRATORS

(1) The parties may agree on a different procedure for appointment of the Arbitral Tribunal than as provided under this Article. In such cases, if the Arbitral Tribunal has not been appointed within the time period agreed by the parties or, where the parties have not agreed on a time period, within the time period set by the Board, the appointment shall be made pursuant to paragraphs (2)–(6).

(2) Where the Arbitral Tribunal is to consist of a sole arbitrator, the parties shall be given 10 days within which to jointly appoint the arbitrator. If the parties fail to make the appointment within this time period, the arbitrator shall be appointed by the Board.

(3) Where the Arbitral Tribunal is to consist of more than one arbitrator, each party shall appoint an equal number of arbitrators and the Chairperson shall be appointed by the Board. Where a party fails to appoint arbitrator(s) within the stipulated time period, the Board shall make the appointment.

(4) Where there are multiple Claimants or Respondents and the Arbitral Tribunal is to consist of more than one arbitrator, the multiple Claimants, jointly, and the multiple Respondents, jointly, shall appoint an equal number of arbitrators. If either side fails to make such joint appointment, the Board shall appoint the entire Arbitral Tribunal.

(5) If the parties are of different nationalities, the sole arbitrator or the Chairperson of the Arbitral Tribunal shall be of a different nationality than the parties, unless the parties have agreed otherwise or unless otherwise deemed appropriate by the Board.

(6) When appointing arbitrators, the Board shall consider the nature and circumstances of the dispute, the applicable law, the seat and language of the arbitration and the nationality of the parties.

ARTICLE 14 IMPARTIALITY AND INDEPENDENCE

(1) Every arbitrator must be impartial and independent.

(2) Before being appointed as arbitrator, a person shall disclose any circumstances which may give rise to justifiable doubts as to his/her impartiality or independence. If the person is appointed as

arbitrator, he/she shall submit to the Secretariat a signed statement of impartiality and independence disclosing any circumstances which may give rise to justifiable doubts as to that person's impartiality or independence. The Secretariat shall send a copy of the statement of impartiality and independence to the parties and the other arbitrators.

(3) An arbitrator shall immediately inform the parties and the other arbitrators in writing where any circumstances referred to in paragraph (2) arise during the course of the arbitration.

ARTICLE 15 CHALLENGE TO ARBITRATORS

(1) A party may challenge any arbitrator if circumstances exist which give rise to justifiable doubts as to the arbitrator's impartiality or independence or if he/she does not possess qualifications agreed by the parties. A party may challenge an arbitrator whom it has appointed or in whose appointment it has participated, only for reasons of which it becomes aware after the appointment was made.

(2) A challenge to an arbitrator shall be made by submitting a written statement to the Secretariat setting forth the reasons for the challenge within 15 days from when the circumstances giving rise to the challenge became known to the party. Failure by a party to challenge an arbitrator within the stipulated time period constitutes a waiver of the right to make the challenge.

(3) The Secretariat shall notify the parties and the arbitrators of the challenge and give them an opportunity to submit comments on the challenge.

(4) If the other party agrees to the challenge, the arbitrator shall resign. In all other cases, the Board shall make the final decision on the challenge.

ARTICLE 16 RELEASE FROM APPOINTMENT

(1) The Board shall release an arbitrator from appointment where:
    (i) the Board accepts the resignation of an arbitrator;
    (ii) a challenge to the arbitrator under Article 15 is sustained; or
    (iii) the arbitrator is otherwise prevented from fulfilling his/her duties or fails to perform his/her functions in an adequate manner.

(2) Before the Board releases an arbitrator, the Secretariat may give the parties and the arbitrators an opportunity to submit comments.

ARTICLE 17 REPLACEMENT OF ARBITRATORS

(1) The Board shall appoint a new arbitrator where an arbitrator has been released from his/her appointment pursuant to Article 16, or where an arbitrator has died. If the arbitrator being replaced was appointed by a party, that party shall appoint the new arbitrator, unless otherwise deemed appropriate by the Board.

(2) Where the Arbitral Tribunal consists of three or more arbitrators, the Board may decide that the remaining arbitrators shall proceed with the arbitration. In making its decision, the Board shall take into account the stage of the arbitration and other relevant circumstances. Before making such decision, the parties and the arbitrators shall be given an opportunity to submit comments.

(3) Where an arbitrator has been replaced, the newly composed Arbitral Tribunal shall decide whether and to what extent the proceedings are to be repeated.

The Proceedings before the Arbitral Tribunal

ARTICLE 18 REFERRAL TO THE ARBITRAL TRIBUNAL

When the Arbitral Tribunal has been appointed and the Advance on Costs has been paid, the Secretariat shall refer the case to the Arbitral Tribunal.

ARTICLE 19 CONDUCT OF THE ARBITRATION

(1) Subject to these Rules and any agreement between the parties, the Arbitral Tribunal may conduct the arbitration in such manner as it considers appropriate.
(2) In all cases, the Arbitral Tribunal shall conduct the arbitration in an impartial, practical and expeditious manner, giving each party an equal and reasonable opportunity to present its case.

ARTICLE 20 SEAT OF ARBITRATION

(1) Unless agreed upon by the parties, the Board shall decide the seat of arbitration.
(2) The Arbitral Tribunal may, after consultation with the parties, conduct hearings at any place which it considers appropriate. The Arbitral Tribunal may meet and deliberate at any place which it considers appropriate. If any hearing, meeting, or deliberation is held elsewhere than at the seat of arbitration, the arbitration shall be deemed to have taken place at the seat of arbitration.
(3) The award shall be deemed to have been made at the seat of arbitration.

ARTICLE 21 LANGUAGE

(1) Unless agreed upon by the parties, the Arbitral Tribunal shall determine the language(s) of the arbitration. In so determining, the Arbitral Tribunal shall have due regard to all relevant circumstances and shall give the parties an opportunity to submit comments.
(2) The Arbitral Tribunal may request that any documents submitted in languages other than the language(s) of the arbitration be accompanied by a translation into the language(s) of the arbitration.

ARTICLE 22 APPLICABLE LAW

(1) The Arbitral Tribunal shall decide the merits of the dispute on the basis of the law(s) or rules of law agreed upon by the parties. In the absence of such agreement, the Arbitral Tribunal shall apply the law or rules of law which it considers to be most appropriate.
(2) Any designation made by the parties of the law of a given state shall be deemed to refer to the substantive law of that state and not to its conflict of laws rules.
(3) The Arbitral Tribunal shall decide the dispute *ex aequo et bono or as amiable compositeur* only if the parties have expressly authorised it to do so.

ARTICLE 23 PROVISIONAL TIMETABLE

After the referral of the case to the Arbitral Tribunal, the Arbitral Tribunal shall promptly consult with the parties with a view to establishing a provisional timetable for the conduct of the arbitration. The Arbitral Tribunal shall send a copy of the provisional timetable to the parties and to the Secretariat.

ARTICLE 24 WRITTEN SUBMISSIONS

(1) The Claimant shall, within the period of time determined by the Arbitral Tribunal, submit a Statement of Claim which shall include, unless previously submitted:
    (i)   the specific relief sought;
    (ii) the material circumstances on which the Claimant relies; and
    (iii) the documents on which the Claimant relies.
(2) The Respondent shall, within the period of time determined by the Arbitral Tribunal, submit a Statement of Defence which shall include, unless previously submitted:
    (i)   any objections concerning the existence, validity or applicability of the arbitration agreement;
    (ii) a statement whether, and to what extent, the Respondent admits or denies the relief sought by the Claimant;

(iii) the material circumstances on which the Respondent relies;

(iv) any counterclaim or set-off and the grounds on which it is based; and

(v) the documents on which the Respondent relies.

(3) The Arbitral Tribunal may order the parties to submit additional written submissions.

ARTICLE 25 AMENDMENTS

At any time prior to the close of proceedings pursuant to Article 34, a party may amend or supplement its claim, counterclaim, defence or set-off provided its case, as amended or supplemented, is still comprised by the arbitration agreement, unless the Arbitral Tribunal considers it inappropriate to allow such amendment or supplement having regard to the delay in making it, the prejudice to the other party or any other circumstances.

ARTICLE 26 EVIDENCE

(1) The admissibility, relevance, materiality and weight of evidence shall be for the Arbitral Tribunal to determine.

(2) The Arbitral Tribunal may order a party to identify the documentary evidence it intends to rely on and specify the circumstances intended to be proved by such evidence.

(3) At the request of a party, the Arbitral Tribunal may order a party to produce any documents or other evidence which may be relevant to the outcome of the case.

ARTICLE 27 HEARINGS

(1) A hearing shall be held if requested by a party, or if deemed appropriate by the Arbitral Tribunal.

(2) The Arbitral Tribunal shall, in consultation with the parties, determine the date, time and location of any hearing and shall provide the parties with reasonable notice thereof.

(3) Unless otherwise agreed by the parties, hearings will be held in private.

ARTICLE 28 WITNESSES

(1) In advance of any hearing, the Arbitral Tribunal may order the parties to identify each witness or expert they intend to call and specify the circumstances intended to be proved by each testimony.

(2) The testimony of witnesses or party-appointed experts may be submitted in the form of signed statements.

(3) Any witness or expert, on whose testimony a party seeks to rely, shall attend a hearing for examination, unless otherwise agreed by the parties.

ARTICLE 29 EXPERTS APPOINTED BY THE ARBITRAL TRIBUNAL

(1) After consultation with the parties, the Arbitral Tribunal may appoint one or more experts to report to it on specific issues set out by the Arbitral Tribunal in writing.

(2) Upon receipt of a report from an expert appointed by the Arbitral Tribunal, the Arbitral Tribunal shall send a copy of the report to the parties and shall give the parties an opportunity to submit written comments on the report.

(3) Upon the request of a party, the parties shall be given an opportunity to examine any expert appointed by the Arbitral Tribunal at a hearing.

ARTICLE 30 DEFAULT

(1) If the Claimant, without showing good cause, fails to submit a Statement of Claim in accordance with Article 24, the Arbitral Tribunal shall terminate the proceedings provided the Respondent has not filed a counterclaim.

(2) If a party, without showing good cause, fails to submit a Statement of Defence or other written statement in accordance with Article 24, or fails to appear at a hearing, or otherwise fails to avail itself of the opportunity to present its case, the Arbitral Tribunal may proceed with the arbitration and make an award.

(3) If a party without good cause fails to comply with any provision of, or requirement under, these Rules or any procedural order given by the Arbitral Tribunal, the Arbitral Tribunal may draw such inferences as it considers appropriate.

ARTICLE 31 WAIVER

A party, who during the arbitration fails to object without delay to any failure to comply with the arbitration agreement, these Rules or other rules applicable to the proceedings, shall be deemed to have waived the right to object to such failure.

ARTICLE 32 INTERIM MEASURES

(1) The Arbitral Tribunal may, at the request of a party, grant any interim measures it deems appropriate.

(2) The Arbitral Tribunal may order the party requesting an interim measure to provide appropriate security in connection with the measure.

(3) An interim measure shall take the form of an order or an award.

(4) Provisions with respect to interim measures requested before arbitration has been commenced or a case has been referred to an Arbitral Tribunal are set out in Appendix II.

(5) A request for interim measures made by a party to a judicial authority is not incompatible with the arbitration agreement or with these Rules.

ARTICLE 33 COMMUNICATIONS FROM THE ARBITRAL TRIBUNAL

Article 8 shall apply to communications from the Arbitral Tribunal.

ARTICLE 34 CLOSE OF PROCEEDINGS

The Arbitral Tribunal shall declare the proceedings closed when it is satisfied that the parties have had a reasonable opportunity to present their cases. In exceptional circumstances, prior to the making of the final award, the Arbitral Tribunal may reopen the proceedings on its own motion, or upon the application of a party.

Awards and Decisions

ARTICLE 35 AWARDS AND DECISIONS

(1) When the Arbitral Tribunal consists of more than one arbitrator, any award or other decision of the Arbitral Tribunal shall be made by a majority of the arbitrators or, failing a majority, by the Chairperson.

(2) The Arbitral Tribunal may decide that the Chairperson alone may make procedural rulings.

ARTICLE 36 MAKING OF AWARDS

(1) The Arbitral Tribunal shall make its award in writing, and, unless otherwise agreed by the parties, shall state the reasons upon which the award is based.

(2) An award shall include the date of the award and the seat of arbitration in accordance with Article 20.

(3) An award shall be signed by the arbitrators. If an arbitrator fails to sign an award, the signatures of the majority of the arbitrators or, failing a majority, of the Chairperson shall be sufficient, provided that the reason for the omission of the signature is stated in the award.

(4) The Arbitral Tribunal shall deliver a copy of the award to each of the parties and to the SCC without delay.

(5) If any arbitrator fails without valid cause to participate in the deliberations of the Arbitral Tribunal on an issue, such failure will not preclude a decision being made by the other arbitrators.

ARTICLE 37 TIME LIMIT FOR FINAL AWARD

The final award shall be made not later than six months from the date upon which the arbitration was referred to the Arbitral Tribunal pursuant to Article 18. The Board may extend this time limit upon a reasoned request from the Arbitral Tribunal or if otherwise deemed necessary.

ARTICLE 38 SEPARATE AWARD

The Arbitral Tribunal may decide a separate issue or part of the dispute in a separate award.

ARTICLE 39 SETTLEMENT OR OTHER GROUNDS FOR TERMINATION OF THE ARBITRATION

(1) If the parties reach a settlement before the final award is made, the Arbitral Tribunal may, upon the request of both parties, record the settlement in the form of a consent award.

(2) If the arbitration for any other reason is terminated before the final award is made, the Arbitral Tribunal shall issue an award recording the termination.

ARTICLE 40 EFFECT OF AN AWARD

An award shall be final and binding on the parties when rendered. By agreeing to arbitration under these Rules, the parties undertake to carry out any award without delay.

ARTICLE 41 CORRECTION AND INTERPRETATION OF AN AWARD

(1) Within 30 days of receiving an award, a party may, upon notice to the other party, request that the Arbitral Tribunal correct any clerical, typographical or computational errors in the award, or provide an interpretation of a specific point or part of the award. If the Arbitral Tribunal considers the request justified, it shall make the correction or provide the interpretation within 30 days of receiving the request.

(2) The Arbitral Tribunal may correct any error of the type referred to in paragraph (1) above on its own motion within 30 days of the date of an award.

(3) Any correction or interpretation of an award shall be in writing and shall comply with the requirements of Article 36.

ARTICLE 42 ADDITIONAL AWARD

Within 30 days of receiving an award, a party may, upon notice to the other party, request the Arbitral Tribunal to make an additional award on claims presented in the arbitration but not determined in the award. If the Arbitral Tribunal considers the request justified, it shall make the additional award within 60 days of receipt of the request. When deemed necessary, the Board may extend this 60 day time limit.

Costs of the Arbitration

ARTICLE 43 COSTS OF THE ARBITRATION

(1) The Costs of the Arbitration consist of:
    (i)   the Fees of the Arbitral Tribunal;
    (ii) the Administrative Fee; and
    (iii) the expenses of the Arbitral Tribunal and the SCC.

(2) Before making the final award, the Arbitral Tribunal shall request the Board to finally determine the Costs of the Arbitration. The Board shall finally determine the Costs of the Arbitration in accordance with the Schedule of Costs (Appendix III) in force on the date of commencement of the arbitration pursuant to Article 4.

(3) If the arbitration is terminated before the final award is made pursuant to Article 39, the Board shall finally determine the Costs of the Arbitration having regard to when the arbitration terminates, the work performed by the Arbitral Tribunal and other relevant circumstances.

(4) The Arbitral Tribunal shall include in the final award the Costs of the Arbitration as finally determined by the Board and specify the individual fees and expenses of each member of the Arbitral Tribunal and the SCC.

(5) Unless otherwise agreed by the parties, the Arbitral Tribunal shall, at the request of a party, apportion the Costs of the Arbitration between the parties, having regard to the outcome of the case and other relevant circumstances.

(6) The parties are jointly and severally liable to the arbitrator(s) and to the SCC for the Costs of the Arbitration.

ARTICLE 44 COSTS INCURRED BY A PARTY

Unless otherwise agreed by the parties, the Arbitral Tribunal may in the final award upon the request of a party, order one party to pay any reasonable costs incurred by another party, including costs for legal representation, having regard to the outcome of the case and other relevant circumstances.

ARTICLE 45 ADVANCE ON COSTS

(1) The Board shall determine an amount to be paid by the parties as an Advance on Costs.

(2) The Advance on Costs shall correspond to the estimated amount of the Costs of Arbitration pursuant to Article 43 (1).

(3) Each party shall pay half of the Advance on Costs, unless separate advances are determined. Where counterclaims or set-offs are submitted, the Board may decide that each of the parties shall pay the advances on costs corresponding to its claim. Upon a request from the Arbitral Tribunal or if otherwise deemed necessary, the Board may order parties to pay additional advances during the course of the arbitration.

(4) If a party fails to make a required payment, the Secretariat shall give the other party an opportunity to do so within a specified period of time. If the required payment is not made, the Board shall dismiss the case in whole or in part. If the other party makes the required payment, the Arbitral Tribunal may, at the request of such party, make a separate award for reimbursement of the payment.

(5) At any stage during the arbitration or after the Award has been made, the Board may draw on the Advance on Costs to cover the Costs of the Arbitration.

(6) The Board may decide that part of the Advance on Costs may be provided in the form of a bank guarantee or other form of security.

General Rules

ARTICLE 46 CONFIDENTIALITY

Unless otherwise agreed by the parties, the SCC and the Arbitral Tribunal shall maintain the confidentiality of the arbitration and the award.

ARTICLE 47 ENFORCEMENT

In all matters not expressly provided for in these Rules, the SCC, the Arbitral Tribunal and the parties shall act in the spirit of these Rules and shall make every reasonable effort to ensure that all awards are legally enforceable.

ARTICLE 48 EXCLUSION OF LIABILITY

Neither the SCC nor the arbitrator(s) are liable to any party for any act or omission in connection with the arbitration unless such act or omission constitutes wilful misconduct or gross negligence.

Appendix I Organisation

ARTICLE 1 ABOUT THE SCC

The Arbitration Institute of the Stockholm Chamber of Commerce (the "SCC") is a body providing administrative services in relation to the settlement of disputes. The SCC is part of the Stockholm Chamber of Commerce, but is independent in exercising its functions in the administration of disputes. The SCC is composed of a board of directors (the "Board") and a secretariat (the "Secretariat").

ARTICLE 2 FUNCTION OF THE SCC

The SCC does not itself decide disputes. The function of the SCC is to:

(i)   administer domestic and international disputes in accordance with the SCC Rules and other procedures or rules agreed upon by the parties; and

(ii) provide information concerning arbitration and mediation matters.

ARTICLE 3 THE BOARD

The Board shall be composed of one chairperson, a maximum of three vice-chairpersons and a maximum of 12 additional members. The Board shall include both Swedish and non-Swedish nationals.

ARTICLE 4 APPOINTMENT OF THE BOARD

The Board shall be appointed by the Board of Directors of the Stockholm Chamber of Commerce (the "Board of Directors"). The members of the Board shall be appointed for a period of three years and are eligible for re-appointment in their respective capacities for one further three year period only, unless exceptional circumstances apply.

ARTICLE 5 REMOVAL OF A MEMBER OF THE BOARD

In exceptional circumstances, the Board of Directors may remove a member of the Board. If a member resigns or is removed during a term of office, the Board of Directors shall appoint a new member for the remainder of the term.

ARTICLE 6 FUNCTION OF THE BOARD

The function of the Board is to take the decisions required of the SCC in administering disputes under the SCC Rules and any other rules or procedures agreed upon by the parties. Such decisions include decisions on the jurisdiction of the SCC, determination of advances on costs, appointment of arbitrators, decisions upon challenges to arbitrators, removal of arbitrators and the fixing of arbitration costs.

ARTICLE 7 DECISIONS BY THE BOARD

Two members of the Board form a quorum. If a majority is not attained, the Chairperson has the casting vote. The Chairperson or a Vice Chairperson may to take decisions on behalf of the Board in urgent matters. A committee of the Board may be appointed to take certain decisions on behalf of the

Board. The Board may delegate decisions to the Secretariat, including decisions on advances on costs, extension of time for rendering an award, dismissal for non-payment of registration fee, release of arbitrators and fixing of arbitration costs. Decisions by the Board are final.

ARTICLE 8 THE SECRETARIAT

The Secretariat acts under the direction of a Secretary General. The Secretariat carries out the functions assigned to it under the SCC Rules. The Secretariat may also take decisions delegated to it by the Board.

ARTICLE 9 PROCEDURES

The SCC shall maintain the confidentiality of the arbitration and the award and shall deal with the arbitration in an impartial, practical and expeditious manner.

Appendix II Emergency Arbitrator

ARTICLE 1 EMERGENCY ARBITRATOR

(1) A party may apply for the appointment of an Emergency Arbitrator until the case has been referred to an Arbitral Tribunal pursuant to Article 18 of the Arbitration Rules.

(2) The powers of the Emergency Arbitrator shall be those set out in Article 32 (1)-(3) of the Arbitration Rules. Such powers terminate when the case has been referred to an Arbitral Tribunal pursuant to Article 18 of the Arbitration Rules or when an emergency decision ceases to be binding according to Article 9 (4) of this Appendix.

ARTICLE 2 APPLICATION FOR THE APPOINTMENT OF AN EMERGENCY ARBITRATOR

An application for the appointment of an Emergency Arbitrator shall include:

(i) a statement of the names and addresses, telephone and facsimile numbers and e-mail addresses of the parties and their counsel;

(ii) a summary of the dispute;

(iii) a statement of the interim relief sought and the reasons therefor;

(iv) a copy or description of the arbitration agreement or clause on the basis of which the dispute is to be settled;

(v) comments on the seat of the emergency proceedings, the applicable law(s) and the language(s) of the proceedings; and

(vi) proof of payment of the costs for the emergency proceedings pursuant to Article 10 (1)-(2) of this Appendix.

ARTICLE 3 NOTICE

As soon as an application for the appointment of an Emergency Arbitrator has been received, the Secretariat shall send the application to the other party.

ARTICLE 4 APPOINTMENT OF THE EMERGENCY ARBITRATOR

(1) The Board shall seek to appoint an Emergency Arbitrator within 24 hours of receipt of the application for the appointment of an Emergency Arbitrator.

(2) An Emergency Arbitrator shall not be appointed if the SCC manifestly lacks jurisdiction over the dispute.

(3) Article 15 of the Arbitration Rules applies except that a challenge must be made within 24 hours from when the circumstances giving rise to the challenge of an Emergency Arbitrator became known to the party.

(4) An Emergency Arbitrator may not act as an arbitrator in any future arbitration relating to the dispute, unless otherwise agreed by the parties.

ARTICLE 5 SEAT OF THE EMERGENCY PROCEEDINGS

The seat of the emergency proceedings shall be that which has been agreed upon by the parties as the seat of the arbitration. If the seat of the arbitration has not been agreed by the parties, the Board shall determine the seat of the emergency proceedings.

ARTICLE 6 REFERRAL TO THE EMERGENCY ARBITRATOR

Once an Emergency Arbitrator has been appointed, the Secretariat shall promptly refer the application to the Emergency Arbitrator.

ARTICLE 7 CONDUCT OF THE EMERGENCY PROCEEDINGS

Article 19 of the Arbitration Rules shall apply to the emergency proceedings, taking into account the urgency inherent in such proceedings.

ARTICLE 8 EMERGENCY DECISIONS ON INTERIM MEASURES

(1) Any emergency decision on interim measures shall be made not later than 5 days from the date upon which the application was referred to the Emergency Arbitrator pursuant to Article 6 of this Appendix. The Board may extend this time limit upon a reasoned request from the Emergency Arbitrator, or if otherwise deemed necessary.

(2) Any emergency decision on interim measures shall:
    (i) be made in writing;
    (ii) state the date when it was made, the seat of the emergency proceedings and the reasons upon which the decision is based; and
    (iii) be signed by the Emergency Arbitrator.

(3) The Emergency Arbitrator shall promptly deliver a copy of the emergency decision to each of the parties and to the SCC.

ARTICLE 9 BINDING EFFECT OF EMERGENCY DECISIONS

(1) An emergency decision shall be binding on the parties when rendered.

(2) The emergency decision may be amended or revoked by the Emergency Arbitrator upon a reasoned request by a party.

(3) By agreeing to arbitration under the Arbitration Rules, the parties undertake to comply with any emergency decision without delay.

(4) The emergency decision ceases to be binding if:
    (i) the Emergency Arbitrator or an Arbitral Tribunal so decides;
    (ii) an Arbitral Tribunal makes a final award;
    (iii) arbitration is not commenced within 30 days from the date of the emergency decision; or
    (iv) the case is not referred to an Arbitral Tribunal within 90 days from the date of the emergency decision.

(5) An Arbitral Tribunal is not bound by the decision(s) and reasons of the Emergency Arbitrator.

ARTICLE 10 COSTS OF THE EMERGENCY PROCEEDINGS

(1) The party applying for the appointment of an Emergency Arbitrator shall pay the costs of the emergency proceedings upon filing the application.

(2) The costs of the emergency proceedings include:
   (i) the fee of the Emergency Arbitrator which amounts to EUR 12,000; and
   (ii) the application fee which amounts to EUR 3,000.

(3) Upon a request from the Emergency Arbitrator or if otherwise deemed appropriate, the Board may decide to increase or reduce the costs having regard to the nature of the case, the work performed by the Emergency Arbitrator and the SCC, and other relevant circumstances.

(4) If payment of the costs of the emergency proceedings is not made in due time, the Secretariat shall dismiss the application.

(5) At the request of a party, the costs of the emergency proceedings may be apportioned between the parties by an Arbitral Tribunal in a final award.

Appendix III Schedule of Costs

Arbitration Costs

ARTICLE 1 REGISTRATION FEE

(1) The Registration Fee referred to in Article 3 of the Arbitration Rules amounts to EUR 1 500.

(2) The Registration Fee is non-refundable and constitutes a part of the Administrative Fee in Article 3 below. The Registration Fee shall be credited to the Advance on Costs to be paid by the Claimant pursuant to Article 45 of the Arbitration Rules.

ARTICLE 2 FEES OF THE ARBITRAL TRIBUNAL

(1) The Board shall determine the fee of a Chairperson or sole arbitrator based on the amount in dispute in accordance with the table below.

(2) Co-arbitrators shall each receive 60 per cent of the fee of the Chairperson. After consultation with the Arbitral Tribunal, the Board may decide that a different percentage shall apply.

(3) The amount in dispute shall be the aggregate value of all claims, counterclaims and set-offs. Where the amount in dispute cannot be ascertained, the Board shall determine the Fees of the Arbitral Tribunal taking all relevant circumstances into account.

(4) In exceptional circumstances, the Board may deviate from the amounts set out in the table.

ARTICLE 3 ADMINISTRATIVE FEE

(1) The Administrative Fee shall be determined in accordance with the table below.

(2) The amount in dispute shall be the aggregate value of all claims, counterclaims and set-offs. Where the amount in dispute cannot be ascertained, the Board shall determine the Administrative Fee taking all relevant circumstances into account.

(3) In exceptional circumstances, the Board may deviate from the amounts set out in the table.

ARTICLE 4 EXPENSES

In addition to the Fees of the arbitrator(s) and the Administrative Fee, the Board shall fix an amount to cover any reasonable expenses incurred by the arbitrator(s) and the SCC. The expenses of the arbitrator(s) may include the fee and expenses of any expert appointed by the Arbitral Tribunal pursuant to Article 29 of the Arbitration Rules.

Arbitrators' Fees

Amount in dispute	Fee of the Chairman/Sole Arbitrator	
(EUR)	Minimum (EUR)	Maximum (EUR)
to 25 000	2 500	5 500
from 25 001 to 50 000	2 500 + 2 % on the amount above 25 000	5 500 + 14 % on the amount above 25 000
from 50 001 to 100 000	3 000 + 2 % on the amount above 50 000	9 000 + 4 % on the amount above the 50 000
from 100 001 to 500 000	4 000 + 1 % on the amount above 100 000	11 000 + 5 % on the amount above 100 000
from 500 001 to 1 000 000	8 000 + 0,8 % on the amount above 500 000	31 000 + 2,4 % on the amount above 500 000
from 1 000 001 to 2 000 000	12 000 + 0,5 % on the amount above 1 000 000	43 000 +2,5 % on the amount above 1 000 000
from 2 000 001 to 5 000 000	17 000 + 0,2 % on the amount above 2 000 000	68 000 + 0,8 % on the amount above 2 000 000
from 5 000 001 to 10 000 000	23 000 + 0,1 % on the amount above 5 000 000	92 000 + 0,68 % on the amount above 5 000 000
from 10 000 001 to 50 000 000	28 000 + 0,03 % on the amount above 10 000 000	126 000 + 0,15 % on the amount above 10 000 000
from 50 000 001 to 75 000 000	40 000 + 0,02 % on the amount above 50 000 000	186 000 + 0,16 % on the amount above 50 000 000
from 75 000 001 to 100 000 000	45 000 + 0,012 % on the amount above 75 000 000	226 000 + 0,02 % on the amount above 75 000 000
from 100 000 001	To be determined by the Board	To be determined by the Board

The Costs of the Arbitration may easily be calculated at www.sccinstitute.com

Administrative Fee

Amount in dispute (EUR)	Administrative Fee (EUR)
Up to 25 000	1 500
from 25 001 to 50 000	1 500 + 4 % on the amount above 25 000
from 50 001 to 100 000	2 500 + 2 % on the amount above 50 000
from 100 001 to 500 000	3 500 + 1,6 % on the amount above 100 000
from 500 001 to 1 000 000	9 900 + 0,8 % on the amount above 500 000
from 1 000 001 to 2 000 000	13 900 + 0,5 % on the amount above 1 000 000
from 2 000 001 to 5 000 000	18 900 + 0,1 % on the amount above 2 000 000
from 5 000 001 to 10 000 000	21 900 + 0,14 % on the amount above 5 000 000
from 10 000 001 to 50 000 000	28 900 + 0,02 % on the amount above 10 000 000
from 50 000 001 to 75 000 000	36 900 + 0,02 % on the amount above 50 000 000
from 75 000 001	41 900 + 0,01 % on the amount above 75 000 000 Maximum 60 000

The Costs of the Arbitration may easily be calculated at www.sccinstitute.com

Rules for Expedited Arbitrations of the Arbitration Institute of the Stockholm Chamber of Commerce (2010)

Arbitration Institute of the Stockholm Chamber of Commerce

ARTICLE 1 ABOUT THE SCC

The Arbitration Institute of the Stockholm Chamber of Commerce (the "SCC") is the body responsible for the administration of disputes in accordance with the "SCC Rules"; the Arbitration Rules of the Arbitration Institute of the Stockholm Chamber of Commerce (the "Arbitration Rules") and the Rules for Expedited Arbitrations of the Stockholm Chamber of Commerce (the "Rules for Expedited Arbitrations"), and other procedures or rules agreed upon by the parties. The SCC is composed of a board of directors (the "Board") and a secretariat (the "Secretariat"). Detailed provisions regarding the organisation of the SCC are set out in Appendix I.

Commencement of Proceedings

ARTICLE 2 REQUEST FOR ARBITRATION

A Request for Arbitration shall include:

(i)   a statement of the names, addresses, telephone and facsimile numbers and e mail addresses of the parties and their counsel;
(ii) a summary of the dispute;
(iii) a preliminary statement of the relief sought by the Claimant;
(iv) a copy or description of the arbitration agreement or clause under which the dispute is to be settled; and
(v)   comments on the seat of arbitration.

ARTICLE 3 REGISTRATION FEE

(1) Upon filing the Request for Arbitration, the Claimant shall pay a Registration Fee. The amount of the Registration Fee shall be determined in accordance with the Schedule of Costs (Appendix III) in force on the date when the Request for Arbitration is filed.
(2) If the Registration Fee is not paid upon filing the Request for Arbitration, the Secretariat shall set a time period within which the Claimant shall pay the Registration Fee. If the Registration Fee is not paid within this time period, the Secretariat shall dismiss the Request for Arbitration.

ARTICLE 4 COMMENCEMENT OF ARBITRATION

Arbitration is commenced on the date when the SCC receives the Request for Arbitration.

ARTICLE 5 ANSWER

(1) The Secretariat shall send a copy of the Request for Arbitration and the documents attached thereto to the Respondent. The Secretariat shall set a time period within which the Respondent shall submit an Answer to the SCC. The Answer shall include:
   (i) any objections concerning the existence, validity or applicability of the arbitration agreement; however, failure to raise any objections shall not preclude the Respondent from subsequently raising such objections at any time up to and including the submission of the Statement of Defence;
   (ii) an admission or denial of the relief sought in the Request for Arbitration;
   (iii) a preliminary statement of any counterclaims or setoffs; and
   (iv) comments on the seat of arbitration.
(2) The Secretariat shall send a copy of the Answer to the Claimant. The Claimant shall be given an opportunity to submit comments on the Answer.
(3) Failure by the Respondent to submit an Answer shall not prevent the arbitration from proceeding.

ARTICLE 6 REQUEST FOR FURTHER DETAILS

The Board may request further details from either party regarding any of their written submissions to the SCC. If the Claimant fails to comply with a request for further details, the Board may dismiss the case. If the Respondent fails to comply with a request for further details regarding its counterclaim or set off, the Board may dismiss the counterclaim or set off. Failure by the Respondent to otherwise comply with a request for further details shall not prevent the arbitration from proceeding.

ARTICLE 7 TIME PERIODS

The Board may, on application by either party or on its own motion, extend any time period which has been set for a party to comply with a particular direction.

ARTICLE 8 NOTICES

(1) Any notice or other communication from the Secretariat or the Board shall be delivered to the last known address of the addressee.
(2) Any notice or other communication shall be delivered by courier or registered mail, facsimile transmission, e mail or any other means of communication that provides a record of the sending thereof.
(3) A notice or communication sent in accordance with paragraph (2) shall be deemed to have been received by the addressee on the date it would normally have been received given the chosen means of communication.

ARTICLE 9 DECISIONS BY THE BOARD

When necessary the Board shall:

(i) decide whether the SCC manifestly lacks jurisdiction over the dispute pursuant to Article 10 (i);
(ii) decide whether to consolidate cases pursuant to Article 11;
(iii) make any appointment of arbitrator pursuant to Article 13;
(iv) decide the seat of arbitration pursuant to Article 20; and
(v) determine the Advance on Costs pursuant to Article 44.

ARTICLE 10 DISMISSAL

The Board shall dismiss a case, in whole or in part, if:
(i) the SCC manifestly lacks jurisdiction over the dispute; or
(ii) the Advance on Costs is not paid pursuant to Article 44.

ARTICLE 11 CONSOLIDATION

If arbitration is commenced concerning a legal relationship in respect of which an arbitration between the same parties is already pending under these Rules, the Board may, at the request of a party, decide to consolidate the new claims with the pending proceedings. Such decision may only be made after consulting the parties and the Arbitrator.

The Arbitrator

ARTICLE 12 NUMBER OF ARBITRATORS

The arbitration shall be decided by a sole Arbitrator.

ARTICLE 13 APPOINTMENT OF ARBITRATOR

(1) The parties may agree on a different procedure for appointment of the Arbitrator than as provided under this Article. In such cases, if the Arbitrator has not been appointed within the time period agreed by the parties or, where the parties have not agreed on a time period, within the time period set by the Board, the appointment shall be made pursuant to paragraphs (2)–(4).

(2) The parties shall be given 10 days within which to jointly appoint the Arbitrator. If the parties fail to make the appointment within this time period, the Arbitrator shall be appointed by the Board.

(3) If the parties are of different nationalities, the Arbitrator shall be of a different nationality than the parties, unless the parties have agreed otherwise or unless otherwise deemed appropriate by the Board.

(4) When appointing Arbitrator, the Board shall consider the nature and circumstances of the dispute, the applicable law, the seat and language of the arbitration and the nationality of the parties.

ARTICLE 14 IMPARTIALITY AND INDEPENDENCE

(1) The Arbitrator must be impartial and independent.

(2) Before being appointed as Arbitrator, a person shall disclose any circumstances which may give rise to justifiable doubts as to his/her impartiality or independence. If the person is appointed as Arbitrator, he/she shall submit to the Secretariat a signed statement of impartiality and independence disclosing any circumstances which may give rise to justifiable or independence. The Secretariat shall send a copy of the statement of impartiality and independence to the parties.

(3) The Arbitrator shall immediately inform the parties in writing where any circumstances referred to in paragraph (2) arise during the course of the arbitration.

ARTICLE 15 CHALLENGE TO ARBITRATOR

(1) A party may challenge the Arbitrator if circumstances exist which give rise to justifiable doubts as to the Arbitrator's impartiality or independence or if he/she does not possess qualifications agreed by the parties.

(2) A challenge to the Arbitrator shall be made by submitting a written statement to the Secretariat setting forth the reasons for the challenge within 15 days from when the circumstances giving rise to the challenge became known to the party. Failure by a party to challenge the Arbitrator within the stipulated time period constitutes a waiver of the right to make the challenge.

(3) The Secretariat shall notify the parties and the Arbitrator of the challenge and give them an opportunity to submit comments on the challenge.

(4) If the other party agrees to the challenge, the Arbitrator shall resign. In all other cases, the Board shall make the final decision on the challenge.

ARTICLE 16 RELEASE FROM APPOINTMENT

(1) The Board shall release the Arbitrator from appointment where:
   (i)   the Board accepts the resignation of the Arbitrator;
   (ii) a challenge to the Arbitrator under Article 15 is sustained; or
   (iii) the Arbitrator is otherwise prevented from fulfilling his/her duties or fails to perform his/her functions in an adequate manner.
(2) Before the Board releases an arbitrator, the Secretariat may give the parties and the Arbitrator an opportunity to submit comments.

ARTICLE 17 REPLACEMENT OF ARBITRATOR

(1) The Board shall appoint a new Arbitrator where the Arbitrator has been released from his/her appointment pursuant to Article 16, or where the Arbitrator has died.
(2) Where the Arbitrator has been replaced, the new Arbitrator shall decide whether and to what extent the proceedings are to be repeated.

The Proceedings before the Arbitrator

ARTICLE 18 REFERRAL TO THE ARBITRATOR

When the Arbitrator has been appointed and the Advance on Costs has been paid, the Secretariat shall refer the case to the Arbitrator.

ARTICLE 19 CONDUCT OF THE ARBITRATION

(1) Subject to these Rules and any agreement between the parties, the Arbitrator may conduct the arbitration in such manner as the Arbitrator considers appropriate.
(2) In all cases, the Arbitrator shall conduct the arbitration in an impartial, practical and expeditious manner, giving each party an equal and reasonable opportunity to present its case.
(3) The following shall apply to the proceedings, unless the Arbitrator, for special reasons, decides otherwise:
   (i)   in addition to the Statement of Claim and the Statement of Defence, the parties each may only submit one written statement, including statements of evidence;
   (ii) the statements must be brief; and
   (iii) the time limits within which the documents shall be submitted may not exceed 10 working days.
(4) The Arbitrator may order a party to finally state its claims for relief and the facts relied on as grounds thereof, and the evidence on which the party relies. At the expiration of the time period for such statement, the party may not amend its claim for relief nor adduce additional facts or evidence, unless the Arbitrator, for special reasons, so permits.

ARTICLE 20 SEAT OF ARBITRATION

(1) Unless agreed upon by the parties, the Board shall decide the seat of arbitration.
(2) The Arbitrator may, after consultation with the parties, conduct hearings at any place which the Arbitrator considers appropriate. If any hearing or meeting is held elsewhere than at the seat of arbitration, the arbitration shall be deemed to have taken place at the seat of arbitration.
(3) The award shall be deemed to have been made at the seat of arbitration.

ARTICLE 21 LANGUAGE

(1) Unless agreed upon by the parties, the Arbitrator shall determine the language(s) of the arbitration. In so determining, the Arbitrator shall have due regard to all relevant circumstances and shall give the parties an opportunity to submit comments.

(2) The Arbitrator may request that any documents submitted in languages other than the language(s) of the arbitration be accompanied by a translation into the language(s) of the arbitration.

ARTICLE 22 APPLICABLE LAW

(1) The Arbitrator shall decide the merits of the dispute on the basis of the law(s) or rules of law agreed upon by the parties. In the absence of such agreement, the Arbitrator shall apply the law or rules of law which the Arbitrator considers to be most appropriate.

(2) Any designation made by the parties of the law of a given state shall be deemed to refer to the substantive law of that state and not to its conflict of laws rules.

(3) The Arbitrator shall decide the dispute ex aequo et bono or as amiable compositeur only if the parties have expressly authorised the Arbitrator to do so.

ARTICLE 23 TIMETABLE

After the referral of the case to the Arbitrator, the Arbitrator shall promptly establish a timetable for the conduct of the arbitration. The Arbitrator shall send a copy of the timetable to the parties and to the Secretariat.

ARTICLE 24 WRITTEN SUBMISSIONS

(1) The Claimant shall, within the period of time determined by the Arbitrator, submit a Statement of Claim which shall include, unless previously submitted:
   (i)   the specific relief sought;
   (ii) the material circumstances on which the Claimant relies; and
   (iii) the documents on which the Claimant relies.

(2) The Respondent shall, within the period of time determined by the Arbitrator, submit a Statement of Defence which shall include, unless previously submitted:
   (i)   any objections concerning the existence, validity or applicability of the arbitration agreement;
   (ii) a statement whether, and to what extent, the Respondent admits or denies the relief sought by the Claimant;
   (iii) the material circumstances on which the Respondent relies;
   (iv) any counterclaim or set off and the grounds on which it is based; and
   (v) the documents on which the Respondent relies.

(3) The Arbitrator may order the parties to submit additional written submissions.

ARTICLE 25 AMENDMENTS

At any time prior to the close of proceedings pursuant to Article 34, a party may amend or supplement its claim, counterclaim, defence or set off provided its case, as amended or supplemented, is still comprised by the arbitration agreement, unless the Arbitrator considers it inappropriate to allow such amendment or supplement having regard to the delay in making it, the prejudice to the other party or any other circumstances.

ARTICLE 26 EVIDENCE

(1) The admissibility, relevance, materiality and weight of evidence shall be for the Arbitrator to determine.

(2) The Arbitrator may order a party to identify the documentary evidence it intends to rely on and specify the circumstances intended to be proved by such evidence.

(3) At the request of a party, the Arbitrator may order a party to produce any documents or other evidence which may be relevant to the outcome of the case.

ARTICLE 27 HEARINGS

(1) A hearing shall be held if requested by a party and if deemed necessary by the Arbitrator.
(2) The Arbitrator shall, in consultation with the parties, determine the date, time and location of any hearing and shall provide the parties with reasonable notice thereof.
(3) Unless otherwise agreed by the parties, hearings will be held in private.

ARTICLE 28 WITNESSES

(1) In advance of any hearing, the Arbitrator may order the parties to identify each witness or expert they intend to call and specify the circumstances intended to be proved by each testimony.
(2) The testimony of witnesses or party appointed experts may be submitted in the form of signed statements.
(3) Any witness or expert, on whose testimony a party seeks to rely, shall attend a hearing for examination, unless otherwise agreed by the parties.

ARTICLE 29 EXPERTS APPOINTED BY THE ARBITRATOR

(1) After consultation with the parties, the Arbitrator may appoint one or more experts to report to the Arbitrator on specific issues set out by the Arbitrator in writing.
(2) Upon receipt of a report from an expert appointed by the Arbitrator, the Arbitrator shall send a copy of the report to the parties and shall give the parties an opportunity to submit written comments on the report.
(3) Upon the request of a party, the parties shall be given an opportunity to examine any expert appointed by the Arbitrator at a hearing.

ARTICLE 30 DEFAULT

(1) If the Claimant, without showing good cause, fails to submit a Statement of Claim in accordance with Article 24, the Arbitrator shall terminate the proceedings provided the Respondent has not filed a counterclaim.
(2) If a party, without showing good cause, fails to submit a Statement of Defence or other written statement in accordance with Article 24, or fails to appear at a hearing, or otherwise fails to avail itself of the opportunity to present its case, the Arbitrator may proceed with the arbitration and make an award.
(3) If a party without good cause fails to comply with any provision of, or requirement under, these Rules or any procedural order given by the Arbitrator, the Arbitrator may draw such inferences as it considers appropriate.

ARTICLE 31 WAIVER

A party, who during the arbitration fails to object without delay to any failure to comply with the arbitration agreement, these Rules or other rules applicable to the proceedings, shall be deemed to have waived the right to object to such failure.

ARTICLE 32 INTERIM MEASURES

(1) The Arbitrator may, at the request of a party, grant any interim measures the Arbitrator deems appropriate.
(2) The Arbitrator may order the party requesting an interim measure to provide appropriate security in connection with the measure.
(3) An interim measure shall take the form of an order or an award.

(4) Provisions with respect to interim measures requested before arbitration has been commenced or a case has been referred to an Arbitrator are set out in Appendix II.

(5) A request for interim measures made by a party to a judicial authority is not incompatible with the arbitration agreement or with these Rules.

ARTICLE 33 COMMUNICATIONS FROM THE ARBITRATOR

Article 8 shall apply to communications from the Arbitrator.

ARTICLE 34 CLOSE OF PROCEEDINGS

The Arbitrator shall declare the proceedings closed when the Arbitrator is satisfied that the parties have had a reasonable opportunity to present their cases. In exceptional circumstances, prior to the making of the final reopen the proceedings on the Arbitrator's own motion, or upon the application of a party.

Awards and Decisions

ARTICLE 35 MAKING OF AWARDS

(1) The Arbitrator shall make the award in writing and sign the award. A party may request a reasoned award no later than at the closing statement.

(2) An award shall include the date of the award and the seat of arbitration in accordance with Article 20.

(3) The Arbitrator shall deliver a copy of the award to each of the parties and to the SCC without delay.

ARTICLE 36 TIME LIMIT FOR FINAL AWARD

The final award shall be made not later than three months from the date upon which the arbitration was referred to the Arbitrator pursuant to Article 18. The Board may extend this time limit upon a reasoned request from the Arbitrator, or if otherwise deemed necessary.

ARTICLE 37 SEPARATE AWARD

The Arbitrator may decide a separate issue or part of the dispute in a separate award.

ARTICLE 38 SETTLEMENT OR OTHER GROUNDS FOR TERMINATION OF THE ARBITRATION

(1) If the parties reach a settlement before the final award is made, the Arbitrator may, upon the request of both parties, record the settlement in the form of a consent award.

(2) If the arbitration for any other reason is terminated before the final award is made, the Arbitrator shall issue an award recording the termination.

ARTICLE 39 EFFECT OF AN AWARD

An award shall be final and binding on the parties when rendered. By agreeing to arbitration under these Rules, the parties undertake to carry out any award without delay.

ARTICLE 40 CORRECTION AND INTERPRETATION OF AN AWARD

(1) Within 30 days of receiving an award, a party may, upon notice to the other party, request that the Arbitrator correct any clerical, typographical or computational errors in the award, or provide an interpretation of a specific point or part of the award. If the Arbitrator considers the

request justified, the Arbitrator shall make the correction or provide the interpretation within 30 days of receiving the request.

(2) The Arbitrator may correct any error of the type referred to in paragraph (1) above on the Arbitrator's own motion within 30 days of the date of an award.

(3) Any correction or interpretation of an award shall be in writing and shall comply with the requirements of Article 35.

ARTICLE 41 ADDITIONAL AWARD

Within 30 days of receiving an award, a party may, upon notice to the other party, request the Arbitrator to make an additional award on claims presented in the arbitration but not determined in the award. If the Arbitrator considers the request justified, the Arbitrator shall make the additional award within 30 days of receipt of the request. When deemed necessary, the Board may extend this 30 day time limit.

Costs of the Arbitration

ARTICLE 42 COSTS OF THE ARBITRATION

(1) The Costs of the Arbitration consist of:
   (i)   the Fee of the Arbitrator;
   (ii)   the Administrative Fee; and
   (iii) the expenses of the Arbitrator and the SCC.

(2) Before making the final award, the Arbitrator shall request the Board to finally determine the Costs of the Arbitration. The Board shall finally determine the Costs of the Arbitration in accordance with the Schedule of Costs (Appendix III) in force on the date of commencement of the arbitration pursuant to Article 4.

(3) If the arbitration is terminated before the final award is made pursuant to Article 38, the Board shall finally determine the Costs of the Arbitration having regard to when the arbitration terminates, the work performed by the Arbitrator and other relevant circumstances. The Arbitrator shall include in the final award the Costs of the Arbitration as finally determined by the Board and specify the fees and expenses of the Arbitrator and the SCC.

(4) Unless otherwise agreed by the parties, the Arbitrator shall, at the request of a party, apportion the Costs of the Arbitration between the parties, having regard to the outcome of the case and other relevant circumstances.

(5) The parties are jointly and severally liable to the Arbitrator and to the SCC for the Costs of the Arbitration.

ARTICLE 43 COSTS INCURRED BY A PARTY

Unless otherwise agreed by the parties, the Arbitrator may in the final award, upon the request of a party, order one party to pay any reasonable costs incurred by another party, including costs for legal representation, having regard to the outcome of the case and other relevant circumstances.

ARTICLE 44 ADVANCE ON COSTS

(1) The Board shall determine an amount to be paid by the parties as an Advance on Costs.

(2) The Advance on Costs shall correspond to the estimated amount of the Costs of Arbitration pursuant to Article 42 (1).

(3) Each party shall pay half of the Advance on Costs, unless separate advances are determined. Where counterclaims or set offs are submitted, the Board may decide that each of the parties shall pay the advances on costs corresponding to its claim. Upon a request from the Arbitrator or if otherwise deemed necessary, the Board may order parties to pay additional advances during the course of the arbitration.

(4) If a party fails to make a required payment, the Secretariat shall give the other party an opportunity to do so within a specified period of time. If the required payment is not made, the Board shall dismiss the case in whole or in part. If the other party makes the required payment, the Arbitrator may, at the request of such party, make a separate award for reimbursement of the payment.

(5) At any stage during the arbitration or after the Award has been made, the Board may draw on the Advance on Costs to cover the Costs of the Arbitration.

(6) The Board may decide that part of the Advance on Costs may be provided in the form of a bank guarantee or other form of security.

General Rules

ARTICLE 45 CONFIDENTIALITY

Unless otherwise agreed by the parties, the SCC and the Arbitrator shall maintain the confidentiality of the arbitration and the award.

ARTICLE 46 ENFORCEMENT

In all matters not expressly provided for in these Rules, the SCC, the Arbitrator and the parties shall act in the spirit of these Rules and shall make every reasonable effort to ensure that all awards are legally enforceable.

ARTICLE 47 EXCLUSION OF LIABILITY

Neither the SCC nor the arbitrator are liable to any party for any act or omission in connection with the arbitration unless such act or omission constitutes wilful misconduct or gross negligence.

Appendix I Organisation

ARTICLE 1 ABOUT THE SCC

The Arbitration Institute of the Stockholm Chamber of Commerce (the "SCC") is a body providing administrative services in relation to the settlement of disputes. The SCC is part of the Stockholm Chamber of Commerce, but is independent in exercising its functions in the administration of disputes. The SCC is composed of a board of directors (the "Board") and a secretariat (the "Secretariat").

ARTICLE 2 FUNCTION OF THE SCC

The SCC does not itself decide disputes. The function of the SCC is to:

(i) administer domestic and international disputes in accordance with the SCC Rules and other procedures or rules agreed upon by the parties; and

(ii) provide information concerning arbitration and mediation matters.

ARTICLE 3 THE BOARD

The Board shall be composed of one chairperson, a maximum of three vice chairpersons and a maximum of 12 additional members. The Board includes both Swedish and non-Swedish nationals.

ARTICLE 4 APPOINTMENT OF THE BOARD

The Board shall be appointed by the Board of Directors of the Stockholm Chamber of Commerce (the "Board of Directors"). The members of the Board shall be appointed for a period of three years and are eligible for re appointment in their respective capacities for one further three year period only, unless exceptional circumstances apply.

ARTICLE 5 REMOVAL OF A MEMBER OF THE BOARD

In exceptional circumstances, the Board of Directors may remove a member of the Board. If a member resigns or is removed during a term of office, the Board of Directors shall appoint a new member for the remainder of the term.

ARTICLE 6 FUNCTION OF THE BOARD

The function of the Board is to take the decisions required of the SCC in administering disputes under the SCC Rules and any other rules or procedures agreed upon by the parties. Such decisions include decisions on the jurisdiction of the SCC, determination of advances on costs, appointment of arbitrators, decisions upon challenges to arbitrators, removal of arbitrators and the fixing of arbitration costs.

ARTICLE 7 DECISIONS BY THE BOARD

Two members of the Board form a quorum. If a majority is not attained, the Chairperson has the casting vote. The Chairperson or a Vice Chairperson may take decisions on behalf of the Board in urgent matters. A committee of the Board may be appointed to take certain decisions on behalf of the Board. The Board may delegate decisions to the Secretariat, including decisions on advances on costs, extension of time for rendering an award, dismissal for non payment of registration fee, release of arbitrators and fixing of arbitration costs. Decisions by the Board are final.

ARTICLE 8 THE SECRETARIAT

The Secretariat acts under the direction of a Secretary General. The Secretariat carries out the functions assigned to it under the SCC Rules. The Secretariat may also take decisions delegated to it by the Board.

ARTICLE 9 PROCEDURES

The SCC shall maintain the confidentiality of the arbitration and the award and shall deal with the arbitration in an impartial, practical and expeditious manner.

Appendix II Emergency Arbitrator

ARTICLE 1 EMERGENCY ARBITRATOR

(1) A party may apply for the appointment of an Emergency Arbitrator until the case has been referred to the Arbitrator pursuant to Article 18 of the Rules for Expedited Arbitrations.

(2) The powers of the Emergency Arbitrator shall be those set out in Article 32 (1) (3) of the Rules for Expedited Arbitrations. Such powers terminate when the case has been referred to the Arbitrator pursuant to Article 18 of the Rules for Expedited Arbitrations or when an emergency decision ceases to be binding according to Article 9 (4) of this Appendix.

ARTICLE 2 APPLICATION FOR THE APPOINTMENT OF AN EMERGENCY ARBITRATOR

An application for the appointment of an Emergency Arbitrator shall include:

(i) a statement of the names and addresses, telephone and facsimile numbers and e mail addresses of the parties and their counsel;

(ii) a summary of the dispute;

(iii) a statement of the interim relief sought and the reasons therefor;

(iv) a copy or description of the arbitration agreement or clause on the basis of which the dispute is to be settled;

(v) comments on the seat of the emergency proceedings, the applicable law(s) and the language(s) of the proceedings; and

(vi) proof of payment of the costs for the emergency proceedings pursuant to Article 10 (1) (2) of this Appendix.

ARTICLE 3 NOTICE

As soon as an application for the appointment of an Emergency Arbitrator has been received, the Secretariat shall send the application to the other party.

ARTICLE 4 APPOINTMENT OF THE EMERGENCY ARBITRATOR

(1) The Board shall seek to appoint an Emergency Arbitrator within 24 hours of receipt of the application for the appointment of an Emergency Arbitrator.

(2) An Emergency Arbitrator shall not be appointed if the SCC manifestly lacks jurisdiction over the dispute.

(3) Article 15 of the Rules for Expedited Arbitrations applies except that a challenge must be made within 24 hours from when the circumstances giving rise to the challenge of an Emergency Arbitrator became known to the party.

(4) An Emergency Arbitrator may not act as an arbitrator in any future arbitration relating to the dispute, unless otherwise agreed by the parties.

ARTICLE 5 SEAT OF THE EMERGENCY PROCEEDINGS

The seat of the emergency proceedings shall be that which has been agreed upon by the parties as the seat of the arbitration. If the seat of the arbitration has not been agreed by the parties, the Board shall determine the seat of the emergency proceedings.

ARTICLE 6 REFERRAL TO THE EMERGENCY ARBITRATOR

Once an Emergency Arbitrator has been appointed, the Secretariat shall promptly refer the application to the Emergency Arbitrator.

ARTICLE 7 CONDUCT OF THE EMERGENCY PROCEEDINGS

Article 19 of the Rules for Expedited Arbitrations shall apply to the emergency proceedings, taking into account the urgency inherent in such proceedings.

ARTICLE 8 EMERGENCY DECISIONS ON INTERIM MEASURES

(1) Any emergency decision on interim measures shall be made not later than 5 days from the date upon which the application was referred to the Emergency Arbitrator pursuant to Article 6 of this Appendix. The Board may extend this time limit upon a reasoned request from the Emergency Arbitrator, or if otherwise deemed necessary.

(2) Any emergency decision on interim measures shall:
   (i) be made in writing;
   (ii) state the date when it was made, the seat of the emergency proceedings and the reasons upon which the decision is based; and
   (iii) be signed by the Emergency Arbitrator.

(3) The Emergency Arbitrator shall promptly deliver a copy of the emergency decision to each of the parties and to the SCC.

ARTICLE 9 BINDING EFFECT OF EMERGENCY DECISIONS

(1) An emergency decision shall be binding on the parties when rendered.

(2) The emergency decision may be amended or revoked by the Emergency Arbitrator upon a reasoned request by a party.

(3) By agreeing to arbitration under the Rules for Expedited Arbitrations, the parties undertake to comply with any emergency decision without delay.

(4) The emergency decision ceases to be binding if:
    (i) the Emergency Arbitrator or an Arbitrator so decides;
    (ii) an Arbitrator makes a final award;
    (iii) arbitration is not commenced within 30 days from the date of the emergency decision; or
    (iv) the case is not referred to an Arbitrator within 90 days from the date of the emergency decision.

(5) An Arbitrator is not bound by the decision(s) and reasons of the Emergency Arbitrator.

ARTICLE 10 COSTS OF THE EMERGENCY PROCEEDINGS

(1) The party applying for the appointment of an Emergency Arbitrator shall pay the costs of the emergency proceedings upon filing the application.

(2) The costs of the emergency proceedings include:
    (i) the fee of the Emergency Arbitrator which amounts to EUR 6,000; and
    (ii) the application fee which amounts to EUR 1,500.

(3) Upon a request from the Emergency Arbitrator or if otherwise deemed appropriate, the Board may decide to increase or reduce the costs having regard to the nature of the case, the work performed by the Emergency Arbitrator and the SCC, and other relevant circumstances.

(4) If payment of the costs of the emergency proceedings is not made in due time, the Secretariat shall dismiss the application.

(5) At the request of a party, the costs of the emergency proceedings may be apportioned between the parties by an Arbitrator in a final award.

Appendix III Schedule of Costs

Arbitration Costs

ARTICLE 1 REGISTRATION FEE

(1) The Registration Fee referred to in Article 3 of the the Rules for Expedited Arbitrations amounts to EUR 1 000.

(2) The Registration Fee is non refundable and constitutes a part of the Administrative Fee in Article 3 below. The Registration Fee shall be credited to the Advance on Costs to be paid by the Claimant pursuant to Article 44 of the Rules for Expedited Arbitrations.

ARTICLE 2 FEE OF THE ARBITRATOR

(1) The Board shall determine the Fee of the Arbitrator based on the amount in dispute in accordance with the table below.

(2) The amount in dispute shall be the aggregate value of all claims, counterclaims and set offs. Where the amount in dispute cannot be ascertained, the Board shall determine the Fee of the Arbitrator taking all relevant circumstances into account.

(3) In exceptional circumstances, the Board may deviate from the amounts set out in the table.

ARTICLE 3 ADMINISTRATIVE FEE

(1) The Administrative Fee shall be determined in accordance with the table below.

(2) The amount in dispute shall be the aggregate value of all claims, counterclaims and set offs. Where the amount in dispute cannot be ascertained, the Board shall determine the Administrative Fee taking all relevant circumstances into account.

(3) In exceptional circumstances, the Board may deviate from the amounts set out in the table.

ARTICLE 4 EXPENSES

In addition to the Fee of the Arbitrator and the Administrative

Fee, the Board shall fix an amount to cover any reasonable expenses incurred by the Arbitrator and the SCC. The expenses of the Arbitrator may include the fee and expenses of any expert appointed by the Arbitrator pursuant to Article 29 of the Rules for Expedited Arbitrations.

Arbitrators' Fees

Amount in dispute (EUR)	Arbitrator's Fee (EUR)	
	Minimum	Maximum
to 25 000	2 000	4 000
from 25 001 to 50 000	2 200 + 2% of the amount above 25 000	4 000 + 6% of the amount above 25 000
from 50 001 to 100 000	2 500 + 0,01% of the amount above 50 000	5 500 + 4% of the amount above 50 000
from 100 001 to 500 000	2 500 + 1,5% of the amount above 100 000	7 500 + 1% of the amount above 100 000
from 500 001 to 1 000 000	5 000 + 0,8% of the amount above 500 000	11 500 + 2,2% of the amount above 500 000
from 1 000 001 to 2 000 000	9 000 + 0,3% of the amount above 1 000 000	13 500 + 2% of the amount above 1 000 000
from 2 000 001 to 5 000 000	13 000 + 0,05% of the amount above 2 000 000	33 500 + 0,05% of the amount above 2 000 000
from 5 000 001 to 10 000 000	17 000 + 0,07% of the amount above 5 000 000	35 000 + 0,3% of the amount above 5 000 000
from 10 000 001 to 50 000 000	21 000 + 0,03% of the amount above 10 000 000	50 000 + 0,02% of the amount above 10 000 000
from 50 000 001 to 75 000 000	31 000 + 0,05% of the amount above 50 000 000	58 000 + 0,04% of the amoun above 50 000 000
from 75 000 001	35 000 + 0,02% of the amount above 75 000 000	68 000 + 0,04% of the amount above 75 000 000

The Costs of the Arbitration may easily be calculated at www.sccinstitute.com

Administrative Fee

Amount in dispute (EUR)	Administrative Fee (EUR)
to 25 000	1 500
from 25 001 to 50 000	1 500
from 50 001 to 100 000	1 500 + 2% of the amount above 50 000
from 100 001 to 500 000	2 200 + 0,5% of the amount above 100 000
from 500 001 to 1 000 000	4 500 + 0,7% of the amount above 500 000
from 1 000 001 to 2 000 000	8 000 + 0,2% of the amount above 1 000 000
from 2 000 001 to 5 000 000	10 000 + 0,1% of the amount above 2 000 000
from 5 000 001 to 10 000 000	13 000 + 0,08% of the amount above 5 000 000
from 10 000 001 to 50 000 000	17 000 + 0,01% of the amount above 10 000 000 Maximum 30 000

The Costs of the Arbitration may easily be calculated at www.sccinstitute.com

APPENDIX 3

Procedures and Services under the UNCITRAL Arbitration Rules

In force from April 1, 1999 (new fee in force from April 1, 2004).

Services as Appointing Authority

ARTICLE 1 APPOINTMENT OF SOLE OR PRESIDING ARBITRATOR

When requested to appoint a sole or presiding arbitrator under the UNCITRAL Arbitration Rules (the Rules), the Arbitration Institute of the Stockholm Chamber of Commerce (the SCC Arbitration Institute) will follow the list procedure set forth in Article 6:3 of the Rules unless all parties agree that the list procedure is not appropriate for the case.

In selecting arbitrators, the SCC Arbitration Institute will carefully consider the nature of the case, as described in the Notice of the Arbitration, in order to include in the list persons who are not only experienced in international arbitration but also familiar with the technical and commercial aspects of the matter.

When appointing a sole or presiding arbitrator under the Rules, the SCC Arbitration Institute will, in so far as possible, designate a person of a nationality other than the nationalities of the parties, unless otherwise agreed by the parties.

ARTICLE 2 APPOINTMENT OF A "SECOND" ARBITRATOR IN THREE-ARBITRATOR CASES

Under Article 7 of the Rules, when three arbitrators are to be appointed, each party is to appoint one arbitrator, but if a party fails to do so, the other party may request that the appointment of the second arbitrator be made by the appointing authority.

In accordance with the Rules, the SCC Arbitration Institute, when appointing a second arbitrator, will exercise its discretion and will not utilize the list procedure. Such second arbitrator shall be impartial and independent of either party.

ARTICLE 3 DECISIONS ON CHALLENGES TO ARBITRATORS

Under Article 10 of the Rules, all arbitrators - including those appointed by a party - are required to be impartial and independent. Article 10 provides that any arbitrator may be challenged if circumstances exist that give rise to justifiable doubts as to the arbitrator's impartiality or independence.

Article 12 of the Rules requires that all contested challenges be decided by the appointing authority. When deciding challenges at the request of any party, the SCC Arbitration Institute will do so through its Board.

ARTICLE 4 APPOINTMENT OF SUBSTITUTE ARBITRATORS

The Rules provide that the appointing authority shall appoint a substitute arbitrator if an arbitrator dies or resigns during an arbitration proceeding, or if a challenge against him is sustained (Articles 12(2) and 13). In such cases, the SCC Arbitration Institute will appoint a substitute arbitrator in accordance with Articles 1 and 2 above.

ARTICLE 5 CONSULTATION OF FEES OF ARBITRATORS AND DEPOSITS OF COSTS

The Rules provide that the fees of the arbitrators shall be reasonable in amount, taking into consideration the amount in dispute, the complexity of the subject matter, the time spent by the arbitrators, and any other relevant circumstances of the case (Article 39(1)). The Rules provide that the parties may request the appointing authority to provide to the arbitrators and parties a statement setting forth the basis for establishing fees that is customarily followed in cases in which the appointing authority acts (Article 39(3)).

The SCC Arbitration Institute has a Regulation for Costs of Arbitration and will, at the request of any party, furnish a statement concerning fees based on this regulation and the SCC Arbitration Institute's experience in administering arbitration cases.

Further, at the request of any party, the SCC Arbitration Institute will make any comments it deems appropriate to the arbitral tribunal concerning the amount of any deposits or supplementary deposits to be made under Article 41 of the Rules.

In addition to giving advice as to the amount of deposits as provided for in Article 41 of the Rules, the SCC Arbitration Institute upon request of one of the parties or of the arbitral tribunal is prepared to hold deposits and to render an account thereof to the arbitral tribunal.

Administrative Services

Upon request of the parties or the arbitral tribunal, the SCC Arbitration Institute will provide the following administrative services:

1. Providing, or arranging for, meeting rooms for hearings or deliberations of the arbitral tribunal.
2. Providing secretarial or clerical assistance.
3. Forwarding of written communications of a party or the arbitrators.
4. Arranging for stenographic transcripts of hearings.
5. Arranging for services of interpreters at hearings.
6. Upon request, the SCC Arbitration Institute will consider providing other appropriate administrative services.

APPENDIX 4

UNCITRAL Model Law on International Commercial Arbitration (1985)

(As adopted by the United Nations Commission on International Trade Law on 21 June 1985, and
as amended by the United Nations Commission on International Trade Law on 7 July 2006)

Chapter I. General Provisions

Article 1. Scope of Application[1]

(1) This Law applies to international commercial[2] arbitration, subject to any agreement in force
between this State and any other State or States.

(2) The provisions of this Law, except articles 8, 9, 17 H, 17 I, 17 J, 35 and 36, apply only if the place
of arbitration is in the territory of this State.

(Article 1(2) has been amended by the Commission at its thirty-ninth session, in 2006)

(3) An arbitration is international if:

   (a) the parties to an arbitration agreement have, at the time of the conclusion of that agreement,
their places of business in different States; or

   (b) one of the following places is situated outside the State in which the parties have their places
of business:

     (i) the place of arbitration if determined in, or pursuant to, the arbitration agreement;

     (ii) any place where a substantial part of the obligations of the commercial relationship is to
be performed or the place with which the subject-matter of the dispute is most closely
connected; or

   (c) the parties have expressly agreed that the subject matter of the arbitration agreement relates to
more than one country.

(4) For the purposes of paragraph (3) of this article:

   (a) if a party has more than one place of business, the place of business is that which has the closest
relationship to the arbitration agreement;

   (b) if a party does not have a place of business, reference is to be made to his habitual residence.

(5) This Law shall not affect any other law of this State by virtue of which certain disputes may not be
submitted to arbitration or may be submitted to arbitration only according to provisions other
than those of this Law.

Article 2. Definitions and Rules of Interpretation

For the purposes of this Law:

   (a) "arbitration" means any arbitration whether or not administered by a permanent arbitral
institution;

   (b) "arbitral tribunal" means a sole arbitrator or a panel of arbitrators;

---

[1] Article headings are for reference purposes only and are not to be used for purposes of interpretation.

[2] The term "commercial" should be given a wide interpretation so as to cover matters arising from all relationships of a commercial nature, whether contractual or not. Relationships of a commercial nature include, but are
not limited to, the following transactions: any trade transaction for the supply or exchange of goods or services;
distribution agreement; commercial representation or agency; factoring; leasing; construction of works; consulting;
engineering; licensing; investment; financing; banking; insurance; exploitation agreement or concession; joint venture and other forms of industrial or business cooperation; carriage of goods or passengers by air, sea, rail or road.

(c) "court" means a body or organ of the judicial system of a State;

(d) where a provision of this Law, except article 28, leaves the parties free to determine a certain issue, such freedom includes the right of the parties to authorize a third party, including an institution, to make that determination;

(e) where a provision of this Law refers to the fact that the parties have agreed or that they may agree or in any other way refers to an agreement of the parties, such agreement includes any arbitration rules referred to in that agreement;

(f) where a provision of this Law, other than in articles 25*(a)* and 32(2) *(a)*, refers to a claim, it also applies to a counter-claim, and where it refers to a defence, it also applies to a defence to such counter-claim.

Article 2 A. International Origin and General Principles (As Adopted by the Commission at its Thirty-Ninth Session, in 2006)

(1) In the interpretation of this Law, regard is to be had to its international origin and to the need to promote uniformity in its application and the observance of good faith.

(2) Questions concerning matters governed by this Law which are not expressly settled in it are to be settled in conformity with the general principles on which this Law is based.

Article 3. Receipt of Written Communications

(1) Unless otherwise agreed by the parties:

(a) any written communication is deemed to have been received if it is delivered to the addressee personally or if it is delivered at his place of business, habitual residence or mailing address; if none of these can be found after making a reasonable inquiry, a written communication is deemed to have been received if it is sent to the addressee's last-known place of business, habitual residence or mailing address by registered letter or any other means which provides a record of the attempt to deliver it;

(b) the communication is deemed to have been received on the day it is so delivered.

(2) The provisions of this article do not apply to communications in court proceedings.

Article 4. Waiver of Right to Object

A party who knows that any provision of this Law from which the parties may derogate or any requirement under the arbitration agreement has not been complied with and yet proceeds with the arbitration without stating his objection to such non-compliance without undue delay or, if a time-limit is provided therefore, within such period of time, shall be deemed to have waived his right to object.

Article 5. Extent of Court Intervention

In matters governed by this Law, no court shall intervene except where so provided in this Law.

Article 6. Court or Other Authority for Certain Functions of Arbitration Assistance and Supervision

The functions referred to in articles 11(3), 11(4), 13(3), 14, 16(3) and 34(2) shall be performed by . . . [Each State enacting this model law specifies the court, courts or, where referred to therein, other authority competent to perform these functions.]

CHAPTER II. ARBITRATION AGREEMENT

Option I

Article 7. Definition and Form of Arbitration Agreement (As Adopted by the Commission at its Thirty-Ninth Session, in 2006)

(1) "Arbitration agreement" is an agreement by the parties to submit to arbitration all or certain disputes which have arisen or which may arise between them in respect of a defined legal relationship, whether contractual or not. An arbitration agreement may be in the form of an arbitration clause in a contract or in the form of a separate agreement.

(2) The arbitration agreement shall be in writing.

(3) An arbitration agreement is in writing if its content is recorded in any form, whether or not the arbitration agreement or contract has been concluded orally, by conduct, or by other means.

(4) The requirement that an arbitration agreement be in writing is met by an electronic communication if the information contained therein is accessible so as to be useable for subsequent reference; "electronic communication" means any communication that the parties make by means of data messages; "data message" means information generated, sent, received or stored by electronic, magnetic, optical or similar means, including, but not limited to, electronic data interchange (EDI), electronic mail, telegram, telex or telecopy.

(5) Furthermore, an arbitration agreement is in writing if it is contained in an exchange of statements of claim and defence in which the existence of an agreement is alleged by one party and not denied by the other.

(6) The reference in a contract to any document containing an arbitration clause constitutes an arbitration agreement in writing, provided that the reference is such as to make that clause part of the contract.

Option II

Article 7. Definition of Arbitration Agreement
(As Adopted by the Commission at its Thirty-Ninth Session, in 2006)

"Arbitration agreement" is an agreement by the parties to submit to arbitration all or certain disputes which have arisen or which may arise between them in respect of a defined legal relationship, whether contractual or not.

Article 8. Arbitration Agreement and Substantive Claim Before Court

(1) A court before which an action is brought in a matter which is the subject of an arbitration agreement shall, if a party so requests not later than when submitting his first statement on the substance of the dispute, refer the parties to arbitration unless it finds that the agreement is null and void, inoperative or incapable of being performed.

(2) Where an action referred to in paragraph (1) of this article has been brought, arbitral proceedings may nevertheless be commenced or continued, and an award may be made, while the issue is pending before the court.

Article 9. Arbitration Agreement and Interim Measures by Court

It is not incompatible with an arbitration agreement for a party to request, before or during arbitral proceedings, from a court an interim measure of protection and for a court to grant such measure.

Chapter III. Composition of Arbitral Tribunal

Article 10. Number of Arbitrators

(1) The parties are free to determine the number of arbitrators.

(2) Failing such determination, the number of arbitrators shall be three.

Article 11. Appointment of Arbitrators

(1) No person shall be precluded by reason of his nationality from acting as an arbitrator, unless otherwise agreed by the parties.

(2) The parties are free to agree on a procedure of appointing the arbitrator or arbitrators, subject to the provisions of paragraphs (4) and (5) of this article.

(3) Failing such agreement,

    (a) in an arbitration with three arbitrators, each party shall appoint one arbitrator, and the two arbitrators thus appointed shall appoint the third arbitrator; if a party fails to appoint the arbitrator within thirty days of receipt of a request to do so from the other party, or if the two

arbitrators fail to agree on the third arbitrator within thirty days of their appointment, the appointment shall be made, upon request of a party, by the court or other authority specified in article 6;

(b) in an arbitration with a sole arbitrator, if the parties are unable to agree on the arbitrator, he shall be appointed, upon request of a party, by the court or other authority specified in article 6.

(4) Where, under an appointment procedure agreed upon by the parties,

(a) a party fails to act as required under such procedure, or

(b) the parties, or two arbitrators, are unable to reach an agreement expected of them under such procedure, or

(c) a third party, including an institution, fails to perform any function entrusted to it under such procedure, any party may request the court or other authority specified in article 6 to take the necessary measure, unless the agreement on the appointment procedure provides other means for securing the appointment.

(5) A decision on a matter entrusted by paragraph (3) or (4) of this article to the court or other authority specified in article 6 shall be subject to no appeal. The court or other authority, in appointing an arbitrator, shall have due regard to any qualifications required of the arbitrator by the agreement of the parties and to such considerations as are likely to secure the appointment of an independent and impartial arbitrator and, in the case of a sole or third arbitrator, shall take into account as well the advisability of appointing an arbitrator of a nationality other than those of the parties.

Article 12. Grounds for Challenge

(1) When a person is approached in connection with his possible appointment as an arbitrator, he shall disclose any circumstances likely to give rise to justifiable doubts as to his impartiality or independence. An arbitrator, from the time of his appointment and throughout the arbitral proceedings, shall without delay disclose any such circumstances to the parties unless they have already been informed of them by him.

(2) An arbitrator may be challenged only if circumstances exist that give rise to justifiable doubts as to his impartiality or independence, or if he does not possess qualifications agreed to by the parties. A party may challenge an arbitrator appointed by him, or in whose appointment he has participated, only for reasons of which he becomes aware after the appointment has been made.

Article 13. Challenge Procedure

(1) The parties are free to agree on a procedure for challenging an arbitrator, subject to the provisions of paragraph (3) of this article.

(2) Failing such agreement, a party who intends to challenge an arbitrator shall, within fifteen days after becoming aware of the constitution of the arbitral tribunal or after becoming aware of any circumstance referred to in article 12(2), send a written statement of the reasons for the challenge to the arbitral tribunal. Unless the challenged arbitrator withdraws from his office or the other party agrees to the challenge, the arbitral tribunal shall decide on the challenge.

(3) If a challenge under any procedure agreed upon by the parties or under the procedure of paragraph (2) of this article is not successful, the challenging party may request, within thirty days after having received notice of the decision rejecting the challenge, the court or other authority specified in article 6 to decide on the challenge, which decision shall be subject to no appeal; while such a request is pending, the arbitral tribunal, including the challenged arbitrator, may continue the arbitral proceedings and make an award.

Article 14. Failure or Impossibility to Act

(1) If an arbitrator becomes *de jure* or *de facto* unable to perform his functions or for other reasons fails to act without undue delay, his mandate terminates if he withdraws from his office or if the parties

agree on the termination. Otherwise, if a controversy remains concerning any of these grounds, any party may request the court or other authority specified in article 6 to decide on the termination of the mandate, which decision shall be subject to no appeal.

(2) If, under this article or article 13(2), an arbitrator withdraws from his office or a party agrees to the termination of the mandate of an arbitrator, this does not imply acceptance of the validity of any ground referred to in this article or article 12(2).

Article 15. Appointment of Substitute Arbitrator

Where the mandate of an arbitrator terminates under article 13 or 14 or because of his withdrawal from office for any other reason or because of the revocation of his mandate by agreement of the parties or in any other case of termination of his mandate, a substitute arbitrator shall be appointed according to the rules that were applicable to the appointment of the arbitrator being replaced.

CHAPTER IV. JURISDICTION OF ARBITRAL TRIBUNAL

Article 16. Competence of Arbitral Tribunal to Rule on its Jurisdiction

(1) The arbitral tribunal may rule on its own jurisdiction, including any objections with respect to the existence or validity of the arbitration agreement. For that purpose, an arbitration clause which forms part of a contract shall be treated as an agreement independent of the other terms of the contract. A decision by the arbitral tribunal that the contract is null and void shall not entail *ipso jure* the invalidity of the arbitration clause.

(2) A plea that the arbitral tribunal does not have jurisdiction shall be raised not later than the submission of the statement of defence. A party is not precluded from raising such a plea by the fact that he has appointed, or participated in the appointment of, an arbitrator. A plea that the arbitral tribunal is exceeding the scope of its authority shall be raised as soon as the matter alleged to be beyond the scope of its authority is raised during the arbitral proceedings. The arbitral tribunal may, in either case, admit a later plea if it considers the delay justified.

(3) The arbitral tribunal may rule on a plea referred to in paragraph (2) of this article either as a preliminary question or in an award on the merits. If the arbitral tribunal rules as a preliminary question that it has jurisdiction, any party may request, within thirty days after having received notice of that ruling, the court specified in article 6 to decide the matter, which decision shall be subject to no appeal; while such a request is pending, the arbitral tribunal may continue the arbitral proceedings and make an award.

CHAPTER IV A. INTERIM MEASURES AND PRELIMINARY ORDERS

(As Adopted by the Commission at its Thirty-Ninth Session, in 2006)

Section 1. Interim measures

Article 17. Power of Arbitral Tribunal to Order Interim Measures

(1) Unless otherwise agreed by the parties, the arbitral tribunal may, at the request of a party, grant interim measures.

(2) An interim measure is any temporary measure, whether in the form of an award or in another form, by which, at any time prior to the issuance of the award by which the dispute is finally decided, the arbitral tribunal orders a party to:

(a) Maintain or restore the status quo pending determination of the dispute;

(b) Take action that would prevent, or refrain from taking action that is likely to cause, current or imminent harm or prejudice to the arbitral process itself;

(c) Provide a means of preserving assets out of which a subsequent award may be satisfied; or

(d) Preserve evidence that may be relevant and material to the resolution of the dispute.

Article 17 A. Conditions for Granting Interim Measures

(1) The party requesting an interim measure under article 17(2)*(a)*, *(b)* and *(c)* shall satisfy the arbitral tribunal that:

    (a) Harm not adequately reparable by an award of damages is likely to result if the measure is not ordered, and such harm substantially outweighs the harm that is likely to result to the party against whom the measure is directed if the measure is granted; and

    (b) There is a reasonable possibility that the requesting party will succeed on the merits of the claim. The determination on this possibility shall not affect the discretion of the arbitral tribunal in making any subsequent determination.

(2) With regard to a request for an interim measure under article 17(2)*(d)*, the requirements in paragraphs (1)*(a)* and *(b)* of this article shall apply only to the extent the arbitral tribunal considers appropriate.

Section 2. Preliminary Orders

Article 17 B. Applications for Preliminary Orders and Conditions for Granting Preliminary Orders

(1) Unless otherwise agreed by the parties, a party may, without notice to any other party, make a request for an interim measure together with an application for a preliminary order directing a party not to frustrate the purpose of the interim measure requested.

(2) The arbitral tribunal may grant a preliminary order provided it considers that prior disclosure of the request for the interim measure to the party against whom it is directed risks frustrating the purpose of the measure.

(3) The conditions defined under article 17A apply to any preliminary order, provided that the harm to be assessed under article 17A(1)*(a)*, is the harm likely to result from the order being granted or not.

Article 17 C. Specific Regime for Preliminary Orders

(1) Immediately after the arbitral tribunal has made a determination in respect of an application for a preliminary order, the arbitral tribunal shall give notice to all parties of the request for the interim measure, the application for the preliminary order, the preliminary order, if any, and all other communications, including by indicating the content of any oral communication, between any party and the arbitral tribunal in relation thereto.

(2) At the same time, the arbitral tribunal shall give an opportunity to any party against whom a preliminary order is directed to present its case at the earliest practicable time.

(3) The arbitral tribunal shall decide promptly on any objection to the preliminary order.

(4) A preliminary order shall expire after twenty days from the date on which it was issued by the arbitral tribunal. However, the arbitral tribunal may issue an interim measure adopting or modifying the preliminary order, after the party against whom the preliminary order is directed has been given notice and an opportunity to present its case.

(5) A preliminary order shall be binding on the parties but shall not be subject to enforcement by a court. Such a preliminary order does not constitute an award.

Section 3. Provisions Applicable to Interim Measures and Preliminary Orders

Article 17 D. Modification, Suspension, Termination

The arbitral tribunal may modify, suspend or terminate an interim measure or a preliminary order it has granted, upon application of any party or, in exceptional circumstances and upon prior notice to the parties, on the arbitral tribunal's own initiative.

Article 17 E. Provision of Security

(1) The arbitral tribunal may require the party requesting an interim measure to provide appropriate security in connection with the measure.

(2) The arbitral tribunal shall require the party applying for a preliminary order to provide security in connection with the order unless the arbitral tribunal considers it inappropriate or unnecessary to do so.

Article 17 F. Disclosure

(1) The arbitral tribunal may require any party promptly to disclose any material change in the circumstances on the basis of which the measure was requested or granted.

(2) The party applying for a preliminary order shall disclose to the arbitral tribunal all circumstances that are likely to be relevant to the arbitral tribunal's determination whether to grant or maintain the order, and such obligation shall continue until the party against whom the order has been requested has had an opportunity to present its case. Thereafter, paragraph (1) of this article shall apply.

Article 17 G. Costs and Damages

The party requesting an interim measure or applying for a preliminary order shall be liable for any costs and damages caused by the measure or the order to any party if the arbitral tribunal later determines that, in the circumstances, the measure or the order should not have been granted. The arbitral tribunal may award such costs and damages at any point during the proceedings.

Section 4. Recognition and Enforcement of Interim Measures

Article 17 H. Recognition and Enforcement

(1) An interim measure issued by an arbitral tribunal shall be recognized as binding and, unless otherwise provided by the arbitral tribunal, enforced upon application to the competent court, irrespective of the country in which it was issued, subject to the provisions of article 17 I.

(2) The party who is seeking or has obtained recognition or enforcement of an interim measure shall promptly inform the court of any termination, suspension or modification of that interim measure.

(3) The court of the State where recognition or enforcement is sought may, if it considers it proper, order the requesting party to provide appropriate security if the arbitral tribunal has not already made a determination with respect to security or where such a decision is necessary to protect the rights of third parties.

Article 17 I. Grounds for Refusing Recognition or Enforcement[3]

(1) Recognition or enforcement of an interim measure may be refused only:
   (a) At the request of the party against whom it is invoked if the court is satisfied that:
       (i)   Such refusal is warranted on the grounds set forth in article 36(1)(a)(i), (ii), (iii) or (iv); or
       (ii) The arbitral tribunal's decision with respect to the provision of security in connection with the interim measure issued by the arbitral tribunal has not been complied with; or
       (iii) The interim measure has been terminated or suspended by the arbitral tribunal or, where so empowered, by the court of the State in which the arbitration takes place or under the law of which that interim measure was granted; or
   (b) If the court finds that:
       (i)   The interim measure is incompatible with the powers conferred upon the court unless the court decides to reformulate the interim measure to the extent necessary to adapt it to its own powers and procedures for the purposes of enforcing that interim measure and without modifying its substance; or

---

[3] The conditions set forth in article 17 I are intended to limit the number of circumstances in which the court may refuse to enforce an interim measure. It would not be contrary to the level of harmonization sought to be achieved by these model provisions if a State were to adopt fewer circumstances in which enforcement may be refused.

(ii) Any of the grounds set forth in article 36(1)(*b*)(i) or (ii), apply to the recognition and enforcement of the interim measure.

(2) Any determination made by the court on any ground in paragraph (1) of this article shall be effective only for the purposes of the application to recognize and enforce the interim measure. The court where recognition or enforcement is sought shall not, in making that determination, undertake a review of the substance of the interim measure.

Section 5. Court-ordered Interim Measures

Article 17 J. Court-ordered Interim Measures

A court shall have the same power of issuing an interim measure in relation to arbitration proceedings, irrespective of whether their place is in the territory of this State, as it has in relation to proceedings in courts. The court shall exercise such power in accordance with its own procedures in consideration of the specific features of international arbitration.

CHAPTER V. CONDUCT OF ARBITRAL PROCEEDINGS

Article 18. Equal Treatment of Parties

The parties shall be treated with equality and each party shall be given a full opportunity of presenting his case.

Article 19. Determination of Rules of Procedure

(1) Subject to the provisions of this Law, the parties are free to agree on the procedure to be followed by the arbitral tribunal in conducting the proceedings.

(2) Failing such agreement, the arbitral tribunal may, subject to the provisions of this Law, conduct the arbitration in such manner as it considers appropriate. The power conferred upon the arbitral tribunal includes the power to determine the admissibility, relevance, materiality and weight of any evidence.

Article 20. Place of Arbitration

(1) The parties are free to agree on the place of arbitration. Failing such agreement, the place of arbitration shall be determined by the arbitral tribunal having regard to the circumstances of the case, including the convenience of the parties.

(2) Notwithstanding the provisions of paragraph (1) of this article, the arbitral tribunal may, unless otherwise agreed by the parties, meet at any place it considers appropriate for consultation among its members, for hearing witnesses, experts or the parties, or for inspection of goods, other property or documents.

Article 21. Commencement of Arbitral Proceedings

Unless otherwise agreed by the parties, the arbitral proceedings in respect of a particular dispute commence on the date on which a request for that dispute to be referred to arbitration is received by the respondent.

Article 22. Language

(1) The parties are free to agree on the language or languages to be used in the arbitral proceedings. Failing such agreement, the arbitral tribunal shall determine the language or languages to be used in the proceedings. This agreement or determination, unless otherwise specified therein, shall apply to any written statement by a party, any hearing and any award, decision or other communication by the arbitral tribunal.

(2) The arbitral tribunal may order that any documentary evidence shall be accompanied by a translation into the language or languages agreed upon by the parties or determined by the arbitral tribunal.

Article 23. Statements of Claim and Defence

(1) Within the period of time agreed by the parties or determined by the arbitral tribunal, the claimant shall state the facts supporting his claim, the points at issue and the relief or remedy sought, and the respondent shall state his defence in respect of these particulars, unless the parties have otherwise agreed as to the required elements of such statements. The parties may submit with their statements all documents they consider to be relevant or may add a reference to the documents or other evidence they will submit.

(2) Unless otherwise agreed by the parties, either party may amend or supplement his claim or defence during the course of the arbitral proceedings, unless the arbitral tribunal considers it inappropriate to allow such amendment having regard to the delay in making it.

Article 24. Hearings and Written Proceedings

(1) Subject to any contrary agreement by the parties, the arbitral tribunal shall decide whether to hold oral hearings for the presentation of evidence or for oral argument, or whether the proceedings shall be conducted on the basis of documents and other materials. However, unless the parties have agreed that no hearings shall be held, the arbitral tribunal shall hold such hearings at an appropriate stage of the proceedings, if so requested by a party.

(2) The parties shall be given sufficient advance notice of any hearing and of any meeting of the arbitral tribunal for the purposes of inspection of goods, other property or documents.

(3) All statements, documents or other information supplied to the arbitral tribunal by one party shall be communicated to the other party. Also any expert report or evidentiary document on which the arbitral tribunal may rely in making its decision shall be communicated to the parties.

Article 25. Default of a Party

Unless otherwise agreed by the parties, if, without showing sufficient cause,

(a) the claimant fails to communicate his statement of claim in accordance with article 23(1), the arbitral tribunal shall terminate the proceedings;

(b) the respondent fails to communicate his statement of defence in accordance with article 23(1), the arbitral tribunal shall continue the proceedings without treating such failure in itself as an admission of the claimant's allegations;

(c) any party fails to appear at a hearing or to produce documentary evidence, the arbitral tribunal may continue the proceedings and make the award on the evidence before it.

Article 26. Expert Appointed by Arbitral Tribunal

(1) Unless otherwise agreed by the parties, the arbitral tribunal
(a) may appoint one or more experts to report to it on specific issues to be determined by the arbitral tribunal;
(b) may require a party to give the expert any relevant information or to produce, or to provide access to, any relevant documents, goods or other property for his inspection.

(2) Unless otherwise agreed by the parties, if a party so requests or if the arbitral tribunal considers it necessary, the expert shall, after delivery of his written or oral report, participate in a hearing where the parties have the opportunity to put questions to him and to present expert witnesses in order to testify on the points at issue.

Article 27. Court Assistance in Taking Evidence

The arbitral tribunal or a party with the approval of the arbitral tribunal may request from a competent court of this State assistance in taking evidence.

The court may execute the request within its competence and according to its rules on taking evidence.

Chapter VI. Making of Award and Termination of Proceedings

Article 28. *Rules Applicable to Substance of Dispute*

(1) The arbitral tribunal shall decide the dispute in accordance with such rules of law as are chosen by the parties as applicable to the substance of the dispute. Any designation of the law or legal system of a given State shall be construed, unless otherwise expressed, as directly referring to the substantive law of that State and not to its conflict of laws rules.

(2) Failing any designation by the parties, the arbitral tribunal shall apply the law determined by the conflict of laws rules which it considers applicable.

(3) The arbitral tribunal shall decide *ex aequo et bono* or as *amiable compositeur* only if the parties have expressly authorized it to do so.

(4) In all cases, the arbitral tribunal shall decide in accordance with the terms of the contract and shall take into account the usages of the trade applicable to the transaction.

Article 29. *Decision-Making by Panel of Arbitrators*

In arbitral proceedings with more than one arbitrator, any decision of the arbitral tribunal shall be made, unless otherwise agreed by the parties, by a majority of all its members. However, questions of procedure may be decided by a presiding arbitrator, if so authorized by the parties or all members of the arbitral tribunal.

Article 30. *Settlement*

(1) If, during arbitral proceedings, the parties settle the dispute, the arbitral tribunal shall terminate the proceedings and, if requested by the parties and not objected to by the arbitral tribunal, record the settlement in the form of an arbitral award on agreed terms.

(2) An award on agreed terms shall be made in accordance with the provisions of article 31 and shall state that it is an award. Such an award has the same status and effect as any other award on the merits of the case.

Article 31. *Form and Contents of Award*

(1) The award shall be made in writing and shall be signed by the arbitrator or arbitrators. In arbitral proceedings with more than one arbitrator, the signatures of the majority of all members of the arbitral tribunal shall suffice, provided that the reason for any omitted signature is stated.

(2) The award shall state the reasons upon which it is based, unless the parties have agreed that no reasons are to be given or the award is an award on agreed terms under article 30.

(3) The award shall state its date and the place of arbitration as determined in accordance with article 20(1). The award shall be deemed to have been made at that place.

(4) After the award is made, a copy signed by the arbitrators in accordance with paragraph (1) of this article shall be delivered to each party.

Article 32. *Termination of Proceedings*

(1) The arbitral proceedings are terminated by the final award or by an order of the arbitral tribunal in accordance with paragraph (2) of this article.

(2) The arbitral tribunal shall issue an order for the termination of the arbitral proceedings when:

   (*a*) the claimant withdraws his claim, unless the respondent objects thereto and the arbitral tribunal recognizes a legitimate interest on his part in obtaining a final settlement of the dispute;

   (*b*) the parties agree on the termination of the proceedings;

   (*c*) the arbitral tribunal finds that the continuation of the proceedings has for any other reason become unnecessary or impossible.

(3) The mandate of the arbitral tribunal terminates with the termination of the arbitral proceedings, subject to the provisions of articles 33 and 34(4).

Article 33. Correction and Interpretation of Award; Additional Award

(1) Within thirty days of receipt of the award, unless another period of time has been agreed upon by the parties:

(a) *a party, with notice to the other party, may request the arbitral* tribunal to correct in the award any errors in computation, any clerical or typographical errors or any errors of similar nature;

(b) if so agreed by the parties, a party, with notice to the other party, may request the arbitral tribunal to give an interpretation of a specific point or part of the award.

If the arbitral tribunal considers the request to be justified, it shall make the correction or give the interpretation within thirty days of receipt of the request. The interpretation shall form part of the award.

(2) The arbitral tribunal may correct any error of the type referred to in paragraph (1)*(a)* of this article on its own initiative within thirty days of the date of the award.

(3) Unless otherwise agreed by the parties, a party, with notice to the other party, may request, within thirty days of receipt of the award, the arbitral tribunal to make an additional award as to claims presented in the arbitral proceedings but omitted from the award. If the arbitral tribunal considers the request to be justified, it shall make the additional award within sixty days.

(4) The arbitral tribunal may extend, if necessary, the period of time within which it shall make a correction, interpretation or an additional award under paragraph (1) or (3) of this article.

(5) The provisions of article 31 shall apply to a correction or interpretation of the award or to an additional award.

Chapter VII. Recourse Against Award

Article 34. Application for Setting Aside as Exclusive Recourse Against Arbitral Award

(1) Recourse to a court against an arbitral award may be made only by an application for setting aside in accordance with paragraphs (2) and (3) of this article.

(2) An arbitral award may be set aside by the court specified in article 6 only if:

(a) the party making the application furnishes proof that:

(i) a party to the arbitration agreement referred to in article 7 was under some incapacity; or the said agreement is not valid under the law to which the parties have subjected it or, failing any indication thereon, under the law of this State; or

(ii) the party making the application was not given proper notice of the appointment of an arbitrator or of the arbitral proceedings or was otherwise unable to present his case; or

(iii) the award deals with a dispute not contemplated by or not falling within the terms of the submission to arbitration, or contains decisions on matters beyond the scope of the submission to arbitration, provided that, if the decisions on matters submitted to arbitration can be separated from those not so submitted, only that part of the award which contains decisions on matters not submitted to arbitration may be set aside; or

(iv) the composition of the arbitral tribunal or the arbitral procedure was not in accordance with the agreement of the parties, unless such agreement was in conflict with a provision of this Law from which the parties cannot derogate, or, failing such agreement, was not in accordance with this Law; or

(b) the court finds that:

(i) the subject-matter of the dispute is not capable of settlement by arbitration under the law of this State; or

(ii) the award is in conflict with the public policy of this State.

(3) An application for setting aside may not be made after three months have elapsed from the date on which the party making that application had received the award or, if a request had been made under article 33, from the date on which that request had been disposed of by the arbitral tribunal.

(4) The court, when asked to set aside an award, may, where appropriate and so requested by a party, suspend the setting aside proceedings for a period of time determined by it in order to give the arbitral tribunal an opportunity to resume the arbitral proceedings or to take such other action as in the arbitral tribunal's opinion will eliminate the grounds for setting aside.

CHAPTER VIII. RECOGNITION AND ENFORCEMENT OF AWARDS

Article 35. Recognition and Enforcement

(1) An arbitral award, irrespective of the country in which it was made, shall be recognized as binding and, upon application in writing to the competent court, shall be enforced subject to the provisions of this article and of article 36.

(2) The party relying on an award or applying for its enforcement shall supply the original award or a copy thereof. If the award is not made in an official language of this State, the court may request the party to supply a translation thereof into such language.[4]

(Article 35(2) has been amended by the Commission at its Thirty-Ninth Session, in 2006)

Article 36. Grounds for Refusing Recognition or Enforcement

(1) Recognition or enforcement of an arbitral award, irrespective of the country in which it was made, may be refused only:

(a) at the request of the party against whom it is invoked, if that party furnishes to the competent court where recognition or enforcement is sought proof that:

    (i) a party to the arbitration agreement referred to in article 7 was under some incapacity; or the said agreement is not valid under the law to which the parties have subjected it or, failing any indication thereon, under the law of the country where the award was made; or

    (ii) the party against whom the award is invoked was not given proper notice of the appointment of an arbitrator or of the arbitral proceedings or was otherwise unable to present his case; or

    (iii) the award deals with a dispute not contemplated by or not falling within the terms of the submission to arbitration, or it contains decisions on matters beyond the scope of the submission to arbitration, provided that, if the decisions on matters submitted to arbitration can be separated from those not so submitted, that part of the award which contains decisions on matters submitted to arbitration may be recognized and enforced; or

    (iv) the composition of the arbitral tribunal or the arbitral procedure was not in accordance with the agreement of the parties or, failing such agreement, was not in accordance with the law of the country where the arbitration took place; or

    (v) the award has not yet become binding on the parties or has been set aside or suspended by a court of the country in which, or under the law of which, that award was made; or

(b) if the court finds that:

    (i) the subject-matter of the dispute is not capable of settlement by arbitration under the law of this State; or

    (ii) the recognition or enforcement of the award would be contrary to the public policy of this State.

(2) If an application for setting aside or suspension of an award has been made to a court referred to in paragraph (1)(a)(v) of this article, the court where recognition or enforcement is sought may, if it considers it proper, adjourn its decision and may also, on the application of the party claiming recognition or enforcement of the award, order the other party to provide appropriate security.

---

[4] The conditions set forth in this paragraph are intended to set maximum standards. It would, thus, not be contrary to the harmonization to be achieved by the model law if a State retained even less onerous conditions.

APPENDIX 5

UNCITRAL Arbitration Rules (1976)

Resolution 31/98 Adopted by the General Assembly on 15 December 1976

31/98. ARBITRATION RULES OF THE UNITED NATIONS COMMISSION ON INTERNATIONAL TRADE LAW

Uncitral Arbitration Rules

Section I
Introductory rules

Scope of Application

Article 1

1. Where the parties to a contract have agreed in writing* that disputes in relation to that contract shall be referred to arbitration under the UNCITRAL Arbitration Rules, then such disputes shall be settled in accordance with these Rules subject to such modification as the parties may agree in writing.

2. These Rules shall govern the arbitration except that where any of these Rules is in conflict with a provision of the law applicable to the arbitration from which the parties cannot derogate, that provision shall prevail.

MODEL ARBITRATION CLAUSE

Any dispute, controversy or claim arising out of or relating to this contract, or the breach, termination or invalidity thereof, shall be settled by arbitration in accordance with the UNCITRAL Arbitration Rules as at present in force.

Note - Parties may wish to consider adding:

(a) The appointing authority shall be . . . (name of institution or person);
(b) The number of arbitrators shall be . . . (one or three);
(c) The place of arbitration shall be . . . (town or country);
(d) The language(s) to be used in the arbitral proceedings shall be . . .

Notice, Calculation of Periods of Time

Article 2

1. For the purposes of these Rules, any notice, including a notification, communication or proposal, is deemed to have been received if it is physically delivered to the addressee or if it is delivered at his habitual residence, place of business or mailing address, or, if none of these can be found after making reasonable inquiry, then at the addressees last-known residence or place of business. Notice shall be deemed to have been received on the day it is so delivered.

2. For the purposes of calculating a period of time under these Rules, such period shall begin to run on the day following the day when a notice, notification, communication or proposal is received. If the last day of such period is an official holiday or a non-business day at the residence or place of business of the addressee, the period is extended until the first business day which follows. Official holidays or

non-business days occurring during the running of the period of time are included in calculating the period.

Notice of Arbitration

Article 3

1. The party initiating recourse to arbitration (hereinafter called the "claimant") shall give to the other party (hereinafter called the "respondent") a notice of arbitration.

2. Arbitral proceedings shall be deemed to commence on the date on which the notice of arbitration is received by the respondent.

3. The notice of arbitration shall include the following:

(a) A demand that the dispute be referred to arbitration;
(b) The names and addresses of the parties;
(c) A reference to the arbitration clause or the separate arbitration agreement that is invoked;
(d) A reference to the contract out of or in relation to which the dispute arises;
(e) The general nature of the claim and an indication of the amount involved, if any;
(f) The relief or remedy sought;
(g) A proposal as to the number of arbitrators (i.e. one or three), if the parties have not previously agreed thereon.

4. The notice of arbitration may also include:

(a) The proposals for the appointments of a sole arbitrator and an appointing authority referred to in article 6, paragraph 1;
(b) The notification of the appointment of an arbitrator referred to in article 7;
(c) The statement of claim referred to in article 18

Representation and assistance

Article 4

The parties may be represented or assisted by persons of their choice. The names and addresses of such persons must be communicated in writing to the other party; such communication must specify whether the appointment is being made for purposes of representation or assistance.

Section II
Composition of the Arbitral Tribunal

Number of Arbitrators

Article 5

If the parties have not previously agreed on the number of arbitrators (i.e. one or three), and if within fifteen days after the receipt by the respondent of the notice of arbitration the parties have not agreed that there shall be only one arbitrator, three arbitrators shall be appointed.

Appointment of Arbitrators (Articles 6 To 8)

Article 6

1. If a sole arbitrator is to be appointed, either party may propose to the other:

(a) The names of one or more persons, one of whom would serve as the sole arbitrator; and
(b) If no appointing authority has been agreed upon by the parties, the name or names of one or more institutions or persons, one of whom would serve as appointing authority.

2. If within thirty days after receipt by a party of a proposal made in accordance with paragraph 1 the parties have not reached agreement on the choice of a sole arbitrator, the sole arbitrator shall be

appointed by the appointing authority agreed upon by the parties. If no appointing authority has been agreed upon by the parties, or if the appointing authority agreed upon refuses to act or fails to appoint the arbitrator within sixty days of the receipt of a party's request therefor, either party may request the Secretary-General of the Permanent Court of Arbitration at The Hague to designate an appointing authority.

3. The appointing authority shall, at the request of one of the parties, appoint the sole arbitrator as promptly as possible. In making the appointment the appointing authority shall use the following list-procedure, unless both parties agree that the list-procedure should not be used or unless the appointing authority determines in its discretion that the use of the list-procedure is not appropriate for the case:

(*a*) At the request of one of the parties the appointing authority shall communicate to both parties an identical list containing at least three names;

(*b*) Within fifteen days after the receipt of this list, each party may return the list to the appointing authority after having deleted the name or names to which he objects and numbered the remaining names on the list in the order of his preference;

(*c*) After the expiration of the above period of time the appointing authority shall appoint the sole arbitrator from among the names approved on the lists returned to it and in accordance with the order of preference indicated by the parties;

(*d*) If for any reason the appointment cannot be made according to this procedure, the appointing authority may exercise its discretion in appointing the sole arbitrator.

4. In making the appointment, the appointing authority shall have regard to such considerations as are likely to secure the appointment of an independent and impartial arbitrator and shall take into account as well the advisability of appointing an arbitrator of a nationality other than the nationalities of the parties.

Article 7

1. If three arbitrators are to be appointed, each party shall appoint one arbitrator. The two arbitrators thus appointed shall choose the third arbitrator who will act as the presiding arbitrator of the tribunal.

2. If within thirty days after the receipt of a party's notification of the appointment of an arbitrator the other party has not notified the first party of the arbitrator he has appointed:

(*a*) The first party may request the appointing authority previously designated by the parties to appoint the second arbitrator; or

(*b*) If no such authority has been previously designated by the parties, or if the appointing authority previously designated refuses to act or fails to appoint the arbitrator within thirty days after receipt of a party's request therefor, the first party may request the Secretary-General of the Permanent Court of Arbitration at The Hague to designate the appointing authority. The first party may then request the appointing authority so designated to appoint the second arbitrator. In either case, the appointing authority may exercise its discretion in appointing the arbitrator.

2. If within thirty days after the appointment of the second arbitrator the two arbitrators have not agreed on the choice of the presiding arbitrator, the presiding arbitrator shall be appointed by an appointing authority in the same way as a sole arbitrator would be appointed under article 6.

Article 8

1. When an appointing authority is requested to appoint an arbitrator pursuant to article 6 or article 7, the party which makes the request shall send to the appointing authority a copy of the notice of arbitration, a copy of the contract out of or in relation to which the dispute has arisen and a copy of the arbitration agreement if it is not contained in the contract. The appointing authority may require from either party such information as it deems necessary to fulfil its function.

2. Where the names of one or more persons are proposed for appointment as arbitrators, their full names, addresses and nationalities shall be indicated, together with a description of their qualifications.

CHALLENGE OF ARBITRATORS (ARTICLES 9 TO 12)

ARTICLE 9

A prospective arbitrator shall disclose to those who approach him in connexion with his possible appointment any circumstances likely to give rise to justifiable doubts as to his impartiality or independence. An arbitrator, once appointed or chosen, shall disclose such circumstances to the parties unless they have already been informed by him of these circumstances.

ARTICLE 10

1. Any arbitrator may be challenged if circumstances exist that give rise to justifiable doubts as to the arbitrators impartiality or independence.

2. A party may challenge the arbitrator appointed by him only for reasons of which he becomes aware after the appointment has been made.

ARTICLE 11

1. A party who intends to challenge an arbitrator shall send notice of his challenge within fifteen days after the appointment of the challenged arbitrator has been notified to the challenging party or within fifteen days after the circumstances mentioned in articles 9 and 10 became known to that party.

2. The challenge shall be notified to the other party, to the arbitrator who is challenged and to the other members of the arbitral tribunal. The notification shall be in writing and shall state the reasons for the challenge.

3. When an arbitrator has been challenged by one party, the other party may agree to the challenge. The arbitrator may also, after the challenge, withdraw from his office. In neither case does this imply acceptance of the validity of the grounds for the challenge. In both cases the procedure provided in article 6 or 7 shall be used in full for the appointment of the substitute arbitrator, even if during the process of appointing the challenged arbitrator a party had failed to exercise his right to appoint or to participate in the appointment.

ARTICLE 12

1. If the other party does not agree to the challenge and the challenged arbitrator does not withdraw, the decision on the challenge will be made:

(*a*) When the initial appointment was made by an appointing authority, by that authority;
(*b*) When the initial appointment was not made by an appointing authority, but an appointing authority has been previously designated, by that authority;
(*c*) In all other cases, by the appointing authority to be designated in accordance with the procedure for designating an appointing authority as provided for in article 6.

2. If the appointing authority sustains the challenge, a substitute arbitrator shall be appointed or chosen pursuant to the procedure applicable to the appointment or choice of an arbitrator as provided in articles 6 to 9 except that, when this procedure would call for the designation of an appointing authority, the appointment of the arbitrator shall be made by the appointing authority which decided on the challenge.

REPLACEMENT OF AN ARBITRATOR

ARTICLE 13

1. In the event of the death or resignation of an arbitrator during the course of the arbitral proceedings, a substitute arbitrator shall be appointed or chosen pursuant to the procedure provided for in articles 6 to 9 that was applicable to the appointment or choice of the arbitrator being replaced.

2. In the event that an arbitrator fails to act or in the event of the *de jure* or *de facto* impossibility of his performing his functions, the procedure in respect of the challenge and replacement of an arbitrator as provided in the preceding articles shall apply.

REPETITION OF HEARINGS IN THE EVENT OF THE REPLACEMENT OF AN ARBITRATOR

ARTICLE 14

If under articles 11 to 13 the sole or presiding arbitrator is replaced, any hearings held previously shall be repeated; if any other arbitrator is replaced, such prior hearings may be repeated at the discretion of the arbitral tribunal.

SECTION III
ARBITRAL PROCEEDINGS

GENERAL PROVISIONS

ARTICLE 15

1. Subject to these Rules, the arbitral tribunal may conduct the arbitration in such manner as it considers appropriate, provided that the parties are treated with equality and that at any stage of the proceedings each party is given a full opportunity of presenting his case.

2. If either party so requests at any stage of the proceedings, the arbitral tribunal shall hold hearings for the presentation of evidence by witnesses, including expert witnesses, or for oral argument. In the absence of such a request, the arbitral tribunal shall decide whether to hold such hearings or whether the proceedings shall be conducted on the basis of documents and other materials.

3. All documents or information supplied to the arbitral tribunal by one party shall at the same time be communicated by that party to the other party.

PLACE OF ARBITRATION

ARTICLE 16

1. Unless the parties have agreed upon the place where the arbitration is to be held, such place shall be determined by the arbitral tribunal, having regard to the circumstances of the arbitration.

2. The arbitral tribunal may determine the locale of the arbitration within the country agreed upon by the parties. It may hear witnesses and hold meetings for consultation among its members at any place it deems appropriate, having regard to the circumstances of the arbitration.

3. The arbitral tribunal may meet at any place it deems appropriate for the inspection of goods, other property or documents. The parties shall be given sufficient notice to enable them to be present at such inspection.

4. The award shall be made at the place of arbitration.

LANGUAGE

ARTICLE 17

1. Subject to an agreement by the parties, the arbitral tribunal shall, promptly after its appointment, determine the language or languages to be used in the proceedings. This determination shall apply to the statement of claim, the statement of defence, and any further written statements and, if oral hearings take place, to the language or languages to be used in such hearings.

2. The arbitral tribunal may order that any documents annexed to the statement of claim or statement of defence, and any supplementary documents or exhibits submitted in the course of the proceedings, delivered in their original language, shall be accompanied by a translation into the language or languages agreed upon by the parties or determined by the arbitral tribunal.

STATEMENT OF CLAIM

ARTICLE 18

1. Unless the statement of claim was contained in the notice of arbitration, within a period of time to be determined by the arbitral tribunal, the claimant shall communicate his statement of claim in writing to the respondent and to each of the arbitrators. A copy of the contract, and of the arbitration agreement if not contained in the contract, shall be annexed thereto.

2. The statement of claim shall include the following particulars:

(a) The names and addresses of the parties;
(b) A statement of the facts supporting the claim;
(c) The points at issue;
(d) The relief or remedy sought.

The claimant may annex to his statement of claim all documents he deems relevant or may add a reference to the documents or other evidence he will submit.

STATEMENT OF DEFENCE

ARTICLE 19

1. Within a period of time to be determined by the arbitral tribunal, the respondent shall communicate his statement of defence in writing to the claimant and to each of the arbitrators.

2. The statement of defence shall reply to the particulars *(b)*, *(c)* and *(d)* of the statement of claim (article 18, para. 2). The respondent may annex to his statement the documents on which he relies for his defence or may add a reference to the documents or other evidence he will submit.

3. In his statement of defence, or at a later stage in the arbitral proceedings if the arbitral tribunal decides that the delay was justified under the circumstances, the respondent may make a counter-claim arising out of the same contract or rely on a claim arising out of the same contract for the purpose of a set-off.

4. The provisions of article 18, paragraph 2, shall apply to a counter-claim and a claim relied on for the purpose of a set-off.

AMENDMENTS TO THE CLAIM OR DEFENCE

ARTICLE 20

During the course of the arbitral proceedings either party may amend or supplement his claim or defence unless the arbitral tribunal considers it inappropriate to allow such amendment having regard to the delay in making it or prejudice to the other party or any other circumstances. However, a claim may not be amended in such a manner that the amended claim falls outside the scope of the arbitration clause or separate arbitration agreement

PLEAS AS TO THE JURISDICTION OF THE ARBITRAL TRIBUNAL

Article 21

1. The arbitral tribunal shall have the power to rule on objections that it has no jurisdiction, including any objections with respect to the existence or validity of the arbitration clause or of the separate arbitration agreement.

2. The arbitral tribunal shall have the power to determine the existence or the validity of the contract of which an arbitration clause forms a part. For the purposes of article 21, an arbitration clause which forms part of a contract and which provides for arbitration under these Rules shall be treated as an agreement independent of the other terms of the contract. A decision by the arbitral tribunal that the contract is null and void shall not entail *ipso jure* the invalidity of the arbitration clause.

3. A plea that the arbitral tribunal does not have jurisdiction shall be raised not later than in the statement of defence or, with respect to a counter-claim, in the reply to the counterclaim.

4. In general, the arbitral tribunal should rule on a plea concerning its jurisdiction as a preliminary question. However, the arbitral tribunal may proceed with the arbitration and rule on such a plea in their final award.

FURTHER WRITTEN STATEMENTS

ARTICLE 22

The arbitral tribunal shall decide which further written statements, in addition to the statement of claim and the statement of defence, shall be required from the parties or may be presented by them and shall fix the periods of time for communicating such statements.

PERIODS OF TIME

ARTICLE 23

The periods of time fixed by the arbitral tribunal for the communication of written statements (including the statement of claim and statement of defence) should not exceed forty-five days. However, the arbitral tribunal may extend the time-limits if it concludes that an extension is justified.

EVIDENCE AND HEARINGS (ARTICLES 24 AND 25)

ARTICLE 24

1. Each party shall have the burden of proving the facts relied on to support his claim or defence.

2. The arbitral tribunal may, if it considers it appropriate, require a party to deliver to the tribunal and to the other party, within such a period of time as the arbitral tribunal shall decide, a summary of the documents and other evidence which that party intends to present in support of the facts in issue set out in his statement of claim or statement of defence.

3. At any time during the arbitral proceedings the arbitral tribunal may require the parties to produce documents, exhibits or other evidence within such a period of time as the tribunal shall determine.

ARTICLE 25

1. In the event of an oral hearing, the arbitral tribunal shall give the parties adequate advance notice of the date, time and place thereof.

2. If witnesses are to be heard, at least fifteen days before the hearing each party shall communicate to the arbitral tribunal and to the other party the names and addresses of the witnesses he intends to present, the subject upon and the languages in which such witnesses will give their testimony.

3. The arbitral tribunal shall make arrangements for the translation of oral statements made at a hearing and for a record of the hearing if either is deemed necessary by the tribunal under the circumstances of the case, or if the parties have agreed thereto and have communicated such agreement to the tribunal at least fifteen days before the hearing.

4. Hearings shall be held *in camera* unless the parties agree otherwise. The arbitral tribunal may require the retirement of any witness or witnesses during the testimony of other witnesses. The arbitral tribunal is free to determine the manner in which witnesses are examined.

5. Evidence of witnesses may also be presented in the form of written statements signed by them.

6. The arbitral tribunal shall determine the admissibility, relevance, materiality and weight of the evidence offered.

INTERIM MEASURES OF PROTECTION

ARTICLE 26

1. At the request of either party, the arbitral tribunal may take any interim measures it deems necessary in respect of the subject-matter of the dispute, including measures for the conservation of the goods forming the subject-matter in dispute, such as ordering their deposit with a third person or the sale of perishable goods.

2. Such interim measures may be established in the form of an interim award. The arbitral tribunal shall be entitled to require security for the costs of such measures.

3. A request for interim measures addressed by any party to a judicial authority shall not be deemed incompatible with the agreement to arbitrate, or as a waiver of that agreement.

EXPERTS

ARTICLE 27

1. The arbitral tribunal may appoint one or more experts to report to it, in writing, on specific issues to be determined by the tribunal. A copy of the expert's terms of reference, established by the arbitral tribunal, shall be communicated to the parties.

2. The parties shall give the expert any relevant information or produce for his inspection any relevant documents or goods that he may require of them. Any dispute between a party and such expert as to the relevance of the required information or production shall be referred to the arbitral tribunal for decision.

3. Upon receipt of the expert's report, the arbitral tribunal shall communicate a copy of the report to the parties who shall be given the opportunity to express, in writing, their opinion on the report. A party shall be entitled to examine any document on which the expert has relied in his report.

4. At the request of either party the expert, after delivery of the report, may be heard at a hearing where the parties shall have the opportunity to be present and to interrogate the expert. At this hearing either party may present expert witnesses in order to testify on the points at issue. The provisions of article 25 shall be applicable to such proceedings.

DEFAULT

ARTICLE 28

1. If, within the period of time fixed by the arbitral tribunal, the claimant has failed to communicate his claim without showing sufficient cause for such failure, the arbitral tribunal shall issue an order for the termination of the arbitral proceedings. If, within the period of time fixed by the arbitral tribunal, the respondent has failed to communicate his statement of defence without showing sufficient cause for such failure, the arbitral tribunal shall order that the proceedings continue.

2. If one of the parties, duly notified under these Rules, fails to appear at a hearing, without showing sufficient cause for such failure, the arbitral tribunal may proceed with the arbitration.

3. If one of the parties, duly invited to produce documentary evidence, fails to do so within the established period of time, without showing sufficient cause for such failure, the arbitral tribunal may make the award on the evidence before it.

CLOSURE OF HEARINGS

ARTICLE 29

1. The arbitral tribunal may inquire of the parties if they have any further proof to offer or witnesses to be heard or submissions to make and, if there are none, it may declare the hearings closed.

2. The arbitral tribunal may, if it considers it necessary owing to exceptional circumstances, decide, on its own motion or upon application of a party, to reopen the hearings at any time before the award is made.

WAIVER OF RULES

ARTICLE 30

A party who knows that any provision of, or requirement under, these Rules has not been complied with and yet proceeds with the arbitration without promptly stating his objection to such non-compliance, shall be deemed to have waived his right to object.

SECTION IV
THE AWARD

DECISIONS

ARTICLE 31

1. When there are three arbitrators, any award or other decision of the arbitral tribunal shall be made by a majority of the arbitrators.

2. In the case of questions of procedure, when there is no majority or when the arbitral tribunal so authorizes, the presiding arbitrator may decide on his own, subject to revision, if any, by the arbitral tribunal.

FORM AND EFFECT OF THE AWARD

ARTICLE 32

1. In addition to making a final award, the arbitral tribunal shall be entitled to make interim, interlocutory, or partial awards.

2. The award shall be made in writing and shall be final and binding on the parties. The parties undertake to carry out the award without delay.

3. The arbitral tribunal shall state the reasons upon which the award is based, unless the parties have agreed that no reasons are to be given.

4. An award shall be signed by the arbitrators and it shall contain the date on which and the place where the award was made. Where there are three arbitrators and one of them fails to sign, the award shall state the reason for the absence of the signature.

5. The award may be made public only with the consent of both parties.

6. Copies of the award signed by the arbitrators shall be communicated to the parties by the arbitral tribunal.

7. If the arbitration law of the country where the award is made requires that the award be filed or registered by the arbitral tribunal, the tribunal shall comply with this requirement within the period of time required by law.

APPLICABLE LAW, AMIABLE COMPOSITEUR

ARTICLE 33

1. The arbitral tribunal shall apply the law designated by the parties as applicable to the substance of the dispute. Failing such designation by the parties, the arbitral tribunal shall apply the law determined by the conflict of laws rules which it considers applicable.

2. The arbitral tribunal shall decide as *amiable compositeur* or *ex aequo et bono* only if the parties have expressly authorized the arbitral tribunal to do so and if the law applicable to the arbitral procedure permits such arbitration.

3. In all cases, the arbitral tribunal shall decide in accordance with the terms of the contract and shall take into account the usages of the trade applicable to the transaction.

SETTLEMENT OR OTHER GROUNDS FOR TERMINATION

ARTICLE 34

1. If, before the award is made, the parties agree on a settlement of the dispute, the arbitral tribunal shall either issue an order for the termination of the arbitral proceedings or, if requested by both parties and accepted by the tribunal, record the settlement in the form of an arbitral award on agreed terms. The arbitral tribunal is not obliged to give reasons for such an award.

2. If, before the award is made, the continuation of the arbitral proceedings becomes unnecessary or impossible for any reason not mentioned in paragraph 1, the arbitral tribunal shall inform the parties of its intention to issue an order for the termination of the proceedings. The arbitral tribunal shall have the power to issue such an order unless a party raises justifiable grounds for objection.

3. Copies of the order for termination of the arbitral proceedings or of the arbitral award on agreed terms, signed by the arbitrators, shall be communicated by the arbitral tribunal to the parties. Where an arbitral award on agreed terms is made, the provisions of article 32, paragraphs 2 and 4 to 7, shall apply.

INTERPRETATION OF THE AWARD

ARTICLE 35

1. Within thirty days after the receipt of the award, either party, with notice to the other party, may request that the arbitral tribunal give an interpretation of the award.

2. The interpretation shall be given in writing within forty-five days after the receipt of the request. The interpretation shall form part of the award and the provisions of article 32, paragraphs 2 to 7, shall apply.

CORRECTION OF THE AWARD

ARTICLE 36

1. Within thirty days after the receipt of the award, either party, with notice to the other party, may request the arbitral tribunal to correct in the award any errors in computation, any clerical or typographical errors, or any errors of similar nature. The arbitral tribunal may within thirty days after the communication of the award make such corrections on its own initiative.

2. Such corrections shall be in writing, and the provisions of article 32, paragraphs 2 to 7, shall apply.

ADDITIONAL AWARD

ARTICLE 37

1. Within thirty days after the receipt of the award, either party, with notice to the other party, may request the arbitral tribunal to make an additional award as to claims presented in the arbitral proceedings but omitted from the award.

2. If the arbitral tribunal considers the request for an additional award to be justified and considers that the omission can be rectified without any further hearings or evidence, it shall complete its award within sixty days after the receipt of the request.

3. When an additional award is made, the provisions of article 32, paragraphs 2 to 7, shall apply.

COSTS (ARTICLES 38 To 40)

ARTICLE 38

The arbitral tribunal shall fix the costs of arbitration in its award. The term "costs" includes only:

(a) The fees of the arbitral tribunal to be stated separately as to each arbitrator and to be fixed by the tribunal itself in accordance with article 39;

(b) The travel and other expenses incurred by the arbitrators;

(c) The costs of expert advice and of other assistance required by the arbitral tribunal;

(d) The travel and other expenses of witnesses to the extent such expenses are approved by the arbitral tribunal;

(e) The costs for legal representation and assistance of the successful party if such costs were claimed during the arbitral proceedings, and only to the extent that the arbitral tribunal determines that the amount of such costs is reasonable;

(f) Any fees and expenses of the appointing authority as well as the expenses of the Secretary-General of the Permanent Court of Arbitration at The Hague.

ARTICLE 39

1. The fees of the arbitral tribunal shall be reasonable in amount, taking into account the amount in dispute, the complexity of the subject-matter, the time spent by the arbitrators and any other relevant circumstances of the case.

2. If an appointing authority has been agreed upon by the parties or designated by the Secretary-General of the Permanent Court of Arbitration at The Hague, and if that authority has issued a schedule of fees for arbitrators in international cases which it administers, the arbitral tribunal in fixing its fees shall take that schedule of fees into account to the extent that it considers appropriate in the circumstances of the case.

3. If such appointing authority has not issued a schedule of fees for arbitrators in international cases, any party may at any time request the appointing authority to furnish a statement setting forth the basis for establishing fees which is customarily followed in international cases in which the authority appoints arbitrators. If the appointing authority consents to provide such a statement, the arbitral tribunal in fixing its fees shall take such information into account to the extent that it considers appropriate in the circumstances of the case.

4. In cases referred to in paragraphs 2 and 3, when a party so requests and the appointing authority consents to perform the function, the arbitral tribunal shall fix its fees only after consultation with the appointing authority which may make any comment it deems appropriate to the arbitral tribunal concerning the fees.

ARTICLE 40

1. Except as provided in paragraph 2, the costs of arbitration shall in principle be borne by the unsuccessful party. However, the arbitral tribunal may apportion each of such costs between the parties if it determines that apportionment is reasonable, taking into account the circumstances of the case.

2. With respect to the costs of legal representation and assistance referred to in article 38, paragraph *(e)*, the arbitral tribunal, taking into account the circumstances of the case, shall be free to determine which party shall bear such costs or may apportion such costs between the parties if it determines that apportionment is reasonable.

3. When the arbitral tribunal issues an order for the termination of the arbitral proceedings or makes an award on agreed terms, it shall fix the costs of arbitration referred to in article 38 and article 39, paragraph 1, in the text of that order or award.

4. No additional fees may be charged by an arbitral tribunal for interpretation or correction or completion of its award under articles 35 to 37.

DEPOSIT OF COSTS

ARTICLE 41

1. The arbitral tribunal, on its establishment, may request each party to deposit an equal amount as an advance for the costs referred to in article 38, paragraphs *(a)*, *(b)* and *(c)*.

2. During the course of the arbitral proceedings the arbitral tribunal may request supplementary deposits from the parties.

3. If an appointing authority has been agreed upon by the parties or designated by the Secretary-General of the Permanent Court of Arbitration at The Hague, and when a party so requests and the appointing authority consents to perform the function, the arbitral tribunal shall fix the amounts of any deposits or supplementary deposits only after consultation with the appointing authority which may make any comments to the arbitral tribunal which it deems appropriate concerning the amount of such deposits and supplementary deposits.

4. If the required deposits are not paid in full within thirty days after the receipt of the request, the arbitral tribunal shall so inform the parties in order that one or another of them may make the required payment. If such payment is not made, the arbitral tribunal may order the suspension or termination of the arbitral proceedings.

5. After the award has been made, the arbitral tribunal shall render an accounting to the parties of the deposits received and return any unexpended balance to the parties.

APPENDIX 6

UNCITRAL Arbitration Rules (2010)

(as revised in 2010)

SECTION I
INTRODUCTORY RULES
SCOPE OF APPLICATION*
ARTICLE 1

1. Where parties have agreed that disputes between them in respect of a defined legal relationship, whether contractual or not, shall be referred to arbitration under the UNCITRAL Arbitration Rules, then such disputes shall be settled in accordance with these Rules subject to such modification as the parties may agree.

2. The parties to an arbitration agreement concluded after 15 August 2010 shall be presumed to have referred to the Rules in effect on the date of commencement of the arbitration, unless the parties have agreed to apply a particular version of the Rules. That presumption does not apply where the arbitration agreement has been concluded by accepting after 15 August 2010 an offer made before that date.

3. These Rules shall govern the arbitration except that where any of these Rules is in conflict with a provision of the law applicable to the arbitration from which the parties cannot derogate, that provision shall prevail.

NOTICE AND CALCULATION OF PERIODS OF TIME
ARTICLE 2

1. A notice, including a notification, communication or proposal, may be transmitted by any means of communication that provides or allows for a record of its transmission.

2. If an address has been designated by a party specifically for this purpose or authorized by the arbitral tribunal, any notice shall be delivered to that party at that address, and if so delivered shall be deemed to have been received. Delivery by electronic means such as facsimile or email may only be made to an address so designated or authorized.

3. In the absence of such designation or authorization, a notice is:

(a) received if it is physically delivered to the addressee; or
(b) deemed to have been received if it is delivered at the place of business, habitual residence or mailing address of the addressee.

4. If, after reasonable efforts, delivery cannot be effected in accordance with paragraphs 2 or 3, a notice is deemed to have been received if it is sent to the addressee's last-known place of business, habitual residence or mailing address by registered letter or any other means that provides a record of delivery or of attempted delivery.

5. A notice shall be deemed to have been received on the day it is delivered in accordance with paragraphs 2, 3 or 4, or attempted to be delivered in accordance with paragraph 4. A notice transmitted by electronic means is deemed to have been received on the day it is sent, except that a notice of arbitration so transmitted is only deemed to have been received on the day when it reaches the addressee's electronic address.

---

* A model arbitration clause for contracts can be found in the annex to the Rules.

6. For the purpose of calculating a period of time under these Rules, such period shall begin to run on the day following the day when a notice is received. If the last day of such period is an official holiday or a non-business day at the residence or place of business of the addressee, the period is extended until the first business day which follows. Official holidays or non-business days occurring during the running of the period of time are included in calculating the period.

NOTICE OF ARBITRATION

ARTICLE 3

1. The party or parties initiating recourse to arbitration (hereinafter called the "claimant") shall communicate to the other party or parties (hereinafter called the "respondent") a notice of arbitration.

2. Arbitral proceedings shall be deemed to commence on the date on which the notice of arbitration is received by the respondent.

3. The notice of arbitration shall include the following:

(a) A demand that the dispute be referred to arbitration;
(b) The names and contact details of the parties;
(c) Identification of the arbitration agreement that is invoked;
(d) Identification of any contract or other legal instrument out of or in relation to which the dispute arises or, in the absence of such contract or instrument, a brief description of the relevant relationship;
(e) A brief description of the claim and an indication of the amount involved, if any;
(f) The relief or remedy sought;
(g) A proposal as to the number of arbitrators, language and place of arbitration, if the parties have not previously agreed thereon.

4. The notice of arbitration may also include:

(a) A proposal for the designation of an appointing authority referred to in article 6, paragraph 1;
(b) A proposal for the appointment of a sole arbitrator referred to in article 8, paragraph 1;
(c) Notification of the appointment of an arbitrator referred to in articles 9 or 10.

5. The constitution of the arbitral tribunal shall not be hindered by any controversy with respect to the sufficiency of the notice of arbitration, which shall be finally resolved by the arbitral tribunal.

RESPONSE TO THE NOTICE OF ARBITRATION

ARTICLE 4

1. Within 30 days of the receipt of the notice of arbitration, the respondent shall communicate to the claimant a response to the notice of arbitration, which shall include:

(a) The name and contact details of each respondent;
(b) A response to the information set forth in the notice of arbitration, pursuant to article 3, paragraphs 3 (c) to (g).

2. The response to the notice of arbitration may also include:

(a) Any plea that an arbitral tribunal to be constituted under these Rules lacks jurisdiction;
(b) A proposal for the designation of an appointing authority referred to in article 6, paragraph 1;
(c) A proposal for the appointment of a sole arbitrator referred to in article 8, paragraph 1;
(d) Notification of the appointment of an arbitrator referred to in articles 9 or 10,
(e) A brief description of counterclaims or claims for the purpose of a set-off, if any, including where relevant, an indication of the amounts involved, and the relief or remedy sought;
(f) A notice of arbitration in accordance with article 3 in case the respondent formulates a claim against a party to the arbitration agreement other than the claimant.

3. The constitution of the arbitral tribunal shall not be hindered by any controversy with respect to the respondent's failure to communicate a response to the notice of arbitration, or an incomplete or late response to the notice of arbitration, which shall be finally resolved by the arbitral tribunal.

Representation and Assistance

Article 5

Each party may be represented or assisted by persons chosen by it. The names and addresses of such persons must be communicated to all parties and to the arbitral tribunal. Such communication must specify whether the appointment is being made for purposes of representation or assistance. Where a person is to act as a representative of a party, the arbitral tribunal, on its own initiative or at the request of any party, may at any time require proof of authority granted to the representative in such a form as the arbitral tribunal may determine.

Designating and Appointing Authorities

Article 6

1. Unless the parties have already agreed on the choice of an appointing authority, a party may at any time propose the name or names of one or more institutions or persons, including the Secretary-General of the Permanent Court of Arbitration at The Hague (hereinafter called the "PCA"), one of whom would serve as appointing authority.

2. If all parties have not agreed on the choice of an appointing authority within 30 days after a proposal made in accordance with paragraph 1 has been received by all other parties, any party may request the Secretary-General of the PCA to designate the appointing authority.

3. Where these Rules provide for a period of time within which a party must refer a matter to an appointing authority and no appointing authority has been agreed on or designated, the period is suspended from the date on which a party initiates the procedure for agreeing on or designating an appointing authority until the date of such agreement or designation.

4. Except as referred to in article 41, paragraph 4, if the appointing authority refuses to act, or if it fails to appoint an arbitrator within 30 days after it receives a party's request to do so, fails to act within any other period provided by these Rules, or fails to decide on a challenge to an arbitrator within a reasonable time after receiving a party's request to do so, any party may request the Secretary-General of the PCA to designate a substitute appointing authority.

5. In exercising their functions under these Rules, the appointing authority and the Secretary-General of the PCA may require from any party and the arbitrators the information they deem necessary and they shall give the parties and, where appropriate, the arbitrators, an opportunity to present their views in any manner they consider appropriate. All such communications to and from the appointing authority and the Secretary-General of the PCA shall also be provided by the sender to all other parties.

6. When the appointing authority is requested to appoint an arbitrator pursuant to articles 8, 9, 10 or 14, the party making the request shall send to the appointing authority copies of the notice of arbitration and, if it exists, any response to the notice of arbitration.

7. The appointing authority shall have regard to such considerations as are likely to secure the appointment of an independent and impartial arbitrator and shall take into account the advisability of appointing an arbitrator of a nationality other than the nationalities of the parties.

Section II
Composition of the arbitral tribunal

Number of Arbitrators

Article 7

1. If the parties have not previously agreed on the number of arbitrators, and if within 30 days after the receipt by the respondent of the notice of arbitration the parties have not agreed that there shall be only one arbitrator, three arbitrators shall be appointed.

2. Notwithstanding paragraph 1, if no other parties have responded to a party's proposal to appoint a sole arbitrator within the time limit provided for in paragraph 1 and the party or parties concerned have failed to appoint a second arbitrator in accordance with articles 9 or 10, the appointing authority may, at the request of a party, appoint a sole arbitrator pursuant to the procedure provided for in article 8, paragraph 2, if it determines that, in view of the circumstances of the case, this is more appropriate.

Appointment of Arbitrators (Articles 8 to 10)

Article 8

1. If the parties have agreed that a sole arbitrator is to be appointed and if within 30 days after receipt by all other parties of a proposal for the appointment of a sole arbitrator the parties have not reached agreement thereon, a sole arbitrator shall, at the request of a party, be appointed by the appointing authority.

2. The appointing authority shall appoint the sole arbitrator as promptly as possible. In making the appointment, the appointing authority shall use the following list-procedure, unless the parties agree that the list-procedure should not be used or unless the appointing authority determines in its discretion that the use of the list-procedure is not appropriate for the case:

(a) The appointing authority shall communicate to each of the parties an identical list containing at least three names;

(b) Within 15 days after the receipt of this list, each party may return the list to the appointing authority after having deleted the name or names to which it objects and numbered the remaining names on the list in the order of its preference;

(c) After the expiration of the above period of time the appointing authority shall appoint the sole arbitrator from among the names approved on the lists returned to it and in accordance with the order of preference indicated by the parties;

(d) If for any reason the appointment cannot be made according to this procedure, the appointing authority may exercise its discretion in appointing the sole arbitrator.

Article 9

1. If three arbitrators are to be appointed, each party shall appoint one arbitrator. The two arbitrators thus appointed shall choose the third arbitrator who will act as the presiding arbitrator of the arbitral tribunal.

2. If within 30 days after the receipt of a party's notification of the appointment of an arbitrator the other party has not notified the first party of the arbitrator it has appointed, the first party may request the appointing authority to appoint the second arbitrator.

3. If within 30 days after the appointment of the second arbitrator the two arbitrators have not agreed on the choice of the presiding arbitrator, the presiding arbitrator shall be appointed by the appointing authority in the same way as a sole arbitrator would be appointed under article 8.

Article 10

1. For the purposes of article 9, paragraph 1, where three arbitrators are to be appointed and there are multiple parties as claimant or as respondent, unless the parties have agreed to another method of appointment of arbitrators, the multiple parties jointly, whether as claimant or as respondent, shall appoint an arbitrator.

2. If the parties have agreed that the arbitral tribunal is to be composed of a number of arbitrators other than one or three, the arbitrators shall be appointed according to the method agreed upon by the parties.

3. In the event of any failure to constitute the arbitral tribunal under these Rules, the appointing authority shall, at the request of any party, constitute the arbitral tribunal and, in doing so, may revoke

any appointment already made and appoint or reappoint each of the arbitrators and designate one of them as the presiding arbitrator.

DISCLOSURES BY AND CHALLENGE OF ARBITRATORS**
(ARTICLES 11 TO 13)

ARTICLE 11

When a person is approached in connection with his or her possible appointment as an arbitrator, he or she shall disclose any circumstances likely to give rise to justifiable doubts as to his or her impartiality or independence. An arbitrator, from the time of his or her appointment and throughout the arbitral proceedings, shall without delay disclose any such circumstances to the parties and the other arbitrators unless they have already been informed by him or her of these circumstances.

ARTICLE 12

1. Any arbitrator may be challenged if circumstances exist that give rise to justifiable doubts as to the arbitrator's impartiality or independence.

2. A party may challenge the arbitrator appointed by it only for reasons of which it becomes aware after the appointment has been made.

3. In the event that an arbitrator fails to act or in the event of the *de jure* or *de facto* impossibility of his or her performing his or her functions, the procedure in respect of the challenge of an arbitrator as provided in article 13 shall apply.

ARTICLE 13

1. A party that intends to challenge an arbitrator shall send notice of its challenge within 15 days after it has been notified of the appointment of the challenged arbitrator, or within 15 days after the circumstances mentioned in articles 11 and 12 became known to that party.

2. The notice of challenge shall be communicated to all other parties, to the arbitrator who is challenged and to the other arbitrators. The notice of challenge shall state the reasons for the challenge.

3. When an arbitrator has been challenged by a party, all parties may agree to the challenge. The arbitrator may also, after the challenge, withdraw from his or her office. In neither case does this imply acceptance of the validity of the grounds for the challenge.

4. If, within 15 days from the date of the notice of challenge, all parties do not agree to the challenge or the challenged arbitrator does not withdraw, the party making the challenge may elect to pursue it. In that case, within 30 days from the date of the notice of challenge, it shall seek a decision on the challenge by the appointing authority.

REPLACEMENT OF AN ARBITRATOR

ARTICLE 14

1. Subject to paragraph 2, in any event where an arbitrator has to be replaced during the course of the arbitral proceedings, a substitute arbitrator shall be appointed or chosen pursuant to the procedure provided for in articles 8 to 11 that was applicable to the appointment or choice of the arbitrator being replaced. This procedure shall apply even if during the process of appointing the arbitrator to be replaced, a party had failed to exercise its right to appoint or to participate in the appointment.

2. If, at the request of a party, the appointing authority determines that, in view of the exceptional circumstances of the case, it would be justified for a party to be deprived of its right to appoint a substitute arbitrator, the appointing authority may, after giving an opportunity to the parties and

---

** Model statements of independence pursuant to article 11 can be found in the annex to the Rules.

the remaining arbitrators to express their views: (a) appoint the substitute arbitrator; or (b) after the closure of the hearings, authorize the other arbitrators to proceed with the arbitration and make any decision or award.

REPETITION OF HEARINGS IN THE EVENT OF THE REPLACEMENT OF AN ARBITRATOR

ARTICLE 15

If an arbitrator is replaced, the proceedings shall resume at the stage where the arbitrator who was replaced ceased to perform his or her functions, unless the arbitral tribunal decides otherwise.

EXCLUSION OF LIABILITY

ARTICLE 16

Save for intentional wrongdoing, the parties waive, to the fullest extent permitted under the applicable law, any claim against the arbitrators, the appointing authority and any person appointed by the arbitral tribunal based on any act or omission in connection with the arbitration.

SECTION III
ARBITRAL PROCEEDINGS

GENERAL PROVISIONS

ARTICLE 17

1. Subject to these Rules, the arbitral tribunal may conduct the arbitration in such manner as it considers appropriate, provided that the parties are treated with equality and that at an appropriate stage of the proceedings each party is given a reasonable opportunity of presenting its case. The arbitral tribunal, in exercising its discretion, shall conduct the proceedings so as to avoid unnecessary delay and expense and to provide a fair and efficient process for resolving the parties' dispute.

2. As soon as practicable after its constitution and after inviting the parties to express their views, the arbitral tribunal shall establish the provisional timetable of the arbitration. The arbitral tribunal may, at any time, after inviting the parties to express their views, extend or abridge any period of time prescribed under these Rules or agreed by the parties.

3. If at an appropriate stage of the proceedings any party so requests, the arbitral tribunal shall hold hearings for the presentation of evidence by witnesses, including expert witnesses, or for oral argument. In the absence of such a request, the arbitral tribunal shall decide whether to hold such hearings or whether the proceedings shall be conducted on the basis of documents and other materials.

4. All communications to the arbitral tribunal by one party shall be communicated by that party to all other parties. Such communications shall be made at the same time, except as otherwise permitted by the arbitral tribunal if it may do so under applicable law.

5. The arbitral tribunal may, at the request of any party, allow one or more third persons to be joined in the arbitration as a party provided such person is a party to the arbitration agreement, unless the arbitral tribunal finds, after giving all parties, including the person or persons to be joined, the opportunity to be heard, that joinder should not be permitted because of prejudice to any of those parties. The arbitral tribunal may make a single award or several awards in respect of all parties so involved in the arbitration.

PLACE OF ARBITRATION

Article 18

1. If the parties have not previously agreed on the place of arbitration, the place of arbitration shall be determined by the arbitral tribunal having regard to the circumstances of the case. The award shall be deemed to have been made at the place of arbitration.

2. The arbitral tribunal may meet at any location it considers appropriate for deliberations. Unless otherwise agreed by the parties, the arbitral tribunal may also meet at any location it considers appropriate for any other purpose, including hearings.

LANGUAGE

ARTICLE 19

1. Subject to an agreement by the parties, the arbitral tribunal shall, promptly after its appointment, determine the language or languages to be used in the proceedings. This determination shall apply to the statement of claim, the statement of defence, and any further written statements and, if oral hearings take place, to the language or languages to be used in such hearings.

2. The arbitral tribunal may order that any documents annexed to the statement of claim or statement of defence, and any supplementary documents or exhibits submitted in the course of the proceedings, delivered in their original language, shall be accompanied by a translation into the language or languages agreed upon by the parties or determined by the arbitral tribunal.

STATEMENT OF CLAIM

ARTICLE 20

1. The claimant shall communicate its statement of claim in writing to the respondent and to each of the arbitrators within a period of time to be determined by the arbitral tribunal. The claimant may elect to treat its notice of arbitration referred to in article 3 as a statement of claim, provided that the notice of arbitration also complies with the requirements of paragraphs 2 to 4 of this article.

2. The statement of claim shall include the following particulars:

(a) The names and contact details of the parties;
(b) A statement of the facts supporting the claim;
(c) The points at issue;
(d) The relief or remedy sought;
(e) The legal grounds or arguments supporting the claim.

3. A copy of any contract or other legal instrument out of or in relation to which the dispute arises and of the arbitration agreement shall be annexed to the statement of claim.

4. The statement of claim should, as far as possible, be accompanied by all documents and other evidence relied upon by the claimant, or contain references to them.

STATEMENT OF DEFENCE

ARTICLE 21

1. The respondent shall communicate its statement of defence in writing to the claimant and to each of the arbitrators within a period of time to be determined by the arbitral tribunal. The respondent may elect to treat its response to the notice of arbitration referred to in article 4 as a statement of defence, provided that the response to the notice of arbitration also complies with the requirements of paragraph 2 of this article.

2. The statement of defence shall reply to the particulars (b) to (e) of the statement of claim (article 20, paragraph 2). The statement of defence should, as far as possible, be accompanied by all documents and other evidence relied upon by the respondent, or contain references to them.

3. In its statement of defence, or at a later stage in the arbitral proceedings if the arbitral tribunal decides that the delay was justified under the circumstances, the respondent may make a counterclaim or rely on a claim for the purpose of a set-off provided that the arbitral tribunal has jurisdiction over it.

4. The provisions of article 20, paragraphs 2 to 4, shall apply to a counterclaim, a claim under article 4, paragraph 2 (f), and a claim relied on for the purpose of a set-off.

AMENDMENTS TO THE CLAIM OR DEFENCE

ARTICLE 22

During the course of the arbitral proceedings, a party may amend or supplement its claim or defence, including a counterclaim or a claim for the purpose of a set-off, unless the arbitral tribunal considers it inappropriate to allow such amendment or supplement having regard to the delay in making it or prejudice to other parties or any other circumstances. However, a claim or defence, including a counterclaim or a claim for the purpose of a set-off, may not be amended or supplemented in such a manner that the amended or supplemented claim or defence falls outside the jurisdiction of the arbitral tribunal.

PLEAS AS TO THE JURISDICTION OF THE ARBITRAL TRIBUNAL

ARTICLE 23

1. The arbitral tribunal shall have the power to rule on its own jurisdiction, including any objections with respect to the existence or validity of the arbitration agreement. For that purpose, an arbitration clause that forms part of a contract shall be treated as an agreement independent of the other terms of the contract. A decision by the arbitral tribunal that the contract is null shall not entail automatically the invalidity of the arbitration clause.

2. A plea that the arbitral tribunal does not have jurisdiction shall be raised no later than in the statement of defence or, with respect to a counterclaim or a claim for the purpose of a set-off, in the reply to the counterclaim or to the claim for the purpose of a set-off. A party is not precluded from raising such a plea by the fact that it has appointed, or participated in the appointment of, an arbitrator. A plea that the arbitral tribunal is exceeding the scope of its authority shall be raised as soon as the matter alleged to be beyond the scope of its authority is raised during the arbitral proceedings. The arbitral tribunal may, in either case, admit a later plea if it considers the delay justified.

3. The arbitral tribunal may rule on a plea referred to in paragraph 2 either as a preliminary question or in an award on the merits. The arbitral tribunal may continue the arbitral proceedings and make an award, notwithstanding any pending challenge to its jurisdiction before a court.

FURTHER WRITTEN STATEMENTS

ARTICLE 24

The arbitral tribunal shall decide which further written statements, in addition to the statement of claim and the statement of defence, shall be required from the parties or may be presented by them and shall fix the periods of time for communicating such statements.

PERIODS OF TIME

ARTICLE 25

The periods of time fixed by the arbitral tribunal for the communication of written statements (including the statement of claim and statement of defence) should not exceed 45 days. However, the arbitral tribunal may extend the time limits if it concludes that an extension is justified.

INTERIM MEASURES

ARTICLE 26

1. The arbitral tribunal may, at the request of a party, grant interim measures.

2. An interim measure is any temporary measure by which, at any time prior to the issuance of the award by which the dispute is finally decided, the arbitral tribunal orders a party, for example and without limitation, to:

(a) Maintain or restore the status quo pending determination of the dispute;

(b) Take action that would prevent, or refrain from taking action that is likely to cause, (i) current or imminent harm or (ii) prejudice to the arbitral process itself;

(c) Provide a means of preserving assets out of which a subsequent award may be satisfied; or

(d) Preserve evidence that may be relevant and material to the resolution of the dispute.

3. The party requesting an interim measure under paragraphs 2 (a) to (c) shall satisfy the arbitral tribunal that:

(a) Harm not adequately reparable by an award of damages is likely to result if the measure is not ordered, and such harm substantially outweighs the harm that is likely to result to the party against whom the measure is directed if the measure is granted; and

(b) There is a reasonable possibility that the requesting party will succeed on the merits of the claim. The determination on this possibility shall not affect the discretion of the arbitral tribunal in making any subsequent determination.

4. With regard to a request for an interim measure under paragraph 2 (d), the requirements in paragraphs 3 (a) and (b) shall apply only to the extent the arbitral tribunal considers appropriate.

5. The arbitral tribunal may modify, suspend or terminate an interim measure it has granted, upon application of any party or, in exceptional circumstances and upon prior notice to the parties, on the arbitral tribunal's own initiative.

6. The arbitral tribunal may require the party requesting an interim measure to provide appropriate security in connection with the measure.

7. The arbitral tribunal may require any party promptly to disclose any material change in the circumstances on the basis of which the interim measure was requested or granted.

8. The party requesting an interim measure may be liable for any costs and damages caused by the measure to any party if the arbitral tribunal later determines that, in the circumstances then prevailing, the measure should not have been granted. The arbitral tribunal may award such costs and damages at any point during the proceedings.

9. A request for interim measures addressed by any party to a judicial authority shall not be deemed incompatible with the agreement to arbitrate, or as a waiver of that agreement.

EVIDENCE

ARTICLE 27

1. Each party shall have the burden of proving the facts relied on to support its claim or defence.

2. Witnesses, including expert witnesses, who are presented by the parties to testify to the arbitral tribunal on any issue of fact or expertise may be any individual, notwithstanding that the individual is a party to the arbitration or in any way related to a party. Unless otherwise directed by the arbitral tribunal, statements by witnesses, including expert witnesses, may be presented in writing and signed by them.

3. At any time during the arbitral proceedings the arbitral tribunal may require the parties to produce documents, exhibits or other evidence within such a period of time as the arbitral tribunal shall determine.

4. The arbitral tribunal shall determine the admissibility, relevance, materiality and weight of the evidence offered.

HEARINGS

Article 28

1. In the event of an oral hearing, the arbitral tribunal shall give the parties adequate advance notice of the date, time and place thereof.

2. Witnesses, including expert witnesses, may be heard under the conditions and examined in the manner set by the arbitral tribunal.

3. Hearings shall be held *in camera* unless the parties agree otherwise. The arbitral tribunal may require the retirement of any witness or witnesses, including expert witnesses, during the testimony of such other witnesses, except that a witness, including an expert witness, who is a party to the arbitration shall not, in principle, be asked to retire.

4. The arbitral tribunal may direct that witnesses, including expert witnesses, be examined through means of telecommunication that do not require their physical presence at the hearing (such as videoconference).

Experts Appointed by the Arbitral Tribunal

Article 29

1. After consultation with the parties, the arbitral tribunal may appoint one or more independent experts to report to it, in writing, on specific issues to be determined by the arbitral tribunal. A copy of the expert's terms of reference, established by the arbitral tribunal, shall be communicated to the parties.

2. The expert shall, in principle before accepting appointment, submit to the arbitral tribunal and to the parties a description of his or her qualifications and a statement of his or her impartiality and independence. Within the time ordered by the arbitral tribunal, the parties shall inform the arbitral tribunal whether they have any objections as to the expert's qualifications, impartiality or independence. The arbitral tribunal shall decide promptly whether to accept any such objections. After an expert's appointment, a party may object to the expert's qualifications, impartiality or independence only if the objection is for reasons of which the party becomes aware after the appointment has been made. The arbitral tribunal shall decide promptly what, if any, action to take.

3. The parties shall give the expert any relevant information or produce for his or her inspection any relevant documents or goods that he or she may require of them. Any dispute between a party and such expert as to the relevance of the required information or production shall be referred to the arbitral tribunal for decision.

4. Upon receipt of the expert's report, the arbitral tribunal shall communicate a copy of the report to the parties, which shall be given the opportunity to express, in writing, their opinion on the report. A party shall be entitled to examine any document on which the expert has relied in his or her report.

5. At the request of any party, the expert, after delivery of the report, may be heard at a hearing where the parties shall have the opportunity to be present and to interrogate the expert. At this hearing, any party may present expert witnesses in order to testify on the points at issue. The provisions of article 28 shall be applicable to such proceedings.

Default

Article 30

1. If, within the period of time fixed by these Rules or the arbitral tribunal, without showing sufficient cause:

(a) The claimant has failed to communicate its statement of claim, the arbitral tribunal shall issue an order for the termination of the arbitral proceedings, unless there are remaining matters that may need to be decided and the arbitral tribunal considers it appropriate to do so;

(b) The respondent has failed to communicate its response to the notice of arbitration or its statement of defence, the arbitral tribunal shall order that the proceedings continue, without treating such failure in itself as an admission of the claimant's allegations; the provisions of this subparagraph also apply to a claimant's failure to submit a defence to a counterclaim or to a claim for the purpose of a set-off.

2. If a party, duly notified under these Rules, fails to appear at a hearing, without showing sufficient cause for such failure, the arbitral tribunal may proceed with the arbitration.

3. If a party, duly invited by the arbitral tribunal to produce documents, exhibits or other evidence, fails to do so within the established period of time, without showing sufficient cause for such failure, the arbitral tribunal may make the award on the evidence before it.

CLOSURE OF HEARINGS

ARTICLE 31

1. The arbitral tribunal may inquire of the parties if they have any further proof to offer or witnesses to be heard or submissions to make and, if there are none, it may declare the hearings closed.

2. The arbitral tribunal may, if it considers it necessary owing to exceptional circumstances, decide, on its own initiative or upon application of a party, to reopen the hearings at any time before the award is made.

WAIVER OF RIGHT TO OBJECT

ARTICLE 32

A failure by any party to object promptly to any non-compliance with these Rules or with any requirement of the arbitration agreement shall be deemed to be a waiver of the right of such party to make such an objection, unless such party can show that, under the circumstances, its failure to object was justified.

SECTION IV
THE AWARD

DECISIONS

ARTICLE 33

1. When there is more than one arbitrator, any award or other decision of the arbitral tribunal shall be made by a majority of the arbitrators.

2. In the case of questions of procedure, when there is no majority or when the arbitral tribunal so authorizes, the presiding arbitrator may decide alone, subject to revision, if any, by the arbitral tribunal.

FORM AND EFFECT OF THE AWARD

ARTICLE 34

1. The arbitral tribunal may make separate awards on different issues at different times.

2. All awards shall be made in writing and shall be final and binding on the parties. The parties shall carry out all awards without delay.

3. The arbitral tribunal shall state the reasons upon which the award is based, unless the parties have agreed that no reasons are to be given.

4. An award shall be signed by the arbitrators and it shall contain the date on which the award was made and indicate the place of arbitration. Where there is more than one arbitrator and any of them fails to sign, the award shall state the reason for the absence of the signature.

5. An award may be made public with the consent of all parties or where and to the extent disclosure is required of a party by legal duty, to protect or pursue a legal right or in relation to legal proceedings before a court or other competent authority.

6. Copies of the award signed by the arbitrators shall be communicated to the parties by the arbitral tribunal.

APPLICABLE LAW, *AMIABLE COMPOSITEUR*

ARTICLE 35

1. The arbitral tribunal shall apply the rules of law designated by the parties as applicable to the substance of the dispute. Failing such designation by the parties, the arbitral tribunal shall apply the law which it determines to be appropriate.

2. The arbitral tribunal shall decide as *amiable compositeur* or *ex aequo et bono* only if the parties have expressly authorized the arbitral tribunal to do so.

3. In all cases, the arbitral tribunal shall decide in accordance with the terms of the contract, if any, and shall take into account any usage of trade applicable to the transaction.

SETTLEMENT OR OTHER GROUNDS FOR TERMINATION

ARTICLE 36

1. If, before the award is made, the parties agree on a settlement of the dispute, the arbitral tribunal shall either issue an order for the termination of the arbitral proceedings or, if requested by the parties and accepted by the arbitral tribunal, record the settlement in the form of an arbitral award on agreed terms. The arbitral tribunal is not obliged to give reasons for such an award.

2. If, before the award is made, the continuation of the arbitral proceedings becomes unnecessary or impossible for any reason not mentioned in paragraph 1, the arbitral tribunal shall inform the parties of its intention to issue an order for the termination of the proceedings. The arbitral tribunal shall have the power to issue such an order unless there are remaining matters that may need to be decided and the arbitral tribunal considers it appropriate to do so.

3. Copies of the order for termination of the arbitral proceedings or of the arbitral award on agreed terms, signed by the arbitrators, shall be communicated by the arbitral tribunal to the parties. Where an arbitral award on agreed terms is made, the provisions of article 34, paragraphs 2, 4 and 5, shall apply.

INTERPRETATION OF THE AWARD

ARTICLE 37

1. Within 30 days after the receipt of the award, a party, with notice to the other parties, may request that the arbitral tribunal give an interpretation of the award.

2. The interpretation shall be given in writing within 45 days after the receipt of the request. The interpretation shall form part of the award and the provisions of article 34, paragraphs 2 to 6, shall apply.

CORRECTION OF THE AWARD

ARTICLE 38

1. Within 30 days after the receipt of the award, a party, with notice to the other parties, may request the arbitral tribunal to correct in the award any error in computation, any clerical or typographical error, or any error or omission of a similar nature. If the arbitral tribunal considers that the request is justified, it shall make the correction within 45 days of receipt of the request.

2. The arbitral tribunal may within 30 days after the communication of the award make such corrections on its own initiative.

3. Such corrections shall be in writing and shall form part of the award. The provisions of article 34, paragraphs 2 to 6, shall apply.

ADDITIONAL AWARD

ARTICLE 39

1. Within 30 days after the receipt of the termination order or the award, a party, with notice to the other parties, may request the arbitral tribunal to make an award or an additional award as to claims presented in the arbitral proceedings but not decided by the arbitral tribunal.

2. If the arbitral tribunal considers the request for an award or additional award to be justified, it shall render or complete its award within 60 days after the receipt of the request. The arbitral tribunal may extend, if necessary, the period of time within which it shall make the award.

3. When such an award or additional award is made, the provisions of article 34, paragraphs 2 to 6, shall apply.

DEFINITION OF COSTS

ARTICLE 40

1. The arbitral tribunal shall fix the costs of arbitration in the final award and, if it deems appropriate, in another decision.

2. The term "costs" includes only:

(a) The fees of the arbitral tribunal to be stated separately as to each arbitrator and to be fixed by the tribunal itself in accordance with article 41;

(b) The reasonable travel and other expenses incurred by the arbitrators;

(c) The reasonable costs of expert advice and of other assistance required by the arbitral tribunal;

(d) The reasonable travel and other expenses of witnesses to the extent such expenses are approved by the arbitral tribunal;

(e) The legal and other costs incurred by the parties in relation to the arbitration to the extent that the arbitral tribunal determines that the amount of such costs is reasonable;

(f) Any fees and expenses of the appointing authority as well as the fees and expenses of the Secretary-General of the PCA.

3. In relation to interpretation, correction or completion of any award under articles 37 to 39, the arbitral tribunal may charge the costs referred to in paragraphs 2 (b) to (f), but no additional fees.

FEES AND EXPENSES OF ARBITRATORS

ARTICLE 41

1. The fees and expenses of the arbitrators shall be reasonable in amount, taking into account the amount in dispute, the complexity of the subject matter, the time spent by the arbitrators and any other relevant circumstances of the case.

2. If there is an appointing authority and it applies or has stated that it will apply a schedule or particular method for determining the fees for arbitrators in international cases, the arbitral tribunal in fixing its fees shall take that schedule or method into account to the extent that it considers appropriate in the circumstances of the case.

3. Promptly after its constitution, the arbitral tribunal shall inform the parties as to how it proposes to determine its fees and expenses, including any rates it intends to apply. Within 15 days of receiving that proposal, any party may refer the proposal to the appointing authority for review. If, within 45 days of receipt of such a referral, the appointing authority finds that the proposal of the arbitral tribunal is inconsistent with paragraph 1, it shall make any necessary adjustments thereto, which shall be binding upon the arbitral tribunal.

4. (a) When informing the parties of the arbitrators' fees and expenses that have been fixed pursuant to article 40, paragraphs 2 (a) and (b), the arbitral tribunal shall also explain the manner in which the corresponding amounts have been calculated.

(b) Within 15 days of receiving the arbitral tribunal's determination of fees and expenses, any party may refer for review such determination to the appointing authority. If no appointing authority has been agreed upon or designated, or if the appointing authority fails to act within the time specified in these Rules, then the review shall be made by the Secretary-General of the PCA.

(c) If the appointing authority or the Secretary-General of the PCA finds that the arbitral tribunal's determination is inconsistent with the arbitral tribunal's proposal (and any adjustment thereto) under paragraph 3 or is otherwise manifestly excessive, it shall, within 45 days of receiving such a referral, make any adjustments to the arbitral tribunal's determination that are necessary to satisfy the criteria in paragraph 1. Any such adjustments shall be binding upon the arbitral tribunal.

(d) Any such adjustments shall either be included by the arbitral tribunal in its award or, if the award has already been issued, be implemented in a correction to the award, to which the procedure of article 38, paragraph 3, shall apply.

5. Throughout the procedure under paragraphs 3 and 4, the arbitral tribunal shall proceed with the arbitration, in accordance with article 17, paragraph 1.

6. A referral under paragraph 4 shall not affect any determination in the award other than the arbitral tribunal's fees and expenses; nor shall it delay the recognition and enforcement of all parts of the award other than those relating to the determination of the arbitral tribunal's fees and expenses.

ALLOCATION OF COSTS

ARTICLE 42

1. The costs of the arbitration shall in principle be borne by the unsuccessful party or parties. However, the arbitral tribunal may apportion each of such costs between the parties if it determines that apportionment is reasonable, taking into account the circumstances of the case.

2. The arbitral tribunal shall in the final award or, if it deems appropriate, in any other award, determine any amount that a party may have to pay to another party as a result of the decision on allocation of costs.

DEPOSIT OF COSTS

ARTICLE 43

1. The arbitral tribunal, on its establishment, may request the parties to deposit an equal amount as an advance for the costs referred to in article 40, paragraphs 2 (a) to (c).

2. During the course of the arbitral proceedings the arbitral tribunal may request supplementary deposits from the parties.

3. If an appointing authority has been agreed upon or designated, and when a party so requests and the appointing authority consents to perform the function, the arbitral tribunal shall fix the amounts of any deposits or supplementary deposits only after consultation with the appointing authority, which may make any comments to the arbitral tribunal that it deems appropriate concerning the amount of such deposits and supplementary deposits.

4. If the required deposits are not paid in full within 30 days after the receipt of the request, the arbitral tribunal shall so inform the parties in order that one or more of them may make the required payment. If such payment is not made, the arbitral tribunal may order the suspension or termination of the arbitral proceedings.

5. After a termination order or final award has been made, the arbitral tribunal shall render an accounting to the parties of the deposits received and return any unexpended balance to the parties.

Annex

MODEL ARBITRATION CLAUSE FOR CONTRACTS

Any dispute, controversy or claim arising out of or relating to this contract, or the breach, termination or invalidity thereof, shall be settled by arbitration in accordance with the UNCITRAL Arbitration Rules.

Note — Parties should consider adding:

(a) The appointing authority shall be . . . (name of institution or person);
(b) The number of arbitrators shall be . . . (one or three);
(c) The place of arbitration shall be . . . (town and country);
(d) The language to be used in the arbitral proceedings shall be. . . .

POSSIBLE WAIVER STATEMENT

Note — If the parties wish to exclude recourse against the arbitral award that may be available under the applicable law, they may consider adding a provision to that effect as suggested below, considering, however, that the effectiveness and conditions of such an exclusion depend on the applicable law.

Waiver: The parties hereby waive their right to any form of recourse against an award to any court or other competent authority, insofar as such waiver can validly be made under the applicable law.

MODEL STATEMENTS OF INDEPENDENCE PURSUANT TO ARTICLE 11 OF THE RULES

No circumstances to disclose: I am impartial and independent of each of the parties and intend to remain so. To the best of my knowledge, there are no circumstances, past or present, likely to give rise to justifiable doubts as to my impartiality or independence. I shall promptly notify the parties and the other arbitrators of any such circumstances that may subsequently come to my attention during this arbitration.

Circumstances to disclose: I am impartial and independent of each of the parties and intend to remain so. Attached is a statement made pursuant to article 11 of the UNCITRAL Arbitration Rules of (a) my past and present professional, business and other relationships with the parties and (b) any other relevant circumstances. [Include statement] I confirm that those circumstances do not affect my independence and impartiality. I shall promptly notify the parties and the other arbitrators of any such further relationships or circumstances that may subsequently come to my attention during this arbitration.

Note — Any party may consider requesting from the arbitrator the following addition to the statement of independence:

I confirm, on the basis of the information presently available to me, that I can devote the time necessary to conduct this arbitration diligently, efficiently and in accordance with the time limits in the Rules.

APPENDIX 7*

Requests to set Aside Arbitral Awards on the Basis of Section 33 and/or Section 34 of the SAA

Abbreviations:

The Supreme Court	HD
The Svea Court of Appeal	HS
The Göta Court of Appeal	HG
The Court of Appeal for Western Sweden	HVS
The Scania and Blekinge Court of Appeal	HSB
The Court of Appeal for Lower Norrland	HNN
The Court of Appeal for Upper Norrland	HON

Parties	Date of decision	Case No.	Court	Issue	Outcome
Korsnäs AB ./. AB Fortum Värme	2010-06-09	NJA 2010 p. 317	HD	Challenge of Arbitral Award	Denied
Soyak International Construction & Investment Inc. ./. Hochtief AG	2009-03-31	NJA 2009 p. 128	HD	Challenge of Arbitral Award	Denied
Anders Jilkén ./. Ericsson AB	2007-11-19	NJA 2007 p. 841	HD	Challenge of Arbitral Award	Set aside
Anders Brahme et.al. ./. Johan af Klint	2006-09-21	NJA 2006 p. 530	HD	Challenge of Arbitral Award	Dismissed
Lennart Gustafsson ./. Advokatfirman Björn Lindmar AB	2002-07-03	NJA 2002 A 5	HD	Challenge of Arbitral Award (Invalidity of Arbitral Award)	Dismissed
Silver Lining Finance SA ./. Perstorp Waspik B.V.	2010-06-17	T 1689-09	HSB	Challenge of Arbitral Award (Invalidity of Arbitral Award)	Denied
Baltiysky Zavod JSC ./. Stena RoRo AB	2010-05-20	T 8622-08	HS	Challenge of Arbitral Award	Denied
Johan Bertilsson Consulting i Stockholm AB bankruptcy estate et al. ./. International Hair Studio Limited	2010-04-27	T 5254-09	HS	Challenge of Arbitral Award (Invalidity of Arbitral Award)	Amicable settlement (Set aside)

(Continued)

* This appendix lists all cases that have been tried under Sections 33 and 34 of the SAA and which have become final and binding as at 1 November 2010.

Parties	Date of decision	Case No.	Court	Issue	Outcome
DigiPoS Store Solutions Inc ./. MultiQ Products AB	2010-04-16	T 3174-09	HSB	Challenge of Arbitral Award	Dismissed
Mihai Iovanescu ./. AFA Trygghetsförsäkring	2010-04-06	T 2513-08	HS	Challenge of Arbitral Award	Denied
Gösta Palm Konsult AB ./. Annehem Fastigheter och Projekt AB	2010-03-23	T 3146-08	HSB	Challenge of Arbitral Award	Withdrawn
Ramco AB ./. Posten Express P.EX AB	2010-02-11	T 43-10	HS	Challenge of Arbitral Award	Withdrawn
Profilrestauranger AB ./. Jan Gren et al.	2010-01-27	T 9691-09	HS	Challenge of Arbitral Award	Withdrawn
SwitchCore AB ./. Instream Partners LLC	2010-01-20	T 8441-09	HS	Challenge of Arbitral Award	Withdrawn
Globe Nuclear Services and Supply GNSS, Limited ./. AO Techsnabexport	2009-12-18	T 5883-07	HS	Challenge of Arbitral Award	Denied
AS Luterma ./. AS Alta Foods	2009-12-08	T 7862-09	HS	Challenge of Arbitral Award	Dismissed
Systembolaget AB ./. V&S Vin & Sprit AB	2009-12-01	T 4548-08	HS	Challenge of Arbitral Award	Set aside
Eva Bergman ./.AFA Trygghetsförsäkringsakti ebolag	2009-11-26	T 6358-08	HS	Challenge of Arbitral	Partially denied/ partially dismissed
Carmeuse S.A. ./. SMA International B.V.	2009-11-18	T 7325-08	HS	Challenge of Arbitral Award	Denied
Fastigheten Preppen HB ./. Carlsberg Sverige AB	2009-09-23	RH 2009:91	HS	Challenge of Arbitral Award	Denied (grounds dismissed)
Richard Larsson ./. Rynninge IK	2009-08-28	T 1648-08	HS	Invalidity of Arbitral Award	Denied
Sävsjö municipality ./. Jönköping county council	2009-06-30	Ö 1125-09	HG	Challenge of Arbitral Award	Amicable settlement
Auto Connect Sweden AB bankruptcy estate et al. ./. Consafe IT AB	2009-05-18	T 754-09	HS	Challenge of Arbitral Award	Denied
State Oil Company of the Republic of Azerbaijan ./. Frontera Resources Azerbaijan Corporation	2009-05-04	RH 2009:55	HS	Challenge of Arbitral Award	Denied
Russian Federation ./. RosInvestCo UK Ltd	2009-04-07	T 58-08	HS	Challenge of Arbitral Award (Award on Jurisdiction)	Denied
Joint Stock Company Acron ./. Yara International ASA	2009-04-07	T 7200-08	HS	Challenge of Arbitral Award (Award on Jurisdiction)	Denied

(*Continued*)

Parties	Date of decision	Case No.	Court	Issue	Outcome
Brain Invest International AB ./. Pierre Francois	2009-03-11	T 336-08	HSB	Challenge of Arbitral Award (Invalidity of Arbitral Award)	Denied
Sadkora Energy AB ./. Antonina Tann LLC	2009-03-09	T 7087-08	HS	Challenge of Arbitral Award	Default judgement (partially set aside)
Restaurantholmen Rösunda AB ./. JM AB	2009-02-17	T 841-09	HS	Challenge of Arbitral Award	Dismissed
Republic of Moldova ./. Agurdino-Chimia JSC et al.	2008-11-28	T 745-06	HS	Challenge of Arbitral Award	Dismissed
Klaffbron AB ./. Bostadsrätts föreningen Soleken	2008-11-07	T 9137-07	HS	Challenge of Arbitral Award	Denied
Symaskinscenter Gislaved AB et al. ./. Babyland Sverige AB et al.	2008-11-04	T 5123-08	HS	Challenge of Arbitral Award	Amicable settlement
Nya Animonhus AB ./. Thomas Hagelstam	2008-10-31	T 3976-07	HVS	Challenge of Arbitral Award	Denied
Aita Päts ./. LOT's Living AB	2008-08-25	T 1926-07	HS	Challenge of Arbitral Award	Denied
Berndt Långström ./. Bernt Westlund et al.	2008-06-27	T 3864-08	HS	Invalidity of Arbitral Award	Withdrawn
Oy Karl Fazer Ab ./. Aktiebolaget Malfors Promotor	2008-06-25	T 1612-07	HS	Challenge of Arbitral Award	Amicable settlement
Granada Shipping AB ./. Broström Ship Management AB	2008-06-25	T 4338-07	HVS	Challenge of Arbitral Award	Denied
Luftfartsverket, Stockholm-Arlanda ./. R&M Gerber Schallschutz GmbH	2008-05-22	T 6250-07	HS	Challenge of Arbitral Award	Amicable settlement
ISS Facility Services AB ./. Skanska Sverige AB	2008-05-20	T 1426-08	HVS	Challenge of Arbitral Award	Withdrawn
ABB Handels- und Verwaltungs AG ./. Global Air Movement (Luxembourg)	2008-05-19	T 10112-06	HS	Challenge of Arbitral Award	Withdrawn
Magnus Eklöv et al. ./. Strike Förvaltning AB	2008-05-08	T 1278-08	HVS	Challenge of Arbitral Award	Denied
Vivica Grantén ./. Landstingens Ömsesidiga Försäkringsbolag	2008-04-23	T 1803-07	HS	Challenge of Arbitral Award	Denied

(*Continued*)

Parties	Date of decision	Case No.	Court	Issue	Outcome
NDG i Malmö AB ./. Kungsan AB	2008-04-16	T 734-08	HSB	Challenge of Arbitral Award	Denied
Todd Booth ./. Ericsson AB	2008-04-01	T 1132-08	HS	Invalidity of Arbitral Award	Denied
Matthias Kjellberg ./. Proffice AB	2008-03-20	T 5398-05	HS	Challenge of Arbitral Award	Denied
Georg Carlde ./. Göran Karlsson et al.	2008-02-11	T 8336-07	HS	Challenge of Arbitral Award	Dismissed
Minoritetsaktieägarna i Realia Fastighets AB ./. Realia AB	2008-02-07	T 139-07	HS	Challenge of Arbitral Award	Denied
LLC IKEA MOS (Retail & Property) ./. Skanska East Europe Oy	2008-01-31	T 1824-06; T 4159-07	HS	Challenge of Arbitral Award	Withdrawn
AEB Rör AB ./. PNB Entreprenad Aktiebolags konkursbo	2008-01-23	T 1858-07	HSB	Challenge of Arbitral Award	Withdrawn
Narinder Pal ./. Moncef Layuoni	2008-01-17	T 3473-07	HS	Challenge of Arbitral Award	Denied
Pontus Rangren ./. AFA Trygghetsförsäkringsaktie-bolag	2007-12-21	T 999-06	HS	Challenge of Arbitral Award (Invalidity of Arbitral Award)	Denied
JSC Techsnabexport ./. Palmco Corporation	2007-11-21	T 6793-07; T 6562-07	HS	Challenge of Arbitral Award	Withdrawn
Ecofina Srl ./. Finans AB Marginalen	2007-10-10	T 4018-07	HS	Challenge of Arbitral Award	Withdrawn
Fora AB ./. Bertil Gustavsson	2007-10-02	T 8274-06	HS	Invalidity of Arbitral Award	Default judgement (valid)
XGHY32 Förvaltning AB ./. PNB Entreprenad AB:s konkursbo	2007-09-03	T 3399-07	HVS	Challenge of Arbitral Award	Withdrawn
AO Techsnabexport ./. Globe Nuclear Services and Supply GNSS, Limited	2007-08-31	T 9383-06	HS	Challenge of Arbitral Award	Withdrawn
JSW Steel Ltd ./. Balli Klöckner GmbH	2007-06-04	T 9462-06	HS	Challenge of Arbitral Award	Amicable settlement
Bostadsrättsföreningen Korpen ./. Byggnads AB Åke Sundvall	2007-02-16	T 1649-04	HS	Challenge of Arbitral Award (Invalidity of Arbitral Award)	Denied
Republic of Kirgizistan ./. Petrobart Limited	2007-01-19	T 5208-05	HS	Challenge of Arbitral Award	Denied

(Continued)

Parties	Date of decision	Case No.	Court	Issue	Outcome
Agresso AB ./. Yellow Register On Line AB	2007-01-17	T 5171-05	HS	Challenge of Arbitral Award	Denied
Kronan Progress Kommanditbolag ./. Freshman AB	2007-01-08	T 4683-06	HS	Invalidity of Arbitral Award	Denied
Rapla Invest AB bankruptcy estate ./. TNK Trade Limited	2006-12-07	T 5044-04	HS	Challenge of Arbitral Award	Denied
Richard Larsson ./. Rynninge IK	2006-11-30	T 503-05	HS	Challenge of Arbitral Award	Denied
Advokatfirman WagnssonHB ./. Perotore AB	2006-11-22	T 5998-05	HS	Challenge of Arbitral Award	Denied
Advokatfirman Sjöberg & Strömberg AB ./. Mariestads municipality	2006-11-10	T 197-06	HS	Challenge of Arbitral Award	Denied
Tunika Cosmetics AB ./. Gant AB	2006-10-17	T 7341-04	HS	Challenge of Arbitral Award	Denied
Dahl Sverige AB ./. Skoogs AB	2006-09-21	T 8890-05	HS	Challenge of Arbitral Award	Denied
HL Eriste OY ./. Roxull AB	2006-09-08	T 6072-06	HS	Challenge of Arbitral Award (Invalidity of Arbitral Award)	Denied
Tomas Tjajkovski ./. Proffice AB	2006-06-09	T 5397-05	HS	Challenge of Arbitral Award	Withdrawn
Johan Ullman bankruptcy estate ./. Gylling Invest AB	2006-06-09	T 1526-05	HS	Challenge of Arbitral Award	Denied
MAQS Law Firm Advokatbyrå Kommanditbolag ./. Charlotte Bus	2006-06-01	T 1215-06	HS	Challenge of Arbitral Award	Withdrawn
Inger Jönsson ./. AFA Trygghetsförsäkrings AB	2006-05-31	T 7680-05	HS	Challenge of Arbitral Award	Set aside
Sichuan Province Yun Lu Development Industrial Company ./. PepsiCo Investments (China) Limited	2006-01-25	T 7250-05	HS	Challenge of Arbitral Award	Withdrawn
Sichuan Pepsi-Cola Beverage Company Limited ./. PepsiCo, Inc	2006-01-24	T 1683-05	HS	Challenge of Arbitral Award	Withdrawn
Todd Booth ./. Ericsson AB (EAB)	2006-01-19	T 92-04	HS	Challenge of Arbitral Award	Denied
Kista Galleria KB ./. Skanska Sverige AB	2006-01-12	T 8249-05	HS	Challenge of Arbitral Award	Withdrawn

(Continued)

Parties	Date of decision	Case No.	Court	Issue	Outcome
ALROSA Company Limited ./. Bateman Projects Limited	2006-01-03	T 6716-04	HS	Challenge of Arbitral Award	Denied
Bertil Rasmussen ./. AFA Trygghetsför säkringsaktiebolag	2005-12-19	T 1388-04	HS	Challenge of Arbitral Award	Denied
Johan Adlers ./. Lorry Bygg AB	2005-12-14	T 5863-04	HS	Challenge of Arbitral Award	Denied
If Skadeförsäkring AB ./. Securitas AB et al.	2005-11-03	T 8016-04	HS	Challenge of Arbitral Award	Partially set aside
Dentirol AB ./. SwissCo Services AG	2005-09-30	T 4805-03	HVS	Challenge of Arbitral Award	Denied
Tuve BLK ./. Christoffer Olsson	2005-09-29	T 4750-04	HVS	Challenge of Arbitral Award	Denied
Wirgin Advokatbyrå Handelsbolag ./. If Skadeförsäkring AB	2005-09-12	T 4390-04	HS	Invalidity of Arbitral Award	Partly invalid
Revúcke Koberce Syntetické s.r.o. ./. Cobble Blackburn Ltd	2005-05-23	T 2265-06	HS	Challenge of Arbitral Award	Denied
Republic of Latvia ./. JSC Latvijas Gaze	2005-05-04	T 6730-03	HS	Challenge of Arbitral Award (Invalidity of Arbitral Award)	Denied
Ann Stillström et al. ./. Outokumpu Stainless Steel Oy	2005-04-04	T 2338-05	HS	Challenge of Arbitral Award	Withdrawn
Alucoal Holdings Limited ./. JSC Novokuznetsk Aluminium Plant	2005-03-18	T 5788-04	HS	Challenge of Arbitral Award	Withdrawn
Georg Carlde ./. Fora försäkringscentral AB	2005-03-15	T 5043-04	HS	Challenge of Arbitral Award (Invalidity of Arbitral Award)	Denied
JSC Aeroflot Russian Airlines ./. Russo International Venture, Inc. et al.	2005-02-21	T 1164-03	HS	Challenge of Arbitral Award	Denied
Åke Oscarsson ./. Arla i likvidation	2005-01-26	T 2116-04	HG	Challenge of Arbitral Award (Invalidity of Arbitral Award)	Denied
Peikeracustic GmbH & Co. KG ./. Saab Automobile AB	2004-12-30	T 3488-03	HS	Challenge of Arbitral Award	Denied

(Continued)

461

Parties	Date of decision	Case No.	Court	Issue	Outcome
Panagiotis Motsanos ./. Folksam ömsesidig sakförsäkring et al.	2004-12-08	T 7798-00	HS	Invalidity of Arbitral Award	Denied
Advokatfirman Lennart Hane AB ./. Carita Wesslin	2004-11-08	T 5112-03	HS	Challenge of Arbitral Award	Denied
Fruktbudet i Stockholm AB ./. Rent a Plant Intressenter AB	2004-10-14	T 4162-03	HS	Challenge of Arbitral Award	Denied
Pelle Andersson ./. MTG Holding AB et al.	2004-08-27	T 7866-02	HS	Challenge of Arbitral Award (Invalidity of Arbitral Award)	Denied
7H Förvaltnings AB ./. Kopparbergs Bryggeri AB	2004-08-24	T 2658-03	HG	Challenge of Arbitral Award	Denied
NFB Express och Spedition AB ./. Frontec Affärssystem AB	2004-07-05	T 8283-03	HS	Challenge of Arbitral Award	Withdrawn
DeuCon Deutsche Gesellschaft ./. Firma Eka Chemicals AB	2004-06-30	T 4085-03	HS	Challenge of Arbitral Award	Withdrawn
Relionus Ventures Limited ./. Silmet	2004-06-02	T 1915-04	HS	Challenge of Arbitral Award	Dismissed
Republic of Kazakhstan ./. MTR Metals Ltd	2004-05-25	T 1361-02	HS	Challenge of Arbitral Award	Denied
Bartholomy & Co et al. ./. Kone Corporation	2004-05-13	T 246-02	HS	Challenge of Arbitral Award	Denied
Premiepension smyndigheten ./. CSC Sverige AB	2004-05-11	T 11006-02	HS	Challenge of Arbitral Award	Denied
Björn A Marklund Advokatbyrå AB ./. SvenskReturindustri AB	2004-04-30	T 1249-03	HS	Challenge of Arbitral Award	Denied
Kaklin Konsult Gamla Stans Vinkällare AB ./. Johnny Askervall	2004-04-16	T 6605-03	HS	Challenge of Arbitral Award	Denied
State Property Fund of Ukraine ./. TMR Energy Limited	2004-03-10	T 7948-02	HS	Challenge of Arbitral Award (Invalidity of Arbitral Award)	Denied
Mariestads municipality ./. GE Capital Equipment Finance AB	2004-02-19	T 7627-01	HS	Challenge of Arbitral Award	Denied
Moderna Försäkringar AB ./. Iris AB	2004-01-15	T 4794-03	HVS	Challenge of Arbitral Award	Withdrawn
Koninklijke Ahold N.V. ./. Canica AS et al.	2004-01-13	T 113-04	HS	Challenge of Arbitral Award	Withdrawn

(Continued)

Parties	Date of decision	Case No.	Court	Issue	Outcome
Dirland Télécom S.A. ./. Viking Telecom AB	2003-12-29	T 4366-02	HVS	Challenge of Arbitral Award	Denied
Enskilda Vattenverket i Sverige AB ./. The Water Harvesting AB	2003-11-21	T 823-03	HS	Challenge of Arbitral Award	Denied
Kenneth Borg ./. Britt Kylegård	2003-10-31	T 9673-02	HS	Challenge of Arbitral Award	Denied
Leif Svensson ./. Landstingens Ömsesidiga Försäkringsbolag	2003-10-13	T 1042-03	HS	Challenge of Arbitral Award	Denied
Scand-Pellet AB ./. Ole Valentin	2003-10-08	T 5899-03	HS	Challenge of Arbitral Award	Withdrawn
C.I.S. Information System BV ./. Överstyrelsen förcivilberedskap	2003-08-14	T 6818-02	HS	Challenge of Arbitral Award	Amicable settlement
Ulf Håkansson ./. Comprimé Components AB	2003-07-03	T 33-02	HG	Challenge of Arbitral Award	Denied
Rune Hedenrå ./. Advokatfirman Björn Lindmar AB	2003-06-24	T 1015-03	HS	Challenge of Arbitral Award	Denied
Kronan Progress KB ./. Freshman Flimmer AB	2003-06-02	T 7020-01	HS	Challenge of Arbitral Award	Amicable settlement
Czech Republic ./. CME Czech Republic B.V.	2003-05-15	RH 2003:55	HS	Legal costs (I); Challenge of Arbitral Award (Invalidity of Arbitral Award) (II)	Amicable settlement (I) Denied (II)
Niklas Leverenz m.fl ./. Alf Havstam et al.	2003-02-25	T 3001-02	HVS	Challenge of Arbitral Award	Dismissed
Regular Capital Incorporated ./. AB Custos	2003-01-10	T 8032-00	HS	Challenge of Arbitral Award	Denied
Pensionsanalys i Piteå AB ./. Länsförsäkringaaar Wasa Liv Försäkringsbolag	2002-11-13	T 7785-02	HS	Invalidity of Arbitral Award	Withdrawn
Sea Carriers Inc, Frontline Ltd ./. Blad Foundation	2002-09-16	T 6588-01-79	HS	Challenge of Arbitral Award (Invalidity of Arbitral Award)	Denied
Märit Westin ./. AFA Sjukförsäkringsaktiebolag	2002-08-26	T 7463-02	HS	Challenge of Arbitral Award	Withdrawn
Argo Trading Ltd ./. Quattrogemini Ltd	2002-07-25	T 6211-01	HS	Challenge of Arbitral Award	Denied
Ming Court Limitid ./. Kuehne & Nagel (Hong Kong) Ltd	2002-06-13	T 7007-01	HS	Challenge of Arbitral Award	Amicable settlement

(*Continued*)

Parties	Date of decision	Case No.	Court	Issue	Outcome
Gunnar Johansson et al. ./. Rosellplast AB	2001-06-29	T 150-00	HG	Challenge of Arbitral Award	Denied
Evelin Hjerp ./. Advokatbyrån JuristForum Aktiebolag	2001-05-07	T 1582-01	HS	Challenge of Arbitral Award	Denied
Advokaten Arto Koivuniemi ./. Ritva Kuru	2001-04-20	T 2217-01	HS	Challenge of Arbitral Award	Dismissed
Katrin Lundberg ./. Advokatfirman Jan Olsén AB	2001-04-18	T 1585-01	HS	Challenge of Arbitral Award	Denied
Nils-Erik Thorell ./. Advokatgruppen Lund HB	2001-03-29	T 5781-00	HS	Challenge of Arbitral Award	Denied
Rolf Strandberg ./. Advokatfirman Skarborg & Partners Aktiebolag	2001-02-14	T 2671-00	HS	Challenge of Arbitral Award	Denied

APPENDIX 8

Review of Arbitral Awards on Jurisdiction

Final decisions as per 1 December 2010

Abbreviations:

The Supreme Court	HD
The Svea Court of Appeal	HS
The Göta Court of Appeal	HG
The Court of Appeal for Western Sweden	HVS
The Scania and Blekinge Court of Appeal	HSB
The Court of Appeal for Lower Norrland	HNN
The Court of Appeal for Upper Norrland	HON

Parties	Date of decision	Case No.	Court	Issue	Outcome
Håkan Hederstierna ./. Handelshögskolan i Stockholm	2010-11-30	T 3258-09	HD	Appeal of Arbitral Award on Jurisdiction	Amended/ Partially set aside
Petrobart Limited ./. Republic of Kirgizistan	2008-03-28	NJA 2008 p. 406	HD	Appeal of Arbitral Award on Jurisdiction	Partially set aside
Sadkora Energy AB ./. Aigar Ojaots	2010-04-08	T 7086-08	HS	Appeal of Arbitral Award on Jurisdiction	Default judgement (set aside)
Johan Forsgren ./. AFA Trygghetsförsäkrings AB	2009-03-18	T 5004-08	HS	Appeal of Arbitral Award on Jurisdiction	Denied
Nicolas Persson ./. Onetwocom AB	2007-02-21	T 6762-05	HS	Appeal of Arbitral Award on Jurisdiction	Denied
William Nagel ./. Czech Republic, Ministry of Transportation and Telecommunications	2005-08-26	T 9059-03	HS	Appeal of Arbitral Award on Jurisdiction	Dismissed
Premiepensionsmyndigheten ./. CSC Sverige AB	2004-07-02	T 9036-03	HS	Appeal of Arbitral Award on Jurisdiction	Withdrawn
Tjänstemannaförbundet HTF ./. M7 Borås non-profit association bankruptcy estate	2004-06-28	T 1342-03	HS	Appeal of Arbitral Award on Jurisdiction	Partially set aside

(Continued)

Parties	Date of decision	Case No.	Court	Issue	Outcome
Josef Boberg ./. Norsk Hydro ASA	2004-02-24	T 1747-03	HS	Appeal of Arbitral Award on Jurisdiction (Challenge of Arbitral Award)	Dismissed
Alucoal Holdings Limited ./. JSC Novokuznetsk Aluminium Plant	2004-02-17	T 3226-03	HS	Appeal of Arbitral Award on Jurisdiction	Dismissed

APPENDIX 9

Enforcement of Arbitral Awards

Decisions by Swedish courts since Sweden's ratification of the New York Convention in 1971.

Abbreviations:

The Supreme Court	HD
The Svea Court of Appeal	HS

Parties	Date of decision	Case No.	Court	Issue	Outcome
LenmorniiproektOAO ./. Arne Larsson & Partner Leasing AB	2010-04-16	NJA 2010 p. 219	HD	Enforcement of Arbitral Award	Denied
Carbaque International AB ./. Fabryka Wyrobów Lnianych Swiebodzice Sp. Z.o.o.	2009-03-24	NJA 2009 N 9	HD	Enforcement of Arbitral Award	Enforced
Finn Bjarne Fløjstrup ./. Jens Madsen et al.	2008-05-06	NJA 2008 N 32	HD	Enforcement of Arbitral Award	Enforced
Kalle Bergander i Stockholm AB ./. Société Planavergne S.A.	2003-09-30	NJA 2003 p. 379	HD	Enforcement of Arbitral Award	Partially enforced
Republic of Latvia ./. SwemBalt AB	2002-12-18	NJA 2002 C 62	HD	Enforcement of Arbitral Award	Enforced
Robert Grizila ./. Johnny Letth bankruptcy estate	2002-10-23	NJA 2002 C 45	HD	Enforcement of Arbitral Award	Denied
Maxgraf Aktiebolag ./. Printing House "GUNDARS"	1998-02-26	NJA 1998 C 14	HD	Enforcement of Arbitral Award	Enforced
Moelven Valåsens Sågverk AB ./. Mikko V. et al.	1996-01-01	NJA 1996 C 21	HD	Enforcement of Arbitral Award	Enforced
Richard E. ./. Monimpex	1993-01-01	NJA 1993 C 56	HD	Enforcement of Arbitral Award	Enforced
DatemaAB ./. Forenede Cresco Finans AS	1992-11-23	NJA 1992 p. 733	HD	Enforcement of Arbitral Award	Enforced
Tommy Klatzkow Konsult AB ./. Pevaeche S.A.	1989-01-01	NJA 1989 C 22	HD	Enforcement of Arbitral Award	Enforced
Rederi AB Gustaf Erikson ./. Rederi AB Thule	1988-01-01	NJA 1988 C 28	HD	Enforcement of Arbitral Award	Dismissed
Kvarnabo Timber AB ./. Cordes GmbH & Co	1986-01-02	NJA 1986 C 26	HD	Enforcement of Arbitral Award	Enforced

(*Continued*)

Parties	Date of decision	Case No.	Court	Issue	Outcome
Gräsås Trävaru AB ./. Sodemaco S.A.	1986-01-01	NJA 1986 C 89	HD	Enforcement of Arbitral Award	Enforced
Eagle Navigation Ltd. ./. MD Shipping Line AB	2010-03-30	Ö 9368-09	HS	Enforcement of Arbitral Award	Enforced
Helsingør Boligselskab afdeling 12, Blicherparken ./. Morneon Fasad AB	2009-06-24	Ö 1475-09	HS	Enforcement of Arbitral Award	Enforced
FabrykaWyrobów Lnianych Swiebodzice Sp. z o.o. ./. Carabaque International AB	2008-12-22	Ö 7186-08	HS	Enforcement of Arbitral Award	Dismissed
A/S Bolderaja ./. Bo Andrén AB	2008-06-18	Ö 8421-07	HS	Enforcement of Arbitral Award	Withdrawn
Marian Janowski et al. ./. Appelkvist Fryseri AB	2007-11-19	Ö 2262-07	HS	Enforcement of Arbitral Award	Amicable settlement
Sparebanken Nord Norge ./. Per-Gunnar Svendsen Ballo	2005-09-28	Ö 2321-05	HS	Enforcement of Arbitral Award	Enforced
ORBIS Spólka Akcyjna ./. Prenad International Aktiebolag	2005-06-10	Ö 9735-04	HS	Enforcement of Arbitral Award	Withdrawn
Ekpac International Ltd. ./. RM Rocade Aktiebolag	2004-11-11	Ö 7159-04	HS	Enforcement of Arbitral Award	Amicable settlement
Mekajohtotiet Oy et al. ./. Bo Andersson	2004-04-01	Ö 2235-04	HS	Enforcement of Arbitral Award	Withdrawn
Norske Skog Flooring Holding AS ./. Välinge Aluminium AB	2003-01-03	Ö 9153-02	HS	Enforcement of Arbitral Award	Withdrawn
Sunnywood Group Ltd ./. Joakim Andersson	2002-09-26	Ö 5684-02	HS	Enforcement of Arbitral Award	Enforced
Odfjell Seachemm AS et al. ./. Windsor Chemicals Europe AB	2002-06-11	Ö 6498-01	HS	Enforcement of Arbitral Award	Withdrawn
American Pacific corporation ./. Sydsvensk Produktutveckling AB bankruptcy estate et al.	2001-03-21	Ö 4859-00	HS	Enforcement of Arbitral Award	Enforced
Group 4 Securitas BV ./. Rajiv Mehta	2000-10-31	Ö 4232-00	HS	Enforcement of Arbitral Award	Enforced

INDEX

accountants 4.42

adhesion contracts 3.05

adoption 3.80

affidavits 6.145, 6.146, 6.222
  see also **written witness statements**

affirmations, truth 6.99, 6.100, 6.122
  court assistance 6.170–6.180

agency 2.134–2.140, 2.142, 2.143, 2.181–2.184
  Rome Convention 1980 2.145

aircraft 2.116, 2.127

amiables compositeurs 2.24, 2.27, 2.75, 7.04

anti-suit injunctions 5.38–5.42

antitrust law 2.75–2.76, 2.189
  arbitrability: civil law effects of 3.98–3.110
  invalid arbitral awards 8.41

appeals 6.86, 7.26, 8.06
  jurisdiction 5.18, 7.23, 8.16, 8.205–8.229
  recognition 9.65, 9.66

applicable law 2.01–2.04, 7.04–7.07
  arbitration agreement 2.145, 2.201–2.209, 3.52,
      8.127, 9.25, 9.32
    centre of gravity test 2.209
    legal identity and corporate legal
        succession 2.177–2.178
    separate agreement 2.201
  capacity 9.24
  choice of law by parties 2.14–2.23, 8.127, 9.32
    content of party autonomy 2.24–2.41
    exercising party autonomy 2.42–2.50
    restrictions on party autonomy 2.51–2.96
  classification rules 2.198–2.200
  issues not covered by *lex contractus*
    agency 2.181–2.184
    lex corporationis 2.145, 2.174–2.180
    negotiable instruments 2.185
    property 2.192–2.197
    torts 2.186–2.191
  lex arbitri 2.02, 2.05–2.13, 2.51, 4.48, 6.190
    enforcement 9.32, 9.35
    evaluation of evidence 6.167
    res judicata 7.135
  no choice of law by parties 2.97–2.105, 9.32
    1964 Act: international sale of goods
        2.105–2.117, 2.165
    centre of gravity test 2.104, 2.118–2.143
    characteristic performance of contract 2.112,
        2.128, 2.150, 2.151, 2.156,
        2.169, 2.177
    in dubio rules 2.125–2.128, 2.130,
        2.136, 2.168

Rome Convention 1980 2.104, 2.105, 2.128,
    2.129–2.130, 2.133, 2.138, 2.143–2.162
Rome I Regulation 2.104, 2.105,
    2.163–2.172
procedure 6.205

arbitrability 3.05, 3.77–3.80, 5.08
  challenge of arbitral awards 8.64
  civil law effects of competition law 3.98–3.110
  consent awards 7.40, 7.41
  consumer and labour disputes 3.95–3.97
  court proceedings 3.123–3.125
  disputes capable of settlement 3.81–3.85
  enforcement 9.52
  existence of factual circumstances 3.86–3.91
  filling gaps 3.92–3.94
  invalid arbitral awards 8.29–8.32
  partly 8.57

arbitration agreement 3.01–3.02
  arbitrability 3.05, 3.77–3.110, 8.64
  challenge of arbitral awards 8.63–8.64
  concluding
    by conduct 3.05, 3.14–3.30, 3.146, 6.82
    inactivity 3.28–3.30
    oral agreement 3.05, 3.12–3.13, 3.146, 6.82
    party usage 3.23–3.27, 3.30
    in writing 3.06–3.11
  consumer disputes 3.39, 3.75–3.76, 3.82, 3.95
  drafting of 3.182–3.190
  effects of
    assistance by courts 3.120, 3.126, 3.169
    authority of arbitrators 3.128–3.129, 3.169,
        3.176, 3.177, 3.188, 7.99
    bar to court proceedings 3.112–3.125,
        5.04, 7.105
    confidentiality 3.164–3.167
    rules of organization and procedure 3.127
    third parties 3.130–3.163
  interpretation of 3.31–3.36
  law governing 2.145, 2.201–2.209, 3.52, 8.127,
      9.25, 9.32
    centre of gravity test 2.209
    implied term 2.204
    legal identity and corporate legal
        succession 2.177–2.178
  oral agreements 3.04, 3.05, 3.10, 3.12–3.13,
      3.146, 6.82, 9.25, 9.64
  separability doctrine 3.42–3.47, 3.71–3.73, 3.179
    application of 3.48–3.52
    limited application of 3.53–3.70
    party substitution 3.137

arbitration agreement *(cont.)*
  termination of 3.122, 3.168–3.170, 4.47
    complete 3.178–3.181
    existing dispute 3.171–3.177
  third parties 3.16, 3.35, 3.130
    conduct by 3.146–3.155
    group of companies doctrine 3.22,
      3.148–3.155
    guarantee agreements 3.142–3.145
    party substitution 3.131–3.141
    third-party beneficiary agreements 3.156–3.163
  unenforceability due to Swedish Contracts
    Act 3.37–3.41
  validity of 3.04–3.05, 3.74–3.76, 5.11, 9.25
Arbitration Institute of Stockholm Chamber of
  Commerce 1.10, 1.46–1.51, 2.209
  compensation to 4.136
  jurisdiction 5.44–5.47
arbitrators
  appointment 4.01–4.02
    courts 3.172, 4.09, 4.16, 4.33, 4.38, 4.69, 4.87
    public policy 8.39
    rules 4.18–4.38
    under SAA 4.04–4.17
  arbitration agreement and authority of 3.128–3.129,
    3.169, 3.176, 3.177, 3.188, 7.99
  challenging
    procedure 4.84–4.86
    replacing 4.69, 4.87–4.90, 4.99
    rules 4.91–4.102
    SAA 4.62–4.90
  compensation of 3.40, 4.103–4.124, 7.78–7.83
    advance on 3.118, 4.114, 4.116, 4.117,
      4.134–4.135, 7.37, 9.15
    amending, correcting or interpreting
      awards 7.139
    cancellation fees 4.125
    expenses 4.109–4.111, 4.114
    interest 4.112, 7.77
    place of arbitration 7.88
    rules 4.130–4.137
    security for 3.118, 4.115–4.117
    value added tax 4.126–4.129
  contract theory 4.54, 4.55
  court challenge to proceedings 1.126
  discretion 7.153
    party substitution 3.133
  duties of 4.46, 4.50–4.51, 6.75, 8.198
    case management 6.192–6.195, 8.86
    national mandatory laws 2.78, 2.81–2.84
    national public policy 2.70
    non-participation of party 6.229
  emergency 4.24–4.27
  liability of 4.52–4.61
  powers of 4.46–4.49
    evidence 6.97–6.100, 6.102, 6.103, 6.126,
      6.151, 6.182, 6.183

    interim measures 6.212, 6.213, 6.214
    questions to witnesses 6.131
  qualifications of 4.39–4.45
  relation of arbitrators to parties 4.52–4.61
  replacement 4.69, 4.87–4.90, 4.99
  sovereign immunity and 1.122–1.123
  status theory 4.54, 4.55
assertion, doctrine of 3.33–3.36
auctions 2.117, 2.127
audi alteram partem 6.32–6.34
auditors 4.42
autonomy, party 4.40, 8.22
  award 7.43
  choice of law *see* **choice of law by parties**
  costs 7.83
  procedure 6.02, 6.05, 6.14, 6.15, 6.30
    evidence 6.97, 6.105, 6.108
    main hearing 6.219
award 7.01
  amendment of 3.176, 7.99, 7.100, 7.137–7.139,
    7.146–7.148, 7.152, 7.155, 7.156
  correction of 3.176, 7.137–7.145, 7.152,
    7.153, 7.154
  costs *see separate entry*
  decision or 7.22–7.26, 7.36
  deliberations and voting 7.10–7.21
  dissenting opinions 7.69–7.70
  effects of 7.92
    execution 7.93
    termination of arbitration
      agreement 7.96–7.103
    time starts running 7.94–7.95
  ex parte proceedings 6.227
  formalities 7.43–7.56
  interest 4.112, 7.71–7.77
  interpretation of 7.137–7.139, 7.149–7.151,
    7.152, 7.153, 7.154, 7.155, 7.157
  jurisdiction, lack of 5.18
  prayers for relief 6.74, 6.75, 7.66, 7.146
  principles of decision 7.02–7.03
    dealing with all matters 7.09
    decision according to law 7.04–7.07
    keeping within authority 7.08
  reasons and dissenting opinions 7.49–7.50,
    7.57–7.70, 7.117
  rendering 7.84–7.91
  supplementation of 3.176, 7.100
  types of
    award or decision 7.22–7.26, 7.36
    consent awards 7.38–7.41
    default awards 6.33, 6.227, 6.229, 7.42
    interim awards 7.36–7.37, 9.15, 9.16
    interlocutory awards 7.33–7.35
    partial awards 7.30–7.32, 8.162, 9.14–9.16
    separate awards 7.27–7.35, 9.14–9.16
  voting and deliberations 7.10–7.21
  in writing 4.50

bankruptcy 3.84
  interim award 7.37
  party substitution 3.132, 3.138–3.140
  public policy 9.60–9.62
  qualifications of arbitrators 4.39
banks 2.127
bias *see* **conflicts of interest**
bifurcation of proceedings 6.206–6.207
bills of exchange 2.145, 2.185
bribery 2.94–2.95, 3.85, 4.58, 8.36, 8.44, 9.54
burden of proof 6.168
  challenge of arbitral awards 8.12, 8.14
  enforcement actions 3.27
  invalid arbitral awards 8.12, 8.13
  non-participation 6.228
  oral agreements 3.12

capacity 3.05, 9.23–9.24
carriage of goods 2.156, 2.171
case management 6.192–6.195, 8.86, 8.166–8.175
chairperson
  deliberations 7.15, 7.17, 7.19
  expenses 4.111
  fees 4.108, 4.133
  procedure 6.31, 6.131, 6.191, 6.194, 6.196,
    7.85, 8.81
    decisions 7.10
    voting 7.11
challenge of arbitral awards 7.26, 8.58–8.62
  appointment of arbitrators, improper 4.41,
    8.112–8.113
  chosen law not applied 2.23
  disqualified arbitrator 8.112, 8.114–8.117
  evidence, issues with 6.98, 6.103, 6.167
  ex parte proceedings 6.226, 6.228
  excess of mandate 2.76, 6.73, 7.08, 7.66,
    8.65–8.77, 8.87
    facts or arguments not pleaded 8.78–8.108
    place of arbitration 8.110
    procedural irregularity or 8.121–8.122,
      8.157–8.158, 8.180
  expiry of award period, award after 7.56
  facts or arguments not pleaded 8.78–8.83
    contractual provisions and
      limitations 8.92–8.105
    evaluation of evidence 8.90–8.91
    excess of mandate: influence on
      outcome 8.106–8.108
    legal rules not relied on by parties 8.84–8.86
    procedural instructions to arbitrators
      8.87–8.88
    res judicata 8.89
  introduction 8.01–8.08
    burden of proof 8.12, 8.14
    in dubio pro validitate principle 8.09–8.11
    jurisdiction of Swedish courts 8.19–8.25
    other means of recourse 8.15–8.18

merits of dispute 3.51, 4.57, 6.167, 7.06, 8.01,
  8.160, 8.171–8.172
no arbitration agreement 8.63–8.64
other procedural irregularities 6.193, 7.09, 7.16,
  8.118–8.128
  amendment and dismissal of claims 8.146–8.147
  case management 8.166–8.175
  deviation from mandate or
    instructions 8.157–8.162
  fault of challenging party 8.182–8.183
  lis pendens 8.152–8.156
  mistakes on position of party 8.135–8.145
  non-participation by arbitrators 8.165
  probable influence on outcome 8.87,
    8.176–8.181
  reasons, failure to provide 7.50, 8.88,
    8.163–8.164
  res judicata 8.89, 8.148–8.155, 8.180, 8.181
  violation of due process 8.129–8.134
place of arbitration
  stated in award 7.47, 7.88
  Sweden incorrect place 8.109–8.111
reasons for award 7.50, 8.88, 8.163–8.164
remission of arbitral awards 8.193–8.204
waiver of right to 8.184
  exclusion agreements 4.41, 8.187–8.192
  implied 8.185–8.186
cheques 2.145, 2.185
China 1.17, 1.48, 1.58
  sovereign immunity 1.65–1.74, 1.100
choice of law by parties 2.14–2.23, 8.127
  arbitration agreement and 2.145, 2.201–2.209
  challenging clause 2.48
  content of party autonomy 2.24–2.41, 7.04
    list of options 2.27
  exercising party autonomy 2.42–2.50
  implied 2.45
    arbitration agreement 2.204
  list of options 2.27
  no choice made 2.97–2.105, 9.32
    1964 Act: international sale of goods
      2.105–2.117, 2.165
    centre of gravity test 2.104, 2.118–2.143
    characteristic performance of contract 2.112,
      2.128, 2.150, 2.151, 2.156, 2.169, 2.177
    in dubio rules 2.125–2.128, 2.130, 2.136, 2.168
    Rome Convention 1980 2.104, 2.105, 2.128,
      2.129–2.130, 2.133, 2.138, 2.143–2.162
    Rome I Regulation 2.104, 2.105, 2.163–2.172
  restrictions on party autonomy 2.51–2.54
    international public policy 2.84, 2.89–2.96
    mandatory rules of municipal law 2.71–2.88,
      2.147, 2.158–2.159, 2.172
    national public policy 2.59–2.70, 2.82,
      2.84, 2.161
    no reasonable connection 2.55–2.58
  unclear clauses 2.49–2.50, 8.96–8.104

citations, case 1.23, 1.24
civil law 1.18, 6.10, 6.219, 7.130, 7.135, 8.161
clean hands 8.45
commercial transactions
  definition of 1.83
  sovereign immunity
    Sweden 1.114–1.119
    UN Convention 1.82–1.84, 1.117
commodity trades 4.43
common law 5.38, 6.10, 6.162, 6.219, 7.130
companies
  agreements by conduct: groups of
    companies 3.17–3.18, 3.21–3.22
  alter ego claims 3.153
  capacity 3.05
  conflict of laws
    lex corporationis 2.145, 2.174–2.180, 3.141
  effects of arbitration agreements
    groups of companies doctrine 3.22,
      3.148–3.155
  piercing corporate veil 3.148, 3.153, 3.154
  procedure: payments to third parties 6.85
  reorganizations
    party substitution 3.138, 3.141
  res judicata and investment treaties 7.122–7.128
  residence 5.26
  service of documents 6.54
  shareholders' agreement 2.180, 4.15, 6.84
compensation of arbitrators 3.40, 4.103–4.124,
  7.78–7.83
  advance on 3.118, 4.114, 4.116, 4.117,
    4.134–4.135, 7.37, 9.15
  amendments to awards 7.139
  cancellation fees 4.125
  corrections to awards 7.139
  court challenge 8.212
  expenses 4.109–4.111, 4.114
  interest on 4.112, 7.77
  interpretation of awards 7.139
  place of arbitration 7.88
  rules 4.130–4.137
  security for 3.118, 4.115–4.117
  value added tax (VAT) 4.126–4.129
compétence de la compétence **doctrine** 3.46–3.47,
  3.72, 5.40
competition law 2.75–2.76, 2.189
  arbitrability: civil law effects of 3.98–3.110
  invalid arbitral awards 8.41
computer printouts 6.110
confidentiality
  arbitration 2.03, 3.164–3.167
    deliberations of arbitrators 7.20
  drafting arbitration clause 3.188
  legal profession 1.42
  trade secrets 6.178
conflict of laws 2.01–2.04
  arbitration agreement 2.145, 2.201–2.209, 8.127,
    9.25, 9.32

  legal identity and corporate legal
    succession 2.177–2.178
  separate agreement 2.201
  capacity 9.24
  choice of law clause 2.14–2.23, 8.100, 8.127
    content of party autonomy 2.24–2.36
    excluding conflict of laws rules 2.43
    exercising of party autonomy 2.42–2.50
    international public policy 2.84, 2.89–2.96
    mandatory rules of municipal law 2.71–2.88,
      2.147, 2.158–2.159, 2.172
    national public policy 2.59–2.70, 2.82,
      2.84, 2.161
    reasonable connection 2.55–2.58
    restrictions on party autonomy 2.51–2.96
  classification rules 2.198–2.200
  dépeçage 2.47, 2.146, 2.195
  issues not covered by *lex contractus* 2.25
    agency 2.181–2.184
    lex corporationis 2.145, 2.174–2.180
    negotiable instruments 2.185
    property 2.192–2.197
    torts 2.186–2.191
  lex arbitri 2.03, 2.05–2.13, 2.51
  no choice of law by parties 2.97–2.105
    Swedish rules *see below*
  property
    moveable 2.193–2.197
    real estate 2.192
  renvoi 2.162, 2.195
  Swedish 2.03, 2.47, 2.101–2.105
    1964 Act: international sale of goods
      2.105–2.117, 2.165
    centre of gravity test 2.104, 2.118–2.143
    characteristic performance of contract 2.112,
      2.128, 2.150, 2.151, 2.156, 2.169, 2.177
    classification rules 2.198–2.200
    in dubio rules 2.125–2.128, 2.130,
      2.136, 2.168
    lex arbitri 2.06–2.07, 2.11–2.13
    real estate 2.116, 2.192
    renvoi 2.162, 2.195
    Rome Convention 1980 2.104, 2.105, 2.128,
      2.129–2.130, 2.133, 2.138, 2.143–2.162
    Rome I Regulation 2.104, 2.105, 2.163–2.172
**conflicts of interest/doubts as to impartiality or
  independence**
  arbitrators 4.62–4.84, 4.91, 4.95–4.96, 4.100,
    4.101, 6.31, 6.131
  challenge of arbitral awards 8.114–8.117
  hearings 6.192, 6.194
  remission of awards 8.197
  self-judgment 8.52
consent awards 7.38–7.41
construction contracts 2.127, 4.42, 6.150, 6.206
consumer contracts 2.171
  arbitration agreement 3.39, 3.75–3.76, 3.82, 3.95
contract theory 4.54, 4.55

copyright 2.127, 3.79
corruption 2.94–2.95, 3.85
costs 7.78–7.83
  amendment of or supplement to claims 6.83
  compensation of arbitrators *see separate entry*
  court review of allocation of 8.212–8.214
Council of Europe
  Convention on State Immunity 1.101
counterclaims 6.81
courts
  appeals 6.86, 7.26, 8.06
    jurisdiction 5.18, 7.23, 8.16, 8.205–8.229
    recognition 9.65, 9.66
  arbitration agreements
    assistance by courts 3.120, 3.126, 3.169
    bar to court proceedings 3.112–3.125,
      5.04, 7.105
    challenging 3.46, 3.114, 3.115
    dispute in part non-contractual 3.35
    state immunity and arbitration clauses
      1.125, 1.126
  arbitrators
    appointment of 3.172, 4.09, 4.16, 4.33, 4.38,
      4.69, 4.87
    chairperson 6.191
    challenging appointment 4.85, 4.86, 4.102
    compensation challenge 4.117, 4.119,
      4.120–4.121, 4.122–4.124
  evidence taken with court assistance 6.170–6.180
  foreign
    anti-suit injunctions 5.38–5.42
  interim measures 6.210
  recognition and enforcement 9.12–9.13
    grounds for refusing 9.17–9.63
    recognition procedure 9.64–9.66
    security measures 9.16
  review of arbitrators' jurisdiction 3.46, 5.03, 5.04,
    5.16, 5.17, 5.19–5.20, 7.24
    appeals 5.18, 7.23, 8.16, 8.205–8.229
    concurrent actions 5.34–5.35
    declaratory action 5.21–5.37
    enforcement 9.51
    potential effects of declaratory action 5.36–5.37
    stay on arbitral proceedings 5.20, 5.36
  setting aside arbitral awards *see separate entry*
  system in Sweden 1.21–1.28
    jurisdiction 5.22–5.33
    procedure 6.04, 6.05, 6.09, 6.13, 6.16–6.28
criminal guilt 3.80
criminal offences 6.99, 8.17, 8.36, 9.54
  title of *advokat* 1.36
cross-claims 6.84
currency control regulations 2.88
customary international law
  sovereign immunity 1.78, 1.128

damages 8.93
  liability of arbitrators 4.52–4.61

death
  arbitrator 4.87
  party substitution 3.132
decision or award 7.22–7.26, 7.36
declaratory judgments 6.20, 7.68
  res judicata 7.114
  review of arbitrators' jurisdiction 5.19–5.37
default awards 6.33, 6.227, 6.229, 7.42
defective goods 3.90
delocalization theory 2.09–2.10
demergers
  party substitution 3.132
dépeçage 2.47, 2.146, 2.195
developing countries
  sovereign immunity 1.54, 1.59
diplomatic immunity
  French law 1.128
  Swedish law 1.120
disclosure
  arbitrators 4.70, 4.72, 4.73, 4.91
    compensation 4.106
discovery
  arbitration 6.67, 6.110, 6.113–6.121
  Swedish judicial procedure 6.26–6.28
discrimination 2.96
dissenting opinions 7.69–7.70
divorce 3.80
domicile 8.109, 8.190
  jurisdiction and Brussels I Regulation
    5.30–5.33
drug trafficking 2.96
due process
  grounds for refusing enforcement 9.26–9.30
  setting aside arbitral awards 8.36, 8.38, 8.106,
    8.124–8.134
duress 9.54

East European countries 2.175
Egypt 1.48
electricity 2.116
electronic communication 3.10
emails
  service of documents 6.50, 6.52, 6.62
emergency arbitrations 4.24–4.27, 6.211,
  6.233–6.235
employment contracts 2.171, 3.39
enforcement 3.128, 7.93, 9.01
  arbitrability 8.30, 8.31, 8.57
  arbitration agreements
    unenforceability due to Swedish Contracts
      Act 3.37–3.41
  compensation of arbitrators 4.119
  consent awards 7.39
  delocalization theory 2.09–2.10
  ex parte proceedings 6.226
  foreign awards 9.07, 9.09–9.10
    arbitral award not binding 9.38–9.51
    capacity, lack of 9.23–9.24

enforcement *(cont.)*
  foreign awards *(cont.)*
    composition of tribunal or
        procedure 9.34–9.37
    due process, violation of 9.26–9.30
    excess of mandate 9.31–9.33
    grounds for refusing 9.17–9.63
    invalid arbitration agreement 9.25
    nationality of award 9.08
    New York Convention v SAA 9.11–9.13
    non-arbitrability 9.52
    public policy 9.53–9.63
    separate, partial and interim awards 9.14–9.16
  interim measures 6.213, 7.36, 7.37
  national
    mandatory rules 2.78
    public policy 2.69, 2.70, 2.82, 2.84, 9.04,
        9.53–9.63
  obscure awards 8.56
  sovereign immunity 1.53, 1.55, 1.102, 1.129,
      1.130, 9.19
    French law 1.127–1.128
    Swedish law 1.102, 1.131, 1.135–1.141
    UN Convention 1.88–1.93, 1.130
    US law 1.140
  Swedish awards 9.01, 9.02–9.05
    enforcement abroad 9.06
engineers 4.42
errors
  see also challenge of arbitral awards
  correction of arbitral awards 7.137–7.145
  in dubio pro validitate principle 8.09–8.11
escrow account 6.216
ethical rules
  legal profession 1.40–1.45, 4.50, 4.55
European Court of Justice 2.164
  anti-suit injunctions 5.41–5.42
  Brussels I Regulation: arbitration exception
      5.31–5.32, 8.19
  competition law and arbitration
      3.104–3.110, 8.41
  invalid arbitral awards 8.41–8.43
  VAT and arbitrators' fees 4.127
European Union
  Brussels I Regulation: arbitration
      exception 5.30–5.33
  competition law 2.75–2.76, 3.104–3.110, 8.41
  party autonomy and *lex contractus* 2.17–2.18
  Swedish legislation 1.20, 4.128
evidence
  admissibility 6.68, 6.101–6.108, 6.182
    expert evidence 6.156
  award, transmission of 7.90
  court assistance 6.170–6.180, 8.134
  cross-examination 6.100, 6.127, 6.136,
      6.137–6.143, 6.144, 6.146, 6.222
    experts 6.157, 6.222

direct examination 6.127, 6.132–6.136,
      6.146, 6.222
  documentary 6.100, 6.103, 6.109–6.111, 6.163
    production of documents 6.112–6.121
  evaluation of 6.162–6.169, 8.90–8.91
    non-compliance 6.162, 6.164–6.166, 7.02
  expert 4.110, 5.15, 6.89, 6.93, 6.105,
      6.150–6.157, 6.222
    court assistance 6.170–6.180
    errors in reports 7.143
    foreign law 6.94
    SCC Rules 6.183
    witness conferencing 6.158–6.159
  foreign law 6.94
  hearsay 6.102
  IBA Rules 6.96, 6.107, 6.148, 6.157, 6.164
  introduction 6.89–6.96
  jurisdiction of tribunal, objections to 5.15
  late 6.34, 6.103, 6.143
  post-hearing briefs 6.65, 6.87–6.88,
      6.104, 6.223
  powers of arbitrators 6.97–6.100, 6.102, 6.103,
      6.182, 6.183
  prayers for relief 6.79
  re-direct examination 6.127, 6.144, 6.222
  SCC rules 6.181–6.183
  site inspections 6.160–6.161
  statements of 6.65, 6.79, 6.95, 6.111, 6.134
  Swedish judicial procedure 6.19, 6.21,
      6.23–6.28, 6.149
  written witness statements 6.95, 6.127, 6.132,
      6.138, 6.145–6.149, 6.222, 7.143
ex aequo et bono 2.24, 2.27, 2.64, 2.75, 7.04
ex parte
  interim measures 6.214
  proceedings 6.33, 6.225–6.229
exchange control regulations 2.88
exchanges and auctions 2.117, 2.127
exclusion agreements 4.41, 8.187–8.192
expedited arbitrations 6.230–6.232
  see also emergency arbitrations
export regulations 2.88

fairs 2.127
family law 3.80
faxes
  service of documents 6.49, 6.52, 6.62
fees
  arbitrators *see* compensation of arbitrators
  legal profession 1.44–1.45
force majeure clauses 2.33–2.34, 3.90
foreign procedural law 2.12–2.13
forgery 8.36
formalities: award 7.43–7.56
France 6.10
  equality of the parties 4.31
  sovereign immunity 1.127–1.128

fraud 3.153
freezing clauses 2.33–2.34

general principles of law
   lex contractus 2.27, 2.32, 2.36, 2.37, 2.38,
     2.39–2.40, 2.64
Germany 6.10
   sovereign immunity 1.129
gifts 2.127
groups of companies doctrine 3.22, 3.148–3.155
   see also companies
guarantees 2.127
   arbitration agreement binding
     guarantor 3.142–3.145
guardianship 3.80

hardship clauses 2.33–2.34
hearings 6.184
   case management 6.192–6.195
   chairperson 6.191, 6.194, 6.196
   ex parte proceedings 6.225–6.229
   expedited and emergency
     arbitrations 6.230–6.235
   iura novit curia 6.69–6.70, 6.195, 7.07, 8.84–8.86
   language 4.44, 6.106, 6.197
   main 6.218–6.224
   place of 6.185–6.190
   pre-arbitral referee 6.236
   preliminary matters
     hearings and meetings 6.198–6.200
     other 6.201–6.217
   records 6.196, 6.223
hearsay evidence 6.102
history of arbitration in Sweden 1.01–1.17
Hong Kong 1.48, 1.69
human rights 2.96

illegal contracts 8.41
immovable property 2.156, 2.168
impartiality *see* conflicts of interest
implied choice of law 2.45
   arbitration agreement 2.204
import regulations 2.88
in dubio pro validitate principle 8.09–8.11
in rem, rights 3.83
   universal succession 3.139–3.140
independence *see* conflicts of interest
infra petita 6.192, 7.09, 8.75–8.76, 8.122
injunctions 3.84, 7.36
insurance contracts 2.127, 2.131–2.133,
   2.140–2.141, 2.143
   qualification of arbitrators 4.43
   Rome Convention 1980 2.145
intellectual property
   conflict of laws 2.116, 2.127, 2.189, 2.191
   copyright 2.127, 3.79
interest 7.71–7.76

on arbitrators' fees 4.112, 7.77
   prayers for relief 6.74
interim measures 3.129, 5.41, 6.174, 7.36–7.37
   emergency arbitrations 4.24–4.27, 6.211,
     6.233–6.235
   enforcement 6.213, 7.36, 9.15, 9.16
   ex parte 6.214
   ICC: urgent provisional measures 6.236
   preliminary hearings 6.208–6.217
interlocutory awards 7.33–7.35, 7.100
international public policy 2.78, 2.84, 2.89–2.91
   content of 2.93–2.96
   function of 2.92
   national public policy and 2.92
international trade law/*lex mercatoria* 2.27, 2.31
interpretation of
   arbitration agreements 3.31–3.36
   awards 7.137–7.139, 7.149–7.151, 7.152, 7.153,
     7.154, 7.155, 7.157
invalid arbitral awards 8.26–8.28, 9.04
   formal requirements 8.47–8.49
   introduction 8.01–8.02, 8.04–8.08
     burden of proof 8.12, 8.13
     jurisdiction of Swedish courts 8.19–8.25
     other means of recourse 8.15–8.18
   non-arbitrability 8.29–8.32
   non-statutory grounds 8.50–8.56
   part of award invalid 8.57
   public policy, violation of 8.33–8.35
     procedural 8.36–8.39
     substantive 8.40–8.46
   remission of arbitral awards 8.193–8.204
investment treaty arbitration 2.41, 7.121–7.128
Italy 6.10
iura novit curia 6.69–6.70, 6.195, 7.07, 8.84–8.86

joint and several liability 4.105, 4.118, 4.136, 7.78
judiciary
   generally 1.22, 1.29–1.34
jurisdiction of arbitral tribunal 5.01–5.06
   anti-suit injunctions 5.38–5.42
   appeals 5.18, 7.23, 8.16, 8.205–8.208
     in practice 8.215–8.229
     scope of application 8.209–8.210
     scope of review 8.211–8.214
   arbitrators' determination of 5.13–5.18
   court review of arbitrators' jurisdiction 3.46, 5.03,
     5.04, 5.16, 5.17, 5.19–5.20, 7.24
     appeals 5.18, 7.23, 8.16, 8.205–8.229
     declaratory action 5.21–5.35
     potential effects of declaratory action 5.36–5.37
   decisions 7.24
   issues affecting 5.07–5.12
   positive ruling: alternatives for dissatisfied
     party 5.17
   procedure if challenge to 6.201–6.204
   SCC Rules 5.43–5.47

jurisdiction of Swedish courts
   setting aside arbitral awards 8.19–8.25

kidnapping 2.96
know-how 2.127

labour disputes 3.96–3.97
language 4.44, 6.106, 6.197
leading questions 6.135, 6.139, 6.144
legal profession 1.35–1.45, 4.42
   ethical rules 1.40–1.45, 4.50, 4.55
   fees 7.81, 7.83
   procedure 6.06, 6.08
legal system in Sweden 1.18–1.20
   courts 1.21–1.28
      jurisdiction 5.22–5.33
      procedure 6.04, 6.05, 6.09, 6.13,
         6.16–6.28, 6.149
   judiciary 1.22, 1.29–1.34
   legal profession *see separate entry*
lex arbitri 2.02, 2.05–2.13, 2.51, 4.48, 6.190
   enforcement 9.32, 9.35
   evaluation of evidence 6.167
   res judicata 7.135
lex contractus *see* **choice of law by parties**
lex corporationis 2.145, 2.174–2.180
   party substitution 3.141
lex fori 2.51, 2.56, 2.59, 2.62, 2.72, 9.32
   classification rules 2.198, 2.200
lex mercatoria/**international trade law** 2.27, 2.31
licensing agreements 2.127
limitation periods 7.33, 9.20
lis pendens 5.34, 6.45, 7.104, 7.105, 7.106, 7.107
   challenge of arbitral awards 8.152–8.156
   identity test 7.108, 7.118–7.119
   international arbitration 7.120, 7.122–7.123,
      7.125–7.130, 7.136
   prayers for relief 6.73
loans 2.127
long-term contracts 3.93
   see also **construction contracts**

Macao 1.69
markets 2.127
mergers
   party substitution 3.132
mistakes
   see also **challenge of arbitral awards**
   correction of arbitral awards 7.137–7.145
   in dubio pro validitate principle 8.09–8.11
moveable property
   conflict of laws 2.193–2.197
multi-party situations 4.35
   appointment of arbitrators 4.13–4.17,
      4.28–4.34, 4.38
   drafting arbitration clause 3.190
municipal law *see* **national law**
murder 2.96

national law
   lex contractus 2.27, 2.33–2.41
      mandatory rules 2.75–2.77
   mandatory rules 2.71–2.74
      lex contractus 2.75–2.77
      other national laws 2.78–2.88, 2.147,
         2.158–2.159, 2.172
   sovereign immunity 1.57–1.59
      China 1.65–1.74
      Russia 1.60–1.64
national public policy 2.59–2.62
   competition law 3.103–3.110
   consent awards 7.40
   enforcement 9.04, 9.53–9.63
   equality of the parties 4.31
   forum 2.161
   international public policy and 2.92
   invalid arbitral awards 8.32–8.46
   jurisdiction of arbitrators 5.08
   lex contractus 2.63–2.68
   lis pendens 7.106
   other 2.69–2.70, 2.82, 2.84
   res judicata 7.106
nationalization 3.66–3.69
negotiable instruments 2.145, 2.185
non-signatories *see* **third parties**

oaths 4.49, 6.25, 6.99, 6.100, 6.122, 6.126, 6.145
   court assistance 6.170–6.180, 8.134
objective approach
   no choice of law made: centre of
      gravity 2.122–2.124
oil concession contracts 2.33, 2.36, 2.37–2.39
oral arbitration agreements 3.04, 3.05, 3.10,
      3.12–3.13, 3.146, 6.82, 9.25, 9.64
ordre public *see* **public policy**

partial awards 7.30–7.32, 8.162, 9.14–9.16
parties
   autonomy 4.40, 8.22
   award 7.43
   choice of law *see* **choice of law by parties**
   costs 7.83
   procedure 6.02, 6.05, 6.14, 6.15, 6.30, 6.97,
      6.105, 6.108, 6.219
   multi-party situations 4.35
      appointment of arbitrators 4.13–4.17,
         4.28–4.34, 4.38
      drafting arbitration clause 3.190
   relation of arbitrators to 4.52–4.61
   substitution 3.131–3.133
      singular succession 3.132, 3.133, 3.134–3.137
      universal succession 3.132, 3.138–3.141
partnerships 7.109
patents 3.79
perjury 6.99
permanent place of business 2.111
piracy 2.96

place of arbitration 4.48, 5.10, 6.185–6.190, 8.21–8.22, 8.25
  award 7.47, 7.88, 8.06, 8.49
  challenge of arbitral awards 8.109–8.111
policy *see* **public policy**
post-hearing briefs 6.65, 6.87–6.88, 6.104, 6.223
prayers for relief *see* **written submissions**
pre-arbitral referee 6.236
precedent 1.19
private international law *see* **conflict of laws**
privatization 2.175
  party substitution 3.138, 3.141
procedure before arbitral tribunal 6.01–6.15
  basic principles 6.29–6.34
  commencing proceedings
    request for arbitration 6.35–6.43
    service of documents 6.44–6.63
  conduct of arbitration
    amended or supplemented claims 6.82–6.83
    counterclaims 6.81
    cross-claims 6.84
    documentary evidence 6.100, 6.103, 6.109–6.121, 6.163
    evidence *see separate entry*
    generally 6.64–6.70
    hearings *see separate entry*
    language 6.106, 6.197
    post-hearing briefs 6.65, 6.87–6.88, 6.104, 6.223
    set-off claims 6.81
    witnesses and experts *see* **witnesses**
    written submissions 6.71–6.86, 6.192, 6.193
  foreign procedural law 2.12–2.13
  Swedish judicial procedure, general principles of 6.16–6.28
promissory notes 2.145, 2.185
prospectuses: public offering 2.180
provisional measures *see* **interim measures**
public international law
  lex contractus 2.27, 2.32
public policy
  international 2.78, 2.84, 2.89–2.91
    content of 2.93–2.96
    function of 2.92
  national 2.59–2.62, 4.31, 4.57, 5.08, 7.106
    competition law 3.103–3.110
    consent awards 7.40
    enforcement 9.04, 9.53–9.63
    forum 2.161
    invalid arbitral awards 8.32–8.46
    lex contractus 2.63–2.68
    other 2.69–2.70, 2.82, 2.84

quantification of claims 6.206, 7.33

re-insurance 4.43
real estate
  conflict of laws 2.116, 2.192

recognition 9.01
  foreign award 9.09, 9.10
    grounds for refusing 9.17–9.63
    procedures 9.64–9.66
  public policy 2.82, 9.53–9.63
  sovereign immunity 1.125, 1.135–1.139, 9.19
  Swedish awards 9.02
records 6.196, 6.223
referee, pre-arbitral 6.236
reference clauses 3.08
remedies 4.52–4.61, 6.20, 7.68, 8.93
  injunctions 3.84, 7.36
remission of arbitral awards 8.193–8.204
reorganizations
  party substitution 3.132, 3.141
reports
  arbitration 2.03, 2.103
  court
    Sweden 1.23, 1.24
res judicata 7.23, 7.98, 7.104, 7.106, 7.107
  authority of arbitrators 3.128
  challenge of arbitral awards 8.89, 8.148–8.155, 8.180, 8.181
  consent awards 7.39
  identity test 7.108–7.119
  interlocutory awards 7.35
  international arbitration 7.120–7.136
  jurisdiction of arbitrators 5.12, 8.206
  operative part of award 7.67
  parallel proceedings 5.34
  prayers for relief 6.73
  recognition of award in Sweden 9.10
  withdrawal and limitation of claim 6.86
residence 5.26, 5.29
restitution 7.68
retention of title 2.193–2.195
revision clauses 2.33–2.34
Roman law 1.02, 2.76, 6.10, 8.45
Russia 1.13–1.15, 1.48, 1.58
  privatization 2.175, 3.141
  sovereign immunity 1.60–1.64

securities 2.116, 2.127
  lex corporationis 2.180
security
  costs 3.118, 4.115–4.117
  interim measures 6.217, 9.16
separability doctrine 3.42–3.47, 3.71–3.73
  application of 3.48–3.52
    limited 3.53–3.70
    no agreement in first place 3.55–3.59
    principal agreement: void, voidable or declared invalid 3.60–3.70
  party substitution 3.137
  termination of arbitration agreement 3.179
separate awards 7.27–7.35, 9.14–9.16
service contracts 2.116, 2.168

service of documents 6.44–6.63
  outside Sweden 6.57
set-off claims 6.81
setting aside arbitral awards 3.46, 7.106
  challenge *see* challenge of arbitral awards
  invalid arbitral awards *see separate entry*
  invalid and challengeable awards
    burden of proof 8.12–8.14
    general remarks 8.01–8.08
    in dubio pro validitate principle 8.09–8.11
    jurisdiction of Swedish courts 8.19–8.25
    other means of recourse 8.15–8.18
  partly set aside 8.57, 8.59
  remission of arbitral awards 3.177, 4.46,
    8.193–8.204
  review of jurisdictional awards 5.18, 7.23, 8.16,
    8.205–8.208
    in practice 8.215–8.229
    scope of application 8.209–8.210
    scope of review 8.211–8.214
shareholders' agreement 2.180, 4.15
  cross-claims 6.84
shipping 4.43
ships 2.116, 2.127
silence 6.162, 7.02
slavery 2.96
sovereign immunity
  arbitration and 1.122–1.130
    Swedish law 1.131–1.141
  enforcement 1.53, 1.55, 1.102, 1.129, 1.130, 9.19
    French law 1.127–1.128
    Swedish law 1.102, 1.131, 1.135–1.141
    UN Convention 1.88–1.93, 1.130
    US law 1.140
  generally 1.52–1.56
  national legislation 1.57–1.59
    China 1.65–1.74
    Russia 1.60–1.64
  Swedish law and 1.94–1.121
    arbitration 1.131–1.141
    real property 1.101
  UN Convention 1.57, 1.75–1.80
    arbitration 1.85–1.93
    China 1.74
    commercial transactions 1.82–1.84, 1.117
    execution of arbitral awards 1.88–1.93
    waivers 1.81
Soviet Union, former 1 13–1.15
  privatization 2.175
  sovereign immunity 1.54, 1.56, 1.60–1.64
specific performance 7.68
stabilization clauses 2.33–2.34
standard contracts 2.127, 3.07, 3.08
standard of proof 6.168, 8.177, 9.54
stare decisis 1.19
State contracts
  protection of non-State party 2.33–2.41

status theory 4.54, 4.55
stay proceedings
  arbitrators 7.29
  declaratory action 5.20, 5.36
  invalidity or setting aside 3.177, 4.46,
    8.193–8.204
stock exchanges 2.127
submission agreements 3.03
subpoenas 6.28, 6.99, 6.113
Swedish Bar Association 1.35, 1.36
  ethical rules 1.40–1.45
Switzerland 1.48

termination of arbitration agreement 3.122,
  3.168–3.170, 4.47, 7.56
  complete 3.178–3.181
  existing dispute
    award 3.176–3.177, 7.96–7.103
    by understanding 3.171
    events during proceedings 3.172
    expiration of award period 3.175
    judgment 3.173–3.174
terrorism 2.96
third parties
  arbitration agreements 3.16, 3.35, 3.130
    conduct by 3.146–3.155
    group of companies doctrine 3.22,
      3.148–3.155
    guarantee agreements 3.142–3.145
    party substitution 3.131–3.141
    third-party beneficiary agreements
      3.156–3.163
  interim measures 6.212
  invalid arbitral awards 8.46, 8.53
  procedure
    disclosure of documents 6.180
    payment to third parties 6.85
  res judicata 7.109
time limits
  arbitrators
    appointment of 4.07, 4.09, 4.27, 6.235
    challenging appointment 4.85
    compensation challenge 4.119, 4.122,
      7.94–7.95
    conflicts of interests 4.84
  award
    amendment of 7.148, 7.156
    appeal 6.86
    correction of 3.176, 7.89, 7.94 7.95,
      7.144, 7.154
    interpretation of 7.151
    period 3.175, 5.36, 6.231, 7.52, 7.53–7.56
    supplementation of 3.176, 7.89
  challenging awards 3.128, 7.56, 7.89, 7.94–7.95,
    8.03, 8.60–8.61, 8.206
    separate awards 7.29
  date of service of documents 6.45

enforcement
   court proceedings: invalidity 9.04
   expedited arbitrations 6.231
   limitation periods 7.33, 9.20
torts 5.27
   conflict of laws 2.186–2.191
trade secrets 6.178
trademarks 3.79
transportation companies 2.127
travaux préparatoires 1.19, 1.20, 1.34
turn-key contracts 2.127

ultra petita 3.92, 3.103, 6.73, 6.75, 6.192,
   7.08, 8.74
   interest 7.71
unclean hands 8.45
unconscionability 7.04
United Kingdom 1.48
   state immunity 1.57, 1.101
United Nations
   state immunity Convention 1.57, 1.74, 1.75–1.79
      arbitration 1.85–1.93
      commercial transactions 1.82–1.84
      enforcement 1.88–1.93, 1.130
      Sweden 1.95
      waivers 1.81
United States 1.13–1.15, 1.48
   sovereign immunity 1.57, 1.74, 1.75–1.84,
      1.101, 1.140
usage
   party
      arbitration agreements 3.23–3.27, 3.30
   trade
      arbitration agreements 3.30

validity of
   arbitration agreements 3.04–3.05, 3.74–3.76,
      5.11, 9.25
   contracts 2.160
valuation reports 6.105
value added tax (VAT)
   arbitrators' fees 4.126–4.129
void awards 3.128, 7.101
   principal agreement: void, voidable or declared
      invalid 3.60–3.70
voidable awards 6.75
   principal agreement: void, voidable or declared
      invalid 3.60–3.70
voting and deliberations 7.10–7.21

waivers
   arbitrability 5.08
   arbitration agreements 3.04, 3.14
      drafting 3.188
      right to arbitration and court
         proceedings 3.113, 3.121, 3.173
   arbitrators 8.114
      qualifications of 4.41
   challenge of arbitral awards 8.184
      exclusion agreements 4.41, 8.187–8.192
      implied waiver 8.185–8.186
   jurisdiction 5.28
   sovereign immunity 1.81, 1.85, 1.86–1.87, 1.89
      arbitration clauses 1.124–1.130
      Sweden 1.101, 1.131–1.141
withdrawal of arbitration request and claim 6.86
witnesses 4.49, 4.90, 5.15, 6.90
   duress 9.54
   evaluation of evidence 6.162–6.169, 7.02, 8.90–8.91
   evidence taken with court assistance
      6.170–6.180, 8.134
   expert 4.110, 5.15, 6.89, 6.93, 6.105,
      6.150–6.157, 6.222
      court assistance 6.170–6.180
      errors in reports 7.143
      foreign law 6.94
      SCC Rules 6.183
      witness conferencing 6.158–6.159
   hearing of 6.122–6.131
      cross-examination 6.100, 6.127, 6.136,
         6.137–6.143, 6.144, 6.146, 6.157, 6.222
      direct examination 6.127, 6.132–6.136,
         6.146, 6.222
   independent 6.163
   number of 6.105
   powers of arbitrators 6.97–6.100, 6.102, 6.103,
      6.182, 6.183
   re-direct examination 6.127, 6.144, 6.222
   SCC rules 6.181–6.183
   site inspections 6.160–6.161
   Swedish judicial procedure 6.25
   written witness statements 6.95, 6.127, 6.132,
      6.138, 6.145–6.149, 6.222, 7.143
written submissions 6.71–6.86, 6.192, 6.193
   prayers for relief 6.72, 6.73–6.75, 7.66, 7.146,
      8.76, 8.77, 8.105
written witness statements 6.95, 6.127, 6.132,
      6.138, 6.145–6.149, 6.222
   errors 7.143